From Age to Age

A Living Witness

A Historical Interpretation of Free
Methodism's First Century

By
Leslie R. Marston

First Fruits Press
Wilmore, Kentucky
c2016

From age to age a living witness: a historical interpretation of Free Methodism's first century.
By Leslie R. Marston.

First Fruits Press, ©2016
Previously published by Light and Life Press, ©1960.

ISBN: 9781621715771 (print), 9781621715788 (digital), 9781621715795 (kindle)

Digital version at http://place.asburyseminary.edu/freemethodistbooks/21/

First Fruits Press is a digital imprint of the Asbury Theological Seminary, B.L. Fisher Library. Asbury Theological Seminary is the legal owner of the material previously published by the Pentecostal Publishing Co. and reserves the right to release new editions of this material as well as new material produced by Asbury Theological Seminary. Its publications are available for noncommercial and educational uses, such as research, teaching and private study. First Fruits Press has licensed the digital version of this work under the Creative Commons Attribution Noncommercial 3.0 United States License. To view a copy of this license, visit http://creativecommons.org/licenses/by-nc/3.0/us/.

For all other uses, contact:

First Fruits Press
B.L. Fisher Library
Asbury Theological Seminary
204 N. Lexington Ave.
Wilmore, KY 40390
http://place.asburyseminary.edu/firstfruits

Marston, Leslie Ray, 1894-1979.
  From age to age a living witness: a historical interpretation of Free Methodism's first century / by Leslie R. Marston. Wilmore, Kentucky: First Fruits Press, ©2016.
      608 pages: illustrations, maps; 21 cm.
      Includes bibliographical references (pages 591-596).
      Reprint. Previously published: Winona Lake, Indiana: Light and Life Press, ©1960.
      ISBN - 13: 9781621715771 (pbk.)
      1. Free Methodist Church of North America--History. I. Title.
BX8413 .M35 2016   287.97

Cover design by Jon Ramsay

asburyseminary.edu
800.2ASBURY
204 North Lexington Avenue
Wilmore, Kentucky 40390

First Fruits Press
The Academic Open Press of Asbury Theological Seminary
204 N. Lexington Ave., Wilmore, KY 40390
859-858-2236
first.fruits@asburyseminary.edu
asbury.to/firstfruits

From Age to Age

A LIVING WITNESS

*A Historical Interpretation of
Free Methodism's First Century*

by

Leslie R. Marston

A Bishop of The Free Methodist Church

LIGHT AND LIFE PRESS
WINONA LAKE, INDIANA

Copyright 1960
LIGHT AND LIFE PRESS
Winona Lake, Indiana

Library of Congress catalog card no. 60—10621

PRINTED IN U.S.A.

To the Church of Tomorrow

"That the generation
to come might know"

Psalm 78:6

Preface

In projecting plans for a historical volume to appear during Free Methodism's centenary period, the first thought of the Board of Bishops was to seek completion of the record from 1915 to 1960. This period had not been covered in *History of the Free Methodist Church,* a two-volume account of the origin of the church and its development to 1915, written by the late Bishop Wilson T. Hogue. A third volume was envisioned, to be developed along lines set by Bishop Hogue in his two volumes.

Further consideration, however, led to the decision to leave the earlier work as a completed project, and to seek a distinctively new approach in a historical interpretation of the development of Free Methodism from its origins. The ends to be sought in such an approach were suggested in this statement of the Board of Bishops in September, 1956:

> Whereas the direction of the church's future development depends in large measure on a common understanding of the church's past history, its basic principles, and its mission in the world, we, the Board of Bishops, recommend . . . that a comprehensive volume be prepared and published on Free Methodism's first century, the same to be primarily an interpretation of the church's history, including the issues of its origin, the pertinence of those issues today, the church's history in the past, and its mission to the future; and further, we recommend that Bishop Leslie R. Marston be requested to accept the commission of writing the same.

This proposal was approved by the Board of Administration.

It is customary to write histories of institutions and organizations that have lived out the cycle of a century. To the author, the writing of the present book has been more than such a customary recognition. The currents of his life have flowed for many a decade through the channels of the church, the story of which he has tried to tell. He was born in a Free Methodist parsonage the year following the death of the church's founder, when the church was but thirty-four years old. His memory reaches back sixty or more years to recall events connected with the church in his early childhood. His service to the church covers forty years save one.

It is difficult, even well-nigh impossible, for one whose life so completely has been engulfed by a cause to be objective in the picture he would paint; more difficult when, as in this instance, his leading purpose is interpretation rather than narrative and chronology. It is hoped that the writer's awareness of the problem and his careful study of the sources upon which he has drawn, both for fact and insight, have safeguarded the picture presented herein against any serious distortion.

According to the editor of *Life*, history as merely a record of facts, without a point of view concerning the facts, has no moral and no pattern; it is "a tale told by an idiot." [1] Interpretation is the meaning a person ascribes to the facts with which he deals, and meaning depends in large measure on the writer's point of view. The author of *From Age to Age a Living Witness* frankly acknowledges that he has written from a point of view concerning the place of Free Methodism within the context of historic Methodism. This point of view he briefly defines in the introductory chapter, and develops its implications throughout succeeding chapters.

Those readers will be disappointed who hope to find in the following pages a chronological sequence of Free Methodist history, highlighted by reminiscent anecdotes and eulogy of persons prominent in the church's past or present. With interpretation the primary task, these features have been subordinated. It is true, however, that both John Wesley and Benjamin Titus Roberts are given large place. To understand the background out of which Free Methodism developed, one must know John Wesley and the Methodism he launched. Furthermore, the place of Roberts in the origin and shaping of Free Methodism demands the emphasis this book attempts to give him, if Free Methodists are to understand Free Methodism.

Rarely are persons still living mentioned, except briefly to relate them to present or recent official positions they hold or have held within the church, or on occasion to quote their views pertinent to a topic under consideration. Nor has attention been given to details of conference leadership and development. This area is left, for the present, to research by conference historical committees for conference publication.

---

1. Editorial, *Life*, March 26, 1956; p. 34.

PREFACE

Grateful acknowledgment is made to the many persons who have assisted the writer in so many ways. The libraries of many institutions have been open to him. Competent friends have reviewed different sections of the book in typescript, and have given valued counsel. Others have responded to the call for help in locating or verifying elusive items of fact. The publisher has given encouragement when at times the task has been heavy, and with his staff has generously assisted in planning important features of the book.

Greenville, Illinois   LESLIE R. MARSTON

Copyright Acknowledgments

The many publishers who have so graciously granted permission to quote copyrighted material are here listed:

Abingdon Press, Nashville;
Association of Methodist Historical Societies, New York;
Augsburg Publishing House, Minneapolis;
Beacon Hill Press, Kansas City, Missouri;
Board of Missions and Church Extension, The Methodist Church, New York;
Cambridge University Press, New York;
Columbia University Press, New York;
Cornell University, Ithaca, New York;
Cowman Publications, Inc., Los Angeles;
Duke University Press, Durham, N. C.;
Epworth Press, London;
Harcourt, Brace and Company, Inc., New York;
Harper and Brothers, New York;
Hodder and Stoughton, Ltd., London;
Light & Life Press, Winona Lake, Indiana;
Longmans, Green, and Co., New York;
The Macmillan Company, New York;
David McKay Company, Inc., New York;
H. Richard Niebuhr (author, *The Social Sources of Denominationalism*);
J. Nelson Norwood (author, *The Schism in the Methodist Episcopal Church, 1844*);
Oxford University Press, New York;
Philosophical Library, New York;
Prentice-Hall, Inc., Englewood Cliffs, New Jersey;
Fleming H. Revell Company, Westwood, New Jersey;
Rivingtons, London;
Charles Scribner's Sons, New York;
Sheed and Ward, Inc., New York;
Upper Room, Nashville;
Clarence H. Zahniser (author and publisher, *Earnest Christian*).

Table of Contents

1	Introduction	13
	The Witness	
2	The Darkness of the English Enlightenment	19
3	John Wesley's Quest	27
4	The Witness Received: Aldersgate and Beyond	41
5	Methodism's Conquering Witness: By What Means?	65
6	Methodism's Conquering Witness: By What Message?	85
7	Methodism's Conquering Witness: With What Results?	105
	Transition and Crisis	
8	Methodism Transplanted to America	121
9	The Witness Blurred: In Doctrine and Life	133
10	The Witness Blurred: Social Issues	151
11	"The Lord Sent a Prophet"	171
12	Prophet Without Honor	189
13	Reformation Fails	207
14	Hoping Against Hope	227
15	Free Methodism Is Born	249
	The Witness Maintained	
16	Doctrinal Integrity	273
17	Christian Experience	301
18	Freedom of the Spirit in Worship	329
19	Disciplined Living	359
20	Faith Working by Love	383
	The Witness Extended	
21	The Church as a Channel	409
22	Outreach Through Evangelism	427

23	The Outreach Through World Missions	451
24	Outreach Through Press and Radio	471
25	The Christian Nurture of Childhood	491
26	The Christian Nurture of Youth	511
27	The Christian Nurture of Youth—Continued	535

Conclusion

| 28 | A Century Ends—Another Dawns | 557 |

Appendices:

A. New School Methodism	573
B. General Conference Action on Roberts' Appeals	578
C. Early Free Methodism and National Affairs	579
D. Genesee Methodism Makes Amends	582
E. General Conferences, Secretaries, Treasurers	589

| Bibliography | 591 |
| Index | 597 |

CHAPTER ONE

Introduction

The late Bishop Frederick DeLand Leete of the Methodist Church once wrote the author to express his wonder that such severe and seemingly unjust treatment was accorded leaders of the reform movement in mid-nineteenth century Methodism, out of which came in 1860, of necessity and not by choice, the organization of the Free Methodist Church. "Perhaps, however," he added, "there was a message and a mission which could be fulfilled in no other way than by separation." [1]

In these words Bishop Leete pointed to that interpretation of Free Methodism's origin and mission which this book seeks to develop. Through ecclesiastical conflicts and other strange providences of one hundred years ago, God wrought His purpose in the formation of another Methodist communion to help conserve essential emphases of that earnest Christianity which had been revived under the leadership of John Wesley one hundred years earlier.

Our fathers had a mission

The Free Methodist Church had its origin a century ago as a movement toward Methodist reform and renewed Wesleyan revival. Its founding generation did not quibble about a cause, for very clearly to them their cause was *the spread of Scriptural holiness over these lands*. To that generation of reformers and crusaders, Scriptural holiness meant:

1. The Scriptural doctrine of entire sanctification according to the Wesleyan interpretation;

2. A corresponding inner experience of cleansing and power;

3. Spirituality and simplicity of worship in the freedom of the Spirit;

4. A way of holy living that separates sharply the Christian from the world;

---

1. F. D. Leete, from a personal letter to the author dated May 18, 1943.

5. Full consecration for service to God and man.

These issues were clear and comprehensive, expressed not by some minor segment of Christian belief or practice, but including elements of practically the entire reach of Christian concern. Within this clear-cut channel, the current which carried the humble craft of the young church was swift and strong. Here, indeed, was Christianity in earnest, and those who took passage surrendered status in established and respectable churches to commit themselves to a rugged but worthy cause.

Transition

The earlier intensity of the movement gave it the fervor of a sect, emphasizing more the distinctives of Free Methodism than the features it held in common with other Christian groups. As decades passed, the new church grew in numbers and gained a measure of influence beyond its own membership. Its procedures became established organizationally, and its common heritage with other evangelical bodies came more and more into focus. Thus, it finally came about that this crusading reform movement, set in motion near the middle of the nineteenth century, tended in the early twentieth century to settle into an established denomination. In this, it followed in a measure the trend of reforming sects as outlined by Troeltsch.[2]

During this transition, however, the growing church held to its distinctives with remarkable tenacity, surpassing the fidelity of original Methodism to its distinctives over a like period of years. Such is the judgment once expressed by the late Bishop William Pearce, and accepted a bit doubtfully by the present writer until his research in the preparation of this volume convinced him that Bishop Pearce had spoken correctly.

World perplexity

In the later stages of this transition of Free Methodism to a firm denominationalism, the entire world-order has fallen into confusion. Bewilderment now prevails in all areas—in morals, religion, economics, government, and international affairs. Our age disturbingly fits our Lord's description of a time of "distress of nations, with perplexity,"

---

2. E. Troeltsch, *The Social Teaching of the Christian Churches*, 2 vols. The Macmillan Co., New York.

and "men's hearts failing them for fear, and for looking after those things which are coming on the earth." [3]

A tragic aspect of the widespread uncertainty of recent years has been the confusion of religious leaders who have lost their sense of direction. Many of these once followed the chart of God's Word, but left that well-ordered course for a new freedom and attempted to chart a new course. But their brave adventure did not bring them to the bright harbor of which they had dreamed, and they lost their way in a fog, vast and dense.

Sense of mission needed

The corrective to the paralysis of perplexity that grips our age is a sense of mission. Even in these confused days there are those that have broken away from the swirling eddies of futility to hurl themselves into the sweeping currents of mighty causes. In some instances, the cause to which commitment has been made is unworthy—perhaps communism, possibly some form of fascism, or even Romanism. The commitment, nevertheless, has dispelled frustration in some and has given life motive and direction.

Yet others are turning from their lostness to the Cross of Christ where they find the meaning of their lives in full surrender to His lordship. This is happening in our time under the quickening grace of God, stirring men from their bewilderment, debauchery and apostasy. True today are Paul's words to Rome of old, "But where sin abounded, grace did much more abound." [4] The evangelical tide is rising in different Christian groups, preparing for revival. Helping to lift this tide has been the current of Free Methodism, channeled from its vigorous source in original Methodism across a century to the present crisis. It is time to ask with what resources and how adequately can Free Methodism meet the challenge of revival.

Issues old and new

A century ago issues of great moment led to the founding of the Free Methodist Church. We have noted that these issues concerned doctrine, experience, worship, piety, and stewardship. The same issues concern the church today, but in varied forms and complex

---
3. *Luke* 21: 25, 26.
4. *Romans* 5:20.

relationships that create problems undreamed of by our founders, but to which, were they living today, they would address themselves with that same courage and sacrifice with which they attacked the problems of their age.

The new problems of our age arise principally from two sources, the growing complexity of modern society making new demands on social, economic, civic, and personal ethics; and the urgency of history which more than hints that time and opportunity for the world's evangelization are limited. Our present mission as a church is not only to conserve our heritage, but to share its benefits by applying the ageless principles of our holy religion to the problems of a complex age.

To serve the present age

This, then, is Free Methodism's mission and challenge, "to serve the present age." Because it expresses the point of view from which this book presents the Free Methodist Church at the opening of its second century, we declare here our confidence that from the last mid-century's period of compromise and spiritual decline, God foresaw this mid-century's apostasy and paganism, and purposed to call out, on the issues of that day, a people through whom He might conserve the essentials of the Wesleyan witness for release upon this age of crisis.

Our mission is still to *spread Scriptural holiness over these lands,* and Scriptural holiness still means sound doctrine, an inner experience of cleansing and power, spiritual worship, a way of holy living, and faithful stewardship. The principles of holiness are ever the same; their application must be extended to new reaches of these principles as the enemy of holiness attacks on new fronts. After a hundred years, Free Methodism still has a message and a mission.

The backward look

From these considerations it follows that as Free Methodism girds itself for its second century, it needs to focus the perspective of history on its present and future course. It needs to know what was its heritage in the movement called Methodism; what Free Methodism was in its origin; what it has been in the course of its development to the present; what is its distinctive mission today; and what the century ahead demands if the church is to justify its place in the family of

Christian denominations. These are important considerations for the further chapters of this book.

In those chapters we shall look back to Methodism's and Free Methodism's origins, not for antiques to be displayed in a denominational museum, but for standards by which to judge the church's place and mission in a new age. Reviewing what our heritage cost our founders and to what benefit for us they invested that heritage, will disclose values to be conserved and invested by this generation for the profit of the next. We do not venerate yesterday merely because it belongs to a past we revere, but we seek to understand it that we may improve today and tomorrow. "The farther backward you can look," Winston Churchill somewhere has said, "the farther forward you are likely to see."

In looking backward, our primary concern is not to rediscover old methods to apply without change to today's needs. The values of the past for us lie not in old methods so much as in enduring principles and in the ideals that have inspired generations of devout living, self-sacrificing service, and undying loyalty to a challenging cause. Conservative in matters of principle, the Apostle Paul urged Timothy to "guard the truths" entrusted to him; and yet in method Paul was so flexible and progressive that he would become "all things to all men" that he "might by all means (methods) save some."[5] Methods may be altered to meet present need; principles are to be maintained for all time, for "Truth is forever true."

A look ahead

Let the reader keep in mind the author's point of view as he has attempted to present it in this introductory chapter. Scanning the sequence of chapter headings in the table of contents from time to time will fix in mind the course of our journey.

Chapters Two to Seven follow Wesley's search for the witness, his receiving it, and his charting the way of revival in eighteenth-century England.

Chapters Eight through Fifteen trace the Wesleyan witness to North America, and mark those changes that occurred in American Methodism which stimulated unsuccessful efforts at reform and led to the founding of the Free Methodist Church.

---

5. *I Cor.* 9:22.

Chapters Sixteen through Twenty evaluate the success of the Free Methodist Church in maintaining the Wesleyan witness in the areas of doctrine, experience, worship, piety, and stewardship.

Chapters Twenty-one through Twenty-seven measure the extension of the church's program through the channels of organized Free Methodism, by means of evangelism, foreign missions, publications, radio, and Christian nurture.

In conclusion, Chapter Twenty-eight considers Free Methodism's present status and its prospects as it enters its second century.

CHAPTER TWO

The Darkness of the English Enlightenment

"Our light looks like the evening of the world." This somber observation was reported in 1694 in a proposal for national reform of conduct in England. The "Puritan century" was then drawing to its tired close.

But even darker, morally and spiritually, were the early decades of the century following. The eighteenth century was the century of "the Enlightenment," but what gains the century made in knowledge and the light of reason were more than lost in the deepening spiritual gloom engulfing all England. W. H. Fitchett, able historian of eighteenth-century Methodism, reports, "Christianity under English skies was never, before nor since, so near the death point." [1]

Degraded morals

Judged even by the easy standards of the twentieth century, the morals of the England of the eighteenth century were unbelievably corrupt. The lower classes existed on a brutish level, sodden with drink, rotting in filth, and depraved in their appetites for pleasure and excitement. All historians of this era paint the picture in dark colors. Profanity, bare-fisted pugilism (even women participating), cock-fighting, bull-, badger-, and bear-baiting, gambling, robbery, sexual immorality, and general violence were prevalent. Perhaps the height of popularity in amusements was reached in the spectacle of public hangings, of which there were many in a land where the death penalty was imposed for a variety of offenses, many of them trivial.

Historians report that about one-half of the children of London were born out of wedlock; that every tenth person (among adults, it is to be assumed) sold liquor, and every sixth shop in the metropolis was a gin-shop. The oft-quoted historian, Lecky, has asserted that drinking in the early eighteenth century was the outstanding phenomenon of the era, greater in its influence upon England than any

---

1. W. H. Fitchett, *Wesley and His Century*. Eaton & Mains, New York; p. 4.

political or military event.[2] Piette points out that gross immorality prevailed in London streets in the daytime, and at night conditions reached the level of savagery when to be out was to risk one's life.[3]

Morals of the country gentry and the court likewise were debauched. So corrupt had the theater become by the late seventeenth century that women attending its performance wore masks to hide their blushes—or, as one writer has suggested, to hide the fact they didn't blush! Theaters welcomed street-walkers without charging them admission. It would appear that both on and off stage the member of the all too common triangle who was held in general disdain was neither the clever seducer nor the too-willing victim, but the stupidly faithful spouse. Writing of the middle of the eighteenth century, the historian Green recorded that, "Purity and fidelity to the marriage vow were sneered out of fashion; and Lord Chesterfield, in his letters to his son, instructs him in the art of seduction as a part of a polite education." [4]

Corruption in politics was rampant, the example of atrocious bribery being set in high places by such notables as Walpole and Pelham. On occasion, widespread drunkenness among its members compelled Parliament to discontinue its business early in the day.

Low state of Church and Clergy

Early in the century, Bishop Burnet lamented the "imminent ruin" he saw hanging over the Church, the principal threat being the Church's own inward condition. He complained that candidates for orders knew neither the Catechism nor the Gospels, and far from knowing enough to be ordained, "they would appear not knowing enough to be admitted to the holy sacrament." [5]

More serious than their intellectual deficiency was the moral disease of many clergymen. A clergyman in the latter part of the century is quoted as saying that among "the most distinguished coxcombs,

---

2. Wm. E. H. Lecky, *A History of England in the Eighteenth Century*. D. Appleton & Co., New York; v. 1, 590.
3. Maximin Piette, *John Wesley in the Evolution of Protestantism*. Published by Sheed & Ward, Inc., New York; pp. 113, 115.
4. J. R. Green, *A Short History of the English People*. Harper & Bros., New York; New York; p. 707.
5. Quoted by Thos. Jackson, *Centenary of Wesleyan Methodism*. Mason & Lane, New York; p. 14 *et seq*. (From preface to Burnet's *Pastoral Care*, 3rd ed., 1713.)

drunkards, debauchees, and gamesters who figure at the watering places, and all places of public resort, are young men of the sacerdotal order." [6] Older clergy were slaves to avarice and indolence.

Many parishes seldom saw the hireling engaged to tend the flock, for through political influence or direct purchase he might have acquired several "livings," from most of which he resided at some distance. Piling up "plural livings" from numerous parishes, some clergymen built up immense incomes while others, faithful shepherds serving a small parish, must eke out a marginal existence as best they could.

In A *History of Preaching*, Dargan calls attention to that large group of clergymen in this period whose low morals and lack of spirituality adversely affected their pulpit ministrations, but further adds that even the sermons of "theoretically evangelical" clergymen might be "lifeless and tame." [7] Piette quotes a clergyman of standing as saying to a friend, "Why should I compose new sermons? I have already twenty-four written out by hand." And he added boastfully, "No one of my fellow ministers has so many." [8]

Poor preaching drew small crowds. We are told that when a preacher with a vital message did attract a crowd, especially the poor, the wealthy members of the congregation locked the rabble out of their pews and absented themselves.[9] Under the prevailing type of "lifeless and tame" preaching, the squire could live through the service comfortably enough when supplied with food and wine, Bible and tobacco, which he might enjoy in the semi-seclusion of his pew. If these failed, a nap during the sermon offered a ready escape from boredom.

Other symptoms of the Church's decline were negligence of the Lord's Supper and the dilapidation of church edifices.

An age of reason without wisdom

O world, thou choosest not the better part!
It is not wisdom to be only wise,

---

6. John Stoughton, *Religion in England*. A. C. Armstrong & Son, New York; v. 6, 206.
7. E. C. Dargan, *A History of Preaching*. Baker Book House, Grand Rapids; v. 2, 291.
8. Maximin Piette, *John Wesley in the Evolution of Protestantism*. Published by Sheed & Ward, Inc., New York; p. 138.
9. *Cambridge Modern History*. Cambridge University Press, New York; v. 6, 79.

> *And on the inward vision close the eyes,*
> *But it is wisdom to believe the heart.*[10]

These lines of Santayana spell the blunder of that earthly wisdom by which eighteenth-century England sought to gain the world but lost its soul. The previous century had borne a Newton whose genius discovered principles according to which measurable relationships in the physical world seemed to open to man the entire universe as a plainly written book. So dazzling was the light of Newton's discovery of gravitation's orderly system, that men thought all questions concerning the universe and their own existence had now been answered, or would be at the turn of another page of nature's book. Pope, with his characteristic cleverness, expressed the far-reaching significance the age had attached to Newton's brilliant work in this couplet:

> *Nature and Nature's laws lay hid in night:*
> *God said, Let Newton be! and all was light.*

Every epochal advance in man's conception of the world and its meaning has been extended by the enthusiasm of discovery far beyond its valid application, and made to explain too much. And so in this instance, the order, uniformity and rationality ascribed to the universe without, were read back into man's inner world as well. The shadowy forms of love and fear, of remorse and aspiration, that stirred deep within man were dissolved under the crystal light of reason, and under that chill light the fire of the human spirit subsided to a cold, dark cinder. All sense of mystery was now dispelled.

Matching the verse opening this section in expressing sheer reason's lack of wisdom, is Carlyle's claim that the man with ever so much knowledge of the universe, who does not habitually wonder and worship, is "but a pair of spectacles behind which there is no eye."

Deism and the Church

Some churchmen were disturbed by the development of naturalism, while others rather easily surrendered to that pale religion of deism which sometimes subsists in connection with materialism. Its God was a master-mechanic who in remote aeons past constructed the vast machine of the universe, set it in perpetual motion, and then withdrew to the outer rim of his creation whence he "watches it go," but

---

10. George Santayana, *Poems*. Charles Scribner's Sons, New York; from Sonnet III.

takes no further part in its affairs. According to deism, God has built reason into the universe, and this is His only revelation, the revelation of nature. There is no place for the supernatural in such a closed system of cause and effect. John Wesley equated the religion of such an absentee God with atheism, saying:

> [It is] a plausible way of thrusting God out of the world he has made. They can do business without him; and so either drop him entirely, not considering him at all; or suppose, that since
>
> *He gave things their beginning,*
> *And set this whirligig a spinning,*
>
> he has not concerned himself with these trifles, but let everything take its own course.[11]

It follows, then, that deism's God is far removed from human concern and does not involve Himself in man's fears and failures, his hopes and aspirations. There is no indwelling Spirit, no voice of God in the soul of man, no revelation of God either through prophet or through God's Son. To claim such is "enthusiasm," the eighteenth-century word for fanaticism. And in the eighteenth century enthusiasm was more feared than either heresy or immorality.

Those of the clergy who frankly accepted the principles of deism were the modernists of that day, then called "Latitudinarians." Of their position the Anglican historian, Wakeman, has written:

> ... The weakness of Latitudinarian religion lay in the fact that it appealed too exclusively to the head and too little to the heart and conscience.... It removed God away from the human heart to enthrone Him among the clouds and the snows of an intellectual Olympus. It called upon man to obey His moral law, not because He was Power and could punish, as Puritanism had done; still less because He was Love and could reward, as the Church had done; but because He was Reason, and obedience was a reasonable duty.... Men can obey the orders of authority implicitly, they will follow the leadership of love unreservedly, they never surrender themselves wholly to the guidance of reason.... Argument can confuse as well as enlighten the conscience....[12]

---

11. J. Wesley, *Sermons on Several Occasions*. Phillips & Hunt, New York; v. 2, 434.
12. H. O. Wakeman, *An Introduction to the History of the Church of England*. Rivingtons, London; p. 419 *et seq.*

The influence of deism spread as a blight through the Church (and the churches, for Dissent was in as grievous a state as was the Church of England), affecting all levels of clergy and not alone the Latitudinarians. Even those scholarly divines of orthodox convictions who took up the pen to resist deism were misled to neglect Christianity's tried weapon of Revelation in the attempt to defeat the enemy with reason, the enemy's own weapon.

A well-known example of such an effort (granted! a splendid effort) is Bishop Butler's *Analogy of Religion*. In the intellectual arena, Butler pressed home to materialists the fact that, after all, the book of Nature could not at every point dispose of revealed religion. But ordinary men paid little heed to learned defenders, even if they were on the side of truth. At the same time, they could hardly escape the inference that the great concern of such scholars involved questions rather than affirmations, perplexities rather than certainties, and that at best Christianity was but the least irrational of the religions. The rational method of defending revealed religion had the effect, then, of spreading rationalism and a measure of skepticism downward through the masses. The Christian religion had been wounded in the house of its friends.

The preaching of the period

Sermons of that day lacked definiteness, urgency and unction. The prophet had yielded the pulpit to the priest and the essayist. The prevailing concept of nature's orderly processes and the general prejudice against supernaturalism brought a chill into the pulpit which flowed freely into the pew.

The influence of deism was especially disastrous to spiritual worship, and the doctrines concerning the Holy Spirit were especially repugnant to such as held to deistic principles. Early in the century Abraham Taylor complained that ridicule was commonly directed against the person and work of the Holy Spirit even by those professing a belief in the Scriptures, and that Christians who claimed the Spirit's presence and aid were ridiculed as "enthusiasts." To such grieving of the Holy Spirit, Taylor ascribed the low state of religion in England at the time he wrote.[13]

---

13. Cited by Thos. Jackson, *Centenary of Wesleyan Methodism*. Mason & Lane, New York; p. 22 *et seq.* (From Hurrion, *Sermons on the Holy Spirit*, p. 5, 1734 ed.)

A rationalistic age is critical and formal, and eighteenth-century preachers were therefore cautious in their pulpit utterances. The dissection of sermons was a favorite intellectual exercise, and to be ridiculed for some statement not agreeable to the rationalistic spirit of the age was an ordeal few preachers had the courage to risk. From this ridicule the surest protection was to prepare an innocuous manuscript to be read with no measure of warmth or zeal.

A contemporary of the period made the rounds of several London churches and reported that not one sermon he heard was any more distinctively Christian than were the writings of Cicero, and that from the content of these sermons one could not discern if the speakers were followers of Confucius, Mohammed, or Christ.[14]

To Arnold Nash we owe this concise but comprehensive paragraph on the content of eighteenth-century English preaching:

> The scholarly skepticism of Butler provided the chaff upon which the Whig and Tory preachers alike sought to feed their flocks. The historian of preaching in the Anglican Church, Canon Charles Smyth, points out that in this period "preaching was little more than prudential morality, based rather on reason than on revelation and appealing deliberately to sober common sense." The situation in non-conformity was no improvement. There the economic virtues were canonized with a little doctrine added apologetically by way of sanction. The Presbyterians, who had received the Puritan heritage, were drifting into Unitarianism, and the Congregationalists and Baptists were little better.[15]

Deism and ethics

Saturating both society and religion, naturalism and deism were devastating in their moral effects. Try as they would, rationalistic philosophers were unable to ground an adequate ethics in nature. Just at the fork of the road where self-interest pulled a man one way and the claims of duty pushed another, nature as *reason* failed to mark clearly which way to go, down the left road of "tooth-and-claw" or up the right road of "good will." Then, nature as *passion* stepped in and propelled a man down the way of "tooth-and-claw" to violence and lust. Or when passion slumbered in the absence of any excitant,

---

14. Maximin Piette, *John Wesley in the Evolution of Protestantism*. Published by Sheed & Ward, Inc., New York; p. 1.
15. Arnold Nash, "The England to which Wesley came," in *Methodism*, Wm. K. Anderson, Ed., Methodist Publishing House, Nashville; p. 19.

and the book of nature was ambiguous or inconclusive concerning the right way, a man could only do his best and take a calculated risk. Thus prudence replaced morality.

In his *Essay on Man*, Alexander Pope, literary interpreter of deism, clearly reflected deism's naturalistic ethics in his urge that, "Reason keep to Nature's road," and in such lines as the following:

> *Shew'd erring Pride whatever is is right;*
> *That Reason, Passion answer one great aim;*
> *That true Self-Love and Social are the same.*

With naturalism the foundation of ethics, it is little wonder that English morals in the early eighteenth century presented the dark pictures sketched earlier in this chapter. Well did Carlyle say of England in this century, "Soul extinct; stomach well alive."

Bishop Berkeley, churchman and philosopher of the period, in his *Discourse to Magistrates and Men in Authority*, pleaded with public officials to do something about the moral situation. "The youth," he said, "born and brought up in wicked times, without any bias to good from early principle or instilled opinion, when they grow ripe must be monsters indeed. And it is to be feared, that the age of monsters is not far off." Such language is emphatic, especially when it comes from the mind and pen of a philosopher. Berkeley declared further, "Our prospect is very terrible; and the symptoms grow stronger every day." [16]

Bishop Berkeley published this *Discourse* in 1736, and republished it in 1738, the latter being the very year a fire was kindled in the heart of a clergyman in London's Aldersgate Street that was to become a great light to dark England, from whence the fire would rapidly spread to encircle the globe.

---

16. A. C. Fraser, Ed., *The Works of George Berkeley*. Oxford University Press, New York; v. 4, 505, 506.

CHAPTER THREE

John Wesley's Quest

Its public life corrupt; its clergy discredited; its Church frozen; its Theology exhausted of Christian elements. This was the England of the eighteenth century! It needed a spiritual revolution to save such a people.[1]

In these words Fitchett describes the plight of England when God chose John Wesley to break through the dense darkness with the light and warmth of the gospel to melt the religious frigidity of the age. Born in 1703 when the century was young, not until the age of thirty-five and after he had followed many devious byways to frustration and failure, did Wesley himself come to the full light and warmth of evangelical faith.

Preparation

John Wesley was reared by parents of character and culture. Notwithstanding the poverty of a large family compelled to exist on the sparse "living" of the Epworth parish among the bleak Lincolnshire fens, John was given the best schooling England afforded, as were likewise his elder brother, Samuel, and his younger brother, Charles.

John's formal education began in the home school conducted in the Epworth rectory under the skilled tutelage of his highly intelligent mother, the noble Susanna Annesley Wesley. At the early age of ten he was accepted at the famous Charterhouse School in London. Here he remained until his admission at seventeen years to Christ Church, one of Oxford's most noted colleges. Until his senior year, John Wesley seems to have been only nominally Christian, carefree perhaps, but by no means a profligate. As he neared the completion of his undergraduate course, however, he became serious concerning his future and more concerned with conducting his life within the limits of sober piety.

He was graduated a bachelor of arts from Oxford in 1725 at the age of twenty-two, and the same year was ordained a deacon by

---

1. W. H. Fitchett, *Wesley and His Century*. Eaton & Mains, New York; p. 148.

Bishop Potter in Christ Church Cathedral. Remaining at Oxford, the next year he won appointment as fellow in Lincoln College, and in 1727 received the degree Master of Arts. Then followed a two-year period as curate, or assistant, to his father at Epworth and more particularly at Wroote, a nearby hamlet which for a time was attached to the Epworth parish. During this period, in 1728, he was ordained a presbyter of the Church of England.

In 1729 he was recalled to his duties as fellow, or instructor, in Lincoln College. Here he had been commissioned to direct disputations, to teach philosophy, and to lecture in Greek on the New Testament. For the training he gained in moderating disputations (or debates), Wesley later declared he often had reason to thank God. Peculiarly effective was this discipline in logic for the later period of his life when he must defend evangelical religion against its self-righteous opponents, and proclaim its message to poor and sinful creatures who needed its life-changing power.

Before John's leaving Oxford to assist his father at Epworth and Wroote, a younger brother, Charles, had entered Christ Church and had caused John a measure of brotherly concern because of his lack of religious seriousness. But upon John's return to Oxford to take up his duties again as fellow at Lincoln, he found Charles the leader of a small group of devout young men whose pursuit of earnest Christianity had won for them the derisive campus sobriquet, "Holy Club." Soon John had succeeded his brother as leader of this group, for leadership was ever John's natural role, and in this situation his leadership was quite inevitable by virtue of his seniority and his position on the staff of Lincoln College.

Under John's leadership, the rigid self-discipline and asceticism of the members of the Holy Club, along with their closely scheduled observance of the duties both of devotion and good works, led to their being dubbed "Methodists." The name stuck, and years after the group was dissolved by the scattering of its members from Oxford, the term "Methodist" identified the revival movement that developed under the leadership of three of them, namely the two Wesleys and George Whitefield.

The quest by way of reason

Until his last year as an undergraduate in Oxford, John Wesley had been properly but not ardently religious. With completion of his course drawing near, he gave attention to his future and, upon the urging of his father, deliberated the taking of orders. He finally decided favorably thereon. He carried on sober correspondence with his parents concerning this serious step, and with his mother concerning such weighty theological topics as predestination and the foreknowledge of God.

Continuing at Oxford after his graduation, he studied extensively the philosophies of the day, and for his master's degree wrote dissertations on such diverse themes as *Animal Souls, Julius Caesar,* and *The Love of God.* He took up and abandoned one system of thought after another, leading Piette rhetorically to ask, "Will John Wesley, a searcher of all philosophies then in vogue, give his adherence completely to any one system in this state of intellectual anarchy, so widespread throughout the eighteenth century in England?" [2] As early as 1725 his scholarly father wrote him a word of warning. "I like your way of thinking and arguing," he said; "but nevertheless I ought to say that it frightens me a little. He who believes and yet argues against reason, is half-papist, half-enthusiast. He who wishes to cramp Revelation to his puny reason is half-deist, half-heretic. My dear child, keep your boat between this Scylla and Charybdis." [3]

In a sermon of his later years, Wesley told of his earlier quest for God and the truth of an invisible world by way of reason, "till there was no spirit in me," he said; "and I was ready to choose strangling rather than life." [4] In his sermon on "The use of money," he illustrated from his own experience that one person may not safely for his faith engage himself in certain employments which others find harmless. "So I am convinced," he said, "from many experiments, I could not study, to any degree of perfection, either mathematics, arithmetic, or algebra without being a deist, if not an atheist: and yet others may study them all their lives, without sustaining any inconvenience." [5] Thus he acknowledged late in life the danger in abstract thought to which he was inclined by nature. Fortunately he

---
2. Maximin Piette, *John Wesley in the Evolution of Protestantism.* Published by Sheed & Ward, Inc., New York; p. 267.
3. Quoted by Piette, *ibid.*
4. J. Wesley, *Sermons on Several Occasions.* Phillips & Hunt, New York; v. 2, 129 et seq.
5. *Ibid.,* v. 2, 443.

turned from an undue dependence upon reason in his early maturity, and already in 1727 had reached the conclusion that mere knowledge is not of worth merely for the sake of knowledge or merely to satisfy curiosity. In that year he wrote his mother:

> I am perfectly come over to your opinion that there are many truths it is not worthwhile to know. Curiosity, indeed, might be a sufficient plea for our laying out some time upon them, if we had half a dozen centuries of life to come; but methinks it is great ill-husbandry to spend a considerable part of the small pittance now allowed us in what makes us neither a quick nor a sure return.[6]

Five years later, in another of his many letters to his mother, he announced this farewell to technical scholarship for which, encouraged by his erudite father, he had held high ambitions:

> Shall I quite break off my pursuit of all learning, but what immediately tends to practice? I once desired to make a fair show in languages and philosophy; but it is past; there is a more excellent way: and if I cannot attain to any progress in the one without throwing up all thoughts of the other—why, fare it well! —Yet a little while, and we shall all be equal in knowledge, if we are in virtue.[7]

But John Wesley did not swing to anti-intellectualism at the other extreme, and was ever strong for reason as handmaid of faith. To correct the extravagances of some of his followers in a later period, he warned against discounting reason or belittling knowledge. Long after his Aldersgate experience he wrote "An Earnest Appeal to Men of Reason and Religion," in which he said, "We join you in desiring a religion founded on reason,"[8] and then proceeded to show that the religion of the Methodists was founded on the highest reason.

Preaching before Oxford University on Salvation by Faith less than a month after he had exercised this faith in the little chapel of Aldersgate Street, he could say from recent and vital experience that saving faith "is not barely a speculative, rational thing, a cold, lifeless assent, a train of ideas in the head; but also a disposition of the heart."[9]

---

6. J. Wesley, *Letters*. Epworth Press, London; v. 1, 39 et seq.
7. *Ibid.*, v. 1, 119.
8. J. Wesley, *Works* (Emory ed. 1853). Carlton & Phillips, New York; v. 5, 11.
9. J. Wesley, *Sermons on Several Occasions*. Phillips & Hunt, New York; v. 1, 14.

The quest by way of mysticism and withdrawal

Nearing the time of his graduation from Christ Church in 1725 and about the time of his decision to seek ordination, John Wesley became interested in devotional literature, especially the writings of the mystics, which exerted on him a deep influence, and while tending to introvert his religious interests, did much to enrich his spiritual life. Later, as we shall see, he was to react strongly against the mystics.

The withdrawing and self-centered tendency of both scholar and mystic appeared during Wesley's earlier Oxford term as fellow when, in 1727, he wrote his mother of the seclusion he hoped to find in a teaching position in Yorkshire for which he had applied. The school was located in an almost inaccessible vale between two hills, "so that you can expect little company from without," he wrote, "and within there is none at all." [10]

Evidently he did not secure the position, for later that year we find him at Epworth's desolate outstation of Wroote where he found seclusion indeed. Twice only during this two-year period did he leave the Epworth area, one of those occasions being his ordination as presbyter. During this seclusion he benefited by his mother's counsel and sane views of life and religion, and by the parish duties that fell to him as his father's assistant. And he had his books.

Following his recall to instructional duties at Lincoln College in 1729, he soon became engrossed with the Holy Club, as we have already noted. After four or five years in what to Wesley was a satisfying life of academic seclusion at Oxford, his aged and declining father desired that he apply for the Epworth "living" as his successor. His brother Samuel, now headmaster of a school at Tiverton, had declined to apply for the place but joined in urging John to do so. Samuel used as a principal argument the vows of ordination John had taken. Forthrightly, John appealed to his bishop for an opinion on this claim that he was under obligation because of his ordination to seek a parish. The bishop answered, "No; provided you can as a clergyman better serve God and His Church in your present or some other station" than as parish priest.

---

10. J. Wesley, *Letters*. Epworth Press, London; v. 1, 42 *et seq*.

John had written his father, declining his request that he apply for the Epworth parish, pleading that he could be holier in Oxford. His father replied, "It is not dear self, but the glory of God, and the different degrees of promoting it, which should be our main consideration and direction on any course of life." And then to his thirty-two year old son, the elder Wesley gave this seasoned advice: "God made us for a social life; we are not to bury our talents; we are to let our light shine before men, and not barely through the chinks of a bushel for fear the wind should blow it out." [11]

But in his systematic way, John wrote his father, giving twenty-some reasons for remaining at Oxford, most of them centering in the welfare of his own soul.[12] Another less worthy clergyman succeeded to the Epworth parish following the death of the old rector.

Within a few months, however, John left for Georgia to be a missionary to the Indians, and, strangely enough, this also was for the purpose of saving his own soul! He answered the question, "Cannot you save your own soul in England as well as in Georgia?" by saying, "No; neither can I hope to attain to the same degree of holiness here which I may there." [13]

In this he reminds one of the monastic temper of the Psalmist who longed to escape to wilderness seclusion, and wrote in Psalm 55:

> O that I had wings like a dove! for then would I fly away, and be at rest. Lo, then would I wander far off, and remain in the wilderness. I would hasten my escape from the windy storm and tempest. . . . I have seen violence and strife in the city.

This flight to the American wilderness, "to learn the true sense of the Gospel of Christ by preaching it to the heathen," as Wesley expressed it, reflects the idealization of the state of nature, undisturbed by organized human society, which found expression in the social and political theory of the times.

Wesley took with him to Georgia some of his favorite authors, and perhaps in that select library were volumes from the mystics he had admired. When he had been in Georgia most of a year he wrote his brother, Samuel, giving his analysis of mysticism's errors, and con-

---

11. H. Moore, *Life of Wesley*. John Kershaw, London; v. 1, 210 *et seq.*
12. J. Wesley, *Journal*. Epworth Press, London; v. 2, 159-166.
13. J. Wesley, *Letters*. Epworth Press, London; v. 1, 190.

fessing, "I think the rock on which I had nearest made shipwreck of the faith was the writings of the mystics; under which term I comprehend all, and only those, who slight any of the means of grace." [14]

On another occasion he declared himself even more critically concerning mysticism and those mystics "whose noble descriptions of union with God, and internal religion made everything else appear mean, flat, and insipid." And he added, "But in truth they make good works appear so too; yea, even faith itself, and what not?" Confused by the mystics' teaching that the Christian is released from the commandments of God because, as they said, "Love is all," he "fluctuated between obedience and disobedience"; he "had no heart, no vigor, no zeal in obeying"; and he was continually in doubt and perplexity, and was disturbed in conscience. After being delivered from mysticism's snare, Wesley came to the conclusion, that "all the other enemies of Christianity are triflers; the mystics are the most dangerous of its enemies." [15]

Wesley's longing for solitude continued, and on the return voyage from Georgia to England he wrote in his Journal the following:

> ... I reflected much on that vain desire, which had pursued me for so many years, of being in solitude in order to be a Christian. I have now, thought I, solitude enough. But am I therefore the nearer being a Christian? Not if Jesus Christ be the model of Christianity.[16]

Some insist that in so sweepingly condemning mysticism, Wesley was unfair, and charge that both he and the Methodist movement were strongly tinged with mystical tendencies. Careful reading of Wesley makes clear, however, that his definition of mysticism makes its essential difference from the faith of Christianity a neglect of the objective means of grace and an exaggeration of subjective efforts at union with God. Wesley's emphasis was a personal relationship to God by faith rather than a mystical union with God.[17]

Most fortunately, Wesley was delivered from suffocation by mysticism. His efforts to guard Methodism against its choking grasp

---

14. *Ibid.*, v. 1, 207.
15. H. Moore, *Life of Wesley*. John Kershaw, London; v. 1, 343 *et seq.*
16. J. Wesley, *Journal*. Epworth Press, London; v. 1, 416.
17. For further development of this distinction, see *From Chaos to Character*, by the present writer; especially "What is Faith?", p. 136 *et seq.*

were to begin within eighteen months after Aldersgate in his controversy with the Moravians over "stillness," and would continue for fifty years. His last reference to mysticism in his *Journal* was September 1, 1790, within six months of his death. Without his own deliverance from mysticism prior to his Aldersgate experience, the revival that followed could well have been engulfed by suffocating subjectivism, and Methodism would have gone down in history merely as one of a host of ephemeral fanatical sects that litter the waysides of Christian history.

The quest by way of legalism

John Wesley was cheerful by nature, as the tenor of his life clearly indicated. But when in Oxford days he began to take life and religion seriously, he became morbidly technical and legalistic in his zeal for personal holiness.

His quest during the Holy Club era at Oxford led him to abstemiousness in food, the strictest self-denial in his expenditures, and a rigorous regimen in controlling his hours and minutes. This strenuous program carried through the Georgia period, with fasting three times a week and meticulous parceling of time. Indeed, his going to Georgia to save his own soul seems itself to have been motivated by his legalism quite as much as by his desire to flee from the perplexities of civilization to the serenity and simplicity of the wilderness. He was seeking personal holiness by his own efforts that he might claim full justification before God. As late as January 24, 1738, during his return voyage from Georgia, he reviewed his religious state and sought crumbs of comfort in his own good works. He wrote into his *Journal* this analysis:

> I think, verily, if the gospel be true, I am safe: for I not only have given, and do give, all my goods to feed the poor; I not only give my body to be burned, drowned, or whatever God shall appoint for me; but I follow after charity (though not as I ought, yet as I can), if haply I may attain it. I *now* believe the Gospel is true. "I show my faith by my works," by staking my all upon it.... Whoever sees me, sees I would be a Christian.... But in a storm I think, "What if the Gospel be not true? ... For what art thou wandering over the face of the earth—a dream, a cunningly devised fable! Oh, who will deliver me from this fear of death?" [18]

---

18. J. Wesley, *Journal*. Epworth Press, London; v. 1, 418.

How significant that one who had climbed the rough and difficult steeps of legalism should later come to understand and so clearly define, as did Wesley, the operation of "faith working by love!" In the sermon already mentioned, which he preached before the University in the early weeks of his walk by faith, he courageously spoke from personal experience when he said, "For there is nothing we are, or have, or do, which can deserve the least thing at God's hand." [19]

His treatment of faith and works in *Explanatory Notes Upon the New Testament* [20] is a far step from his own early legalism, and an equal distance on the other hand from antinomianism which, said Wesley, "makes void the law through faith," and for which he held an intense hatred.

The quest by way of ritualism

In his Georgia sojourn John Wesley became extremely sacerdotal and, as he later acknowledged, placed too much credence in the assumed antiquity of certain rites and ordinances. He sought diligently to restore primitive Christianity among the uncultured and often immoral colonists of primitive Georgia, and he was keenly disappointed that his purpose to introduce primitive Christianity to the Georgia savages failed for lack of opportunity to carry on missionary work among them.

On the rude frontier Wesley insisted upon baptism, even of infants, by immersion—trine baptism at that! He refused Christian burial to those not baptized, and refused baptism to children of dissenters. He held two services a day and on occasion floundered through the Georgia wilderness in his clerical robes. In fact, he was looked upon as a papist by some for his extreme sacerdotalism.

His high-church convictions led him to refuse the Lord's Supper to a saintly Moravian pastor, Boltzius by name, because he had not been baptized by an episcopally ordained minister. A dozen years later, and following his own persecution as an "irregular" by the Church of England and his exclusion from most of her pulpits, he received a gracious letter from Pastor Boltzius declaring the increase of his love for Wesley, which had first been kindled during Wesley's

---

19. J. Wesley, *Sermons on Several Occasions*. Phillips & Hunt, New York; v. 1, 13.
20. See Wesley's *Notes* on the Epistle of James. Epworth Press, London; p. 861 et seq.

Savannah ministry! Wesley quotes the letter in his *Journal* and records the Savannah incident. "Can anyone carry High Church zeal higher than this?" he asked; then quaintly exclaimed, "How well have I since been beaten with my own staff!" [21]

Even more appropriately might he have applied this same expression to an even sharper irony. On his visit to the Moravian colonies in Germany following his Aldersgate experience, and only a few months after his high ritualism in Georgia, it is reported (although not established, according to Curnock) that the Moravians refused to admit him to Communion because they deemed that he was not prepared in heart. This exclusion was the more pointed because they did admit his traveling companion, Ingham, who had earlier been with Wesley in the Holy Club and had shared with him the Georgia venture. Ingham later joined the Moravians.

In later years, during the development of the Methodist movement, Wesley so far moderated his former rigidity as to admit penitent sinners and properly instructed children to the Lord's table. According to his later views, the Communion was both a *confirming* ordinance for the believer and a *converting* ordinance for the sincerely penitent. Wesley ever maintained a higher view of the Lord's Supper than would reduce it merely to a symbol or a witness. It was a channel of grace to those who by faith appropriated its benefits, and consistently with this view he communed on an average of every five days for most of his long life. He distinguished the priestly from the prophetic ministry, restricting the administration of the sacraments to ordained clergymen but authorizing laymen to serve in the prophetic office as preachers. This stricture on his preachers was to become the cause of severe tensions, for there were few episcopally ordained clergymen in Methodism, and the growing membership came to demand the Sacraments at the hands of their own pastors. This demand, along with the peculiar needs of American Methodists after the American Revolution, finally led the precise, yet practical, Wesley to ordain a limited number of his preachers, and even to ordain Dr. Coke superintendent of the work in America. He was supported in this irregularity by a conviction of years' standing that the Scriptures make no distinction between bishops and presbyters. This step all but led to

---

21. J. Wesley, *Journal*. Epworth Press, London; v. 3, 434.

rupture with his brother, Charles, who was more ardently Anglican than John. As was Charles' habit on occasions happy or otherwise, he resorted to verse, in this instance to express his disapproval with this bit of sarcasm:

> *How easily are bishops made*
> *By man or woman's whim!*
> *Wesley his hands on Coke hath laid,*
> *But who laid hands on him?* [22]

Charles saw this move as a step away from the Church of England, as indeed it proved to be, although the formal break from the Church did not come during the lifetime of the Wesleys.

Nearing the end of the quest

He had sat at the feet of many instructors and had read many books. He had been a sacerdotalist, a mystic, a legalist, all in turns—nay, all together! And yet, through all these stages, he had persistently misread the true order of the spiritual world. He believed that a changed life was not the fruit of forgiveness, but its cause. Good works, he said, come before forgiveness and constituted the title to it; they did not come after and represent its effects.[23]

Thus does Fitchett summarize Wesley's fruitless quest for rest of soul by devious routes that seemed good to prideful man because they promised salvation through human capacity and effort. Having exhausted himself in all such efforts, Wesley is about to make the discovery that salvation is by grace on God's part, through an answering faith on man's part; and that even this faith is not of man but of God.

The faith by which man finds rest in God, Wesley had now learned, is not the bare, intellectual effort of the Oxford rationalist; nor is it the fuzzy subjectivism of the mystic's moods in which for a period he had floundered; nor yet the Georgia formalist's scrupulous adherence to hoary ritual; nor even the legalist's arduous and compulsive efforts to achieve holiness through asceticism and good works, such as had harried Wesley for a weary decade.

Wesley's tutor in the way of faith was the pious and learned

---

22. Quoted by Gerald Kennedy, *The Methodist Way of Life.* © 1958 by Prentice-Hall, Inc., Englewood Cliffs, New Jersey; p. 52.
23. W. H. Fitchett, *Wesley and His Century,* Eaton & Mains, New York; p. 128.

Moravian, Peter Bohler. The two met in February, 1738, a few days after Wesley's return from his disappointing Georgia venture and during Bohler's stopover in England on his way to Georgia as a missionary.

The first truth Peter Bohler, by the Spirit, conveyed to John Wesley was the basic evangelical fact that salvation is through faith alone. Before giving his assent to this claim, the devout logician, Wesley, demanded proof from Scripture; and empiricist that he was, demanded also the testimony of experience. Both demands were met, and he intellectually accepted the doctrine. Then, upon Bohler's insistance, Wesley reluctantly preached what he had not experienced himself. But he was a sincere seeker and his preaching salvation by faith was effective!

The second lesson Bohler taught Wesley was that the work of faith is instantaneous. Turning again to search the Scriptures, Wesley was astonished to find, as he said, "scarce any instances there of other than instantaneous conversions; scarce any so slow as that of St. Paul, who was three days in the pangs of the new birth." But did instantaneous conversions still occur, or were they reserved to Bible times and personages? Again, Wesley demanded the test of experience, and Bohler produced several witnesses to instantaneous conversion. "Here ended my dispute," Wesley wrote. "I could only cry out, 'Lord, help thou my unbelief.' " [24]

This was in late April of 1738. Dawn was about to break. A month later would come the heart-warming sunburst of faith, perhaps brighter and warmer because Wesley had explored to his own *dis*satisfaction every way by which God is sought but cannot be found, except the fleshly lowlands of naturalism. To him there was no lure in that direction, but the highlands of faith beckoned.

It is difficult to comprehend how Wesley could have met and overcome the many counter-influences that later were to oppose the revival, without the wide and varied explorations he had made by his own efforts to find the way of faith. In an introductory section of the *Journal*, Editor Curnock turns all of Wesley's wandering to the profit of his later ministry, saying:

---

24. J. Wesley, *Journal.* Epworth Press, London; v. 1, 455.

This strange story of pilgrimage had its stages, its discipline, its instruction in faith and righteousness, its prophecies of the future. Nothing in the long journey from the town of Legality to the Cross was lost. Not only Methodism, but the whole Christian Church, is the richer today because of all the ways in which John Wesley, during these years, was led and humbled and proved.[25]

---

25. *Ibid.*, v. 1, 35.

CHAPTER FOUR

The Witness Received: Aldersgate and Beyond

Charles Wesley preceded his brother, John, by three days in finding what John, in reporting Charles' conversion, called "rest to his soul." And in these three days, according to his own testimony, John had "continual sorrow and heaviness of heart." It was during these days that he wrote as follows to a friend who evidently was in like distress:

> I know that I too deserve nothing but wrath, being full of all abominations; and having no good thing in me to atone for them, or to remove the wrath of God. All my works, my righteousness, my prayers, need an atonement for themselves....
> Yet I hear a voice (and is it not the voice of God?) saying, "Believe, and thou shalt be saved. He that believeth is passed from death unto life."[1]

In his *Journal*, Wesley records these three events of Wednesday, May 24, 1738: In the early morning he received encouragement from Scripture, one passage being, "Thou art not far from the Kingdom of God"; in the afternoon at worship in St. Paul's Cathedral he was impressed by the anthem, "Out of the deep have I called unto thee" (*Psalm 130*); the third event we give in the words of Wesley himself:

> In the evening I went very unwillingly to a society in Aldersgate Street, where one was reading Luther's preface to the *Epistle to the Romans*. About a quarter before nine, while he was describing the change which God works in the heart through faith in Christ, I felt my heart strangely warmed. I felt I did trust in Christ, Christ alone for salvation; and an assurance was given me that He had taken away *my* sins, even *mine*, and saved *me* from the law of sin and death.[2]

I believe

But a fourth event of that day is recorded by Charles rather than John. This incident followed John's Aldersgate crisis by about an

---

1. J. Wesley, *Journal*. Epworth Press, London; v. 1, 464 *et seq.*
2. *Ibid.*, v. 1, 475.

hour. Charles was not present at the little service in Aldersgate Street that evening, but was convalescing from an illness in the house of a friend on Little Britain Street, hardly more than a stone's throw away. About ten o'clock that night John and a company of friends came singing up the street to Charles' sick room. Upon entering the room, John announced to his brother, "I believe." [3] As reported above, John wrote of the Aldersgate experience in his *Journal*, "I felt. . . ." Aldersgate involved both the *feeling* of experience and the *believing* of faith, and ever since the synthesis of faith and feeling has been important in the lives of Wesley's spiritual descendants.

After John had made the glad announcement to his brother, Charles records in his *Journal*, "We sang the hymn with great joy," evidently referring to the hymn he had written the day before in celebration of his own conversion the Sunday preceding.[4] Interestingly enough, both phases of Christian experience to which John had witnessed that night, the subjective factor of feeling and the more objective factor of knowledge by faith, had been combined by Charles in the fifth line of a stanza which we quote:

> *O how shall I the goodness tell,*
> *Father, which thou to me hast showed?*
> *That I a child of wrath and hell,*
> *I should be called a child of God,*
> *Should know, should feel my sins forgiv'n,*
> *Blest with this antepast of heav'n.*

And this hymn started Methodism singing its way around the world.

Was Aldersgate important?

Some have belittled the significance of what happened in the soul of John Wesley at Aldersgate. Elmer T. Clark points out that Coleridge suggested a passing "throb of sensibility" was what Wesley there experienced; Southey, that he suffered an attack of indigestion; and others, that the experience came as aftermath of the unhappy termination of Wesley's Georgia romance.[5] It seems that non-evangelical writers especially are prone to attempt to explain away the

---

3. C. Wesley, *Journal of the Rev. Charles Wesley, A.M.: The Early Journal, 1736-1739.* Robert Culley, London; p. 153.
4. Charles Wesley's "Conversion Hymn," rarely found in American hymnals. See *Hymns of the Living Faith*, Light and Life Press, Winona Lake; No. 204.
5. Elmer T. Clark, *The Warm Heart of John Wesley*. Association of Methodist Historical Societies, New York; p. 31.

spiritual significance of Aldersgate, and therefore it brings no surprise that in our century the Catholic scholar-priest, Piette, strongly contends that the Aldersgate event was not a crisis in Wesley's religious life. But Clark, in the book, *The Warm Heart of John Wesley*, carefully and effectively answers Piette and all others who will not admit in Wesley's Aldersgate experience the manifestation of God in the soul of man. In a previous chapter we have noted that Wesley's generation viewed any religion of the Spirit as "enthusiasm," and Clark makes this trenchant comment, "In any century save the deistical 18th and the humanistic 20th, Christians would have said that God touched the man's heart." [6]

Even those who do accept the spiritual significance of Aldersgate differ in their interpretations of what actually happened in that heart-warming crisis. According to the usual interpretation, John Wesley had not been a child of God until he was then converted. But Clark makes Wesley's conviction of sin preceding Aldersgate a conviction of inner sinfulness rather than of sins committed; of his state of sin rather than his acts of sin.

At first thought Clark's interpretation seems to fit the context of Wesley's spiritual pilgrimage to this point. Certainly the evidence is convincing that prior to Aldersgate Wesley had not been delivered from the principle of sin within, and one finds it a bit difficult to maintain that at no time during the decade or more of his earnest quest for holiness did he have that measure of faith and grace sufficient to enable him to overcome temptation by believing upon and obeying his Lord. But further examination of the record suggests that during this period Wesley was living in earnest but futile legalism. One living an outwardly righteous life, as best that is possible without saving grace, may indeed be keenly aware of the inner principle of sin. With Isaiah he may sense that "the whole head is sick, and the whole heart faint"; with no soundness "from the sole of the foot even unto the head," but only "wounds, and bruises, and putrefying sores."

Beating the air before Aldersgate

Searching Wesley's *Journal* for evidence of his state, one is impressed by the great lengths to which Wesley went in self-discipline

---
6. *Ibid.*, p. 64.

and legalistic striving for perfection. At intervals he caught brief flashes of sunshine, but defeat and failure were his prevailing mood. While in Georgia, struggling with the problem of whether he should marry "Miss Sophy" of Savannah, he prayed for resignation to God's will, "whatever that might be," and then he was "in a new world"; but in his very rejoicing he became "exceeding fearful" lest he lose this blessing "by want of thankfulness" or "of care to improve it." [7] When Sophy later had pledged herself to another, he was plunged into despair and could not pray; but finally, without words or even lucid thought, he did look to Christ, who "so far took the cup from me," he wrote, "that I drank so deeply of it no more." [8]

Having promised God he would witness freely and without shame to the gospel of Christ on a visit among strangers in Charleston, Wesley reported that "by God's assistance" he was able to do this in any company.[9] On another occasion ease and idle but harmless conversation had so weakened him that he sensed that he was an easy prey to temptation; but God gave him "new life," he said, "and I again rejoiced in His strength." [10]

Shortly thereafter, on shipboard returning to England, he was for several days oppressed with a foreboding of disaster. But he wrote, "I cried earnestly for help, and it pleased God, in a moment, to restore peace to my soul." He then had the desire not to forget the experience "till I attain another manner of spirit," he said; "a spirit equally willing to glorify God by life or by death"; and he declared this exacting standard, that whoever is uneasy on any account other than physical pain, "carries in himself his own conviction, that he is so far an unbeliever." He proceeded then even further to assert that close examination in such instances will show, that "beside the general want of faith, every particular uneasiness is evidently owing to the want of some particular Christian temper." [11] This position bears the stamp of a legalist, harried by scrupulosity, who condemns himself for not reaching some absolute and humanly unattainable standard.

In the clear light and cheering warmth of his Aldersgate experience,

---

7. J. Wesley, *Journal.* Epworth Press, London; v. 1, 317.
8. *Ibid.*, v. 1, 335.
9. *Ibid.*, v. 1, 349.
10. *Ibid.*, v. 1, 412 *et seq.*
11. *Ibid.*, v. 1, 413 *et seq.*

Wesley recorded his estimate of his religious state throughout all stages of his life to that event. He described himself in the period before Aldersgate as in the condition portrayed by Paul in *Romans* 7, and applied passages therefrom to himself. He said that during that period he was "beating the air." In this synopsis of his religious life which he wrote shortly after Aldersgate, Wesley reported that during his recent years of earnest questing after holiness he was in bondage to sin, serving it unwillingly whereas in earlier years he had served sin willingly. "I fell, and rose, and fell again," he wrote. "Sometimes I was overcome, and in heaviness; sometimes I overcame, and was in joy. For as in the former state I had some foretastes of the terrors of the law, so had I in this, of the comforts of the gospel." He called the struggle one between nature and grace; and admitted many answers to his prayers, especially when he was in trouble, and many "short anticipations of the life of faith." But he insists that he was under the law, not grace, for he was "only striving with, not freed from sin"; nor had he the witness of the Spirit.[12]

It would seem that for more than ten years preceding Aldersgate, Wesley enjoyed no constant or consistent spiritual victory and had no assurance that he was a child of God. His state presents the not unfamiliar picture of the seeker who, in his quest for God, follows now one route and then another through weary months and long years of faithfulness without faith, of duty without victory; catching now and again a glimpse of what victory could mean, only to lapse at once into failure and despair.

Until Aldersgate, servant but not son

In congregations of devoutly earnest people will often be found one or more such honest souls that labor along the difficult path of duty, striving in their own strength to serve God but, for all their arduous efforts—or because of them—failing to break through the barrier of doubt to faith's victory. Their problem is not the doubt that arises from wilful disobedience; seldom is it intellectual doubt concerning the claims of Scriptural Christianity. They live above outbroken sin and have an orthodox faith, but a trusting faith eludes their worried search. This seems to have been the religious state of John Wesley before that night in Aldersgate in late May of 1738.

---

12. *Ibid.*, v. 1, 470 *et seq.*

But there is reason to suspect that Wesley may have painted the picture of his religious state before Aldersgate in colors too somber, both in the repeated observations he made in his *Journal* while in his periods of legalistic distress, and in his retrospective evaluations of the valleys he had traversed, viewed from the spiritual hilltop of Aldersgate. At any rate, in later life he moderated some rather extreme statements he had written on the high seas when homeward bound from Georgia in January of 1738, smarting under the failure of his mission. Then he had lamented that he who had gone to America to convert others was not converted himself; decades later he wrote, "I am not sure of this." Then he had asserted that notwithstanding his outwardly righteous life and his ardent devotion, he was without faith in Christ; later he wrote, "I had even then the faith of a servant, though not of a son." Then he had declared, "I am a child of wrath"; later when making these revisions, he tersely added, "I believe not." [13]

The second of these revisions is illuminated by a sermon on faith that Wesley preached in his eighties, wherein he modified the absolute position he had held fifty years earlier by allowing now that a man might lack the assurance of sins forgiven and not be "a child of the devil"; that he might rather be a servant, accepted as one "who feareth God, and worketh righteousness," and who will receive one day the adoption of a son unless he "halt by the way." [14] The faithful without faith, then, will receive faith *if he continues faithful.*

In the mellower light of life's late afternoon Wesley seems to have discerned that in his pre-Aldersgate floundering he had indeed been on the way, although he had not yet arrived; that he had been a dutiful servant but not a trusting son. And the Aldersgate experience had brought him into his inheritance as a son.

Struggles after Aldersgate

Many who ascribe to Aldersgate the revolutionary change in John Wesley from a floundering priestly legalist to a well organized, confident and intense prophet and evangelist, overlook his period of strug-

---

13. These three comments, made by Wesley in correcting an edition of his *Works*, were missed by the printer but later included in Jackson's edition of 1829-31. See *Journal*, v. 1, 422-423, and Editor Curnock's footnotes thereto.
14. J. Wesley, *Sermons on Several Occasions.* Phillips & Hunt, New York; v. 2, 385, *et seq.*

gle and vacillation that soon followed his heart-warming. His sins committed had been forgiven, but the roots of sin remained to trouble him with hot temptation, moods of depression and sore testing of faith, under which once he so far broke as to assert that he no longer had the assurance he received at Aldersgate.

He had early to learn that his relationship as a child of God did not depend upon constant joy. The very evening of his conversion he had to fight the battle of faith against feeling. Of this conflict he reported:

> But it was not long before the enemy suggested, "This cannot be faith; for where is thy joy?" Then was I taught that peace and victory over sin are essential to faith in the Captain of our salvation; but that, as to transports of joy that usually attend the beginning of it, especially in those who have mourned deeply, God sometimes giveth, sometimes withholdeth them, according to the counsels of His own will.[15]

After reaching home that night, he was "much buffeted with temptation," which he drove away with prayer again and again. The following comment on the difference between the former struggles and the present is revealing: "And I herein found the difference between this and my former state chiefly consisted. I was striving, yea, fighting with all my might under the law, as well as under grace, but then I was sometimes, if not often, conquered; now, I was always conqueror." [16]

As on the day of his conversion, John Wesley the next day received great blessing from the anthem at St. Paul's. This anthem began, "My song shall be always of the loving-kindness of the Lord." Wesley wrote, "Yet the enemy injected a fear, 'if thou doest believe, why is there not a more sensible change?'" To this he replied, "That I know not. But this I know, I have 'now peace with God.' And I sin not today, and Jesus my Master has forbid me to take thought for tomorrow." To meet the tempter's suggestion that any sort of fear proved that he believed not, he turned to Paul's statement, "Without were fightings, within were fears," and concluded, "well may fears be within me; but I must go on, and tread them under my feet." [17]

---
15. J. Wesley, *Journal.* Epworth Press, London; v. 1, 476.
16. *Ibid.*, v. 1, 476 *et seq.*
17. *Ibid.*, v. 1, 478.

Friday, the second day after his conversion, his soul "continued in peace, but yet in heaviness because of manifold temptations." A Moravian friend to whom he appealed advised him, "You must not fight with them, as you did before, but flee from them the moment they appear, and take shelter in the wounds of Jesus." And again he was encouraged by the anthem at St. Paul's.[18]

On Saturday he discovered that the want of prayer explained his want of joy, and by prayer his "spirit was enlarged" and he was "more than conqueror." Sunday he "waked in peace, but not in joy," and in the evening when attacked by friends as an enthusiast and seducer, he "was not moved to anger," but confessed that he had not a properly tender concern for his attackers.[19]

On Monday he was in company with Peter Bohler's first convert in England whose spiritual state was so advanced that Wesley said he was "tempted to doubt whether we had one faith"; but he steadied himself by maintaining that he knew by the fruits that God had given him a degree of faith. "For I have constant peace," he said, "not one uneasy thought." "And," he added, "I have freedom from sin; not one unholy desire."[20] But such a testimony was not sustained, as we shall see.

Wednesday, one week after Aldersgate, he had grieved the Spirit by lack of prayer, "and by speaking with sharpness instead of tender love of one that was not sound in the faith." His heaviness was not relieved until Thursday morning when, in helping another, God brought comfort to him.[21] There is no Friday entry, but the record shows that on Saturday came one of his old temptations, and he had scarce strength to pray, but upon praying "faintly" the temptation left him.[22]

Sunday was a day of great blessing which included among its activities, "calling sinners to repentance." There is no report for Monday, but on Tuesday his comfort, peace and joy were increased, which, he feared, had led him to presumption for in the evening a letter from Oxford threw him into great perplexity by its claim that "who-

---

18. *Ibid.*, v. 1, 478 *et seq.*
19. *Ibid.*, v. 1, 479 *et seq.*
20. *Ibid.*, v. 1, 481.
21. *Loc. cit.*
22. *Ibid.*, v 1, 482.

ever at any time felt any doubt or fear was not weak in faith, but had no faith at all." Turning to the Scriptures, Wesley found that Paul called the carnal Corinthians "babes in Christ" and even "the temple of God." He argued, then, that they must have had "some degree of faith; . . . though their faith was but weak." Scripture and prayer comforted this "babe in Christ," but a soreness at his heart told him the wound had not healed.[23]

On Wednesday, June 7, exactly two weeks after his conversion, he resolved that the time had come to visit the Moravians in Germany because, as he said, "My weak mind could not bear to be thus sawn asunder." His purpose in making the journey was to find help from "those holy men who were themselves living witnesses of the full power of faith." [24]

Before leaving England, Wesley went to Salisbury to take leave of his widowed mother, and on Sunday, June 11, preached his manifesto on "Salvation by Faith" to the University at St. Mary's Church, Oxford. Strange it is that Wesley made no mention of this event in his *Journal*. From Oxford he proceeded to London where he met his old friend, Ingham, and with him embarked for Germany.

Sin remains, but does not reign

The Aldersgate experience had brought Wesley the clear consciousness of the forgiveness of sins, but it had not brought freedom from sin's strivings within. Evidently he was not as yet clear, in terms of experience, in the distinction between justification and entire sanctification as successive operations of the Holy Spirit in the soul. But while at Herrnhut that amazing example of saintly spiritual insight among the Moravians, Christian David, told him, "the being justified is widely different from having the full assurance of faith," and notwithstanding the fact that the Moravian leader, Count Zinzendorf, held that justification and sanctification were one event (as the Count was later to tell Wesley), Christian David testified to Wesley that after his own justification he found that sin, "though it did not reign in me, did remain in me," as he so succinctly expressed it; and added, "I was continually tempted, though not overcome." [25]

---

23. *Loc. cit.*
24. *Ibid.*, v. 1, 482 et seq.
25. *Ibid.*, v. 2, 30.

John Wesley was keen in discrimination and could not but relate Christian David's experience after justification to his own post-Aldersgate condition when, at times, he was "in heaviness through manifold temptations," was in want of joy, tempted to doubt, had grieved the Spirit through failure to pray or through sharpness in speech, and was so "sawn asunder" by contending forces within him that he had to seek help in Germany if he were to "go on from faith to faith and 'from strength to strength.' " [26]

Among the Moravians Wesley gained insight and made discoveries that helped him, but he was not blinded to certain weaknesses within the movement by his admiration for the spirituality of some of its members. This spirituality, he was later to find, was too subjective and experience-dominated to be contained within any consistent doctrinal pattern.

Wesley returned to England in mid-September. He had received steadying instruction and for a time gave little if any evidence of inner struggles. In fact, he records little concerning his moods, either of joy or depression. He preached to different religious societies and in churches the pulpits of which were still open to him. Newgate Prison also received his ministry. Between the glow of Aldersgate and the heights of revival power that were manifested later in his labors, this period of his ministry was rather ordinary.

Struggles increase after Herrnhut

He had been in England less than a month, however, when again inner conflict was precipitated, to become even more severe than before his sojourn in Germany. On October 14, while on a visit in Oxford, he fell into a state of distressing spiritual perplexity. Heeding the command, "Examine yourselves, whether ye be in the faith," he resorted to Paul's standard, "If any man be in Christ, he is a new creature: old things are passed away; behold, all things are become new." From this examination he concluded that he was created anew in his judgments, his designs, his conversation, his actions, and that God had begun but had not finished making his desires new. Nevertheless, the old desires contrary to a new creature in Christ did not reign. Christian David had made this clear enough: after justification, sin *remains* but does not *reign*.

---

26. *Ibid.*, v. 1, 482.

Wesley then proceeded to a new test: Did he manifest the fruits of the Spirit? He found in his life a measure of some of them, but lack of others. Here are the results of his relentless self-examination:

> ... I cannot find in myself the love of God, or of Christ. Hence my deadness and wanderings in public prayer; hence it is that even in the Holy Communion I have frequently no more than a cold attention.
>
> Again, I have not that joy in the Holy Ghost; no settled, lasting joy. Nor have I such a peace as excludes the possibility either of fear or doubt. When holy men have told me I had no faith, I have often doubted whether I had or no. And those doubts have made me very uneasy, till I was relieved by prayer and the Holy Scriptures.
>
> Yet, upon the whole, although I have not yet that joy in the Holy Ghost, nor the full assurance of faith, much less am I, in the full sense of the words, 'in Christ a new creature;' I nevertheless trust that I have a measure of faith, and am 'accepted in the Beloved'; I trust 'the handwriting that was against me is blotted out,' and that I am 'reconciled to God' through His Son.[27]

A few days later he wrote to his brother in answer to Samuel's inquiry as to what he meant by being made a Christian. This letter is a bit more confident, but quite in line with the discouraging results of his self-analysis although approaching nearer a statement of the distinction between his present justified state and the fullness of the Spirit toward which he was striving. Here in part is his letter to Samuel:

> By a Christian, I mean one who so believes in Christ as that sin hath no more dominion over him; and in this obvious sense of the word I was not a Christian till May 24th last past. For till then sin had the dominion over me, although I fought with it continually; but, surely then from that time to this, it hath not, such is the free grace of God in Christ.... If you ask by what means I am made free? I answer, by faith in Christ; by such a sort or degree of faith as I had not till that day.... Some measure of this faith, which bringeth salvation or victory over sin, and which implies peace or trust in God through Christ, I now enjoy by His free mercy; though in very word it is in me but as a grain of mustard seed: for the ... seal of the Spirit, the love of God shed abroad in my heart, and producing joy in the Holy Ghost,

---

27. Ibid., v. 2, 89-91.

'joy which no man taketh away, joy unspeakable and full of glory,' —this witness of the Spirit I have not; but I patiently wait for it.[28]

The entry in Wesley's *Journal* for December 16, 1738, refers to and reviews his self-analysis of two months earlier in terms even less optimistic than either the original analysis or his letter to Samuel. The October analysis had said that he had the mark of a new creature because he judged himself to have no good thing abiding in him; now he says, "But I feel it not. Therefore there is in me still the old heart of stone." Then he had said he judged of happiness only in the enjoyment of God; now he writes, "But I still hanker after creature happiness. . . . I have more pleasure in eating and drinking, and in the company of those I love, than I have in God. I have a relish of earthly happiness. I have not a relish for heavenly. . . . Therefore there is in me still the carnal heart." Then he had said that his designs were those of a new creature; but now he confesses, "But a thousand little designs are daily stealing into my soul. This is my *ultimate* design—but *intermediate* designs are continually creeping in upon me. . . . Therefore my eye is not yet single; at least, not always so." The concluding paragraph graphically represents the presence within of the "double mind" that made him "unstable in all his ways":

> Again, my desires, passions, and inclinations in general were mixed; having something of Christ and something of earth. I love you, for instance. But my love is only partly spiritual and partly natural. Something of my own cleaves to that which is of God. Nor can I divide the earthly from the heavenly.[29]

On January 4, 1739, he reached the depths. Friends, he said, had called him mad for saying he was not a Christian a year ago, but on this day he bluntly wrote, "I am not a Christian now." He did not disclaim the experience of Aldersgate, but out of his despair he plaintively cried, "Indeed, what I might have been I know not, had I been faithful to the grace then given, when . . . I received such a sense of forgiveness of my sins as till then I never knew." He confessed to a love for the world, a lack of joy in the Holy Ghost, the absence of the peace of God, and concluded in utter discouragement, with this lament, "My works are nothing, my sufferings are nothing; I have

---

28. J. Wesley, *Letters.* Epworth Press, London; v. 1, 262 *et seq.*
29. J. Wesley, *Journal.* Epworth Press, London; v. 2, 115 *et seq.*

not the fruits of the Spirit of Christ. Though I have constantly used all the means of grace for twenty years, I am not a Christian." [30]

This entry of January 4 is introduced impersonally, thus, "One who had the form of godliness many years wrote the following reflections . . . ," and some might conclude therefore that Wesley was not giving his own but another's testimony. But his introduction to the December 16 entry likewise is impersonal, but so worded that its author is positively identified as Wesley. There can be no reasonable doubt that Wesley in the January 4 entry wrote of himself.

It may be that Wesley was suffering the rather normal reaction from his spiritual exaltation of the all-night love feast reported in his *Journal* for January 1.[31] Sixty of the brethren engaged in this service, and about three in the morning, the record says, "the power of God came mightily upon us, insomuch that many cried out for exceeding joy, and many fell to the ground." These latter may well have been Moravians, prostrating themselves before the Lord as was their custom.

Tyerman's explanation of the confession of failure would have it that Wesley had been too much among the Moravians, both in England and in Germany, and due to his high regard for Moravian piety had given too much credence to their experiences, some of them being genuinely spiritual but others of them plainly fanatical. He was caught in a labyrinth, said Tyerman, and must find his way out as best he could.

Strangely enough, with no further word about conflict, or of victory following the breaking of his grip of faith on January 4, the *Journal* proceeds objectively and briefly to record Wesley's activities, such as preaching in churches and the religious societies of London. And still we find no evidence of such success as was shortly to result from his labors.

Beyond Aldersgate

Something had happened to John Wesley at Aldersgate, as he then confidently announced and was later to confess, even out of his despair. His heart was strangely warmed, he trusted in Christ, and an

---

30. *Ibid.*, v. 2, 125 *et seq.*
31. *Ibid.*, v. 2, 121 *et seq.*

assurance was given him that even his sins were forgiven. But something happened after Aldersgate also, delivering him from the unexpected but entirely normal inner struggle between the old mind to sin and the newly implanted mind to righteousness—something that resolved the inner conflict and released his moral and spiritual energies for joyful and effective service. We are not able to point to a specific time or to circumstantial details marking this second deliverance, but there is evidence that the event occurred not long after Aldersgate—probably a matter of months, not years.

The evidence is two-fold. In the first place, there seems suddenly to have occurred, about ten months after Aldersgate, a marked change in the direction of Wesley's energies from inner conflict and strained service to tireless, irresistible and successful achievement in evangelism and in organizational generalship. Contrary to the usual claim of writers on John Wesley, Aldersgate did not mark the end of the too intense self-concern of his religion. The outward direction of his religious concern came a few months later, as study of his *Journal* makes clear. According to the evidence, this change took place somewhere between his sense of complete failure on January 4, 1739, and his self-committing response to Whitefield's call to the Bristol area late in March of the same year. Probably the change occurred in connection with his response to the call or his actual entry upon the task. What is the evidence?

The summons to Bristol was viewed, both by John Wesley and his Fetter Lane friends, as crucially affecting his future life. Curnock makes clear in a footnote to the March 27 entry in the *Journal* that Wesley at this period had premonitions of an early death.[32] The *Journal* itself reports several scriptures to which Wesley had opened in his search for guidance, and these in his mind connected death with his removal to Bristol. However, he cautiously noted, "whether this was permitted only for the trial of our faith, God knoweth, and the event will show." [33]

His entry for the next day, March 28, opens with the statement, "My journey was proposed to our society in Fetter Lane." Such, it should be explained, was in line with one of the orders of the Society

---

32. *Ibid.*, v. 2, 157, n. 1.
33. *Ibid.*, v. 2, 157.

which stipulated, "that any person who desires or designs to take a journey, shall first, if it be possible, have the approbation of the bands."[34] Evidently Wesley's own mind by this time was inclined toward Bristol, but Charles opposed the step. John's *Journal* states, "But my brother Charles would scarce hear the mention of it; till, appealing to the oracles of God, he received those words as spoken to himself, and answered not again: 'Son of man, behold, I take from thee the desire of thine eyes with a stroke: yet shalt thou not mourn or weep, neither shall thy tears run down.' "[35]

Because of division of opinion, the Fetter Lane group resorted to the lot, and it fell out that Wesley should go. May we observe that it is not inconceivable that God, even in the present dispensation in rare instances, might accommodate His dealings to the weakness of a man's faith, even as he did with Gideon in his age. The very splendid index to the Standard Edition of Wesley's *Journal*, it is interesting to note, lists no participation by Wesley in decisions by lot subsequent to this occasion. In this instance, the lot at least had served the purpose of achieving unanimity of consent that Wesley should respond to the Bristol call. But let it be remembered that all resorting to signs such as Gideon's fleece, the lot, or chance opening of Scripture to find God's will, is not the exercise of sturdy faith as some would boast, but is rather the symptom of spiritual immaturity.

It is not without significance that later, in preparing his *Journal* of this period for publication,[36] Wesley included in his March 28 entry the several thousand words he wrote his father four years earlier to justify his remaining in Oxford seclusion for the good of his own soul, rather than applying for the Epworth parish that he might minister to the needs of others as his father desired.[37] How different now his commitment to Bristol and the nearby Kingswood miners, from that callousness with which he had written his father concerning the Epworth parishioners, saying, "And He that took care of those poor

---

34. *Ibid.*, v. 2, 157, *n*. 3.
35. *Ibid.*, v. 2, 157 *et seq.*
36. John Wesley's *Journal* is not a record of daily happenings as they occurred, but an account in retrospect based upon his minutely detailed diary, his memory, and his subsequent observations; and sometimes it includes letters he wished to insert in the record. On occasion, even brief homilies were included. The *Journal* was published in sections, at intervals.
37. J. Wesley, *Journal*. Epworth Press, London; v. 2, 159-166.

sheep before you were born will not forget them when you are dead." It is clear from his *Journal* that John Wesley now contrasted his earlier self-centeredness with the Bristol venture, for by way of introducing the letter at this point, four or more years after its writing, Wesley said, "Perhaps it may be a satisfaction to some if, before I enter upon this new period of my life, I give the reasons why I preferred for so many years an University life before any other. . . . I have here, therefore, subjoined the letter I wrote several years ago. . . ." [38]

Wesley now sensed that his energies, heretofore restrained and even selfishly introverted—in Oxford, perhaps Georgia and even Fetter Lane—are to be redirected to the task of saving souls other than his own. What he had refused his dying father he now yields to his Lord and Master. Irrelevant indeed was this letter's insertion at this point if his Oxford self-centeredness and his recent reluctance to leave Fetter Lane safety, had not contrasted sharply in his own mind with his entering *"upon this new period of my life,"* which had begun with what we conceive was his full self-commitment to God for unreserved service.

Quite in line with such a crucial step as we believe was the Bristol decision, are these terse comments of Charles on John's departure: "A great power was among us. He offered himself willingly to whatsoever the Lord should appoint. The next day he set out, commended by us to the grace of God. He left a blessing behind. I desired to die with him." [39]

The Spirit of the Lord is upon me

With the beginning of John Wesley's Bristol ministry came a noticeable change, both in the tempo and the melody of his life. Herein is our most convincing evidence of a second profound spiritual event in Wesley's pilgrimage at this point. We have suggested other considerations which point to such a revolution within the soul of John Wesley, but they are of little weight apart from the change that took place in his life and ministry. From the somewhat ordinary ministry that had been his since Aldersgate, the record changes abruptly to action, courage, confidence, sermon on sermon of revival power; moodiness and self-analysis are gone; there is no hint now of soul

---

38. *Ibid.*, v. 2, 159.
39. Charles Wesley, *The Early Journal*, 1736-1739, Robert Culley, London; p. 227.

struggle, and soul saving becomes dominant over controversy. Events moved rapidly in a succession of climaxes after Wesley's open-air sermon in the Bristol brick yard on April 2, 1739.

Later that month, after preaching three times in one day in the fields to an estimated aggregate of fourteen thousand people, and after preaching twice in church services and leading a love feast in the evening, he could write in his *Journal*, "Oh how has God renewed my strength! who used ten years ago to be so faint and weary with preaching *twice* in one day!" [40] The following month the consciousness of power so came upon him that of one occasion in his ministry at that time he said, "methought I could have cried out (in another sense than poor vain Archimedes), 'Give me where to stand, and I will shake the earth!'" [41] It was about this time that, in explaining his irregularly preaching in others' parishes, he said, "I look upon all the world as my parish." [42]

After mid-June of 1739 he continued his vigorous evangelism, with periods in London and journeyings in the west of England and in Wales. The first suggestion of a flagging of his energies that we glean from his *Journal* appears in his account of going to a society in the London area on June 15, as he said, "weary in body and faint in spirit." But even in that service revival power was present.[43] After returning to Bristol after a London journey of eight days, he found spiritual decline, but quickening came with his return. Again he went to a preaching appointment with no lift of inspiration. "I . . . had no life or spirit in me," he said, "and was much in doubt whether God would not lay me aside and send other labourers into his harvest." He began the service in weakness, but found that God could use him in power.[44] On both of these occasions his distress seems to have resulted from declining strength and a feeling of ineffectiveness, and not from any disorder in his spiritual condition or personal relationship with God. And revival continued!

November of 1739 and the months following brought serious concern for the Fetter Lane Society because of the poison of Moravian

---

40. J. Wesley, *Journal*. Epworth Press, London; v. 2, 186.
41. Ibid., v. 2, 201.
42. Ibid., v. 2, 218.
43. Ibid., v. 2, 221.
44. Ibid., v. 2, 226 *et seq.*

mysticism and the doctrinal confusion which were spreading from it to other areas. But Wesley held steady and maintained a consistent position, with no sign of spiritual perplexity or inner confusion. Of a service near Bristol, he said, "I took occasion to describe that wilderness state, that state of doubts, and fears, and strong temptation, which so many go through, though in different degrees, after they have received remission of sins." [45] How well he understood this wilderness from which he had so recently emerged! Wesley was qualified through experience to guide those in despair because of the Moravian teaching that one weak in faith *has no faith*, and that everything is done for one when he is justified without need of a further work of grace.

Finally, in June of 1740 he preached at the Foundery a series of sermons by which he sought to meet the Moravian issue and steady the faith of those who were wavering under the influence of false teaching. In one of these sermons he urged those who sensed sin still within, and had been shaken by the teaching that therefore it could not be they were justified, not to cast away their confidence. This sermon so clearly reflected Wesley's own earlier post-conversion condition and so confidently promised deliverance to his distraught hearers as to bring assurance that Wesley had traversed the road himself and already had come into his full liberty.[46]

The break with the Moravians came July 20, 1740, when John Wesley and about a score of others who agreed with him in doctrine and experience withdrew to the Foundery, leaving to the Moravians the Fetter Lane Society which Wesley had organized shortly before Aldersgate. Throughout this distressing transition Wesley maintained inner constancy and steady faith.

Introducing the question of Wesley's second crisis on page 54 we suggested two lines of evidence. One line, the course of personal Christian experience as reflected in his mood and his ministry, we have now traced in some detail. The other line of evidence may seem to be less striking in its contrasts with Wesley's past beliefs, but it is significant. That line follows the development of Wesley's doctrinal distinctions concerning two works of grace, a development beginning

---
45. *Ibid.*, v. 2, 339.
46. *Ibid.*, v. 2, see p. 359.

soon after Aldersgate. The discussion of the doctrinal aspect belongs logically to Chapter Six where it will be found in the section, *Is there deliverance from sin?*

Blazing the trail of Christian experience

There has been much speculation about Wesley's own experience of the believer's deliverance from the principle of sin within. These are the questions that are raised: Did Wesley ever reach that deliverance? If so, at what point in his life? The present writer believes that his thesis, according to which the deliverance came in connection with Wesley's Bristol venture and the attending release of unprecedented power along with deliverance from his former introspective agonizings, is better supported by all the facts than those speculations which seek to identify the event with some nebulous moment of intensified emotional exaltation. We do not date the event, but it is documented by the *Journal* which reflects the change from strain to poise in his inner life, and from casual success to deep-moving and far-reaching revival through his ministry.

Throughout Wesley's pre-Aldersgate and post-Aldersgate period, up to and even beyond the turning-point of Bristol, one gathers that he was clearer in his intellectual comprehension and more explicit in preaching the truths of inward religion, than he was in apprehending those truths in his own experience by a living faith in Christ. Most of the distinctive truths that later characterized his teachings were at least implicit in his earlier preaching.

That the truths of religion were thus clearer to Wesley in doctrine than in experience is understandable. Both the culture of Wesley's age and his own education in that culture maintained that religion is moderate and gradual, and to claim divine assurance of the consummation of salvation in the forgiveness of sin or of sin's cleansing was rankest fanaticism. While it is true that the church distinguished the two doctrines of justification and sanctification, their sequence had been confused even by Wesley who for years had diligently sought holiness that he might merit justification. He was later to clarify the distinction between sin as an act to be forgiven in justification, and sin as a corrupting inner condition to be cleansed in entire sanctification subsequently to justification.

An idea of the distance Wesley must travel from Oxford to Aldersgate is caught from reading the following fragment from Jeremy Taylor's *Holy Living and Holy Dying,* one of Wesley's favorite books at the period in his life when his questing led him the way of legalism:

> No man is to reckon his pardon immediately upon his return from sin to the beginnings of a good life, but is to begin his hopes and degrees of confidence according as sin dies in him, and grace lives, as the habits of sin lessen, and righteousness grows. . . .
>
> . . . For we must know, that God pardons our sins by parts; as our duty increases, and our care is more prudent and active, so God's anger decreases: and yet it may be the last sin you committed made God unalterably resolve to send upon you some judgment. . . .
>
> A true penitent must all the days of his life pray for pardon, and never think the work completed till he dies. . . . And whether God hath forgiven us or no, we know not, and how far we know not; and all that we have done is not of sufficient worth to obtain pardon: therefore still pray, and still be sorrowful for ever having done it, and for ever watch against it; and then those beginnings of pardon which are working all the way, will at last be perfected in the day of the Lord.[47]

Not until shortly before Aldersgate, and then not through personal experience, but by new light on Scripture struck for him by the teaching and testimony of Moravians, could Wesley believe that an instantaneous work of grace in the human heart is possible, or that the Christian may have the assurance within his own consciousness that such a work has been wrought in him. Aldersgate made these truths, recently accepted by his intellect, immediate and living facts of his experience.

But Wesley, even after Aldersgate, seems not clearly to have distinguished the stages of Christian experience which later he would so clearly sketch for others. He had not made his own journey to Aldersgate—and beyond—by any such chart as outlines for us since Wesley the pattern of a developing Christian experience. May we say that having made the journey, Wesley looked back over the route by which he had found so full and satisfying a salvation, and carefully studied in the light of Scripture his own and the experiences of many

---

47. *The Whole Works of the Right Rev. Jeremy Taylor, D.D.* Longmans, Green & Co., New York; v. 3, 210 *et seq.*

Methodist converts. His empirical data factually and logically fitted Scripture's teaching; and from his Biblical knowledge, his empirical observations, his personal knowledge of inward religion, and his logical analyses, the Wesleyan formulation of the progress of Christian experience took shape.

Familiar to us after two centuries of the Wesleyan tradition is this pattern of Christian experience which begins with the crisis of conversion; proceeds by growth in grace to a second crisis of full deliverance from the inward principle of sin, and continues in a process of "perfecting holiness in the fear of God." But how remarkable a providence it was that Wesley, with no marked trail to guide his quest, should find in the maze of criss-crossing paths of rationalism, mysticism, ritualism, and legalism, the way of faith to lead him out of the spiritual darkness and religious frigidity of eighteenth-century England to the light and warmth of Aldersgate!—and from that point, through the hazards of the faltering walk of a "babe in Christ," to the full stride of Christian maturity.

Could it be that his own uncharted course to Aldersgate, and beyond to the fulness of faith, contributed to his later reticence to open his soul's deepest crisis to public scrutiny, lest his early flounderings through the tangled wilderness be judged by the test of his own mature formulations of the normal progress of the Christian?

Conclusion

There are those who liken what happened to Wesley at Aldersgate to what happened to the disciples of Jesus at Pentecost seventeen centuries earlier. In this, they are mistaken. The resemblance of Wesley's life and ministry to the disciples following Pentecost appears, not in London's Aldersgate on May 24, 1738, but somewhere near the date of Wesley's commitment to field-preaching in Bristol's brickyard on April 2, 1739, when he spoke from that text of peculiar significance for the occasion, "The Spirit of the Lord is upon me." The results in Wesley's life from that event are unsurpassed in any life since martyrdom of the Apostle Paul.

Wesley's crisis of Aldersgate is dated and documented; we have noted that the later crisis is not dated but is fully documented in the detailed record of his subsequent achievements. Without the Aldersgate crisis, the later full surrender could not have been made, even as without that surrender Wesley could never have become what he was or have achieved what he did. Although yielding qualified assent to biographers who label Aldersgate the continental divide in Wesley's life, and to historians such as Lecky who have made it a turning point in history, we still remember that only after Bristol did Wesley "shake the earth."

Summary

In this and the preceding chapter, John Wesley's religious and spiritual development has been sketched in these four stages:

1. *Indifference.* This was his early, religiously carefree period when he was Christian in name, but had little more than a form of godliness. This period extended roughly to his senior year in the University. He was a generally good church member, but without a saving knowledge of God, which lack caused him little concern.

2. *Anguished quest.* In his last year as an undergraduate, he faced the choice of his life's work and began to think more seriously on life and religion. For a decade or more to come he would be seeking holiness by devious routes of his own planning by which to achieve a goodness that would justify him before God. These routes included reason, mysticism, legalism, ritualism—all of which led him only to despair.

3. *Discovery, but inner conflict.* At thirty-five years of age John Wesley passed through the crisis of conversion and received the assurance of sins forgiven in response to faith, but was dismayed then to find that conflict continued with alternating victory and failure. He was many times in anguish of spirit because of sin within which, although it did not *reign*, did *remain*. And he earnestly sought full deliverance.

4. *Spiritual conquest.* Some time after the Aldersgate conversion experience, Wesley's *Journal* reveals a quite complete redirection of his energies from inner conflict to outer conquest. Cleansed of that inner principle of sin that had exhausted his energies in a civil war within him, Wesley's life at long last could direct the energies of body, mind and soul to the great task of Kingdom building. The isolated event when this revolutionary redirection of his life forces

occurred eludes our search, but the evidence in his life's fruitage points to its appearance in connection with his full commitment to the call to Bristol in the spring of 1739, about ten months after Aldersgate.

Chapter Five

Methodism's Conquering Witness: By What Means?

Wesley . . . had personally gone through the whole gamut of religious exercise. He was familiar with all schools of religious thought. . . . He was familiar, indeed, with every school of theology and every variety of ecclesiastical use. He knew men, cities, books, churches, history. No development of human nature and no turn of ecclesiastical polity found him unprepared.[1]

Such was the remarkable preparation by schooling and experience of the man who was destined after thirty-five years of disappointing mediocrity to begin a world-shaking and world-shaping career that has rarely been equaled. The author of the above paragraph is Fitchett who points to the puzzling but significant fact that as his father's curate at Wroote for two years, a decade before Aldersgate, John Wesley had "all the human qualifications for success as a minister in at least as high a degree as at any stage in his whole life. And yet he failed . . . !"[2] And Wesley himself wrote of his insipid ministry at Wroote, "I preached much but saw no fruit of my labors."[3]

John Wesley, a man of exceptional abilities and opportunities but of ordinary attainments until thirty-five years of age, reached the heights of sustained achievement only after his spiritual journey from Aldersgate to Bristol. This fact convincingly argues for the truth of Fitchett's claim that his secret of success was spiritual, and lay not in any combination of transcendent natural abilities that made him a genius.[4] By the well-known words he uttered on his deathbed, "The best of all is, God is with us," he declared the truth, not alone of God's presence and power in that hour, but as well during the fifty-three glorious years he had lived since Aldersgate and Bristol.

---

1. W. H. Fitchett, *Wesley and His Century*. Eaton & Mains, New York; p. 304.
2. *Ibid.*, p. 71.
3. As quoted by Tyerman, *The Life and Times of the Rev. John Wesley*. Harper & Bros., New York; v. 1, 57.
4. W. H. Fitchett, *Wesley and His Century*. Eaton & Mains, New York; p. 9.

It is the purpose of this chapter to review in brief certain outstanding events and features of the powerful witness of Methodism that developed so largely under John Wesley's direct authority and influence.

By all means save some

In the *First Corinthian* letter the Apostle declares his passion to save others by preaching the gospel and ministering God's grace, not in a constrained and fixed fashion that would limit it to a particular class of men, but with a freedom of method adapting it to every man's condition and station. Although free, Paul made himself the servant of all; to gain those under the law, he discarded the law (nevertheless being obedient to Christ's law of love); to gain the weak, he became weak. He sums it all up by saying, "I am made all things to all men, that I might by all means save some."

A long succession of preachers stretches across the centuries from the Apostle Paul to our day. In this succession, too few have followed Paul's example of flexibility and adaptability in method and emphasis, and at the same time have held fast "the form of sound words." Many, including even some who would guard the truths committed to them, have sought to constrain the life of the Spirit within fixed forms, and to control it by humanly prescribed procedures. Now and again in history the quickening Spirit has broken through the forms to bring revival, but after a time priestly uniformity and what John Wesley called "painted fire" have succeeded again in subduing prophetic fire.

In the early eighteenth century three men appeared with Paul's passion to reach lost men and "by all means save some." As noted in in an earlier chapter, icy regularity was the order of all things religious in eighteenth-century England, with "enthusiasm" a cardinal evil to be suppressed by legal decree or illegal persecution. All of them Oxford graduates and ordained clergymen of the Church of England, these three men were called mad enthusiasts because they would free the gospel from the confining gothic arches of established religion and release it to the masses in street and field, to the sick and unclean in hovel and gutter, to the wretched and condemned in Bedlam and prison. These "irregulars" were John and Charles Wesley, and George Whitefield.

A light shined in the prison

One morning in July, 1738, the brutal London mob that had gathered at Tyburn to witness the popular spectacle of public hangings beheld a strange event. As the death-cart bearing its ten victims arrived below the gallows after its long parade through crowded streets from Newgate prison, a young clergyman left his carriage on the outskirts of the throng and pressed his way to the death-cart. Climbing upon it, he was received with deep and tender feeling by the condemned felons. When the prison chaplain would follow the clergyman, the prisoners begged him to stay away, and the mob accommodatingly forced him back.

For days preceding the execution, the clergyman had visited these felons in prison, had counseled them and prayed with them, and, after instruction, had administered to all save one the Lord's Supper; for most of them under his ministry had given evidence of a change of heart and of hope in Christ. Only last night, he and a humble layman had suffered themselves to be locked in the death-cell with the condemned men to comfort them with prayer and song. And now the clergyman stood with them under the gallows to support them in their last tragic moments. In his *Journal* he reported concerning them:

> They were all cheerful, full of comfort, peace, and triumph. . . . None showed any natural terror of death; no fear, or crying, or tears. . . . I never saw such calm triumph, such incredible indifference to dying.

And of himself he said, "That hour under the gallows was the most blessed hour of my life." [5]

This "prison evangelist" was none other than Charles Wesley, Oxford graduate and master of arts, and an ordained Anglican clergyman. Already he had been on a mission to Georgia with General Oglethorpe. Notwithstanding these facts of his life, he had found assurance of his own salvation only two months before winning to Christ these ten condemned felons! An earlier chapter noted his conversion on Whitsunday, 1738.

Charles' zeal to save those in prison continued to his old age.

---

5. C. Wesley, *The Early Journal*, 1736-1739. Robert Culley, London; see pp. 191-194.

Nearly a half-century after the gallows incident related in this chapter, he published a collection of "Prayers for Condemned Malefactors," upon one copy of which the author in his distinctive hand had written, "These prayers were answered, Thursday, April 28th, 1785, on nineteen malefactors, who had all died penitent." And he had added, "Not unto me, O Lord, not unto me." [6] He was then seventy-eight years of age!

Interestingly enough, a few months earlier than the gallows scene in which Charles Wesley was a principal figure, another prison conversion had occurred under the ministry of his brother, even before John himself had received the clear assurance of faith. This was during John's tutelage under Peter Bohler who had advised him, now intellectually convinced of the doctrine, to preach salvation by faith. Wesley drew back from offering to others that of which he himself had no assurance deep in his own consciousness. But Bohler urged him further, saying, "Preach faith until you have it; and then, because you have it, you will preach faith." [7] Reluctantly following this advice, John offered salvation by faith to a condemned prisoner in St. George's Tower, Oxford; and this man, Clifford by name, believed on Christ. On the day of Clifford's execution John Wesley heard him testify, "I am now ready to die. I know Christ has taken away my sins, and there is no more condemnation for me." But not until two months later could Wesley testify in like confident words, ". . . an assurance was given me, that he had taken away *my* sins, even *mine*, and saved *me* from the law of sin and death." [8]

The third member of this trio who would "by all means save some," was George Whitefield. He had been a member of Oxford's "Holy Club" with John and Charles Wesley. For a time at Oxford, Whitefield, a tavern boy who was working his way through Pembroke College, had observed the severe piety and devotion of this much-ridiculed group on the Oxford campus, and he shrank from the persecution he knew would come if he joined their ranks. He was finally won to the "Holy Club" by the efforts of Charles Wesley, and once he had cast his lot with the group he courageously maintained its standards.

---

6. Elmer T. Clark, *Charles Wesley, Singer of the Evangelical Revival*. The Upper Room, Nashville; p. 28.
7. J. Wesley, *Journal*. Epworth Press, London; v. 1, 442.
8. *Ibid.*, 448.

METHODISM'S CONQUERING WITNESS: BY WHAT MEANS?

After a period of severe asceticism and emotional upheaval, Whitefield was converted—three years before the conversion of his older friends, the Wesleys! Following that greatest event of his life, Whitefield rapidly rose to great renown as an effective and dramatic preacher, and many doors were opened to him in England while the Wesleys were in Georgia. He resolutely turned from every opening that he also might go to Georgia, challenged thereto by a letter from that far-off place from his old Oxford friend, John Wesley.

But before Whitefield's arrival in Georgia, Wesley had fled for England, and shortly thereafter was to come to his "heart-warming" at Aldersgate.

In December of the same year Whitefield returned to England to enlist interest in and support of his Georgia orphanage project. This was to be but one of his many return visits to England over the span of thirty-one years. Now he was received by some with their former favor, but by others—and their number quickly grew—with deep prejudice. Churches were closed against him, and finally he was barred even from preaching in Bristol's prison, Newgate. For he too, with the Wesleys, was a "prison evangelist."

Look on the fields . . . white already to harvest
> *God moves in a mysterious way*
> *His wonders to perform.*

With churches and even prisons closed against his preaching, Whitefield now turned to the depraved colliers of the Kingswood area near Bristol, preaching to them in the fields. His first such service was on February 17, 1739, which drew an audience of two hundred. On this occasion he wrote in his *Journal*, "Blessed be God, I have now broke the ice; I believe I was never more acceptable to my Master than when I was standing to teach those hearers in the open fields." Eight days later 20,000 gathered to hear him, and soon he could say, "I now preach to ten times more people than I should if I had been confined to the churches." [9]

But America was calling him to return, and he could not long remain in the Bristol-Kingswood area. He would leave his converts in

---

9. S. C. Henry, *George Whitefield*. Abingdon, Nashville; p. 48. (Quoting Whitefield's *Journal*, v. 1, 205.)

the care of John Wesley, who then was but ten months beyond Aldersgate, and to whom one church after another had been closed because of his preaching faith in Christ as the only way of salvation. Wesley was now the center of a nucleus of believers in London and, as we have noted, was reluctant to answer Whitefield's call.

Upon arriving in Bristol, Wesley was disturbed to observe Whitefield's "strange way of preaching in the fields . . . having been all my life (till very lately)," he said, "so tenacious of every point relating to decency and order that I should have thought the saving of souls a sin if it had not been done in church." [10]

Whitefield's lack of the cultural restraints that had been Wesley's all his life, and Whitefield's flair for the dramatic and spectacular made him the readier to break with tradition. He was indeed the one to "break the ice," but the marvel is that John Wesley then plunged into the water's chilly depths. Wesley was orderly, systematic, and by temperament inclined to high-church sentiments. We have seen that before his conversion he had long been a legalist. His teaching responsibilities at Lincoln College had included debate and logic, but notwithstanding his logical preciseness and ritualistic predilections, the next day after observing Whitefield's open-air methods, he followed his example and reported thus in his *Journal* for that April 2 of 1739: "At four in the afternoon, I submitted to be more vile, and proclaimed in the highways the glad tidings of salvation, speaking from an eminence in a ground adjoining to the city, to about three thousand people." [11]

The *Cambridge Modern History* marks this event, John Wesley's first field-preaching, as the beginning of "a new era in the religious history of England." [12] Regularly, now, John Wesley preached in the fields, large crowds attending upon his well-ordered and intellectual gospel declarations, even as formerly they had flocked to hear the dramatic and emotionally charged utterances of Whitefield.

There is reason to believe that Whitefield did not expect from the orderly and restrained Wesley such evangelistic fruitage as his own labors had produced, but rather a pastoral and teaching ministry.

---
10. J. Wesley, *Journal*. Epworth Press, London; v. 2, 167.
11. *Ibid.*, 172 *et seq.*
12. *Cambridge Modern History*. Cambridge University Press, New York; v. 6, 83.

METHODISM'S CONQUERING WITNESS: BY WHAT MEANS?

Upon his departure from Bristol, Whitefield wrote in his *Journal*, "What gives me the greatest comfort is the consideration that my dear and honoured friend, Mr. Wesley, is left behind, to confirm those that are awakened." [13] Wesley promptly demonstrated his ability to confirm the awakened by organizing the converts into bands his first week in Bristol. Wesley was an evangelist as was Whitefield, but more—Wesley had the genius for organization and administration so lacking in the latter.

John Wesley's alert mind and readiness of speech prepared him for the rough-and-tumble of field-preaching. Notwithstanding his primness, he was at home with all levels of society and culture. And what a distance in culture from Kingswood to Bath, although separated geographically but a few miles! Two months after Wesley's first outdoor sermon in the Bristol "brickyards," he had carved out a circuit that took him on Tuesdays to Bath, the English capital of worldly fashion.

In Bath, Wesley encountered Beau Nash, Bath's "cock of the walk," leader in fashion and vice. Friends tried to dissuade Wesley from preaching in the open, fearing that there would be trouble. But Wesley was not easily diverted from plans once laid. A great crowd had gathered, sensing that there would be excitement. The rich and fashionable were present, and the preacher told them that the Scriptures included all under sin. This surprised the social set, and some were becoming serious when Nash appeared and pushed his way through the throng to Wesley. After trying in vain to frighten Wesley by accusing him of violating the Act of Parliament against conventicles, Nash took another course and told Wesley that his preaching "frightened the people out of their wits." Here is Wesley's account of the dialogue from this point:

> I asked if he had heard me preach. If not, how could he judge of what he had never heard? He said, "By common report, for he knew my character." I then asked, "Pray, sir, are you a justice of the peace or the mayor of this city?" Answer: "No, I am not." "Why then, sir, pray by what authority do you ask me these things?" Here he paused a little, and I went on: "Give me leave, sir, to ask, Is not your name Nash?" Answer: "Sir, my name is

---

13. As quoted by Mabel Richmond Brailsford, *A Tale of Two Brothers*. Oxford University Press, New York; p. 126.

Nash." "Why then, sir, I trust common report is no good evidence of truth." Here the laugh turned full against him, so that he looked about and could scarce recover. Then a bystander said, "Sir, let an old woman answer him." Then, turning to Mr. Nash, she said, "Sir, if you ask what we come here for, we come for the food of our souls. You care for your body: we care for our souls." He replied not one word, but turned and walked away.[14]

Field-preacher poet

Even as all three of the great leaders of the Wesleyan Revival we have introduced were prison evangelists, so all were field-preachers. Charles Wesley in the London area had been disturbing church authorities by preaching his favorite doctrine of salvation by faith. Churches were closing against him as they had closed against John Wesley and Whitefield. Finally Charles was excluded from the pulpit of the church he served as curate. About this time a farmer invited him to preach in his field, and he accepted the opportunity on May 29, 1739. After the service he wrote, "I returned to the house rejoicing." Other open-air preaching followed, but it is clear that Charles went through excruciating struggles over field-preaching such as John seems not to have known after his first plunge at Bristol. Facing the ordeal of preaching at Moorfields on June 23, 1739, Charles committed to his *Journal* the following, "My inward conflict continued. I perceived it was the fear of man; and that, by preaching in the field next Sunday, as George Whitefield urges me, I shall break down the bridge and become desperate." But after preaching to "ten thousand helpless sinners," he reported that the Lord was with him, "His meanest messenger." During this summer of 1739 his *Journal* tells of large crowds and great success attending his field-preaching, but of intense spiritual struggle. As he expressed it, "God continues to work *by* me but not *in* me." [15]

During this troublous period, his Moravian friends of Fetter Lane on the one hand were slipping into fanaticism, and the Anglican Church on the other hand was opposing and rejecting his ministry. But he continued to observe the ordinances and forms of worship of the Anglican Church, holding steadily but painfully his course between the extremes of fanaticism and frigidity. From preaching to

---
14. J. Wesley, *Letters*. Epworth Press, London; v. 1, 320.
15. C. Wesley, *The Early Journal*, 1736-1739. Robert Culley, London; p. 245.

Moorfield's milling mob one Sunday, this remarkable man proceeded to Oxford the next, to preach before the University in St. Mary's. Severe tensions strained the soul of this poet, caught between contrasting situations and contending forces.

When Charles was happily married, he tried to reassure John that having a wife would not interfere with his ministry, but not long thereafter he left the itinerancy and its field-preaching to become a settled pastor, first at Bristol and in later years at London. But this change by no means ended his usefulness to Methodism and the Kingdom. Had he continued the itinerant ministry, he could hardly have made the contribution to hymnody that a settled life made possible. Moreover, none can estimate the value of his pastoral ministry in two of the greatest centers of Methodism during the formative period of the movement. "By all means" includes the pastoral as well as the evangelistic ministry, and hymnody as well as homiletics.

John Wesley and George Whitefield also married, the one unhappily and the other with doubtful benefit. Both continued the itinerant ministry with its arduous field-preaching. A month after his marriage, John wrote in his *Journal*, "I cannot understand how a Methodist preacher can answer it to God to preach one sermon or travel one day less in a married than in a single state." [16] One may judge the domestic bliss of our trio by a letter the vicar of Everton wrote Lady Huntingdon which contained the devastating comment, "No trap so mischievous to the field preacher as wedlock. Matrimony has quite maimed poor Charles, and might have spoiled John and George if a wise Master had not graciously sent them a brace of ferrets." [17]

Once John Wesley had decided that field-preaching was a divinely approved means of evangelism, he committed himself unwaveringly to it, without the inner struggles that beset Charles. He became convinced that field-preaching was more than a temporary device for bridging the gap between the exclusion of Methodists from Anglican pulpits and the building of Methodist preaching-houses. The growth and vitality of the Revival were to depend upon this means of "saving

---

16. J. Wesley, *Journal*. Epworth Press, London; v. 3, 517.
17. As quoted by Brailsford, *A Tale of Two Brothers*. Oxford University Press, New York; p. 230.

some," long after Methodists had their own chapels. In fact, the Revival had been in progress a quarter-century when Wesley ascribed the spiritual dearth in a certain place to want of field-preaching. Then, speaking of the place of field-preaching in the Methodist movement, he said, "If ever this is laid aside, I expect the whole work will gradually die away." [18]

John Wesley welcomed the opportunity to preach in churches also, and in his later years, after the Revival had extended its warming influence, again was welcomed to Anglican pulpits. To him, "all means" included both, church and open field. After preaching from a tombstone in a churchyard, he once said, "How wisely does God order things! Some will not hear even the Word of God out of a church: for the sake of these we are permitted to preach in a church. Others will not hear it in a church: for their sakes we are often compelled to preach in the highways." [19]

But John Wesley did not take to the fields by personal preference. In his mid-fifties he wrote, "What marvel the devil does not like field-preaching? Neither do I: I love a commodious room, a soft cushion, an handsome pulpit. But where is my zeal, if I do not trample all these under foot, in order to save one more soul?" [20] Again, when nearly seventy, he said, "To this day, field-preaching is a cross to me. But I know my commission, and see no other way of 'preaching the gospel to every creature.'" [21]

That he did not take to field-preaching by natural temperament or acquired taste, appears in the following statement addressed to fellow clergymen of the Church of England in "A Further Appeal to Men of Reason and Religion":

> Who is there among you, brethren, that is willing (examine your own hearts) even to save souls from death at this price? Would not you let a thousand souls perish rather than you would be the instrument of rescuing them thus? Can you bear the summer sun to beat upon your naked head? Can you suffer the wintry rain or wind, from whatever quarter it blows? Are you able to stand in the open air without any covering or defence

---

18. J. Wesley, *Journal*. Epworth Press, London; v. 5, 79.
19. *Ibid.*, v. 3, 290.
20. *Ibid.*, v. 4, 325.
21. *Ibid.*, v. 5, 484.

when God casteth abroad his snow like wool, or scattereth his hoar-frost like ashes? And yet these are some of the smallest inconveniences which accompany field-preaching. Far beyond all these, are the contradiction of sinners, the scoffs both of the great, vulgar, and small; contempt and reproach of every kind; often more than verbal affronts, stupid, brutal violence, sometimes to the hazard of health, or limbs, or life. Brethren, do you envy us this honour? What, I pray, would buy you to be a field-preacher? Or what, think you, could induce any man of common sense to continue therein one year, unless he had a full conviction in himself that it was the will of God concerning him? [22]

The witness through song

When John and Charles Wesley sang their conversion hymn that night of Aldersgate in 1738, no one could foresee the distinguished place hymns and hymn-singing would have in the revival that soon would break. Until his conversion Charles had been little concerned with writing poetry and song—in fact, less concerned than John had been. Already, in Georgia, John had prepared the first book of hymns published in the American colonies. But from his conversion until his death there flowed from Charles Wesley's pen and out of his poetic heart 6,500 hymns! The quantity forbade high excellence in all of them, but enough of Wesley's hymns have survived the test of two centuries to establish the author in a major position in the hymnals of today. Checking nineteen contemporary hymnals of different communions in England and America, the present writer has found that other than *The Methodist Hymn Book* of England (which alone includes 238 hymns by Charles Wesley!) the average of the thirteen books with author-index is twenty-one hymns by this famed hymn-writer. Interestingly enough, the Protestant Episcopal *Hymnal 1940* includes eighteen by Charles Wesley, which is a larger number than it carries of any other author, save one.

All nineteen hymnals include what has been called the greatest heart-hymn, "Jesus, Lover of My Soul." Henry Ward Beecher said he would rather have written that hymn than "have all the fame of all the kings that ever lived." Today's self-contained sophisticate may scorn its sentiment, but pilgrims and strangers on earth still find in

---

22. *Ibid.*, v. 5, 163.

it comfort in loneliness, strength for the journey, and hope for eternity.

All nineteen hymnals also include what one writer has characterized as Charles Wesley's "lofty and glowing lyric on perfect love." Indeed, one of the noblest expressions of God as love and of what man through Christ may become is the hymn "Love Divine, All Loves Excelling."

Other favorites among these hymnals include that great nativity hymn, "Hark, the Herald Angels Sing" (included in eighteen of the nineteen); the song of resurrection triumph, "Christ the Lord is Risen Today" (included in seventeen); that swelling paean of praise, "O for a Thousand Tongues to Sing" (included in fifteen); the sober yet stirring call to faithfulness, "A Charge to Keep I Have" (included in fifteen).

The rapid blossoming of Charles Wesley's poetic genius after his conversion is cause for marvel. "Hark, the Herald Angels Sing" and "Christ the Lord is Risen Today" appeared only one year after his conversion; "O for a Thousand Tongues to Sing" was written for the first anniversary of his conversion; "Jesus, Lover of My Soul" was published two years after his spiritual rebirth; and that masterpiece, "Love Divine, All Loves Excelling," appeared within the first decade of his life under grace.

In a class by itself is the stirring lyrical drama, "Wrestling Jacob." Its length hinders its general use, but the English *Methodist Hymn Book* carries twelve stanzas, and *Hymns of the Living Faith*[23] includes six. Isaac Watts, Charles Wesley's older contemporary and contestant for first place in volume of hymns produced, said that this poem was worth all the verses Watts himself had written. Shortly after Charles Wesley's death at eighty-one years, John, then eighty-five, was lining this hymn in a Methodist chapel. At the couplet,

> *My company before is gone,*
> *And I am left alone with Thee—*

this man of normally complete self-command broke into tears and, overwhelmed by emotion, sat down and hid his face in his hands. The congregation of several hundred worshipers became silent, sensing

---

23. *Hymns of the Living Faith*. Light & Life Press, Winona Lake; hymn 309.

the tragic drama these lines had precipitated in the soul of the revered saint.[24]

Several of Wesley's hymns have been set to music derived from the composer of the famous oratorio, *The Messiah*. It is quite certain that Handel knew the Charles Wesley family, and some think Handel may have been influenced by the Evangelical Revival when, in the early years of that revival, he turned from secular music to writing sacred oratorios. *The Messiah* was written in 1742. It is said that he composed four tunes for hymns written by Wesley.

Through his hymns Charles Wesley did more to shape the doctrinal thinking of Methodism's converts than did John through his able preaching. After relating how Charles "breathed the breath of life and of song" into the prosily tame words of Matthew Henry's comments on Leviticus 8:35, and made them immortal in the hymn "A Charge to Keep I Have," Bishop Ledden adds that what Charles did for Matthew Henry's *Commentary* he did also for his brother's sermons.[25] Another has said that the compendium of John Wesley's theology is not his sermons but Charles' hymns. These hymns, moreover, made clear the doctrinal and devotional teachings of Scripture and are filled with scriptural terms and allusions. Dr. Henry Betts has been quoted as claiming that practically every paragraph of Scripture is somewhere reflected in them. In the preface to one of his later hymnbooks, John Wesley published the following:

> It is large enough to contain all the most important truths of our most holy religion, whether speculative or practical; yea, to illustrate them all, and to prove them both by Scripture and reason.... In what other publication of the kind have you so distinct and full an account of scriptural Christianity? such a declaration of the heights and depths of religion, speculative and practical? so strong cautions against the most plausible errors ...? and so clear directions for making our calling and election sure; for perfecting holiness in the fear of the Lord?[26]

With common folk, Methodism won its battle against Calvinism by the warmth and glad assurance of its hymns more than by the logic

---

24. L. Tyerman, *Life and Times of John Wesley*. Harper & Bros., New York; v. 3, 527.
25. W. E. Ledden, "The hymnal as a means of grace," in *Proceedings of the Ninth World Methodist Conference*. The Methodist Publishing House, Nashville; p. 146.
26. J. Wesley, *Works* (Jackson's 3rd ed.); v. 14, 353.

of its preachers. "Calvinism had no song; it produced singers but they could not sing about Calvinism." So writes W. Bardsley Brash, who then explains, "It is impossible to become lyrical about fractions, or to sing with full-throated ease about decimal points and the limited love of God. The Calvinist singers, when they sang, were the singers of the songs of the free grace of God." [27]

Until the Wesleys, there had been little hymn-singing in England. The Anglican Church had its chants, anthems and paraphrases of the Psalms. Dissent had its Psalms and some hymns, such as those of Watts. But hymn-singing did not become popular until the Revival when Charles Wesley's lyrical verse, set to bright and moving music, started a conflagration of profound religious feeling that spread from heart to heart, and swayed vast congregations to accept the good news of salvation for all.

The witness of the printed page

John Wesley was one of the most prolific writers of all time. Beginning to publish when he was thirty-three years old, he averaged about six volumes a year for fifty-five years. His titles cover a wide field, including school texts, home remedies, devotional reprints and digests, theology, moral and social problems, controversy, hymnbooks (in cooperation with Charles Wesley), the *Arminian Magazine*, his voluminous letters, and his extensive *Journal*. His original works have been estimated at 233, his edited and abridged reprints a like number.

His style was simple, and consequently his writings, although voluminous, are not diluted with verbiage. He said that if angels wrote books, the books would have few folios. Should he find what he called a "stiff" expression in his copy for the press, he threw it out "neck and shoulders." He sought clarity because, he said, he must "instruct people of the lowest understanding," and would "no more write in a fine style than wear a fine coat."

One of his amazing literary achievements was the translation of the New Testament and the writing of his *Explanatory Notes* thereon. Much of the work for this large volume was done during an illness in 1754, and the book was completed and published in 1755. He long had desired to undertake the task, and when stricken with a

---

27. W. B. Brash, *Methodism*. Harper & Bros., New York; p. 101.

serious ailment that forbade his traveling or preaching, he said, "But, blessed be God, I can still read and write and think." He had a premonition that his death was near, and desired to finish the task and his life together. He lived thirty-six years after the book's publication, but his illness served the purpose of launching him on this major undertaking.

The aim of the translation and its related notes was to provide a means by which people of little learning could gain a full understanding of the essentials of the New Testament. His rendering of the New Testament was not merely his version or paraphrase of the King James or any other version, but was a fresh translation from the Greek. For the task, he was well-fitted by his careful study of the New Testament in the original over a period of many years. While a fellow at Lincoln College, as noted in Chapter Three, he had lectured in Greek on the New Testament. It is estimated that in his translation of the New Testament he made twelve thousand changes from earlier translations, nine thousand of which were retained in the scholarly Standard Version whose preparation was begun in 1870.[28]

Ralph Earle has checked Wesley's translation against the new Revised Standard Version, and finds that in more than 6,500 instances Wesley anticipated RSV variations from the King James Version. "It remains to be seen," writes Earle, "whether anyone can furnish us today a translation which combines in such high degree conservatism and criticism, spirituality and intellectuality, common sense and scholarship, simplicity and profundity, as did John Wesley's *New Testament* two hundred years ago." [29]

For the accompanying *Notes*, Wesley levied extensively on the writings of others, especially the learned and pious Bengel of Germany. To those from whom he borrowed, he gave due credit. The translation and the *Notes* made a volume of approximately one thousand pages,[30] and went through five editions during Wesley's lifetime. It came to be recognized as a part of English Methodism's doctrinal standards, along with Wesley's doctrinal sermons.

---

28. *John Wesley's New Testament.* Winston Anniversary Edition, The John C. Winston Co., Philadelphia; pp. ix-xiv.
29. Ralph Earle, "John Wesley's New Testament," *The Seminary Tower.* Kansas City, Mo., Spring, 1959.
30. J. Wesley, *Explanatory Notes on the New Testament.* Epworth Press, London.

Wesley's publishing ministry after the launching of the Methodist movement began at the Foundery, the first London headquarters of Methodism. There, books were sold in the room used for band meetings. From this beginning, English Methodism's publishing enterprise has developed into the great publishing plant and Book Room across Tabernacle Street from the site of its embryonic beginnings in the old Foundery.

Wesley told his preachers, "Read the most useful books, and that regularly and constantly," at least five hours a day. His reply to any who might offer the objection, "But I read only the Bible," was this severe rebuke, "Then you ought to teach others to read only the Bible, and, by parity of reason, to hear only the Bible: But if so," he added, "you need preach no more. . . . If you need no book but the Bible, you are got above St. Paul," who asked Timothy to bring to him in prison his books and his parchments. To those who protested, "But I have no taste for reading," his answer was curt enough, "Contract a taste for it by use, or return to your trade." [31]

Such was the advice to his preachers of one who declared that he was a man of one book! In a letter to his niece, Sally, he made clear what he meant by this claim when, advising her on her reading and submitting a broadly cultural list of books, he placed the Bible first and central with the injunction that all she learned should be related to the Bible, "either directly or remotely."

Near the end of his life he wrote, "It cannot be that the people should grow in grace, unless they give themselves to reading." [32] Thus, he was more than a friend of learning, he was its ardent promoter, insisting that Methodists, both preachers and people, read both widely and wisely. And as a practical man, he undertook to encourage the same by supplying a wide range of good literature at low cost. In this he succeeded. Most of the considerable profit derived from the sale of his publications went into the work so near his heart. In his sermon, "On the Danger of Riches," he said:

> Two and forty years ago, having a desire to furnish poor people with cheaper, shorter, and plainer books than any I had seen, I wrote many small tracts, generally a penny a-piece; and afterwards

---

31. J. Wesley, *Works* (Jackson's 3rd ed.); v. 8, 315.
32. J. Wesley, *Letters*, Epworth Press, London; v. 8, 247.

several larger. Some of these had such sale as I never thought of; and by this means, I unawares became rich. But I never desired or endeavoured after it. And now that it has come upon me unawares, I lay up no treasures upon earth: I lay up nothing at all.[33]

The witness through organization and discipline

The swelling number of converts through the Revival soon demanded a group structure and a regimen of discipline if this fruitage was to be conserved and the converts be nurtured to Christian maturity. Organization and discipline soon took shape under the guiding mind and hand of John Wesley. Thus, the distinctive witness of Methodism in the area of Christian living was brought into clear focus.

The organization of the United Societies began with the formation of a society in London in 1739 which Wesley defined as, "a company of men having the form and seeking the power of godliness, united in order to pray together, to receive the word of exhortation, and to watch over one another in love, that they may help each other to work out their salvation."

For such a religious society there was ample precedent. Piette says that religious societies began in England in 1678, and, following an initial period of suspicion and opposition, they developed rapidly. By the time of Wesley's birth in 1703, a quarter-century after the first was formed, there were one hundred religious societies in the London-Westminster area alone. From this point, decline began, but such societies were far from extinction when Wesley began organizing the followers and converts of Methodism. In fact, Wesley already had been active in such societies at Oxford, Aldersgate, and Fetter Lane, the last named having been organized by Wesley himself a year before he organized the first Methodist society.

Those who know Methodism only as it functions today tend to think of the movement as a denomination from the beginning. But as with societies generally in Wesley's time, his societies were not units of an established church organization, but were voluntary cells not sponsored or governed by the church, but largely made up of members thereof. They were associations of earnest and devout people, mostly

---

33. J. Wesley, *Sermons on Several Occasions*. Phillips & Hunt, New York; v. 2, 254.

Anglicans, seeking through the society a more vital spiritual life. Although trends toward separation of the United Methodist Societies from the Church of England appeared in Wesley's lifetime, we have previously noted that the final break did not come until after his death.

Not long after the organization of the first Methodist society, Wesley adopted the system of dividing societies into smaller groups called classes. This was valuable for closer counseling by leaders and more intimate fellowship and mutual helpfulness among the members of a family-size circle of not more than twelve. Some of the societies grew to memberships numbering hundreds, and without subdivision into classes, would have been unwieldy and undisciplined congregations. Although the pattern of organization by classes was developed in Bristol early in 1742 as a means of liquidating the debt on the New Room, Wesley saw in the plan a means of spiritual nurture and moral discipline. Accordingly, he introduced classes throughout all Methodism. Both the spirituality and the discipline of the societies were greatly strengthened by the class organization and the class meeting, and the system developed a sturdy corps of lay workers whose official designation was class leader. The decline of the class meeting in Methodism in later years, with consequent decline in the importance of spiritual leadership drawn from the laity, has brought decline likewise in Methodist discipline and spiritual nurture.

For a time the societies continued with no formally declared standards of conduct for their members, but the need that privileges of membership carry a reciprocal duty of righteous conduct became painfully apparent in the large New Castle society of nearly a thousand members. Between visits of Wesley, separated only by two months, seventy-six members had dropped out because of persecution, family opposition, and like causes, and nearly as many more had been expelled for such misconduct as drunkenness, selling liquor, profanity, Sabbath desecration, lying, wife-beating, and other less easily graded offences such as quarreling, railing, laziness, lightness, and carelessness (twenty-nine for the last-named!) Two months later, May 1, 1743, the Society Rules were published, signed by John and Charles Wesley. David Sherman, an authority on the American Methodist *Discipline*, declared that this first attempt at law-making in Methodism was "the most remarkable uninspired code for the regulation of a spiritual body on record." [34]

The General Rules of the United Societies are well known if not so well practiced throughout Methodism today. Many consider the rules irksome restrictions on personal liberty that impose the burden of law upon those whose right it is to enjoy the freedom of grace. But honest scrutiny of the rules discloses that they are based on essential principles of the gospel of love, and that they carefully seek the glory of God, man's own welfare, and the good of society. More detailed consideration must await the discussion of personal discipline in a later chapter.

Other features of Methodism's discipline than those we have noted at society and class levels reach upward, through the ranks of the ministry in particular, to the annual conference and, in America, to the general conference. The connectional system of Methodism still exerts a strong organizational discipline long after the decline of its personal discipline.

* * * * *

The means noted in this chapter by which Methodism's witness was established include prison evangelism, field-preaching, hymn-singing, the printed page, the organization of converts, and personal discipline. The next chapter surveys the doctrinal message to which Methodism witnessed.

---

34. David Sherman, *History of the Revisions of the Discipline.* Nelson & Phillips, New York; p. 15.

Chapter Six

Methodism's Conquering Witness: By What Message?

Early Methodism's most important means of "saving some" was the message to which its preaching, personal testimony, song and printed word so convincingly witnessed. The doctrinal framework of this message was the nominally accepted declaration of beliefs set forth in the Articles of Religion of the Church of England. Opinions on Wesley's doctrinal contribution agree that his distinctiveness lay in his rediscovery and fresh application of historically established and sometimes forgotten truths, rather than in doctrinal innovation or deviation.

Beliefs are important

Notwithstanding an increasingly prevalent idea that doctrinal distinctives meant little to him, John Wesley held without wavering to the great central themes of revealed religion interpreted in line with conservative Arminianism. The late Dr. J. A. Faulkner of Drew has been quoted as saying that Wesley "was the greatest doctrinal preacher of the eighteenth century." That he did not "play down" doctrine is conclusively settled by Bishop Neely whose summary statement on the issue is this:

> For anyone to assert that John Wesley was indifferent as to doctrines and that he put little or no stress on doctrinal matters, is to assert that which is absolutely untrue, and no well-informed and candid student of the history would venture such a suggestion. . . . He always had his essential creed, though he conceded there were some non-essentials on which brother Christians might differ and not disagree.[1]

Neely's placing in context some much-quoted, isolated statements of Wesley, such as "We think and let think," and "If thine heart be as my heart, give me thy hand," will repay anyone interested in look-

---

1. T. B. Neely, *Doctrinal Standards of Methodism.* Fleming H. Revell Co., Westwood, N. J.; p. 77.

ing up Neely's book to read page 81 alone. He will then be intrigued to read more on this subject of Wesley's concern for definitive doctrine.

One who has accepted the current view that John Wesley was doctrinally broad should note what he wrote on the catholic or liberal spirit, by which he meant universal love. This spirit, is "not speculative latitudinarianism," he said. "It is not an indifference to all opinions: this is the spawn of hell, not the offspring of heaven." And further, "A man of a truly catholic spirit, has not now his religion to seek. He is fixed as the sun in his judgment concerning the main branches of Christian doctrine." [2]

Upon what authority did Wesley base his beliefs?

Much is made today of Wesley's "Theology of experience." The phrase would have displeased him greatly if used to suggest that the basis of his doctrine was in man himself, as some intend who use those words. The subjectivist who seeks God's revelation of Himself mirrored in man's inner experience tends to an error not unlike that of the deist who looks outward to find God's revelation of Himself only in the reasonableness of the universe.

The late Bishop Paul B. Kern traced the emphasis on experience from Bacon through Descartes to Kant, contemporary of Wesley, and on to Schleiermacher, and characterized the movement as the shift "from dogmatism to experience." He called experience "the central authority in life" and asked, "Is reality to be accepted, handed down predetermined; or is it to be inward, experimental, warmly personal? Methodism's answer to this," he continued, "is fortified by all the developments of historical criticism and of inductive reasoning." [3] It would seem, then, that today's Methodism derives more from the subjectivism of Schleiermacher than from Wesley's emphasis on experience as an authority subordinate to Scripture.

But for Wesley, dogma and experience checked each other. He would seek the truth in neither alone, but in both racial experience expressed as dogma, and in personal experience. Throughout his life he firmly held to the doctrines of the Church of England, with which he judged Christian experience to be in accord. But he held

---

2. J. Wesley, *Sermons on Several Occasions.* Phillips & Hunt, New York; v. 1, 353.
3. P. B. Kern, *Methodism Has a Message.* Abingdon-Cokesbury, Nashville; p. 23.

that there is a higher standard of truth than either, namely, the revelation of Scripture. By that standard Wesley checked the testimony of both racial and personal experience.

In 1762, when the revival in the London area suffered from the erratic and fanatical beliefs of certain Methodist leaders who relied too much on inner experience, Wesley published a tract warning against such extravagances as were developing and holding high the Scriptures as the standard. "Do not hastily ascribe things to God," he said. "Do not easily suppose the dreams, voices, impressions, visions, or revelations to be from God. They may be from Him. They may be from nature. They may be from the devil." He then plainly advised, "try all things by the written word, and let all bow down before it." He warned, "You are in danger of enthusiasm every hour, if you depart ever so little from Scripture; yea, from the plain, literal meaning of any text, taken in connection with its context." [4] Again, he made the Scriptures basic in his notes on I John 4:1. "We are to try all spirits by the written word," he asserted. " 'To the law and the testimony!' If any man speak not according to these, the spirit which actuates him is not of God." [5] In 1756 he wrote to Rev. Dodd, taking his stand on Scripture as highest and final authority, saying that he regulated all his opinions thereby according to his best understanding.[6]

That Wesley perceived danger in viewing Scripture merely in an objective and intellectual fashion, with no inner spiritual response to its truth, we infer from his reply to the rationalistic Conyers Middleton on the nature and evidences of Christianity. Unless the formal traditionalists "do not obey the loud call of God, and lay far more stress than they have hitherto done on this internal evidence of Christianity," suggested Wesley, they will "one after another, give up the external, and (in heart at least) go over to those they are now contending with." Then, "in a century or two the people of England will be fairly divided into real Deists and real Christians." [7] Tenney notes that this had already happened in Wesley's own day in deism's

---

4. J. Wesley, *A Plain Account of Christian Perfection*. Epworth Press, London; p. 88.
5. J. Wesley, *Explanatory Notes Upon the New Testament*. Epworth Press, London; p. 913.
6. J. Wesley, *Letters*. Epworth Press, London; v. 3, 157.
7. J. Wesley, *Works*. (Emory ed. 1853) Carlton & Phillips, New York; v. 5, 759.

invasion of the Church.[8] Perhaps in voicing this warning Wesley foresaw just such a development as later was to lead New England to react from Calvinism to Unitarianism.

Wesley included reason also, along with experience and dogma, as a ground of belief subordinate to Scripture. To a critic charging him with being an enthusiast, and claiming that an enthusiast rejects reason by resolving "all his religious opinions and notions into immediate inspiration," Wesley replied that by the critic's own definition he was not an enthusiast, "for I resolve none of my notions into immediate inspiration," and he added, "I am ready to give up every opinion which I cannot by calm, clear reason defend."[9] In his "Appeal to Men of Reason and Religion," Wesley sought to show that the faith he claimed, far from being enthusiasm, was the highest form of reason, resting not on speculation but on certainty.

And thus the basis of Wesley's certainty was faith, contributing to which were experience, dogma, reason, and Scripture, the last named being the central authority with veto power over all the rest, faith included.

Wesley did not make the Bible a mechanical guide needing neither intelligent study nor active faith. This is made clear in the following beautiful passage from his facile pen:

> I am a creature of a day, passing through life as an arrow through the air. I am a spirit come from God, and returning to God: just hovering over the great gulf; till, a few moments hence, I am no more seen! I drop into an unchangeable eternity! I want to know one thing—the way to heaven: how to land safe on that happy shore. God Himself has condescended to teach the way; for this very end He came from heaven. He hath written it down in a Book! Oh give me that Book! At any price, give me the Book of God! I have it: here is knowledge enough for me. Let me be *homo unius libri*. Here, then, I am, far from the busy ways of men. I sit down alone. Only God is here. In His presence I open, I read this book; for this end, to find the way to heaven. Is there a doubt concerning the meaning of what I read? Does anything appear dark and intricate, I lift up my heart to the Fa-

---

8. M. A. Tenney, *Blueprint for a Christian World*. Light & Life Press, Winona Lake; p. 99.
9. Umphrey Lee, *The Historical Backgrounds of Early Methodist Enthusiasm*. Columbia University Press, New York; p. 146.

ther of Lights: "Lord, is it not Thy word, 'If any man lack wisdom, let him ask of God?' Thou 'givest liberally and upbraidest not.' Thou hast said, 'If any be willing to do my will, he shall know.' I am willing to do: let me know thy will." I then search after, and consider parallel passages of Scripture, "comparing spiritual things with spiritual." I meditate thereon, with all the attention and earnestness of which my mind is capable. If any doubt still remains, I consult those who are experienced in the things of God; and then, the writings whereby, being dead, they yet speak. And what I thus learn, that I teach.[10]

The doctrine of assurance

In his sermon on "The Witness of the Spirit," Wesley defined the testimony of the Spirit as "an inward impression on the soul, whereby the Spirit of God directly witnesses to my spirit, that I am a child of God; that Jesus Christ hath loved me, and given Himself for me; and that all my sins are blotted out, and I, even I, am reconciled to God."[11]

To the deists who disbelieved every claim that man can experience God other than through Nature, such preaching was irrational and fantastic; and to formal religionists who had never known the crisis of conversion and the assurance that follows, such preaching was rank enthusiasm. S. D. McConnell has frankly explained the Church of England's rejection of the Wesleyan Revival on the ground that for bishops or other clergymen to identify themselves with the movement, meant either to declare that they had previously been consciously converted, or to confess that until now they had been outside the kingdom of God—either admission being one few of them would make.[12] Wesley's emphasis on assurance as the normal experience of every Christian, combined with his irregular modes of preaching (which clergymen claimed violated their parish rights) made the clergy of the Church of England one of Wesley's most powerful obstacles to the promotion of the revival.

In August of 1739 Wesley was being interviewed closely by Joseph Butler, Bishop of Bristol and author of the *Analogy*, who asked him what he meant by faith. In reply Wesley defined justifying faith in

---

10. J. Wesley, *Sermons on Several Occasions*. Phillips & Hunt, New York; v. 1, 6.
11. *Ibid.*, v. 1, 87.
12. S. D. McConnell, *History of the American Episcopal Church*. Thomas Whitaker, New York; p. 169.

terms very similar to his definition of the witness of the Spirit as quoted above. When asked further by the Bishop, "But how do you prove this to be the justifying faith taught by our Church?" Wesley answered, "My lord, from her Homily on Salvation, where she describes it thus: 'A sure trust and confidence which a man hath in God that, through the merits of Christ, his sins are forgiven and he reconciled to the favor of God!'" This reply confirms the claim that Wesley was not an innovator in doctrinal teaching, even as the Bishop's reply "Why, see, this is quite another thing," discloses how void of vital meaning the doctrines of a church may become when formalism has taken over.

The examination was pressed further, the Bishop bringing up the pretending "to extraordinary revelations and gifts of the Holy Ghost," and said of such, "a horrid thing—a very horrid thing!" Wesley rejoined, "I pretend to no extraordinary revelations, or gifts of the Holy Ghost; none but what every Christian may receive and ought to expect and pray for." Wesley, of course, included the witness of the Spirit as the right of every Christian!

The Bishop shortly told Wesley he had no business in Bristol, and asked him to leave. Wesley declared in turn that his business on earth was to do all the good he could, and where he could do most good, there he must stay: just now that place was Bristol! He knew his authority, and reminded the Bishop that, having been ordained as a fellow of Lincoln College, he was not limited to a particular parish but had "an indeterminate commission to preach the gospel in any part of the Church of England." [13]

The sequel to this interview, involving as it did the doctrine of assurance, is the incident thirteen years later when the Bishop, approaching death without assurance of salvation, told his chaplain he was afraid to die. The chaplain would encourage him with the thought of Christ as Saviour, but the Bishop plaintively asked how he could know Christ was *his* Saviour. The chaplain quoted the passage, "Him that cometh unto me I will in no wise cast out." "True," said the Bishop, "and I am surprised that though I have read that Scripture a thousand times, I never felt its virtue till this moment." Then he added, "And now I die happy."

---

13. J. Wesley, *Journal*. Epworth Press, London; v. 2, 256 *n, et seq.*

In relating this dying incident Bishop Kern noted "the startling contrast between the sunlit certainty of Wesley's experience and the shadowed insecurity of a bishop's soul who could prove the existence of God by analogies from nature but who knew him not in the peace of an inward, mystical and redeeming fellowship." [14]

The assurance that one is a child of God comes, said Wesley, as the Holy Spirit "so works upon the soul by His immediate influence, and by a strong, though inexplicable operation, that the stormy wind and troubled waves subside, and there is a sweet calm; and the heart resting as in the arms of Jesus, and the sinner being clearly satisfied that God is reconciled, and all his 'iniquities are forgiven, and his sins covered.'" [15]

This doctrine of assurance, although it had been carried through generations in the Homilies of the Church of England, had long been a dead letter until Wesley experienced that witness of the Spirit at Aldersgate, and thereafter preached it everywhere as a promise of joy and peace and inner rest to multitudes who had never known that deliverance is possible from the guilty sense of sin. And that witness of the Holy Spirit was the warmth in the heart that moved the lips of Methodist converts to convincing testimony and glad song.

Is salvation for all?

A second doctrinal conflict also engaged John Wesley, in this instance against his friend and fellow-Methodist, George Whitefield. The issue was the atonement, whether effective for all who would accept it, or only for those elected to be saved. As early as 1725, Wesley had challenged the doctrine of election; but Whitefield was an ardent Calvinist, although not in any sense an able theologian who had arrived at his position by careful study, or one who could defend his position against Wesley's scholarly logic. "Alas, I never read anything that Calvin wrote," he once admitted to Wesley; ". . . my doctrines I had from Christ and his Apostles. I was taught them of God!" [16] Needless to say, his evangelistic preaching was not Calvin-

---

14. P. B. Kern, *Methodism Has a Message*. Abingdon-Cokesbury, Nashville; see p. 16 for this quotation and a fuller account of the death-bed incident to which it relates.
15. J. Wesley, *Sermons on Several Occasions*. Phillips & Hunt, New York; v. 1, 94.
16. S. C. Henry, *George Whitefield*. Abingdon, Nashville; p. 96. (Quoted from Whitefields *Works*, v. 1, 205.)

istic—as the preaching of Calvinist evangelists seldom is! Stuart C. Henry, a recent biographer of Whitefield and source of the foregoing quotation, has pointed out that Whitefield's creed and his faith were at variance: in creed he was Calvinistic, but not in the faith by which he lived.

The occasion of the outbreak of the conflict was a sermon Wesley preached at Bristol on "Free Grace." This happened in 1739, early in Wesley's evangelistic ministry after Aldersgate, and while he was caring for the revival in the Bristol area after Whitefield had left on his second voyage to America. After Whitefield's arrival in America a copy of Wesley's sermon came to his hand, and the controversy was on, first by an answer published in America and by letters, and at closer range upon Whitefield's return to England in 1741. His first letter of protest, addressed to Wesley personally, was pirated and published—it is thought by a Whitefield follower. This aggravated the situation, and upon Whitefield's arrival he published a reply to Wesley's sermon.

In this sermon on "Free Grace," Wesley had devoted his keen logic to prove, according to the doctrine of election, that "by virtue of an eternal, unchangeable, irresistible decree of God, one part of mankind are infallibly saved, and the rest infallibly damned; it being impossible that any of the former should be damned, or that any of the latter should be saved." [17] The inescapable conclusion was that all preaching is vain, since no man's eternally decreed destiny can be changed. He inveighed against the doctrine in words of far sharper severity than those just noted, as when he charged that it represents God "as more cruel, false, and unjust than the devil!"

After a year or two, however, reconciliation was effected; but efforts to carry out an agreement by which both sides would refrain from further controversial preaching on the principal issues causing division were never fully satisfactory, even as Charles had predicted when, in affixing his signature to the document, he added, "Vain agreement." After thus making what would seem to be unwarranted concessions for the sake of peace, perhaps doing this also because at that early date he had not sufficiently clarified his own thinking, John Wesley

---

17. J. Wesley, *Sermons on Several Occasions*, Phillips & Hunt, New York; v. 1, 483.

in his first Conference with his preachers, held in 1744, admitted that he had "unawares leaned too much towards Calvinism."

Antinomianism, nurtured by Calvinism, was swelling to such a tide that by 1770, more than a quarter-century later, it was carrying away many Calvinistic and not a few Wesleyan Methodists. In the Conference that year Wesley referred to his admission, in his very first Conference twenty-six years earlier, that he "had leaned too much towards Calvinism," and gave reasons for that judgment in even plainer terms than in 1744. A conflict ensued with Lady Huntingdon's Calvinistic Methodists that lasted several years and still further separated the two Methodist branches.

Whitefield was in America at this time, and was not a party to this new outbreak of controversy. Shortly after the 1770 Conference he died, and according to a long-standing agreement between the two friends, John Wesley delivered his funeral message. The sermon paid tribute to Whitefield's staunch preaching everywhere on the two great fundamental doctrines of the new birth and justification by faith, and took occasion to plead for harmony and a forgiving spirit. But the Calvinists were effronted that Wesley had not mentioned also Whitefield's doctrines of election and the final perseverance of the saints—doctrines which Whitefield was not wont to preach even though they were in his creed. Wesley answered critics of his sermon, declaring that in all the times he had heard Whitefield preach, he never had heard him mention either doctrine.

Whitefield's magnanimity towards John Wesley, whom he dearly loved for all their contention over doctrine, is high-lighted by the narrative ascribed to Lecky by Henry, according to which a critical and unbending Calvinist asked Whitefield if he thought they would ever see John Wesley in heaven. Whitefield answered, "I fear not, he will be so near the throne, and we shall be at such a distance, that we shall hardly get a sight of him." [18]

Lady Huntingdon declared against the Minutes of the 1770 Conference, and took such a severe stand that Joseph Benson, noted teacher of the classics at her Trevecca College, and Trevecca's more famous president, John Fletcher, were compelled to leave the service

---

18. S. C. Henry, *George Whitefield*. Abingdon, Nashville; p. 80.

of the institution. The issue, now so sharply drawn, brought Fletcher into the controversy with his renowned *Checks to Antinomianism.*

The late Professor Cell of Boston University has attempted to relate Wesley more closely to the Calvinism of the Reformation period than to the Arminianism of the Church of England of Wesley's day which, it is true, had been disastrously affected by the humanism of the eighteenth century.[19] John Wesley was in firm accord with certain central gospel principles of the Reformation but, as previously noted, could never accept the doctrine of election that would, by God's infallible decree, from all eternity to all eternity fix the damnation of any soul. Furthermore, it became increasingly clear to Wesley that the natural trend of Calvinism was towards antinomianism.

When seventy-five years of age, in the ripeness of his thinking after he had corrected the confessed earlier leaning "too much towards Calvinism," he wrote a revealing letter to a teacher, Miss Bishop, who apparently was contemplating leaving the Church of England for some dissenting group. Answering Miss Bishop's argument that Anglican clergymen do not preach the gospel, Wesley said, "Neither do the independent or Anabaptist ministers. Calvinism is not the gospel; nay, it is farther from it than most of the sermons I hear at the Church. These are very frequently unevangelical; but those are anti-evangelical. . . . Few of the Methodists are now in danger from imbibing error from the Church ministers; but they are in great danger of imbibing the grand error—Calvinism, from the Dissenting ministers." After admitting there were difficulties in remaining with the Church, he added, "yet, I advise all our friends to keep to the Church."

Until reading in this letter the full context of what not infrequently is quoted as from Wesley's pen, the present writer had been puzzled by his statement, "I find more profit in sermons on either good temper, or good works than in what are vulgarly [commonly] called gospel sermons." The closing statement in this connection of Wesley's thought provides the key. It is this: "We know no gospel without salvation from sin." Wesley here emphatically declares in a half-dozen sentences that he prefers the Anglican preaching of

---

19. G. C. Cell, *The Rediscovery of John Wesley.* Henry Holt & Co., New York; Preface, pp. v-xi.

morality and manners to the prevalent Calvinistic preaching of antinomianism, miscalled the gospel, which makes the blood of Christ a cover for sin. Pointedly he says, "Surely Methodists have not so learnt Christ." [20]

While the dependent and secondary doctrine of the perseverance of the saints continues today in neo-Calvinism's doctrine of "eternal security," the primary doctrine of election, upon which perseverance rested in original Calvinism, has now yielded in most Reformed groups to the warming influence of Methodism's joyous declaration of "free grace." But John Fletcher warned that there are dangers in going too far in either direction. "As there is but a step between high Arminianism and self-righteousness," he declared in his *First Check to Antinomianism*, "so there is but one between high Calvinism and Antinomianism. I charge you to shun both, especially the-latter." And again in the same letter of the *First Check* he said, "I repeat it once more, warp not to Antinomianism, and in order to this, *take heed, O! take heed to your doctrine.*" [21]

Is there deliverance from sin?

In Chapter Four it was noted that John Wesley, following Aldersgate, passed through a period of alternating struggle and victory, with now and then an overwhelming sense of defeat. He had sought help in a journey to the Moravian settlements of Germany, and after returning to England had continued in fellowship with the London Moravians. Several of these were members of the Fetter Lane Society which Wesley had organized shortly before the Aldersgate event on the advice of Peter Bohler who, although present in the organizing meeting, was then about to embark for America.

A few months after Wesley's return from Germany, Whitefield called him to the Bristol-Kingswood area to take charge of the revival in progress there. This was in late March, 1739. During the next several months, Wesley made occasional visits to London. In the fall of 1739 trouble developed in the Fetter Lane Society through a Moravian brother named Molther, recently from Germany, who taught "stillness." By this was meant refraining from the ordinances of the Church, from reading the Scriptures and other means of grace,

---

20. J. Wesley, *Letters*. Epworth Press, London; v. 6, 326 *et seq.*
21. J. Fletcher, *Checks to Antinomianism*. Phillips & Hunt, New York; v. 1, nos. 21, 23.

and from good works. Molther and his followers condemned the exercises of devotion and good works in seekers especially, and discouraged them in believers as well; for such would not help but rather hinder the former, and the latter had no need of them.

Wesley attempted to correct this fanaticism over a period of months as his visits to London would allow, but the blight had struck deeper than even his logic and winsome presence could reach. He finally gave up all hope of restoring the group, and on July 20, 1740, withdrew from the society he had organized more than two years earlier, taking with him nearly a score of followers with whom he was soon to establish Methodist headquarters for London in the Foundery, even as already he had built the New Room as Methodist headquarters in the Bristol area. The Fetter Lane Society, after the withdrawal of Wesley, was reorganized as a Moravian society, and Fetter Lane became the London headquarters of the Moravians until the bombings of World War II had devastated Fetter Lane, after which the headquarters were moved to the suburbs of London.

Personal relationships among members of the Wesleyan and Moravian groups continued close, however, and difficulties were bred in consequence. Even Charles Wesley barely escaped the toils of the spiritual death of "stillness," and in April of 1741 John wrote him a letter of serious counsel. John's reasons for not joining in with the Moravians, he told Charles, included the following: their teachings were mystical rather than scriptural; they rejected self-denial and cross-bearing; they were not open and guileless in conversation and conduct; they conformed to the world in dress; they were not zealous for good works; they made inward religion swallow up outward religion.[22]

In September of 1741 Count Zinzendorf, the head of the Moravians who was then in London, desired an interview with John Wesley. This was granted. In this interview, Zinzendorf was emphatic that there can be no inherent perfection in this life, only imputed. He would not concede to Wesley's definition of Christian perfection in terms of love, but asserted that increase of love does not increase holiness: one is sanctified the instant he is justified, and holiness is neither increased or decreased until death. Zinzendorf also rejected

---

22. J. Wesley, *Letters*. Epworth Press, London; v. 1, 352 *et seq.*

self-denial, and maintained that no purification precedes perfect love. And believers, he said, may do what they will.

The Moravian or Zinzendorfian view of sanctification as occurring simultaneously with justification bothered Methodism for a long time, and we shall meet it later in considering nineteenth-century Methodism in America. In 1772, Wesley said that this view strikes "at the root of perfection; it leaves no room for it at all. If we are never sanctified in any other sense than we are sanctified then [in justification], Christian perfection has no being." [23]

And in Zinzendorf's teachings appears another element to which Wesley was fundamentally opposed. In Moravianism, stark antinomianism came into conflict with Wesleyan principles in Methodism's infancy, but from quite a different quarter than came the later antinomian attack by Calvinism which we noted in the preceding section. "The making void the law through faith," as Wesley defined antinomianism, may accompany either a subjective or an objective religious emphasis. The deeply experiential subjectivism of the Moravians led some of them, with Count Zinzendorf, to assume that the imputed holiness of Christ delivers a man from the demands of the moral law. The doctrinal objectivism of Calvinism led some to what in effect became a contract, previously signed by Christ in His blood and needing only a man's believing on Christ to validate an arrangement whereby he may draw at will on Christ's righteousness to pay the penalty of his sins—past, present, and future.

But all this was most repugnant to John Wesley whose problem of sin had been not alone its satisfaction or forgiveness, but the further restoration of the sinner to holiness. After he had come to justification by faith as the first step towards the goal, Wesley must continue the earnest pursuit of complete holiness.

In Chapter Four two lines of evidence were suggested, pointing to Wesley's reaching that goal within the first year after Aldersgate. One is the evidence of the abrupt turn in the direction of his religious concern from himself and inner turmoil to others and to outer conquest. This appeared about the time of the opening of his ministry of field-preaching in the Bristol-Kingswood revival in the spring of

---

23. *Ibid.*, v. 5, 325.

1739. The other line of evidence is the apparent increase in Wesley's comprehension of the stages of religious experience in the Christian's normal progress in grace, the clear pattern of which may be discerned in essential details. Note the following citations:

> With the Moravians at Herrnhut in the summer of 1738, Wesley learned from Christian David, with reference to indwelling sin after justification, that "though it did not reign, it did remain." [24]

> By September 13, 1739, Wesley had so far defined his position on inward holiness that he could declare as one of the distinctives of his position, "I believe justification to be wholly distinct from sanctification and necessarily antecedent to it." [25]

> In June of 1740, in a series of expositions at the Foundery in which he had struck, as he said, "at the root of the grand delusion" [meaning thereby Moravian "stillness" and its antinomianism], he turned his course to offer encouragement to those with sins forgiven but still in a condition he described in terms that accurately fitted his own condition in the period following Aldersgate: loss of joy; love waxed cold; peace assaulted; doubt and fear; strong and uninterrupted temptation; the body of sin still remaining within. Such teaching was necessary to steady and reassure "babes in Christ," weak in faith and discouraged by the Moravian teaching that if one's faith is not complete, one has no faith at all. "Your finding sin remaining in you," he said, "still is no proof that you are not a believer. Sin does remain in one that is justified though it has not dominion over him. . . . But fear not, though you have an evil heart. Yet a little while, and you shall be endued with power from on high, whereby you may 'purify yourselves, even as He is pure'; and be 'holy, as He which hath called you is holy!' " [26] The steady confidence and crystal clarity of this message of hope convey the strong if not compelling impression that Wesley had already passed from his post-conversion civil war within, to his lifelong campaign to establish the Kingdom of righteousness in the world without.

> In the preface to the 1740 hymnbook, Wesley declared against what Zinzendorf later was to tell him, saying, "Neither dare we affirm, as some have done, that *all this salvation is given at once.*" Then, admitting both an instantaneous and a gradual work, Wesley continued, "But we do not know a single instance, in any place, of a person's receiving in one and the same moment,

---

24. J. Wesley, *Journal*. Epworth Press, London; v. 2, 30.
25. *Ibid.*, v. 2, 275.
26. *Ibid.*, v. 2, 352-359.

remission of sins, the abiding witness of the Spirit, and a new, clean heart.[27] Wesley's careful study of the religious experiences of others was already under way.

Attempting to correct the claim of an enthusiast in the 1762 London revival that the doctrine of perfection as love excluding sin and attainable instantly by faith, had only recently been preached among Methodists, Wesley wrote the extremist a letter which dates his teaching the doctrine back to 1742 and earlier. "You have over and over denied instantaneous sanctification to me," said Wesley; "but I have known and taught it . . . above these twenty years." [28]

That the mature Wesley distinguished clearly the condition of the justified Christian from his entirely sanctified state, while recognizing progression from one condition to the other, is a fact settled conclusively by Wesley's sermon, "The Scripture Way of Salvation," first published in 1765.[29] The following statements are found therein:

"And at the same time that we are justified, yea, in that very moment, sanctification begins."

"They [the justified] now feel two principles in themselves, plainly contrary to each other; 'the flesh lusting against the Spirit'; nature opposing the grace of God."

"From the time of our being born again the gradual work of sanctification takes place."

"Exactly as we are justified by faith, so are we sanctified by faith."

"But what is perfection? . . . It is love excluding sin; love filling the heart, taking up the full capacity of the soul."

"But does God work this great work in the soul gradually or instantaneously? Perhaps it may be gradually wrought in some; I mean in this sense, they do not advert to the particular moment wherein sin ceased to be. But it is infinitely desirable, were it the will of God, that it should be done instantaneously. . . . And so he generally does: a plain fact, of which there is evidence enough to satisfy any unprejudiced person."

Crisis and process in Christian perfection

Some have maintained that in the development of the doctrine of Christian perfection in the earlier period of the Revival, Wesley emphasized the distinctiveness of entire sanctification as a crisis, but

---

27. J. Wesley, *Works.* (Jackson's 3rd ed.); v. 14, 339.
28. J. Wesley, *Journal.* Epworth Press, London; v. 4, 536.
29. J. Wesley, *Sermons on Several Occasions.* Phillips & Hunt, New York; v. 1, 384.

in later years moderated this position in favor of a gradual process. The problem has been carefully investigated by George A. Turner who has found in Wesley's writings that the trend was rather from earlier indefiniteness to later unequivocal clarity on the crisis character of the experience.[30] Another contemporary authority on the history of this distinctive doctrine of Methodism, J. L. Peters, discovers that throughout Wesley's maturity to the end of his life, both in preaching and writing, "he continued to stress perfection as available 'now and by simple faith.' " Peters says, "In fact, if any appreciable change is to be noted, it is that such exhortations become more frequent and explicit. At the point of emphasis, then," he adds, "the instantaneous view must be recognized as clearly Wesleyan."[31] And thirty years ago Merrill Gaddis took this position in his masterly dissertation on *Christian Perfectionism in America* when he said:

> Modern Methodists who are embarrassed by the "second blessing" holiness movements among the small sects of Methodist derivation, are inclined to deny that Wesley gave any support to such interpretation. In this their wishes prevail over their historical judgments. Wesley gave full support to the "second blessing" or "second work of grace" principle and technique; and the small holiness sects are far more "Wesleyan" than their critics. It is possible, of course, to interpret some of Wesley's isolated statements otherwise, but not his complete and connected presentation of the subject.[32]

But Wesley's emphasis on the crises of Christian experience did not mislead him to overlook the importance of the daily process of growing in grace. Again and again he emphasized the necessity of advancing in inward holiness and outward righteousness. When an aged man of eighty-six years he wrote, "Those who do already enjoy it [perfect love] cannot possibly stand still. Unless they continue to watch and pray and aspire after higher degrees of holiness, I cannot conceive not only how they can go forward but how they can keep what they already have received. Certainly, therefore," he continued, "this is a point which must be insisted on . . . that all who have tasted

---

30. G. A. Turner, *The More Excellent Way*. Light & Life Press, Winona Lake; see especially Chapter 7.
31. J. L. Peters, *Christian Perfection and American Methodism*. Abingdon, Nashville; p. 50.
32. M. E. Gaddis, *Christian Perfectionism in America*. University of Chicago Thesis; p. 143 et seq.

of the pure love of God should continually grow in grace."[33] And again he said that however far one might have attained, he needs still to advance in knowledge and love.

Wesley maintained to the end that the pattern of normal Christian growth is progress in holiness from the new birth to the crisis of entire cleansing, and, from that event, continuously perfecting holiness to life's close. Some who look with disfavor upon the crisis doctrine of entire sanctification may charge its advocates with holding to a static, once-for-all work of grace, but nothing could be farther from Wesley's idea, nor does such a view appear in the writings of representative Wesleyan scholars from his day to this. Wesley himself was aware of the problem even in using the phrase, "state of grace," and defined that problem in 1771 as follows:

> Does not talking of a justified or sanctified *state* tend to mislead men? Almost naturally leading them to trust in what was done in one moment, whereas we are every hour and every moment pleasing or displeasing to God *according to our works*, according to the whole of our inward tempers and our outward behaviour.[34]

Thus Wesley would not reduce Christian experience to two plateaus, one elevated above the other by a perpendicular cliff separating sharply the two levels. A figure more accurately representing his view employs a lifelong incline, rising from the crisis of the new birth and extending to life's close, with the crisis of entire sanctification marking an intermediate point at which the angle of ascent sharply accelerates.

Even as Wesley sought diligently to make clear that by the doctrine of perfection he meant no absolute or final perfection beyond which a man cannot advance to higher attainments in holiness, so he sought to protect the same against the teaching that it admits no falling below absolute perfection in conduct. In 1759 he defined Christian perfection as, "The loving God with all our heart, mind, soul, and strength. This implies that no wrong temper, none contrary to love, remains in the soul; and that all the thoughts, words, and actions are governed by pure love." But this perfection, Wesley in-

---
33. J. Wesley, *Letters*. Epworth Press, London; v. 8, 184.
34. *Ibid.*, v. 5, 265.

sisted, does not deliver from infirmities, ignorance and mistakes in judgment, all of which may be the occasion of mistakes in practice. He held that "where every word and action springs from love, such a mistake is not properly *a sin.*" But since a mistake falls short of God's perfect law, he warned that "it cannot bear the rigour of God's justice, but needs the atoning blood," and "it follows that the most perfect have continual need of the merits of Christ." [35]

About the time of the fanatical extravagances of Maxwell, Bell and others in the London Revival of 1762, John Wesley wrote the Anglican clergyman, Samuel Furley:

> I know no persons living who are so deeply conscious of their needing Christ both as Prophet, Priest, and King as those who believe themselves, and whom I believe, to be cleansed from all sin—I mean from all pride, anger, evil desire, idolatry, and unbelief. These very persons feel more than ever their own ignorance, littleness of grace, coming short of the full mind that was in Christ, and walking less accurately than they might have done after their divine pattern; are more convinced of the insufficiency of all they are, have, or do to bear the eye of God without a Mediator; are more penetrated with the sense of the want of Him than ever they were before.[36]

Elsewhere the present writer has sought to express Wesley's limitation of the perfection the Christian can know in this life in these words:

> Our perfection, then, is not a legal perfection but a perfection of heart, of motive, of intent, of love. Fully willing the perfect law of God, our failure to meet that law comes, not from any rivalry within of sin or self set against God's will, but from infirmities entailed by the blight of sin in the race and our own unregenerate years.[37]

* * * * *

This chapter has emphasized the fact (contrary to a prevailing point of view) that John Wesley had a hearty respect for doctrine, the final

---

35. J. Wesley, *A Plain Account of Christian Perfection.* Epworth Press, London; pp. 42, 43.
36. J. Wesley, *Letters.* Epworth Press, London; v. 4, 189.
37. L. R. Marston, "What it means to love God perfectly," in *The Holiness Pulpit*, James McGraw, Compiler. Beacon Hill Press, Kansas City, Mo.; p. 46.

test of the validity of which, as of all grounds of belief, he maintained was Scripture.

Three doctrines prominent in his thought and ministry have been reviewed:

1. The doctrine of assurance, which he maintained against the rationalistic deists and the formal churchmen of his day;

2. The doctrine of free grace, which he opposed to the fatalism of Calvinistic election and predestination;

3. The doctrine of Christian perfection or entire sanctification as a second crisis in Christian experience, which he opposed to the Moravian teaching that sanctification is simultaneous with justification and to the antinomian development both of Moravianism and Calvinism.

The combination of crisis and process in normal Christian experience as taught by Wesley has been presented, and note made of Wesley's teaching that Christian perfection does not deliver from human infirmities, and therefore absolute perfection of conduct is not guaranteed by perfection of love. Hence it follows that the most saintly Christian still needs the atonement.

CHAPTER SEVEN

Methodism's Conquering Witness: With What Results?

John Wesley was a practical man who did not rest his case when he had awakened his hearers and stirred in them Christian aspirations but, as we have observed, promptly gathered them into Society and Class. The effects of his organizing genius continue to this day in a world Methodism of nearly fifteen million members. Our present concern with results, however, goes back of organization and numbers to the impact of the Wesleyan message and method, both on individuals and on society.

Lives were changed

Lives were changed—this was the result of first importance in eighteenth-century England. From the beginning there were many who criticized and some who cautioned Wesley concerning the spectacular physical accompaniments of religious fervor. To Samuel, his elder brother, John finally wrote, affirming that he had seen "many persons changed in a moment from the spirit of fear, horror, despair, to the spirit of love, joy, and peace; and from sinful desire, till then reigning over them, to a pure desire of doing the will of God." He added that the change wrought in these persons appeared, "not from their shedding tears only, or falling into fits, or crying out," but "from the whole tenor of their life, till then many ways wicked; from that time holy, just, and good." And he could produce exhibits. "I will show you," he said, "him that was a lion till then, and is now a lamb; him that was a drunkard, and is now exemplarily sober; the whoremonger that was, who now abhors the very 'garment spotted by the flesh.' These are my living arguments . . ."[1]

And they were telling arguments. Instances need not be multiplied, but we cite one which won the verdict of a magistrate in favor of the defendants, "a whole wagon-load of these heretics," the Meth-

---
1. J. Wesley, *Journal*. Epworth Press, London; v. 2, 202.

odists. The justice asked the accusers what were their charges against them, and there was a heavy silence. As Wesley said, "that was a point their conductors had forgot." One of the persecutors asserted that these Methodists claimed to be better than other people, "and, besides, they prayed from morning to night." The justice pressed for further charges and an old man spoke up to complain, "they have *convarted* my wife, who before had such a tongue! And now," he added, "she is as quiet as a lamb." The magistrate ordered, "Carry them back, carry them back, and let them convert all the scolds in town." [2]

Society was changed

Wesley's first concern was the salvation of sinners, but his evangelism brought outstanding social consequences. Within a few months after the outbreak of Revival early in 1739 among the colliers of Kingswood, Wesley reported the following:

> Few persons have lived long in the West of England who have not heard of the colliers of Kingswood, a people famous, from the beginning hitherto, for neither fearing God nor regarding man; so ignorant of the things of God that they seemed but one remove from the beasts that perish; and therefore utterly without the desire of instruction, as well as without the means of it.
> ... The scene is already changed. Kingswood does not now, as a year ago, resound with cursing and blasphemy. It is no more filled with drunkenness and uncleanness, and the idle diversions that naturally lead thereto. It is no longer full of wars and fightings, clamor and bitterness, of wrath and envyings. Peace and love are there." [3]

The report proceeds to an account of the building of the nearly completed Kingswood School—a perfectly normal social consequence of evangelism.

A similar change came to West Cornwall, which long had been a region of smugglers, fighters, and those who lured ships on the rocks to plunder them. A year after revival came to that neighborhood there was not one felon in its prison, a condition Charles Wesley declared had not been known in the memory of man.

The social benefits of religious revival were more than local; they

2. *Ibid.*, v. 3, 20.
3. *Ibid.*, v. 2, 323.

were national. As reviewed in Chapter Two, the times were morally desperate. England had been caught in the current that would sweep France to violent revolution before the century's close. How explain England's escape from such a blood-bath as came to France? Even Lecky, who had no great sympathy with earnest religion, set the pattern for succeeding historians in his claim that Wesley and the Revival saved England from a similar revolution. This happy outcome resulted, not from applying peripheral patches to England's open sores, but from the changing of individual hearts to bring social healing through personal soundness.

Wesley's welfare concern

We have said that Wesley's first concern was the salvation of souls, but we cannot overlook his very genuine and even passionate interest in helping the unfortunate. He established the first free dispensary in London, opened workshops for the unemployed poor, organized a benevolent loan society, and collected a charity fund to aid the needy who might be members of no Methodist Society. And his good works were personal as well as corporate: one cold winter, when he was past eighty, he trudged the streets of London in ankle-deep slush to collect two hundred pounds with which to buy warm clothes for the poor, and became ill from the exposure.

John Wesley was active in social reform as well as aiding the needy. He promoted temperance, opposed slavery, condemned political corruption, related the poverty of some to the luxury of others, exposed the folly of war, and maintained Christian standards against such common evil practices as gambling and smuggling.

Faith and works

Wesley was attacked vigorously in his day because of his insistence that the Christian must validate his faith by a life of service to God and man. By some he was charged with legalism, by others accused of being a papist. Unlike Martin Luther, he accepted fully the Epistle of James. Commenting thereon, he summarized in one terse statement the relationship of faith and works, saying, "Works do not give life to faith, but faith begets works, and then is perfected by them." [4]

---

4. J. Wesley, *Explanatory Notes Upon the New Testament*. Epworth Press, London; p. 863.

To correct a critic's misunderstanding of one of his preachers as teaching salvation by works, he wrote, "None of us talk of being accepted for our works; that is a Calvinist slander. But we all maintain we are not saved without works, that works are a condition (though not the meritorious cause) of final salvation." [5] He defended another of his preachers against the charge of teaching sanctification by works in these sane words: "Probably the difference between you and others lies in words chiefly. All who expect to be sanctified at all expect to be sanctified by faith. But meantime they know that faith will not be given but to them that obey. Remotely, therefore, the blessing depends on our works, although immediately upon simple faith." [6]

While he made much of the social direction of the Christian religion, insisting that good works must be the fruit of a living faith and a condition of one's continuing in saving relationship to God, he protested forcefully against the teaching that works can yield merit for one's salvation. At St. Mary's of Oxford he preached his sermon on "Salvation by Faith," shortly after Aldersgate. Therein he forthrightly declared, "there is nothing we are, or have, or do which can deserve the least thing at God's hand. . . . And whatever righteousness may be found in man, this is also the gift of God." [7]

Perhaps never did Wesley more pointedly declare the social character of Christianity than when he said, "The gospel of Christ knows of no religion but social; no holiness but social holiness." His further assertion in this context probes the conscience of all who profess the distinctive experience in grace that Wesley taught: *"Faith working by love* is the length and breadth and depth and height of Christian perfection." [8] And again in one of his several discourses on the Sermon on the Mount, he declared, "Christianity is essentially a social religion; and . . . to turn it into a solitary one is to destroy it." [9] The extension of his religious interests to include political concerns he expressed by saying, "There is the closest connection . . . between my religious and my political conduct." [10]

---

5. J. Wesley, *Letters.* Epworth Press, v. 6, 76.
6. *Ibid.,* v. 4, 71.
7. J. Wesley, *Sermons on Several Occasions.* Phillips & Hunt, New York; v. 1, 13.
8. J. Wesley, *Works* (Jackson's 3rd ed.); v. 14, 334.
9. J. Wesley, *Sermons on Several Occasions.* Phillips & Hunt, New York; v. 1, 211..
10. J. Wesley, *Letters.* Epworth Press, London; v. 6, 267.

Wesley spoke out on social issues

Wesley was outspoken on social evils of his day. In "Thoughts on the Present Scarcity of Provisions" he charged lack of bread to the use of corn in distilling liquor; the lack of oats to feeding the horses of the rich; the lack of mutton and beef to breeding horses for the aristocracy and for export to France; the lack of such provisions as pork, poultry and eggs to large-scale farming which displaced small land-holders. He proposed these remedies, with others: prohibit distilling grains; heavily tax luxury goods; discontinue useless pensions; reduce the national debt.[11]

He warned against unfair trade practices. "We cannot, consistent with brotherly love," he said, "sell our goods below market price; we cannot study to ruin our neighbor's trade, in order to advance our own." [12] Against the liquor traffic he wrote, "Neither may we gain by hurting our neighbor in his body. Therefore we may not sell anything which tends to impair health; such is, eminently, all that liquid fire, commonly called drams, or spirituous liquors." [13]

Thirteen years before the Abolition Committee was organized to combat slavery, and while this evil was flourishing under the law, Wesley wrote "Thoughts on Slavery" wherein he said:

> Can [human law] turn darkness into light, or evil into good? ... Notwithstanding ten thousand laws, right is right, and wrong is wrong still.... I deny that villainy is ever necessary.... A man can be under no necessity of degrading himself into a wolf.... Give liberty to whom liberty is due, that is, to every child of man, to every partaker of human nature. Let none serve you but by his own act and deed, by his own voluntary choice.[14]

The last letter Wesley wrote, only six days before his death, was directed to the great philanthropist and advocate of emancipation of the slaves, William Wilberforce. He urged the reformer, "Go on, in the name of God, and in the power of His might, till even American slavery (the vilest that ever saw the sun) shall vanish away before it." [15]

---

11. J. Wesley, *Works* (Emory ed. 1853). Carlton & Phillips, New York; v. 6, 274 et seq.
12. J. Wesley, *Sermons on Several Occasions*. Phillips & Hunt, New York; v. 1, 443.
13. *Loc. cit.*
14. J. Wesley, *Works* (Emory ed. 1853). Carlton & Phillips, New York; v. 6, 286 et seq.
15. J. Wesley, *Letters*. Epworth Press, London; v. 8, 265.

In the following indictment of the War of the American Revolution, Wesley indicted all wars:

> But a matter is in dispute relative to the mode of taxation. So these countrymen, children of the same parents, are to *murder* each other in all possible haste, to *prove* who is in the right. Now what an argument is this! What a method of proof! What an amazing way of deciding controversies! [16]

Modern critics of Wesley's social principles

Notwithstanding the generally acknowledged benefits accruing to society from the Wesleyan Revival, there are severe critics today of Wesley's social views and methods. In *After Wesley*, Maldwyn Edwards decries the conservative effect of Wesley's teaching on Christian perfection in terms so exclusively personal as not to provoke in his followers a proper concern for society.[17] This criticism is difficult to support as applied to Wesley's definition and elaboration of the doctrine and the experience of Christian perfection, however well it may have applied to some of the followers of Wesley, especially after his death. Wesley himself emphasized the social direction of Christianity with a force and clarity few modern prophets have achieved. Both in principle and in application, he held love in sharp focus. His making I Corinthians 13 the pattern of Christian perfection, his exposition of works in their relationship to faith in his *Notes* on the Epistle of James, his General Rules for the United Societies, his sermons, his personal example—all these give vigorous thrust to the social reach of religion as "faith working by love."

And yet Richard Niebuhr has given Wesley little credit for possessing a sensitive social conscience. Here is his criticism:

> The social ethics of Methodism was an ethics of philanthropy and humanitarianism, which regarded movements toward equality as concessions made out of love rather than as demands of justice, and this philanthropy suffered the constant danger of degenerating into sentimental charity. But the typical social ethics of the poor is an ethics of reconstruction whose excrescences appear in violence rather than in sentimentality.[18]

It is disturbing that those who criticize Wesley's social concern

---

16. J. Wesley, *Works* (Emory ed. 1853). Carlton & Phillips, New York; v. 6, 323.
17. Maldwyn Edwards, *After Wesley*. Epworth Press, London; p. 22.
18. H. R. Niebuhr, *The Social Sources of Denominationalism*. Henry Holt & Co., Inc., New York; p. 69.

should discount Christian love in favor of violence and revolution as the method of social reform. Certainly, for Christians the Sermon on the Mount gives solid support to Wesley's method of outgoing love rather than the method of violent and vindictive revolution. And Wesley's statement on slavery, sketched above, settles any issue concerning his recognition of justice as the basis for the structure of the social order. Upon that *just social basis* Wesley maintained that *love* should operate in the sphere of *personal relationships*.

Mary Alice Tenney has called attention to a letter Wesley wrote Bishop Secker pointing out that even before Wesley came under censure for preaching, and before he had even known "salvation by faith," he had been excluded from several pulpits for preaching love to God and man as the substance of religion.[19] We venture to suggest that had Wesley's emphasis at that early date in his ministry, or later, been mere philanthropy, his preaching could hardly have aroused such antagonism as it did provoke. As a prophet of righteousness and justice, his realism pricked the sensibilities of favored groups in society and aroused their active hostility.

In an exciting book on John and Charles Wesley, Mabel Richmond Brailsford charges that under Wesley's teachings "Resignation became a prime virtue and restiveness under suffering a major crime," and the author casts aspersion on early Methodism for the social consequences of its alleged other-worldliness in these words:

> It has been said that when the Wesleys began their work, England was ripe for revolution, but by preaching the duty of obedience to rulers and of patience under affliction, and by representing this earthly life, with its negations and miseries, as the indispensable training ground for the heavenly, they lulled asleep the restlessness and resentment of the deeply wronged poor.[20]

To support her claim, Brailsford gives an account of the response of the colliers of Kingswood to the plea of Charles Wesley when, because of the high price of bread during a period of scarcity, they were moving on Bristol as a mob. Some of them, especially converts of the Kingswood revival, turned aside to join Charles Wesley in

---

19. M. A. Tenney, *Blueprint for a Christian World*. Light & Life Press, Winona Lake; p. 35.
20. M. R. Brailsford, *A Tale of Two Brothers*. Oxford University Press, New York; p. 149.

prayer. In due time the rioters returned from Bristol where no violence had occurred, the mob satisfying itself that some of its leaders had presented their grievances to Bristol's mayor.

What does Brailsford prefer, riots or orderly negotiations? Perhaps her severest criticism of early Methodism is this claim that its teachings made the lower classes docile. On this ground, in fact, she charges that the Methodist Revival must bear a part of the responsibility for the economic and social evils attending England's Industrial Revolution of the nineteenth century.[21]

But John Wesley's love was far from that docile, placid variety which lacks the strength and fiber of a sanctified will to pass judgment on evils in society or to rebuke sin in the individual. He records in his *Journal*, with no hint of disapproval, instances of popular uprisings against economic injustice. That his influence was effective in promoting positive reforms, even the critics we have quoted concede. Richard Niebuhr adds to criticism this acknowledgment, "Methodism largely represented the religious aspect of that great revolutionary movement of the eighteenth century which placed the individual at the center of things and so profoundly modified all existing institutions." [22] He notes further, "The Methodist revival was the last great religious revolution of the disinherited in Christendom," [23] by which he indicates that thereafter social reforms were to be secular, even as the revolution we know today as Communism.

Maldwyn Edwards grants that "John Wesley helped to make England conscious of its social obligations," [24] and further says:

> . . . The revival of religion did leaven society in a clear and unmistakable manner. Gross brutality in sport disappeared; there came an improvement in the tone of the drama, and J. R. Green was able to speak of the fresh spirit of moral zeal which at the end of the eighteenth century purified our literature and our manners.[25]

Even Brailsford brought herself to acknowledge that Wesley "raised

---

21. *Ibid.*, p. 292.
22. H. R. Niebuhr, *The Social Sources of Denominationalism.* Henry Holt & Co., Inc., New York; p. 65.
23. *Ibid.*, p. 72.
24. Maldwyn Edwards, *After Wesley. Epworth Press*, London; p. 117.
25. *Ibid.*, p. 138.

the standard of morals of the working classes, and so, almost automatically, improved their living conditions," which he accomplished "by inculcating the virtues of thrift and honesty." [26]

Other evaluations of Wesley as reformer

Declarations of leaders in church and state, and letters to the greatness of Wesley's achievements and the social benefits of the Wesleyan Revival would fill a volume. We cite but a few.

The Cambridge Modern History, after describing eighteenth-century conditions in England, asserts that with the advent of Methodism, "A governing class, intent only on pleasure or politics, a Church occupied chiefly with patronage and controversy, were now to feel the force of a great religious wave which was to beat on every wall of privilege." [27] That wave was effective, for again we read from the same source, "The earlier half of the eighteenth century was an age of materialism, a period of dim ideals, of expiring hopes; before the middle of the century its character was transformed; there appeared a movement headed by a mighty leader, who brought forth water from the rocks to make a barren land live again." After noting the self-complacency, materialism and rationalism of the period and the men therein who sought reform—Chatham in politics, Thomson in poetry, Berkeley in philosophy, and Law in divinity, the writer asserts that, "more important than any of these in universality of influence and in range of achievements were John Wesley and the religious revival to which he gave his name and his life." [28]

August Birrell, the essayist, evaluated Wesley's influence in these high terms:

> If you want to get into the last century, to feel its pulses throb beneath your finger, be content sometimes to leave the letters of Horace Walpole unturned ... and ride up and down the country with the greatest force of the eighteenth century in England. No man lived nearer the centre than John Wesley, neither Clive nor Pitt, neither Mansfield nor Johnson. You cannot cut him out of our national life. No single figure influenced so many minds,

---

26. M. R. Brailsford, *A Tale of Two Brothers*. Oxford University Press, New York; p. 292.
27. *The Cambridge Modern History*, Cambridge University Press, New York; v. 6, 80.
28. *Ibid.*, v. 6, 77.

no single voice touched so many hearts. No other man did such a life's work for England.[29]

A *New History of Methodism* cites M. Taine, French historian, as recording his judgment that John Wesley and Methodism saved England from revolution,[30] and the English historian, Lecky, is frequently quoted to the same effect. The same volume ascribes great economic improvement in England to the influence of the Revival on shopkeepers and laborers. Before the Revival, "both time and money had been recklessly wasted in drinking, gambling, roystering, and sporting." But due to the Revival, "crowds of these became productive instead of wasteful elements in the national life."[31]

According to Green the eighteenth-century revival "changed in a few years the whole temper of English society." This change was expressed in the following ways:

> The Church was restored to life and activity. Religion carried to the hearts of the poor a fresh spirit of moral zeal, while it purified our literature and our manners. A new philanthropy reformed our prisons, infused clemency and wisdom into our penal laws, abolished the slave-trade, and gave the first impulses to popular education.[32]

Bready quoted Lloyd-George when prime minister in 1922 as claiming that "Wales owed more to the movement of which Wesley was the inspirer and leader, than to any other movement in the whole of its history."[33]

According to Fitchett, John Wesley "set in motion forces that changed the religious history of England."[34] T. R. Glover, Baptist scholar of Cambridge, ranked Wesley with Paul, Augustine, and Luther as "one of the four intellectuals through whom God put a new heart into Christendom on both sides of the Atlantic."[35]

---

29. A. Birrell, *Essays and Addresses*. Chas. Scribner's Sons, New York; p. 35.
30. Townsend, Workman & Eayrs, Editors, *A New History of Methodism*. Hodder & Stoughton, London; v. 1, 371.
31. *Ibid.*, 374.
32. J. H. Green, *A Short History of the English People*. Harper & Bros., New York; p. 707 *et seq.*
33. Quoted by J. W. Bready, *This Freedom—Whence?* Light & Life Press, Winona Lake; p. 96.
34. W. H. Fitchett, *Wesley and His Century*. Eaton & Mains, New York; p. 8..
35. Quoted by J. R. Joy; *John Wesley's Awakening*. The Methodist Book Concern, New York; p. 114.

The estimates of John Wesley by representative men of the Church of England are worthy of note. Archbishop Davidson has been quoted as pronouncing Wesley "one of the greatest Englishmen that ever lived," and saying that he "practically changed the outlook and even the character of the English nation." [36] Wakemen, historian of the English Church, wrote, "John Wesley must always stand out in English Church History as the greatest religious figure in the eighteenth century." Nothwithstanding the separation that finally came, Wakeman grants that Wesley and the Methodists "warmed the chilled blood of the Church of England once more into activity by the doctrine of love." [37] Finally, we cite *A History of the English Church*, in the index to which volume John Wesley's entries exceed all others, including Anglican bishops and archbishops.[38]

But it remained not alone for subsequent generations to honor and to praise Wesley. He lived to see hostility and personal hatred pass, and to be welcomed and revered wherever he went. In July, 1789, a few months before his death, he wrote, "We now fear greater danger from honor than dishonor." [39] On the last page he ever wrote in his *Journal*, he reported preaching at Lynn with all clergymen of the town present save one, who was lame. "They are all prejudiced in favor of the Methodists; as indeed are most of the townsmen," Wesley said. The next day he was at Diss with no place to preach until the bishop, asked if he had any objection to Wesley's preaching in the church, reassured the timorous minister by saying, "None at all." On that day, one of the largest churches in all England was filled to hear Wesley.[40]

A final word on Wesley's social witness

Viewed against the background of his century, John Wesley was far advanced in social sensitiveness, economic and social insights, and in his practical applications of principles to the needs of society. Although some of his critics today would have had him seek reform

---

36. Quoted by J. W. Bready, *This Freedom—Whence?* Light & Life Press, Winona Lake; p. 96.
37. H. O. Wakeman, *An Introduction to the History of the Church of England*. Rivingtons, London; pp. 437, 438.
38. J. H. Overton and F. Relton, *A History of the English Church*, 1714-1800. The Macmillan Co., Ltd., London.
39. J. Wesley, *Letters*. Epworth Press, London; v. 8, 152.
40. J. Wesley, *Journal*. Epworth Press, London; v. 8, 108, 109.

by fomenting revolution, Wesley was both reformer and philanthropist. Too many reformers, concerned with abstract justice, can let multitudes about them suffer while they fight for a "cause." But the reformer who is moved by a sincere and intelligent Christian love, not for a particular class or order of men, but for all men as neighbors, combines philanthropy with reform by moving to help the unfortunate victim while he works for a radical corrective through social justice.

Wesley was a man of balance, well poised in his positions on most vital issues for all his Tory leanings politically. His political conservatism strengthened the grip he held in the area of discipline, so remarkable in one of such passion for justice to the unfortunate and commitment to perfect love as the standard in all human relationships. He accepted in principle and applied in practice the scriptural synthesis of "faith working by love," both in its upward reach to God and in its outward reach to all men; and especially in the latter was he far in advance of his age.

According to Carter, Wesley's "doctrine of stewardship has undiminished relevance for Christians in all generations." [41] Even in this day of the welfare state with its impersonal administration of assistance to the underprivileged, there is need for Wesley's principle of personal sharing by which both recipient and benefactor are benefited. Dr. Tenney states the case well when she says, "Early Methodism stood for something more than the bland sentimental humanitarianism of the nineteenth century, which stooped as it gave; and something far more than the impersonal and secularized administration of welfare work in the twentieth century. It demanded personal identification with the deepest needs of mankind." [42]

Wesley was not an ascetic, esteeming poverty and self-affliction virtues in themselves. He believed in a life to which every worthy interest is tributary, and was in full accord with Paul's repeated "whatsoevers" of Philippians 4:8. We see the wide range of Wesley's sympathies and his proper humanism in a sermon in which he pictured the man of God as a man of love, saying of him:

---

41. H. Carter, *The Methodist Heritage*. Abingdon-Cokesbury, New York; p. 122.
42. M. A. Tenney, *Blueprint for a Christian World*. Light & Life Press, Winona Lake; p. 268.

Indeed, good in general is his glory and his joy, wherever diffused throughout the race of mankind. As a citizen of the world he claims a share in the happiness of all the inhabitants of it. Because he is a man, he is not unconcerned in the welfare of any man; but enjoys whatsoever brings glory to God and promotes peace and good-will among men.[43]

Elsewhere we find him refusing to agree with Pascal that man should avoid all pleasure on the ground that this is impossible without destroying the body; that far from requiring it, God rather " 'giveth us all things to enjoy,' so we enjoy them to his glory." [44]

Troeltsch has pointed out that the early Christian dealt neither with hopes of improving the social order nor with the healing of social ills, and that the summons of Jesus was not to a program of social reform but to individual preparation for the Kingdom of God. But nevertheless, the development of a social order out of the Christian message was inevitable.[45] In a remarkable way Wesley saw the social bearing of the Christian religion of love and established a healthy relationship of the vertical and horizontal, of the personal and social in Christian living.

In a letter written in his advancing eighties as he faced the setting sun, Wesley repeated to a friend a paraphrase of what a respected counselor had told him fifty or sixty years before. "It is a blessed thing to have fellow travelers to the new Jerusalem," he said. "If you cannot find any, you must make them; for none can travel that way alone." [46]

* * * * *

Wesley a guide for today

Up to this point John Wesley has dominated our study, for any clear understanding of Methodism is impossible without an understanding of the underlying qualities of character, the principal traits of personality, and the deep-rooted convictions of truth which its founder projected into the movement he organized and capably led for half a century. Not only his leadership during fifty years, but also the wanderings of his earlier life in other paths than the way of faith

---

43. J. Wesley, *Sermons on Several Occasions*. Phillips & Hunt, New York; v. 1, 196.
44. J. Wesley, *Works* (Jackson's 3rd ed.); v. 11, 461 *et seq.*
45. E. Troeltsch, *The Social Teaching of the Christian Churches*. The Macmillan Co., New York; v. 1, p. 40.
46. J. Wesley, *Letters*. Epworth Press, London; v. 8, 198.

make him the surer guide to those who would follow him, even as he came at last to follow Christ. Wesley's life and character have a message for a bewildered age.

There are those who warn that one should follow the Bible, not Wesley, Calvin, Luther, or any man. We agree that the Bible is our sufficient standard both of faith and practice, but do not agree with the underlying assumption that ordinary piety and ordinary intellects can claim such insight into Biblical and spiritual truth as men of Wesley's stature have manifested, both in their writings and in their influence on the course of human events. Too frequently the advice to follow the Bible and not man is parroted by those who readily accept the interpretations of Scripture by some man of lesser piety and scholarship than any of those named, and depend upon the pre-digested thought-patterns of "Bible helps" that fall pathetically short of such devout and scholarly use of the Bible as Wesley described so beautifully in that literary gem quoted on page 88 and following.

We do well to consider the steps of a wise and good man who found his way to the Scriptural standard of faith after trying the many and devious routes men are prone to take in their quest for God, only to be disappointed, disillusioned, and brought to despair; or, which is worse, to be lulled to sleep in a false confidence that they have found the way. The Wesley Society, a contemporary group of Methodist scholars seeking to rediscover John Wesley, declares that today the danger is not that we *canonize* but that we *ignore* him.

One of the marvels of all biography is the way John Wesley was delivered from false leads, without thereafter reversing himself to the opposite extreme to renounce those very powers of mind and personality upon which he had been misled to place undue dependence in his search for God. Wesley was delivered from the icy grip of reason, and yet thereafter was ever the friend of learning and sought the counsel of reason, without submitting to its absolute reign. He was delivered from the heavy chains of legalism, and nevertheless ever after declared the imperatives of righteous living and of good works. He was delivered from an asceticism that had renounced even life's good things, but still maintained the discipline of spirit over the strivings of physical desire. He broke from the bondage of ritualism, but never renounced church order for chaos. He broke through the fog of mysticism, but came to a vital, heartfelt personal experience, safeguarded against the riot of subjectivism by the restraints of social discipline and by the Bible as the standard by which to judge personal experience itself. Without such balance in the center of the conflicting forces of the eighteenth century, John Wesley could not have been the effective instrument by which God moved England into new channels of faith, hope, and love, and set in motion a current of spiritual warmth and power to encircle the earth.

CHAPTER EIGHT

Methodism Transplanted to America

Early beginnings in America

George Whitefield had been laboring in the American Colonies in evangelism and philanthropy, except for intervals he spent in England, from 1738 to 1770. He had not organized the results of his fruitful evangelistic labors, but left his converts to the care of the existing churches—or without care. Consequently, the history of organized Methodism in America usually begins, not with Whitefield's first visit in 1738, but with a small nucleus of Irish immigrants in New York about 1766. These were of German descent whose ancestors had emigrated to Ireland to escape persecution under Louis XIV in the later seventeenth century.

These immigrants in America had been under the influence of the Wesleyan revival in the county of Limerick, Ireland. One of them was a local preacher named Philip Embury. He had become religiously discouraged and morally passive in the New World, but his cousin, Barbara Heck, finally shamed him for his lack of religious concern in the face of the growing wickedness of the immigrant group, and challenged him to resume his preaching. This he did, opening his own home and having in his first service a congregation of five.

The interest grew, and suddenly one day there appeared in the service a colorful character in the uniform of an army officer who called himself "Captain Thomas Webb, of the king's service, and also a soldier of the cross and a spiritual son of John Wesley." Captain Webb was shortly assisting Philip Embury with the preaching, dramatically laying his sword across stand or table before him as he spoke. Before long, the congregation moved to a sailing-loft, and then, under the stimulus and generous support of Captain Webb, bought a lot and built Wesley Chapel on John Street. The building was dedicated on October 30, 1768, the preacher of the occasion being none other than the humble yet capable Philip Embury.

Methodism in the southern colonies likewise had its inception by way of Ireland. Robert Strawbridge was an ebullient son of the Emerald Isle and a Methodist convert who had settled in Maryland and opened his house for services until he could provide a meetinghouse. Without ordination, he assumed many powers thereof. Notwithstanding his independent spirit, he was instrumental in bringing hundreds into the Methodist movement.

The Methodist family magazine, *Together*, in its issue commemorating the 175th anniversary of the organization of the Methodist Episcopal Church in 1784, carries an article by Elmer T. Clark which presents facts concerning Methodist developments pointing to priority of each of the three afore-mentioned men and associated places as representing the origin of organized Methodism in America. Which was first: the outcome of Whitefield's labors in Philadelphia? Philip Embury in New York? Robert Strawbridge and the Baltimore area? Clark writes, "I but note the facts revealed by research and leave the answers to you!" [1]

Another Irish Methodist came to America in 1769, with Wesley's approval but not supported by the Conference. This was Robert Williams who ministered with zeal and effectiveness until his early death, the first Methodist preacher to give up his life in America. Urged by American Methodists and especially by Captain Webb, the English Conference began officially to send itinerant preachers to the American colonies. The first of these were Richard Boardman and Joseph Pilmoor, sent in 1769. One of those sent in 1771 was Francis Asbury, a young itinerant who was destined to shape the course of early American Methodism more than any other man.

With the outbreak of the Revolution, several preachers returned to England, and the Conference sent no more until after the war had ended. Out of the Revolutionary War period, during which he had endured persecution and enforced seclusion because suspected of Tory sympathies, Francis Asbury emerged to become a strong and wise leader.

Before the War, American Methodists had looked to the Anglican Church for the sacraments, as had been their custom in England. But after the War the Anglican Church no longer existed in the newly

---

1. E. T. Clark, "The three roots of American Methodism," *Together*, v. 3, Nov. 1959, p. 25.

independent nation, and its successor, The Protestant Episcopal Church, had not been organized. The need for ordained ministers was acute. Wesley attempted without success to persuade a bishop to ordain one of his preachers for ministry in America. Then, in his characteristically practical way in an emergency, he broke with tradition and took it upon himself to ordain the learned Dr. Thomas Coke as a superintendent of American Methodism, with authority to ordain deacons and elders in America, including Francis Asbury whom Wesley appointed also a superintendent to serve with Dr. Coke.

Shortly after Dr. Coke's arrival in America, the famous "Christmas Conference" of 1784 was summoned. In this conference the preachers voted to organize the Methodist Episcopal Church, for which John Wesley had provided Articles of Religion, revised largely by abbreviation from the Thirty-nine Articles of the Church of England, and also a revision of the liturgy of the Church of England called *The Sunday Service*. These were adopted, but the latter never became popular and soon fell into discard without having been revoked by official act. The Articles of Religion, however, continue to this day as Methodism's statement of doctrine.

Asbury would not accept appointment as superintendent by Wesley without election by his fellows to that office. This accomplished, Asbury received on three successive days ordination as deacon, ordination as elder, and consecration as bishop.

To Asbury's consecration as "bishop" Wesley strongly objected, as also he objected to the decision of the Conference to establish a school with such an ambitious designation as "Cokesbury College." On these matters he wrote to Asbury in these plain words:

> But in one point, my dear brother, I am a little afraid both the Doctor [Coke] and you differ from me. I study to be little: you study to be great. I creep: you strut along. I found a school: you a college! nay, and call it after your own names! . . .
>
> One instance of this, of your greatness, has given me great concern. How can you, how dare you suffer yourself to be called Bishop? I shudder, I start at the very thought! Men may call me a knave or a fool, a rascal, a scoundrel, and I am content: but they shall never by my consent call me Bishop! For my sake, for God's sake, for Christ's sake put a full end to this! [2]

---

2. J. Wesley, *Letters*. Epworth Press, London; v. 8, 91.

But the episcopal title has continued in American Methodism from that day to this, a period of 175 years.

Early American Methodism: its doctrines

Chapter Six stated the three distinctive doctrinal emphases of John Wesley to be an unlimited atonement, assurance, and Christian perfection. The scholarly historian of American Methodism, Abel Stevens, in his account of the organization of the Methodist Episcopal Church by the "Christmas Conference," states that in addition to those doctrines in its Articles of Religion which it shares with the universal church, Methodism "preaches, especially, Universal Redemption, Assurance and Perfection." [3] Thus, the Methodism transplanted to the American Continent in the period 1768-1784 was unmistakably Wesleyan in doctrine.

A rare personality connected with Methodism in Colonial America was the Anglican clergyman, Devereux Jarratt, of Virginia. Interestingly enough, E. Clowes Chorley begins the first chapter of his official history of the Protestant Episcopal Church with Jarratt. He gives considerable space to Jarratt's hearty cooperation with Robert Williams and other Methodists, with whom he identified himself by using the pronoun "we" in reporting on Christian perfection as one of the doctrines of the revival in the South which united the influence of his own spiritually productive ministry with the Methodist movement. It is noteworthy that such a clear statement of the doctrine came from an American Anglican of the colonial period, and that in 1946 it is quoted in an official history of the Protestant Episcopal Church. The following from Jarratt's pen could have been taken directly from the writings of John Wesley:

> One of the doctrines, as you know, which we particularly insist upon, is that of a present salvation; a salvation not only from the guilt and power, but also from the root of sin; a cleansing from all filthiness of the flesh and spirit, that we may perfect holiness in the fear of God; a going on to perfection, which we sometimes define as loving God with all our hearts.

He reported having seen several "who had been happy in a sense of God's pardoning love, as much convicted on account of the remains of sin in their hearts, and," he said, "as much distressed for a

---

3. A. Stevens, *A Compendious History of American Methodism.* Eaton & Mains, New York; p. 194 *et seq.*

total deliverance from them, as ever I saw any for justification." In truly Wesleyan phrasing, he added, "They all testify that they have received the gift instantaneously, and by simple faith."

It is little wonder that this Anglican divine was disturbed by what seemed to him certain emotional excesses of the revival. There was "some wild fire mixed with the sacred flame," he said, but declared himself better reconciled thereto after reading President Edwards' judgment that, "Wherever these [excesses] most appear, there is always the greatest and deepest work," and, "It requires much wisdom to allay the wild, and not damp the sacred fire." [4]

Jarratt traveled great distances to administer baptism and the Lord's Supper to scattered Methodists whose unordained preachers could not properly serve them in these ordinances. During the Revolutionary War when few ordained clergymen could be found in the colonies, and certain unordained itinerants took it upon themselves to administer the sacraments, Jarratt's relationships with the Methodists became strained. Chorley notes that this breach of order occurred only in the south—Asbury and the northern itinerants being opposed to such unauthorized ministries.

No doubt Strawbridge was the chief offender, for as Stevens said, "Robert Strawbridge contended sturdily for the right of the people to the sacrament, and could not be deterred by Asbury or Rankin from administering them." [5] When the first American Conference was held in 1773, the preachers adopted a rule on the issue, keeping in mind when they voted that Strawbridge was to be an exception. Stevens makes this claim on the authority of Asbury.

The evidence is convincing that the Methodism transplanted to America was the clear-cut pattern of Wesley's mature conception of a definite crisis of entire sanctification. In 1774, the year after sending Rankin to America, Wesley wrote his superintendent urging that the preachers press converts at once to go on to perfection. To the question in the 1784 *Discipline*, "What can be done to revive the work of God where it is decayed?" this answer by Wesley appears,

---

4. Devereux Jarratt, *Sermons on Various and Important Subjects in Practical Divinity.* (Quoted by E. C. Chorley, *Men and Movements in the American Episcopal Church.* Charles Scribner's Sons, New York; p. 14.)
5. A. Stevens, *A Compendious History of American Methodism;* pp. 75, 76.

"Strongly and explicitly exhort all believers to 'go on to perfection.' ... The Papists say, 'This cannot be attained till we have been refined by the fire of Purgatory.' The Calvinists say, 'Nay, it will be attained as soon as the soul leaves the body.' The old Methodists say, 'It may be attained before we die.'" The same *Discipline* asked candidates for the ministry, "Are you going on to perfection?" and "Do you expect to be made perfect in this life?" And, moreover, *Wesley's Plain Account of Christian Perfection* was published in the *Discipline*. During the first year of the Methodist Episcopal Church, John Wesley wrote Freeborn Garretson, "The more strongly and vigilantly you press all believers to aspire after full sanctification as attainable now by simple faith the more the work of God will prosper." [6]

Both Coke and Asbury were ardent advocates of the doctrine of entire sanctification. In 1789 Dr. Coke wrote, "Whether this be wildfire or not, I do most earnestly wish that there was such a work at this present time in England," and mentioned the revival in Maryland where twenty-five received "full sanctification" in one meeting, and where commonly twenty or twenty-five were justified in a day.[7]

On different occasions Asbury reproached himself for not sufficiently pressing the people on the issue, and in 1793, while struggling with illness but pursuing his work nevertheless, he wrote in his *Journal*, "I have found by secret search, that I have not preached sanctification as I should have done: if I am restored, this shall be my theme more pointedly than ever, God being my helper." [8]

Peters summarizes as follows his well-grounded conclusion that the Methodism transplanted to America was clearly Wesleyan in doctrine:

> The data appear to support the conclusion that American colonial Methodism in its standards and—more specifically—in its preaching made the doctrine of Christian perfection one of its characteristic features. The type of perfection so taught was the later Wesleyan view which included the concept of an experience attainable "now and by simple faith" and which at the same time made ample provision for corporate Christian nurture.

---

6. J. Wesley, *Letters*. Epworth Press, London; v. 7, 276.
7. Quoted by John Atkinson, *Centennial History of American Methodism*. Phillips & Hunt, New York; p. 234.
8. F. Asbury, *Journal*. Lane & Scott, New York; v. 2, 207.

It is reasonable to assume that it was with this connotation that the doctrine was embodied in the first Discipline of the Methodist Episcopal Church.[9]

Early American Methodism: its discipline

The first Conference held in America (Philadelphia, 1773) asked the question, "Ought not the doctrine and discipline of the Methodists, as contained in the Minutes [Wesley's *Large Minutes*], to be the sole rule of our conduct, who labor in the Connection with Mr. Wesley in America?" The answer was, "Yes." [10] By this question and its answer the Conference officially declared that in doctrine and in discipline, both organizational and individual, American Methodism was to be built on the Wesleyan pattern.

From the beginning in 1766, it had been taken for granted that Wesley's General Rules governed the conduct of a Methodist. The organizing Conference of 1784 gave special attention to the rule forbidding superfluous adornment. In answer to the question, "How shall we prevent superfluity of dress among our people?" the *Minutes* records the following answer, "Let the preachers carefully avoid everything of this kind in themselves, and speak frequently and faithfully against it in all our societies." The first *Discipline* based upon that Conference contained the following:

> *Quest.* 18. Should we insist on the rules concerning dress?
> *Ans.* By all means. This is no time to give any encouragement to superfluity of apparel. Therefore give no tickets to any till they have left off superfluous ornaments. In order to do this, 1. Let every assistant [pastor-in-charge] read the "Thoughts on Dress" at least once a year, in every large society. 2. In visiting the classes, be very mild, but very strict. 3. Allow no exempt cases, not even of a married woman. Better one suffer than many. 4. Give no tickets to any that wear high heads, enormous bonnets, ruffles or rings.[11]

In his recent book on Methodism, Bishop Gerald Kennedy responds to such seeming rigidity with the comment, "There was no nonsense

---

9. J. L. Peters, *Christian Perfection and American Methodism*. Abingdon Press, Nashville; p. 88 *et seq.*
10. Quoted by Sherman, *History of the Revision of the Discipline;* Nelson & Phillips, New York; p. 16.
11. Quoted by Emory, *History of the Discipline of the Methodist Episcopal Church.* Carlton & Porter, New York; p. 36.

about this, and every Methodist accepted certain standards of behavior as the price of membership." [12]

The first *Discipline* also enjoined simplicity and economy in the architecture of preaching houses and gave a pointed reason: "Let all our Chapels be built plain and decent; but not more expensively than is absolutely unavoidable: Otherwise the Necessity of raising Money will make Rich Men necessary to us. But if so, we must be dependent upon them, yea, and governed by them. And then farewell to the Methodist Discipline, if not Doctrine too." [13]

This *Discipline* carried no prohibition of pew rentals, but pewed churches were well understood to be contrary to Methodist principles. "From the beginning," says Barclay, "everyone knew that the Methodist chapels were open to all without financial obligation of any kind." [14]

Beginning with the Philadelphia Conference of 1773 and for several years thereafter, the early conferences were engaged in the conflict over the right of unordained preachers to administer the sacraments of baptism and the Lord's Supper, the South contending for and the North opposing the practice. Notwithstanding the greater numerical strength of the South, the North's position officially prevailed in the main, but without complete exclusion of the practice in the South. Relief came in 1784, as we have seen, by the arrival of Dr. Coke with authority as superintendent to ordain others, an authority that was extended to Asbury after his own ordinations by Coke, and his election to the superintendency along with Coke.

Preoccupation with the contention over the ordinances may have prevented attention to matters of conduct having a vital relationship to the welfare of society during the years following 1773, but the Baltimore Conference of 1780 came to grips with two contemporary forces that were destructive of society, namely intemperance and slavery. This Conference disapproved "the practice of distilling grain into liquor" and would disown all who would not renounce it. It

---

12. Gerald Kennedy, *The Methodist Way of Life*. © 1958 by Prentice-Hall, Inc.; Englewood Cliffs, New Jersey; p. 190.
13. Quoted by W. C. Barclay, *Early American Methodism, 1769-1844*: Vol. 2. *To Reform the Nation*. Board of Missions and Church Extension of the Methodist Church, New York; p. 5.
14. W. C. Barclay, *ibid.*, p. 6.

further resolved, "that slavery is contrary to the laws of God, man, and nature, and hurtful to society; contrary to the dictates of conscience and pure religion, and doing that which we would not that others should do unto us and ours"; and declared, "we do pass our disapprobation on all our friends who keep slaves, and advise their freedom." Traveling preachers owning slaves must "give promises to set them free." These positions on distilling and slavery inclined definitely towards Wesley's standards as declared in the General Rules.

These same problems received more serious attention in the Baltimore Conference of 1783 which pronounced, not only the manufacture, but also the sale or use of ardent spirits as "drams" to be "wrong in its nature and consequences," and directed preachers to instruct the people to refrain from the evil. Further, this Conference went beyond that of 1780 in its action on slavery by requiring, in addition to traveling preachers, local preachers also to free their slaves in states permitting emancipation.

Two conferences were held in Baltimore in 1784, the earlier one directing that members, previously warned, who bought slaves to hold them as such were to be expelled, and on no consideration were members to sell slaves; that local preachers not complying with the order to emancipate their slaves, where state laws permitted, were to be suspended—except in Virginia, where they were given another year to make adjustments; and that traveling preachers who refused to free their slaves be employed no longer. The "Christmas Conference" of the same year declared the following strong position against slavery:

> We view it as contrary to the golden law of God, on which hang all the law and the prophets, and the inalienable rights of mankind, as well as every principle of the Revolution, to hold in the deepest abasement, in a more abject slavery than is perhaps to be found in any part of the world except America, so many souls that are all capable of the image of God. We, therefore, think it our most bounden duty to take immediately some effectual method to extirpate this abomination from among us.[15]

By action of this "Christmas Conference" members were given one year after notice to emancipate slaves of specified ages in their pos-

---

15. Quoted by A. Stevens, *A Compendious History of American Methodism*; p. 189.

session. Failure to comply meant leaving the church or being excluded. Slaveholders might not join the church or be admitted to the Lord's Supper. Concession again was made to Virginia by allowing its members two years to decide their course, and again the regulations were effective only in states permitting owners to free their slaves.

Early in 1785 and not long after the "Christmas Conference," Coke and Asbury dined with President Washington at Mount Vernon, after which in a private interview they solicited his signature for a petition in behalf of emancipation. The President replied that he did not think it proper for him to sign, but he was favorable to the sentiment of the petition and would communicate his position to the Assembly should the question of emancipation come before that body.

The legislation of the "Christmas Conference" aroused great hostility, and another Conference called within six months suspended the rules which were so obnoxious to those involved with slavery. Thus, a brave idealism was clouded in its incipiency, and from this point the record of American Methodism concerning this ghastly moral and social evil is one of regrettable indecision and compromise. But that account belongs to the next chapter.

Resources of a transplanted Methodism

The new church in a new nation had a message and a method well adapted to the rugged frontier. The itinerant system permitted the church to move with the frontier, and the Methodist circuit-rider who inevitably found his way to the lonely settler's cabin in the remotest wilderness became proverbial.

Methodism's message was one of hope. Unlike the usual predestinarian fatalism of the older churches that had established themselves in America, Methodism declared salvation for all, and proclaimed that one could know by inner experience that he had been saved. Moreover, Methodism told the rough pioneer, contending with hitherto unrestrained forces within, as well as primeval forces without, that by the power of God's grace he could rule the one, even as by physical strength and wilderness cunning he could tame the other.

Men and neighborhoods had been changed by its message. Two years after the Virginia revival under Rector Jarratt and his itinerant

Methodist associates, a justice of the peace in a certain community declared that before the Methodists came, "There was nothing but drunkenness, cursing, swearing, and fighting most of the time the court sat: whereas now nothing is heard but prayer and praise, and conversing about God, and the things of God." [16]

With the organization of the Methodist Episcopal Church in 1784, Methodism in America was thenceforth to be largely on its own. From Wesley and the parent English church it had a goodly heritage in the itinerants who had come to America as evangelists; in such leaders as Asbury and Coke whom Wesley had commissioned as superintendents; in the *Large Minutes* and General Rules for organizational order and individual discipline; in the Articles of Religion and Wesley's *Notes* and *Sermons* as standards of doctrine.

Moreover, the new church began its independent existence with from 15,000 to 18,000 members, more than 60 chapels, 104 traveling preachers, several hundred local preachers and exhorters, and a constituency of regular attendants estimated at 200,000. The Methodist Episcopal Church was soon to surpass in every measurable respect its English parent, and one day would be the largest Protestant denomination in America.

It is our purpose in following chapters to trace its stewardship of this rich heritage during the seventy-five years following the "Christmas Conference."

---

16. Quoted by J. L. Peters, *Christian Perfection and American Methodism*. Abingdon Press, Nashville; p. 84. (From Thos. Rankin, A Brief Narrative of the Revival in Virginia; pp. 7, 8.)

CHAPTER NINE

The Witness Blurred: In Doctrine and Life

Concerning John Wesley's tolerance in matters of opinion, Umphrey Lee has said, "Let it be repeated that Wesley was not proposing a home for refugees from conviction." [1] For with all his open-mindedness, Wesley was firm on the great essentials of the Christian faith. It was to be expected, therefore, that his religious descendants would hold to his central doctrinal teachings.

Doctrinal decline in English Methodism

Chapter Eight noted that Wesley's three most distinctive doctrinal emphases were assurance, an unlimited atonement, and Christian perfection. The last named of the three has been the great doctrinal touchstone of historic Methodism, especially in view of the fact that the other two doctrines have pretty thoroughly permeated evangelical Protestantism generally.

Disturbingly enough, the doctrine had come under question among some of the Methodists of England, even during the lifetime of Methodism's founder. According to Mary Alice Tenney, the preaching of the doctrine had come into disrepute in some quarters, or was considered only "a 'counsel of perfection,' a spiritual experience to be enjoyed only by 'elect' souls, such as might live in seclusion, but not the criterion for everyday ethical conduct." She adds that, "even some of the preachers are said to have laughed behind his back about *Wesley's* doctrine of perfection." [2]

In 1772 John wrote his brother Charles, "I find almost all our preachers in every circuit have done with Christian perfection. They say they believe it; but they never preach it, or not once in a quarter.

---

1. Umphrey Lee, "Freedom from rigid creed," in *Methodism*, Wm. K. Anderson, Ed. The Methodist Publishing House, Nashville; p. 137.
2. M. A. Tenney, *Blueprint for a Christian World*. Light & Life Press, Winona Lake; p. 270.

What is to be done? Shall we let it drop, or make a point of it?"[3] The record is clear that John continued to "make a point of it."

He visited Launceston in 1776, and was disturbed because the work there had not advanced since his previous visit. He diagnosed the difficulty as due to failure of the preachers to declare the doctrine of Christian perfection, and wrote in his *Journal*:

> Here I found the plain reason why the work of God had gained no ground in this circuit all the year. The preachers had given up the Methodist testimony. Either they did not speak of Perfection at all (the peculiar doctrine committed to our trust), or they spoke of it only in general terms, without urging believers to "go on unto perfection," and to expect it every moment. And wherever this is not earnestly done, the work of God does not prosper.[4]

Peters has expressed the opinion that Wesley's statement concerning Launceston described a large area of Methodism in the latter part of the eighteenth century.[5] In fact, even Wesley had made strikingly similar explanations of the spiritual death he found in Cornwall in 1762, and in Bristol in 1765.

Christian perfection in America

That Wesley committed the doctrine of Christian perfection to the new church in America, and that the early leaders of that church heartily accepted it, we observed in the preceding chapter. We are now to review the course of the doctrine to the middle of the nineteenth century.

Valuable investigations in this field have been made by Merrill E. Gaddis, "Christian Perfectionism in America" (1929); John L. Peters, *Christian Perfection and American Methodism* (1956); and Timothy L. Smith, *Revivalism and Social Reform* (1957). For thirty years the splendid work of Gaddis has been basic, and will continue as a classic in tracing and interpreting spiritual movements. Unfortunately, this doctoral dissertation has never been published as a book, and dissemination of its story has been sharply restricted until in recent years it has been made available in micro-film to those with a serious interest

---

3. J. Wesley, *Letters*. Epworth Press, London; v. 5, 314.
4. J. Wesley, *Journal*. Epworth Press, London; v. 6, 120.
5. J. L. Peters, *Christian Perfection and American Methodism*. Abingdon Press, Nashville; p. 70.

in the field it covers. The other two studies are recent, the one by Peters limiting itself closely to the course of the doctrine in American Methodism; that by Smith including the broader field of evangelism, perfectionism, and social reform in all denominations, but restricting its account largely to the period 1840-1865. The three studies are not in accord at every point, Smith especially diverging from Gaddis and Peters. Our summary draws upon all three sources, and at the appropriate point suggests an explanation of the divergence.

Christian perfection was a vital doctrinal and experiential factor during the early years of the Methodist Episcopal Church; and the Second Great Awakening, which began in Kentucky in 1800 and immediately engaged several denominations of divergent traditions, caused a quickening of concern among Methodists for their distinctive doctrine. Moreover, this was the era of persistent preaching on the theme by the far-ranging Bishop Asbury.

Both Peters and Smith suggest that frontier preaching normally would direct its message to warning sinners to flee from wrath, rather than urging believers toward perfection; and both agree that during the early period the doctrine of entire sanctification was not the dominant theme of preaching, but a corollary. But Smith, more than Peters and Gaddis, discounts the usual estimate of the place of the doctrine in early Methodism. This is in line with Smith's thesis that the mid-century period saw the great flowering of perfectionistic teaching and striving in American Protestantism generally—not alone among Methodists.

Peters connects the decline of Methodist emphasis on heart holiness, which followed its quickening after the revival of 1800, with the removal from the *Discipline* in 1812 of the section devoted to the doctrinal tracts. These included, among other treatises vital to Methodism, Wesley's *Plain Account of Christian Perfection*. When the removal from the *Discipline* was made, the plan was to publish these tracts in a separate volume, but for some unaccountable reason the publication was delayed until 1832. This delay of twenty years tended further to the doctrine's decline during that interval.

According to Gaddis, the period of the forties and fifties was one of general decline of the doctrine in Methodism. In this claim he has been supported by the late William Warren Sweet, an authority on American church history and Methodist history in particular. "In the two decades previous to the Civil War," wrote Sweet, "Wesley's doctrine of Christian perfection was largely neglected and had become little more than a creedal matter among Methodist bodies." [6]

Gaddis ascribed the decline to several factors. One was the autocratic pressure of episcopal Methodism which tended to crowd out of the church the more strongly perfectionistic, and consequently the more democratically inclined minorities. As Gaddis remarked, "Perfectionism and expediency do not go well together." [7] Other factors included the passing of the frontier itinerancy, the decline of the class meeting and the camp meeting, and slavery.

In the period of the twenties and thirties, according to Peters, Christian perfection was an acknowledged but neglected standard of Methodism. Then came a quickening of holiness teaching and promotion in the late thirties and the early forties which stirred up a measure of opposition, to be followed by vigorous controversy in the late forties. The quickening included the development of the famed Tuesday holiness meetings, begun in New York City by Mrs. Phoebe Palmer in 1835, which were maintained for years and won the patronage of several prominent Methodists; the successful evangelistic labors of Dr. and Mrs. Palmer; the establishment in 1839 by Timothy Merritt of *Guide to Holiness*, a journal of the deeper life that had a long and successful period of publication and at one time reached a circulation of 40,000; and the open advocacy of Christian perfection by such Methodist leaders as Bishops Morris, Hedding, Janes, and Hamline; such distinguished scholars and educators as Fisk and Olin; and such masterly preachers and writers as Nathan Bangs, George Peck, R. S. Foster, and Jesse T. Peck—the last two later to become bishops.

But notwithstanding the quickening of holiness teaching and its revivalistic results, all was not favorable to the cause, according to Peters' analysis of Methodist literature of the period, and in the late

---

6. W. W. Sweet, *Methodism in American History*. Methodist Book Concern, New York; p. 340.
7. M. E. Gaddis, "Christian Perfectionism in America." University of Chicago, unpublished thesis; p. 426. See Chapter 10 for the account of decline in perfectionism within Methodism.

forties active disagreement with the traditional Wesleyan teaching on Christian perfection was expressed by such writings as Merritt Caldwell's *Philosophy of Christian Perfection* (1848) and articles in Methodist periodicals. Caldwell, a professor in Maine Wesleyan Seminary, set forth the view that sanctification is a rectifying of tangled and conflicting tendencies of human nature in consequence of earlier sin, rather than a cleansing or eradication of an innate sin principle.[8]

The year after the appearance of Caldwell's book, what was essentially the Zinzendorfian view of the identity of regeneration and sanctification was presented by W. C. Hosmer in the *Methodist Quarterly Review*. Peters summarizes Hosmer's argument as follows:

> All that is necessary to salvation is given in regeneration. If sanctification is necessary to salvation, as its proponents claim, then sanctification is given in regeneration. If sanctification is given in regeneration, then there is no essential difference between the two. Therefore sanctification and regeneration are for all *real* purposes identical.[9]

In 1854 D. W. Clark expressed the Zinzendorfian view in *The Ladies Repository*, and caused little disturbance. However, he became a target for severe criticism the next year when his *Life and Times of Elijah Hedding, D.D.* was published. Therein he left in doubt Bishop Hedding's claiming the experience of perfect love. Controversy blazed, and a compilation of quotations from Clark's writings was published to show that he had abandoned the Wesleyan doctrine. But Clark survived the ordeal, and in 1864 was elected bishop.[10]

The controversy of this general period led to an exhortation in the Pastoral Address to the General Conference of 1852, that the established views on Christian perfection be maintained and the phraseology of Wesley and Fletcher be employed, for such is "not

---

8. T. L. Smith, *Revivalism and Social Reform*. Abingdon Press, Nashville; p. 127. Smith interprets Caldwell as holding to a "second blessing" in which harmony is restored to the warring tendencies within man. But Peters interprets Caldwell as denying any essential difference between regeneration and sanctification. See Peters, p. 122.
9. J. L. Peters, *Christian Perfection and American Methodism*. Abingdon Press, Nashville; p. 122.
10. See T. L. Smith, *Revivalism and Social Reform*. Abingdon Press, Nashville; pp. 128, 133.

superseded by the more recent writers on this subject." The address urged, "Avoid both new theories, new expressions, and new measures on this subject, and adhere closely to the ancient landmarks." [11]

Against the claim of Gaddis, supported by Sweet, that the period 1840-1860 saw definite decline in the doctrine of Christian perfection in American Methodism, and against Peters' claim of no consistent increase of the doctrine's acceptance, but only brief intervals of quickening that stimulated reaction and controversy, Smith maintains the view that the period was one of general and sustained revival of the doctrine. After reviewing such emphases on the doctrine as characterized Peters' period of quickening that brought opposition and controversy, Smith says, "The gospel of Christian holiness thus became a chief strain in the melody of mid-century Methodism." [12]

Explanation of divergence in views

The divergence of Smith from Gaddis and Peters no doubt arises from the different contexts in which they view the picture. Gaddis and Peters measure the Methodist perfectionism of the period against the background of the historic Wesleyan tradition, and find decline or deviation rather than revival. Smith, on the other hand, includes in the sweep of his survey all denominations, and discerns a groundswell of perfectionistic hope and striving. But he does not make clear the distinction between the *reformers*, such as the Methodist Palmers and Pecks, Hamline and Janes, Foster and Bangs, and the *discoverers*, such as Baptist Earle, Presbyterian Boardman, Congregationalist Bushnell, Lutheran Schmucker, Episcopalian McIlvaine, and Unitarian Huntington,[13] all of whom Smith connects with the revival movement of mid-century, and most of them with the revival's perfectionist corollary.

Let us grant Smith's thesis that the period 1840 to 1865 saw a general quickening of concern for the Christian's possibilities in grace; and further, let us accept his interpretation of the same as the common man's evangelical equivalent of mid-century transcendental-

---

11. Quoted by J. L. Peters, *Christian Perfection and American Methodism*. Abingdon Press, Nashville; p. 123 *et seq.*
12. See T. L. Smith, *Revivalism and Social Reform*. Abingdon Press, Nashville; chap. 8. The quoted portion is found on page 124 *et seq.*
13. Huntington forsook the Unitarian Church in 1860 and united with the Protestant Episcopal Church. See T. L. Smith, chapter 6.

ism. But at the same time let us be clear that such a diffuse movement, strongly tinged with humanism at points, could operate against the Methodist version of Christian perfection quite as disastrously as direct opposition might hinder it. In fact, it may very well be that Methodism's controversy over Christian perfection, just at the period in question, was stimulated in measure by the very spirit then stirring most of Protestantism; and, for example, that Merritt Caldwell's heresy against historic Methodist doctrine in *The Philosophy of Christian Perfection* may have been influenced by the Unitarian transcendentalism surrounding this New England professor.

Briefly then, one interpreter of the period, looking principally at the general increase in perfectionist concern, would include Caldwell's book with the evidence of that increase; but another interpreter, intent on discerning the direction of Methodism's perfectionism, could interpret Caldwell's book as an evidence of decline and deviation.

The testimony of Nathan Bangs

Nathan Bangs was perhaps the most representative Methodist of the early half of the nineteenth century. He held high positions in the denomination, and according to Abel Stevens had twice been offered its highest honor, election to the office of bishop.[14] In the midst of the period in question he wrote two books, each having something to say on the course Methodism had taken with reference to the doctrine and experience of entire sanctification.

Prospects and Responsibilities of the Methodist Episcopal Church appeared in 1850, dealing with all angles of the church's program and mission. In the portion devoted to doctrine, Bangs claimed that Christian perfection is the chief of Methodism's distinctive doctrines. In the beginning, he said, Methodists generally preached the doctrine, but then as now, many of them, both preachers and people, did not profess to enjoy the experience. Preachers too often set forth the doctrine merely as a theory rather than a personal reality. Confidently, but with moderation, he expressed his opinion that the work of holiness had revived in the six or seven years past, with more than the usual number seeking and finding "the blessing of perfect love."

---

14. As quoted by J. L. Peters, *Christian Perfection and American Methodism.* Abingdon Press, Nashville; p. 114. (From A. Stevens, *Life and Times of Nathan Bangs,* p. 15.)

Near the book's close, he urged Methodists to make entire sanctification "the mark at which they constantly aim," and ministers, "from a deep conviction of its attainableness to press the necessity of this home upon themselves and all their people." [15]

In 1851 *The Necessity, Nature, and Fruits of Entire Sanctification* was published, reflecting less optimism concerning the doctrinal integrity of the church. The purpose of the former book, as its title indicates, was to display the church's advantages along all lines, and accordingly it was geared to the building of morale. But this book on entire sanctification realistically focused the doctrinal issue in order to accomplish certain purposes the author had in mind in writing it. His principal purpose was to reaffirm the doctrine of sanctification for the benefit of those who were indifferent or antagonistic toward it. We give his words:

> I was well aware that many of our preachers and people had become lukewarm, to say no more of it, upon the subject of entire sanctification. For though it is a prominent doctrine of our Church, taught by all our standard writers, Wesley, Fletcher, Clarke, and others, yet, from my intercourse with them, I found many that appeared quite indifferent respecting it, while a few manifested a decided hostility to the doctrine of entire sanctification; and although I could not hope to add much new light to what had been shed upon it by those able divines, yet I thought I could revive the doctrine in their recollection, by first giving a synopsis of what Wesley had written; and then, secondly, I might stir up their minds, by way of remembrance, by the use of some arguments which had not been employed by others. . . . [16]

He gave as a further reason for writing the book, that he could not now be long for this world and wished to commit his witness to print "for the benefit of my children, and all others who may condescend to read what I have written." He continued, "They will here find my most matured thoughts upon one of the most vital truths of Divine revelation." [17]

The book is directly in line with the best holiness teachings of our

---

15. Nathan Bangs, *Prospects and Responsibilities of the Methodist Episcopal Church.* Lane & Scott, New York; p. 288.
16. Nathan Bangs, *The Necessity, Nature, and Fruits of Entire Sanctification.* Phillips & Hunt, New York; p. 10 *et seq.*
17. *Ibid.,* p. 12.

day, and effectively refutes both the "gradualism" and the Zinzendorfiian doctrine which, in the Methodism of Bangs' day, were blurring Wesley's clear teachings that so effectively united process and crisis in the work of sanctification.

Inseparable from the doctrine of entire sanctification is the corresponding experience of cleansing and power. Whenever the teaching and preaching of the doctrine subside, the experience declines in frequency and constancy among the people. We call Dr. Bangs to witness concerning the uncertain standing of the experience of Christian holiness in mid-century Methodism, even as we have called him as witness to the decline in doctrine. His humble testimony in his own reverent phrasing is first given:

> If I do not misunderstand the promptings of my own heart, I think I can say that in these letters [18] I have expressed its genuine sentiments of affectionate attachment to all those who "love our Lord Jesus Christ in sincerity and also love one another with a pure heart fervently"—the whole springing from the "love of God spread abroad in the heart by the Holy Ghost."

This nineteenth-century Methodist saint wrote from a compelling sense of urgency about his own deep Christian experience, well aware that for his testimony he would be harshly criticized. He said further:

> I know, indeed, that this profession will subject me to the severity of criticism; but I cannot well avoid it; for if I were to withhold this testimony in favor of the abundant grace of God in Christ, vouchsafed to a sinner like myself, "the stones," the stony hearts of sinners, "would cry out against me." [19]

That a great Methodist preacher and denominational leader a century ago must thus steel himself against the criticism that could follow his testimony to inward holiness, bespeaks loudly mid-century Methodism's weak esteem for that experience which was so clearly proclaimed by Methodism's founder a century earlier.

Peter Cartwright was a contemporary of Nathan Bangs, but slightly the younger of the two. Both men were active in the development of American Methodism throughout the first half of the nineteenth century. Bangs' sphere of service was in the east, and at the very

---

18. *Loc. cit.* The book is set up as a series of letters to a friend.
19. *Ibid.*, p. 13.

center of denominational life. Cartwright was a circuit-rider of the Kentucky, Ohio and Illinois frontiers. Naturally, therefore, they differed in cultural tastes and outlook. They were further dissimilar in their degree of concern for the doctrine and experience of entire holiness of heart and life. We have noted Bangs' deep interest, both for himself and the church. Cartwright the pioneer, although he denounced pewed churches, organs, choirs, standing or sitting during prayer, personal adornment, and seminary-trained preachers, is strangely silent concerning sanctification throughout the several hundred pages of his *Autobiography*. Therein he has said not a word of having experienced a "second blessing"; in all his doctrinal remarks, this doctrine is not once mentioned; nor does he make comment on the experience; and although he reports hundreds converted in camp meetings and revivals, he gives not a single instance of seekers for full cleansing. The closest approach to the subject the writer can recall in Cartwright's account of his life is his ascribing any man's ambition to be presiding elder to "the outcropping of fallen and unsanctified human nature." [20] Certainly Cartwright's case tends to confirm the observation cited earlier in this chapter that Christian perfection was not the normal preaching theme on the rough frontier.

Declining simplicity of worship

But none can deny that Cartwright's preaching supported Wesley's General Rules and his discipline requiring simplicity in worship and plainness of dress. A few fragments from his *Autibiography* concerning matters of worship declare his convictions thereon:

> There was no standing among the members in time of prayer, especially the abominable practice of sitting down during that exercise was unknown among early Methodists. [21]
>
> Lord, save the Church from desiring to have pews, choirs, organs, or instrumental music, and a congregational ministry like other heathen Churches around them! [22]
>
> May the day be eternally distant, when camp meetings, class-meetings, prayer-meetings and love-feasts shall be laid aside in the Methodist Episcopal Church.[23]

---

20. Peter Cartwright, *Autobiography*. Abingdon Press, Nashville; p. 92.
21. *Ibid.*, p. 61.
22. *Ibid.*, p. 86.
23. *Ibid.*, p. 340.

THE WITNESS BLURRED: IN DOCTRINE AND LIFE

In these statements Cartwright touched upon worship practices of the forties and especially the fifties that were innovations which disturbed many Methodists. That he was not alone in his prejudices will appear from the following accounts concerning his contemporaries.

Instrumental music was never prohibited by the *Discipline* of the Methodist Episcopal Church, but in the earlier period it had not been approved practice and on different occasions General Conference had admonished against its introduction.

In 1841 the brilliant editor of the *Christian Advocate*, Thomas E. Bond, wrote extensively on the question of instrumental music. He maintained that the question was not one of wrong or right, but of expediency, and that instrumental music was not "the more excellent way." He concluded his editorial, "Whether we have instrumental music in our churches or not, let us follow peace with all men; and holiness, without which no man shall see the Lord." [24]

In 1846 the committee on the state of discipline of the Genesee Conference dealt comprehensively with the problem of instruments and choirs. It defined the problem by stating the extremes on both sides of the question, contrasting the advocates of scientific performance in music who are insensitive to piety and devotion, with those who care not for scientific music, deem the use of instruments sinful, choirs objectionable, and tune books out of place in worship. The committee declared there was right on both sides, and compromises must be made by each. It urged classes for training in music, from which a "company of singers" (the term "choir" being studiously avoided) should be selected to sit apart and lead congregational singing, using principally the familiar tunes. The committee made clear that it would not condemn the use of instruments as sinful, but declared its preference for vocal music, and recommended the discontinuance of instrumental music, except "where expedient for regulating the key, or assisting those parts which are weak and unreliable." [25]

But the advent of choirs and instruments for general use was

---

24. T. E. Bond, *Christian Advocate*; Sept. 15, 1841. (As quoted in Centennial issue of *Christian Advocate*, Sept. 9, 1926.)
25. See F. W. Conable, *History of the Genesee Conference of the Methodist Episcopal Church*. Nelson & Phillips, New York; p. 532.

inevitable. The domination of "scientific" music in the services, use of difficult and unfamiliar tunes, the increased formality and the greater programming of the services, and the leading participation of worldly and even ungodly singers in the choir, were soon sadly to reduce the power and inspiration of Methodist worship. The unfortunate effect of all this on Methodist singing was pungently expressed by the noted Congregational preacher, Henry Ward Beecher. In his magazine, *The Independent*, he published in 1857 an editorial prompted by his attendance upon a Methodist service near his summer retreat. The article is too long for full reproduction, but we quote a part of it:

> I expected a treat of good hearty singing. Imagine my chagrin when, after reading the hymn, up rose the choir from the shelf at the other end of the church, and began to sing a monotonous tune of the modern music-book style. The patient congregation stood up meekly to be sung to, as men stand under rain when there is no shelter. Scarcely a lip moved. No one seemed to hear the hymn, or to care for the music. How I longed for the good old Methodist thunder! One good burst of old-fashioned music would have blown this modern singing out of the window like a wadding from a gun.
>
> We missed the old fervor—the good old-fashioned Methodist fire. We have seen the time when one of Charles Wesley's hymns, taking the congregation by the hand, would have led them to the gate of heaven. But yesterday it only led them up as far as the choir, about ten feet above the pews. Brethren! You are in the wrong way. It will never do for you to silence the people. Your fire will go out, if you rake it up under the ashes of a false refinement. Oh, that there might be a rain of righteousness upon them [the Methodists] which will swell their hearts to overflowing, and cleanse their sanctuary from all formalism, especially from the formalism of pedantic music.[26]

The span of time from the cautiously mediating report of the Genesee committee in 1846 to Beecher's heavy castigation of Methodism for squandering its musical heritage in 1857, was but little more than a decade, although the change in Methodist music it witnessed would seem to measure a century.

The historic revival of 1858, which broke out in laymen's prayer meetings in New York City and spread across the nation through all

---

26. Quoted in *Northern Independent*, v. 2, Sept. 10, 1857.

denominations, brought with it a revival of congregational singing. In 1860 a Methodist commented that when congregational singing was unfashionable, Methodists held to it, but now, "Since it has become fashionable, they quietly leave it, and adopt choir singing." The writer continues with this razor-edged witticism:

> It does appear strange, going into a Methodist Church, and when the minister announces one of our inimitable hymns, with the remark that "we will *join* in singing," to hear, after due deliberation, a very select choir, at a very select distance from the audience, discourse a new-fangled tune that nobody knows—to the edification of nobody.[27]

In other ways, the simplicity of Methodist worship was being affected by change. In 1859 a Brooklyn contributor to the *Northern Independent* wrote of the unfortunate bondage to prevailing custom by which spiritual freedom was lost. Although living in the great American metropolis, it seems that the writer had the urge to worship as did her fathers; but she had been told by a friend that it was no longer the custom to kneel in their church and she would appear "singular" to do so. "I kept my seat," she said, "but lost my independence and self respect." [28]

In the same issue of this journal a member of the Philadelphia Conference reported his travels in New York, noting that the New Yorkers were not as emotionally demonstrative in worship as Methodists in his area, and that he found more musical instruments in the churches of New York, of which there were but few in his conference. He added, "and from the increase of their number, good Lord, deliver us." Then he declared his dislike for the New York custom of sitting during prayer, "and on the announcement of the hymn, the congregation turning their rear part to the pulpit, to pay their devotions to the choir." [29] For as may have been gathered from Beecher's account, the choir in those days was placed in a gallery at side or back of the sanctuary.

Gaddis quotes Gorham's *Camp-Meeting Manual* of 1854 to the effect that a decade earlier Methodists were "silently and gradually" abandoning the camp meeting. And Gaddis further claims that the

---
27. *Northern Independent*, v. 4, March 29, 1860.
28. *Ibid.*, v. 4, Aug. 11, 1859.
29. *Ibid.*, v. 3, Feb. 15, 1859.

class meeting was on the defensive in 1851, when Bishop Morris wrote in his introduction to Miley's *Treatise on Class-Meetings* that not to require class attendance "would be practically to abolish the institution itself; and to abolish class meeting would be virtually to abandon Methodism." [30]

The love feast was still a Methodist institution, but in this period of change it was moving from a closed service to one all might attend; and the complaint was made that in a certain area the use of bread and water as symbols of Christian love and fellowship had departed from this historic observance.

Decline in plainness of dress

Turning from declining simplicity and from historic customs in religious worship to changes in the Methodist standard of dress, we find that extravagance and fashion were likewise the target of Peter Cartwright's peppery pen.

It was seldom necessary in primitive Methodism for preachers to mention the evils of worldly dress, Cartwright said, for even the wicked knew it was wrong and condemned it.[31] When he joined the church, a Methodist preacher could be recognized by his plain garb as far as one could see him; and the members wore no jewelry, superfluous ornaments, or extravagant dress—and this, he said, was the rule for all, "whether poor or rich, young or old." He readily granted, that "the religion of Jesus Christ did not consist in dress, or the cut of the garment," but early Methodists knew that fashion engendered pride; and the cost equivalent of rich clothes and expensive adornment might carry the gospel to hundreds of thousands.[32]

The manner in which a Christian dressed was thus for Cartwright more than a hobby, but involved substantial Christian principles. And so it was also with Allen Wiley, Hoosier circuit-rider and Cartwright's contemporary. Wiley lamented both the introduction of rented pews and the finery displayed by women in the better pews as tending to discourage humble folk from attending church.[33]

---

30. M. E. Gaddis, "Christian Perfectionism in America"; p. 393.
31. Peter Cartwright, *Autobiography*. Abingdon Press, Nashville; p. 61 *et seq.*
32. *Ibid.*, p. 334.
33. E. K. Nottingham, *Methodism and the Frontier*. Columbia University Press, New York; p. 83.

It is an interesting coincidence that Cartwright's *Autobiography* was published the same year in which General Conference changed the long-standing rule prohibiting specific items of dress, and substituted for the prohibitions an exhortation to follow the general apostolic directive concerning adornment. Since the organizing conference of 1784 there had been no substantial change, the rule in 1856, just prior to the change, reading:

> *Quest.* Should we insist on the rules concerning dress?
> *Ans.* By all means. This is no time to encourage superfluity in dress. Therefore receive none into the church till they have left off superfluous ornaments. In order to this, 1. Let everyone who has charge of a circuit read Mr. Wesley's "Thoughts on Dress" at least once a year in every society. 2. In visiting the classes, be very mild but very strict. 3. Allow no exempt case. Better one suffer than many. 4. Give no tickets to any that wear high heads, enormous bonnets, ruffles or rings.

The 1856 General Conference changed the rule to read:

> *Quest.* Should we insist on the rules concerning dress?
> *Ans.* By all means. This is no time to encourage superfluity in dress. Therefore, let all our people be exhorted to conform to the spirit of the apostolic precept, "not to adorn themselves with gold, and pearls, and costly array."—I Tim. 2:9.[34]

How rapidly beyond its former excess under stipulated prohibitions, "superfluity in dress" increased under mere exhortation, we do not know. But an article in the *Northern Independent* in 1860 had discoursed on worldly dress in New England, along with formality in worship and neglect of preaching Christian perfection.[35] In due time there appeared in subsequent issues two replies denying the last two charges but admitting the first. One of the defenders of New England Methodism admitted worldliness in women's dress, *as elsewhere in Methodism*; the other admitted extravagance in dress and gaudy display *as in every other part of the country where members do not obey the rules.* Extremes in dress had indeed become established custom when the only answer to criticism was the small boy's impudent rejoinder, "And so are you!"

---

34. See Sherman, *History of the Revision of the Discipline.* Nelson & Phillips, New York; p. 122.
35. *Northern Independent;* v. 4, Feb. 16, 1860. See replies in issues of Mar. 15 and Mar. 22.

In 1859 another writer in the same journal revealed a social conscience on extravagant dress, saying, "Excessive dress has become a dead letter in our church government," in consequence of which, "Sister A or B may put from $15 to $50 on her head, and $500 on her person, and God's creatures starving, almost within reach of her hand." [36]

Within a quarter-century of this period a bishop's wife who, with her husband, moved in wealthy Methodist lay circles of the "gilded age" following the war, was to set the pattern of elegance in attire. A recent biography of the bishop reports concerning Mrs. Matthew Simpson, "Much more fashionably dressed than some people expected the wife of a Methodist preacher to be, she made a striking figure in a Methodist gathering." [37]

An incident is related by the biographer which suggests Mrs. Simpson may have been as influential in changing the styles in dress among Methodist women by example, as Bishop Simpson was in setting the pace for magnificent churches by his ardent advocacy of Gothic architecture during the same period. Here is Biographer Clark's account of the incident:

> On one occasion she brought consternation to a Presbyterian banker's wife who was entertaining them during the conference session. Thinking of the Methodists as plain, illiterate people, the hostess, wishing not to overawe her guests at their first dinner, twisted her hair in a tight knot, took off her rings, wore a "big-flowered tycoon-rep wrapper" and a white apron. She had not yet seen her guest, who had been shown to her room by a servant. At dinnertime Mrs. Simpson swept down the stairs, a tall, stately woman in black silk ruffled to the waist, with expensive laces and jewelry, and her hair done in the latest style. The banker's wife, embarrassed and chagrined, sat silent through the meal while Mrs. Simpson, a splendid talker, "charmed everybody." [38]

In the sophistication of the mid-twentieth century, it is easy to shrug off New Testament injunctions concerning the Christian's dress as inconsequential, and with a superior air smile at the Methodist simplicity of four or five generations ago; but, with Wesley, these early Methodists took seriously the instructions of Paul, discerning

---
36. *Ibid.*, v. 4, Aug. 11, 1859.
37. R. D. Clark, *The Life of Matthew Simpson*. The Macmillan Co., New York; p. 164.
38. *Ibid.*, p. 276.

in them more than eccentric scruples of an uncultured mind. Rather, they would heed them as a witness to their Christian profession. In connection with the "other-worldliness" of the people of God, Dr. Harold Roberts in the Conference Sermon of the World Methodist Conference at Lake Junaluska in 1956, said that John Wesley preached to his people on dress, because he would have their attire give evidence of the way of life they sought to represent. At this point Roberts suggested that Wesley would have something pertinent to say about the attire of Methodists of both sexes today.[39]

Amusements and general discipline

The Methodist Episcopal Church at mid-century had only the General Rules and Methodism's unwritten standards to define the bounds of legitimate amusements and recreational activities. Specific legislation had not been needed in the beginning, but the inroads of questionable amusements began long before the legislation of 1872 specifically forbade dancing, cards, gambling, the theater, and the like.

On a New England pastorate in 1829, Elijah Hedding could preach on the evils and perils of dancing, adroitly bring in condemnation of other objectionable practices, and have the city paper give an extended account of the same.[40] In his editorship of the *Western Christian Advocate* during the quadrennium before he was elected bishop in 1852, Matthew Simpson vigorously editorialized against the theater, state licensing of liquor, Sabbath desecration, and the licentiousness which he claimed was stimulated by the exhibition of Hiram Powers' sculptured nude, "The Greek Slave." [41]

But questionable amusements already were a disturbing problem at this time. The Genesee Conference in 1849 adopted resolutions approving a communication from the Board of Bishops condemning the prevalence of sinful amusements among Methodists. The Conference requested publication of the bishops' message in the *Northern Christian Advocate*, and asked pastors to read the message in their congregations. Ten years later a correspondent reported in the *North-*

---
39. H. Roberts, "The people of God," in *Proceedings of the Ninth World Methodist Conference*. The Methodist Publishing House, Nashville; p. 103 *et seq.*
40. D. W. Clark, *The Life and Times of Elijah Hedding, D.D.* Carlton & Phillips, New York; p. 462.
41. R. D. Clark, *The Life of Matthew Simpson*. The Macmillan Co., New York; p. 154.

ern Independent that whereas formerly to be seen at a theater meant separation from the Methodist Episcopal Church, "now *custom* sanctions it to a great extent, . . . and so with all other amusements of that stamp." [42]

As early as 1846 the decline of discipline in the Genesee Conference had been observed by a committee which reported laxity and lack of uniformity among preachers in administering discipline, which might prove, the committee said, "subversive of order if not destructive to the distinguishing characteristics of our beloved Methodism." The committee reported also departures by the people "from those landmarks which once so clearly and satisfactorily bounded and defined our limits as a heritage of God," to which they must return, "or our once fruitful field will be turned to a broken waste." [43]

*   *   *   *   *

This chapter has presented evidence that belief and practice are interrelated; that decline in doctrine and the easing of discipline proceed in step together; that by the middle of the nineteenth century American Methodism had begun its deviation from earlier distinctive principles and practices of personal religion and piety.

The chapter following traces the course of Methodism in areas of social concern during the seventy-five years closing with 1860.

---

42. *Northern Independent*; v. 4, Aug. 11, 1859.
43. Quoted by Conable, *History of the Genesee Conference*, p. 531.

CHAPTER TEN

The Witness Blurred: Social Issues

In commemorating one hundred years of organized Methodism in America in 1884, Bishop R. S. Foster indulged the characteristic Methodist optimism of that era in a fulsome eulogy on the perfections of his church, saying:

> It is fair that it should be said that Methodism has not been a temporizing Church. The vast host of its converts have not been won by pandering to their prejudices and vices. From the first she has been thorough, outspoken, and uncompromising. There never has been a moral issue, or political issue involving principle, before the people that she has not been bold in her allegiance to the right. She has invariably taken the highest ground and the front rank. No cause of doubtful nature has ever looked to her for support. From the first she recorded her protest against slavery, and incorporated it in her organic law. Her testimony and her laws have ever been unequivocal against the theater, the dance, and all gaming. Against intemperance she has been a burning wrath. No public or private sin has ever escaped her scourge. Mere formalism she has unsparingly denounced. She has demanded a thorough-paced spiritual experience, and a consistent and holy life. Her habit in all these respects has branded her as extreme, even Puritanical, not to say fanatical, and the straitest of the sects. It is her glory that intense religiousness, separation from the world, and self-denial have always been branded as Methodistic.[1]

Today's historians of Methodism are more realistic than such good men as was Bishop Foster who, when he addressed the above words to The Pulpit, was under the spell of America's "Gilded Age" of the late nineteenth century, with its expansive prosperity and mushrooming culture. His tribute honors the high idealism of Methodist beginnings and the church's general course through a century, but its sweeping generalizations and categorical assertions reckon not with

---

1. R. S. Foster, *Centenary Thoughts for the Pew and Pulpit.* Phillips & Hunt, New York; p. 30.

those pragmatic compromises that now and again betrayed the Wesleyan witness. But even Bishop Foster was in a more sober mood when, in the same volume, he addressed The Pew and moderated his optimism several degrees, saying:

> Our great dangers, as we see them, are: assimilation to the world, neglect of the poor, substitution of the form for the fact of godliness, abandonment of discipline, a hireling ministry, an impure gospel, which, summed up, is a fashionable Church. That Methodism should be liable to such an outcome, and that there should be signs of it in a hundred years from the "sail-loft," seems almost the miracle of history; but who that looks about him today can fail to see the fact? [2]

A good begining

We do not overlook the glorious course of Methodism's evangelizing, reforming and nurturing influence during the early and rustic generations of this new nation—an influence unsurpassed by any other religious movement of that period. Its growth in numbers was phenomenal, from about 18,000 members in 1784 to an estimated 2,350,000 members in 1884; from one Methodist in 200 of the country's population in 1784, to one in 20 in 1884.

As during the colonial period in America, the Methodist itinerant followed the shifting tides of population, and adherents grew in numbers to leaven with righteousness the rough and wicked frontiers. Most effective in the leavening process was the Methodist revival spirit which, in the unsettled conditions of rapid migration, pressed the urgency of salvation *now*; for many of those hearing the gospel one day would have moved with the advancing frontier by the time the itinerant could make his round and back to this point another day, weeks later. And by that time, someone converted on his former visit might be a missionary in some settlement of a new frontier.

Methodists at first were a despised people. For the most part, they were poor. They worshiped in private houses, in barns, in groves, and after a time in their log meeting-houses, and in the country schools that were being built on the edge of the wilderness. Pioneer Methodist preachers depended upon native vigor, self-education, common sense, and the help of the Holy Spirit, but lacked the formal

---

2. *Ibid.*, p. 166.

training of ministers of the older American churches.

Within a few decades the status of Methodism changed. Churches were built; schools, colleges and seminaries were established; literary and publication agencies were expanded. Through frugality and industry Methodists prospered; many of them achieved middle-class comfort; a few amassed sizable fortunes. Methodists came also to wield a considerable measure of political influence, and many officeholders were drawn from their ranks to fill places of authority in local, state and national councils. Methodism was now a force to be reckoned with on the American scene.

The problem of prosperity

But the progress of Methodism to middle-class status brought problems in America as it had already done in England. John Wesley in his old age had said, "I give you one more advice before I sink into the dust. Mark those words of St. Paul: 'Those that desire' or endeavor 'to be rich' that moment 'fall into temptation': Yea, a deep gulf of temptation, out of which nothing less than almighty power can deliver them." [3]

One of the heaviest burdens of Wesley's declining years was the loss of spirituality he saw in English Methodism, associated closely in his mind with growing wealth and its accompanying culture and worldliness. The blurring of original Methodist patterns led him to question if revivals are not born to destroy themselves. When eighty-seven years of age he wrote the following solemn warning that may well be pondered by all branches of Methodism today, the world around:

> The Methodists grow more and more self indulgent, because they *grow rich*. . . . And it is an observation that admits of few exceptions, that nine in ten of these [who become rich] decreased in grace, in the same proportion as they increased in wealth. . . .
>
> But how astonishing a thing is this! How can we understand it? Does it not seem (and yet this cannot be) that Christianity, true, scriptural Christianity, has a tendency, in process of time, to undermine and destroy itself? For, wherever true Christianity spreads, it must cause diligence and frugality, which, in the nat-

---

3. J. Wesley, *Sermons on Several Occasions*. Phillips & Hunt, New York; v. 2, 490 et seq.

ural course of things, must beget riches. And riches naturally beget pride, love of the world, and every temper that is destructive of Christianity. . . .

But is there no way to prevent this? . . . I can see only one possible way: find out another who can. Do you gain all you can, and save all you can? Then you must in the nature of things grow rich. Then if you have any desire to escape the damnation of hell, *give* all you can; otherwise I can have no more hope of your salvation, than that of Judas Iscariot.[4]

This threat of wealth to undermine the Christian integrity of a church calls to mind the claim of Niebuhr that social and economic factors have been more significant than doctrinal tenets in determining the rise of denominations, and also his calling denominationalism "the accommodation of Christianity to the caste system of society."[5] He speaks uncomfortable words when, concerning the churches and the crisis of American slavery, he points out that, "various denominations, as was to be expected, showed themselves to be mouthpieces of the economic and sectional groups represented."[6]

The purpose of this chapter is to survey what happened within the Methodist Episcopal Church in areas of social concern during its first seventy-five years, closing with the outbreak of the Civil War in 1860, precipitated by the slavery issue.

The problem of American slavery

From its suspension of the 1784 rule which made slaveholding a bar to church membership, the course of American Methodism in dealing with what John Wesley called, "that execrable sum of all villainies," is an embarrassing record of successive compromises and bald betrayals of the church's loudly proclaimed ideals. Economic interest in the South and ecclesiastical prudence in the North alike exerted damaging pressures against moral principle.

Representative Methodists of more recent years unite in criticism of the church's course on slavery. J. Minton Batten of Vanderbilt University has noted that, "until the issuance of the Emancipation Proclamation Methodists compromised in dealing with the evil in all

---

4. *Ibid.*, v. 2, 441.
5. H. R. Niebuhr, *The Social Sources of Denominationalism.* Henry Holt & Co., Inc., New York; p. 6.
6. *Ibid.*, p. 24.

sections where slavery existed."[7] Luccock and Hutchinson likewise declare that the church retreated from its high stand of 1784 until "it had nothing to say against slaveholding by its individual members, and only refused to admit slaveholders to official positions where they failed to emancipate their slaves when the laws made that possible."[8] The late Dr. Faulkner of Drew reported estimates indicating that in 1843 in the Methodist Episcopal Church, 200 traveling preachers owned an average of 8 slaves each, 1,000 local preachers owned an average of 10 slaves each, and 25,000 members held an average of 8 each—an aggregate of well over 200,000 souls held in captivity by those who called themselves Methodists![9]

Peter Cartwright, who lived through practically all of the struggle of Methodism over slavery, in his shrewd way set forth the specious rationalizations by which even preachers, when personal financial interests were involved, were able to persuade themselves of the righteousness of holding slaves. In the beginning, Methodist preachers were too poor to possess slaves, but in time some of them acquired slave property through marriage, or possibly by inheritance. At first these preachers would apologize for owning slaves; next, they would justify slaveholding on legal grounds; and finally, "lo and behold! it is not an evil, but a good! it is not a curse, but a blessing!" and, "to hear them tell the story, if you had the means and did not buy a lot of them, you would go to the devil for not enjoying the labor, toil, and sweat of this degraded race. . . ."[10]

Compromise versus principle

The record of the struggle over slavery shows that the architects of the church's policy of compromise, Northern ecclesiastics in the main, too often were more disturbed by the threat of division over the slavery issue than by the injustices suffered by the enslaved blacks. A recent historian has noted that after the organization of state and national anti-slavery societies in the early thirties, the leaders in the North developed concern, not so much because of the evils of slavery

---

7. J. M. Batten, "Divisions in American Methodism," in *Methodism*, Wm. K. Anderson, Ed. Meth. Pub. House, Nashville; p. 62.
8. Luccock & Hutchinson, *The Story of Methodism*. Abingdon Press, Nashville; p. 328.
9. J. A. Faulkner, *The Methodists*. Eaton & Mains, New York; p. 168 *et seq*.
10. Peter Cartwright, *Autobiography*. Abingdon Press, Nashville; p. 111.

as because of the growing number of preachers now agitating for abolition. And this was a serious matter, tending to dissension and disruption.[11] A recent biographer of Matthew Simpson says of him, in that same period when the church was determined to silence anti-slavery agitation and before Simpson became bishop, "Matthew did not doubt the evil of slavery," but, "he feared the abolitionists even more than the fire-eating southerners," and "came to believe that the only hope for the glory of God and the unity of the church lay in the conservative party." [12] Also, "He approved abolishing slavery so long as it did not injure the institution of Methodism." [13]

The measures resorted to in the thirties and early forties to suppress abolitionism in Northern Methodism were unbelievably extreme. The General Conference of 1836 condemned abolitionism, denied the right of the church to concern itself with relations between master and slave, and censured two of its members who, while at the seat of the Conference, took part in an anti-slavery meeting. The 1840 General Conference declared, "We should regard it as a sore evil to divert Methodism from her proper work of spreading scriptural holiness over these lands to questions of temporal import involving the rights of Caesar." The same General Conference resolved that owning slaves was no legal barrier to admission to any level of the ministry, and refused to hear a minority report on abolition.

In the annual conferences, the bishops in the North resorted to vigorous ecclesiastical measures in the effort to stifle every appearance of abolitionism, allowing no discussion of anti-slavery petitions and refusing to recognize disturbing motions. In 1837 the Philadelphia Conference began asking candidates for the ministry if they were abolitionists, and refused to admit them if they were. Three preachers in the New York Conference were tried and suspended for circulating an anti-slavery tract—someone has asked if it was Wesley's—and for attending an anti-slavery convention.

The outcome of such attempts to suppress the declaration of the convictions of determined men that slavery was sinful and should be

---

11. Elizabeth K. Nottingham, *Methodism and the Frontier*. Columbia University Press, New York; p. 139.
12. R. D. Clark, *The Life of Matthew Simpson*. The Macmillan Co., New York; p. 56.
13. *Ibid.*, p. 69.

abolished, was the secession of several thousand abolitionists in the North, and their organization in 1843 as the Wesleyan Methodist Connexion. Such a warning, that compromise on slavery to hold the South in the church could wreck the church in the North, brought strength to the abolition forces remaining in the church, and caution to the strategists of compromise.

In the General Conference of 1844, the North was therefore firm in its insistence that slaveholding Bishop Andrew should refrain from episcopal duties so long as he had slaves in his possession. But the South would hold to the church's traditional policy of compromise. The great schism ensued. Compromise had failed.

But the issue was not yet settled in the Northern church, which now continued its policy of compromise on slavery in order to hold the Border conferences, even as it had formerly compromised to hold the Southern conferences. In fact, it is difficult at this distance from the firing line to discern any great valor in the position taken by the North in the case of Bishop Andrew, notwithstanding the claim of Bishop Simpson that no other church in the country had made "such sacrifices for its stern devotion to principle." [14] For as Dr. Batten has pointed out: (1) The South demanded only that program of compromise in the case of Bishop Andrew which the church had followed for decades; (2) after separation, both the Northern and the Southern churches continued the same rule on slavery as the united church had before separation; and, (3) until the Civil War both churches retained slaveholders in communion.[15] In fact, not until 1864, when there was not a legally owned slave anywhere in the nation, did the Northern church vote in General Conference to restore to its General Rules a clear-cut prohibition of slaveholding, and refer the same for ratification to the annual conferences.

Ought the church challenge Caesar?

The slavery problem with which the Methodist Episcopal Church was disturbed throughout the first seventy-five years of its history was not one easily solved, and honest and devout men were found in both

---

14. M. Simpson, *One Hundred Years of Methodism*. Nelson & Phillips, New York; p. 14.
15. J. Minton Batten, "Divisions in American Methodism," in *Methodism*, Wm. K. Anderson, Ed. Methodist Publihing House, Nashville; p. 61 *et seq.*

camps. Even the saintly Bishop Asbury, holding a perfect hatred for the institution of slavery, nevertheless expressed perplexity in words that could not but supply the policy of compromise with the argument that the spiritual welfare of slaves was, after all, more important than their freedom. He said:

> We are defrauded of great numbers by the pains that are taken to keep the blacks from us; their masters are afraid of the influence of our principles. Would not an *amelioration* in the condition and treatment of slaves have produced more practical good to the poor Africans than any attempt at their *emancipation?* . . . Who will take the pains to lead them into the way of salvation, and watch over them, that they may not stray, but the Methodists? . . . What is the personal liberty of the African, which he may abuse, to the salvation of his soul; how may it be compared? [16]

It is undoubtedly true that many were sincere in their belief that only through a moderate course with reference to slavery would it be possible to reach either master or slave with the ministry of the gospel, and that these sincerely believed that the evils of slavery as an institution were not the responsibility of the church, but of Caesar. But against these moderates were determined men who held, with William Hosmer, one-time editor of the *Northern Christian Advocate* who, in 1853, during the post-separation period of compromise, wrote the following:

> But it may be said, "this belongs to Caesar—the Church has nothing to do with the evil." We deny it utterly. The Church has everything to do with slavery, if slavery is sin. Caesar belongs to Christ. Sins of the State are to be reproved and extirpated as truly as sins of individuals. It is not enough for the Church to say, "it is the State, it is the State," and deem her own responsibility ended. The State must be rebuked for its wickedness. If our Christianity cannot do this—cannot remonstrate against iniquity in the high places of our semi-Christian government—how is it fit to grapple with legalized sins of pagan nations? Our religion is not worth exporting to foreign countries, if it is thus impotent at home.[17]

That the "hands-off-slavery" policy did unfavorably affect missions

---
16. F. Asbury, *Journal*. Lane & Scott, New York; v. 3, 298.
17. W. Hosmer, *Slavery and the Church*. William J. Moses, Auburn, New York; p. 199, *et seq.*

is supported by Barclay's claim that the anti-slavery movement in America failed to stimulate Christian missions as did the corresponding movement in England, largely because of "the long course of compromise in relation to slavery pursued by Methodism in common with other evangelical churches." [18]

Another factor aggravating the slavery problem for Methodism was the far-flung operation of the church as a close connectional system throughout the nation. Sectional churches, and churches less closely knit denominationally, were less seriously threatened by the slavery issue. And less affected, likewise, were other strongly organized churches of wide extent which, however, had not the emotional susceptibilities characteristic of Methodism.[19]

As a close connectional system, the organizational discipline of Methodism has always been strong—and is today, even after Methodism's surrender of much of its historic discipline of individual conduct. Hence, organizational unity, enforced by its leaders, has been a powerful factor in keeping divergent elements in line with general policy. Norwood gives an example of Methodist organizational discipline as wielded by Bishop Waugh when the New England Conference pressed the issue against slavery compromise in 1837. The bishop wrote the Conference in part as follows:

> Will you, brethren, hazard the unity of the Methodist Episcopal Church ... by agitating those fearfully exciting topics, and that too, in opposition to the solemn decision and deliberate conclusion of the General Conference? ... Are you willing to contribute to the destruction of our beautiful and excellent form of civil and political government, after it has cost the labor, treasure and blood of our fathers to establish it? ... I would that it [slavery] were obliterated from the earth; but in view of the terrific consequences that are likely to follow the agitation of those exciting topics at the present I cannot consent to be participant in any sense or degree, in those measures which are advocated by modern abolitionists.[20]

The motives and methods of the Northern strategists from the

---

18. W. C. Barclay, *Early American Methodism, 1769-1844*: Vol. 2. *To Reform the Nation.* Board of Missions and Church Extension of the Methodist Church, New York; p. 111.
19. See J. N. Norwood, *The Schism of the Methodist Episcopal Church, 1844.* The Alfred Press, Alfred, N.Y. Preface.
20. *Ibid.*, p. 35. (Quoted from *Zion's Herald*, June 28, 1837.)

great schism of 1844 to the Emancipation Proclamation in 1863 are well represented by Bishop Simpson's position as stated by his biographer, Robert D. Clark:

> His position was moderate and cautious, one of watchful waiting. Despising slavery—perhaps as much for the dissension and strife it brought into the church as for what it did to bind men's souls—he dared not strike at it lest he destroy the unity of Northern Methodism. He believed that his first task was to preserve the church. In due course, the states along the border would abolish slavery of their own accord. Was it not wise in the meantime, while bearing witness to the evil, to avoid action which would drive border Methodism into the proslavery southern church? [21]

It is a sobering observation that the church took no vigorous, consistent, and unwavering stand against slavery compromise during the entire period of organized Methodism's history up to the outbreak of the Civil War. The cautiously prudential and pragmatic approach to the slavery issue failed, after all, to maintain its great objective, the unity of Methodism. Two divisions had occurred, the abolitionist secession that led to the founding of the Wesleyan Methodist Church in 1843, and the schism of 1844 that led to the organization of the Methodist Episcopal Church, South in 1845. And the same consistent policy of compromise had a bearing on the final separation from Methodism of those who in 1860 organized the Free Methodist Church. That development will be reviewed in a later chapter.

The problem of intemperance

The use of intoxicants is a social evil as well as a matter of personal morals, as indeed are all social evils. John Wesley saw this clearly when he said, "Neither may we gain by hurting our neighbor in his body. Therefore we may not sell anything which tends to impair health. Such is eminently, all that liquid fire, commonly called drams, or spirituous liquors." [22] He saw in the use of corn for distilling liquor one cause of the scarcity of bread and proposed as remedy the prohibition of distilling.

---

21. R. D. Clark, *The Life of Matthew Simpson*. The Macmillan Co., New York; p. 213.
22. J. Wesley, *Sermons on Several Occasions*; v. 1, 443.

In 1743 the necessity of expelling sixty-four members of the large Newcastle Society for various types of misconduct proved to Wesley the need for clearly defining the standards of Christian living to be required of society members, and the General Rules were promptly formulated and published. Seventeen cases of drunkenness had been among those expelled from society at Newcastle, and two cases of selling spirituous liquors—30 per cent of the total! One must bear in mind the appalling prevalence of drinking in eighteenth-century England, to which, contrary to the tendency of too many churches today, Wesley steadfastly refused to adjust the Christian standard. Accordingly, his General Rule on temperance forthrightly forbade "Drunkenness, buying or selling spirituous liquors, or drinking them, unless in cases of extreme necessity." At its organization in the "Christmas Conference" of 1784, American Methodism adopted this rule, omitting the excepting clause.

In the period following Wesley's death, English Methodism departed far from Wesley's standard and came even to oppose the cause of total abstinence. And as American Methodism followed the rough frontier, it compromised with pioneer culture and came to accept the drinking of liquor without serious protest. In 1790 the church inserted the excepting clause, and strangely enough, struck out the prohibition of "buying or selling." Not until 1848 was the rule restored as Wesley had formulated it in 1743, and so it stands in the *Discipline* of the Methodist church today.

Evidently the omission of "buying and selling" from the restrictions on liquor in 1790 had opened the way for the development of disorderly taverns operated by Methodists, for the 1796 General Conference adopted a resolution according to which a member of the church who sold or gave spirituous liquors and "anything disorderly be transacted under his roof on this account," the preacher in charge was to proceed against such member "as in the case of other immoralities."

It would seem that local preachers availed themselves of the loophole caused by the deletion of the prohibition of "buying and selling" spirituous liquors, for a resolution was presented to the General Conference of 1812 proposing, "That no stationed or local preacher shall retail spirituous or malt liquors without forfeiting his ministerial character among us." The resolution was voted down, but when presented to the next General Conference (1816) without the inclusion of malt liquors in the prohibition, it was passed.

Deeks Pickett attributed the defeat of the 1812 resolution to the state of public opinion at that time, when temperance sentiment called only for moderation in the use of hard liquors and seldom disapproved malt liquors.[23] Both the defeat of the resolution of 1812 and the passage thereof in 1816 with "malt liquors" excluded, disturbingly confirm Dr. Sweet's opinion that "the church does not lead public opinion on such matters as the slavery issue, but, rather, tends to follow public opinion." [24]

Cartwright reports the occasion when on the way to the 1824 General Conference with other preachers, he protested against the practice of two of the brethren in ordering spirits with their meals at wayside inns, and demanded that these brethren quit the practice, or part with his company.[25] The lax standards on temperance during the twenties also appears in the fact that two of the larger Methodist churches on Manhattan in that period rented their basements for the storage of beer and ale.

Gradually, temperance sentiment gathered strength within Methodism. The 1820 General Conference elected a committee on temperance. Wilbur Fisk was a pioneer in promoting General Conference concern for the cause, and in 1828 he offered a resolution against drinking and offering drinks to one's visitors and workmen. He preached a temperance sermon to the General Conference of 1832 that prompted an order for the publication and distribution of temperance tracts. It is thought that this was the first General Conference sermon on the theme. Although the 1840 General Conference refused to pass a proposal to restore the General Rule on temperance as originally phrased by Wesley, the following Conference did so; and with the concurrent votes of annual conference members during the quadrennium intervening, the restoration became basic law in 1848.

Writing in 1850, Nathan Bangs admitted that when the American

---

23. D. Pickett, *The Christian Advocate* (Centennial Number, Sec. 2); Sept. 9, 1926.
24. W. W. Sweet, *Methodism in American History*. Methodist Book Concern, New York; p. 232.
25. Peter Cartwright, *Autobiography*. Abingdon Press, Nashville; p. 180.

THE WITNESS BLURRED: SOCIAL ISSUES

Temperance Society was formed in 1826, "many of us, both preachers and people were in the habit of drinking, if not to excess, yet drinking moderately cider, beer, wine, and brandy," and, he wrote, "The rule had become almost a dead letter and the Church had fallen asleep upon this subject...." Writing two years after the restored rule, he believed that it and the steady efforts of preachers and people, "will finally gain a complete triumph over alcoholic drinks...." [26]

The General Conference of 1860 went on record as endorsing total abstinence and the prohibition of the sale of liquor. Methodism was now launched upon its crusade for temperance reform. After compromising the Wesleyan witness for many decades, it had restored the standard for its members and then, more than any other denomination, undertook to promote a national reform that climaxed in the federal prohibition amendment of 1920.

But again, Methodism betrayed the Wesleyan witness. Writing of the lower standards of discipline than formerly prevailed in the Methodist Church, Bishop Gerald Kennedy has said, "Unless some flagrant crime has been committed, the Church seldom acts to remove a member...." Mentioning no other restrictions on personal conduct, he adds, "We do have a specific prohibition against any Methodist engaging in the liquor business." [27] In a later section he admits that, notwithstanding the reputation of Methodists as *teetotalers*, "it is obvious that many of our laymen no longer live up to it." [28]

Pewed churches and the poor

The *Discipline* of 1784, as noted in Chapter Eight, carried no instruction concerning "pewed" churches, for "free" churches were then taken for granted. It was not many years, however, before the pew system was introduced in New England.

In England, even before Wesley's death, a few Methodist chapels rented pews. In fact, it would appear from Wesley's *Journal* that City Road Chapel and West Chapel in London were financed in part by pew rents, but Wesley insisted that no one paying pew rent could

---

26. N. Bangs, *Prospects and Responsibilities of the Methodist Episcopal Church.* Lane & Scott, New York; p. 125 *et seq.*
27. Gerald Kennedy, *The Methodist Way of Life.* © 1958 by Prentice-Hall, Inc.; Englewood Cliffs, New Jersey; p. 141.
28. *Ibid.*, p. 145.

claim a particular pew. When the trustees tried to force the issue in 1787, Wesley wrote in his *Journal* that for families of men and women to sit together and those taking pews to claim particular places as their own, would overthrow "at one blow, the discipline which I have been establishing for fifty years." [29] Apparently those who had not taken pews had inferior accommodations, and it is to be inferred that the point of Wesley's discipline he would not have overthrown was the separation of the sexes. But anyway, the trustees graciously yielded to his will.

Around 1805 those not pewholders had difficulty finding places in the more popular chapels in London, and Maldwyn Edwards reports that a stranger, after waiting some time to be offered a seat, spied a notice which read, "It is expected that those who have attended at this chapel a sufficient time to ascertain whether they like the preaching do take tickets as they cannot be accommodated with seats without them." That pew rents had become an accepted method of church support among Methodists in early nineteenth-century England, Edwards points out, meant that the Methodist Church was no longer the church of the poor.[30] What Thomas Jackson, writing in 1839, intended as praise of English Methodism for its generous treatment of the poor in its chapels, tended rather to emphasize the discrimination against them by the pew system then prevailing in England. He said: "In Leeds alone the chapels contain four thousand free sittings for the accommodation of the poor; and in many other places the spiritual necessities of the lower classes of society are met in the same liberal manner." [31]

Growing membership and wealth, with the development of urban culture, early brought the pewed church into New England Methodism, and later into New York and elsewhere in the United States. Pewed churches came into New England about 1808, much to the grief of that pioneer of the area, Jesse Lee. When, on a return visit to New England some time after his ministry there, he found men and women seated together in pews, he asked, "Is this not a violation of Methodist rules?" Visiting the Bromfield Street Church

---
29. J. Wesley, *Journal*. Epworth Press, London; v. 7, 349 *et seq.*
30. M. Edwards, *After Wesley*. Epworth Press, London; p. 91 *et seq.*
31. T. Jackson, *The Centenary of Wesleyan Methodism*. Mason & Lane, New York; p. 173.

in Boston, he granted the beauty and spaciousness of the sanctuary and added, "but it is not on the Methodist plan, for the pews are sold to the highest bidder." [32]

Bishop McKendree wrote in his *Journal* after the 1813 session of the New England Conference, expressing his fear that Methodists in that area were "building very expensive and ornamental houses; selling pews, so that it is made difficult for the poor to hear the gospel; and fixing the government in the hands of such as may become owners of pews; so that our itinerant preachers, as well as the poor, may be excluded when men of the world may choose to do so." [33]

Bishop Asbury was more emphatic, declaring, "We have made a stand in the New England Conference against steeples and pews; and shall probably give up the houses unless the pews are taken out, and the houses made sure to us exclusively." [34]

The General Conference of 1816 refused to take other action than a vote of disapprobation, but in 1820 there was added to the original rule of the *Discipline* on simplicity and economy of architecture the words, "and with free seats." The following paragraph also was added:

> As it is contrary to our economy to build houses with pews to sell or rent, it shall be the duty of the several Annual Conferences, to use their influence to prevent houses from being so built in the future; and as far as possible to make those houses free which have already built pews.

Because of the new paragraph's lack of a clear-cut mandate, quibbling resulted and out of it came in 1833 the first pewed church in New York City, financed on the joint-stock plan, and therefore virtually owned by the pewholders. A precedent had been set, and another pewed church was soon erected in New York City.

According to Timothy L. Smith, "competition in impressive edifices toppled even Baptist and Methodists prejudices against pew rents," [35] and Nottingham placed the renting of pews along with building colleges, erecting churches, and "the habit of attending Sun-

---

32. D. W. Clark, *Life and Times of Rev. Elijah Hedding, D.D.* Carlton & Phillips, New York; p. 177 et seq.
33. Robert Paine, *Life and Times of William McKendree.* Publishing House of M. E. Church, South, Nashville; v. 1, 285.
34. F. Asbury, *Journal;* v. 3, 416.
35. T. L. Smith, *Revivalism and Social Reform.* Abingdon Press, Nashville; p. 164.

day services in the most elegant apparel," as manifestations of the desire for prestige as Methodists became prosperous.[36]

The whole matter of pewed churches came to an issue in the General Conference of 1852, meeting in fashionable Boston, the center of pewed-church influence. This conference refused to sustain the Ohio Conference in its censure of a preacher for building a pewed church. In consequence, and, according to Smith, with the aid of prominent New Yorkers, the rule requiring seats to be free was amended by adding, "wherever practicable," thus virtually annulling restrictions against pew rentals and sales. And this, notwithstanding the pastoral address to that Conference which "deplored the growing love of riches and advised that Wesley's followers should avoid costly buildings." [37]

Thereafter, pewed churches rapidly multiplied until a "free" Methodist church might not be found even in some of the larger cities with several Methodist churches. When, three years after the Boston Conference, Bishop Osmond C. Baker published his *Guide-Book in the Administration of the Discipline*, he devoted six pages therein to pew rentals and pew ownership, giving various angles of civil law and citing several court decisions in different states.

Elias Bowen in 1863 condemned the practice of churches repudiating the claims of pewholders in order to increase revenue by compelling these holders to rent the pews they once owned, and called it a "downright swindle" because it violated a binding contract.[38]

In America in the beginning, even as with Wesley in England, it appears that the deterrent to pewed churches had been as much their violation of the historic Methodist rule which divided the seating of men and women, as the social discrimination inherent in the system. In fact, not until restrictions against pews were removed, was the requirement of separate seating of men and women removed. But the action of 1852 concerning pews, and the resulting multiplication of pewed churches, would shortly bring into sharp focus the unchristian principle of discrimination within the church on the basis of

---

36. E. K. Nottingham, *Methodism and the Frontier*. Columbia University Press, New York; p. 83 *et seq.*
37. T. L. Smith, *Revivalism and Social Reform*. Abingdon Press, Nashville; p. 164.
38. *Northern Independent*, v. 7, April 2, 1863.

THE WITNESS BLURRED: SOCIAL ISSUES

wealth. The Christian principle of freedom of rich and poor alike to gospel privileges, and as well the slave's claim to civil and political freedom, were soon to play an important part in the formation of the Free Methodist Church and would principally determine its name.

The problem of secrecy

A problem of social import with which John Wesley dealt only implicitly, albeit very clearly in principle, is the secret, oathbound lodge. During the period now under survey, the first seventy-five years of American Methodism, this issue was raised now and again in annual conferences but stirred little concern in the General Conference, for secrecy has long enjoyed a fair degree of favor in the higher administrative circles of Methodism.

Prior to 1860, the Genesee Conference of the Methodist Episcopal Church had acted on the issue, both in general and in application to specific cases. Conable reports that in 1811 a preacher was continued on trial rather than ordained, and reproved by the Chair for two offenses, one of which was his having joined the Masonic Lodge. In 1841 another preacher's ordination was withheld, in part for the same offense. In 1829, shortly after the Morgan abduction and murder, allegedly by the Masons and within the borders of the Genesee Conference, the following resolution was adopted:

> That we will admit no person on trial, continue none on trial, nor admit any into full connection in this Conference—neither elect any either to deacons or elders orders, whether traveling or local—who shall have ever belonged to the Masonic fraternity, who will not renounce all connection with Masons as such, by withdrawing from the institution, and promising to have no further connections with Masons.[39]

The *Journal* records further action indicating that at this conference a group of preachers, former Masons, renounced Masonry and asked that their statements be filed.

The murder of Morgan in 1826 had serious consequences for Masonry, greatly depleting its membership and deeply stirring the indignation of the nation against secret orders. W. R. Cross com-

---

39. Quoted by Conable, *History of the Genesee Annual Conference*. Nelson & Phillips, New York; p. 302.

ments as follows on Methodism's tolerance concerning the issue at this time:

> ... Methodists appear to have been the least disturbed denomination throughout the episode. Petitions from local conferences for a church disciplinary rule on the Masonic affiliation entertained no hope of passage, while in several localities individuals excluded from Presbyterian congregations on this point joined the Methodists with impunity.[40]

And true it is that the General Conference of 1828, which followed by only two years the Morgan episode, refused to condemn Masonry; and the Conference of 1832 refused even to examine the question of secret societies. The struggle to rise above humble origins and frontier culture may have led many in Methodism just at this period to seek status by *belonging*, whereas older denominations such as the Presbyterians, which already had achieved status, needed not the lodge to bolster a sense of importance with its cabalistic ritual, closed-group chumminess, and pompous pageantry.

The General Conference in 1852 ruled that the *Discipline* does not authorize an annual conference to censure a preacher for belonging to a secret society unless it is known that the society is in conflict with the rules of the church. But who can know if such is the case except a member of the secret society in question?—*and he has sworn himself to secrecy!*

In the developments leading to the organization of the Free Methodist Church in 1860, the lodge played a prominent part, as will be related in a later chapter.

Conclusion

In this and the preceding chapter has been sketched the blurring, by mid-century, of American Methodism's witness concerning Christian doctrine and experience, simplicity in worship, purity of personal living, and certain areas of social relationship. Recent decades had been a period of many and rapid changes in Methodism, not all of which were in themselves evil so much as indicative of a carelessness that could throw aside seemingly minor features of a great heritage without discerning their relationship to the vital core of that heritage.

---

40. W. R. Cross, *The Burned-Over District*. Cornell Press, Ithaca, N. Y.; p. 121.

In his old age John Wesley had warned that the "circumstantial" features of Methodism were necessary to the "essential" features. In "Thoughts Upon Methodism" in 1786 he had said:

> Methodism is only plain, Scriptural religion, guarded by a few prudential regulations. The essence of it is holiness of heart and life; the circumstantials all points to this. And as long as they are joined together in the people called Methodists, no weapon formed against them shall prosper. But if even the circumstantial parts are despised, the essential will soon be lost. And if ever the essential parts should evaporate, what remains will be dung and dross.[41]

Methodism continued after mid-century as a great moral and evangelistic force, but through individual and official compromises the Methodist way of life had declined from the high level set by the General Rules and early Methodist practice.

There were sincere members in the church—many of them—who loved it and longed to see its restoration to its earlier purity and spiritual power. The unsuccessful efforts of some of them to secure those ends are to be traced in following chapters.

---

41. J. Wesley, *Works* (Emory ed. 1853); v. 7, 317.

CHAPTER ELEVEN

"The Lord Sent a Prophet"

How churches are born

As Christianity moves with the centuries, it tends now and again to wander from the founding principles of the New Testament Church. God then calls forth a prophet to lead in a restoration or reformation. Frequently also it happens that a particular church or denomination of the Christian movement loses or compromises the witness for which God called it into being, and again God calls a man to lift the standard that has fallen. Often these reforms lead, not to the reformation of the original group, but to the organization of a new movement to perpetuate the witness renounced or neglected by the parent church.

The Roman Catholic Church had dominated the Middle Ages, corrupting the simplicity and purity of original Christianity in many ways. It had elevated the authority of the Church above the Bible, and held that salvation depends upon man's merit gained through penance and good works. In the early sixteenth century, God called Martin Luther to uncover again the New Testament foundation of salvation through faith as a personal relationship of man to God through Christ. Luther was a man of learning and power, and under his influence more than any other, Protestantism became the bearer of the Christian message which the Roman Church had so sadly distorted.

After its early heroic beginnings in England, the Protestant Reformation there became more of a political matter involving the King's break with the Pope, than the spiritual movement in which it had begun. Consequently, by the eighteenth century the religious state of England was at low tide, and immorality and wretched social conditions were rotting the fiber of English character, as set forth in Chapter Two.

But God had his man in John Wesley, a graduate, Master of Arts and Fellow of Oxford University. We have seen how, in a ministry of more than half a century, John Wesley led a revival of religion that changed lives, raised the moral tone of society, and brought a great spiritual quickening to the churches of that day. This revival movement produced in England the Wesleyan Methodist Church, and in America the Methodist Episcopal Church. One of the younger of the major Protestant movements, Methodism rapidly spread around the world to become one of the largest.

In former chapters we have also seen how, with the growth of the American nation and the development of American life, Methodism on this continent tended to make concessions that compromised some of the standards that were vital to the Wesleyan witness. And again, God had a man, university trained as were Luther and Wesley before him, firm in purpose and strong in his convictions of God's will. He was Benjamin Titus Roberts, graduate of Wesleyan University and Master of Arts, a young and successful pastor in his conference. But as in other instances of history, the church this reformer sought to restore to its first principles rejected him and his earnest followers, and a new denomination was born.

The present chapter proceeds with an account of this man who, by strange providences and quite apart from personal intent, became the symbol of reform and then the leader of those who sought to hold Methodism to its historic course. The facts upon which this chapter's brief account of Roberts' early life is based are found in large part in a biography written by his son, Benson H. Roberts, a few years after the father's death, under the title, *Benjamin Titus Roberts: A Biography*.

Spiritual quickening

One winter in the late forties of the nineteenth century, a Methodist revival swept Middletown, Connecticut, including the campus of Wesleyan University situated in that city. The evangelist was a medical doctor and local preacher, John Wesley Redfield.

The president of the University at the time was Stephen A. Olin, distinguished scholar and saint. Hearing reports concerning the revival, he arose from a sickbed to learn what was happening on the campus. He was quickly convinced of the soundness of the preaching and the genuineness of the results, and said, "This, brethren, is Methodism, and you must stand by it." [1]

Dr. Olin was one of the greatest men of Methodism in his century Bishop Hamline, after hearing him preach on the witness of the Spirit and the experience of perfect love, declared, "I doubt not that Dr. Olin is the greatest man on the continent, and simple as great." [2] Consequently, when a man of Dr. Olin's competence endorsed the Redfield revival, his word carried weight. Leading members of his faculty humbled themselves in confession and prayer, and the revival moved on with power.

One of the students stirred by the Redfield revival was young Roberts. He had earlier been converted, an event that turned him from the study of law when he was nearly ready for admission to the bar, to preparation for the Christian ministry. It was for this preparation that he was in Wesleyan University at the time of the Redfield revival. The profound effect of that meeting remained with him through the years.

Early interest in reform

Even before entering Wesleyan University, Roberts had been interested in both temperance and slavery reform. His first public message had been on the subject of abolition while he was studying law. His interest in the colored race was expressed in a practical way while he was in college. He reported in a letter to his sister that on Sundays he no longer was lonesome since he had begun teaching a class of young women at the African church. He added this observation:

> They have too much of the slavery spirit even here among the descendants of the Puritans, to worship the Universal Father in the same temple with their sable brethren. They have, therefore, here in Connecticut, not Negro slips [galleries], but Negro churches, Negro preachers, presiding elders and conferences.[3]

This letter was written in 1846, shortly after the abolitionist seces-

---

1. B. H. Roberts, *Benjamin Titus Roberts*. Earnest Christian Office, N. Chili, N. Y.; p. 20.
2. F. G. Hibbard, *Biography of Rev. Leonidas L. Hamline*. Eaton & Mains, New York; p. 155.
3. B. H. Roberts, *Benjamin Titus Roberts*; p. 17.

sion of 1843 that led to the organization of the Wesleyan Methodist Church, and the separation of the Southern Church in 1845. Abolitionism was an explosive subject in Northern Methodism in 1846 because of tensions due to the church's compromise, previously noted, for the purpose of holding the Border conferences and avoiding further depletion in members and loss of territory. Already Roberts' convictions were clear, and the course he would later take was predictable.

University success

Roberts was compelled by financial need to teach district school for a few terms during his University course, and while doing so, he carried on his own studies as well, without the advantage of class instruction. As a lad he had begun Latin without a teacher, and had mastered algebra before he knew anyone else that understood it. And now he had some of his district school pupils, of which there were seventy in all, studying algebra, geometry, Latin—and he was planning to offer Greek! [4]

Notwithstanding the stiff competition of able classmates and the handicap of only part-time residence on the campus, Roberts succeeded in achieving university honors. He was chosen one of three for the "Junior Exhibition" orations. Those honored with him were Daniel Steele, later to become president of Syracuse University and an able writer on Christian perfection, and William C. Kendall who became a brilliant and saintly preacher, and who met an untimely death while sharing Roberts' sufferings in the Genesee Conference troubles. The orations were on the following subjects:

Benjamin Titus Roberts, "Genius of Saxon Literature."
William C. Kendall, "Mission of the American Scholar."
Daniel Steele, "The Moral, the Perfection of the Intellectual." [5]

A year later, at graduation, honors came again to Roberts in his being chosen to deliver the metaphysical oration. Before leaving the campus, he was faced with that choice between Christian education and a pastorate which so frequently confronts earnest and scholarly candidates for the ministry. He was invited to the presidency of Wyoming Seminary of Kingston, Pa., a secondary institution of the

---
4. *Ibid.*, p. 23.
5. *Ibid.*, p. 26.

Methodist Episcopal Church. He turned for counsel to President Olin, who told him, "There are more who are ready to teach than to preach." [6]

Full of hope and in happy ignorance of what awaited him within a decade, B. T. Roberts decided to cast his lot with the Genesee Conference; and a month after his graduation from Wesleyan University in 1848, when he was twenty-six years of age, he was admitted to the Genesee Conference on trial.

Marriage and early ministry

Roberts went to his first pastoral charge a single man, but was married the following May to Ellen Lois Stowe, niece of Rev. George Lane, Book Agent of the Methodist Episcopal Church in its New York office. Four bishops were guests at the wedding supper at the Lane home—Bishops Morris, Waugh, Hedding and Janes.

On his first pastorate, his first sermon was on heart purity. The young preacher wrote his father, "I am trying to give myself wholly to the work of the Lord, to be a man of one calling, of one work." [7] He was well liked by his people, and had a revival in the winter which, as he expressed it, "did not survive the spring fashions." At year's close he wrote in his journal:

> I had a pleasant year at Caryville. Was favored with some success. Received during the year about forty members into the society. Enlarged and repaired the church at an expense of about six hundred dollars, and paid an old debt on the parsonage. I came out myself at the end of the year $60 in debt for board. The people expressed a strong desire for our return. Stationed at Pike.[8]

He had done well for a first year, but for a time was deeply discouraged with Pike, his second appointment. In the beginning, the people didn't want him, but had hoped for an older man. After two or three months at Pike, young Roberts wrote his father, telling him of his dissatisfaction with the place and the poor support. He confessed:

> I have been looking the wrong way altogether. I should have

---

6. *Ibid.*, p. 29.
7. *Ibid.*, p. 32.
8. *Ibid.*, p. 37.

looked at the Savior more and at the people less. As a necessary consequence I have not been able to preach with any degree of satisfaction. . . . But I am now giving myself up wholly to the Lord, repenting of my sin, and I feel better, and I believe preach better.[9]

He then reported encouraging signs of better church attendance and a deepening spirituality in his members. In January came a revival.

At the 1850 annual conference he was admitted to full membership, ordained a deacon by Bishop Waugh, and returned to Pike. During this year Roberts found a deeper level of consecration and enduement for service at the Collins camp meeting, where the theme of holiness was strongly emphasized under the leadership of a presiding elder of deep spirituality, Eleazer Thomas. Mrs. Phoebe Palmer and Dr. Palmer were present and active in pressing the work of holiness of heart. Convictions received under Redfield's preaching at Middletown had never left him, Roberts said, and these were now deepened. It was at this camp meeting that he received the blessing of holiness.[10]

Years later, in his magazine, *The Earnest Christian*, he reported that at this camp meeting he saw before him clearly two ways, one of popularity but with a profitless ministry that would end in the loss of his own soul; the other a "narrow way" with persecution, but preaching full truth with a thorough work resulting, and heaven at the end. Then, in his words:

The Spirit fell upon me in an overwhelming degree. I received a power to labor such as I had never possessed before. This consecration has never been taken back. I have many times had to humble myself before the Lord for grieving his Spirit. I have been but an unprofitable servant. It is by grace alone that I am saved. Yet the determination is fixed, to obey the Lord and take the narrow way, come what will.[11]

This humility concerning his own merit, even when declaring a great spiritual victory, was characteristic of Roberts even in later years while he was bearing the heavy responsibility of leadership.

---

9. *Ibid.*, p. 46.
10. B. T. Roberts, *Why Another Sect*. Earnest Christian Publishing House, Rochester; p. 54.
11. B. T. Roberts, *The Earnest Christian*, v. 9, Jan. 1865, p. 6.

When he had completed two years at Pike, according to the Methodist itinerancy of that day, it was time for a change. Accordingly, at the annual conference of 1851 the bishop appointed him to the Rushford charge.

In a letter to his wife's aunt, Mrs. Lane, he noted that Rushford was strong in numbers, wealth and social standing, "and a stranger among us," he wrote, "would imagine that they enjoyed a good degree of the life and power of religion. They did years ago. The words that then expressed their feelings they still use, but the feelings are gone." His honest humility then led him to add, "I have been endeavoring to arouse them but fear that I am no more than half awake myself. I am complaining of the stupidity of others, when I ought to be shaking off my own. I have far too little power of doing good." [12]

And yet he had only recently been called to Pike for a revival—the place where he had not been wanted two years before when sent there as a pastor. His successor at Pike was his university friend, William C. Kendall. Roberts reported in this letter, "over a hundred have professed conversion and about ninety had united with our church when I left." His anguished pastor's heart prays, "Oh! may it break out in Rushford, and in the regions round about." [13]

Evidences of the young pastor's diligence, but withal his dissatisfaction with himself, appear in diary entries for December of this year. The following excerpts are given by Benson Roberts in the biography of his father:

> December 3rd.—Visited among the unconverted most of the day. Preached in the evening; many forward for prayers and some converted. The Spirit of God powerfully manifest.
>
> December 7th.—Preached in the morning from Matt. 1:21. The Lord graciously assisted. Between twenty and thirty received into the church.
>
> December 10th.—Rose at five. Read in the Hebrew and Greek Bible. Very busy all the forenoon in accomplishing nothing. Visited, and feel the need of more religion.[14]

In February a revival did come to Rushford, some time after which he wrote in his journal, "Twenty-three have joined this quarter. An

---
12. B. H. Roberts, *Benjamin Titus Roberts*; p. 61.
13. *Loc. cit.*
14. *Ibid.*, p. 60.

immense congregation today." The year closed with success, the people at last anxious to build a new church for which the pastor had labored.

The Niagara Street appointment

At the Lockport Conference of 1852, Bishop Morris ordained B. T. Roberts an elder. To his wife from the seat of conference, Roberts wrote, "O, what solemn vows are upon me." He shared with her a conference rumor that he might be sent to Niagara Street Church in Buffalo, but commented, "I would rather not go there now; but the will of the Lord be done." [15]

When the appointments were read, this young man of only four years' pastoral experience and now but thirty years of age, was promoted to Niagara Street, a central church of the district and oldest church in Buffalo. At this time, everything pointed to his full favor with conference leadership, and he need only be "a regular" to continue in favor and to advance in position. His name had already been mentioned as an early prospect for the presiding eldership. But principles which had been firmly established in his mind and conscience were quickened to forceful expression by what he observed and experienced in a popular city church, and soon would involve him in difficulties with the ruling order.

As we have noted above, from the 1852 Conference he had written his wife that he preferred another appointment, and years later he wrote as follows concerning his reluctance to accept the appointment to Niagara Street:

> ... It was the only appointment made for us with which we ever tried to interfere. We felt deeply our lack of ability, experience and grace, to fill so important a position. We entreated the Bishop not to send us there. But when we were sent, we resolved to do our duty faithfully. God kept us from compromising, and gave us a good revival of religion.[16]

After several weeks on his new charge, Roberts wrote his father that congregations and interest were increasing, but added, "you have no idea of the low state of Methodism in this city. Nothing but the power of the Lord can save us." [17] To quicken the church by revival,

---
15. *Ibid.*, p. 66.
16. B. T. Roberts, *Why Another Sect*; p. 104 *et seq.*
17. B. H. Roberts, *Benjamin Titus Roberts*; p. 67.

he engaged Dr. Redfield as evangelist, with other helpers. The meeting was well under way, with encouraging evidences of great victory, when it was interrupted for several days by the general anniversary of the Missionary Society which was held in Niagara Street Church. Roberts wrote later that, "the aid of eloquence and wit, and personal, and church rivalry was invoked to raise money." In consequence, "a spirit of levity prevailed, and conviction was dissipated." [18] The occasion also brought prominent preachers into contact with the members, some of whom prejudiced the people against the meeting and the spiritual program the pastor had undertaken. When the meetings were resumed, the revival spirit had left and strong opposition became apparent. Three members came to the pastor with their protests: one said the standard was too high; another objected to "measures" (presumably meaning close preaching on certain evils); the third contended for growth *into* holiness. When Dr. Redfield asked some of his critics if he were not preaching according to Scripture, the answer was "Yes! but we cannot live up to it." When Dr. Redfield left, the church made no provision even for his expenses, and the pastor had already borrowed money to assist another worker to proceed on his way.

The preceding May, Roberts had been a visitor at the 1852 General Conference in Boston, and there may have heard the debate concerning pewed churches, the outcome of which was the elimination of the restriction against the same. But if not before, Roberts now saw by direct observation in his own church the evils of the pew system, and he began to use his influence against such commercializing of the church and discrimination against the poor. He offered to see the debt against Niagara Street Church lifted if it were made a "free" church, but to no avail. And by that debt, increased by extravagant remodeling under a subsequent pastor, the church was to be lost to Methodism within a few years and become a Jewish synagogue.

Having failed to convert Niagara Street into a "free" church, Roberts next sought to enlist his congregation in the building of a "free" church elsewhere in Buffalo that the poor might have a place of worship without embarrassment. Considerable interest developed, and at one point the society voted approval of the project, but for some

---

18. B. T. Roberts, *The Earnest Christian*, v. 7, Feb. 1864; p. 38.

reason plans were never carried through. Several years later, through his initiative and sacrifice, Roberts saw established a "free" church in Buffalo as one of the early congregations of the newly organized Free Methodist denomination.

The spirit of the prophet now stirred Roberts to action. His own spiritual deepening at the Collins camp meeting of 1851 when he dedicated himself completely to preach the whole truth; the spiritual desolation and appalling worldliness he found in the Niagara Street congregation; his people's stubborn resistance to the rugged preaching of Dr. Redfield; the discrimination of the pewed church against the poor; and what he knew of conference conditions generally, all combined to commit him to the course of reform. He began to wield his incisive pen against the evils he believed God would have him oppose in an effort to restore the Conference to its former course in historic Methodism's clear-cut channel.

Apparently his first article on reform was published in the *Northern Christian Advocate*, February 16, 1853, shortly after the Redfield meeting in Niagara Street Church. As summarized by C. H. Zahniser, the article analyzed the membership statistics of the conference to show an actual loss in a decade of 1,139 members, and a loss relative to population increase during the decade of 4,269. He interpreted the loss as due to lack of spiritual life and power. The conditions described by Roberts we give in the words of Dr. Zahniser:

> He then specifically judged that not one half of the members enjoyed justifying grace, that the Discipline was a dead letter, and that Biblical injunctions against fashionable sins and 'duties irksome to the carnal heart' had been virtually repealed, and that a tide of worldliness was threatening to sweep away the boundaries between the Church and the world.[19]

Such an article was not designed to court favor with conference leaders. Some controversy followed in the columns of the *Northern Christian Advocate*. According to Roberts, the article also "called forth some sneering remarks in the *Buffalo Advocate*." His diary for March 25 discloses that he sent that day an article against pewed churches to the *Northern Christian Advocate*. He comments, "The system is doing mischief."

---

19. C. H. Zahniser, *Earnest Christian: Life and Works of Benjamin Titus Roberts*; p. 59.

Zahniser's thumb-nail sketch well summarizes Roberts' year at Niagara Street Church:

> That year's pastorate gives a glimpse of the man fasting and praying, studying "as usual" in the mornings, reading Irving's *Life of Mohammed* and commenting, "The style is too diffusive to suit me"; attending a lecture on gesture by Taverner, another on elocution; calling on his members, laboring in the jail and occasionally at the hydraulics; preaching in his stock church and working for a free church; writing for the church paper to correct what he considered errors; encouraged and discouraged; denounced and lauded; having little to get along on and yet buying a house which afterward became the means for the first free church in Buffalo.[20]

The gathering storm

Roberts' appointment by the conference of 1853 was a vexing problem. In the end he was removed from Niagara Street, no doubt very largely because of the issue over a "free" church, and was placed at Brockport. At the conclusion of the conference, he wrote in his journal, "I have never felt less anxiety about my appointment or prayed more. I receive it gratefully as from the Lord."[21]

Again he found worldliness in the church, and long-standing feuds made revival difficult; but at last it came. In the midst of the year's revival progress, this pastor of earnest but humble spirit, who so persistently urged others to higher spiritual levels, confessed in his journal, "I have commenced to seek earnestly a higher state of religious experience than I have ever enjoyed before."[22] Near the close of the year he reported, "The Conference year is closing up well. Out of sixty-six who have joined on probation during the year we have had to drop but ten."[23] The next day was Sunday, and he preached in the morning on "Methodism"; baptized four adults and two children, received eighteen into full membership, and in the evening had two forward for prayer. No wonder he described it in his journal, "A pleasant day."

Roberts was returned to Brockport for another prosperous year. But conference developments were ominous for those not inclined to

---

20. *Ibid.*, p. 65.
21. B. H. Roberts, *Benjamin Titus Roberts*; p. 79.
22. *Ibid.*, p. 88.
23. *Ibid.*, p. 97.

accept the prevailing order in control of the Conference. It was clear in the 1854 Conference that there were two opposing parties, the compromising, latitudinarian group which readily took up with new measures and little heeded the witness of early Methodism, and the conservative group which urged the Conference to "ask for the old paths."

During the year party feeling became strong. In July of 1855 the *Buffalo Advocate* accused the minority group of organizing a secret society called the "Nazarite Union," basing the charge on a document that had come into the hands of Editor Robie, and which had been prepared by the unpredictable Joseph McCreery, Jr. It is true that McCreery did design an organization to combat the "Buffalo Regency," as the controlling faction came to be called. But McCreery emphatically declared that the so-called "Nazarite Union" existed only on paper, and said, "*I alone was responsible for the whole concern.*" Nevertheless, much was made of the affair and the 1855 Conference adopted a resolution which assumed the actual existence of such a union and passed disapprobation thereon.[24] The term "Nazarite" came to designate the reform group for several years, but B. T. Roberts never accepted the designation.

In this Conference of 1855, the party lines were clearly drawn. The division was well defined by Benson H. Roberts in his biography of his father, and a part of his analysis of the situation in the Conference is worthy of reproduction.

> The Conference at Olean saw two sentiments clearly defined.... The one sentiment was liberal in its utterances, its theology was non-Methodistic and anti-Wesleyan. Its adherents saw no necessity for the rigid rules of the discipline upon the subject of worldliness It was friendly to the world and would have the world friendly to it. Rented pews, church fairs, sociables were quite in favor with these, and as for the class-meeting they made little use of it, or of the prayer-meeting. The other sentiment that had a strong hold on many of the ministers, and more of the laity, was staunch in its adherence to old time Wesleyan Methodism, both in doctrine and experience. It believed in the church rules in respect to worldly conformity and in enforcing them. With this sentiment the practice of supporting churches by the sale or

---

24. W. T. Hogue, *The History of the Free Methodist Church*. Free Methodist Publishing House, Winona Lake; v. 1, 60.

rental of pews was at variance. Spiritual life and power were sought and taught as the privilege and duty of God's children.[25]

Those of the liberal program in doctrine and worldly policy were now largely in control of conference officers and appointments. Many of them were secret society men, the numbers and influence of whom had grown since Roberts was admitted to the Conference on trial in 1848. In that year a pamphlet, written by a preacher of the Conference to show the evils of secrecy, created a great stir. To keep peace and avoid schism, conciliatory resolutions were adopted which were a far cry from the unequivocal action of the Genesee Conference nineteen years earlier.[26] The outcome of the 1848 incident was a signal victory for the secrecy group, and by it they had learned that, "all they had to do to carry their points was to stand together and assume a threatening attitude, and enough 'union savers' would rally to their support to give them a majority." But the issue proliferated far beyond secrecy as such, its tentacles bringing the world into the church. Around the secrecy nucleus, Chesbrough observed, "gathered those whose religious sympathies and experiences led them to place dependence on worldly policy for the advancement of the Church." [27]

Having served two years at Brockport, B. T. Roberts was appointed to Albion by the 1855 Conference, to follow William C. Kendall who had left the charge in good condition.

The newly appointed presiding elder of the Genesee District, in which Albion was located, was a gifted young man of superior culture, a graduate of the Biblical Institute of Concord, New Hampshire. According to B. T. Roberts, Loren Stiles, Jr., had been appointed to the position to correct or quell the so-called extremes of the reform group. But Stiles was soon convinced of the genuineness of the reform movement and, recognizing his own spiritual need, he sought and entered into the experience of sanctification. He then became an outstanding advocate of reform in the Conference.

A second presiding elder, appointed to the Niagara District, also disappointed the Regency by concluding that the charge of fanaticism against the reform group was unfounded. I. C. Kingsley had been a

---

25. B. H. Roberts, *Benjamin Titus Roberts*; p. 105 et seq.
26. See Chapter 10 of this book under "The problem of secrecy," p. 167.
27. S. K. J. Chesbrough, *Defence of Rev. B. T. Roberts, A.M.* The Morning Express Office, Buffalo; p. 4.

Presbyterian, and now found in the Genesee reform movement what he had expected to find when he came into the Methodist Episcopal Church. But pressure having been brought by Regency men in the 1856 Conference, who threatened that they would not take work under Stiles or Kingsley if they were reappointed, the two were granted transfers to the Cincinnati Conference. But their standing in the Genesee Conference was such that more than fifteen hundred members petitioned for their return, and in 1857 they were transferred back to the Genesee Conference.

The most significant event of Roberts' pastorate at Albion occurred in the second year. This was his publication of the fateful article, "New School Methodism." In giving an account of the whole matter later, Roberts stated his purpose in publishing the article as follows:

> ... Our opponents had, from time to time, in the *Buffalo Advocate* and other papers, in neither truthful nor respectful language, set forth their version of matters. We thought the time had come for us to set ourselves right before the public. This we endeavored to do in the following article which was published over our well known signature in the *Northern Independent*, of which I was at the time, a corresponding editor.[28]

The Northern Independent

The Northern Independent was a religious news journal, devoted principally to slavery reform, but its columns were open as well to other causes agitating Methodism in Western New York in the late fifties and early sixties. William Hosmer, the editor, had previously been editor of the *Northern Christian Advocate* but his zeal for slavery reform[29] made him unacceptable to the pro-slavery forces of the 1852 General Conference. He was therefore replaced by F. G. Hibbard, a moderate. The anti-slavery men of the Methodist conferences in the area served by the *Northern Christian Advocate*, not satisfied with the action of the General Conference, established the *Northern Independent* with Hosmer as editor. It won a large following.

The publication began in January, 1857, and from the beginning served well the cause of the reform party in Genesee. For years, until

---

28. B. T. Roberts, *Why Another Sect*; p. 85.
29. William Hosmer wrote *Slavery and the Church* while editor of the *Northern Christian Advocate*. The preceding chapter carries a quotation from this book which discloses the effectiveness of his trenchant style.

he resigned to establish his own journal, *The Earnest Christian*, B. T. Roberts was an associate or corresponding editor. With his resignation, S. K. J. Chesbrough, a prominent layman of the reform group who was later to become prominent in the Free Methodist Church, took Roberts' place on the editorial staff.

The present writer has covered the approximately two hundred and thirty extant issues of the *Northern Independent*, which are to be found, and then in broken series, only in the libraries of the following institutions:

Garrett Biblical Institute, Evanston, Illinois;
University of Wisconsin (Wisconsin State Historical Library), Madison, Wisconsin;
University of Minnesota, Minneapolis, Minnesota.

Additional issues may be lodged in private attics, but no others are listed as available to the public. These extant issues abound in items of intense interest concerning Genesee Conference troubles of the period, out of which eventually came the organization of the Free Methodist Church. Editor Hosmer courageously espoused the cause of the so-called "Nazarite" reformers against what he claimed was ecclesiastical tyranny and injustice. After the Free Methodist Church was organized, and before it had a publication of its own, the columns of the *Northern Independent* freely carried news and announcements concerning the new denomination. B. T. Roberts said of the editor, "In intellect and courage, Hosmer was the John Knox of his day." [30]

Significant is the fact that Editor Hibbard of the *Northern Christian Advocate*, to whom Roberts first offered "New School Methodism" for publication, returned it with a letter which in effect approved what Roberts had said, but rejected it for reasons of prudence and to avoid controversy. The letter follows:

Dear Brother Roberts: I return your communication as you requested, not feeling it prudent to publish. I presume you can not see things as I do from my stand point. Your communication would involve me in hopeless controversy, which would make me much trouble and perplexity, with no hope as I view it, of doing substantial good to the church, or the cause of Christ. I do not speak this against your article considered by itself, but of

---

30. B. T. Roberts, *Why Another Sect*; p. 47.

the controversy which your article would occasion. *Your article appears to me to be written in as mild and candid a tone as such facts can be stated in.* Be assured, my dear Brother, that in the doctrine of holiness, in the life and power of religion, in the integrity and spirit of Methodism, I have a deep and lively interest. I labor to promote these. But I could not feel justified in taking sides in the question that now unhappily divides the Genesee Conference. May the Lord bless you and all his ministers, and give peace and prosperity to the churches.

Ever yours in Christ,

Auburn, Aug. 10, 1857.   F. G. Hibbard[31]

Later, Hibbard did take sides. "After it was clear that we were in the minority," said Roberts, "Dr. Hibbard wrote against us with great zeal and, as we think, unfairness."[32]

In his crisp and incisive phrasing, pungent yet dignified, B. T. Roberts in his article dealt with the departure of the Genesee Conference from the Wesleyan witness in the five areas detailed in our introductory chapter as distinctive emphases of Free Methodism as a bearer of the Wesleyan heritage. The article is too long to quote in full, but the following excerpts will set forth some of the applications the article makes to problems in these areas.[33]

DOCTRINE. B. T. Roberts wrote, "The New School Methodists affect as great degree of liberalism as do Theodore Parker and Mr. Newman." The article in the *Buffalo Advocate* which had subordinated devotion to beneficence had said, "Christianity is not, characteristically, a system of devotion. It has none of those features which must distinguish a religion grounded on the idea that to adore the Divine character is the most imperative obligation resting upon human beings. It enjoins the observance of but very few sacred rites; nor does it prescribe any particular mode for paying homage to the Deity. It eschews all exterior forms, and teaches that they who worship God, must worship him in spirit and in truth." Thus the article stated what Christianity is not, according to those whom Roberts called New School Methodists. The following is the statement of what Christianity is, according to the same article: "The characteristic idea of this system (Christianity) is benevolence; and its practical realization is achieved in beneficence. It consecrates the principle of charity,

---

31. *Ibid.*, p. 96 *et seq.*
32. *Loc. cit.*
33. For the full text of "New School Methodism," see Appendix A.

and instructs its votaries to regard good works as the holiest sacrifice, and the most acceptable which they can bring to the Almighty."—*May 14, 1857.*

DOCTRINE AND EXPERIENCE. B. T. Roberts said, "The New School Methodists hold that justification and entire sanctification, or holiness, are the same—that when a sinner is pardoned, he is at the same time made holy—that all the spiritual change he may thenceforth expect is simply a growth in grace. When they speak of 'holiness,' they mean by it the same as do evangelical ministers of those denominations which do not receive the doctrines taught by Wesley and Fletcher on this subject."

EXPERIENCE. According to Roberts' article, New School ministers "treat with distrust all professions of deep Christian experience."

WORSHIP. "The following sneer is not unworthy of Thomas Paine himself. It falls below the dignity of Voltaire." Such was Roberts' response to this statement in the *Advocate* article: "Christianity in no wise gives countenance to the supposition that the great Jehovah is so affected with the infirmity of vanity, as to receive with peculiarly grateful emotions, the attentions and offerings which poor, human creatures may pay directly to Him in worship." Further concerning worship, Roberts quotes the same article as evidence that New School Methodists frankly acknowledge that their teaching is critical of the Church. "So in the exercises and means of grace instituted by the Church, it is clearly apparent that respect is had, rather to the excitation of the religious sensibilities, and the culture of emotional piety, than the development of genial and humane dispositions and the formation of habits of active, vigorous goodness." Roberts suggests, then, that to secure New School ends, "The Lodge must supersede the class-meeting and the love-feast; and the old-fashioned prayer-meeting must give way to the social party."

WORSHIP AND STEWARDSHIP. Roberts' observation in this area was that New School Methodists, "build stock Churches, and furnish them with pews to accommodate a select congregation; and with organs, melodeons, violins, and professional singers, to execute difficult pieces of music for a fashionable audience."

CHRISTIAN CONDUCT. According to Roberts' article, New School ministers "encourage by their silence, and in some cases by their own example, and that of their wives and daughters, 'the putting on of gold and costly apparel. . . .' "

CHRISTIAN CONDUCT AND STEWARDSHIP. Roberts declared that

when New School Ministers "desire to raise money for the benefit of the Church, they have recourse to the selling of pews to the highest bidder; to parties of pleasure, oyster suppers, fairs, grab-bags, festivals, and lotteries. . . ."

For each of the above items, Roberts set forth in his article the opposite belief or practice of "Old School Methodists," and concluded the article with Jeremiah 6:16:

Thus saith the Lord, Stand ye in the ways, and see, and ask for the old paths, where is the good way, and walk therein, and ye shall find rest for your souls.

With the publication of "New School Methodism," the storm broke in its fury. And the Annual Conference would convene within a few days.

In 1843, five years before B. T. Roberts received from it his first pastoral appointment, Dr. Olin had visited the Genesee Conference to enlist its support of Wesleyan University. Later Olin wrote of Genesee, "It is an interesting conference, youthful, ardent, a little mercurial, strong in resources and talent. I hope they will prove to have ballast for all weathers." [34] We shall soon learn that their ballast was inadequate and poorly placed to keep the conference on an even keel.

---

34. Quoted by Conable, *History of the Genesee Conference of the Methodist Episcopal Church*. Nelson & Phillips, New York; p. 501.

CHAPTER TWELVE

Prophet Without Honor

In August of 1957 there came into the writer's hands, by a strange providence, a bundle of old books and documents from a New England source, some of the material dealing with the origins and early history of Free Methodism. In the lot was one item of exceptional interest—an old pocket diary published by Carlton and Porter of the Methodist Episcopal Book Room in New York. Stamped in gold on the cover-flap in Old English lettering is the inscription, "Diary 1857." The flyleaf bears the name and residence of the owner, "W. C. Kendall, North Chili."

Upon the pages of this diary William C. Kendall, pastor at North Chili, had poured his heart-longings, heartaches, and heartbreaks of that fateful year of 1857 in "Old Genesee." Interestingly enough, I had received this diary, which had survived a full century, on August 28, 1957, during the period of the centenary of the Annual Conference held in LeRoy August 26 to September 5, 1857.

Here, indeed, was a prize discovery! This little book carried the words describing the doings of the LeRoy Conference by a reporter who was a member of the body and who no doubt recorded some of the events from his seat as they occurred in his presence. Before the Conference was to end, the reporter himself would be thrust into the white-hot coals, with another of like metal, to be hammered on the anvil of persecution to shape the destiny of a movement whose pattern was a segment of God's providential plan.

The LeRoy Conference of 1857

The diary discovers Kendall at the LeRoy Conference a day early, it would appear for the purpose of assisting in examining ministerial candidates. On that day he wrote, "Our conference is in a very disturbed state. Two classes, one called Nazarites, the other Buffalo Regency. The former for the old 'landmarks' of Methodism, the other for policy and progress."

The next day, Wednesday, the conference opened at nine o'clock.

"Bishop Waugh administers the Sacrament with the unction. A tussle over secretary—Fuller 45, Roberts 40. A good strong Committee on tobacco. The forces are fairly arrayed."

The contest over the secretaryship of the Conference gave a measure of the relative strength of the parties. Had laymen in those days had a vote, the outcome of the election and of Roberts' trial later in the session, could have been quite different. Reform sentiment was strong among the laity of the conference. As it was, a shift of three votes from Fuller to Roberts would have elected Roberts secretary.

Thursday's entry reported that one of the preachers "read transcendentalism in the evening." Just at that time Emerson was the literary, and Theodore Parker the religious leader of unitarian transcendentalism. Kendall's cryptic entry does not make it clear that he was alert to the tragic significance of "reading transcendentalism" in an evening service of a Methodist annual conference. However, it is reasonably safe to assume that its portent was sensed by the honors orator at Wesleyan University of a decade earlier, whose subject had been, "Mission of the American Scholar." Kendall's college oration had followed by twenty years Emerson's famed oration of similar title, "The American Scholar."

Several days later Kendall wrote, "We shall have, I see clearly, a baptism of suffering. May God make us able." How true was his prediction! His entry for Wednesday, September 2, reads: "Charges were presented against B. T. Roberts. A motion to entertain the Bill was passed. A commission is sent to Buffalo to take testimony."

The next day his own character was arrested. He reported: "I receive a bill of one charge and thirteen specifications." Later, another bill of charges was preferred against him. He discovered what his opponents desired. "The design," he writes, "is to locate me." The nature of the charge against him comes to light in Friday's entry. "Brother Brainerd[1] comes to conference with 8 or 10 brethren to defend me from the charge of 'inacceptability.'" An unusual complaint against a man who had repeated revivals on his pastorates, and had taken into the church from one revival as many as one hundred members!

---

1. One of the Laymen from North Chili, W. C. Kendall's charge.

On this same day, Friday, September 4, the diary records the crisis. "Brother Roberts' case comes on. Great unfairness. Brother R—— declines proceeding. By solicitation of friends makes a plea in his [own] defense. Is condemned guilty of immorality by a vote of 53 affirmative to 43 negative. Is sentenced to a reproof and caution by the Bishop. God blesses him. The Regency are determined to crush the cause of Jesus. God forbid!" Note that a switch of five votes, by a tie, would have prevented conviction.

The Conference was now in its tenth day, and time failed to dispose finally of Kendall's case. He said, "My character passes with [a word has been omitted, evidently 'charges'] against me. Strange work this." So closes the record for Friday. The appointments were read, and at 1:30 Saturday morning the Conference adjourned. Kendall's entry for Saturday reports, "I am sent to West Falls, a starvation appointment some seventy miles away. The Lord will bring good out of this intended evil."

The following Sunday found Kendall preaching on his new charge. He found himself at the wrong point of the circuit for morning preaching, but a few gathered when they heard of his presence. Then he went to another point and preached to "a small sleepy congregation," and at five "to a crowded house at West Falls." While engaged in pastoral calling two days later he visited his predecessor who, as Kendall wrote in his diary, "has been about half fed here for two years. The people however," he added, "many of them are quite wealthy. This ought not to be. The Lord help me to do my duty." This entry, dated September 15, is the last in the book. Later will be noted the events of Kendall's last six months on earth, for on February 1, 1858, one of the well educated, most holy and most loved but shamefully persecuted preachers of Genesee died in the triumph of the faith.

Roberts' Trial of 1857

Only a few days after the appearance of "New School Methodism," in the *Northern Independent*, the Annual Conference convened in LeRoy. The Regency was greatly exercised by the return to the Conference of Stiles and Kingsley, some of them possibly the more so because in 1856 Stiles had tried to get the conference to appoint a committee to investigate business dealings of a partnership or firm made up of three prominent preachers of the Conference. In this he had not been successful, but for him to return to the Conference no doubt increased the uneasiness of these brethren, and, according to Roberts, prompted the Regency to extra concern to crush the "Nazarites."[2] The "New School" article provided a handle by which they sought to reach Roberts, and charges were brought against him for writing and publishing it.

At the time of the LeRoy trial, it was not known to Roberts that the Regency party had convened secret meetings, both at Medina in 1856 and now at LeRoy in 1857. Some of the devastating facts of those meetings came out in Roberts' second trial at Perry in 1858. Better to understand the compromise of justice at LeRoy, some of these facts are reviewed at this point.[3]

When charges against him were to be prosecuted at Perry, Roberts petitioned for trial by committee, explaining that he had no reason to expect a fair trial before a conference that included those that had met in secret to prejudice his case at LeRoy. He further pointed out that members of the Conference claiming personal injury from the article in question would have a prejudiced interest in the outcome of the trial. Arguing against his request had been Thomas Carlton, a leader in the Regency party and successor to George Lane (Mrs. Roberts' uncle) as denominational book agent in the New York office. Carlton denied that secret meetings were held, calling them rather "select" meetings. He said he had attended three such meetings at Medina in 1856, and "some of the select meetings in LeRoy." He estimated that in one at LeRoy there were present about forty, in another, sixty. But he insisted that no vote was taken to condemn Roberts: rather, the vote was that he should have a fair trial. At this point Roberts produced and read the record of proceedings of one of these "select" meetings which had providentially come into his possession since the LeRoy trial. It is here quoted—note that the document is dated the day before Roberts' conviction at LeRoy.

2. See B. T. Roberts, *Why Another Sect*. The Earnest Christian Publishing House, Rochester; p. 197.
3. Our account is drawn from S. K. J. Chesbrough, *Defence of Rev. B. T. Roberts, A.M., before the Genesee Conference*. Office of the Morning Express, Buffalo. This booklet was based upon notes and testimony taken at the second trial of B. T. Roberts at the Conference session in Perry, N.Y., in 1858. A more accessible account is that found in *Why Another Sect*, Chapter 8.

LeRoy, September 3rd, 1857.
Meeting convened according to adjournment, Bro. Parsons in the chair.

Brethren present pledged themselves by rising, to keep to themselves the proceedings of this meeting.

Moved, that we will not allow the character of B. T. Roberts to pass, until he has had a fair trial.—Passed.

Moved, that we will not pass the character of Rev. W. C. Kendall, until he has had a fair trial.—Passed.

Moved, that Bro. Carlton be added to the committee on Bro. Kendall's cases.—Passed.

Having read these minutes, Roberts pointed out that, "this secret Conclave assumed to act in a judicial manner upon the cases of absent brethren," and pointedly asked, "What right had this Conclave to say that any Brother should have a trial at all?"

The petition for trial by committee was denied, 48 to 39. A switch of five votes would have granted the petition. Again, as at LeRoy, Roberts was to be tried with the plaintiffs seated on the jury!

Although read in Conference at the time of the Perry trial, and repeatedly published, the genuineness of the document reporting the proceedings of a secret meeting during the LeRoy trial was never challenged. That such meetings were held, both at LeRoy in 1857 and at Medina in 1856, was confirmed in the Perry trial by reluctant witnesses who had participated in the same.[4]

Knowing nothing of such meetings at the time of his first trial, however, Roberts arose in the LeRoy Conference and said:

> I have no intention to misrepresent any one. I do not think I have. I honestly think that the men referred to, hold just the opinions I say they do. But if they do not, I shall be glad to be corrected. If they will say they do not, I will take their word for it, make my humble confession, and, as far as possible, repair the wrong I have done. I will publish in the *Northern Independent*, and in all the church papers they desire me to, from Maine to California, that I have misrepresented them."[5]

But in response to this challenge, there was no charge of misrepresentation. Roberts observed, "They had been at great pains to

---
4. See B. T. Roberts, *Why Another Sect*; p. 65.
5. *Ibid.*, p. 148.

get their majority, and now they must use it. As one of the preachers said, '*Nazaritism must be crushed out, and we have the tools to do it with!*' " [6] In his own defense, Roberts showed that, (1) the precise language of the alleged libel must be set forth in the indictment; (2) a man cannot be made responsible for the construction his enemies place upon his words; and (3) the charges against him were perversions of statements in his article. But the Conference voted his conviction by a narrow margin and sentenced him to reproof by the Chair. Having received the reproof, Roberts appealed to the General Conference that would sit three years later. Then, Roberts, a man convicted of "immoral and unchristian conduct," was appointed to the Pekin charge!

Three days before Roberts' conviction for immorality in the writing and publishing of "New School Methodism," a presiding elder of a neighboring conference wrote him, "I am gratified with your exposure of the 'New Divinity,' that is cursing our church. It is creeping into our Conference and doing immense mischief. Keep the monster in the light." It was evidently after his conviction that he received from a prominent minister the commendation, "If you had belonged to our Conference we would have given you a vote of thanks for writing that article." [7]

"New School Methodism" not overdrawn

That Roberts' "New School Methodism" was not the primary issue, but only the convenient occasion against him as a leader of the reform party, seems clear from the fact that there were at this period other criticisms of contemporary Methodism's worldly and unspiritual state as severe as was Roberts' article. One of the most severe was by none other than Editor Robie, of the *Buffalo Advocate*, concerning the religious state in Buffalo in 1859. Robie's editorial was promptly republished by Dr. Stevens in the New York *Christian Advocate and Journal*. In *Why Another Sect* Roberts points out that his own article "dealt more with speculative opinions—but this article," he said, "accuses [church members] of a want of experimental and practical piety."[8]

---

6. *Ibid.*, p. 149.
7. *Ibid.*, both quotations p. 97.
8. *Ibid.*, p. 99.

The following is Roberts' quotation of Robie's editorial:

RELIGIOUS INTEREST IN BUFFALO

We have none; we have no more than is usual through the year. We do not intend to convey the idea by the above heading that there is any special movement among us, or that there is any marked efforts toward getting souls converted, or keeping those converted who are already in the Church. The great movement among us is, we judge, to determine how far the church can go back to the world, and save its semblance to piety, devotion, and truth. Hence, many, many Church members have become the most frivolous and pleasure-loving, and folly-taking part of our towns people. They love, give and sustain the most popular, worldly amusements, such as dancing parties, card parties, drinking parties, masquerade and surprise parties, and have no disposition to come out from the world and be separate from it. All this may be seen, read and known in more or less of the Buffalo churches.[9]

Roberts questioned if these were not more serious charges than any in his article. Evidently "New School Methodism" had not been overdrawn.

In the light of Robie's editorial in the *Buffalo Advocate*, the veracity of the *Buffalo Courier*, a secular paper, can the more readily be accepted in its greatly extended and glowing account of a church festival, from which account we glean a few disturbing facts. The feature of the festival, held on spacious picnic grounds, was a "Clam Bake and Chowder." The *Courier* editor's account suggests a street fair or carnival. After enlarging on the varied gustatory attractions offered, he described a dance where "a large crowd had collected, and to the music of two bands were jumping about and perspiring to their heart's content," at ten cents per dancer. But, "The air in this place was so intensely hot and high flavored," said the editor, "that we positively failed to get the programme of the dances." Gate receipts were $400, which meant 4,000 admissions at ten cents each. Several hundred dollars were received in addition at the various booths. "The proceeds," reported the *Courier*, "are for the benefit of the Niagara Street Church, and will prove a great assistance to them in paying off the debt of the church." [10]

---

9. *Ibid.*, p. 98 *et seq.*
10. The account is given as quoted in *The Earnest Christian*, v. 1, Sept. 1860; p. 289 *et seq.*

The reader will recall that this church was the one served by B. T. Roberts in Buffalo in 1852-53, the debt on which he had offered to liquidate if it were made a "free" church. Roberts now comments editorially as follows:

> This Church, once highly prosperous, when 'holiness' was a common theme among its members, has been declining for several years. The members were taught that this lack of prosperity was not occasioned by a decline of spirituality, but by the want of a better edifice. The church was remodeled, and made one of the most splendid in the city. All the money was raised that could be raised by the sale of pews—by taxing the members to the utmost of their ability, and by making one of the largest liquor dealers in the city trustee and treasurer.[11]

Conable's *History of the Genesee Conference* records that about the year 1860 the Niagara Street Church was in severe financial straits and the Conference passed a resolution of sympathy, promising to help financially and otherwise. Conable's explanation of the cause of the difficulty differs from Roberts'—it was due, he said, to monetary disasters in Buffalo and the death of prominent members. Writing in 1876, Conable could report what had not yet happened in 1860 when Roberts republished the *Courier* account of the clambake and chowder festival, the final loss of the church and its use as a Jewish synagogue.[12] Roberts did complete the tragic account in 1878 when he wrote *Why Another Sect*.[13]

The Pekin pastorate

The reputation of Pekin's new pastor preceded him. A preacher of the Regency faction had carried the startling news to Pekin before his arrival, that the new pastor had just been convicted of immoral conduct. Shortly after Conference the *Buffalo Advocate* spread the word abroad, with no explanation of the unusual meaning attached to "immorality" in this instance. No wonder his reception at Pekin was a chilly one. "We doubt if any itinerant ever had a colder reception," wrote Roberts of his introduction to his parish. "Even Father Chesbrough, one of the noblest of men, and staunchest and most

---

11. *Ibid.*, p. 290.
12. F. W. Conable, *History of the Genesee Conference of the Methodist Episcopal Church*. Nelson & Phillips, New York; p. 667.
13. B. T. Roberts, *Why Another Sect*; p. 106.

loyal of Methodists, at first thought he would not even go to hear me preach. 'What have we done,' he exclaimed, 'that a man convicted of immoral conduct should be sent as our pastor?' " [14]

But this sturdy gentleman, a man of wide experience and significant responsibilities in the business world, went to church that first Sunday as usual. On the way home he said to his son, after they had journeyed in silence for some distance, "Well, Sam, I know nothing about the man, but I do know that what we have heard today is Methodism as I used to hear it in the old Baltimore Conference, and as I have not heard it preached in western New York." [15]

The new pastor was distressed that the people knew so little of heartfelt religion, but as usually occurred on his charges, a revival soon came and the work began to prosper. In late winter he wrote his father of seekers numbering ten or twenty every night of a revival series, and of calls for meetings in many places. Among these calls was one from the Congregational Church at LeRoy, the community in which a few months before he had been convicted of "immorality." It is apparent that the people in these places understood the partisan significance of his difficulties in the Conference, and that the unjust conviction had not besmirched his name in places where he was known.

During this year a local preacher of the Clarkson charge, George W. Estes by name, republished "New School Methodism" in a pamphlet with an account of the trial and attending events. B. T. Roberts was suspected by the Regency of responsibility for what seemed to be frank defiance of his conviction by the Conference for the article's original publication, and likewise defiance of his censure by the bishop. Accordingly, plans were formulated for a second trial at the forthcoming Conference at Perry.

During the Perry Conference an article appeared in the *Northern Independent* paying high tribute to the Pekin pastor. The author was S. K. J. Chesbrough, son of the Father Chesbrough above cited. After acknowledging the strange conditions under which B. T. Roberts had been sent to Pekin after conviction for "unchristian and immoral conduct," the author reported that, "the Church has

---
14. *Ibid.*, p. 155.
15. *Loc. cit.*

prospered through the blessing of God through the year." Between fifty and sixty had professed conversion, and about forty had joined the church. "The preaching," said the reporter, "has been plain, simple, and pointed, and in accordance with the doctrines and discipline of the Church." Many of the members had been seekers at an altar of prayer, some for justification and others for entire sanctification. The Sunday noon class meeting had grown from fifteen to seventy-five or eighty, with prayer meeting and Sunday-school attendance high.[16]

Wm. C. Kendall summoned before a higher court

We left Wm. C. Kendall at West Falls, after the 1857 Conference had adjourned with charges pending against him which, he had been assured, would be tried at the 1858 Conference. He had been found weeping in his room by Mrs. Kendall after the LeRoy Conference adjourned. Upon her persistent entreaty, he told her what was wrong. "Oh, it is not because they have sent me to a poor appointment, or an obscure place," he said, "but to look back and think how they have hunted me from one post to another, *because* I have conscientiously toiled to the extent of my powers to keep my ordination vows, and bring the church to *discipline and holy living!* They know this is all I have tried to do, and I have not half done that. Why is it? O! It makes me wish I was in *heaven;* and I believe I shall be soon." [17]

Before Conference the presiding elder had told the West Falls people that he doubted if a pastor small enough for them could be found. When Kendall was appointed, it was apparently with the thought that it was so small nothing could hurt it; and he was informed that the support was so small that he could not maintain a home, but might make out by living among the people. But Wm. C. Kendall went to his obscure appointment with faith and courage, a loyal itinerant obeying the order of his Conference.

At West Falls, Kendall found a cordial people, but formal in

---

16. *Northern Independent*, v. 3, Oct. 14, 1858.
17. A. A. Phelps, "Memoir of Rev. Wm. C. Kendall, A.M." in *Guide to Holiness*, v. 34, August, 1858. The author had been an intimate friend of Wm. C. Kendall. The complete Memoir appeared in four installments of this historic journal. *The Earnest Christian* ran eight installments on the life and work of Wm. C. Kendall during 1861.

worship, "the idol of which," according to Phelps, "was a well-drilled *exclusive choir*, that for years had been a fruitful source of jealousies and divisions—eating out the life of the church." Supported by a heavy vote of the congregation, and aided in securing the same, no doubt, by the singing school he had established, he restored congregational singing. Kendall had a beautiful voice, and had employed the singing school as a means of revival as early as his university days when he conducted such schools during winter vacation, and saw most of those in his classes converted. Another of his restorations was the closed-door love feast.

Even more than was true of Roberts, revivals came to Kendall's charges. And revival came to West Falls circuit that winter. His effectiveness was never greater, and his burning passion for the salvation of his people kept him from sleep. But fever struck in January. He was too ill to meet his appointments one Sunday, but would make the effort. He left the pulpit with a chill after preaching at his first appointment. Mrs. Kendall tried to prevail upon him to give up his next appointment and return home. "Let me preach at least twenty minutes," he pleaded; "I want to say something to the people of Potters's Corner, which they will remember. I have not done my full duty there, on conformity to the world." He went to Potter's Corner and preached, not twenty, but thirty minutes. His text was, "Be not conformed to this world." He was a very sick man and suffered intensely on the ride home. He had to be assisted into the house, and was never again to leave it alive.

On his deathbed he told Mrs. Kendall,[18] "I have no fear of death, but this conflict in the Conference I want to see ended." Then he added, "Well, Jesus can do without *any* of us. I will give it all up." There came periods of darkness and faith's testing, always followed by faith's triumph. Near the last, he rallied and sang, "Could I meet with angels, I'd sing them a song."

---

18. Many readers will be interested to know that Martha Wallace Kendall later married the Rev. T. S. LaDue, a young minister who had been a pastor in the Congregational Church but joined the Free Methodist Church in Northern Illinois within one year of the organization of the denomination. He became one of Free Methodism's greatest pioneer preachers. The late Professor John LaDue, noted teacher and preacher who for many years shaped the minds and characters of young ministers in Greenville College, was born of this union.

Wm. C. Kendall died at the age of thirty-five, having been God's instrument in revival after revival on his own pastorates. Following Roberts at Pike, he saw one hundred and fifty conversions in one year, and took more than one hundred into the church. He preceded Roberts at Albion where more than two hundred were converted in one year, and one hundred and thirty joined the church. And now at West Falls he had gone to his eternal reward from a blazing revival that changed the community for miles around. In every house for eight miles along the main road there were converts from this revival, and it was said that all but three homes in West Falls had established a family altar.

We recall his confidence when, upon learning of his cruel appointment, he declared, "The Lord will bring good out of this intended evil," and we add the appropriate words of the Apostle Paul, "whether it be by life or by death."

Strange doings!

Instead of trying William C. Kendall on the charges preferred against him at the LeRoy Conference, which had been held over for trial at the 1858 Conference, this Conference held a memorial service honoring his memory. To do this, the Conference suspended Roberts' second trial, then in progress, *and unanimously elected Roberts to preach the memorial sermon!* Roberts did so, with two bishops with him on the platform. The trial was resumed later, and ended in the conviction of Roberts, again for "unchristian and immoral conduct," and his expulsion from Conference and church. It might be added to this strange account that on another occasion during the trial Roberts was given a place of responsibility, if not of honor, as chairman of a public anniversary service of the American Bible Society.

In the bibliographic essay at the close of *Revivalism and Social Reform*,[19] Smith notes that Conable gives a "bitterly prejudiced account of Free Methodist origins" in his *History of the Genesee Annual Conference*. With this claim the present writer fully agrees. Because of his prejudice, Conable's favorable dealing with William C. Kendall is the more significant. Kendall was one of the group that had been dubbed "Nazarite." His retrogression by one-year appoint-

---

19. T. L. Smith, *Revivalism and Social Reform*. Abingdon Press, Nashville; p. 242.

ments to lower and lower Conference status, and the plans of the Conference to locate him in 1857 had been due to his stand on "Nazarite" issues. But Conable nowhere connects him with the "Nazarites" or refers to *the charge of inacceptability* brought against him less than six months before his death and which hung over his head until his summons to appear before the Supreme Court of the Universe. After a brief statement of Kendall's earlier connections, Conable said, "*he had preached with success* on the Cambria, Royalton, Pike, Covington, Albion, Brockport, and Chili charges, and next and last, on the West Falls Circuit, he finished his course." [20] Conable then devoted an extended section to the report of the committee which brought to the Conference a high tribute to the memory of this holy and beloved man of God.

Kendall's life and character had been so untouched by evil of any kind, and his ministry had won so many to Christ who now revered his memory, that only truth could stand the light he had kindled throughout the Conference. And who but Kendall's friend, although even then under trial a second time for alleged "unchristian and immoral conduct," could so fittingly bring the memorial sermon? To do honor to the deep spirituality and fearless devotion of a Kendall, called for a Roberts who was known by all to have the same qualities of life and character. And had Roberts been the deceased, his selfless devotion and sterling character should have inclined even a Conable to deal graciously with his memory, as did the Genesee Conference a half-century later in a way we have yet to record.

Let us recall at this point that an Irish jury once brought these findings against Charles Wesley:

> We find and present Charles Wesley to be a person of ill-fame, a vagabond, and a common disturber of His Majesty's peace, and we pray he may be transported.[21]

The Perry trial of 1858

The charge against B. T. Roberts at the Perry Conference again, as at LeRoy the previous year, was "unchristian and immoral con-

---

20. F. W. Conable, *History of the Genesee Conference*; p. 626 *et seq.* (Italics supplied by present writer.)
21. *Northern Independent*, v. 4, May 3, 1860. This event is also cited by L. Tyerman. *Life and Times of the Rev. John Wesley, A.M.*; v. 2, 40.

duct." The specifications were: (1) Contumacy in disregarding the action against him in the previous trial; (2) Re-publishing and circulating the original article, "New School Methodism"; (3) Publishing and circulating an offensive document attached to "New School Methodism" and signed "George W. Estes."

Roberts requested the privilege of employing counsel from outside the Genesee Conference. This was refused. Roberts requested that B. I. Ives, with his consent, be transferred to the Genesee Conference that he might assist in his defense. The bishop denied this request likewise. The defendant offered to stand trial in a civil court where an oath could be administered, with pledge of full security to pay all costs and damages that might be charged against him in consequence of such civil trial. He further requested that his offer be recorded in the Journal of the Conference. Both offer and request were refused. Roberts then asked for change of venue, and his transfer to the Oneida Conference to be tried there. He pointed out the impossibility of securing a fair trial with the Genesee Conference which was rife with partisanship over his case. The bishop ruled that change of venue was not possible. Last of all, Roberts asked for a trial by committee, pointing out that a fair trial by the entire Conference could not be expected in view of the secret meetings that a large segment of the Conference had held, to his prejudice, during the LeRoy trial. Roberts gave a further reason for trial by committee: those with responsibility for the decision would hear the testimony and examine the case, whereas in the LeRoy trial, he feared, some were absent when the evidence was taken. Chesbrough added this illuminating comment to his report of the proceedings at this point: "This was actually the case. While the examination of witnesses was going on, some of the preachers were away in the woods gathering chestnuts, others were lounging about the door, and in the lecture room. But care was taken to have them present in time to vote." [22] As noted earlier, the Conference voted against this request for trial by committee. And thus, privileges and rights that might have been his in a civil court were denied Roberts in this ecclesiastical court.

We digress here to observe that the unfair procedures against both ministers and laymen who were thrust out of the church beginning

---

22. S. K. J. Chesbrough, *Defence of the Rev. B. T. Roberts, A.M.*; pp. 10-16.

with the Perry Conference, explain the strong safeguards of membership established by the Free Methodist Church, founded shortly thereafter by men who had suffered unjust and summary dismissals from the parent body.

The principal witness called by the defense was George W. Estes whose testimony was as follows:

> George W. Estes called.—Brother Roberts had nothing to do with publishing or assisting in publishing the document under consideration, to my knowledge, and I presume to know. He had nothing to do with the writing of the part that bears my name; I do not know that he had any knowledge that its publication was intended; he never gave his consent that the part entitled 'New School Methodism,' should be re-published by me or any one else to my knowledge; he was never responsible for the payment of its publication, in whole or in part; he never contributed anything to the expenses of its publication to my knowledge; I intended that so far as sold, it should go to defray expenses of publication; I never sold any to him.
>
> Cross Examination.—I never forwarded or caused to be forwarded any of them to Brother Roberts; I never gave any to him personally; I do not know of anyone giving or forwarding him any. *I never gave orders* to anyone to forward Brother Roberts any, to my knowledge.[23]

A. D. Wilbor, presiding elder of the area where Estes resided, was called. He stated that Estes was an exhorter and that his license had been renewed at the last Clarkson quarterly conference. As presiding elder, Wilbor had signed it.

In a footnote, Chesbrough asked how A. D. Wilbor could license Estes as an exhorter, knowing he had published the pamphlet (for previously Estes had told him), and yet lend his influence against Roberts and vote for his expulsion for simply circulating it. A pertinent question.

The principal witness for the prosecution was the Rev. John Bowman, who stated that B. T. Roberts had met him on the train, handed him a bundle of the pamphlets to be distributed, and had said he had been at considerable expense to get them printed and would like to get enough to cover the cost, but to circulate them anyway. Russell

---
23. *Ibid.*, p. 17.

Wilcox, a local deacon of the Pekin charge was called; he stated that he was intimately acquainted with B. T. Roberts [his pastor], and said, "I do not know that he has ever circulated this pamphlet anywhere; I first saw it after I left home, on my way to this Conference." The Rev. J. P. Kent testified that he had asked B. T. Roberts for a copy of the pamphlet, and that Roberts said "he did not circulate them, but had no objection to my seeing the one that he had."

Bowman's testimony concerning the pamphlets was countered in measure by Estes' testimony that Roberts had nothing whatever to do with the publication of the same, and that he had never delivered any of the pamphlets to Roberts. And the testimonies of Wilcox and Kent offered no corroboration of the claim that Roberts had distributed them. Bowman's own reliability as a witness was later further weakened when, during testimony on another point having to do with events at the Medina Conference, he gave a different version of an incident than several witnesses declared he had given them at the time it occurred.

The only evidence upon which conviction was based was Bowman's questionable testimony. Even granting its validity, other members of the Conference in both parties had been circulating the pamphlet freely but, other than Joseph McCreery, were not tried for the same. The vote stood 54 to 34, of a total conference membership of 116. Several present had not voted, no doubt some refraining to avoid placing in jeopardy their standing with the ruling party of the Conference.

The same Conference expelled Joseph McCreery on similar grounds. The reader will recall his authorship of the "Nazarite" documents. The vote for his conviction was 50 to 17. Both Roberts and McCreery gave notice of appeal to the General Conference which would meet in 1860.

Several points of prejudice in Conable's *History of the Genesee Annual Conference,* which was published in 1876, are answered by Roberts in *Why Another Sect,* published in 1878. We cite only one. Conable on page 646 claimed that the printer of the pamphlet which was signed "George W. Estes," "refused to testify as to the authorship, and we have no law to oblige attendance at an ecclesiastical court." But B. T. Roberts had in writing from H. N. Beach of Brockport, the printer, the declaration that, "Rev. E. M. Buck got me to go to Perry in the case, at the time of the Conference; but I was not called to testify, because, I suppose, my evidence was not what was wanted." [24]

Roberts asserted that Conable had crowded "two known, great falsehoods into one short sentence." These were, (1st) The printer did attend the court. (2nd) He did not refuse to testify! [25] Roberts, trained as he was in law, must have been sure of his ground, for he printed this charge of serious falsehood in 1878 while Conable was alive to answer it if he chose, either by his pen or by resort to the courts. Both Conable and Roberts were to live yet many years. Although answering Conable's misstatements therein, B. T. Roberts in fact wrote *Why Another Sect*, a book of well over three hundred pages, specifically to correct the prejudiced misrepresentation of Free Methodist origins that had appeared in Bishop Simpson's *Cyclopedia of Methodism* in 1877.

As B. T. Roberts left the Conference at Perry in 1858, Bishop Janes, who was present at his trial although Bishop Baker was president of the Conference, cordially shook his hand and said, "Do not be discouraged, Brother Roberts—there is a bright future before you yet." That this prophecy was not soon to be fulfilled, the next chapter will disclose.

Principle versus ambition

When difficulties develop such as vexed the Genesee Conference, mistakes will be made by members of both factions. Human infirmities in some good people do not bear the strain of opposition and injustice, and life does not afford even the strong enough opportunities to gain the skill that comes by experience to enable them always to handle perfectly major crises. Some of the oppressed at the time under consideration, no doubt, responded to unfair treatment unwisely and provocatively. We shall later see that Roberts himself was unwise to accept the advice of friends to rejoin the church on probation as a layman while awaiting General Conference to act on his appeals. It was imprudent, because jeopardizing his case with General Conference, for him to engage in a public ministry of exhortation and

---

24. B. T Roberts, *Why Another Sect*, p. 309.
25. *Loc. cit.*

evangelism after expulsion, even though he carefully refrained from exercising the sacerdotal functions conveyed by ordination.

Let all this be granted, it still remains that the essential causes of the disturbance were betrayal of the Wesleyan witness, violation of elemental justice, and tyrannical domination of the conference by a secrecy-shrouded faction. The course of Roberts' life does not substantiate the charge of ambition by which some have sought to place responsibility on him for the troubles in Genesee at this period. The restraint of Roberts when under heavy pressures and his fairness to those who differed with him, were outstanding characteristics of the man. The course he later took as leader of the denomination that had its origin in this conflict was far from demagoguery. The measures he promoted were not always adopted by the councils of the church he led, and he suffered some crushing defeats; but it was said that to oppose Roberts was to make him your friend. Confidence in his integrity was such that every General Conference continued him in office from the founding convention of 1860 until his death in 1893.

CHAPTER THIRTEEN

Reformation Fails

Resolutions of Protest

There followed the 1858 expulsions of Roberts and McCreery a series of resolutions from local church bodies, condemning the proceedings against these men and denouncing those responsible for the expulsions. Many such resolutions were published in the *Northern Independent* which had asked concerning the expulsions, "Expelled for what?" The editor predicted, "The public verdict will be that these men were expelled, not because they had done wrong, but because they were in a minority." [1]

From Perry, where the trials had been held, came resolutions in which it was declared, "the public verdict here rendered by almost all the citizens who heard the trial, we fear is but too true, to wit, that 'Mr. Roberts was condemned before he came here.'" The official members at Olean adopted resolutions endorsing Roberts and censuring those who voted his conviction. Similar resolutions were voted by the Gowanda charge, further specifying that the presiding elder was not entitled to support and rejecting his official ministry. The Collins resolutions disapproved the presiding elders, preachers and superannuates who voted against Roberts and McCreery, and declared refusal of support until confession and reformation.[2]

There is no way to determine how many such resolutions were adopted throughout the Conference. After publishing several, the editor of the *Northern Independent* announced that he would publish no more. "What have already appeared are sufficient," he said, "to indicate the drift of public opinion in that region." Then he added, "The articles published by Bro. Roberts were met by majorities, not with facts and arguments." Editor Hosmer further expressed his doubt that withholding ministerial support was the best method of seeking redress, but granted that "all Methodist authorities on Church

---

1. *Northern Independent*, v. 3, Oct. 21, 1858.
2. See *Northern Independent*, issues appearing in November and December, v. 3, 1858.

Discipline agree our laity have the right." He concluded, "The preachers legislate, the people pay.—If the right of withholding support thus belongs to the people, none can blame them for using it when they think proper." [3]

Ecclesiastical domination just then was a warm issue in the Methodist Episcopal Church, with growing agitation for lay representation in the councils of church government. Dr. Abel Stevens had said in *Church Polity*, a book included in the course of study for preachers at that time, that adequate check on the clerical control of church government in Methodism resided in the laymen through their control of finances.

> ... It is clear that as the preachers appoint the Bishops, and the Bishops distribute the preachers, the people should check the whole plan by a counter-balance upon the whole ministerial body. This is provided in the most decisive form that it could possibly assume, namely, the power of pecuniary supplies. . . .
>
> A Methodist Church has no necessity, in order to control or remove the preacher, to prosecute him by a tedious and expensive process of law, but simply to signify that after a given date *his supplies cease*. He cannot live on air; he must submit or depart.
>
> This would be a sufficient guarantee, certainly; and this check applies not merely to a specific prerogative of the ministry, but the *whole* ministerial system. . . .[4]

Stevens quoted Bishop Emory to support this position, and both Stevens and Emory, along with Bond and Fillmore, were cited later by the Albion Laymen's Convention of December 1, 1858, to support their recommendation that the people take recourse to withholding support of preachers as a legitimate check upon the abuses they had suffered.

A layman again

But what was B. T. Roberts to do? He was a Methodist in belief, in experience, in fellowship, and in loyalty. Furthermore, he had no sense of release from his call to go to those needing him, for God had not withdrawn his commission to preach the gospel. He was assured a superior charge in Brooklyn, but he would not leave those with whom he had been laboring for reform in Genesee.

---

3. *Ibid.*, v. 3, Dec. 2, 1858.
4. B. T. Roberts, *Why Another Sect*. Earnest Christian Publishing House, Rochester; p. 196 *et seq*.

A fellow-minister in the Genesee Conference asked Bishop Janes if joining the church on probation would impair the appeal of an expelled minister, and the bishop answered, "I do not think it would." But others counseled Roberts against such a step lest it becloud his appeal to the General Conference. A presiding elder in a neighboring Conference took this position, but did encourage Roberts to continue to preach. He should do so, advised this friend, under no authority of the Methodist Episcopal Church but solely by authority of his divine call, and should perform no such functions in his public ministry as officiating at meetings or administering the sacraments.

But Roberts followed other counsel on the matter of joining the church, and was admitted on probation in his last pastoral charge, Pekin. Undoubtedly, this was an error. Later, a letter to the Pekin pastor from Bishop Baker, in restrained but plain phrasing, advised that both relationships granted Roberts by the Pekin charge, membership on probation after expulsion and license as an exhorter, were anomalous.[5]

As a layman, B. T. Roberts now, even as when a minister, continued to be subject to public criticism and attack. One of his severest critics in this period was Dr. Hibbard, editor of the *Northern Christian Advocate*. The reader will recall that Hibbard at least implicitly had approved the sentiments Roberts had expressed in "New School Methodism" in 1857, but by now Hibbard had lined up with the majority and had proclaimed his vigorous opposition to the "rebellious party," against which he bravely promised to do his full duty. Rev. J. A. Wells, who was to be expelled by the Genesee Conference at its next session, answered Hibbard's threats in the *Northern Independent*. Wells pointed out that at the Medina Conference of 1856 Hibbard was understood to favor the "Nazarites," but "no sooner are the party lines strictly drawn, and the majority proves to be on the pro-slavery side," Wells said, "than he goes to that side to work with all his energy." According to Wells' opinion, Hibbard hounded the "Nazarites" in order to strengthen the pro-slavery faction whose support Hibbard was anxious to have. Wells added,

---

5. See C. H. Zahniser, *Earnest Christian*; p. 119. This letter from Bishop Osmond C. Baker, an authority on ecclesiastical law, is one of the interesting sidelights uncovered by Dr. Zahniser in his search among the personal documents of the Roberts family in the old home in North Chili, N. Y.

"These men who are called 'Nazarites,' are favorites with the people, because they stand firm for truth and righteousness." [6]

In this same issue of the *Northern Independent*, Editor Hosmer took a hand in the hassle with Editor Hibbard and declared that the latter "should know that the man at whom his shafts are principally aimed, is his equal in every way, and his superior in learning, in talents, and in all the higher elements of ministerial character." He could so speak, said Hosmer, because he never had been a defender of the "Nazarites," who were well able to defend themselves.

Hosmer's rating of Roberts' ability was confirmed at least in measure not long after by the clarity and incisive logic with which Roberts met Hibbard's reasoning on the matter of appeals to a higher court. In criticism of Roberts, Hibbard had said, "He that appeals to a superior court, makes his appeal to justice, and denies the equity of the court below; he that confesses makes his appeal to mercy, and admits the equity of the first court." To this, Roberts replied, "The defect of this argument is its foundation. It rests upon a false maxim, 'A majority can do no wrong.' . . . It supposes that no one can, by any possibility, be condemned when innocent; who may in such a case be restored without confession!" He then quoted Bishop Baker's *A Guide-Book to the Administration of the Discipline* as follows:

> When a member or preacher has been expelled according to due form of Discipline, he cannot afterwards enjoy the privileges of society and sacraments in our Church, without contrition, confession and satisfactory reformation; but if, however, the society become convinced of the innocence of the expelled member, he may again be received on trial without confession.[7]

Roberts had proceeded to join the church on the basis of this construction of Discipline by Bishop Baker. The Pekin society, convinced of his innocence, had unanimously received him on probation and had granted him a license to exhort. Principally for these two acts, receiving Roberts on probation and issuing him an exhorter's license, the Pekin pastor, C. D. Burlingham, was expelled on the charge of "contumacy" at the following session of the Genesee Annual Conference. Roberts' joining the church on probation on Bishop

---

6. *Northern Independent*, v. 3, Jan. 20, 1859.
7. *Ibid.*, v. 3, March 3, 1859.

Baker's interpretation of the Discipline presumably would have been held valid by the bishops, but for the fact that Roberts had previously appealed his case to the ensuing General Conference.

The first Laymen's Convention

In the midst of the agitation throughout the Conference over the expulsion of Roberts and McCreery, Isaac M. Chesbrough proposed a convention of those laymen in the various societies who desired to protest against the tyranny of the Regency. There was a ready response to the suggestion, and nearly two hundred responded to the call to meet at Albion on December 1, 1858. Hon. Abner I. Wood was made chairman, and S. K. J. Chesbrough headed the very important committee on resolutions. Denied a voice in the affairs of the Conference by the church's strongly clerical government, these determined laymen purposed to speak out clearly against the evils of partisan control of the Genesee Conference.

The convention condemned the recent expulsions, and commended the candor and spirit of B. T. Roberts' article, "New School Methodism," the publication of which had started a train of such tragic events. The committee pointed out that in all efforts to vindicate those voting the expulsions, none had claimed that the evidence justified the action. Those who nevertheless would justify the expulsions explained that the encouragement of enthusiasm and fanaticism by Roberts and McCreery was reason enough. The committee asked, "Where is the justice of trying men for one thing, and condemning them for another?"

The committee then evaluated the charge of fanaticism. It claimed for its members reliable means of information through close contacts with those called "Nazarites" in the camp meetings and the general quarterly meetings which had been criticized as "hot-beds of enthusiasm," and through familiarity with the preaching of the men involved. "*We know what Methodism* is; some of us were converted, and joined the church under the labors of her honored pioneers," the committee said; and then pronounced *"utterly false and groundless"* the charge that the expelled men promoted fanaticism.

One of the grievances cited in the report was the inability to secure investigation by the conference of complaints against members of the ruling faction, whatever the alleged offense.

The resolutions adopted by the convention included: (1) A declaration of full confidence in the expelled brethren; (2) An emphatic assertion of attachment to the Methodist Episcopal Church, with refusal to acknowledge the policies of the Regency faction as those of the church, or to submit to them; (3) A disavowal of any intention to secede, and approval of the course of the expelled brethren in rejoining the church; (4) A condemnation of discrimination against devoted and spiritual members by pastors in the administration of local church affairs; (5) A plea for greater respect for and recognition of lay opinion by Conference leaders; (6) A pledge to support financially the expelled brethren; (7) A recommendation that the expelled brethren travel at large and labor for the salvation of souls; (8) Refusal to support any member of the Genesee Conference who participated in the expulsion of B. T. Roberts and Joseph McCreery until their reinstatement.

The convention made it clear that neither of the expelled brethren nor any preacher of the Conference had anything to do with calling the same. The *Orleans American*, a newspaper of Albion and Orleans County, gave the convention a favorable report, remarking, "It was composed of able men who had set themselves to work in earnest to correct what they believed to be a great evil in the administration of church affairs."

The Convention based resolution "8" above on the full legality of taking recourse to withholding support as the direct and effective remedy against oppression by the clergy, according to the declarations of such authorities on Methodist polity as previously cited.[8] This action of the Convention was peculiarly odious to the Regency, although as we have previously noted, several local churches had already resorted to this measure. But the reformers declared another reason for the procedure: the claim of faithful stewardship that their financial support should not go to unworthy men "to put down the work of the Lord."[9]

Reprisals and reaction

Reprisals against those participating in the Albion Laymen's Con-

---

8. *Supra*, p. 208.
9. See *Why Another Sect*, Chap. 9, for a full account of the Albion Laymen's Convention of 1858.

vention were prompt and severe. Claudius Brainerd of North Chili, an ordained local preacher of sterling character, was expelled. Although the charges against him seem to have been conveyed in terms not explicitly or solely limited to his participation in the Albion Convention, his contemporaries very well discerned that such was the essential ground of his expulsion. His own statement in the *Northern Independent* was, "Yesterday, I was expelled from the M. E. Church for attending the Laymen's Convention. No other charge was preferred." [10] Brainerd carried his appeal to the 1859 Annual Conference which refused to entertain it. When he asked a ministerial friend why he had voted against considering his appeal, the preacher promptly replied, "Because Bishop Simpson told me to." [11]

The Brainerd case prompted Editor Hosmer to say in the *Northern Independent*, "When ecclesiastical persecution assumes a judicial form, it is one of the most tremendous scourges let loose upon society." [12]

Claudius Brainerd was a godly man whose religion was attractive. Explaining the radiance of his home-going, Daniel Steele, a relative of Brainerd's, said, "As he entered heaven, the glory shone through the gates and rested on his face." [13]

Others were tried and expelled for similar cause, and as the persecutions continued many laymen of the reform party were read out as "withdrawn," although they had made no such request and had no opportunity to contest such illegal proceedings.

At one point, a warrant for the arrest of a member of the church was secured on trumped up charges early in the week and held for service on the victim while he was in church Sunday morning. The brother was arrested, handcuffed and hauled away to jail in a wagon like a criminal. Of this outrage, the *Niagara City Herald* of October 8, 1859, said, "Thus have our free institutions been disgraced by an act of religious persecution that would be better

---

10. B. T. Roberts, *Why Another Sect*; p. 208.
11. *Ibid.*, p. 209.
12. Quoted in *Why Another Sect*, p. 211.
13. Quoted by Hogue, *History of the Free Methodist Church*, F. M. Pub. House, Winona Lake; v. 1, 212.

befitting Italy or Rome. The Christians arrested are as quiet and inoffensive men as can be found." [14]

Another brother, expelled for attending the Albion Convention, was defended before his fellow-townsmen in the *Olean Advertiser* in part as follows:

> James H. Brooks, Esq., a resident of Olean these thirty odd years, a man of unblemished private character, a member of the Methodist Episcopal Church ever since he was fifteen years old, a Christian of acknowledged worth and usefulness, and a citizen against whom the breath of calumny never breathed until now, has been expelled from the church. . . .
>
> James H. Brooks has grown up in our midst from boyhood; his private worth is as familiar to our citizens, as a 'thrice told tale.' Generosity, integrity, honesty, and living piety, are eminent characteristics of the man. . . .
>
> The trial and expulsion of such a man, naturally produces in the public mind, a supposition that he has been guilty of some heinous offence, either against good morals or the peace of society, and that the proceedings were necessary to purify the church, and to warn the world against an unchristian example.
>
> We however learn, and are gratified in being able to say that such is not the case, that he has neither adopted a spurious faith, nor has been guilty of any heresies condemned by the doctrine of his church, nor has he indulged in any impropriety of conduct that would warrant, under any ordinary circumstances, his expulsion from the church.
>
> In every human mind there is an innate sense of justice which is offended and aroused at acts of oppression and palpable wrongs. We confess we partake of the general feeling pervading this community, that grievous wrong has been done Mr. Brooks.[15]

Poor public relations which hindered evangelism and recruitment from without, wholesale excommunications bleeding the church from within, and the voluntary withdrawals of those who had lost hope, all added up to a sad decline in the membership of Genesee. There were 10,999 members in 1859, but successive losses reduced their number to 7,593 by 1865, a decline of over 30 per cent in six years. Not until 1878 did the Conference regain its 1859 membership level.[16]

---

14. Quoted by B. H. Roberts, *Benjamin Titus Roberts*, Earnest Christian Office, North Chili, N. Y.; p. 195.
15. Quoted in *Why Another Sect*, p. 214 et seq.
16. See Ray Allen, *A Century of the Genesee Annual Conference*; p. 10.

In labors more abundant

Early in November of 1858, the Roberts family left the parsonage at Pekin to make way for the incoming pastor, C. D. Burlingham. Several homes were open to the Robertses, and he had his call to a pastorate in Brooklyn. But he decided to remain in the field of reform activities with those who had so loyally stood together in the cause. Buffalo was finally chosen as the place of residence. From that center, he carried on a busy speaking schedule in many sections of the Conference. Depending for the support of a family upon collections taken at the meetings in which he labored was a hazardous pecuniary venture; but it seems that the Robertses were good managers. Anyway, they survived this crucial period, and in the years following made a success of editing and publishing the *Earnest Christian* through a third of a century, the journal rivaling in longevity and, some would claim, in format and content, the *Guide to Holiness* which enjoyed such distinguished patronage.

In March of 1859 B. T. Roberts journeyed to St. Louis, Missouri, where Dr. Redfield was pastoring a group of approximately 150 people. These, without Redfield's promoting the separation, had withdrawn from a leading church that had closed its pulpit against him. Already the reform movement had begun to stir the "West," as the Chicago-St. Louis axis was then called. And Dr. Redfield was the impetus to revival and reform at both ends of this axis. B. T. Roberts was much challenged by the stirring metropolis of St. Louis, through which pioneers were pouring into the western plains and beyond.

It was in this month, March of 1859, that Roberts reported in the *Northern Independent* his being discontinued from the church as a probationer, obviously in consequence of Bishop Baker's letter to Pastor Burlingham, cited above.[17] Roberts' statement presents an interesting angle on his busy evangelistic life, and we report here the portion he reprinted later in *Why Another Sect:*

> It seems to be a question among the doctors, whether I belong to the church or not. I did the best I could to stay in; and when I was thrust out without my fault, I tried to get back, and really thought I had accomplished it, but the president of a recent

---

17. P. 209.

church trial [Bishop Baker had presided at both of his trials], which trials, by the way, are becoming quite numerous in Genesee Conference, decided that I was not a member, even 'on probation.' As this was a 'judicial decision,' an 'act of administration,' of course it settles the question. But in or out, I trust I may still be permitted to entertain 'a desire to flee from the wrath to come.' Our excellent discipline specifies as among the fruits of this desire, 'instructing, reproving, and exhorting all we have any intercourse with.' This, then, is what I am doing. The Lord has opened a wide door, into which I have entered. I disclaim all authority from man, but simply 'instruct, reprove and exhort,' because I believe he has called me to it, and he blesses me in it. Everywhere we go, large and attentive congregations listen to the word with apparently deep interest.[18]

Another laymen's convention was called on June 20, 1859, in connection with the Bergen camp meeting. The call, issued by the Hon. Abner I. Wood as chairman, and others, was freighted with a seriousness intended to steel these courageous men for any outcome their participation in the convention might bring. "*Important* interests are at stake," the summons said; "we feel the iron heel of oppression heavily laid upon us as laymen. We feel unwilling to become the slaves of any power." After referring to those of their brethren who had met with expulsion for attending the Albion convention, the summons challenged all to full devotion to the cause even at a similar price, saying, "the fear of expulsion or removal from office should never drive a Methodist from doing his duty." [19]

A preacher in the Oneida Conference, J. F. Crawford, present at the Bergen camp meeting, said of the laymen's convention, "We did not see anything in their proceedings, but what we could endorse. These laymen are men of intelligence, power and prudence." [20]

Little business is reported from this convention, but it ordered a third meeting, known as the Second Annual Convention, to convene at Albion November 1, 1859. But before that event, four preachers of the reform group were to be expelled by the 1859 Conference.

The expulsions of the 1859 Conference

In *Earnest Christian,* Zahniser has sketched an editorial by John

---
18. B. T. Roberts, *Why Another Sect;* p. 201 *et seq.*
19. *Ibid.,* p. 216 *et seq.*
20. *Ibid.,* p. 123.

Robie in the *Buffalo Advocate* which indicates that full preparations had been made by the dominant party to terminate the "Nazarite" plague at the 1859 Conference. Since this sketch reveals the low esteem in which the rabid editor of the "Regency" held the "Nazarites," and since it undoubtedly represents likewise the opinion of many who read the *Buffalo Advocate* and other journals that borrowed therefrom, we give Zahniser's summary:

> The Genesee Annual Conference convened in Brockport in October, 1859, with Bishop Matthew Simpson in the chair. The report found in the *Advocate* of October 13 stated that the Conference was determined to rid itself of the factional element of Nazaritism. The editor doubted not that the societies generally throughout the work would be glad to learn that fact, and would rejoice that they were no longer to suffer 'the disgrace arising from one of the worst scandals which ever pestered a denomination of Christians.' For years past, he continued, the Conference had borne with its abettors, advising and even entreating them to be loyal to church order, and to cease their 'disgraceful proceedings.' But, he opined, 'crazy men will not be orderly'; and since they were bent on their own destruction, the Conference had wisely concluded to let them have their own ways, and cut them off from all connection with the church. . . . Others undoubtedly would be expelled; 'having coveted martyrdom, they will have it.' [21]

During the Conference the lawyer-evangelist, Fay Purdy, conducted a huge tent meeting at the edge of the village of Brockport, not far from the church where the Conference was held. The pavilion seated three thousand, and around it were numerous family and society tents. The daily attendance was from three to five thousand, with many coming from a distance and some from other denominations. The editor of the *Northern Independent* said that this meeting was intended to be an olive branch, Purdy hoping that the conflicting parties would be drawn together and tensions be relaxed.[22]

But Bishop Simpson could hardly have accepted such an interpretation. To him and the conference body generally, the tent meeting was a most annoying irritant. And little wonder! For preachers from other conferences who were not answerable to Genesee had come

---
21. C. H. Zahniser, *Earnest Christian*; p. 133.
22. *Northern Independent*, v. 4, Oct. 13, 1859.

to assist in the meeting, and Purdy scheduled B. T. Roberts to preach on one occasion. Bishop Simpson dealt with some of the visiting preachers, but not all heeded his instructions, among them the Rev. D. W. Thurston, a presiding elder in the Oneida Conference. The bishop expressed his irritation in a letter to Mrs. Simpson which he wrote from Brockport on October 9: "Women have come by troops —one crowd by a canalboat, others from Utica, and some, it is said, from St. Louis. They are in attendance in the galleries, and some have their knitting busily employed. They are all Nazarites, and use, in their conversation, many epithets denunciatory of the Conference." [23]

Early in the Conference at Brockport, five resolutions were adopted, penalty for violations being attached. Thus, contrary to Methodist polity, the Genesee Conference had become a legislative body, usurping the powers reserved to the General Conference. The restrictions imposed by these resolutions were intended to whip the reformers into line, or bring them to trial and expulsion. Four were tried and expelled, the basic charge being "contumacy." These four were J. A. Wells, who later entered the Presbyterian Church; Loren Stiles, Jr., who took no appeal but proceeded to establish an independent "Congregational Free Methodist Church" at Albion, the same becoming a part of the Free Methodist denomination when it was organized a year later; C. D. Burlingham, who appealed to the General Conference and ceased all public ministry, his case then being remanded by General Conference for a new trial by the Genesee Conference; and William Cooley, who was a member of the organizing convention of the Free Methodist Church, and later became a leading member of the Susquehanna Conference. The Conference further located two members of the reforming group, J. W. Reddy and H. H. Farnsworth. But the former was later expelled by his quarterly conference without even written charges against him, and shortly joined the Eastern Convention (later known as the Genesee Conference) of the Free Methodist Church. The latter was a member of the convention at which the new denomination was organized, but he thought organization at that time was premature. We find no further record of his connection with Free Methodism, but he became identified

---

23. Geo. R. Crooks, *The Life of Bishop Matthew Simpson*. Harper & Bros., New York; p. 359.

with the extremists who later associated themselves together under their chosen name, "Nazarite."

History repeats itself

Editor Hosmer expressed his judgment that the Genesee Conference was on the wrong track to seek peace through ecclesiastical trials. Concerning the charge that some of the reform group were disorderly, he made the pointed observation that, "Methodism grew up in spite of order—not without order in itself, nor contrary to the order of God, but in spite of the order of the established Church, in whose bosom its founder lived and died." He continued: "A system which owes its existence to an irregularity of this kind, should be tolerant of irregularities, especially where even prejudice itself can impute no crime." [24]

At a much later period, Luccock and Hutchinson have remarked on the irony of the fact that Methodist secessions have originated largely "as protests against legalistic interpretations of church custom and order," although Methodism itself had its origin in just such a protest and was "the child of irregularity." These authors point out that, "with Methodism once established, it soon solidified into a regularity, an institutionalism of its own," and this process was well under way less than a decade following Wesley's death.[25]

Even before Wesley's death, the O'Kelly faction in 1792 separated from the American church in protest against the denial of the right of appeal to the Conference by preachers not satisfied with the bishop's appointment.

The Methodist system in the early nineteenth century has been called more autocratic than any other in Protestantism. In the twenties, pressures for reform were insistent, but counter-pressures were vigorous and unrelenting. In 1828 John Emory (later bishop) published *Defence of the Fathers* in which he opposed reformers who sought greater democracy in church government. The General Conference of that year was adamant against change. The Baltimore Conference the preceding year had suspended Dennis B. Dorsey for promoting the circulation of *Mutual Rights*, the magazine of the reformers. And now the General Conference sustained the action of the Baltimore

---

24. *Northern Independent*, v. 4, Oct. 13, 1859.
25. Luccock and Hutchinson, *The Story of Methodism*. Abingdon Press, Nashville; p. 333 *et seq.*

Conference, denying Dorsey's appeal. J. Minton Batten of Vanderbilt University has charged that in this conflict "church authorities depended upon the heavy hand of discipline as the most effective means of crushing the reform movement," and further, "Many persons were expelled from the church without strict regard for due process of law." To students of the history of Free Methodism's beginnings, strikingly familiar is Dr. Batten's statement, "The Methodist Protestant Church had its genesis in the expulsion of reform advocates from the Methodist Episcopal Church." [26]

Again, in the origin of the Wesleyan Methodist Church during the contention over abolitionism in the forties, authoritarianism played a decisive role. Centralized power was so unchecked that a bishop presided at the trial of an abolitionist editor charged with slandering him (the bishop). The editor was convicted, and was disciplined but not expelled.[27] In Chapter Nine mention was made of the "gag-rule" applied by the bishops to abolitionists, the denial of conference membership to abolitionists, discrimination against abolitionists already conference members, and other oppressive measures.

It happened also in England

Alexander Kilham is known as England's "first Methodist reformer." He was expelled from the Wesleyan Methodist Conference as an irregular, principally because he had written a pamphlet calling for reform in church government that would grant to laymen certain democratic rights. According to *A New History of Methodism*, "No charge was alleged against his character, teaching, abilities, or diligence." And further, "None doubted his piety." [28] High-handed expulsions of members by the Conference followed, and brought into being the Methodist New Connexion. This occurred in 1797, only six years after the death of John Wesley.

The Primitive Methodist Church and the Independent Methodist Churches resulted from authoritarian moves of the dominant Methodist body to control religious fervor and evangelistic outreach by

---

26. J. M. Batten, "Divisions in American Methodism," in *Methodism*, Wm. K. Anderson, Ed., Meth. Pub. House, Nashville; p. 58.
27. See Norwood, *The Schism of the Methodist Episcopal Church, 1844.* Alfred Press, Alfred, N.Y.; p. 41 *et seq.*
28. Townsend, Workman & Eayrs, *A New History of Methodism*. Hodder & Stoughton, London; v. 1, pp. 493, 497.

restricting and opposing camp meetings (which were a variation of John Wesley's field-preaching), and cottage meetings. The leaders of such "irregularitis" were numbered with those early nineteenth century problem-children of English Methodism called "Revivalists." Whereas the main direction of English Methodism thus early in the church's history was toward regularity and restraint, the Revivalists were principally concerned with the salvation of souls and freedom in government and worship. "As between the Revivalists and the constituted authorities it was a question of church statics *versus* church dynamics." [29] In other words, tension and final rupture came from the conflict of letter and spirit. The Independent Methodist Churches developed from the cottage meeting, the Primitive Methodist Church from camp meeting revivalism, both methods of revival and outreach then being considered "irregular" by official Methodism.

The organization of the Primitive Methodist Church was precipitated by an expulsion, as in the case of the Methodist New Connexion. In 1808 Hugh Bourne was expelled on the technical charge of nonattendance at class meeting, but the actual cause was his evangelism, of which his nonattendance was merely the result that provided the authorities with a convenient handle. Edwards has called it, "a sad commentary on the history of religious revivals that within twenty-five years of Wesley's death [seventeen, to be exact] Hugh Bourne was thrust out of the parent Society for his irregular methods in evangelism." [30]

Another expulsion contributing to the beginnings of the Primitive Methodist Church was that of William Clowes, who was denied his class-ticket on the charge of violating Methodist discipline by attending camp meetings! It is interesting that in May of 1860, the very month in which the General Conference of the Methodist Episcopal Church made inevitable the organization of the Free Methodist Church by refusing to review the appeal of B. T. Roberts, Roberts wrote and published in *The Earnest Christian* a six-page article on William Clowes. After noting that probably no other church had been founded in greater irregularities than Methodism, Roberts trenchantly observed:

---
29. *Ibid.*, p. 556.
30. M. Edwards, *After Wesley*. Epworth Press, London; p. 53.

Yet strange to say, the church he [Wesley] thus founded, expelled from her communion, within twenty years after the death of Wesley, a pious and useful preacher, for the crime of attending camp or field meetings, "contrary to the Methodist discipline!" [31]

These two men, Bourne and Clowes, became closely associated in the development of the Primitive Methodist Church. The movement continued for a decade or more, its fruitage being garnered largely by the parent church, until in 1820 the first annual conference was held.

Of British Methodism's rapid subsidence to regularity, Edwards has said:

> In so short a time the organization of Methodism had become rigid. . . . The meetings on Mow Cop [site of early camp meetings] seemed as dangerous and irregular a proceeding to the [Methodist] ministers of Burslem and district as Wesley's open-air preaching seemed to the [Anglican] clergy of his day.[32]

A third English Methodist secession took the name Bible Christians. Its first conference was held in 1819. It, too, was precipitated by the expulsion of an ardent and therefore "irregular" evangelist. William O'Bryan of Cornwall had been denied the itinerant relationship because he had a family to support, but nevertheless he itinerated on his own responsibility among the desolate and unchurched of Cornwall's neglected areas. For this he was discontinued, without trial, after twenty years a Methodist! Later he rejoined the Methodists in Devon but again was excluded, this time for nonattendance at class from which he had been absent on his far-ranging tours of evangelism. One historian has commented, "Martinets often make short work of such fervid irregulars as O'Bryan." [33]

In the late twenties of the nineteenth century, the Protestant Methodists seceded over difficulties attending the installation of an organ at Leeds. Certain trustees favored the organ, but the pastor and the people generally opposed it. Irregular procedures secured the sanction of the Conference, the approval of which at that time was

---
31. B. T. Roberts, *The Earnest Christian;* v. 1, May 1860, p. 138.
32. M. Edwards, *After Wesley;* p. 53.
33. Townsend, Workman & Eayrs, *A New History of Methodism.* Hodder & Stoughton, London; v. 1, 505.

necessary to such a step. This led a local preacher who opposed the building of the organ to attack the questionable procedures, and he was suspended from his office as local preacher. Supporting the suspended brother's cause, seventy other local preachers of Leeds refused to labor on the circuit. A special District Meeting of doubtful authority sustained the suspension. Conference authorities, high among them the redoubtable Jabez Bunting, favored an organ for Leeds, and contrary to established procedures it was built—at a cost "£1,000 and one thousand members!" From these thousand members came the nucleus of the Protestant Methodists, organized during the very period of struggle in America out of which came the Methodist Protestant Church. The Wesleyan Methodist Association was organized in 1836, and the Protestant Methodists combined therewith.

The Wesleyan Methodist Association grew out of protests against autocracy in the Wesleyan Methodist Conference, these protests, according to the usual pattern, having been met with expulsions. The Association united with the Methodist Reform Union in 1857 to form the United Methodist Free Churches.

During this mid-century period there developed within the Wesleyan Methodist Conference a dominant party that rigidly controlled conference affairs, often under a cloak of secrecy that bred suspicion and unrest. Strongly suggesting the Regency in the Genesee Conference of American Methodism that took shape near the same date, is this characterization of the dictatorship of the English Wesleyan Methodist Conference:

> Unhappily at this period, as all now admit, the Wesleyan Conference seemed often to be animated by a spirit that ill-brooked opposition. Honors, indulgence, tolerance fell stintedly, it was thought, to any but those of the dominant party.[34]

According to Eayrs, a growing temperance sentiment also challenged the policy of the Conference, few of whose preachers were abstainers. Many and complex dissastisfactions in time erupted in a series of four anonymous pamphlets called *Fly Sheets*. Replies to these blistering publications were published, but attempts at an official answer to the charges carried in the *Fly Sheets* were slow in appearing. In fact, the Secretary of the Conference, although he disapproved the agitation

---
34. *Ibid.*, v. 1, 528.

resulting from these publications, said, "I am asked to declare that the *Fly Sheets* are wicked lies. I cannot, for it is well known that many of the sentiments therein have been mine for years." [35] Jabez Bunting was a prominent target of the reform criticism.

Drastic efforts to identify the writers of the *Fly Sheets* failed, but finally in 1849 the Conference expelled James Everett for "contumacy" and two others for refusing to discontinue their writing and publishing on reform issues. Several were censured and the following year another was expelled. But no charge against the character or efficiency of these preachers was made. Eayrs reports, "They were amongst the most eminent and laborious; some were beloved by all." [36]

Wholesale expulsions and secessions followed, and the societies were depleted thereby nearly one-third, or more than one hundred thousand members. Some of these first united to form the Methodist Reform Union, which in turn joined with the Wesleyan Methodist Association in 1857 to form the United Methodist Free Churches, as previously noted. But during this period all Methodist bodies suffered losses.

We cite one more instance of authoritarian rigidity giving rise to a new movement in English Methodism. As already noted, the Methodist New Connexion was separated from the Wesleyan Methodist Conference by the latter's autocracy in 1797. In turn, the New Connexion's refusal to accept or adjust to William Booth's program of evangelizing the poor led to his withdrawal from the Connexion in 1861 and to the development of the Salvation Army under his organizing genius. "That Methodism could forget her own grievance against the Church of England so easily," writes Bishop Kennedy, "must have made John Wesley weep in heaven." [37]

Letter against spirit

It appears from the foregoing instances of over-reaching authority, both in England and America, that Methodism's strength has also been its weakness. The rigidity of its administrative control has maintained Methodism's organizational discipline, it is true; but now and

---
35. *Ibid.*, v. 1, 530.
36. *Ibid.*, v. 1, 531.
37. Gerald Kennedy, *The Methodist Way of Life.* © 1958 by Prentice-Hall, Inc.; Englewood Cliffs, New Jersey; p.89.

again conflicts have developed between authority and democratic impulses in the area of church polity on the one hand, and, on the other, between authority and personal convictions that have their roots deep in historic Methodism. These conflicts have led to fractures and even to open schism and separation. Furthermore, concentrated power tends to an opportunism that is prone to sacrifice principle in order to maintain intact the organization through which that power is exerted. An outstanding example is American Methodism's course of compromise with slavery which, as we have seen in Chapter Ten, at points placed the interests of organizational Methodism above human freedom. Compromise likewise appeared in the areas of corporate worship and personal Christian conduct. As previously noted, those attempting reform or restoration usually have met with ecclesiastical discipline of the severest order. "Irregularity" seems to have been regarded by both English and American Methodism as the cardinal sin.

Nottingham explains Methodism's contradiction of its own irregular beginnings by its later efforts to enforce disciplined regularity, as owing to the incorporation within Methodism by its founder of the contradictory principles which Sabatier has called "the religion of the spirit" and "the religion of authority." "This conjunction of belief in the authority of an organized church with insistence upon the value and reality of individual experience as the final test," Nottingham observes, "is peculiar to Wesley and to Methodism." [38]

Eayrs similarly ascribed Methodism's conflict between spiritual freedom and organizational authoritarianism to Wesley's transmitting these contrasting principles to his followers. He states the issue: "When the soul has been awakened to spiritual realities, and believes that its intuitions and experiences are next in value to the teachings of Holy Scripture, it is impossible to circumscribe its movements in matters of religion by the commands of external authority." Eayrs notes that in consequence, "The constitutional history of Methodism is a record of the interplay of authority and freedom." [39]

Notwithstanding the more rapid growth and vastly greater numbers

---

38. E. K. Nottingham, *Methodism and the Frontier.* Columbia University Press, New York; p. 130.
39. Townsend, Workman & Eayrs, *A New History of Methodism.* Hodder & Stoughton, London; v. 1, p. 486.

in American Methodism than in English, the fractures of the former were fewer over the period closing with mid-century. Nottingham's interpretation of Methodism on the American scene may explain this interesting fact. She points out that as Methodist churches in a settled area of America moderated their evangelistic zeal and achieved social and economic status, the unsettled frontier "provided a legitimate outlet for the energies of potential schismatics," [40] that is, of reformers and irregulars. England however was more closely settled from the time of Methodism's beginnings, and had no frontiers to which its irregulars and reformers might turn as an arena for the exercise of their zeal and earnestness. Tensions developed between settled authority and reforming irregulars, and division resulted.

Interesting in this connection, and perhaps significant, is the case of B. T. Roberts. After serving successfully four years in rural pastorates of western New York, where there were generous opportunities to exert his deep Christian earnestness in revival and in the restoration of Methodist principles and practices, he was sent to a fashionable church in the metropolis of the Conference where his revival efforts met with only moderate success and where the people were irresponsive to his call to personal piety and social righteousness. Here his reforming zeal was fanned to a blaze by the indifferent and worldly attitudes he encountered, and the conflict between authority and freedom soon was joined.

It is normally thus, that the spirit of earnest Christianity is aroused by Laodicean complacency, and the reformer's zeal disturbs that complacency into vigorous antagonism against the disturber of the peace. Expulsion of the disturber often follows, and Laodicea settles again into its false security. In this fashion a movement that has lost its first earnestness comes in time to oppose and crush the very forces still lingering within it that seek to arouse and promote its original purposes.

And reformation fails!

---

40. E. K. Nottingham, *Methodism and the Frontier*. Columbia University Press, New York; p. 144.

CHAPTER FOURTEEN

Hoping Against Hope

It was impossible for B. T. Roberts and his fellow reformers to accept even their expulsion from the Conference and the wholesale exclusion of devoted members from many local churches as the end of their hope that the parent would finally vindicate the justice of their cause and own them as faithful children. Was not the conflict one between children? General Conference was approaching—would not the parent set everything right?

Efforts were now directed to holding together in Bands and Societies the detached groups; to maintaining the cause of reform within the church in places where the reformers still had access; to extending their numbers through evangelism; and to holding their groups in readiness for acceptance by the church when the General Conference should have acted to confirm their rights as loyal Methodists. That General Conference would so act was their confidence. Even in perplexity, they were not in despair.

But this hope was not shared by all of the reformers. One of those was Dr. Redfield who for years, unlike B. T. Roberts, had held the conviction that separation was inevitable. However, he did not expect separation to come in his day, nor did he attempt to force it ahead of schedule. In July of 1856 he wrote his close friends, the Kendalls, opening to them his heart on the matter of separation. He saw the sharp cleavage between the reformers and the regulars in the Methodist Episcopal Church, and was convinced that the two groups could not be brought to agreement. "As God lives," he wrote, "there is no rational hope but separation; and yet I would by no means hoist the banner of separation, for you cannot then keep out the spirit of carnal warfare, and that will be the death to spirituality." [1]

Developments in the western field

Revivals began in the western area as early as 1856 when Dr. Red-

---

1. J. G. Terrill, *The Life of Rev. John Wesley Redfield, M.D.* F. M. Pub. House, Chicago; p. 309, *et seq.*

field was called to St. Charles, Illinois, by the Methodist Episcopal pastor of that city who had known of Redfield's work in the East. The remainder of this revivalist's ministry was spent largely in the West, and the story of the early development of the cause of revival and reform in that area is closely associated with that ministry.

A stirring revival in St. Charles brought many to repentance and led many church members into the experience of Christian holiness. The success of this meeting brought Redfield invitations to other points in the area, such as Elgin, Marengo, and Woodstock. Especially in Woodstock, the revival reached community leaders—professional men, representative citizens, and even the sheriff of the county.[2]

In June, 1857, the presiding elder of the district engaged Dr. Redfield as evangelist in a camp meeting near St. Charles. In this meeting preachers as well as laymen were stirred to seek a deeper experience in grace. Conference opposition to the movement seems not yet to have developed. Somewhat later, the Rev. Seymour Coleman of the Troy Conference in the East providentially came to visit a son in the region and was asked to supply a vacancy in Aurora First Church until Conference. A revival broke out under his ministry.

In 1858 and 1859 opposition to the spreading revival arose within the Rock River Conference, and persecutions began which followed the eastern pattern of wholesale expulsions. At St. Charles in the fall of 1859, where three years earlier Dr. Redfield had held his first western revival, the pastor took drastic action against several members of his church for attending Redfield meetings in another St. Charles church after he had denied their request that Redfield be invited back to the Methodist pulpit.

Bishop Simpson had only recently passed through the Nazarite ordeal of the 1859 Genesee Conference at Brockport. Apparently the St. Charles pastor sought the advice of the Bishop who about that time moved to nearby Evanston. Anyway, he quoted Bishop Simpson as saying that the official board had authority to determine if those had withdrawn who had attended the Redfield services. This advice agreed with the counsel the Bishop had given in the western New York area—advice which was used by pastors there to validate their

---

2. See J. G. Terrill, *The St. Charles Camp Meeting.* T. B. Arnold, Chicago; p. 6.

"reading out of the church" those members who were cooperating with the reformers. This acceptance as law of Bishop Simpson's unofficially declared opinion led the 1860 General Conference to direct that bishops' decisions, except when given judicially in an annual conference, do not have the force of law, and that no member of the church can be pronounced withdrawn without at least his verbal consent.[3] But before that restraining action of 1860, many good Methodists suffered the injustice of losing their membership in the church, with no opportunity to defend themselves by exercise of their constitutional right of trial.

And this is what happened in St. Charles. The official board declared fourteen persons withdrawn, but by mistake included a nonmember. Of the thirteen members declared withdrawn, several were on the official board and five were members of the board of nine trustees. When the thirteen were "read out" on prayer meting night, about fifty others called for their letters, but refused them when offered letters of withdrawal instead of transfer. Hoping that the conflict would be resolved before long, the group rented a hall as temporary quarters for their services, and called as pastor a young local preacher from Elgin, J. G. Terrill by name. This young man was to become a prominent personality in the western area of the new denomination which was later organized, and at the time of his death he was its general missionary secretary. Revival came, and some hard cases were among those converted. A "Band" was then organized which adopted the General Rules of the Methodist Episcopal Church, except the compromise rule on slavery. Finally, on April 27, 1860, convinced at last that there was no hope of redress within the parent congregation, the group of now 112 members organized as an independent congregation, taking the name "Free Methodist Church." In concluding this incident, we note that the Rock River Conference endorsed the course taken by the St. Charles pastor, but advised against such a course in the future![4]

Near Marengo occurred the trial and expulsion of the Bishop

---
3. See *Northern Independent*, v. 4, May 31, 1860.
4. For a fuller account of the St. Charles case, see *Why Another Sect*. Earnest Christian Pub. House, Rochester; pp. 274-277.

family of five members, the complaint against them being their neglect of public worship at the Franklinville church where they held membership. They had been disturbed by the weak stand of the pastor on doctrine, and were wearied always to be the target of his sermons when they did attend. Moreover, they had supported schoolhouse revivals in the area which had been highly productive. Also, they had gone to Marengo to hear Dr. Redfield. As B. T. Roberts commented on the case, "If their neglect had been from worldly motives, no notice would have been taken of it; but as they gave their money and influence—not to fight holiness—but to promote it, they were expelled from the church."[5] When expelled, the Bishop family and those of like earnest spiritual concern formed the "Earnest Christian Band." The daughter married Edward Payson Hart, a young Methodist preacher reared in the same region. Shortly after the organization of the Free Methodist denomination, E. P. Hart accepted a pastoral charge at Belvidere in the Western Convention (Illinois Conference). In 1874 he became the colleague of B. T. Roberts as junior general superintendent of the young church.

We have made mention of Dr. Redfield's St. Louis congregation in Chapter Thirteen. The separation of this congregation from Ebenezer Methodist Church in St. Louis and its establishment as an independent congregation brought to Dr. Redfield the severest pressures of his entire career, and well may have contributed to his break not long thereafter. When all efforts at reconciliation with the regular Methodist program of St. Louis had been abandoned, Dr. Redfield wrote the now widowed Mrs. Kendall as follows:

> Now the question comes up: Where shall we attach ourselves? We have offered ourselves to the Methodist Episcopal Church, and they spurn us. We cannot go to the Methodist Church South on account of slavery. We are Methodists, and cannot be anything else. I said to them, [his congregation] "Perhaps the pilgrims of Western New York will receive you, and look after you."
>
> So they have organized congregationally until they can open up negotiations with the East. We have written to Brother Roberts to come on and take charge. There are a number of other places where matters are somewhat as they are here. . . .

---

5. *Ibid.*, p. 277 *et seq.*

The opposition have sent for Bishop Janes to come and help them out of their difficulty. He is expected today. But it is too late. The new church voted night before last, to make no further attempt at reconciliation.

I have for years seen that we must come to this; but never once supposed that it would be done in my day. But we are forced into it.[6]

This letter was dated February 17, 1859. It was in March that B. T. Roberts arrived. This group also took the name "Free Methodist Church," and adopted, in the main, the rules and regulations of the Methodist Episcopal *Discipline* so far as applicable to an independent church. B. T. Roberts, who assisted in completing the organization, saw to it that a rule was adopted making slave-holding an insurmountable barrier to membership. Heartily supporting this measure was a member of the church who from firm conviction had recently freed all his slaves, valued at thirty thousand dollars.

According to one report, at one time the St. Louis church numbered about 275 members. But a pastor of sensational methods, overreaching ambition and faulty character scattered many of the flock. About one hundred members survived until Dr. Redfield's return to St. Louis in the fall of 1859.

It is interesting to note that the St. Louis Free Methodist Church received a pastor by appointment of the first Laymen's Convention in the West on July 1, 1860, anticipating by eight weeks the Pekin Convention in New York at which the Free Methodist denomination was formally organized. By the time of this Western Convention, the General Conference had cut off all avenues of restoration to the parent church. The pastor appointed to St. Louis by this convention was Joseph Travis who later became editor of *The Free Methodist*. Several other points, most of them in Illinois, received pastors also by appointment of the same convention. But more later about this forward-looking assembly.

When asked what to do with the fruits of revivals in the western area, Dr. Redfield advised organizing the converts as Societies, after the pattern of St. Louis. He hoped thereby to influence the approaching General Conference to correct the abuses to which the reformers

---

6. J. G. Terrill, *Life of Redfield;* p. 376.

had been subjected and, as he said, "give us guarantees that the preaching of living Methodism would be maintained." [7] Apparently he believed, after all, that there was still some hope of reconciliation, and that organized but independent and self-directing societies ready to come directly into the parent church should grievances be remedied, would exert a pressure in the direction of reform and reconciliation not possible with unorganized groups whose members might scatter in many directions.

Such a society, for example, was organized at Clintonville, a village across the Fox River from Elgin where a Methodist Episcopal appointment had been abandoned some years before. But local preachers had recently stirred up a revival which resulted in many conversions, and a church was needed. A subscription blank was prepared, a facsimile of which shows reference to "the Free Methodist Society of Clintonville." This is dated April 19, 1860, four months before the organization of the Free Methodist denomination.[8]

Having sketched the development of the venturesome western child of the reform movement to the eve of its "coming of age," we now turn to the unfolding events of reform in the East that were leading both East and West to their separation from the parent church, not by the choice of the reformers but by the necessity of their rejection by the General Conference of 1860.

The Second Annual Laymen's Convention in the East

The interim convention held on the Bergen campground in June, 1859, had ordered a convention at Albion for November 1. This second annual convention opened on the ordered date in the Albion Baptist Church, and adopted a series of resolutions declaring confidence in the expelled ministers; affirming loyalty to Methodist doctrines and usages but refusing to recognize the actions of the Regency as actions of the church; recommending that the expelled and located preachers continue to labor in the Lord's work, and promising support; providing for organizing into "Bands" under districts those unjustly thrust out of their churches; calling for regular collections from these Bands for supporting the ministers; renewing the advice

---

7. *Ibid.*, p. 421 *et seq.*
8. For facsimile of the Clintonville subscription blank, see *The Free Methodist*, July 25, 1950.

of the First Annual Convention to withhold support from ministers who had aided in unjust expulsions; repudiating the course of preachers whose actions were inconsistent with their pulpit pronouncements; declaring against the ecclesiastical tyranny of the 1859 Conference at Brockport in devising and applying its own test-resolutions as laws of the church; appealing to the forthcoming General Conference against the "contumacy" expulsions of the Genesee Annual Conference.

The convention declared that the charge of "contumacy" was "generally resorted to for the purpose of oppressions," and further asserted, "Let whatever the dominant power in the Church may be pleased to call 'contumacy' be treated as a crime, religious liberty is at an end. There is not an honest man in the Conference but may be expelled for 'contumacy', whenever, by any means, a majority can be obtained against him. . . . Let some mandate be issued that cannot in conscience be obeyed, and the guilt of contumacy is incurred."

The convention declared its loyalty to Methodism in these vigorous words: "Our attachment to Methodism was never stronger than it is at present, and our sympathy and our means shall be given to the men who toil and suffer to promote it. We cannot abandon, at the bidding of a majority, the doctrines of Methodism, and the men who defend them." [9]

It is clear that this Second Annual Convention in the East, by organizing the work into Bands and the area into districts, and by planning financial assistance to the workers, had taken a long step toward the advanced position the Western Laymen's Convention was to take eight months later. Providentially, whether or not by design on the part of the convention, the East was being prepared for separation if the reformers' hopes for redress of grievances by the forthcoming General Conference were not realized.

But the declared purpose of the reformers was against separation. In an article in the *Northern Independent* the month of the convention and soon following the Brockport Conference of 1859, B. T.

---
9. For full report of the Second Laymen's Convention, see v. 1, Chap. 26, of W. T. Hogue, *History of the Free Methodist Church*. F. M. Pub. House, Winona Lake.

Roberts reported the surprise of candid observers at the readiness with which Bishop Simpson gave his influence to the Regency cause in the Brockport trials. "We heard an able lawyer," wrote Roberts, "who attended all through the so-called trials, and who had no bias in favor of either party, deliberately state that he had never before, in all his experience, seen such partiality manifested by the presiding officer of a judicial tribunal." This apparent prejudice puzzled Roberts whose impression of Bishop Simpson heretofore had been favorable. "But the mystery is solved," he wrote. "The good Bishop was made to believe that the so-called Nazarites, or Old School Methodists of the Genesee Conference, really intended to secede!" For Simpson, after the Genesee Conference, had reported that he had in his possession a printed plan of the secession to form a new church to be called "Associate Methodists." Roberts explains that the Bishop, no doubt sincere himself, had been duped by designing men. Then Roberts declared, "The trouble is, we will not 'secede'. We are Methodists from conviction . . . We say to our people everywhere, 'Cling to the Church. Do not withdraw, nor suffer yourselves to be withdrawn.' The temporary organizations we effect, are necessary to keep our people from being scattered, till the General Conference has had opportunity to correct the wrongs and redress the outrages inflicted upon us. . . . We form no 'Free Churches' save where 'Free Churches' are needed, and those are ready to come into the Conference as soon as wrongs are made right." [10]

The reformers alleged that the cry of secession was designed by their opponents to precipitate the same, and the concocted "plan" was intended to prejudice the Bishop.

Local developments in the East

The recommendation of the Second Annual Laymen's Convention that Bands be organized is good evidence that such were already in existence, and it can be assumed that such a recommendation encouraged their extension. Moreover, in the East as well as in the West, Societies and independent "free" Methodist churches were established in this period prior to the organization of the Free Methodist denomination.

---

10. B. T. Roberts, "Secession—Bishop Simpson," *Northern Independent*, v. 4, Nov. 17, 1859.

In *The Earnest Christian*, March, 1860, the editor published a brief article on "Salvation Bands," stating their purpose "to induce those in sympathy with earnest Christianity to put forth direct, systematic and persevering efforts for the salvation of souls." That the reformers patterned these Bands on old Methodist lines appears from the instructions Roberts gave in this article: "Wherever there are three or more believers in Christ, of one heart and one mind, who feel the worth of souls, let them form a Band, adopting the directions to the Band Societies, found in all the Methodist Disciplines published prior to 1852." He gave further directions concerning leaders, holding services in localities especially needing revival, and the features of an appropriate service.[11]

Zahniser finds in the diary of Mrs. Roberts an entry dated February 8, 1860, reporting that her husband had organized "a Free Methodist Society" in Syracuse [12]—probably the group that later became the First Free Methodist Church of Syracuse, from which Mrs. Roberts received a letter of transfer dated December 6, 1860, and signed by Charles Hicks.[13] This Mr. Hicks was the leader of a Syracuse group that had withdrawn from the Third Methodist Episcopal Church. He was a prominent public official of Onondaga County for many years, and became a leading layman of the Susquehanna Conference of the Free Methodist Church.

Returning from Syracuse, probably on the occasion of organizing the Society in that city, B. T. Roberts stopped off at Rochester between trains. On January 30, 1860, he wrote his wife (whom he had left in Syracuse) about a meeting he had attended during his evening in Rochester at which a Band was organized, as a step toward later establishment of a Free Methodist Church in that city.[14] And so the movement progressed.

A mission type of "free" Methodist Episcopal Church had been serving poor people in an outlying section of Buffalo, housed in a building provided without charge by a Congregationalist. When B. T. Roberts moved to Buffalo following his expulsion, he accepted an invitation one midweek evening to speak in this church. It was

---
11. B. T. Roberts, "Salvation Bands," *The Earnest Christian*; v. 1, March 1860, p. 97.
12. C. H. Zahniser, *Earnest Christian*; p. 150.
13. *Ibid.*, p. 147, 147 n. 6.
14. *Ibid.*, p. 148.

not a service scheduled by the Methodists, but Methodist authorities took the position that if Roberts used the church, they would withdraw both pastor and missionary appropriation from the project. The man in charge of the building replied that they could do as they liked, but the house was open for Mr. Roberts' use. Thereafter, Roberts conducted services in the place which became known as Thirteenth Street Free Methodist Church. *The Eastern Christian* of April, 1860, reported that a year after Roberts had taken over the church, a revival was in progress, and fifty or sixty persons were remaining for class. This congregation became one of the early churches of the new denomination following its organization.

But B. T. Roberts was not satisfied with but one "free" church in Buffalo and soon undertook to secure a second. The Thirteenth Street Church was in a location then far from the center of the city, and he desired a downtown location as well. This man, one-time pastor of a fashionable "pewed" church of Buffalo, now expelled and persecuted by the church he loved, carrying the burden of supervising widely scattered groups of earnest Christians likewise without a church home, editing and publishing a religious journal of high literary and devotional merit, and with no stable source of support for his family, would now assume the spiritual and financial responsibility of two "free" churches that the poor of Buffalo might have the gospel preached to them.

On April 19, 1860, he wrote his father of "an opening by which we can preach the Gospel in the central portion of the city." An old theater building on Pearl Street was available, and he was perplexed to find a way to meet the down payment. But when he was pastor of Niagara Street Methodist Church a few years earlier, that Society providing no parsonage, Roberts had purchased a humble home which now he sold to secure the Pearl Street Theater as a downtown "free" church. Like Wesley's, his social conscience was practical in its operations.

The capacity of the building was six or eight hundred. "Soon the church was packed, floor and galleries. Many lost souls here found life and salvation. Free churches were an established fact in Buffalo." [15]

---

15. B. H. Roberts, *Benjamin Titus Roberts*. Earnest Christian Office, North Chili, N.Y.; p. 218 *et seq.*

The most significant interim organization, East or West, that came into the Free Methodist denomination at its founding was the Congregational Free Methodist Church of Albion, New York. When Loren Stiles, Jr., was expelled for contumacy in 1859, he was more realistic in his grasp of the true situation in the parent church than were his fellow expellees, and he had less confidence than had they that the General Conference would enact remedial measures against injustices the reformers had suffered. Unlike them, he made no appeal from the decision of the Conference, but went his way to establish in the community of his last pastorate under the Methodist Episcopal Church an independent church, Methodist and free. In this venture he had the confidence of the people, and was able soon to complete and dedicate a spacious edifice, free of debt. Reporting the dedication, which occurred May 18, 1860, the Buffalo *Morning Express* said:

> ... The Rev. L. Stiles, who, with others, was expelled by the Genesee Conference, at its last session, for doing his duty as a Christian minister, was invited by the great majority of the Church at Albion, which he had served with great acceptability for the two previous years, to continue his labors among them, as a minister of Jesus Christ, and he accepted the invitation. Rather than have any disturbance, they gave up the Church property, to which they were legally entitled, and proceeded at once to purchase a lot, and erect a house of worship. This house was yesterday dedicated to the worship of God by the Rev. E. Bowen, D.D., of the Oneida Conference of the Methodist Episcopal Church. ... The house was crowded to its utmost, some 1,300 being present, and many left, unable to get in. ... Mr. Stiles has collected a large and intelligent congregation, a devoted, pious, working Church, and with their present facilities for doing good, the best results may be anticipated. ...[16]

The *Northern Independent* carried reports of the dedication in two of its issues,[17] and from these accounts we glean the following interesting facts: The seating capacity of the church was 1,300; one reporter claimed that 1,500 crowded into the edifice for the dedicatory service, and the other said that people were turned away for lack of room. Dr. B. I. Ives of the Oneida Conference officiated at the laying of the cornerstone. Dr. Elias Bowen of the same Conference de-

---

16. Quoted by Hogue, *History of the Free Methodist Church;* v. 1, 132 et seq.
17. *Northern Independent,* v. 4, May 31 and June 14, 1860.

livered the dedicatory message, and Dr. Ives offered the dedicatory prayer. In the general quarterly meeting that followed the day of dedication, 440 communicants were served the Sacrament of the Lord's Supper, and in the evangelistic service of the closing evening several penitents responded to the gospel invitation.

Such organized independent "free" churches are pretty well matters of historical record, but the number of Bands and larger Societies that came into existence during this period we have no way of knowing. That many of the earlier Free Methodist churches grew out of these Bands and Societies, we do know. Hogue says:

> No sooner was the infant organization born and christened than the scattered remnants of Methodism—scattered by the hand of ecclesiastical tyranny and despotism—began to turn toward the new Church as a place of refuge from oppression, and as an organization specially committed to the work for which John Wesley said the early Methodist societies were raised up—"to spread Scriptural holiness over these lands." One after another the Bands, Societies, and Churches which had been organized here and there as a temporary expedient, united with the new denomination by the adoption of its Discipline, no longer to be mere fragmentary and isolated groups, but societies of a regularly constituted Christian Church, united in one body, laboring together for the advancement of the kingdom of God under one and the same ecclesiastical organization.[18]

Third Laymen's Convention of the East

The Third Laymen's Convention was held February 1 and 2, 1860, in Olean. With the General Conference only three months away, this gathering was a most significant one, and was attended by representatives from every charge in the Genesee Conference. A surprising degree of reform interest in the Conference was indicated by such far-reaching attendance.

The convention was to have been held in the Methodist Episcopal Church, but an injunction had been secured against the use of the building for this purpose. In the emergency, the Presbyterian Church of Olean offered its facilities.

The convention petitioned the General Conference to investigate the judicial actions of the Genesee Annual Conference in the

---
18. W. T. Hogue, *History of the Free Methodist Church*; v. 1, 327.

expulsion of six named members, and, further, so to amend the church's judicial procedures as to give the right of trial by an impartial committee. Before reaching the General Conference, this petition had received the signatures of more than fifteen hundred laymen,[19] further proving the widespread concern for reform throughout the Genesee Conference.

A third petition to General Conference asked that legislation be enacted to exclude from the church's communion all "who shall be guilty of holding, buying or selling, or in any way using a human being as a slave."

The following resolution was adopted:

> *Resolved*, That we reiterate our unfaltering attachment to the M. E. Church, while we protest against, and repudiate its abuses and iniquitous administration, by which we have been aggrieved, and the Church scandalized. Our controversy is in favor of the doctrines and Discipline of the Church, and against temporary maladministration. And we exhort our brethren everywhere not to secede, or withdraw from the Church, or be persuaded into any other ecclesiastical organization; but to form themselves into Bands, after the example of early Methodism, and remain in the Church until expelled.

The convention adopted a cogently reasoned "Preamble" which sought to establish certain principles of reform and concluded with two resolutions (which also were adopted), one resolution reaffirming the positions taken in the 1858 and 1859 Albion conventions, and a second resolution protesting the "reading out" of members as withdrawn from the church, when not even the form of a trial had been followed, "as an act of outrage upon our rights as members of the Church."

Steps were taken establishing an executive council for each district, which should schedule and supervise camp meetings, general quarterly meetings, and other general gatherings; and between conventions these councils were to exercise general oversight within their respective districts.

A resolution was adopted highly commending the new journal published by B. T. Roberts, *The Earnest Christian*.

---

19. *Ibid.*, v. 1, 287.

The following resolution of interest in and good will toward the newly organized Albion Church was adopted:

> *Resolved,* That we look with lively interest on the denominational position of the Free Methodist Church of Albion, under the care of Rev. L. Stiles, Jr.; that we rejoice in her prosperity; that we hail her as a welcome co-laborer in the vineyard of our common Master, and as a worthy member in the sisterhood of Evangelical Churches.

The foregoing digest of proceedings of the convention is based upon Bishop Hogue's gleanings from the extended account of the convention that appeared at the time in the Olean *Advertiser*.[20]

The General Conference of 1860

It seems that Mrs. Roberts had written her friend, Mrs. W. C. Kendall, shortly before or during the General Conference which extended throughout the month of May, declaring her confidence that the conflict would be resolved and the reformers re-established in the church. No doubt this confidence had been borrowed from her husband. But Mrs. Kendall, then in the West and under Dr. Redfield's influence, wrote Mrs. Roberts on May 19, 1860, saying, "You think there is hope of restoration to the church. I wish I could say I believe it would be so. . . . But God will be glorified in either way. I believe, however, that it is God's will to raise up another people whose God is the Lord, and among whom dwelleth righteousness, peace and joy in the Holy Ghost."[21] As it turned out, Mrs. Roberts' hopes were not fulfilled.

The General Conference met in Buffalo, the center of Regency strength. At its adjournment, it seemed to leave the reformers no alternative but to organize another Methodist communion to conserve and maintain the Wesleyan witness. Briefly stated, here is what happened:[22]

> 1. *The Genesee Conference and the conferences along the southern border, reversing their historic positions, were united*

---

20. *Ibid.,* v. 1, 289-293.
21. C. H. Zahniser, *Earnest Christian;* p. 146 *et seq.*, quoting a personal letter found among the documents of the Roberts family.
22. See *General Conference Journal,* 1860; Carlton & Porter, New York; pp. 98, 147, 148, 220 *et al.,* also W. T. Hogue, *History of the Free Methodist Church,* v. 1, 295 *et seq.*

on the major isssues of this Conference, slavery and Nazaritism.

Observers noted that the delegates of historically anti-slavery Genesee voted with the pro-slavery Border delegates against a stiff anti-slavery rule, and the delegates of the doctrinally conservative Border voted with the liberal Regency on Genesee Conference matters. An editorial in the *Northern Independent* speculated in the following ironical strain:

> It may be that men who, four years ago took the stump to keep slavery out of the territories, have suddenly become convinced that it should be nestled and fostered in the bosom of the Church! We should like to know by what arguments they were converted, and when it was done! Was this a part of the scheme to keep slave-holders in the Church? Did the border understand that if they voted as desired by the Genesee delegates, they would reciprocate the favor? Or did the strange coincidence come about by chance? [23]

2. *The effort to investigate Genesee difficulties was defeated.*

The flood of petitions signed by a multitude of Genesee laymen asking for investigation of the judicial procedures by which six members of the Genesee Conference had been expelled, was referred first to a committee composed of one delegate from each conference delegation, making a committee of forty-seven members. When, some days after its appointment, it was proposed to instruct this committee to seek the origin and nature of the Genesee trouble that lay back of the expulsions, with right of access to all Genesee documents, the Regency forces offered stiff resistance and the proposal was tabled by a small margin, 97 to 84. It was then proposed to dismiss the special committee and transfer papers in its possession to appropriate standing committees. After several had spoken for the proposal and before a representative of the petitioners had the floor, the vote was ordered to be taken without further debate, and the special committee was discharged by a vote of 104 to 81.[24]

A clever bid for Border support of the Regency is reported in the following quotation by Smith in which he sets forth the retention of the Border to the Methodist Episcopal Church as the foremost purpose of the 1860 General Conference:

---

23. *Northern Independent*, v. 4, June 14, 1860.
24. *General Conference Journal*, 1860; p. 148.

... A chief concern of the General Conference of 1860 was to keep the "Border conferences" in Kentucky, Maryland, West Virginia, and Missouri within the denomination, and hence to contribute—so its leaders hoped—to the campaign to prevent the secession of those states from the national union. Sustaining an appeal from abolitionists, even sanctified ones, would hardly serve this purpose. The motion to dismiss the committee appointed to consider the difficulties in Genesee was, in fact, carried after one of the Buffalo group proclaimed his adherence to states' rights in politics and conference rights in the church, and a delegate from the Baltimore Conference responded with an appeal which set off a wave of speeches in its support! [25]

The petitions and resolutions bearing on Genesee difficulties were transferred to the committee on itineracy where they probably were submerged under routine business. Hogue may be right in suspecting that the chief memorial was not even read before that committee. An article in the *Northern Independent* states that the committee on itinerary claimed it had no jurisdiction in the case of these petitions, inasmuch as the records gave no evidence that the complaints contained therein had first come before the Genesee Conference! [26]

3. *The committee on appeals by a tie vote sustained Genesee against Roberts' first appeal, and refused to hear his second appeal or the appeals of his associates, one excepted.*

The appeal from the 1857 sentence of reproof was entertained by the Court of Appeals, and when the vote was taken it turned out to be a tie. The bishop ruled that the decision of the lower court against B. T. Roberts was sustained. This presumably was on the parliamentary ground that a tie vote changes nothing.

The appeal from the 1858 sentence of expulsion was presented, but the Court voted not to entertain it. [27] In the opening procedures of the Court, such unfairness was exhibited toward the appellant that, according to Roberts' claim of reliable information, the presiding bishop retired from the chair rather than have a part in such injustice.

---

25. T. L. Smith, *Revivalism and Social Reform*. Abingdon Press, Nashville; p. 131. Smith cites Hogue's *History of the Free Methodist Church*, v. 1, 295, as source of the states' rights—conference rights incident.
26. *Northern Independent*, v. 4, July 19, 1860.
27. See Appendix B of this book for a copy of the General Conference record on the two appeal cases of B. T. Roberts.

He was replaced by a bishop of pro-Border leanings on the slavery issue. To Roberts it was always an unsolved mystery why the same committee should hear one appeal and refuse to hear the other. By the Court's refusal to consider his appeal, Roberts was left outside the Methodist Episcopal Church by expulsion from the Genesee Conference.

It should be explained that the Court refused likewise to hear the appeals of all others associated with Roberts, C. D. Burlingham excepted. In his case, as pointed out in the *Northern Independent*, the Court did a strange thing in remanding it to Genesee for retrial when neither side had requested it, no irregularities in the original trial were alleged, and there had developed no new evidence. In fact, Burlingham in his trial had admitted the alleged grounds of his expulsion, but had appealed from the sentence imposed as too severe for the acts committed. It seemed clear that the Court was dodging the issue.[28]

During the General Conference an editorial in the *Northern Independent* commented on what the editor took to be a possible obstacle to the restoration of the expelled brethren, namely, their having continued to preach after their expulsion. He said, "Personally we have always regretted that our brethren, so unwarrantedly expelled, did not see it consistent with duty to refrain from preaching until their appeals could be tried. Not that we doubted their still being empowered by the Great Head of the Church to preach, but that refraining for the time being would enable the General Conference to take hold of their appeals with less embarrassment. . . . Their course, though anomalous, is not without precedent. Luther, after his expulsion, kept on preaching to the end of life." [29]

Following the General Conference, when these brethren had no further hope of restoration, Editor Hosmer published another editorial in which he acutely analyzed the refusal of the Court of Appeals to try the cases appealed. The *Discipline*, he pointed out, guarantees the right of appeal in a "restrictive" rule which limits the powers of the General Conference in these words: "They shall not do away with the privileges of our ministers or preachers of trial by a commit-

---

28. *Northern Independent*, v. 4, June 14, 1860.
29. *Ibid.*, v. 4, May 17, 1860.

tee, or of appeal. . . ." Hosmer declared in his examination of the handling of the appeals, that when General Conference refuses to hear an appeal because of anything the appellant has done since the decision from which he appeals, it assumes power it does not possess. "In doing this," he says, "they must first try the appellant on his general conduct since his trial . . . in order to determine whether his appeal should be entertained or not! But the Discipline does not give the General Conference original jurisdiction over any of the ministers except the Bishops. . . ." If through appeal to General Conference a man is restored to the ministry of the Conference which expelled him, he is then answerable to that Conference and not to the General Conference, for his actions since his expulsion. "The General Conference," continued Hosmer, "is authorized to try *appeal cases,* but not preachers." [30]

This editorial points out that in the case of B. T. Roberts, the trial in the lower court was prejudged before complaint was made or charges were preferred. Certainly such a case should be heard by an appeal court.

Which way from here?

The General Conference closed on June 4, after nearly five weeks in session, leaving the reformers without hope of restoration and with no church home. B. T. Roberts devoted approximately a page in *The Earnest Christian* to the activities of the General Conference, the page being divided equally between the feeble and futile admonitory action on the slavery issue and the fate of the appeals of the reformers. With great restraint he gave the following account of his own disappointment and his protest concerning the refusal to hear the appeals:

> We must confess that we felt greatly disappointed. The hope had been indulged that these difficulties would be investigated with such thoroughness and impartiality, as would entitle the decision to respect. If we have been wrong in our teaching or spirit or practice, we feel anxious to know it. No person can possibly be as anxious as we are, to be convinced that we are out of the way, if this is really the case. But such proceedings con-

---

30. *Ibid.,* v. 4, June 28, 1860.

vince us only that there is in certain quarters a great dread of light, and that other considerations weigh more heavily with the authorities of the Church than the disposition to do justice, and to judge righteous judgment.

We trust our friends will give us their sympathies and their prayers, and we will do the best we can under the disadvantageous circumstances we are placed in, to promote the Redeemer's kingdom, waiting for the revelation of the last day to set all right.[31]

He then offered a copy of his trial and of the proceedings of the Laymen's Convention to those desiring particulars involved in the difficulties and who would send twenty-four cents in postage.

Thus, with an influential magazine at his command for purposes of demagoguery, were he tempted in that direction as so often is true of reformers, he quietly handled a crisis in his personal and public life, brought on by heavy injustice, with a few direct statements requiring less than one and a half *per centum* of the magazine's space. Such was the composure and the sober sincerity of B. T. Roberts.

This restraint under pressure and steadiness of purpose were to be needed in the momentous days ahead. What they held in store, Roberts knew not.

Looking backward

In the perspective of a century it is clear that great principles were involved in the Genesee conflict of the 1850's, and that the reformers were seeking sincerely to restore and maintain the Wesleyan witness. It is also clear that some good men did not join forces with them. In the very nature of the case reformers are provocative, and in this instance their attack on the established order seemed to threaten the unity of the Conference. Those whose control of the Conference was challenged by this attack could hold in line even sincere and pious men who loved peace and hoped that even growing evils might be checked in some other way. As with slavery, so with other areas of reform, conflicting interests confused even honest men concerning what was basic in principle and what after all might be marginal and secondary. And intertwining all issues, as ever, the web of

---

31. *The Earnest Christian*, v. 1, July 1860, p. 226.

Methodist organizational discipline exerted its steady pull of loyalty to the ruling order.

Free Methodists do not dwell upon the injustices of that era with rancor, but do take legitimate satisfaction in the fact that the parent Conference fifty years later acknowledged error and did what it could to make amends. In 1910 the Genesee Conference of the Methodist Episcopal Church celebrated the centennial of its organization. Looking back to the century's turbulent mid-point, the Conference voted to restore their parchments to the brethren expelled for party differences in 1858 and 1859.

A service of dignity and sincere Christian fellowship marked the restoration of the parchments of B. T. Roberts, then deceased seventeen years, into the hands of his son, the Rev. Benson H. Roberts. Introducing his address as fraternal delegate of the Genesee Conference of the Free Methodist Church, Professor Roberts handled skillfully what could have been an embarrassing moment with these words: "The child of fifty years, begotten amid the stress and storm of divided opinion and stern antagonisms, of reluctant parentage, greets today the mother who has attained the century mark." The scholarly message that followed courageously faced the issues of the mid-century tempest with a challenge to both denominations to unite as Methodists with a common heritage in facing those issues in the present. This address is deemed of sufficient importance to reproduce in the appendix to the present work. [32]

At this centennial Conference, Dr. Ray Allen, Conference Secretary and Historian, reviewed the century, devoting major attention to the crucial mid-century period. The portion of his paper dealing with the fifties follows in full:

> This is a period worth study. For Genesee Conference these years and the few immediately following, were more momentous than any other in all her history. How it all came about is difficult if not impossible to understand. But two parties arose, both containing good people, and both needing all the good they had. There is no name, mutually agreed upon, by which these two parties can be distinguished. For lack of better terms they are here called the Regulars and the Nazarites—both honorable words, and neither used here with the slightest tinge of aught else.

---

32. Appendix D.

Some subjects came up for consideration—Secret societies, and the right of Methodists to join them; Church pews, whether they should be sold, rented, or free; Dress; Holiness; Demonstrativeness in religious meetings; Old-time Methodism, and its essentials.

On these subjects there was sufficient difference of opinion naturally, but as party lines became drawn men took positions, or seemed to take positions, which otherwise they never would have taken, or appeared to take.

When the first test votes came the parties were not very unequal in numbers—the Regulars somewhat the more numerous. Things went rapidly from bad to worse. The Regulars seemed to have ecclesiastical power on their side, and this added to their strength and to their numbers. After much self-control on both sides, and after many painful episodes in the Conference sessions and throughout its bounds, the lamentable controversy came to a climax in the expulsion of two of the leading Nazarites in 1858, and four more in 1859. It is not surprising that the one Conference sat for seventeen days, and the other for twelve. Would that they had continued in session long enough to work out some other solution!

This heroic treatment might have seemed necessary at the time, but looked at half a century later it seems unjust, and therefore exceedingly unwise. Those expelled brethren were among the best men the Conference contained, and scarce anyone thought otherwise even then. Some of the cases were appealed to the General Conference of 1860, held in Buffalo, but that body failed to right the wrong, and in the most conspicuous case did not get far enough to even entertain the appeal, because of a technicality. A few weeks after decision by the court of last resort some of these expelled brethren, with others who left Genesee Conference of their own accord, organized the Free Methodist Church, which now has forty Annual Conferences, and a little more than 30,000 members.

But the troubles of Genesee Conference were not cured by a surgical operation. Following 1859 came the darkest years in her life, and her membership steadily fell year by year until in 1865 it was at the lowest level ever reached. She then had only 7,593— a sadly wasted figure! In 1866 she began to amend, but the territory which in 1859 held 10,999 members never got back to that number again for nineteen years. Truly she came out of great tribulation, and it is to be hoped she washed her robes white.[33]

---
33. Ray Allen, *A Century of the Genesee Annual Conference*; p. 9 et seq.

With this review of the unfortunate ecclesiastical conflict and resulting division of a century ago in mind, it may be appropriate to recall these words of Bishop Leete, quoted in the opening paragraph of Chapter One of this book: "Perhaps, however, there was a message and a mission which could be fulfilled in no other way than by separation." [34] We have followed developments to separation. The next chapter sketches the first steps taken by the reformers to insure fulfillment of the message and mission committed to them.

---

34. P. 13.

CHAPTER FIFTEEN

Free Methodism Is Born

The East ponders the future

The Genesee reformers met in a session of the Laymen's Convention on June 23, 1860, at West Sweden to survey the field and plan a course of action. This was less than three weeks after the adjournment of General Conference. A report of the proceedings of the convention appeared in the *Northern Independent*. The spirit of restraint exhibited by the actions of the assembly is the more remarkable in view of the recent termination of all prospect of restoration to the fold of the parent church. Note the following resolution which the convention adopted:

Resolved, That we reiterate our unfaltering attachment to the doctrines and proper usages of the M. E. Church, and exhort our people everywhere to adhere to the same, where such adherence is tolerated by the administration. But where such adherence is not permitted without continual strife and opposition, it is recommended, for the sake of Christian peace and order, that they form themselves into bands and societies, under the name "Free Methodist Societies." [1]

This convention looked toward greater stability and permanence of organization by appointing a committee, "to prepare some code of General Rules and Regulations, by which the principles, usages and spirit of primitive Methodism be restored and secured." A significant step toward ecclesiastical independence was taken by a vote to recognize as valid, "the ordination of the ordained preachers, traveling and local, who have been expelled from the Genesee Conference" on party issues, and to recommend "their administration of the sacraments as usual."

It was directed that the next convention be a delegated body, and the basis of representation of every Band, Society or Charge was fixed in terms of the number of members represented. Step by step the East was drawing its organizational bonds more closely, and one

---
1. *Northern Independent*, v. 4, July 12, 1860.

day soon a decision must be made concerning the launching of a new Methodist denomination. Not all thought the time for such had arrived.

The West organizes—and acts!

The reform movement in the East had begun among conference preachers of ability and influence. From them it spread to responsive and capable laymen throughout the Conference. The expulsion of Roberts and McCreery over the issues of reform had precipitated the first Laymen's Convention at Albion in December, 1858.

The movement in the West, however, was more local, following Dr. Redfield's itinerant revivalism from community to community, without creating a clear-cut issue that divided preachers at the conference level. The spiritual quickening that came to several preachers through Redfield's labors at the camp meeting of 1857 seems to have subsided under official opposition within a year or so. Dr. Redfield was a powerful revivalist, but lacked the administrative and leadership qualities of B. T. Roberts. Moreover, Redfield was a local, not a conference preacher. Seymour Coleman, gifted and powerful as he was, was older than is usual among leaders of reform, and as member of a distant conference in the East he had no official standing in the West. Such may have been factors delaying organized, area-wide action against the reformers in the West until the General Conference of 1860 had closed and bolted the door against restoration and reform. When this happened, the West appears to have moved more rapidly toward an independent church than did the East.

The Western Laymen's Convention met in conjunction with the St. Charles camp meeting on July 1, 1860, eight days after the West Sweden convention in the East. B. T. Roberts had been invited to attend, and was elected president of the assembly. A secretary was chosen, and a roll was established of twenty-one members from eight localities, mostly in Illinois. The convention proceeded to transact business much as though it were an annual conference.[2]

B. T. Roberts, so recently from the West Sweden convention, formulated and presented early in this convention a resolution pat-

---

2. For a full account of the Western Convention of 1860, see *Life of Redfield*, by J. G. Terrill; pp. 449-451.

terned after the Eastern resolution, which was unanimously adopted. It was worded as follows:

> *Resolved*, That our attachment to the doctrines, usages, spirit, and discipline of Methodism, is hearty and sincere. It is with the most profound grief that we have witnessed the departure of many of the ministers from the God-honored usages of Methodism. We feel bound to adhere to them, and to labor all we can, and to the best possible advantage, to promote the life and power of godliness. We recommend that those in sympathy with the doctrine of holiness, as taught by Wesley, should labor in harmony with the respective churches to which they belong. But when this cannot be done, without continual strife and contention, we recommend the formation of Free Methodist churches, as contemplated by the convention held in the Genesee Conference, in New York.[3]

The business transacted by the Western Convention included the granting of a license to preach; recommending a Methodist Episcopal minister "to take work in the itineracy of the convention"; appointing a standing stationing committee to function until the next convention; passing J. W. Redfield's character and appointing him superintendent over the Western work; instructing the stationing committee to employ all local preachers under its charge; recognizing the ordination of ministers who had affiliated with the convention; electing B. T. Roberts "general superintendent of the work"; ordering a camp meeting in early September, and another the June of 1861.

The appointment of Dr. Redfield to superintend the Western work undoubtedly conveyed supervisory authority over existing Societies, whereas the election of B. T. Roberts as "general superintendent" may have had in view his directing the expansion of the work into new western fields not yet touched. It could hardly be that this Western Convention assumed the responsibility of electing Roberts general superintendent over the East—and the less likely with him in the chair!

The stationing committee made appointments to Ogle Circuit, St. Charles, Clintonville, Coral, Queen Ann, Big Rock, Elgin, St. Louis Circuit, St. Louis Mission, Iowa Mission, and Michigan Mission.

---

3. *The Earnest Christian*, v. 1, August 1860; p. 260.

The following month two delegates would represent the Western Convention at Pekin, N.Y., to deliberate the question of forming a new denomination. J. W. Redfield and Daniel Lloyd were those delegates.

Although taking strong initiative in setting up a program of its own for conserving and extending the work of revival in the West, this convention flexibly adjusted its plans to developments in the East, looking forward to united action. It adopted no discipline by which its member churches and individuals should be governed, and therefore did not precipitate a new denomination. Here was the courageous venture of an association of local Christian groups to accept pastors by appointments of a central committee, and of preachers to go where sent, either to embryo Societies or to virgin territory where they would be expected to raise up new Societies. Such indeed, was the spirit of the West!

The challenge

The call for a convention at Pekin, N. Y., to be held in conjunction with a camp meeting at that place, appeared in the August (1860) issue of *The Earnest Christian*. Significantly enough, this call sounded the challenge on items involving the five issues of Free Methodism's origin as analyzed in our introductory chapter and as reflected in Roberts' epochal article, "New School Methodism." The statement of these issues is repeated here for a clearer understanding of the relevance thereto of the call.

1. *Doctrine:* The Scriptural doctrine of entire sanctification according to the Arminian-Wesleyan interpretation;

2. *Experience:* A corresponding experience of cleansing and power;

3. *Worship:* Spirituality and simplicity of worship in the freedom of the Spirit;

4. *Piety:* A way of holy living that separates the Christian from the world;

5. *Stewardship:* Full consecration for service to God and man.

It will be observed that item "1" of the call which follows is a comprehensive statement, touching upon all five of the above. Item "3" deals further with matters of Stewardship as understood by a sensitive social conscience. Item "2" is related to the broad concept of Stewardship, involving as it does a call to democratic reform in church government. The particulars listed in the call by no means exhaust the above five principles, but represent some of the areas of more acute and immediate concern to the reformers.

The call read as follows:

> A convention will be held at Pekin, for the purpose of adopting a Discipline for the Free Methodist Church, to commence at the close of the camp meeting, August 23rd. All societies and bands that find it necessary, in order to promote the prosperity and permanency of the work of holiness, to organize a Free Church on the following basis, are invited to send delegates:
>
> 1. Doctrines and usages of primitive Methodism, such as the Witness of the Spirit, Entire Sanctification as a state of grace distinct from justification, attainable instantaneously by faith. Free seats, and congregational singing, without instrumental music in all cases; plainness of dress.
>
> 2. An equal representation of ministers and members in all the councils of the Church.
>
> 3. No slaveholding, and no connection with secret and oath bound societies.
>
> Each society or band will be entitled to send one delegate at least; and an additional one for every forty members.[4]

Delegates responding to the call numbered fifteen preachers and forty-five laymen. In this connection it is interesting to note that the Pekin Convention, which launched a new denomination with a provision for "equal representation of ministers and laymen in all the councils of the Church," had three times as many lay as ministerial members.

Reaching an important decision

Some of the delegates to the convention, and others of the reformers not delegates, were opposed to organizing a church at this time. Among the latter was S. K. J. Chesbrough who had been prominent in the Laymen's Conventions that preceded Pekin. He had refused to be a delegate to the Pekin Convention and did not attend its deliberations. He later reported that some of the leaders had met under an apple tree in his back yard before the convention

---

4. *Ibid.*, p. 259 *et seq.*

opened, while he listened to them from his back door. They agreed among themselves to proceed with the organization of a church, and then returned to the campground in a nearby grove on his father's farm where the convention was held. Although the Sunday following the convention, B. T. Roberts organized in Pekin the first class under the new Discipline, Mrs. Chesbrough being included therein, her husband held off a few weeks until convinced he was in error. He then joined the Free Methodist Church, of which he was to become a distinguished leader as general publisher and as treasurer.

His father, I. M. Chesbrough, who first proposed the Laymen's Convention of 1858, was made chairman of the Pekin Convention at its organization. Several delegates opposed organization of a new church as premature, holding that at a later date more members of the Methodist Episcopal Church would be ready to join. In the meantime, they held, the movement should continue to function in local Bands.

But recent events had convinced Dr. Redfield that the time for a new church, the eventual necessity of which he had foreseen for years, had now arrived. He is reported to have said, "Brethren, when fruit is ripe, it had better be picked, lest on falling it bruise. In the West we are ready for an organization. If in the East you are not ready, wait until you are."

The ties binding the East to the parent church were perhaps more closely drawn than the ties in the newer West, making the irrevocable step more difficult for the former. Anyway, as we have seen earlier in this chapter, the more aggressive West had already ventured far toward organization. Had the East withheld action to organize, permitting the West to proceed to independence alone, the history of Free Methodism would be far different. Fortunately the two areas moved together. Each needed the other, the vigorous, pioneering and more impulsive West and the deliberate and determined but more seasoned East.

After long months and even years of "hoping against hope" that reform of the parent church would come, B. T. Roberts had reached his decision—that morning under the apple tree, if not before. Following the remarks of Dr. Redfield noted above, he arose and said, "We are ready, and the West and the East should move in the matter simultaneously." The proposal to organize then carried.[5]

Dissenting from the decision were five preachers and two laymen, seven in all. Some of the dissenters went their own way to become the nucleus of what they chose to call "Nazarite Bands." These tended to be the extremists of the reform element, and later harassed the young church by creating fanatical disturbances in Free Methodist meetings and stirring up contention. Their withdrawal to form their own loosely organized Bands was fortunate for the church which, organized as it was with freedom of the Spirit in worship as one of its principles, faced the task of safeguarding against demonstrations "in the flesh" under the guise of an assumed spiritual freedom.

Two of the preachers who withdrew at Pekin later joined the new church. One was Rev. W. Cooley, a minister expelled by the Genesee Conference in 1859 and whose appeal was denied by the General Conference. He seems at first to have leaned toward the Nazarite Bands, but the Rev. M. N. Downing, an early pioneer of Free Methodism in the East who was a member of the Pekin Convention, has reported as follows concerning him and the Bands: "The Nazarite faction went to seed completely at a camp meeting in East Shelby, N. Y. Rev. W. Cooley and wife were at this meeting, and seeing fanaticism in some of its wildest features coming in, fled to the Free Methodist Church for refuge, and were useful workers therein."

Another dissenter from the Pekin decision to organize the Free Methodist Church was Joseph McCreery, author of the troublesome "Nazarite Documents" of some years earlier. He had been expelled from the Genesee Conference with Roberts, and likewise was denied an appeal by the General Conference. After a time with the Nazarite faction, McCreery also joined the Free Methodist Church and labored in its ministry.

There was general accord among the delegates of the Pekin Convention on the adoption of a Discipline by which the new church should be governed. This harmony was the more remarkable in view of the fact that it prevailed among eager reformers, all of whom were seeking to embody their moral, religious and ecclesiastical ideals in such a document as the Discipline of a new church, just coming to

---

5. B. H. Roberts, *Benjamin Titus Roberts*. Earnest Christian Office, North Chili, N.Y.; p. 232.

birth. B. T. Roberts wrote in his account of the convention, "It was as surprising as delightful to notice the similarity of views entertained by men who think for themselves coming from different parts of the country." [6] We cite a few outstanding provisions of the Discipline adopted by the convention:

Greater democracy in church government

A church that had developed from a lay movement, the origin of which was a protest against ecclesiastical tyranny, would naturally seek to provide greater lay participation in its government. Some movements react against the rigid clerical control of the body from which they had separated by going to the other extreme of congregationalism. To the founders of Free Methodism, however, abuses in church government presented only one of several issues calling for reform, and their concern at the point of government was to provide a polity for the new church that would insure justice to individuals, whether laymen or ministers, and also protect the church's principles of doctrine and Christian living. Accordingly, the Pekin Convention moderated the episcopal system of major Methodism without adopting congregationalism.

Free Methodism's major reform in church polity was the firm establishment of equal lay and ministerial representation in the church's annual and quadrennial bodies. Lay delegates in the Pekin Convention, we have noted, greatly outnumbered ministerial delegates, and Roberts expressed his satisfaction with the capable performance of these laymen in carrying on the business of the convention. In the editorial just referred to he said, "The deep interest and close scrutiny of the intelligent laymen who were present as delegates must have convinced anyone that that church is a great loser which excludes them from her counsels."

In granting equal lay representation, the infant church moved far ahead of its parent. From its origin in 1784, the Methodist Episcopal Church had refused representation in General Conference to its laymen, and was not to grant that right for twelve years after Free Methodism's founding. In fact, those M. E. preachers who favored lay representation were regarded as dangerous radicals by their breth-

---

6. *The Earnest Christian*, v. 1, Sept. 1860; p. 291.

ren, and they could expect no preferences from their conferences in appointments or offices. It is told that near mid-century, a minister of the Philadelphia Conference protested the admission of a candidate because he was a delegation man, and, said the objector, "I had as lief travel with the devil as with a lay delegation man."

Laymen were first seated in a Methodist Episcopal General Conference in 1872, but even then and until 1900 lay and ministerial representations were not equal, for lay representation was limited to two delegates from each Conference. Lay representation in Annual Conference came even later, and not for many years would full and equal lay representation be achieved in the Methodist Episcopal Church—a principle that had been firmly established by the Free Methodist Church at its founding.

Other moves of the Pekin Convention toward greater democracy in church government included provisions for election by the General Conference of general superintendents for a term of four years with re-election possible, rather than election of bishops for life with consecration or ordination; election by the Annual Conference of district chairmen who might also be pastors, rather than appointment of presiding elders by the bishop; and election of class leaders by the members rather than their appointment by the pastor.

The general structure of government, however, was taken over from the Methodist Episcopal Church, and although the titles of general superintendent and district chairman have been changed to bishop and district (or conference) superintendent respectively, the powers still remain more restricted than those inhering in the corresponding offices of the Methodist Church.

The Articles of Religion changed by four deletions and two additions

The new church adopted the Articles of Religion which the parent church had received at its founding in 1784 (edited and abridged for it by John Wesley from the Thirty-nine Articles of the Church of England), save three and a portion of another. These were deletions of declarations against Romanism with which the founders of Free Methodism certainly agreed, but which they probably thought unnecessary. The Articles deleted were, "Of Purgatory," "Of Both Kinds," "Of the Marriage of Ministers," and all but the first paragraph of the Article, "Of the Sacraments." Also deleted by the Pekin Convention was the Article added by the Christmas Conference of 1784, "Of the Rulers of the United States of America." Accordingly, Free Methodism retained as a part of its heritage from the parent church, twenty-one of the twenty-five Articles of Religion of the Methodist Episcopal Church.

The founders of Free Methodism added two Articles, "Entire Sanctification," and "Future Rewards and Punishment." Historians have noted Wesley's unaccountable omission of any statement on entire sanctification in the Articles of Religion he prepared for American Methodism. The Pekin Convention sought to supply this lack by inserting a statement on the subject taken largely from the writings of Wesley. This procedure had its limitations, for Wesley might have phrased the doctrine differently had he been writing for such a purpose. It is easy to believe, for example, that Wesley would have omitted the first word of the opening statement which, as originally adopted, read, "Merely justified persons. . . ." "Merely" was deleted in 1870 as tending to ascribe too low a status to the first work of justifying grace. The Article now reads:

> Justified persons, while they do not outwardly commit sin, are nevertheless conscious of sin still remaining in the heart. They feel a natural tendency to evil, a proneness to depart from God, and cleave to the things of earth. Those who are sanctified wholly are saved from all inward sin—from evil thoughts and evil tempers. No wrong temper, none contrary to love, remains in the soul. All their thoughts, words, and actions are governed by pure love.
>
> Entire sanctification takes place subsequently to justification, and is the work of God wrought instantaneously upon the consecrated, believing soul. After a soul is cleansed from sin, it is then fully prepared to grow in grace.

Since the crucial doctrinal issue between the reformers and the parent church had centered on entire sanctification, it seemed a necessary safeguard to the founders of Free Methodism to affirm the new church's position in its constitutional declaration of beliefs, the Articles of Religion. But there was at least a mild difference of opinion over the statement that should be approved. Loren Stiles had desired greater latitude which would allow a more gradualistic interpretation along with the instantaneous view, but Dr. Redfield objected. Downing has summarized his remarks as follows: "Brethren, I would not make a threat, but unless we go straight on the question of holiness in the Discipline, we had better halt where we are. The gradualistic theory is what has made so much mischief. We are John Wesleyan Methodists. We must not dodge that point." [7]

Perhaps Stiles had hoped to emphasize process more strongly than did the proposed statement, as well as crisis, but was misinterpreted by the zealous evangelist (and Downing) as intending to make the experience of entire sanctification possible through process without crisis. B. T. Roberts was one of the clearest and sanest teachers of growth, both before and after the crisis of complete cleansing; but as a mediator of differences in the young and vigorous church, he may have allowed the Doctor to carry his point lest the revision Stiles had proposed produce confusion and general misunderstanding at this crucial stage. After all, the issue with the parent church was on the crisis, not the process of sanctification.

The other Article of Religion added by the Pekin Convention was made necessary by the encroachments of Universalism at that period, and the too-ready cooperation of Methodist preachers in its services. The Article stands in the *Discipline* today, unchanged from the writing of the fathers.

> God has appointed a day in which He will judge the world in righteousness by Jesus Christ, according to the gospel. The righteous shall have in heaven an inheritance incorruptible, undefiled, and that fadeth not away. The wicked shall go away into everlasting punishment, where their worm dieth not, and the fire is not quenched.

Establishing standards of church membership

The Free Methodist Church continued the two levels of church membership existing in the parent church at the time of the former's origin. However, the requirements for each level were made more stringent. Rather than merely giving evidence of a "desire to flee from the wrath to come" as the condition of probationary membership, the candidate was required to "give satisfactory evidence of Scriptural conversion," and the 1866 General Conference of the Free Methodist Church further required "consent to be governed by the General

---

7. B. H. Roberts, *Benjamin Titus Roberts*, p. 232 *et seq.*

Rules." Thus, even probationary membership was based upon saving faith in Christ and, after 1866, upon a pledge to maintain the church's standard of Christian living. By such safeguards the early church sought to avoid having the church filled with unconverted members, which the reformers claimed had crippled the spiritual life of the parent church.

The questions asked those seeking membership in full connection were even more specific and exacting. After a period of six months on probation, one could become a candidate for full membership in the church on recommendation of the official board. He must then declare his covenant before the Society and be accepted by three-fourths of the members present. Declaring his covenant would place personal responsibility on the candidate to lead a consistent Christian life, and thereby protect the purity of the church. He made his covenant by answering affirmatively the following questions:

(1) Have you the witness of the Spirit that you are a child of God?

(2) Have you that perfect love which casteth out fear? If not, will you diligently seek until you obtain it?

(3) Is it your purpose to devote yourself the remainder of your life wholly to the service of God, doing good to your fellow men, and working out your own salvation with fear and trembling?

(4) Will you forever lay aside all superfluous ornaments, and adorn yourself in modest apparel, with shamefacedness and sobriety, not with broidered hair, or gold, or pearls, or costly array, but, which becometh those professing godliness, with good works?

(5) Will you abstain from connection with all secret societies, keeping yourself free to follow the will of the Lord in all things?

(6) Do you subscribe to our articles of religion, our general rules, and our discipline, and are you willing to be governed by the same?

(7) Have you Christian fellowship and love for the members of this society, and will you assist them as God shall give you ability in carrying on the work of the Lord?

The place of discipline in the development of the Free Methodist Church is treated in a later chapter, but we note in passing that for a century this covenant has remained without other than editorial change, except for the recent addition of an eighth question calling for Christian stewardship of time, talents, and possessions, and the deletion in (4) of the words, "with shamefacedness and sobriety" and "with broidered hair."

For further guidance of members, both in avoiding wrong and pursuing right, the General Rules of the parent church, substantially as formulated by Wesley in 1743, were adopted by the Free Methodist Church at its founding. By virtue of a member's affirmative answer to question (6), the General Rules become a part of his covenant. It should be noted that the rule against slavery of the parent church was unsatisfactory to Free Methodism's founders, and accordingly they rephrased it in these unequivocal terms: *The buying, selling, or holding of a human being as a slave.*

In answering question (6) affirmatively, the member likewise declares his acceptance of the cardinal beliefs of the Free Methodist Church as set forth in its Articles of Religion. Membership in the Free Methodist Church was therefore to mean both the confession of Christian faith and the testimony of a Christian life.

Establishing standards for local churches

The early Free Methodist Church went beyond the formulation of rules of individual conduct, to define standards as well for the corporate group or local congregation. The reformers saw that evils had developed in the practices of many churches which were detrimental to spirituality and Christian ideals. They took precautions against the development of these practices early in the church's history by formulating restrictions to guide local churches.

The very first *Discipline,* adopted by the Pekin Convention in 1860, declared, "In no case let there be instrumental music or choir singing in our public worship." This rule reflected the reformers' reaction to the rapid deterioration in congregational singing and the parallel increase in formality that had come with the introduction of instrumental music and choirs in Methodist worship. One should not permit these strictures against instruments and choir to overshadow the reformers' intelligent concern for the improvement of congregational singing. The *Discipline* advised that hymns be selected that suited the occasion, with tune suited to the sentiment of the words. It directed every Society to give proper attention to the cultivation of sacred music. Where pastor was not qualified, leaders were to be appointed; and all in the congregation were urged to sing, "not one in ten." It is significant that the only official reversal by the Free Methodist Church of a major position of the Pekin Convention has been its acceptance of instruments and choirs in public worship. The steps taken by the church over a period of many years which finally led to this reversal are traced in Chapter Eighteen.

Apparently neither the organizing convention of 1860 nor the first General Conference, held in 1862, thought it necessary to legislate specifically for free seats and simplicity in church structures. However, the *Disciplines* of both 1860 and 1862 very clearly discountenanced the practice of renting pews in the historical preface to the *Discipline* which gave an account of the origin of the Free Methodist Church. As evidence of the worldly drift of the parent church, recent changes in the Methodist Episcopal Church were cited. One of these citations reads as follows:

> In 1852 the rule requiring our houses of worship to be built "plain and with free seats," was effectually neutralized by adding the words, "wherever practicable."

The foregoing appeared in both 1860 and 1862 *Disciplines*, but the preface to the 1866 *Discipline* and several following was more specific. We find the following:

> All their churches are required to be as free as the grace they preach. They believe that their mission is two-fold—to maintain the Bible standard of Christianity—and to preach the Gospel to the poor. Hence they require that all seats in their houses of worship should *be free*. No pews can be rented or sold among them.

Such a requirement means little today when "pewed" churches are exceedingly rare; but when the Free Methodist Church was founded, as previously noted, there were many cities and larger towns in this country where a "free" church did not exist.

The 1866 and following *Disciplines*, likewise in the preface, took a position against commercial methods of raising money to support the church, declaring of Free Methodists, "They do not believe in resorting to worldly policy to sustain the Gospel," and adding, "There is no more virtue in giving to the cause of God, for carnal pleasure, than there is in any other purely selfish action." Raising money for the church by means of suppers, fairs, bazaars, entertainments, and other merchandising methods was held to be dishonoring to the Gospel and corrupting to the church. "To say that the church cannot be sustained without these contrivances to beguile the world into its support, is to confess that professing Christians are 'lovers of pleasure more than lovers of God.' It is to pronounce Christianity a failure." This is still the standard of the Free Methodist Church for the support of the Gospel.

A Biblical rather than a popular standard

The stringent standards we have reviewed make it clear that the founders of Free Methodism did not have in mind as a major objective the gathering of a large membership. The introduction to the new *Discipline* plainly stated, "We have no desire to get up simply a large church; but we do hope that our societies will be composed, exclusively, of those who are in earnest to gain heaven, and who are determined, by the grace of God, to live up to the requirements of the Bible." To understand the subsequent course of Free Methodism demands a clear grasp of this position of its founders. In an editorial on the Pekin Convention, Roberts pointed out that such a church as had been launched must come to naught without God's approval. He wrote:

> We have this consolation—and it is a great one—that if our effort is not for the glory of God, and does not receive His approbation, *it cannot succeed*. And if it is not for His glory, we most devoutly pray that it may fail in its very incipiency. We would rather be covered with any amount of dishonor than have the cause of God suffer. We have no men of commanding ability and influence to help on the enterprise—no wealth, no sympathy from powerful ecclesiastical, political, or secret societies; but all these against us—so that if we succeed, it must be by the blessing of Heaven upon our feeble endeavors. We cannot avail ourselves of any popular excitement in favor of a reform in Church government—or against slavery; but we are engaged in the work, always unpopular, and especially so in this age, in trying to persuade our fellow-men to tread in the path of self-denial—*the narrow way that leadeth unto life.*[8]

---
8. *The Earnest Christian*, v. 1, Sept. 1860; p. 292.

B. T. Roberts made general superintendent

The man of leading influence in the convention was B. T. Roberts. The new *Discipline* was largely his work, for the delegates made very few changes in the plan he proposed. At one point, however, the convention over-ruled his plan. He had proposed a standing committee of three to have general charge of the church's administration. "But the convention judged best to have a general superintendent," he entered in his diary of the convention, August 23, 1860. The record continues, "To my surprise the choice fell on me. Lord, give me heavenly wisdom to guide me!" The position would mean heavy responsibilities and sharp criticism. Foreseeing this, again he prayed, "Let me have Thy presence and help, O God of power!" [9]

It is altogether likely that Roberts related the shadowy glimpse he now caught of a dark and difficult future to that choice he had made at the Collins camp meeting in 1851, when he resolutely turned from the appeal of popularity by way of compromise, to the "narrow way," with persecution for faithful preaching of the full counsel of God.

The young church has a name and a constituency

We find no record of debate in the Pekin Convention on the question of naming the new denomination. Probably there was none. Had not the call for the convention declared its purpose to be the adoption of a Discipline for "the Free Methodist Church"? As with many children, the church seems to have been named before it was born! Puzzled as are many today to understand the significance of the name *Free* Methodist, there was no question about its relevance a century ago. The issues of the church's founding included so many freedoms that it would have been difficult to attach to it any other name. Free seats in their houses of worship had already given independent churches of the reform group the name "Free Methodist," as in the cases of St. Louis, St. Charles, and Albion. Freedom from slavery was also a well-known issue of the reformers. And there were other freedoms for which the reformers were noted; such as, freedom from the oath-bound lodge, freedom from ecclesiastical domination, the gospel of freedom from sin, and freedom of the Spirit in worship.

---

9. B. H. Roberts, *Benjamin Titus Roberts*, p. 235.

FREE METHODISM IS BORN

The church came by its name legitimately and appropriately.[10]

Bishop Hogue has well described the drawing into the new organization of scattered fragments of the reform movement to comprise the beginnings of a denominational constituency.[11]

Organizations at the regional level, uniting local groups or Societies of the same area into Annual Conferences[12] under the General Church, followed promptly. According to Terrill, the West met in Aurora, Illinois, the month following the Pekin Convention and adopted the *Discipline*, but the Illinois Annual Conference was not officially organized under the *Discipline* until June 1, 1861. The Genesee Annual Conference was the first to organize under the *Discipline*, doing so at Rushford, N. Y., at a session beginning November 8, 1860—less than three months after the Pekin Convention.

The first session of the first Annual Conference

The members of this, the first Annual Conference session convened in the new denomination, numbered fourteen preachers and fourteen laymen. The nineteen appointments were divided between a northern or Genesee District, and a southern or Allegany District. Pastors were assigned to fifteen charges, leaving four appointments to be supplied. The district chairmen were authorized to secure ten more preachers.

Prior to the Conference, the editor of the *Northern Independent* had commented briefly on the information that, "a new paper designed exclusively for the use of the Free Methodist Church, is contemplated." [13] We find that the Rev. A. A. Phelps, secretary of the Pekin Convention and a man of journalistic bent, who had been a departmental editor of *The Guide to Holiness*, had promoted the idea of a denominational weekly among Free Methodist preachers,

---

10. See W. T. Hogue, *History of the Free Methodist Church*. F. M. Pub. House, Winona Lake; v. 1, 326 *et seq.*, for C. D. Brooks' account of his proposing the name "Free Methodist" for Stiles' church at Albion. The term "free Methodist church" was already in use by the time of the Pekin Convention to designate Methodist churches with free seats.
11. *Supra*, p. 238.
12. Regional and general levels of organization were called "Conventions" until the first General Convention, held in 1862, reverted to the traditional Methodist term, "Conference." Throughout the present volume, "Conference" is used.
13. *Northern Independent*, v. 5, Oct. 18, 1860.

265

and with their encouragement had issued a prospectus proposing the launching of such a paper beginning January, 1861.

In the meantime the Annual Conference considered the project and decided to defer the establishment of a paper, but appointed a committee to raise the necessary funds. Following Conference, Phelps published an explanation of the change of plans in the *Northern Independent*,[14] and called for a response from those favoring such a publication, promising it as soon as prospective patronage would warrant. "Meanwhile," he said, "let all our friends take *The Earnest Christian*, edited by Rev. B. T. Roberts, and published in Buffalo, N. Y.; and also the *Northern Independent*, prince of the weeklies in America!"

For some time thereafter, the *Northern Independent* served in effect as the denominational organ of Free Methodism, carrying its official notices and appointments. *The Free Methodist* did not make its appearance until 1868, and then, as for some years following, was a privately owned publication. In the meantime the *Northern Independent* had ceased publication. Through all this period, from January, 1860, and to his death in 1893, B. T. Roberts successfully edited and published *The Earnest Christian* as an independent Christian monthly of high literary and journalistic merit, free from controversy, and devoted to the cause of vital personal piety, interdenominational ideals, and worthy social causes.

In reporting the first session of the Genesee Annual Conference in *The Earnest Christian*, Roberts set forth the arguments against initiating a denominational paper at that time. One factor was the cost, but he gave a more significant reason which further confirms the Christian restraint of the man who had been chosen to lead the new church. He said:

> A weekly paper at the present time would almost unavoidably involve us in controversy. Those who are leaving no means untried to destroy us, have put so many weapons into our hands, that might be employed to our advantage and their discomfiture, that the temptation to use them would, we fear, be irresistible. But to beget and foster a controversial spirit among the people of God would be a great calamity. What we most need is, *a general, deep, and thorough revival* of religion. A rehearsal of the wrongs

---
14. *Ibid.*, v. 5, Nov. 22, 1860.

we have suffered, and of the misdeeds of others, will not be very likely to save souls.[15]

Another absorbing theme of quite a different character engaged this first Annual Conference. Loren Stiles presented a resolution on "miraculous gifts" which declared that the members of that body did not believe that such gifts "in the commonly received theological sense of the term, are for us Christians at the present day, to be obtained or exercised." No doubt the resolution was intended to safeguard the young church against extravagant claims of enthusiasts, within or without its membership. The resolution passed, but B. T. Roberts in his editorial report on the Conference in *The Earnest Christian* attempted to clear up misunderstandings by distinguishing "miracle" in the theological from the philosophical meanings of the term. He agreed with the Stiles resolution as directed against the claim of the present possibility of "theological miracle," that is, a miracle attesting a doctrine or the authority of some person. But Roberts did insist upon the present possibility of miracle in its philosophical meaning, defined by Richard Watson as "an effect which does not follow from any of the regular laws of nature."[16] A leading article relevant to this problem on "Spiritual Gifts" was published in the following number of *The Earnest Christian*, and was continued in the next, by Dr. Elias Bowen who later joined the Free Methodist Church but at that time was a minister in the Oneida Conference of the Methodist Episcopal Church.

The Illinois Annual Conference organized

Nearly a year after the Pekin Convention had organized the new denomination, the Illinois Annual Conference was organized as a part of the Free Methodist Church. This was in June of 1861. Immediate organization had not been urgent inasmuch as a month after the Pekin Convention the Western Laymen's Convention had met to adopt the new *Discipline*, which act committed the work of the reformers in that area to the Free Methodist Church.

The session was held in connection with the St. Charles camp meeting on the Laughlin place, and the Conference transacted its business on the famous rail pile. Twenty preachers and twenty dele-

---

15. *The Earnest Christian*, v. 1, December 1860; p. 392.
16. *Ibid.*, v. 1, 393 *et seq.*

gates were on the roll of this, the first Illinois Conference convened under the Free Methodist Discipline. The appointments numbered fourteen, all of them circuits, each of which was expected to have at least six points. In reporting on the Conference, B. T. Roberts said:

> Ten preachers were admitted to the traveling connection. All the preachers profess and we believe enjoy the blessing of entire sanctification. They are devotedly pious, laborious young men, capable of doing a great deal of service in the cause of Christ upon a very small salary. One of them during the year walked 1,600 miles, visited and prayed with 1,000 families, and received thirty dollars. Such men are not easily to be put down when engaged in spreading holiness, with the Holy Ghost sent down from heaven.[17]

Re-enforcements

The *Northern Independent* of March 14, 1861, carried a long article on the withdrawal of the Rev. Asa Abell and the Rev. C. D. Brooks from the Methodist Episcopal Church and their joining the Free Methodist Church. The editor took occasion to review some of the difficulties of late years in the Genesee Conference of the former church, and explained: "These brethren, though neither tried nor expelled for Nazarite leanings, have felt themselves too much embarrassed by the action of the Conference to allow of their remaining longer in the M. E. Church. But they have left in deep grief, and without the slightest feeling of bitterness towards their former associates. They have joined the new organization, not to war with the M. E. Church, but to throw off the hindrances, which, in their locality, are a fatal incubus upon Methodism." Then follows Asa Abell's moving statement which we later reproduce.

The Earnest Christian likewise reported the reception of Asa Abell into the Free Methodist Church at a Quarterly Meeting in Albion, N. Y. It was a significant occasion, with about 340 communicants at the Lord's Supper. Roberts wrote in his editorial:

> One of the most thrilling scenes we ever witnessed took place in the Quarterly Convention when the Rev. Asa Abell joined the Free Methodist Church. For forty years he has been a traveling preacher in the M. E. Church. He has been a delegate to four General Conferences, and for eighteen years he filled the office

---

17. *Ibid.*, v. 2, July 1861; p. 225.

of Presiding Elder. He is generally known and deeply beloved. There was scarcely a dry eye in the Convention when he announced his conviction that the time had come when he must change his church relations.

We reproduce this distinguished minister's remarks as he took this crucial step, quoting them from *The Earnest Christian*:

> I have long been a member of the Methodist Episcopal Church. It is with great reluctance that I leave. I owe my salvation under God to the M. E. Church. She is my mother. I cannot turn against it. It is not in my heart, and I trust it is not in the hearts of any of us to make war upon it. My sympathies are with those brethren who have been branded as Nazarites. The heel of oppression has been placed upon them. Some of them have been, as I believe, unjustly excluded, and all redress denied them. It has been thought that they could be easily annihilated. I thought otherwise. The great revival of holiness in Genesee district was branded as fanaticism. I believed it to be a genuine work of God. My sympathies have been with this class of persons. I must go with one or the other. I have made up my mind to cast in my lot with you. I could sit down and cry for an hour. I wish there had been no occasion for this step. But we are sundered in feeling. The fellowship is gone. So I must come among you if you will take me.[18]

He was accepted, and promptly was made Chairman of the Genesee District.

We have had occasion earlier in this volume to refer to the bitterly prejudiced account given of the "Nazarites" by F. W. Conable in his *History of the Genesee Annual Conference*. The withdrawal of Asa Abell from the M. E. Church to join the Free Methodist Church was a difficult matter for him to explain, but which nevertheless he attempted by throwing out the hint that there must have been concealed in this seasoned Methodist divine a vein of fanaticism. Conable wrote as follows:

> As to the venerable and venerated Asa Abell, who joined the Genesee Conference in 1821, and who had for many years been a champion defender and promoter of Episcopal Methodism— it seemed one of the things that ought not to be, that from any real or fancied wrongs committed against him, or existing, or

---

18. *Ibid.*, v. 2, March 1861; p. 98.

supposed to exist, in the Conference or Church, he should feel forced or drawn away from all his old into such new and strange connections and associations. It is believed that Elder Abell never intended to be fanatical, though it was next to certain he was too much under the fanatical influence of others. May he live to die in the Methodist Episcopal Church! [19]

Among the documents referred to in the opening of Chapter Twelve is a letter Asa Abell had written, a year after his joining the Free Methodist Church, to a convert of Wm. C. Kendall's last revival. This man, at the time Abell wrote the letter, was planning to enter the ministry, and the purpose of Abell's lengthy epistle was to advise him along many lines, one of them being a warning against fanaticism. The discovery of this document effectively settles Conable's aspersion against Abell's religious balance, for none could better handle the problem of fanaticism than did Abell in this letter.[20]

The Rev. Levi Wood of the East Genesee Conference of the M. E. Church also came into the Free Methodist Church at the Albion Quarterly Meeting at which Asa Abell had joined. Of this likewise remarkable man, Bishop Hogue declared, "He was great in body, great in intellect, great in soul. He was great as a preacher and as a writer. He was a deep and original thinker." [21] Levi Wood was to become the founder of *The Free Methodist*.

Another seasoned recruit was the Rev. Dr. A. F. Curry, formerly a medical practitioner and later a preacher of the Genesee Conference of the M. E. Church. He had withdrawn from the Methodist ministry and established a Congregational Free Methodist Church at Allegany, but in 1860 joined the Genesee Conference of the Free Methodist Church, bringing with him most of his congregation. He was made chairman of the Allegany District.

The Rev. C. D. Brooks and 160 laymen had left the M. E. Church in Genesee about the time of the Pekin Convention, and a few months thereafter came into the Free Methodist Church as a body.

---

19. F. W. Conable, *History of the Genesee Annual Conference*. Nelson & Phillips, N.Y.; p. 691.
20. For extensive quotations from this letter, see "A voice from 1862," by L. R. Marston in *The Free Methodist*, v. 90, Oct. 18, 1957; p. 649.
21. W. T. Hogue, *History of the Free Methodist Church*; v. 1, 244.

These accessions of capable and experienced ministers, and in some cases their parishioners, who had escaped the purge but had nevertheless made their deliberate decision to join forces with the Free Methodist Church, were a great encouragement and source of strength to the young but vigorous child among the denominations.

Editorial greetings to the new church

Shortly after the Pekin Convention, the *Northern Independent* carried an editorial acknowledgment of the organization of the Free Methodist Church, conceding that whereas the group had been hopelessly barred from the Methodist Episcopal Church, "and were compelled to provide for themselves nothing less was to be expected." [22] A statement appeared in another issue a few weeks later which, without naming the new church, pointed out that those severed from the M. E. Church "will not be lost to the Church general." [23] The editor said further:

> Those expelled ones are so many sparks struck out to kindle new fires, and thus enlarge the sphere of evangelical operation. God will use these men, so strangely separated from their brethren, for His own glory—they are clay in His hand, out of which He will make vessels unto honor. It is yet too early to comprehend the results of such an unusual providence as that which has set these men adrift, but we may rest assured that He who "makes all things work together for good to them that love Him," will overrule these seemingly adverse movements to beneficent ends.

The purpose of the following chapters is to trace God's working of good through the Free Methodist Church over the course of a century.

---

22. *Northern Independent*, v. 5, Sept. 6, 1860.
23. *Ibid.*, v. 5, Oct. 25, 1860.

Chapter Sixteen

Doctrinal Integrity

This chapter and the four following trace the issues of Free Methodism's origin through the church's first century to assess its faithfulness in maintaining its founding principles. These principles have been stated earler in this account as having to do with (1) doctrine, (2) experience, (3) worship, (4) piety, and (5) stewardship. The present chapter traces the record of Free Methodist doctrine.

Doctrinal emphases in Free Methodism's beginnings

That doctrine was important in the minds of the founders of the Free Methodist Church has been disclosed in the record of events leading to the organization of the church, and in the founders' adding two doctrines to the Articles of Religion inherited from Wesley through the parent church, namely, the doctrines of future rewards and punishment and of entire sanctification.

In 1854, six years before the organization of the church, a book had been published in western New York in which the author, after discussing the doctrines of the Methodist Episcopal Church as embodied in its Articles of Religion, proceeded to consider the four important creedal points of Methodism not included therein, but clearly taught in standard Methodist writings. These four doctrines were, (1) the witness of the Spirit; (2) the sanctification of believers; (3) the possibility of falling from grace; and (4) eternal rewards and punishment.[1]

Members of the Pekin Convention who revised the Articles for the new church may well have been acquainted with this treatise, and have received from it the idea of extending the Articles of Religion for the new church to cover (2) and (4). But why, then, did they not include (1) and (3), which they fully accepted and which the church for a century since has never questioned? They knew that Methodist standards of doctrine had included, other than the Articles,

---

1. P. D. Gorrie, *Episcopal Methodism As It Was and Is*. Miller, Orton & Mulligan, Auburn, N.Y.

Wesley's fifty-two doctrinal sermons and his *Explanatory Notes Upon the New Testament*. Perhaps they were content to let this new child of Methodism proceed on a similar basis, except for the two doctrines of eternal rewards and punishment and of entire sanctification which, for reasons of contemporary urgency, they would protect by placing them in the formally stated Articles of Religion.

Other than the second-crisis emphasis of Free Methodism's article on entire sanctification, Free Methodist doctrines, even as the doctrines of historic Methodism set forth in its Articles, are the common tenets of evangelical Arminianism. These have met with little question and no serious challenge among Free Methodists during the entire century. From the event of its founding, the touchstone of Free Methodism's doctrinal integrity has been its faithfulness to the Wesleyan witness to entire sanctification as a distinct work of grace.

Roberts' leadership in holiness doctrine

The character and abilities of B. T. Roberts provide a context in which to evaluate his competence for leadership of a movement to renew and maintain the crucial doctrine of Christian holiness. Earlier pages have recorded his career as an honors student in Wesleyan University, where he shared scholarship distinctions with such men as William C. Kendall and Daniel Steele, and later as a young pastor who rapidly rose in the ranks of the Genesee Conference to a prominent pastorate.

Mention has been made also of Roberts' able editorship of the monthly magazine, *The Earnest Christian*, of which he was likewise owner and publisher for more than three decades. This journal had wide circulation, which it merited on the basis of its attractive format; its competent contributors who wrote on a wide variety of topics—doctrine, devotion, practical godliness, revival news on the worldfront, biography, reform; its content further enriched by excerpts and longer reprints of some of the very best of the Christian classics; and its general editorial excellence.

The maiden issue of January, 1860, carried this declaration of editorial policy: "We shall endeavor to keep free from controversy, and to avoid all offensive personalities. We hope never to infringe upon the sacred right of private judgment." This was a high standard, indeed, for a magazine pledged to such emotionally charged causes as religious revival on Bible lines of conversion and Christian holiness, and to unpopular reforms. The preceding chapter recorded an example of the editor's success in maintaining this standard, even under severe personal stress when he could have used the columns of his magazine in self-defense and in sharp criticism of his ecclesiastical enemies.

The successive issues of *The Earnest Christian* displayed an editorial dignity, a graciousness of spirit, and a literary quality in character with Roberts' desire, expressed as follows in the magazine's first issue:

> We hope by our catholic spirit, by an uncompromising advocacy of "righteousness, peace and joy in the Holy Spirit," to make our magazine a favorite and welcome visitor to every family where pure religion and morality are inculcated.

The new magazine was highly acclaimed by secular and religious exchanges alike, both as to content and appearance.

As writer and preacher B. T. Roberts was logical in thought, forceful in style and manner, terse and pungent in phrasing. His aim was to simplify and elucidate profound themes rather than to dazzle and mystify by a display of learning. Writing Mrs. Roberts, he reported on one occasion the help of the Spirit in his morning preaching, but said, "In the evening there was too much learning and too little salvation." [2]

A. B. Hyde in his well-known account of Methodism said, "He was a brilliant and effective speaker, and a concise, clear, energetic writer," [3] and N. S. Gould in the *Cyclopedia of Biblical, Theological and Ecclesiastical Literature* characterized him as "a writer of considerable power" whose "editorials, tracts, and essays display argumentative ability, and the faculty of uttering truth concisely." [4]

In his recent book referred to in Chapter Nine, Timothy L. Smith makes a significant observation concerning the doctrinal sanity of Roberts—the more significant because Smith is by no means prejudiced in favor of Roberts and early Free Methodism. Smith answers

---

2. B. H. Roberts, *Benjamin Titus Roberts*. Earnest Christian Office, North Chili, N.Y.; p. 469.
3. A. B. Hyde, *The Story of Methodism*. M. W. Hazen Co., New York; p. 319.
4. N. S. Gould, "Free Methodists," in *Cyclopedia of Biblical, Theological and Ecclesiastical Literature*, Harper & Bros., New York; v. 6, pp. 187-189.

the official Methodist version of the Genesee controversy which, he says, "alleged that the holiness leaders were fanatics," with the assertion, "Roberts' later writings on the doctrine of sanctification were certainly far from fanatical. They emphasized the ideal of perfect character, toward which he believed perfect love and all other authentic religious experiences tend."[5]

Such was the man who set the pattern for the Free Methodist Church, the doctrinal *motif* of which pattern he developed in his publications, principally *The Earnest Christian*. Immediately after Roberts' death his son compiled thirty-eight articles on themes related to Christian holiness that had flowed from his father's pen onto the pages of *The Earnest Christian* within the period 1860 to 1893, and published these articles as a book under the title, *Holiness Teachings*.

Smith cites this book as his source on B. T. Roberts' views of sanctification. Apparently he missed the fact that the book represents Roberts' views covering a third of a century, and not alone his later years.

The following section draws upon *Holiness Teachings* for representative features of Roberts' doctrinal concepts of entire sanctification and related themes. Chapter Seventeen will deal primarily with Christian experience, but Roberts' treatment of doctrine is so practical that we must encroach at points upon the sphere of experience in this chapter likewise.

Holiness Teachings[6]

1. *Holiness begins in regeneration and is consummated in entire sanctification.*

Roberts made clear the beginnings of sanctification or holiness in the newborn Christian but, unlike Zinzendorf's claim that all is received in regeneration, he maintained with Wesley that the process of sanctification is consummated in a second event of entire sanctification. Roberts wrote:

Many appear to think that they can possess saving grace with-

---

5. T. L. Smith, *Revivalism and Social Reform*. Abingdon Press, Nashville; p. 131.
6. The page references in this section are citations to B. T. Roberts' *Holiness Teachings*. Earnest Christian Publishing House, North Chili, N.Y. Paragraph divisions of *Holiness Teachings* are not always maintained in the portions here quoted.

out any measure of holiness. This is a fundamental error. When God forgives, he says, with power, "Go, sin no more." Such a change is wrought, instantaneously, in the moral nature of one whom God forgives, that from that moment he has power over his sinful appetites and passions. We must never lose sight of the great truth that "He that committeth sin is of the devil."—I John 3:8.... An unwashed sinner, wallowing in his sins, is not justified. When forgiven he is sanctified not only in the sense of consecrated—that is set apart to do God's will—but in the sense of made holy.... From being a sinner he has become, in an important sense, a holy man.... He is so far sanctified that he has power over sin.... Sin does not have dominion over him as it once did. But he feels sinful tendencies remaining in his heart. He has, at times, to repress pride, to keep it down. He does not yield to anger, but sometimes he feels it, and suppresses it. He comes to God, confesses and bewails these inbred sins and is cleansed from them.... He is sanctified wholly. (p. 138 *et seq.*)

Thus did Roberts explain the Wesleyan distinction between conversion, with its initial sanctification whereby the Christian receives power to live without committing sin, and the consummation of entire sanctification whereby the corrupting inner impulses to sin are cleansed away and the Christian is enabled to love God from a pure heart, and his neighbor as he loves himself.

By holding to this fact of an initial sanctification of the newly converted Christian, Roberts has denied a "sinning religion" to the first stage of the Christian life, unlike some holiness teachers in their efforts to magnify the later stage. Nor did Roberts, while holding to an initial holiness of the believer, make the highest degree of holiness a state of absolute perfection. "Some," he said, "make holiness comprise attributes which are entirely beyond the reach of a human being in our present condition. They give a meaning to the term which the Scriptures do not warrant," and "make no allowance for lack of judgment or imperfect training." (p. 18.)

   2. *Entire sanctification is the full cleansing of man's nature and his complete surrender of every power and passion to the Spirit's control, so that all his motives are promptings of perfect love toward God and all men.*

Roberts followed the traditional Wesleyan interpretation of entire sanctification, which term expresses the cleansing phase of complete holiness, even as the term perfect love expresses the positive. He employed the terms synonymously, although they differ in connotation.

Roberts held that entire sanctification is more than a change in one's standing with God, more than the achievement of excellence through long practice of good behavior. He maintained that it is a radical change at the core of a man's being, supernaturally wrought by the Holy Spirit. Accordingly he wrote:

> But, that sanctification is not merely a change in our condition or relation but also a change in our nature, in our character and conduct, the Scriptures plainly teach. (p. 176.)
>
> It is the work of the Holy Spirit. No education however Scriptural, no training however religious, can produce it. He who is truly holy is sanctified by the Holy Ghost. (p. 159.)
>
> No matter how much refinement or self-government a man may acquire by discipline—this self-control is not true holiness. Some of the old heathen philosophers lived according to the most rigid rules of morality. Here is found one fault of much that is taught for holiness in these days. It strives to make men *do better*, without telling them how to *be better*. It lays great stress upon their doing holy things, without insisting on their being holy. (p. 22.)

Roberts was specific in naming evil propensities of the regenerated but unsanctified man, from which he must be cleansed if he is to have the mind that was in Christ. Note a few crisp statements, each expressing the theme of a chapter in *Holiness Teachings*: "Holiness implies deliverance from pride. . . . Pride cannot dwell in a holy soul." (p. 35.) "Holiness implies deliverance from selfishness. A selfish person cannot, at the same time, be a holy person. (p. 40.) "Holiness implies deliverance from all hatred of any human being." (p. 52.) "Scriptural holiness implies hatred of sin." (p. 59.)

Such propensities to pride, selfishness, hatred of enemies, love for pet sins, are commonly recognized as evidences of lingering carnality in the Christian; but Roberts does not call the unsanctified "carnally minded," a term which stands in the Scriptures for spiritual death (Rom. 8:6), when in fact the unsanctified Christian has spiritual life. Roberts would grant, however, that the unsanctified Christian is "carnal," that is, has lingering roots of bitterness "along side the new life" (to use another's figure). Let Roberts speak for himself, first of the sinner, who is carnally minded and therefore spiritually dead:

> A man has but one mind, one intellect, one soul. He may have many thoughts, inclinations, and purposes. If he is in his natural state, unrenewed by the grace of God, his mind taken up with worldly thoughts, and plans, and purposes, he is *carnally minded,*—in a state of spiritual death. (p. 241)

Then of one not sanctified wholly:

> If he has been duly converted to God, his mind is taken up with spiritual things. Whatever may engage his attention for the time, God is never lost sight of in all his plans and purposes. The bent of his mind is toward God. . . . But if, while he is devoted to Christ on the whole, he at the same time is partisan in his spirit, . . . he is in a measure carnal, though still a babe in Christ.
>
> "And I, brethren, could not speak unto you as unto spiritual, but as unto carnal, even as unto babes in Christ." "For ye are yet carnal: for whereas there is among you envying, and strife, and divisions, are ye not carnal, and walk as men?"—I Cor. 3:1, 3.
>
> But as they were not wholly given up to this spirit of strife and division, they had not yet reached the state of being *carnally minded*—that is, a state of death, though they were on their way to it. (p. 242)

He describes the entirely sanctified:

> If one is sanctified wholly his mind, his will, is so changed that earthly things lose their attraction, and he sets his affections on things above, not on things in the earth. Such persons follow the Lord fully. But their minds are not destroyed. The "carnal mind" is never so destroyed as to do away with the freedom of the will. (p. 242)

In the last sentence Roberts can easily be misunderstood, and although Roberts was seldom less than clear, we must agree at this point with Smith that his terminology is confused. One familiar with the total context of the sentence and with the book's consistent insistence upon full deliverance from sin, will understand that Roberts was pleading for no least remain of carnality in the sanctified personality. Taken with a sentence quoted earlier, "A man has but one mind, one intellect, one soul," the perplexing portion means that the "carnal mind" is not an entity which, through any operation of divine grace, is replaced by another mind-entity unrelated to the former. Such a condition is found, it is true, in abnormal cases of dual or multiple personality in which the earlier mind is dissociated and another mind with different aims, different likes and dislikes and even different moral purposes, takes over without the faintest memory of the former self.

In other words, Roberts intended to convey the truth that the mind which develops from birth, and spiritually speaking is dead until grace has infused spiritual life, is the same mind one possesses after the entire sanctification of the nature, and retains its identity throughout all the natural and spiritual changes of existence. His point, certainly a valid and an important one, could better have been made by some such fuller statement as we have here attempted:

> If one is sanctified wholly, his mind, his will, is so changed that earthly things lose their attraction, and he sets his affections on things above, not on things in the earth. Such a person follows the Lord fully. But his mind as the conscious core of his abiding existence, endowed with freedom of moral choice, was not destroyed in the sanctification of his nature to be replaced by a new mind that could do only right. Rather, the evil propensities of that mind were cleansed by the Spirit of God, and the inner conflict of good and evil impulses was resolved by his full choice of righteousness, bringing moral harmony into all areas of his heart and life.

But Roberts would have revised his statement with fewer words!

3. *The holiness of the entirely sanctified may be replaced by corrupting tendencies to sin again invading the nature, and these inner propensities may lead to the outward transgressions of a backslidden state.*

What Roberts said immediately following the perplexing statement noted under "2" above, confirms the interpretation and amplification attempted in our revision. He warned against a Christian's assuming that, once entirely sanctified, he will be rid of the possibility of sin, and drives home the fact that even with sinful propensities removed, the dangerous possibility of sin remains. Here is the caution:

> There is need to constantly watch and pray. Things that may be lawful in themselves may easily be run to sinful excess. The love that begins in the Spirit may end in the flesh. Eating "their meat with gladness" may degenerate into a desire for luxuries. "Diligence in business" may easily run into a love of the world. Even a fixed determination "to follow the Lord fully" may unconsciously slide into a consecration to one's own will, so that those

will be fellowshipped who indorse us and our methods, and those who do not will be unchristianized. (p. 243.)

Thus Roberts was clear on the possibility of an entirely sanctified person's reversion to an unsanctified and even a completely backslidden condition, a conclusion John Wesley reached after an initial period in which he held to the security of the entirely sanctified from all dangers of lapse. Here is a bit of Roberts' terse logic:

> Holiness is voluntary. It is a moral state. But a moral action implies freedom of choice.... Therefore a holy person is holy from choice.
>
> But a voluntary state may be lost. The helm that can be turned in a right direction can also be turned in a wrong direction.
>
> One who has walked in the way of holiness for a season, may yield to temptation and turn aside.... It is evident then, that one who has experienced the blessing of holiness, can lose it. He need not; he should not—but still he may. (p. 134 *et seq.*)

Roberts maintained that a man who loses the blessing of holiness through giving way to doubts concerning his experience or through failure to bear witness to the cleansing grace of God may still remain justified if he has not fallen into sin.

> He may still truly love God and faithfully endeavor to keep His commandments. Such a person in losing the blessing of holiness has not lost his justification. He is still a child of God. He is sensible of what he has lost and strives to regain it. To do this it is not necessary that he should throw up all profession of religion and begin anew. He is not unholy; but he is holy only in part. He should pray to be sanctified wholly. (136 *et seq.*)

With one who has committed sin in open disobedience it is different, for:

> When one falls into actual sin he loses both justification and sanctification. He falls into condemnation. He is no longer a saint; he becames a sinner. If he gets back to God, he must come confessing like any other sinner. (p. 155 *et seq.*)

Although doing so carries us rather far afield from the consideration of doctrine, this seems the appropriate point to quote the following sane advice Roberts gave on dealing with those who have lost ground in their Christian experience:

> It is not best, unnecessarily, to discourage those who have lost some of the grace they once enjoyed. When they are on their

backs the way to recover them is not to cut off their heads. Encourage them to hold fast that which they have, and to seek for more.... Be more ready to build up than to tear down. To lead on than to drive back. (p. 141 *et seq.*)

The present writer ventures the suggestion that failure to follow this counsel may account for much of the "altar turn-over" of holiness revivalism within Free Methodism and in other groups.

4. *The process of sanctification, either initial or entire, does not make a man one whit less human.*

Roberts held and taught no strained view of a grace that eradicates from human nature any essentially human quality or trait with which God endowed it in creation. His view is in accord with Wesley's claim that Christian meekness "does not destroy but balances the affections, which the God of nature never designed should be rooted out by grace, but only brought and kept under due regulations."[7] Following are excerpts from Roberts:

> Holiness implies *deliverance from all wrong dispositions, tempers, and desires;* and from all inclinations to indulge those that are right, in an unlawful manner, or to an inordinate degree. There are dispositions of the soul that are wrong in themselves, such as *anger, pride, and covetousness*.... Other desires become sinful only when indulged in an unlawful manner, or to an inordinate degree. (p. 3.)

> The natural appetites were given us for a good purpose. They are not in themselves sinful.... They are to be brought into subjection to reason, to conscience, and the word of God. No holy person can be under the dominion of appetite. (p. 45)

> The bodily appetites undergo a great transformation. Those that are unnatural are removed. Those that are natural and right within proper limits are subdued and brought into subjection to reason and conscience. The reins of government have passed from the carnal to the spiritual. He is still in the body, but not in the flesh. The flesh no longer dominates and controls. A blessed harmony prevails throughout his entire being. One thus saved is no longer at war with himself. (p. 222 *et seq.*)

The following paragraph is of a kind with Wesley's observation that, "It is not possible to avoid all pleasure, even of sense, without destroying the body. Neither doth God require it at our hands; it is

---

7. J. Wesley, *Sermons on Special Occasion.* Phillips & Hunt, New York; v. 1, 188.

not his will concerning us," but, "On the contrary, he 'giveth us all things to enjoy,' so we enjoy them to his glory." [8] Here is Roberts' version:

> The second great command is, "Thou shalt love thy neighbor as thyself."—Matt. 19:19. This certainly supposes that we are, within proper limits, to love ourselves. The Scriptures not only allow, but command us, to have a due regard for our own happiness. Every promise of the Bible is based upon the principle that it is right for us, within proper limitations, to pursue our own welfare.... Self-love is a principle which God gave man for his own preservation: selfishness is the sinful substitute which man at the fall adopted. The one is the alcohol which maddens: the other is the corn that gives strength, and the delicious grape that gives health to man. (p. 41.)

Some of these quoted fragments disclose that there is in the teachings of Roberts no hint of that asceticism which holds the body to be essentially evil and needing to be cudgeled into submission or —an even worse fanaticism—allowed to run its own course into excess of riot because disowned by the soul which claims no responsibility for the sins of the body. A further hint of Roberts' breadth of interests, so necessary to stabilize earnest devotion against narrow zeal, is the following from his pen:

> The truly devout also take delight in ascertaining the will of God as shown in the physical laws by which our bodies and other material substances are governed. A lover of God is likely to be a lover of nature. (p. 76.)

5. *The core principle of holiness is perfect love to God and man.*

With John Wesley, Roberts places love at the center, seeking its expression upward to God and outward to others. This centrality of love has been emphasized in previous paragraphs, but further emphasis will re-enforce the principle.

> We have seen that there can be no true holiness without the love of God. Neither can there be without love for our fellow men. The two are joined together. (p. 85.)

> The holy Spirit will enable us to hate sin, and love the sinner. It will make us kind to them, but not indulgent to their faults. Holiness is not blind. It has eyes as well as heart. It never mis-

---
8. J. Wesley, *Works* (Jackson 3rd ed.); v. 11, 461 *et seq.*

takes darkness for light. To one who has true holiness it is not hard to obey the command, "If thine enemy hunger, feed him; if he thirst, give him drink; for in so doing thou shalt heap coals of fire on his head."—Rom. 12:20. (p. 89.)

In the statement below, Roberts brings to mind the claim of Wesley that the man of God, as "a citizen of the world," is "not unconcerned in the welfare of any man." Roberts put the truth this way:

A holy person feels a lively interest in the well-being of his fellow men. His heart is large—it takes in mankind. His arms are long—they carry assistance to the perishing in the ends of the earth. (p. 85.)

Again and again, in presenting the many facets of holiness in its applications to life, Roberts hinged the same in love, and it is in the realm of love that we encounter the realizable perfection of entire holiness or entire sanctification. Roberts was very clear at this point.

"Be ye therefore perfect, even as your Father which is in heaven is perfect."—Matt. 5:48. This is a plain command. But many err in supposing that this perfection is one of knowledge or of judgment. It is no such thing. In this sense God only is perfect. The perfection which God requires is a perfection of love.

In many things we are necessarily imperfect, and always shall be. But, by the grace of God, we may become perfect in love. Our capacity for this kind of perfection does not depend upon our talents or our circumstances. He who has but one dollar can give all the money he has, just as well as he who has a million. I can love God with all *my* heart; an angel can love God with no more than with all *his* heart. . . . Whatever our defects, we may have the "love of God shed abroad in our hearts by the Holy Ghost given unto us."—Rom. 5:5. When this is the case—when we love God with all the heart, mind and strength, and our neighbor as ourselves—then have we perfect love. Not that it is incapable of increase. As our capacities enlarge, our love will increase, but as we now are we can do no better; and it is accepted according to what a man hath, and not according to what he hath not. (p. 213 *et seq.*)

Is not this "perfect love" what is meant by Christian perfection? In part, yes; but the term "perfect love" does not exhaust the meaning of the term Christian perfection. According to Roberts, the two terms are not synonymous, as he makes clear in quotations under "6" following.

6. *"Christian perfection" is a broader term than "entire sanctification" or "perfect love," applicable to any stage of a sincere Christian's development toward full maturity.*

We reach here a point in which Roberts diverges from the traditional Wesleyan usage of terms describing progress in grace toward "the measure of the stature of the fullness of Christ." Much of the confusion over the term "Christian perfection" in Wesley's time (and since!) might have been avoided had Wesley maintained the clear distinction in terms that Roberts made a century later. To guard against misunderstanding Roberts, we permit him to speak at length.

Roberts held that the Biblical command to be perfect refers not to any specific step in the Christian life, but to its every phase and stage. He said:

> The command "be perfect," does not express any well known, definite act like the command "repent"; nor any particular experience like being "born again." It is taken in a wider sense; with a greater latitude of meaning. It applies to a child of God in various stages of his experience. A blade of corn may be said to be perfect in a dozen different stages of its growth. But if, before it is ripe, it stopped growing, it would not be perfect. So, at a certain period of his experience, a person may be said to be a perfect Christian, and yet his attainments in piety be small in comparison with what they are after years of toil and sorrow. (p. 209 *et seq.*)

He illustrated further by drawing upon the increasing perfection of the intellectual powers, which may be perfect at one stage but reach higher perfections with growth and discipline:

> A young man leaves the district school for the academy. He has studied hard and begins to reap some of its fruits. The teacher, proud of his pupil, says: "He is perfect in his mathematics. He can solve every problem in the hardest arithmetic." After three years in the academy with a lesson every day in mathematics, he is sent to college, recommended as "perfect in mathematics." He is well versed in algebra, geometry and trigonometry. After studying mathematics in college four years, having completed his course, he graduates with the highest honors of the mathematical department. He then goes to some special school and spends perhaps three more years in studying mathematics as applied to astronomy or to civil engineering. Then again he is

pronounced perfect in his well-mastered study. At the close of a life of unremitting study, we hear him say with the immortal Sir Isaac Newton, "I seem like a child standing upon the shore of the ocean gathering pebbles. I have picked up here and there a pearl, while the great ocean of truth lies unexplored before me." (p. 210.)

And now his pointed application:

So when one becomes a Christian his conversion may be perfect; when his heart is purified by faith he may be perfectly sanctified; and still after years of growth in grace we hear him saying with Job when he got a sight of God, "Wherefore I abhor myself and repent in dust and ashes." Yet God had twice pronounced him perfect. (p. 210 *et seq.*)

Thus Roberts would show that Christian perfection is not a definite step to be taken by faith, as regeneration or entire sanctification, but is a continuous process involving day by day obedience and discipline. And therefore:

We must not confound the perfection which the Gospel requires with perfect love or entire sanctification. The Scriptures do not use these terms as synonymous. (p. 212.)

And further:

We never read in the Bible of any being made perfect by faith. We read of persons being "justified by faith."—Rom. 9:30; Rom. 5:1; Gal. 3:24; "Sanctified by faith."—Acts 15:9; Acts 26:18; but never once a person being made perfect by faith. Quite another element enters into the making of the saints perfect. "For it became him, for whom are all things, and by whom are all things, in bringing many sons into glory, to make the captain of their salvation perfect through sufferings."—Heb. 2:10. (p. 211.)

The final perfection of the Christian is no instantaneous gift of God's grace to be obtained alone by the prayer of faith, but the lifetime process of a ripening Christian character. In his late maturity Wesley had said there are two ways "wherein it pleases God to lead his children to perfection: doing and suffering." [9] It therefore follows, as Roberts declared:

We are not to seek Christian perfection so much by praying for it as a blessing to be received in an instant of faith, as by "patient continuance in well-doing." We are to seek it as a well-

---

9. J. Wesley, *Letters*.

disposed boy seeks a vigorous manhood by shunning the vices and overcoming the temptations to which he is exposed, and by doing faithfully the duties to which he is called. (p. 212.)

From this viewpoint, Christian perfection is not static, something given once for all, a state in which the Christian placidly rests; it is a conquest, achieved through faithful service and patient endurance. Roberts warned:

> We must not conclude that we shall by any natural process grow out of our imperfections and become perfect Christians, without any special effort in that direction. (p. 212.)

In leaving this feature of Roberts' teaching, we call attention to an observation made by a recent author who has caught a glimpse in Wesley's *Plain Account* of the same concept of Christian perfection that was developed by Roberts. In Wesley's summary of his position he affirmed concerning Christian perfection:

> It is improvable. It is so far from lying in an indivisible point, from being incapable of increase, that one perfected in love may grow in grace far swifter than he did before.[10]

John L. Peters says that in this statement, "Wesley implies a distinction which he generally fails to maintain . . . between entire sanctification as an event and Christian perfection as a continuing process of which that event is a part." Peters further asserts that here Wesley "displays one of the most significant, *and neglected*, facets of his teaching." [11]

The present writer questions if Wesley was as clear even in his own thinking as is Peters in his terse statement or Roberts in his fuller development of the distinction, else he would have made it as clear in words as have they, and thus have ended much of the agitating discussion and pointless criticism his use of the term "Christian perfection" as synonymous with "entire sanctification" and "perfect love" has provoked.

A distinction in terms, not doctrine

The distinction between Wesley and Roberts concerning entire sanctification and Christian perfection is not one of doctrine but of

---
10. J. Wesley, *A Plain Account of Christian Perfection*, Epworth Press, London; p. 106.
11. J. L. Peters, *Christian Perfection and American Methodism*. Abingdon Press, Nashville; p. 52.

terms, this difference, however, having a direct bearing upon the clarity of doctrine and its meaning in experience. The difference between the two may most clearly be stated in terms of II Corinthians 7:1, ". . . let us cleanse ourselves from all filthiness of the flesh and spirit, perfecting holiness in the fear of God." For both Wesley and Roberts, the cleansing is consummated in cleanness, a finished act as signified by the aorist tense of "cleanse" *(katharisomen)* used in the Greek. For both of them this cleansing meant the removal of everything contrary to perfect love in the Christian's heart. This event of cleansing is the negative aspect of the positive possession of the heart by naught but love which, while perfect in quality, increases in degree and in breadth of its application to wider and wider areas of life's relationships as the Christian follows the exhortation of Peter to "grow in grace, and in the knowledge of our Lord and Saviour Jesus Christ." (II Peter 3:18.)

For both Wesley and Roberts, then, beyond the event of complete cleansing which they called "entire sanctification" and its positive corollary which they called "perfect love," there is in the normal course of Christian experience a continuous progress in holiness toward final completeness, the present participle for "perfecting" *(epitelountes)* being used in II Corinthians 7:1. This final completeness is that perfection of eternity when the Christian shall come "unto a perfect man, unto the measure of the stature of the fulness of Christ." (Ephesians 4:13.)

The difference between Wesley and Roberts lies in the latter's explicit recognition of what is implicit in Wesley's teaching, that the progression of the Christian life toward complete and final perfection in the glorified state may properly be called "Christian perfection" at any stage of the Christian's walk in full obedience and faith. Roberts teaches no doctrine of "gradualism" that denies the crisis of entire sanctification and the full possession of the nature by perfect love. On the contrary, he is most emphatic concerning the crisis nature of the cleansing. But he does make clear the unbroken progression that should characterize the newly converted Christian's growth to the mature saint, and its further continuance to final completeness in the resurrection, by his applying the term Christian perfection, not as beginning with a particular crisis, but as belonging to every stage of the Christian's walk of full obedience and faith toward the final perfection of the fully redeemed.

These six approaches to Roberts' teachings on holiness, although incompletely developing his concepts, make it abundantly clear that he was in the Wesleyan tradition, but not so strait-jacketed thereby that his logic could make no refinements in terms, or his constructive thinking reach no new insights. Smith was right when he denied all evidence of fanaticism in Roberts' holiness teachings, and characterized them as emphasizing "the ideal of perfect character, toward which he believed perfect love and all other authentic religious experiences tend." [12]

Changes in the Discipline relating to doctrine[13]

Articles of Religion. The official acts and opinions of the church in the area of doctrine began with the adoption of the Articles of Religion in the Pekin Convention of 1860. Only minor changes have been made in these Articles in the course of a century. In 1870 the word "merely" as a modifier of "justified" in the beginning of Article xiii was dropped, as noted in the preceding chapter. In 1874, "enabling" was substituted for "preventing" as modifier of "grace" in Article viii. This in no wise changed the meaning of the Article, but made it more intelligible to that generation—and ours. Also in 1874, the proposal was made to delete Article xxiii, "Of a Christian man's oath," but it failed to carry. However, this effort led to the Article's modification so that at present a footnote declares that the Article does not bar from membership those with conscientious scruples against the taking of an oath under the authority of the state. In 1882 the proposal to substitute for "reconcile his Father to us," the words "effect reconciliation between God and man" in Article ii was deferred for action to four years later, and then it failed to carry.

These few changes, largely editorial in nature, and these few unsuccessful efforts to change the Articles, have left the basic, constitutional doctrines of the church quite undisturbed throughout the church's first century.

---

12. T. L. Smith, *Revivalism and Social Reform.* Abingdon Press, Nashville; p. 131.
13. The numbers of paragraphs cited in the *Discipline* are not given. The interested reader should be able to locate a desired paragraph by means of the table of contents or the index of the *Discipline* for the edition indicated.

But doctrinal trends in the church may be reflected in actions of the General Conference in no wise altering the Articles of Religion, such as amending other sections of the *Discipline*, principally the ritual, the membership covenant, and the regulations governing the educational institutions of the church. Unlike changes in the Articles, which require concurrent action by the annual conferences, these sections may be changed by action of General Conference alone.

Ritual. The earliest changes in the *Discipline* bearing on doctrine had largely to do with the ritual, especially the Lord's Supper and baptism. A church's ritual involves both its worship and its doctrine, but the changes attempted in the ritual of early Free Methodism reflected more a doctrinal than a devotional concern. Most efforts to change the ritual, successful and unsuccessful, have had little crucial bearing upon serious questions of doctrine.

Changes in the ritual of the Lord's Supper were first proposed in the second General Conference, that of 1866. This body refused to remove the rubrics accompanying the prayer of consecration, or to delete the prayer for forgiveness, the collect, and the prayer of humble access. Again in 1878 unsuccessful efforts were made to delete the general confession and the prayer for forgiveness. The nature of the proposed deletions suggests that the objectors may have been seeking to remove from the service of Communion principally those elements which give it significance as a channel of grace and a converting ordinance, leaving in the service its memorial and confirming features. The rubrics accompanying the consecration of the elements may have seemed to some to incline to high-church ritual. The confession of unforgiven and uncleansed sin and the plea for forgiveness could well have been objectionable as in seeming conflict with the church's profession of the standard of holiness. Nevertheless, the young church held to its pattern of practice and belief against those whose Christian fervor would go beyond the restraints of historic Methodism, and of its founder who had said that, "the most perfect have continual need of the merits of Christ, even for their actual transgressions, and may say, for themselves, as well as for their brethren, 'Forgive us our trespasses.' "[14]

But changes in the Communion ritual were made in the General

---

14. J. Wesley, *Plain Account*; p. 43.

Conference of 1882. The invitation to the Lord's table was modified by substituting for "Ye that do truly and earnestly repent of your sins . . .," the words, "Ye that do truly present the sacrifice of a broken and contrite heart . . . ." For a series of Scripture passages was substituted an address by the elder on the authority, gracious preservation and meaning of the ordinance. This Conference also deleted the general confession and substituted the Lord's Prayer.

But the following General Conference (1886) struck from the ritual the elder's address and restored the invitation to its historic wording. This Conference further restored the general confession, permitting the elder to choose it or the Lord's Prayer. It amended the prayer of humble access by substituting for the clause, "that our sinful souls and bodies may be made clean by his death," the words, "that we may ever live and grow thereby." After holding firm against radical changes in the ritual for a quarter-century, the church now began to revise the stronger suggestions of a "sinning religion" to meet a reasonable standard of holiness.

In 1898 the instructions to the elder on guarding the table were moderated in a measure to make immorality and disreputable practices the bar against admission to the Communion, rather than all unchristian practices that disqualified one for membership in the Free Methodist Church.

In 1907 the general confession was amended by substituting for "our manifold sins and wickedness," the words, "the manifold sins and wickedness of our past lives"; and the word "past" was inserted in the phrase, "for these our misdoings," [15] These also were changes justified by the church's holiness witness. Proposals for other changes in the ritual of the Lord's Supper were rejected by this Conference, and no further changes therein, other than editorial, have been made during the past half-century.

The church has offered less resistance to changes in the ritual of baptism than in the ritual of the Communion. In 1866 an examination of parents presenting children for baptism was introduced, and a vow by the parents was required. In 1882 a solemn passage was deleted from the same ritual which had stressed the child's inherited

---

15. These changes were omitted in the 1907 *Discipline*. The omissions were noted by the 1911 General Conference which ordered again the insertions.

sin and its consequent need of the grace of God if it were not to be led astray; but another revision in the same section made clear that only by being made partaker of the divine nature could the child "grow up into Christ." The amendment's softer phrasing did not blur the doctrine that man can be saved only through Christ.

In 1955 a set of questions was introduced for use in the baptism of children above infancy and below the age of twelve, these questions being more suited to youthful understanding than the questions asked adult candidates. This step expressed the concern, growing in the church in recent years, for Christian conversion and nurture of the young.

The minister's charge to adult candidates was changed in 1882 by striking, "to release you of your sins," probably to emphasize the church's position that baptism is a sign of forgiveness and not its accompanying cause. Proposals to revise the adult ritual in 1907 were rejected, but somewhat extensive revisions were adopted in 1911 which in general indicated more clearly than did the original ritual that baptism witnesses to the inner change of conversion rather than being a means of conversion. By these changes the Free Methodist Church was seeking to resolve the strange inconsistency of John Wesley in whom, at this point at least, high-church influence had tinged with a suggestion of sacerdotalism his otherwise strongly evangelical convictions. Since these changes of 1911, the adult ritual has remained unchanged.

Changes and attempted changes in other areas of the ritual, such as burial of the dead, matrimony, and ordinations, have little relevance for our present concern with the church's doctrine. But before leaving the ritual, we would note the proportionately large space devoted thereto in the early *Disciplines*, which bespeaks the concern of the young church for order in its solemn and contractual acts. The first *Discipline* of 1860 and the second of 1862 gave 30 per cent of their pages to the ritual, and the 1866 *Discipline* gave 36. With organizational growth through the years, the relative emphasis on government and administration necessarily increased, and such interests have required more and more space until only 8 per cent of the pages of the 1955 *Discipline* are required for the ritual. The denominational stability of Free Methodism and its sense of historic church-hood, unusual for a youthful reform movement, no doubt have come in some measure from its strong commitment to church order, both in its ritual and in its fundamental ecclesiastical law.

Changes of the *Discipline* in the membership covenant which bear on the church's doctrinal positions have been few. In 1878 the revisions committee approved substituting for the question asked candidates for full membership, "Have you that perfect love which casteth out fear?" the following: "Have you entire sanctification as taught in Article xiii of our Articles of Religion?" The General Conference rejected the change, but the 1951 General Conference approached the 1878 proposal by adopting this wording: "Have you now the experience of entire sanctification?" Still not satisfied, the 1955 General Conference returned to the original term, "perfect love," and tied the same to Scripture, as follows: "Do you have that perfect love for God and man which is taught in the Holy Scriptures?"

Doctrinal standards for educational institutions. The remaining area in which changes of the *Discipline* concern doctrine is the field of education. The relationships of secondary schools and colleges to the church, and the bearing of the instruction offered therein on Christian belief, came before the General Conference of 1923. It is worthy of note that the church's concern at that time went beyond doctrines related to Christian holiness to include items of basic evanglical faith. The section of the *Discipline* on the schools was changed in 1923 to include the following:

> All instruction in the various departments, particularly in science and the social sciences, shall be positively in harmony with the teachings of the Scriptures as generally interpreted by the Free Methodist Church and set forth in her Discipline, and no textbooks or periodicals shall be adopted for classroom use, the general influence of whose teachings tends to destroy belief in the Bible as the revealed Word of God or to undermine faith in Christ as the divine Son of God and the all-sufficient Savior of the world.
>
> No presidents, principals, professors or teachers shall be employed or retained in our seminaries or colleges who are not in harmony with the above rule, and any, . . . upon evidence of conduct or teaching to the contrary, shall be subject to dismissal.

A further safeguard was established by this General Conference, requiring that two-thirds of the members of the boards of trustees and of the faculties of the church's schools belong to the Free Methodist Church.

In 1935 the declaration concerning textbooks and periodicals quoted above was deleted, but the main principles guiding the schools remained. In 1943 the chapter of the *Discipline* on Christian Education was rewritten, but the doctrinal safeguards of the previous *Discipline* remained except for the omission of the resolution on organic evolution, first adopted in 1923 and covered in essential meaning by the more inclusive declaration requiring all instruction to be in harmony with the teachings of the Scriptures—a requirement that still stands.

The 1943 General Conference directed that all instructors in the theological departments of the schools must sign a statement of agreement with the church's position on the doctrine and experience of entire sanctification, and the *Discipline* of 1947 clarified this stipulation by including the full text of Article xiii (on entire sanctification) in the declaration these instructors must make in affirming their belief in the Wesleyan position.

The foregoing record shows that, with the growth of the church and its educational program, and the melting of barriers of isolation that formerly had protected the young church from the mounting liberalism in theology and secularism in general culture, safeguards to the church's doctrine were sought through General Conference legislation governing church schools. The regulations established seem unwarranted strictures to many in the educational world, but such have been common in the school ventures of minority and pietistic groups throughout America's history. That minority religious and cultural groups shall have freedom to maintain their own religious and educational programs is guaranteed by our democracy; that these groups in turn have made worthy contributions to the American genius is generally acknowledged.

Reports and resolutions on doctrine

Indicating still further the doctrinal alertness of the church are certain resolutions adopted by the General Conference and such official reports to the General Conference as the pastoral messages of the bishops, and the declarations of the committee on the state of the work.¹⁶ Two cases of erroneous teaching also have come before the General Conference for action, and these we report first.

In one hundred years there has been but one appeal to the General Conference from the expulsion of a minister by his annual conference on the charge of erroneous teaching. D. W. Thurston had been a presiding elder in the Oneida Methodist Episcopal Conference during the troubles in Genesee. After the Free Methodist Church was organized he transferred into its Susquehanna Conference and was elected a district chairman. Later he was charged with erroneous teaching and was expelled by his annual conference. He appealed to the 1870 General Conference which sustained the Susquehanna action. However, the alleged "erroneous teaching" involved primarily practical rather than doctrinal matters, and therefore will be reviewed in its bearing on disciplined living in Chapter Nineteen. Strictly speaking, not in one hundred years has the General Conference handled an appeal from the decision of an annual conference against any preacher on specifically doctrinal grounds.

The second case involved both doctrine and practice, but reached the General Conference by another route. Richard Watson Hawkins had been a presiding elder in the Erie Conference of the Methodist Episcopal Church. He was a man of unusual talents who was led into the experience of entire sanctification under Free Methodist influence. Afterward he became a minister of the denomination and in time was elected district chairman in the Pittsburgh Conference. However, confusion resulted from his teaching the redemption of the body in such a way as to lead some into the snare of "spiritual affinity" and into the license naturally following. Hawkins himself vigorously condemned both, the "affinity" and the license. When he published his views in a book, *Redemption, or the Living Way*, his conference memorialized the General Conference, calling in question the teachings of the same. General Conference referred the matter to the committee on the state of the work, which reported portions of the book "unsound, and unscriptural, and consequently misleading and dangerous," and recommended that "its circulation be discountenanced by our people" and that the author withdraw it from sale.

---

16. Reports of the actions of the General Conference in this and following chapters are based upon the unpublished journals of the General Conferences cited.

A minority report by B. T. Roberts was more moderate in its demands. He declared the portions of the book on justification and sanctification "clear and instructive," but the treatment of redemption unscriptural. Even the author's warnings against "spiritual affinity," Roberts said, gave to some readers the impression that the temptations to "spiritual affinity" are especially severe to those in a high state of grace. He recommended that Hawkins insert an appendix which in unequivocal terms should declare against "spiritual affinities," but that, since the church had established no dogma on the translation of the body, the author was not properly subject to ecclesiastical censure for writing *Redemption*. But the majority report prevailed.

Hawkins suffered deeply under this action of the General Conference. Shortly thereafter he transferred to the Wesleyan Methodist Church, was elected its missionary secretary, but soon died.[17] From the copy of *Redemption* in the writer's possession, it appears that Hawkins heeded not the request of the General Conference to withdraw the book from sale, but chose rather to follow B. T. Roberts' minority recommendation; for the copy in hand carries a four-page "tipped-in" folder headed "Appendix." This insert is dated October 31, 1890, two years after the book's publication and less than a month after the General Conference that ruled against the doctrinal soundness of the book. The inserted Appendix, under five points, defends the book as adequately safeguarded against any hint favorable to false affinities, and declares that the author "is positively and unequivocally opposed" to them.

It is noteworthy that a church of such strong doctrinal conservatism has had but these two cases of doctrinal or didactic deviation to come before its General Conference in an entire century.

The 1890 General Conference appointed a committee to prepare a catechism which should incorporate Scripture to support the church's doctrines. Its use was contemplated in the home, the Sunday school and the boarding school. Thus was recognized, albeit belatedly, the importance of formal doctrinal instruction in the early years.

---

17. See W. T. Hogue, *History of the Free Methodist Church*. F. M. Pub. House, Winona Lake; v. 2, 72-75. His account supplements the General Conference Journal.

The pastoral address to the 1894 General Conference urged that, "while we would be severely orthodox, we would do well to remember that orthodoxy cannot inspire and maintain spiritual life, but that our spiritual life must intensify and maintain our orthodoxy." The committee on the state of the work reported, "We do not discover any marked tendencies to depart from the much loved doctrines of Methodism." Such was the verdict after the church had been in existence a third of a century.

Doctrinal integrity was included in the concern, expressed in the bishops' address of 1898, that the church guard the door both to membership and to the ministry in order that Free Methodism might "escape the rocks of formality and worldliness, and pride and false doctrines on which others have wrecked."

According to the bishops' address of 1907, for nearly a half-century the church had "unfalteringly borne faithful testimony through all the land to the great fundamental truths of Christianity, and particularly regarding the privilege and obligation of believers to be sanctified wholly in the present life." The report proceeded further, touching upon contemporary doctrinal issues, saying:

> Moreover, in the midst of prevalent assaults of "higher criticism" upon the integrity and inerrancy of the holy scriptures, and of the consequent decline of faith in the supernaturalism of the Bible so common in many other religious bodies of today, it is a source of great satisfaction to us to know that, so far, Free Methodists unquestionably accept the whole Bible as the inspired Word of God, and maintain in simplicity and incorruptibility their faith in Christianity as a supernatural religion.

The bishops' address of 1939 called for a strong doctrinal orthodoxy as one restraining bank of the church's channel, and a strong piety as the other bank, through which channel the power of the Spirit as a mighty current might be directed to the great end and purpose of the church.[18]

We noted above the move of the 1923 General Conference to bring the colleges into closer relationship to the church, in order to secure which, changes in the *Discipline* were made governing educational institutions. This same Conference also adopted resolu-

---

18. *Our Church in This Age*, Pastoral Address to the 1939 General Conference (a pamphlet).

tions against erroneous teachings in the attempt to fortify the church against contemporary influences opposed to evangelical faith, declaring its "utter dissonance with evolution, theistic and atheistic, Higher Criticism, Materialism, German Rationalism, and the whole trend of modern theology," and pledging resistance to such influences wherever in evidence. The resolutions further approved the efforts of The Honorable William Jennings Bryan and others, "to reestablish public faith in the scriptural account of creation and the origin and development of man."

This was the period of great activity of conservative and fundamentalist forces, and these resolutions placed the Free Methodist Church uncompromisingly in opposition to liberal theology and naturalistic philosophy. But while always strongly conservative in doctrine, the Free Methodist Church has never been characterized in any general sense by the temper of a belligerent fundamentalism.

Millennial doctrine

It is not surprising that Methodism, which holds that the life of God can animate the soul of man here and now, cleansing it from sin and uncleanness in this world, should lay less emphasis on the time schedule of last things than do those who hold to man's inescapable sinfulness in the present dispensation. The latter view at least logically calls for a purgatorial deliverance from sin for believers who escape death by Christ's millennial return. The Methodist movement never has been strongly premillennial and throughout its history the Free Methodist Church has included those who could not accept the premillennial position, even when premillennialism was sweeping through the conservative Christian world in earlier decades of the present century.

The two groups are nearer together now than a few years ago. Few in the church today hold the hope that by its inherent power, apart from the fiat of a Sovereign God, righteousness shall reign and "the earth shall be full of the knowledge of the Lord, as the waters cover the sea." And premillennialists of the church generally have never been so dazzled by the prospect of "Rapture" as to dull their concern for a general judgment; nor have they held that the Holy Spirit will be withdrawn from the earth before Christ comes; nor that there will be a post-tribulation opportunity for sinners to repent after His return.

Those inclining to the premillennial position have generally been moderate in their millennial interpretations, and such today probably comprise the majority of the church on the millennial issue.

In the hundred years of its history the Free Methodist Church has made no specific doctrinal pronouncement on the issue, nor has it been pressed to do so. The church holds firmly to the position that belief in the Lord's return is essential, and both in its Articles of Religion and in its burial ritual places that coming at the last day.[19]

We may not be fully agreed on all the details of a Kingdom that is to come among men, but we are agreed that the Kingdom that has already come within men's hearts is the complete reign of righteousness in every area of life and personality.

A concluding word

The Free Methodist Church for a century past has stood firmly for evangelical doctrine in the Wesleyan tradition. Its doctrinal emphasis has not been strident or eccentric, for as noted repeatedly in these pages Free Methodism's range of vital concerns has included not only Christian doctrine, but also the wide range of Christian experience, worship, life, and stewardship.

The church has maintained its doctrinal integrity against the inroads of the various "modernisms" of its period of history, with Christian holiness a central doctrinal theme. To this emphasis the church is still firmly committed. If there is a doctrinal weakness, it is not decline in acceptance of the doctrine so much as lack of clarity in defining it and lack of forcefulness in proclaiming it. In this area Wesley and Roberts are still up-to-date, and a renewed interest in their sane and scriptural teachings should clarify the doctrine for this generation and make more effective the church's approach to Christian holiness, both in the inner experience of this grace and in its expression in daily living.

---

19. See Articles of Religion iii and xiv, and the rituals of baptism and burial in the *Discipline*.

Chapter Seventeen

Christian Experience

In the preceding chapter we have attempted to measure the success of the Free Methodist Church in maintaining its doctrinal witness, especially its position on the Wesleyan doctrine of Christian holiness. We have traced that doctrine's continuing validity in the church to the close of the church's first century.

Listed second among the church's founding principles in Chapter One was the validity of the Christian's inner experience of cleansing and power. This is a principal theme of the present chapter, but along with it is considered the various emotional expressions of religious experience, both legitimate and extravagant, and their relationship to Christian worship. The two, Christian experience and Christian worship, are so inextricably interwoven that they are best treated together. In the next chapter we shall deal primarily with worship, but again its relationship to Christian experience will be included.

In uniting the discussion of these two themes, experience and worship, we do not ignore the bearing of doctrine on both, but doctrine is more objective and self-contained, as contrasted with the warmly subjective quality that melts experience and worship into one.

Historic Methodism, beginning with John Wesley's Aldersgate experience, has allowed due place to "the heart" in personal devotion and in corporate worship. Free Methodism has likewise been characterized by fervor in its religious moods and expressions. An effort to clarify certain facts of the religious consciousness and the place of emotion in religion is here made to aid in the understanding of Methodism's religion of the heart.

Most doctrines are inaccessible to the test of personal experience because, drawing their authority from revelation, reason, tradition, and ecclesiastical councils, the truths they assert are beyond the reach of the believer's direct participation other than his intellectual assent. But two distinctive doctrines of Methodism are affirmations of what occurs in human experience under certain operations of divine grace. They are the doctrines of assurance and of entire sanctification. These, with other facts of Christian experience, are now to be noted.

Assurance

The truth of the doctrine of assurance became John Wesley's at Aldersgate as a personal reality. Assurance is the Christian's consciousness of God's justifying grace in the conversion of his life from sin to righteousness. Testifying to the experience that came to him, Wesley said, "I felt I did trust in Christ, Christ alone for salvation; and an assurance was given me that he had taken away *my* sins, even *mine*, and saved *me* from the law of sin and death." [1] His fuller statement of what he meant by assurance was given on page 89.

Religious conversion is an incontestable fact of experience, to which multitudes who have been "born again" confidently testify. Conversion is admitted alike by believer and skeptic. Even naturalistic psychologists who flout its supernatural cause and its eternal consequences are unable to dislodge its reality in the experience of the Christian, and are compelled to admit that through this experience called the "new birth," men and women bound for years by vicious and antisocial habits, are suddenly and permanently transformed in life and conduct.

Inner conflict

But there is another indisputable fact of Christian experience, not itself the basis of a doctrine but tending to support the doctrine of original sin. This fact is the post-conversion struggle of conflicting impulses, by which conflict Wesley in his post-Aldersgate period said he was "sawn asunder"; and which Christian David explained to him as due to sin's *remaining* but not *reigning* in the justified state.

This is the common experience of those who have entered the Christian way through forgiveness of sins committed, and regeneration or the "new birth." Notwithstanding their assurance of the Divine favor, Christians sooner or later discover within them a *mind to sin* opposing the *mind to righteousness*, and waging therewith almost incessant civil war. E. Stanley Jones has well stated the fact of conflict and illustrated its cause by a graphic figure:

---

1. J. Wesley, *Journal*. Epworth Press, London; v. 1, 475.

Conversion introduced new life, but not full life. As the first flush of the new life ebbs a bit we find things within us we did not dream could survive the inrush of the new. . . . The rank growth has been cut down, but roots have remained. And we are uneasy with old roots alongside new life, and cry out for full deliverance.[2]

Inner cleansing

We have stated that two distinct doctrines of Methodism are attested in human experience, and proceeded to consider the doctrine of assurance as one of these. We then stated the fact of a post-conversion inner conflict between righteousness and sin. Now we come to the second distinctive doctrine of Methodism that directly involves personal experience.

The doctrine of entire sanctification proclaims a work of divine grace whereby the Christian's inmost nature is cleansed of sin, and perfect love becomes the motive of all his relationships to God and his fellows. True, not all Christians testify to this resolution of the inner conflict by the cleansing away of the impulse to sin, for some have never proceeded to the point of full surrender to the claims of holiness. Nevertheless, the witnesses are many, sufficient to establish firmly deliverance from the consciousness of inward sin as a fact of Christian experience.

Wesley's witnesses

John Wesley, influenced by Locke's empiricism, was a pioneer in the investigation of the religious consciousness. As reports came to him of those who claimed an experience of full deliverance from sin, both its inward principle and its outward transgression, he placed these persons on the witness stand for close examination. Many are the cases he reported in his *Journal*. The testimony of some he could not accept, but the number of them was large who satisfied him that their testimony to full deliverance was valid.

For example, at Leeds in 1760 he received many professors of the experience of perfect love from the city and the surrounding towns, and examined them one by one. Some testimonies were not convincing, but of most he examined he thought it clear, "(unless they could be supposed to tell wilful and deliberate lies), (1) that they feel

---
2. E. S. Jones, *Victorious Living*. Abingdon Press, Nashville; p. 82.

no inward sin, and to the best of their knowledge commit no outward sin; (2) that they see and love God every moment, and pray, rejoice, give thanks evermore; (3) that they have constantly as clear a witness from God of sanctification as they have of justification." To this report Wesley added quaintly, "Now in this I do rejoice, and will rejoice, call it what you please; and I would to God thousands had experienced thus much, let them afterward experience as much more as God pleases." [3]

Wesley, fortunately, was open to conviction of the sincerity of those he so closely questioned, for skepticism on the part of one of his revered standing could have thrown many of these simple Methodists into confusion and doubt. He thought it unwise to wait a few months "to see if the gift be really given," insisting rather, "If a man says, 'I now feel nothing but love,' and I know him to be an honest man, I believe him." [4] Even those whose testimony left doubt in his own mind concerning their degree of grace, he dealt with charitably.

In London in 1761 he reported:

We had a comfortable love-feast, at which several declared the blessings they had found lately. We need not be careful by what *name* to call them, while the *thing* is beyond dispute. Many have, and many do daily experience an unspeakable change. After being deeply convinced of inbred sin, particularly of pride, anger, self-will, and unbelief, in a moment they feel all faith and love—no pride, no self-will, or anger; and from that moment they have continual fellowship with God, always rejoicing, praying, and giving thanks. Whoever ascribes such a change to the devil, I ascribe it to the Spirit of God.[5]

Also in London he called to the Foundery those claiming to be perfect in love that he might, as he said, "be perfectly satisfied." Assisting him in interrogating these witnesses was the learned Thomas Walsh. "They answered every one without hesitation and with the utmost simplicity, so that we were fully persuaded they did not deceive themselves," wrote Wesley. Every one of these and many others, Wesley affirmed, "declared that his deliverance from sin was instantaneous; that the change was wrought in a moment." [6]

---
3. J. Wesley, *Journal*. Epworth Press, London; v. 4, 372.
4. *Ibid.*, v. 5, 17.
5. *Ibid.*, v. 4, 480.
6. J. Wesley, *Works* (Jackson 3rd ed.); v. 6, 490 *et seq.*

The followers of Wesley have a rich heritage in his extensive investigations of the experience of Christian holiness, augmented by subsequent generations of Wesleyan piety and scholarship.

The testimony of the Christian church

There are those who mistakenly assume that the doctrine of Christian holiness or entire sanctification is a recent development, dating from Wesley and coming to extravagant expression in the "holiness movement" of the past two or three generations. But the goal of Christian perfection has dominated areas of Christian life and thought from the birth of Christianity itself. Jesus commanded perfection, and through the ages there have been His followers who agonized for Godlikeness. Every age has had its groups which maintained the doctrine, and its saints who witnessed by word and life to the experience of perfect love. For convincing evidence at this point, let the reader study that scholarly work by R. Newton Flew, *The Idea of Perfection in Christian Theology*. Reading this book yields historical perspective on the part perfection has played in the church, and demonstrates that in all ages the doctrine has been vital to the church's health, and with its neglect, that the church has become feeble and lame.[7]

Summary of the facts of Christian experience

The facts of Christian experience briefly reviewed to this point are four, namely:

1. The assurance that comes with forgiveness of sins in Christian conversion, and the consciousness of power to live a new life of outward righteousness;

2. The post-conversion struggle in consciousness of the impulse to righteousness implanted by grace and the impulse to evil arising from human nature's propensity to sin;

3. The consciousness of inner cleansing from sin and the focal integration of the entire life about righteousness, as the Christian yields to the full control of the Holy Spirit;

4. The experience of the Christian church through the centuries, as recorded in the history of individuals and groups that have sought—and ofttimes found—full deliverance from the inner pollution of sin, and have come into victorious Christian living.

---

7. R. N. Flew, *The Idea of Perfection in Christian Theology*. Oxford University Press, London.

The response of faith

Even as John Wesley, after following in vain the devious ways of rationalism, mysticism, legalism, and ritualism, had finally to address God by faith to find Him in the forgiveness of his sins, so must one in quest of Christian holiness turn from all his own ways, and by faith accept full deliverance from inward sin by the cleansing of the Holy Spirit. "Exactly as we are justified by faith," said Wesley, "so are we sanctified by faith." [8]

Faith, Wesley found after his much wandering, is other than the assent of reason, the intuitions of feeling, the good works of legalism, the meticulous observances of all the ordinances of ritualism. It goes deeper than any or all of the particular functions or powers that man may claim, to the very core of his existence. Faith is the response of man to God in his inmost, utmost being, in his essential self; in what the Scriptures in Luke 10:27 call "the heart" as the seat of conscience and the center of moral and spiritual capacity. Faith is man's trusting yet active commitment of his total being to the truth of God revealed by His Spirit and His Word in Christ Jesus as Lord and only Saviour.

And even this faith as the self's total response to God is "not of yourselves: it is the gift of God," for not only does man seek God, but God seeks man; and when the downward reach of His saving hand grips the groping upward reach of man's helplessness, faith is a reality. Then man knows God, not by the intellect or reason alone; not merely in his emotional consciousness; nor by his dutiful obedience in service and devotion: but man knows God in that supreme experience of faith by which he possesses "the assurance of things hoped for, a conviction of things not seen."

When this adjustment of man to God has once been made through the outreach of "the heart" in faith, man's worship of God and his service both to God and man are then expressed in love, channeled through what the same Scripture passage (Luke 10:27) calls, (1) "the soul" as the moving, dynamic, striving, affectional aspect of personality; (2) "the strength" as the direction of all man's energies in moral conduct and in all his conscious behavior; and (3) "the mind," repre-

---

8. J. Wesley, *Sermons on Several Occasions.* Phillips & Hunt, New York; v. 1, 388.

senting the full range of man's intellectual and rational powers.[9]

If held in balance through the sustained operation of steadfast faith, all these channels of worship and service will strengthen and confirm faith itself, and lead on through time and (as Wesley held) into eternity in an increasing perfection of Christian character, till we come "unto the measure of the stature of the fulness of Christ." But if there develops either neglect or undue prominence of any of these three channels of feeling, action, or thought, faith becomes weak and may lose its hold on God; and Christian character becomes eccentric, and may lose its balance and collapse.

These extended observations on faith are made because the discussion now turns to the manifestations of emotion in religion which sometimes have led to charges of fanaticism against spiritual Christianity. When are such charges valid?

A religion of the heart

Enthusiasm, the eighteenth century term for fanaticism, early was charged against the Methodists, if on no other ground than their claim of joyous assurance that they were saved. Such a profession was not in accord with the prevailing deism which would limit all knowledge of God to an inference from His creation, and with the chill religious formalism of a day which was exceedingly annoyed by any manifestation or profession of inward religion.

As early as 1739, writing a defense of Methodism against charges of religious vagaries, Wesley assured a critic that when a man has experienced a living faith, he will in consequence experience much else, such as "the love of God shed abroad in his heart, the peace of God which passeth all understanding, and joy in the holy Ghost." [10]

The tract, *Letters Against Fanaticism*, written by an Anabaptist pastor, brought from Wesley this protest against labeling as fanaticism all religious feeling:

> The very thing which Mr. Sinstra calls fanaticism is no other than heart-religion; in other words, "righteousness, peace, and

---
9. For interpretation of Luke 10:27 supporting this approach, see *Explanatory Notes Upon the New Testament*, by John Wesley; Epworth Press, London; p. 240; but more especially *The New Testament in Modern Speech*, R. F. Weymouth; Pilgrim Press, Boston; p. 166 *et seq.*
10. J. Wesley, *Journal.* Epworth Press, London; v. 2, 250, 251.

joy in the Holy Ghost." These must be *felt*, or they have no being. All, therefore, who condemn inward feelings in the gross, leave no place either for joy, peace, or love in religion; and consequently reduce it to a dry carcase.[11]

A feature of Methodism that led to more serious charges of fanaticism was the peculiar and even spectacular physical effects which the preaching and praying of the revivalists had on unbelievers, even on some who had come to scoff. Strangely enough, these effects at first were more pronounced under John Wesley's restrained and orderly sermons than under Whitefield's dramatic oratory, and when they first developed in Wesley's meetings, Whitefield took issue with him for not vigorously suppressing them. Later such physical demonstrations also accompanied Whitefield's preaching. They were common in early American Methodism for generations, but in time gradually subsided.

But revivals have had sensational physical effects in older denominations as well. The Anglican clergyman, Devereux Jarratt of Virginia, who cooperated with early Methodist itinerants in a vigorous revival in the south just before the Revolutionary War, was disturbed by some of the revival's manifestations, as could well be expected. This is what he wrote:

> It has been frequently observed, that there never was any remarkable revival of religion, but some degree of enthusiasm mingled with it—some wild fire mixed with the sacred flame. It may be doubted whether this is not unavoidable in the nature of things. And notwithstanding all the care we have taken, this work has not been quite free from it; but it never rose to any considerable height, neither was of long continuance.... I have no doubt but the work now carrying on is genuine: yet there were some circumstances attending it which I disliked; such as loud outcries, tremblings, fallings, convulsions. But I am better reconciled since I read President Edwards on that head, who observes, "That wherever these most appear, there is always the greatest and deepest work."[12]

The devout Jarratt, who had once been a Presbyterian, was reassured by Jonathan Edwards' unswerving acceptance of marked physical

---
11. *Ibid.*, v. 5, 426.
12. Devereux Jarratt, *Sermons on Various and Important Subjects in Practical Divinity.* (Quoted by E. C. Chorley, *Men and Movements in the American Episcopal Church.* Charles Scribner's Sons, New York; p. 14 *et seq.*)

agitations as inseparable from deep conviction for sin and the profound stirring of religious sensibilities in the unsaved under revival excitement. In our age of moderate preaching and flexible morals, we witness less of the desperate conviction of lostness that gripped sinners under the definite preaching of absolutes and categorical imperatives in an earlier day. The strong appeal of the gospel as presented a century ago is glimpsed in the following fragment from the pen of B. T. Roberts:

> Every part of man's nature that can be moved—his fears and his hopes, his affections and his sympathies, his judgment, his sense of duty, his love of happiness, and his dread of suffering, of exposure and of shame—each and all are appealed to in the strongest manner by the Gospel of Christ, to lead erring mortals to return to their allegiance to God.[13]

Other than the abiding inner joy of the believer and the occasions of uncontrollable seizures under conviction for sin during revivals, early Methodism was noted likewise for spontaneous outbreaks of joy in its services, expressed by loud exclamations, jumping, running and other manifestations of freedom from the restraints of the usual forms of worship. Thus came the descriptive expression, "a shouting Methodist."

Religious emotion is a characteristic of worship in all groups. In some, the expression of emotion is ordered by a pattern or ritual which engages all the worshipers in unison. Although all groups normally worship within a general structure or order of service, in some of them individuals may readily break away from the order to "assert their liberty" along individual lines in prayer, ejaculatory praise, song, testimony, exhortation, and the like. Historic Methodism held to such free worship, but with restraints on license, for Wesley would have all things done decently and in order.

Overshooting sober Christianity

But at times extravagance developed and liberty was carried into license. These occasions taxed the leaders' tact and skill, for fanaticism explodes under opposition and the flames spread afar. The most serious outbreak was in London during the great revival there of the

---

13. B. T. Roberts, "Religious Sensibility," *The Earnest Christian;* v. 1, July, 1860; p. 197.

early 1760's, when Thomas Maxfield and George Bell led many off into harmful extremes. It was at this time that John Fletcher said, "Many of our brethren are overshooting sober Christianity. . . . The corruption of the best things is always the worst of corruptions."[14]

This was one of the most trying periods of Wesley's leadership of Methodism and the revival, but out of it came his tract in which he gave most valuable advice against deviations into fanaticism, and directed believers to balanced Christian living.

The effect of the outbreak had spread far. In June of 1763 Wesley wrote:

> The wildness of our poor brethren in London has put it [Christian perfection] out of countenance above two hundred miles off; so these strange advocates for perfection have given it a deeper wound than all its enemies together could do.[15]

In October of that year he reported his efforts in London "to confirm those that had been shaken as to the important doctrine of Christian Perfection, either by its wild defenders, or wise opposers, who much availed themselves of that wildness."[16]

During 1763 alone, 106 members left Society in London on account of the fanatical outbreak, but in the same entry in his *Journal* where this is reported, Wesley still could claim great progress in the revival:

> Nor has it [the revival] ceased to this day in any of its branches. God still convinces, justifies, sanctifies. We have lost only the dross, the enthusiasm, the prejudice, the offence. The pure gold remains, faith working by love, and, we have good ground to believe, increases daily.[17]

Bangs has quoted Wesley as saying, "That there have been a few warm-headed men, is no reproach to the work itself, no just ground for accusing a multitude of sober-minded men, who are patterns of strict holiness."[18] Wesley's venture to maintain the spirit and practice

---

14. See L. Tyerman, *The Life and Times of the Rev. John Wesley, A. M.* Harper & Bros., New York; v. 2, 464.
15. J. Wesley, *Journal*. Epworth Press, London; v. 5, 17.
16. *Ibid.*, v. 5, 35.
17. *Ibid.*, v. 5, 41.
18. N. Bangs, *The Necessity, Nature and Fruits of Sanctification*. Phillips & Hunt, New York; p. 50.

CHRISTIAN EXPERIENCE

of free worship throughout a prolonged period of revival urgency meant risking shipwreck on the rocks of fanaticism, but the outcome justified his courage. We ask, with Leslie Church, "Whatever the dangers Wesley had to face, who shall say that he was not wise in accepting the risk rather than rejecting or ignoring the living realities?" [19]

Mysticism and fanaticism

The basis of much fanaticism is a mysticism in which the worshiper claims direct union with God. This assumed union may be achieved either by such introvertive techniques as those of the Sufi mystic of India, who in absolute quiet fixes his gaze on his navel; or by such extrovertive techniques as employed by the whirling dervish of Islam, with his mechanical repetition of "Allah! Allah!" In either case the principle is the same: in his ecstatic swoon into that ALL which is nothingness the worshiper loses the distinction of "I" and "Thou," the self and the not-self. Such is the opposite of these valid experiences of God in which the sense of self-hood is maintained through communion with God—and more, is enlarged and strengthened.

There have been Christian saints who were mystical in temperament, but "Christian" and "mystic" are far from equivalent adjectives. When "holy men" of all world-faiths but of unholy morals experience the mystic ecstasy, one must seek a source for it other than the God of the Christian. Some of the mystics of Christendom have been so carried way by their assumed exalted spirituality and their consequent delusion that they had a "private wire" to heaven, that they have rebelled against all authority but their own inner impulses which they mistake for the voice of God. Most accurate is that description of the fanatic which makes him one who "takes the emotions of his own passions for those of grace." [20]

For Wesley, man's experience of God was not *mystical*, but a *personal* relationship of God and man maintained on man's part by faith through the indwelling Spirit. Some insist that such a relationship after all is mystical, and that Wesley unjustly condemned all varieties of mysticism without distinction. The present writer inclines

---
19. Leslie F. Church, *The Early Methodist People*. The Philosophical Library, New York; p. 130.
20. *The Earnest Christian*, v. 4, Dec. 1862, p. 183.

to Wesley's usage or refinement of the term mysticism, and would describe historic Methodism as a *personal* rather than a *mystical* relationship to God, except for those deviations on one hand into Moravian "stillness," and on the other hand into rhapsodic exhibitionism. Both of these were unfortunate aberrations from the balance of valid faith, caused by undue weighting of the emotions.

Briefly stated, the distinction we draw between *personal* and *mystical* is this: In the response of the "heart" or essential self to God in the personal commitment of faith, the accompanying feeling or emotion is *the human response to the experience of God*; but in the mystical quest for God, feeling is placed at the center as *the means by which the seeker would find God*. Mysticism thus substitutes feeling for faith, the response of a part of the self for the response of the total being, and thereby prepares the way for the distortions of fanaticism.

Manifestations of religious feeling

In preceding pages have been noted briefly four varieties of emotional manifestation in religion. Examples follow in order of our previous introduction of the types.

1. *The sustained, joyous assurance of the Christian that he is a child of God.*

Representing humble folks of her kind, well did an unnamed "poor Methodist woman" of the eighteenth century express the joy of heartfelt religion, even in her ordinary life's most common circumstances:

> I do not know when I have had happier times in my soul, than when I have been sitting at work, with nothing before me but a candle and a white cloth, and hearing no sound but that of my own breath, with God in my soul and heaven in my eye. ... I rejoice in being exactly what I am,—a creature capable of loving God, and who, as long as God lives, must be happy. I get up and look for a while out of the window, and gaze at the moon and stars, the work of an Almighty hand. I think of the grandeur of the universe, and then sit down, and think myself one of the happiest beings in it.[21]

Richard Trewarvas had been converted and living a consistent

---

21. Mary W. Tileston, Compiler, *Daily Strength for Daily Needs*. Little, Brown, and Co., Boston; p. 19.

CHRISTIAN EXPERIENCE

Christian life for ten years when he found full deliverance from sin within. His inner consciousness of this deliverance he expressed in convincing terms of joyous confidence:

> God has at last given me the victory through faith in Christ Jesus my Lord. O happy change! . . . I enjoy his constant smile, and peaceable reign in my soul. . . . He hath implanted that divine principle in my soul, whereby I am enabled to govern my affections, to subject my will and desires and keep within due bounds all the passions of my soul. God hath now taught me that most excellent lesson, in every circumstance of life, and under every dispensation of his providence, to be content. . . . Praised be the God of my salvation; he hath delivered my soul from every painful anxiety of life, and gloomy idea of death.[22]

2. *Profound bodily effects of the terror of sinners "under conviction" for their sins.*

The following from Wesley's *Journal* of 1739 confirms our earlier statement that Whitefield protested against the crying out and other physical manifestations accompanying the preaching of Wesley. The two paragraphs are for successive days, July 6 and 7.

> In the afternoon I was with Mr. Whitefield, just come from London, with whom I went to Baptist Mills [near Bristol], where he preached concerning "the Holy Ghost, which all who believe are to receive"; not without just, though severe censure of those who preach as if there were no Holy Ghost.
>
> I had an opportunity to talk with him of those outward signs which had so often accompanied the inward work of God. I found his objections were chiefly grounded on gross misrepresentations of matter of fact. But the next day he had an opportunity of informing himself better: for no sooner had he begun (in the application of his sermon) to invite all sinners to believe in Christ, than four persons sunk down close to him, almost in the same moment. One of them lay without either sense or motion; a second trembled exceedingly; the third had strong convulsions all over his body, but made no noise, unless by groans; the fourth, equally convulsed, called upon God, with strong cries and tears. From this time, I trust, we shall suffer God to carry on His own work in the way that pleaseth Him.[23]

Whitefield's *Journal* for July 7 refers to "a useful conference about

---
22. Leslie F. Church, *The Early Methodist People*. The Philosophical Library, New York; p. 133. (Quoted from *Memoirs of Richard Trewarvas, Senr.*)
23. J. Wesley, *Journal*. Epworth Press, London; v. 2, 238-240.

many things with my honored friend, Mr. Wesley." No doubt, prominent among the topics of the conference were the outbreaks during Wesley's preaching of which he had heard, and which were so annoying to him. Interestingly enough, he comments on the Baptist Mills congregation most favorably, saying:

> The congregation I observed to be much more serious and affected than when I left them, and their loud and repeated *Amens*, which they put up to every petition, as well as the exemplariness of their conversation in common life, plainly show that they have not received the grace of God in vain.[24]

Already hearty Methodist *Amens* from believers were accepted by Whitefield with approval. It was the next day he was to have demonstrations under his own preaching of the seizures that sometimes gripped sinners, which Wesley that day had explained to him.

3. Spontaneous outbreaks of joy or of deep heart-concern during Christian worship, usually but not always in a group of believers.

Outbursts, both of joy and sorrow which struck congregations suddenly, are described by that early itinerant of American Methodism, Jesse Lee. Reporting on the revival in the southern colonies in which the Anglican clergyman, Devereux Jarratt, so cordially cooperated, Lee wrote:

> Some of the assemblies resembled the congregation of the *Jews* at laying the foundations of the second temple in the days of *Ezra*. Some wept for grief; others shouted for joy; so that it was hard to distinguish one from the other. So it was here. The mourning and distress were so blended with the voice of joy and gladness, that it was hard to distinguish the one from the other. But the voice of joy prevailed, the people shouted with a great shout, so that it might be heard afar off.[25]

More than a half-century later an untried president of a frontier Methodist college, a stranger from the east who was unknown to his constituency and was yet to be inaugurated the president of their Indiana Asbury University, accepted an invitation to preach at the

---

24. J. Wesley, *Journal*. Epworth Press, London; v. 2, 239 n. (Editor Curnock quotes this from Whitefield's *Journal* for Saturday, July 7, 1739.)
25. Jesse Lee, *A Short History of the Methodists in the United States of America*. Cokesbury Press, Nashville; p. 59. (Originally published in 1810 by Magill & Clime, Baltimore.)

annual conference a centenary sermon commemorating the organization of the Methodist United Societies. He chose as his subject Ezekiel's rising river which he made a symbol of the growth and spread of Methodism. So eloquent was his presentation that he was only well started with his message when a woman of a well-known family of the community was overpowered with feeling and arose and walked to the center aisle with hand upstretched, and cried out, "Sun, stand thou still and let the moon pass by." A recent biographer of Matthew Simpson continues the account of the service as follows:

> When Simpson resumed his theme the resistance of the audience was broken, and emotion was at a new high level. With every "fresh unfolding of the subject," every new interpretation of the symbol, came a "fresh gust of tears and shouting." The preachers were so overcome as almost to drown out the voice of the speaker.[26]

John Wesley himself was a participant in an outbreak of religious feeling on the first New Year's day after Aldersgate. Here is his account:

> 1739. Jan. 1, Mon.—Mr. Hall, Kinchin, Ingham, Whitefield, Hutchins, and my brother Charles were present at our love-feast in Fetter Lane, with about sixty of our brethren. About three in the morning, as we were continuing instant in prayer, the power of God came mightily upon us, insomuch that many cried out for exceeding joy, and many fell to the ground. As soon as we were recovered a little from that awe and amazement at the presence of His majesty we broke out with one voice, "We praise Thee, O God; we acknowledge Thee to be the Lord." [27]

4. *Exaggerations of the emotional or temperamental functions to the point of disrupting faith and leading to erratic ideas and fanatical behavior.*

In behavior, such extravagances as these are well described by John Wesley in his sermon, "On Knowing Christ After the Flesh," at the point where he warns against the use of what he calls fondling terms of familiar endearment applied to Deity—expressions, by the way, which were freely used by the Moravians.

> Perhaps some may be afraid, lest the refraining from these warm expressions, or even gently checking them, should check

---
26. Robert D. Clark, *The Life of Matthew Simpson*. The Macmillan Co., New York; p. 78.
27. J. Wesley, *Journal*. Epworth Press, London; v. 2, 124, 125.

the fervor of our devotion. It is very possible it may check, or even prevent, some kind of fervor which has passed for devotion. Possibly it may prevent loud shouting, horrid, unnatural screaming, repeating the same words twenty or thirty times, jumping two or three feet high, and throwing about the arms or legs, both of men and women, in a manner shocking not only to religion, but to common decency.[28]

In the matter of ideas, a picture of the fanatic is given in a letter John Wesley wrote Thomas Maxfield, detailing what he disliked in his and his fellows' "doctrine, spirit, or outward behavior." We give some of the unfavorable features according to Wesley, who tactfully included favorable comments which we omit.

> I dislike your supposing man may be as perfect as an angel; that he can be absolutely perfect; that he can be infallible, or above being tempted; or that the moment he is pure in heart he cannot fall from it.
>
> I dislike your saying that one saved from sin [meaning one entirely sanctified] needs nothing more than looking to Jesus; needs not to hear or think of anything else; believe, believe, is enough; that he needs no self-examination, no times of private prayer; needs not mind little or outward things; and that he cannot be taught by any person who is not in the same state.
>
> ... I dislike something which has the appearance of pride, of overvaluing yourself and undervaluing others; particularly the preachers; your speaking of yourself as though you were the only men who knew and taught the gospel; and as if not only all the clergy, but all the Methodists, were in utter darkness.
>
> I dislike your overvaluing feelings and inward impressions; mistaking the mere work of imagination for the voice of the Spirit; expecting the end without the means; and undervaluing reason, knowledge, and wisdom in general.
>
> I dislike something that has the appearance of Antinomianism, not magnifying the law, and making it honorable; not enough valuing tenderness of conscience and exact watchfulness in order thereto; using faith rather as contradistinguished from holiness than as productive of it.
>
> But what I most of all dislike is, your littleness of love to your brethren; to your society; ... your impatience of contradiction; your counting every man your enemy that reproves or admonishes you in love; your bigotry ... ; your censoriousness. ...[29]

---
28. J. Wesley, *Sermons on Several Occasions;* v. 2, 444.
29. J. Wesley, *Journal.* Epworth Press, London, v. 4, 535-537.

Charity and wisdom

It is evident from the foregoing four-fold classification that not all types of religious emotion can be called fanatical in nature, nor can all degrees or traits of any type be so judged.

No devout person will charge him who experiences the sustained joy of assurance with being, for that reason, fanatical. Would that Christians everywhere had that full assurance which is the secret of the joy of the Lord!

The bodily seizures of those deeply convicted of their sins are the physical effects of profound emotion, stirred and quickened by the operation of the Spirit upon the conscience. Such seizures are abnormal, yes, even as is the sin which is their essential cause. Some victims have symptoms that are hysterical in nature, incited by suggestion under intense group emotion. For this reason, if for no other, leaders of religious assemblies should not seek to incite the seizures. Recent authorities have refuted the claim of many historians that in early revivalism physical demonstrations were "worked up" by the leaders.[30]

The spontaneous outbursts of joy and of deep heart-concern on the part of believers, if in the Spirit, are the legitimate physical expressions normally resulting from genuine experiences of God at times of His especially manifested presence. Such human expressions may be expected to vary in the forms they take, according to the temperamental individuality of the worshipers. A tradition of Methodism is this freedom of spontaneous rather than the rigidity of ritualistic expression of fervor in religion. Fanatical perversion of this freedom occurs when "bodily exercise" becomes a technique for inducing an imagined experience of God rather than serving as a normal expression of spiritual emotion.

Obviously, the more extravagant exaggerations of the emotional life, which disrupt rather than strengthen true faith, are very properly to be classed as fanaticism. But one must allow a charitable margin for the lesser eccentricities of mind and behavior in those whose early training or present culture predisposes them to religious ideas which

---

30. See M. E. Gaddis, "Christian Perfectionism in America," University of Chicago doctoral thesis; p. 212. Also W. W. Sweet, *Methodism in American History*. Methodist Book Concern, New York; p. 159.

deviate in measure from those generally accepted, and to physical responses of the emotions of lesser restraint than is normally expected.

Although Wesley's course in meeting fanaticism was not to attempt forthright suppression at the first appearance of its symptoms, when other methods failed he did assert his authority. Out of his unfortunate experiences with the Maxfield-Bell outbreak, he proposed in particular three safeguards: to seek higher degrees of love; to heed the Scriptures as a check on impressions; to hold a proper respect for knowledge and intelligence.

Early Methodists were fervently religious, and Wesley therefore warned them that the very desire to grow in grace provided an opening through which fanaticism might enter, by leading them "to seek something else new, besides new degrees of love to God and man," such as special gifts. This, then, was a primary safeguard, in all one's seeking to seek more love. If you seek any other gift, he said, "you are looking wide of the mark, you are getting out of the royal way." [31]

Wesley emphasized the Scriptures as a further safeguard against fanaticism, especially against ascribing "dreams, voices, impressions, visions, or revelations" to God as their source. "They may be from Him," he said. "They may be from nature. They may be from the devil." And he urged, "Try all things by the written Word, and let all bow down before it. You are in danger of enthusiasm every hour, if you depart ever so little from Scripture; yea, or from the plain, literal meaning of any text, taken in connection with context." [32]

Another safeguard against fanaticism Wesley sought to erect was a proper regard for human knowledge and scholarship. "I advise you," he said, "never to use the words wisdom, reason, or knowledge, by way of reproach. On the contrary, pray that you yourself may abound in them more and more. If you mean worldly wisdom, useless knowledge, false reasoning, say so; and throw away the chaff, but not the wheat." [33]

For a religion as fervent as that represented in early Methodism, its personal, rather than mystical center, was its essential strength against dangerous emotional extravagance and fanaticism. According

---

31. J. Wesley, *A Plain Account of Christian Perfection.* Epworth Press, London; p. 90.
32. *Ibid.*, p. 88.
33. *Ibid.*, p. 89.

to Troeltsch, the Methodist revival was not at core mystical, but did seek to establish through emotional revivalism a personal relationship to God, the inherent danger of anarchy from such individualism being checked by Methodism's strong organization and discipline.[34]

Umphrey Lee's research in the field of early Methodist fervor leads him to conclude that Methodism as a whole avoided the mystic's passive quietism and the fanatic's unrestrained individualism. He sets forth as follows Methodism's subjective and emotional impulses and their counteracting forces that kept the movement from disastrous excesses:

> Such was the character of Methodist "enthusiasm": unusual and disturbing religious practices carried on in defiance of 'taste' and propriety, and with joyous disregard of ecclesiastical law; an insistence upon immediate communion of the individual with God, restricted, however, to a change of the individual's inner life, a certainty of personal relation with Deity, and to such experiences as did not conflict with the Bible or "Reason" and did not exceed the privileges of every Christian.[35]

A further factor, to which has been ascribed a measure of Methodism's stability notwithstanding its fervor, was the channeling of the energy of ardent religious emotions into whole-souled singing of gospel hymns. This provided not only emotional release but had a socializing effect in relating each worshiper to the group. The social check of class meeting and love feast tended to protect against moral and religious hazards of a deviating and too assertive individualism.

Abel Stevens pointed out the effectiveness of organizational discipline for checking and removing fanaticism in the ministerial ranks of early American Methodism. He admitted that a few eccentrics found their way into the group, "but the rigorous discipline and exhaustive labors of the denomination controlled or expended their morbid energy," said Stevens; "or, if these failed," he added, "the rapid but steady motion of its ecclesiastical system threw them off, and so far off that they ceased to be dangerous." [36]

---

34. Ernst Troeltsch, *The Social Teaching of the Christian Churches*. The Macmillan Co., New York; v. 2, 784.
35. U. Lee, *The Historical Backgrounds of Early Methodist Enthusiasm*. Columbia University Press, New York; p. 146.
36. A Stevens, *A Compendious History of American Methodism*. Carlton & Porter, New York; p. 268.

Genesee reformers: fervent or fanatical?

Against the background now sketched, we examine the character of the emotional manifestations of the reformers of western New York in the fifties of the nineteenth century. These were charged with fanaticism by the Regency party of the Genesee Conference, and yet, as was noted in Chapter Sixteen, Timothy L. Smith has given his judgment that Roberts' writings on sanctification "were certainly far from fanatical." The analysis of these writings, reported in the same chapter, confirms Smith's claim.

Furthermore, seventeen ministers of the Genesee Conference, identified with the alleged "Nazarite Union" which had been charged with promoting fanaticism, signed the following statement which was published in the *Northern Independent*:

> Connected with the charge of association [in a "Nazarite Union"], is that of encouraging fanaticism, and extravagance in religious exercises and worship. This charge we declare to be as groundless as the other. We have never encouraged excesses, and with them we have not the *least* sympathy.

That they were fully committed to the promotion of earnest Christianity, however, they boldly affirmed:

> But while we stand opposed to all improprieties in religious exercises and worship, we declare ourselves in favor of a consistent and vitalized religion; not a dead formalism, but the power of godliness.[37]

Among the signers of this document, which was dated in September 1857, were the following representative preachers:

Asa Abell, who had joined the Genesee Conference in 1821, had served for eighteen years as presiding elder, and four times had been a delegate to General Conference.

C. D. Burlingham, a presiding elder at the time of signing the document, who had represented Genesee at the immediately preceding General Conference.

I. C. Kingsley, who also had been a delegate to the last General Conference, and recently for four years had been a presiding elder.

S. C. Church, who had served four years as presiding elder, and after his passing would be memorialized in the records of the Genesee Conference by these two statements, highly significant in view of his relation to the

---

37. B. T. Roberts, *Why Another Sect*. The Earnest Christian Publishing House, Rochester, New York; p. 24 *et seq.*

Genesee troubles of the fifties: "His conscientiousness would not allow him to be neutral. His good sense and generosity kept him from mere partisanship."

John P. Kent, of blameless character, who served in the conference until he became an honored superannuate.

Amos Hard, who was to be reported in the records of the Genesee Conference "as a Christian . . . thorough and earnest," who "tolerated nothing superficial in himself or others," but with a devotion in spiritual things that caused him to present "one of the most vivid pictures of a Christian in earnest."

Loren G. Stiles, Jr., who recently had been a presiding elder in high favor with laymen and the reformers, but a disappointment to the Regency because of his conversion to the cause of reform.

B. T. Roberts, who needs no further comment at this point.[38]

In Chapter Thirteen was cited the declaration of the First Laymen's Convention (December 1858) protesting the charge of fanaticism against the reformers and the criticism that their general quarterly meetings and their camp meetings were "hot-beds of enthusiasm." According to Roberts, the Bergen camp meeting of 1858, held shortly before his second trial and expulsion, was so branded.[39] But quite a different evaluation of that camp meeting was reported in the *Northern Christian Advocate* by an observer from outside Genesee bounds. William Reddy, for many years a presiding elder in the neighboring Oneida Conference and author of a book, *Inside Views of Methodism* (probably then in preparation, for it was published by the Methodist Episcopal Church the following year) had this to say of the meeting:

> I heard old Methodists from Boston and Connecticut say, with streaming eyes and bounding hearts, "This is as it used to be forty years ago." . . . The doctrine of sanctification after the Wesley Standard, the definite way of seeking the blessing, the spontaneous confessions of having obtained it, on the part of intelligent and mature persons, the duty of exemplifying it by self-denial and universal obedience, and keeping the rules of the Discipline, "not for wrath, but for conscience' sake," the patient and loving endurance of opposition and persecution for Christ's sake, if

---

38. The statistical facts concerning these men have been compiled from *A Century of The Genesee Annual Conference of the Methodist Episcopal Church, 1810-1910*, by Ray Allen. The evaluations of the men are taken largely from *Why Another Sect*, p. 31 et seq.
39. B. T. Roberts, *Why Another Sect*; p. 118.

need be, were all earnestly taught and enforced, and many were the witnesses.[40]

Another observer was Rev. B. I. Ives, D.D., likewise of the Oneida Conference, who said the meeting was the biggest by far he had ever attended, with at least five thousand present on Sunday. He was impressed by "the number of intelligent business and influential men" who with their families tented on the ground throughout the meeting. "I saw nothing," said Dr. Ives, "that appeared 'like wildfire,' or mere 'animal excitement,' during the entire meeting. The motto was: 'order and power.' "[41]

The Bergen camp meeting the following year, 1859, again was reported by a member of the Oneida Conference, Rev. J. F. Crawford. He listed among those preaching in the camp meeting such men as B. T. Roberts, J. W. Redfield, B. I. Ives, C. D. Brooks, Fay Purdy, William Reddy—all of whom have earlier appeared in these pages. Particularly effective refutation of the charge of fanaticism against B. T. Roberts was Crawford's account of Roberts' ministering in the spirit of love, with no reference whatever to his enemies —which is hardly the spirit of a fanatic!

> B. T. Roberts preached at ten o'clock. What was remarkable in this sermon, the speaker did not so much as refer to his troubles, but the sweetest and most heavenly spirit seemed to reign through the whole discourse. If he continues to maintain the spirit he now possesses, his foes must fall powerless at his feet.

Crawford reported twelve thousand present on Sunday, but "perfect order prevailed during the whole day." Of the people, he said: "They are as intelligent a class of people as you will find in the State of New York. They are clear in their views of holiness, according to our standard authors, and according to Scripture."[42]

That the Genesee reform leaders were earnest and fervent, but as a group not fanatical, is the conclusion to which the character of these leaders and the opinions of observers of their assemblies clearly point. And such a conclusion is confirmed by evidences of contemporary fervor which was similar to theirs, according to the Methodist

---
40. *Ibid.*, p. 118 *et seq.*
41. *Ibid.*, p. 119 *et seq.*
42. *Ibid.*, p. 122 *et seq.*

literature of that period, indicating that these manifestations were then accepted as legitimate in Methodist quarters.

Methodist fervor of mid-century

In 1859 an article appeared in the *Methodist Quarterly Review* on religious catalepsy which was far from condemnatory, but, on the contrary, was reasonably tolerant. The writer represented such a condition as "an accompaniment of the work of grace, to be viewed rather as a blemish than an ornament." The account seemed to deal with contemporary cases of religious catalepsy, which apparently were not rare.[43]

The same volume carried also a book review on physical manifestations in religious excitement of various types. If the reviewer, who was not in full accord with the book, represented the general attitude of Methodism in his statement quoted below, we conclude that at this period emotional manifestations were accepted but not encouraged. He said:

> We thank God for the religion which has in all ages made men weep and shout, and has even resulted, through human infirmity, in jerks and catalepsies; but we desire no effort to promote the weeping, shouting, jerking, and catalepsies as a distinct institution.[44]

Bishop Hamline, the first year of his ministry in the episcopal office while at the Troy Conference of 1844, wrote:

> But the preachers are coming in, and I am told that some of them are warm and sunny and fiery, and can weep and shout. Oh, I bless God for religion and for Methodism. But when Methodism affects the dignity and silence and stiffness and corpse-like aspect of formalism, it makes me weep.[45]

In *The Life of Rev. John S. Inskip* we read of a university lad of high Christian character who in 1871 was stricken in a meeting during which he had been a seeker for a clean heart. He performed violent contortions which led to fear that he would seriously injure himself, but he came quietly out of the seizure and testified that he was cleansed. Instead of harming, this peculiar manifestation seemed to

---

43. *Methodist Quarterly Review*, v. 41, 1859; p. 227.
44. *Ibid.*, p. 666 *et seq.*
45. F. G. Hibbard, *Biography of Rev. Leonidas L. Hamline*. Eaton & Mains, New York; p. 154 *et seq.*

benefit the meetings, and at the close of the series resolutions of appreciation were presented to the leaders. These were signed by two Methodist presiding elders, the president and two professors of the Methodist university located in the community of the meetings, and many pastors.[46]

Bishop Simpson participated in the first National Camp Meeting at Vineland, New Jersey, held in 1867, and wrote the preface to the book reporting this and other National holiness camp meetings in which he had preached. In this book is found the account of a service in which the preacher had spoken on spiritual diseases of the heart, and had pointed to worldly fashion in dress as one symptom. At the close of the message intense enthusiasm blazed, with resounding shouts, followed by spontaneous singing. We read what happened next:

> Then the congregation was invited to come closer towards the stand, and under the fearful excitement to which the exercises had led, the most appalling shouts for mercy were heard, and the most earnest supplications uttered.[47]

A traveler through central New York in 1859, who resided within the Philadelphia Conference, reported in the *Northern Independent* the differences he had observed between Methodism in his home conference and in New York. Among other differences, he noted the greater restraint he found in the north, where "there is not that excitement and physical demonstration attending their devotions as characterize the meetings of the latitude of the Philadelphia Conference."[48] Even the contrast indicated the fact of Methodist fervor in the late fifties, and the lower religious temperature in New York may have extended to Genesee to explain its intense opposition to a fervor normal to Methodism elsewhere.

As reflecting the attitude toward religious fervor in the Methodism of his childhood and youth, beginning about 1875 (for he was born in 1864), a few passages from Bishop Cannon's fair description and wholesome evaluation of revivals and camp meetings deserve a place in our inquiry. It hasn't been many years since he wrote the following:

---

46. W. McDonald and John E. Searles, *The Life of Rev. John Inskip*. McDonald & Gill, Boston; p. 246 et seq.
47. A. McLean and J. W. Eaton, *Penuel; or, Face to Face with God*. W. C. Palmer, Jr., New York; p. 77.
48. *Northern Independent*, v. 3, Feb. 17, 1859.

Criticism has gone so far as to speak in derogatory terms of the outbursts of joy on the part of saved sinners and their happy friends.... If, as the Master says, there is joy in heaven over one sinner that repenteth, why should there not be joy expressed at the altar on earth where repentance is professed? If the mission of the church is to seek and to save the lost, the preaching and the methods used in my little home church, while accompanied with emotion, were neither fanatical nor hysterical.[49]

Concerning camp meetings:

That there was some excitement, I will not deny. Some mothers and fathers sometimes shouted praises to God at the conversion of their children. Sometimes there was a sweeping burst of hallelujahs followed by prayer and song, when some well-known sinner made profession of faith, but I never saw ... anything not entirely warranted by the Scriptural idea of joy over repentance and salvation of sinners.... The camp meetings of those days were a religious factor of great value, and we have nothing now to take their place and few occasions where there are manifestations of such moral and spiritual power.[50]

The graver danger

Fanaticism has done damage to the cause of spiritual religion by the prejudice it has created against commendable zeal. John Fletcher recognized this, and while cautioning against the false zeal of fanaticism, urged the true zeal of the pious which, he said, "differs as much from fanaticism as vigor, accompanied by health, differs from a delirium produced by a burning fever." Thus did this scholarly saint encourage a proper Christian earnestness.[51]

Arnold Toynbee asserts that the attitude of mind which ridiculed Christianity in the deistic and materialistic eighteenth century, "sterilized fanaticism at the cost of extinguishing faith." This attitude, Toynbee says, began in the seventeenth and persists in the twentieth century, and is at last being recognized "as the supreme danger to the spiritual health and even to the material existence of the Western social body...." And this interpreter of history declares further, "It will be hard indeed to refill the spiritual vacuum which has been hollowed in our Western hearts by the progressive decay

---

49. Richard L. Watson, Editor, *Bishop Cannon's Own Story*. Duke University Press, Durham, N. C.; p. 14.
50. *Ibid.*, p. 21.
51. *The Earnest Christian*, v. 4, Dec., 1862; p. 183.

of religious belief that has been going on for some two-and-a-half centuries." [52]

In our fear of religious fervor, it is possible to lean too far on the other side, tipping the boat into the chilly currents of the dangerously close icebergs of dead formalism. Even Horace Bushnell a century ago, noting the oscillations of Christian history between ardent religion with its signs, gifts and miracles at one pole, and the rigid rationality of a religion with no "expectation" at the other, placed the two in opposite pans of a balance and found the scales all but tipping in favor of fervor against formalism. "But whoever ponders thoughtfully the question will find ample room to doubt," he said, "which is really widest of a just respect; the excesses of fanaticism and false fire, or the comatose and dull impotence of a religion that worships without expectation." [53]

A generation later William James detected the beginning of Methodism's swing of the pendulum from fervor to non-expectant rationalism, which has an affinity for formal religion—if for any whatever! In *Varieties of Religious Experience* he remarked that "the intellect, everywhere invasive, shows everywhere its shallowing effect," and added by way of illustration, "See how the ancient spirit of Methodism evaporates under those wonderfully able rationalistic booklets ... of a philosopher like Professor Bowne." [54]

In the Boston Lowell Lectures of 1900, Geo. C. Lorimer spoke up in defense of the camp-meeting revivalism of the period around 1800, even with its excess of religious emotion run riot. The alleviation brought by that revival to the desperately low moral and spiritual state then prevalent, in Lorimer's judgment, far out-weighed any damage resulting from fanaticism. He said he deplored the sensational phenomena that accompanied the meetings, but would ask of the critics who magnify the evils thereof, "Whether these incidental physical excesses were not as the mere automatic action of the eyelids in comparison with the more appalling moral and spiritual blindness of

---

52. Arnold Toynbee, *A Study of History*. Oxford University Press, New York and London; pp. 486, 487.
53. *The Earnest Christian*, v. 5, April, 1863; p. 126. (Quoting *Nature and the Supernatural*, by Horace Bushnell.)
54. William James, *Varieties of Religious Experience*. Longmans Green, and Co., New York; 502 n.

the age?" Remarks from such a source deserve further quotation:

> Was it not infinitely better to incur the possibility of such momentary exhibitions of nervousness than to have continued permanently in the blank, heartless atheism which was blighting and blasting every human hope? Better that people should lose their wits for a season than that they should lose their souls. The choice seems to have been between the revolutionary methods of the French and the revival methods of the Saxon. . . .[55]

The graver danger of formalism has been piquantly stated by B. T. Roberts: "Fanaticism is the devil arrayed in the righteousness of the saints; and he wears the robes so awkwardly, that the cloven foot is soon discovered." But, "Temptations that present an attractive appearance, under the garb of sanctity, are doubly dangerous"—and formalism is attractively clothed in that garb. "Formalism is dangerous, because it is contagious"; and, moreover, it begets the complacency of the Laodicean church.[56]

A century ago Roberts reported a Presbyterian revivalist of international reputation who warned against setting the limits of order within which the Spirit must work in a revival,[57] expressing the thought of John Wesley who would "suffer God to carry on His own work in the way that pleaseth Him."

Summary

The chapter we now conclude has sought to provide the background principles of Christian experience and worship as exhibited in early Methodism, in terms of which will be drawn, in the following chapter, the lines of Free Methodism's development in the same areas over the past one hundred years.

The early portion of the chapter outlined the four facts of Christian experience, (1) the Christian's assurance in consciousness of forgiveness; (2) the convert's consciousness of inner conflict between impulses to righteousness and impulses to sin; (3) the consciousness of inner cleansing the Christian reaches through the crisis of entire sanctification; and, (4) the long record of the experience of the Chris-

---

55. G. C. Lorimer, *Christianity in the Nineteenth Century*. Griffith & Rowland Press, Philadelphia; p. 31 *et seq.*
56. *The Earnest Christian*, v. 6, Sept. 1863; p. 66.
57. *Ibid.*, v. 1, June 1860; p. 167.

tian church in the quest for perfection, and the meaning of this to the health and progress of the church. In connection with the third item in the foregoing list, Wesley's examination of witnesses to heart cleansing was reviewed.

Briefly reviewed was the Christian's response to God by faith as the trusting yet active commitment of his total being to God, in consequence of which he will come, in Christian holiness, to experience perfect love to God and man. This love he will show forth in worship and service through the channels of his thought life, his affectional nature, and his conscious behavior. Through neglect of, or undue emphasis on, any one of these channels, imbalance results which, if extreme, may wreck both faith and character.

The varieties of emotional experience and its outward expression which characterized the worship and devotion of early Methodism were summarized as, (1) sustained joyous assurance of the religion of the heart; (2) profound bodily seizures caused in sinners by their deep terror and conviction for their sins; (3) spontaneous outbreaks of joy or deep heart-concern on the part of believers, usually in group worship; and (4) exaggerations of emotional response which disrupt or damage faith and lead to fanaticism. Illustrations or descriptions of these four varieties were presented.

The need for the exercise of charity and wisdom in dealing with strongly emotional and fanatical manifestations was pointed out, and methods of safeguarding against extremes were reviewed, especially methods recommended by John Wesley. The factors within historic Methodism that made for balanced control of its fervent religious life and worship were reviewed. The religious zeal of the Genesee reformers of the mid-nineteenth century, viewed in the perspective of the foregoing considerations and in the light of contemporary Methodist fervor, would appear to be earnest but not extravagant.

A final caution was expressed concerning today's graver danger of veering too far from religious fervor into dead formalism.

CHAPTER EIGHTEEN

Freedom of the Spirit in Worship

In this chapter we are to review the problems of religious experience, sometimes overwrought, with which Free Methodism had to deal both within and without its own ranks; to note the steadying influence of the ritual, especially the sacraments, upon the church's worship; to trace the movement from early restrictions against instrumental music and choir to freedom in terms of principle, and from simple beginnings to the development of an excellent hymnody; to consider church architecture in relation to the conservative principles of the denomination; to define the place of believers' meetings in earlier times and now; and to conclude with an evaluation of spiritual as against liturgical worship in their relation to the future of the Free Methodist Church.

A zeal not according to knowledge

The existence of religious extremists who operated as a loosely organized band under their chosen name, Nazarites, was referred to in Chapter Fifteen. These Nazarites are not to be confused with the earlier leaders of reform in Genesee who were dubbed "Nazarites" by the Regency after its discovery of the fictitious "Nazarite Documents" written by Joseph McCreery, setting forth the purpose and program of an organization that existed only in his own mind. In the chapter preceding this, the sane but earnest religious fervor of this earlier group of leaders of reform was well established.

Joseph McCreery had been one of the men at the Pekin Convention who dissented from the judgment of the majority to organize a new denomination. With others he withdrew from the majority and became one of the leaders of the organization which chose to be called Nazarites or Nazarite Band. It is fairly safe to assume that McCreery yet hoped that some such movement as he earlier had concocted in his highly fanciful imagination might flourish and reform Methodism. At least now he had the name of the organization of which he had dreamed. But in this hope he was to be disappointed, for the Nazarite movement came to naught, and McCreery finally entered the ministry of the Free Methodist Church in Kansas in 1869. According to Rev. M. N. Downing, however, he never was in full sympathy with the church.[1]

Although not Free Methodists, these Nazarites did not hesitate to flock to Free Methodist assemblies where, on occasion, they caused unpleasant disturbances. In a camp meeting near Allegany in 1861, Nazarites were in attendance and affairs were in confusion, the difficulty having been augmented, perhaps, by the efforts of some of the preachers to discourage extremes. The Nazarites tended to withdraw to themselves even for separate services which sometimes they continued during the regular services "at the stand." One evening B. T. Roberts went to their place of assembly, a tent located outside "the circle," and in a kind manner asked that they close their service and "go to the stand," assuring them that they could again assemble after the regular service and continue as long as they wished. He was greeted with such insolent refusals as, "We shall close when God tells us to," and, "The Holy Ghost began the meeting, and let Him close it." One man confronted Roberts and sang the Nazarite song, "If you can't stand the Nazarite fire." The Nazarites continued until their service was subdued by rowdies, who could make more noise than they! Strange to say, Roberts could report, "In spite of this, we had a good meeting at the stand . . . and several were saved."[2]

At the Pekin camp meeting which followed Allegany, there were five or six tents labeled "Nazarites," and their inmates were there to cause commotion. In a public service, one of the women reported that the Lord would have her say that Brother Roberts had a devil, and she further claimed that Brother Abell had been preaching for the devil from the opening of the camp meeting. Even the more sober Nazarites were ashamed of their own crowd's efforts to stir up trouble.[3]

By the time this camp concluded, it was little wonder that at the next, the Lyndon camp meeting, restraint should have come upon the

---

1. B. H. Roberts, *Benjamin Titus Roberts*. Earnest Christian Office, North Chili, New York; p. 232.
2. *Ibid.*, p. 320.
3. *Ibid.*, p. 322 *et seq.*

Free Methodists. Roberts wrote, "Many of our best people in this section have been frightened by the cry of 'fanaticism.'" [4]

Shortly after the outrages perpetrated by the Nazarites in the Allegany camp meeting, Roberts wrote an account of the movement in his diary, adding an analysis that strikingly resembles Wesley's description of the fanaticism that broke out under Maxfield, Bell and others in London precisely a century earlier. He said:

> There is among those who set out with us a class who style themselves Nazarites, in distinction from the Free Methodists. . . . They are pious, devoted, and some of them profess strong faith. They are—some of them at least—opposed to church organization, especially the Free Methodist Church. Others do not join for fear the church will come under the influence of Brothers Stiles and Abell, and in a short time become as formal as the M. E. Church.

Roberts proceeded to point out four respects in which he thought they were wrong: (1) Their meetings aimed, not "at the salvation of sinners and the sanctification of believers," but at having "'a free time,' that is, throwing off all restraint, and shouting, jumping, etc." (2) They placed the Spirit's leadership above the Bible, "sometimes claiming Divine inspiration for doing things which the Word of God especially forbids." (3) "They appear to seek reproach and to glory in it rather than purity and power." (4) Some of them "indulge in a wrong spirit," resenting even mild reproof as persecution, and "are exclusive, and do not fellowship fully any who do not appear to endorse their peculiar measures." [5]

The above entry in Roberts' diary has peculiar interest in the light of an editorial he published in *The Earnest Christian* long after. From that editorial it would seem that the fanatical elements in the following of the reformers had been a major factor in Roberts' decision to organize a church. There had been no intention to start a new denomination, he explained, because the reformers were confident that the General Conference would redress the wrongs the Genesee Conference had inflicted on them. But after the General Conference, they knew not what to do. No other existing denomination agreed with the reformers on the issues involved in their exclusion from the

---
4. *Ibid.*, p. 323.
5. *Ibid.*, p. 321 *et seq.*

Methodist Episcopal Church. But the need was clear—there must be an organization to control—or exclude!—the explosive elements that adhered to the reform group. This need led Roberts at last to join with those who favored organizing, even should only a microscopic minority submit to control by joining a duly established denomination. Note his own words:

> Some who had been clearly saved, unconsciously gave way to spiritual pride and self-will. A spirit of fanaticism . . . was exhibited by some. They would neither be instructed nor controlled. No one had any authority over them. In the eyes of the public we were all held responsible for their unscriptural conduct. The conviction was forced upon us that there must be an organization, even if there were not a dozen to join it. We felt clearly called of God to take the stand we took.[6]

Wise restraint of undue fervor

In time the Nazarite movement disintegrated, but a measure of the spirit it had exhibited did continue, and that there were extremists in early Free Methodism, as in early Methodism a century earlier, cannot be denied. The evidence appears in articles and letters by the church's leaders, and in other historical sources. With its emphasis on earnest Christianity, the new church attracted some whose zeal was not according to knowledge, and fringe remnants of the reforming element took advantage of the freedom promised by the church's name.

The policy of B. T. Roberts in handling the problems of excessive fervor was one of wise moderation rather than the somewhat rigid efforts at suppression to which other reform leaders were inclined to resort. In the summer of the acute difficulties with the Nazarites, he gave this caution:

> We do not fear any of the manifestations of the Spirit of God. But let the emotions you manifest be an effect produced by the Divine Spirit. We may shout until shouting becomes a habit. . . . There may be a formal noise as well as a formal silence. What we want is not noisy meetings, not still meetings—but the *spirit of the living God* in all our worshiping assemblies.[7]

A few years later he clearly stated his policy in an article on "Steadying the ark," in which he advised:

---

6. *The Earnest Christian*, v. 47, May 1884; p. 161.
7. *Ibid.*, v. 2, July 1861; p. 226 *et seq.*

Do not lay stress on any physical manifestations, as though the work of God could not go on without them; and do not magnify their importance by opposition.—Many a healthy child has been killed by giving it medicine instead of nourishment. Keep the true light shining and it will eclipse the false. . . . God is mightier than the devil.[8]

But Roberts' policy of moderation was not one of weakness, for he could be firm in his kindness. He wrote an extremist during the period of Nazarite annoyance in the summer of 1861, whether a Nazarite or another we do not know; but he called in question this man's disturbing a meeting with his fervor when it would have been better, Roberts suggested, had the people left "with the solemn truths to which they had listened ringing in their ears." He explained his position: "I believe in the Holy Ghost and I would not on any account grieve Him, or have others do so; but I think I have seen times when the devil used good people to hinder the work of God." He asked that the brother take this letter kindly, lay the matter before the Lord and no one else, and not call it persecution. "I love you," said Roberts, "and I want you should be more useful than you have ever been." But Roberts is not yet done with reproof! He continues, "I thought you did not take in a right spirit what Brother ——— said to you Sunday. You were too excited. You did not seem to me to take it patiently as you should. See I Peter, 2:20." His master strategy came in his closing paragraph: "Now, I want you should pray for me, for I do want to be right. Let me hear from you, and believe me ever, Your Brother in Jesus, B. T. Roberts." [9]

And there were problems also in the western field. In 1860 E. P. Hart, then a Methodist but later to become the second bishop of the Free Methodist Church as Roberts' junior, visited the St. Charles camp meeting which was destined to become famous throughout northern Illinois. This was the occasion, referred to in Chapter Fifteen, when the Illinois Conference or Western Convention was organized two months before the denomination itself had been organized. When in his later years Bishop Hart wrote *Reminiscences of Early Free Methodism*, he very frankly declared his estimate of that camp meeting, saying, "That there was much of divine power mani-

---

8. *Ibid.*, v. 14, March 1867; p. 95.
9. B. H. Roberts, *Benjamin Titus Roberts*; p. 327 *et seq.*

fested no one could question," but at once added, "and that there was a good deal of the rankest fanaticism no one in his right senses could deny."[10] To one who complained to Redfield about the extravagances, the good Doctor whimsically replied that "he thought there was full as much mercy for those who served God a little too hard as for those who did not serve him at all!"[11]

Because it was not Redfield's nature to hold a stiff rein, which fact his remark on the occasion just cited well indicated, it is the greater surprise to find that he wrote the preachers under him in the West a letter of most serious caution against permitting emotional excesses among the people. The letter was dated August 28, 1860, five days after the organizing convention at Pekin and while he was yet in the East where he had been representing the West in that assembly. Portions of his timely letter follow:

> I wish you and all your preachers, kindly but firmly, to set your powers against allowing the people's mind to be turned away from soul saving and a present Jesus, to something they know not what. . . . But do persuade them to preach repentance to the ungodly rather than gifts, and holiness to believers rather than tongues.

Doctor Redfield at this point perhaps recalled the tragedy of Edward Irving only a quarter-century earlier, whose deep learning, electric eloquence, princely personality and deep devotion only increased the confusion that came to his Presbyterian congregation from his encouraging *tongues* as evidence of God's breaking through in revival upon London. But to resume Redfield's advice to his preachers:

> May the Lord help you to keep all our people to the Bible rather than to impressions; to the love of Jesus rather than to the love of wonders. . . . If we cannot bring the people to the legitimate work of soul saving, both East and West, we will suffer shipwreck. . . . Give a mild but effectual check to the undue forwardness of the irresponsible.[12]

Possibly Dr. Redfield was sobered by an increasing sense of responsibility, now that an organized church was an accomplished fact—and

---

10. E. P. Hart, *Reminiscences of Early Free Methodism.* Free Meth. Pub. House, Chicago; p. 45.
11. J. G. Terrill, *The St. Charles Camp Meeting.* T. B. Arnold, Chicago; p. 13.
12. B. H. Roberts, *Benjamin Titus Roberts*; p. 331 et seq.

in no small measure due to his influence. Anyway, it was fortunate that the three stalwarts of this untried organization—a child of irregularity as Methodism itself had been—were level in judgment and firm in purpose to shape the new church according to Methodist principles of order in experience and worship, as well as in doctrine. These stalwarts were B. T. Roberts, John Wesley Redfield, and Loren G. Stiles, Jr. A fourth stalwart, Asa Abell, would soon join them.

Reported in Chapter Fifteen was a letter in Abell's hand that came to us by a strange providence during our research in preparation for the writing of this book. In reporting that discovery earlier, we stated that the letter effectively refuted the sly hint of a historian of Genesee that Asa Abell must have had in his nature a predisposition to fanaticism which explained the step he took in leaving the Methodist Episcopal Church for the Free Methodist. Let the reader judge for himself the religious balance of Asa Abell from the following brief excerpts from his advice to a prospective minister:

> Religious errors and especially such as highly excite the human mind, are pretty sure to produce some monstrosity or other in Christian character. Be careful then to keep within the Divine Records. Study the Holy Scriptures; and get all the help you can to a right understanding of them. Consult the writings of able and devout men, especially such as are well approved by the great Methodist bodies of Christians.
>
> Look for the guidance of the Holy Spirit but not in such a way nor in such a degree as to preclude the proper exercise of your own reason and judgment. . . . The idea which some appear to have embraced, that the mind of the highly spiritual person is inaccessible to the devil, has led within a few years to the wildest fanaticism. . . .
>
> In some cases of fanaticism which I have noticed, I have observed a lack of holy love and joy, but the presence of what appeared to me, to be a fiery and bitter zeal, an unteachable, ungovernable insubordinate spirit; and all I have no doubt under the idea of being beyond the reach of the devil, and of being led by an inner voice or impression from the Holy Ghost. . . .
>
> If you can, discourage all praying for miraculous gifts or for any gifts not belonging to the common Christian character. It is God's prerogative to bestow them if he pleases, but I cannot see that they are to be prayed for.

After much more advice on these and other problems of the

preacher, he closed with these words: "Be all the while learning—all the while disciplining and mending yourself. And my prayer is that you may be a much wiser and better man than your friend and brother in Christ, A. Abell."

Wise restraint was applied by Roberts during the early years of the church through *The Earnest Christian*. In 1862 he urged the importance of sanctified reason, and in the same editorial warned against that cardinal sin of the extremist, pride of opinion.

> Look with distrust upon all requirements to throw away your reason. This is one of the noblest faculties God has given to man. ... But the reason should be sanctified. And when it is, it should be listened to with attention. ...
>
> Look to it then that you are meek and lowly in heart—sufficiently humble to confess mistakes when you are left to make them. A subtle, unperceived pride of opinion that makes us unwilling to confess we are ever wrong, often leads us astray, and then keeps us from coming back into the right path.
>
> We must not throw away the doctrine of the leading of God's Spirit, because it is abused. But let us seek to understand it. God will give us wisdom if we humbly implore it.[13]

The battle to restrain excesses was not won in a year or two, but to the close of his life Roberts sought on the one hand to warn against the dangers of a zeal not according to knowledge, and on the other to encourage spiritual worship as against dead formalism. In a letter to his wife written in 1877 has been found this plaintive note concerning a conference he had just administered: "I should have enjoyed it better had not some of our good brethren felt that it was necessary to be noisy in order to be free."[14] Not long before his last General Conference he described "fanatical holiness" in the following discerning manner:

> *There is a fanatical holiness.* It lays great stress upon that for which it has least reason and Scripture for its support. Its self-denial is great, and is only equalled by its self-will. It has in it an element of sincerity, but it is vitiated by being consecrated to its own will, rather than the will of God. It lacks the great quality of submission. It does not know how to yield, even in matters the smallest and most indifferent. It must have its own

---

13. *The Earnest Christian*, v. 4, July 1862; p. 28 *et seq.*
14. B. H. Roberts, *Benjamin Titus Roberts;* p. 514.

way in everything. Every one must submit to its dictates or receive its fiery condemnation.[15]

About a year before his death he published an article entitled "Fanaticism," [16] from which we excerpt the following:

> Nothing pleases the devil more than to push devoted Christians over into fanaticism.
>
> It makes honest people afraid of Holy Ghost power. It takes one or two generations to get over the dread it occasions. Churches composed of sincere, earnest Christians become so afraid of fanaticism that the least manifestation of the Spirit's presence, out of the regular order, stirs them up to the most determined opposition.
>
> It gives great occasion for the enemies of spiritual religion to triumph.... For fear of it some go to the opposite extreme. Worldliness takes possession of preachers and churches.
>
> A spirit of self-sufficiency is the highway on which Satan enters the soul.

And then to set everything in perspective, he holds up spiritual religion as the center of Christianity:

> We must never forget that the essence of our Christianity is not doctrinal beliefs, nor observance of forms, but the indwelling Spirit.

Progress and problems

But progress was being made. As early as 1876 in *Cyclopedia of Biblical, Theological and Ecclesiastical Literature*, N. S. Gould reviewed this progress in the following words:

> During the first years of its history [the Free Methodist Church] had to encounter some of the difficulties which beset early Methodism in the form of wild fanaticism and a spirit of insubordination to proper church regulations, and it suffered considerably from the doings of some who were never members of the Church, but who, taking advantage of the circumstances under which it was formed, and acting somewhat in connection with its movements, promulgated ideas and encouraged practices contrary to pure Gospel; but the young denomination has had power to shake off these parasites, and free itself from these encumbrances, and bids fair to march on its way successfully in the mission of spreading scriptural holiness as understood by Wesley

---

15. *The Earnest Christian*, v. 62, Sept. 1891; p. 70.
16. *Ibid.*, v. 63, Feb. 1892; pp. 37-40.

and his immediate coadjutors. The religious services of the Free Methodists are generally characterized by the warmth and power so noticeable among early methodists.[17]

Shortly after the above was published, Bishop Simpson—by no means an impersonal or impartial judge of Free Methodism—after commenting in his *Cyclopedia of Methodism* (1878) on earlier excesses, added, "As the denomination has progressed, and has extended its boundaries, though their services are still attended by much fervor, there is less of these manifestations." [18] Writing a decade later, and also after noting earlier extravagances, A. B. Hyde said, "These have worn off, and in twenty-six years energy and zeal have come to be joined to charity, sobriety and decorum." [19]

But the church itself in this period was not unaware of continuing excesses. In the General Conference of 1886 the committee on the state of the work warned against "an egotistical holiness" that makes self the center and is harsh toward any who hold different opinions. It also warned against placing the standard of holiness either too low or too high—if too high, some will claim an imaginary holiness and be led into delusion.

The same committee in the General Conference of 1894 faced realistically the difficulties that had prevented greater growth in the church. It recognized deepening spirituality in some places, but pointed to "more or less fanaticism here and there;" the dissemination of wild and utterly unscriptural doctrine by would-be leaders;" the "spirit of insubordination . . . manifested in the various independent movements among us . . . eating like a canker;" "a woeful lack of prudence in presenting our issues" which had "created a tremendous amount of unnecessary prejudice." No wonder the committee exclaimed, "O when shall we learn wisdom?"

In the General Conference of 1907, the bishops in their address spoke out plainly. They declared strong confidence that the church as a whole was maintaining its spirituality and that "the large majority

---

17. N. S. Gould, "Free Methodists," in *Cyclopedia of Biblical, Theological and Ecclesiastical Literature."* Harper & Bros., New York; pp. 187-189.
18. Matthew Simpson, *Cyclopedia of Methodism*. Everts & Stewart, Philadelphia; pp. 379, 380.
19. A. B. Hyde, *The Story of Methodism*. M. W. Hazen Co., New York; p. 320 of "The Story in America."

of both preachers and laymen profess to be in 'the fulness of the blessing.'" However, the work was hindered by excessive emphasis on negative issues by some, and also by "ambitious and schismatic pretenders to a more spiritual leadership" than the church had chosen, who "claimed to promote a type of experience far in advance of anything 'possessed' by the regularly constituted leaders of the church or by the rank and file of its membership."

In time, with the growth of the church and stabilization of its government, the more vexatious manifestations of spiritual pride, extravagant emotionalism, and delusions of the flesh were allayed. Along with growing moderation of religious fervor, the church maintained the freedom of the Spirit and accepted manifestations of spiritual life and power as an essential quality of earnest Christianity. In this, Free Methodism has been in accord with the injunction of Nolan B. Harmon, Jr., who has said, "Above everything else let us keep clear the old Methodist and Protestant contention that the individual must have perfect liberty as he meets his God." [20]

Worship through ritual and the sacraments

From the problem of emotion and its spontaneous expression in worship, our inquiry turns abruptly to the officially recognized and directed channels which worship has followed in the Free Methodist Church. As is true of groups generally that hold to the tradition of free worship, ritual has occupied but a minor place in its worship. However, the special occasions when ritual is the order have made a contribution of value to the stability and the spiritual depth of the congregation.

Most important of the church's ritual services is the Communion of the Lord's Supper, which in Free Methodism follows historic Methodism in essentials of content, form, and rubrics. The high regard in which the church has held its heritage in this area is disclosed in the resistance would-be innovators have encountered from the General Conference in their attempts to make changes in the ritual of the Communion. Something of this faithfulness to our rich past was reviewed in Chapter Sixteen on doctrine.

The established posture in receiving the Sacrament of the Lord's

---

20. Nolan B. Harmon, "Methodist Worship and Ideals," in *Methodism*, Wm. K. Anderson, Ed. The Methodist Publishing House, Nashville; p. 237.

Supper is stipulated in the invitation by the words, "meekly kneeling"; and the earlier words, "draw near," directed to the worshipers, imply a group response at the communion rail. In recent years, serving in the pews has tended in places to disrupt this solemn Methodist tradition of a communion group surrounding the Lord's table, and sometimes a visitor might conclude he had entered the service of a congregational or independent group. The mangling of a beautiful service by borrowing from other traditions or attempting innovations on one's own, has been unfortunate. Members of an earlier generation who sturdily stood for their freedom in the Spirit in an ordinary service, would be deeply disturbed today by what to them would appear violence to a hallowed rite in which their turbulence of spirit was quieted by His presence as they partook of the emblems of His broken body and shed blood. Freedom of the Spirit? Yes!—in the regular services. In the Lord's Supper, let it be the solemnity of His passion and the deep unutterable joy of His salvation into which His free Spirit leads the communicants.

With the scholarly and devout Dr. Harold Roberts, president of the World Methodist Council, Free Methodists can heartily agree that "the service of Holy Communion is something more than a memorial service since He who is commemorated returns in the fulness of His power." [21]

The ritual of baptism is important as that Sacrament by which one becomes identified with the visible body of Christ. Great joy has come upon recipients and the assembled congregations in this service which symbolizes and proclaims Christian victory.

God is present in this sacramental rite to minister His grace to candidates ready through the atonement to receive it. The atonement covers infant as well as saved adult, qualifying both for baptism. The adult recipient's part is to witness to his personal faith and declare his vows of obedience, a part that parents take in behalf of the infant or small child. After the child's conversion and in connection with his joining the church, he is then to declare for himself the vows made in his behalf by his parents at the time of his baptism.

---

21. Harold Roberts, "The People of God," in *Proceedings of the Ninth World Methodist Conference*, Elmer T. Clark and E. Benson Perkins, Editors. The Methodist Publishing House, Nashville; p. 102.

It is significant that when the concept of baptism comprehends its nature as a sacrament in which God is active in ministering grace to the recipient, even Baptists in Ceylon have been able to unite with Episcopalians, accepting both infant and adult baptism. "Conceiving baptism primarily as a sacrament, one is unable to argue that God cannot act upon a child." [22]

This is quite in line with Wesley who said, "If infants ought to come to Christ, if they are capable of admission into the Church of God, and consequently of solemn sacramental dedication to him, then they are proper subjects of baptism." The virtue of the rite, said Wesley, is ascribed not "to the outward washing, but to the inward grace, which, added thereto, makes it a sacrament." [23]

The Free Methodist Church maintains that the grace ministered in baptism is not regenerating grace, either in adult or in child; and the church firmly stands opposed to the doctrine of baptismal regeneration. It does, however, with open arms receive into the fellowship and nurture of the Christian community, through baptism, such little children as Jesus blessed and declared to be of the Kingdom of God. The church's Article of Religion on baptism declares, "The baptism of young children shall be retained in the church."

The ordination of ministers (deacons and elders) follows a dignified and prescribed ritual, with the laying on of hands. This ritual is uniformly observed. Rituals for services of dedication of churches and for the solemnizing of marriage are provided, but these, being in nature neither sacraments nor investiture with ministerial authority, are less strictly followed, the officiating minister being allowed greater freedom in choosing the order he will use.

Early restrictions on music in worship

The call for the organization of the Free Methodist Church in 1860 listed as one issue upon which the proposed church should be established, the requirement of "congregational singing, without instrumental music in all cases."

Unaccompanied singing in divine worship is no novelty even today,

---

22. Eugene L. Smith, "New United Churches and Suggested Plans of Union," in *ibid.*, p. 277.
23. See Ralph Kirby, Compiler, *The Methodist Bedside Book*. David McKay Co., Inc., New York; p. 318.

one hundred years after Pekin. There still are denominations that refuse instrumental accompaniment to singing in their churches. One group, numbering several hundred thousand members, holds that the use of musical instruments in the church is contrary to New Testament Christianity, and widely advertises its position even in the secular press.

Methodism, including Free Methodism, has been less absolutist. Both have sought to settle the problem on the basis of what is "the more excellent way," rather than to reject either as forthrightly wrong. But this is not to say that many individuals who have been opposed to instrumental music in Methodism and Free Methodism have not claimed that its use is wrong.

We need not follow the steps toward choirs and instrumental music taken by the Methodist Episcopal Church. This was sufficiently reviewed in Chapter Nine. But we should recall that the issue had not long before been settled in the parent church when the Free Methodist Church was launched. Even in 1860, the matter was still being agitated through such reform channels as the *Northern Independent*.

Early Free Methodist *Disciplines* carried over from the Methodist Episcopal *Discipline* a section entitled "Of the Spirit and Truth of Singing," but with the following restrictions added: "In no case let there be instrumental music or choir singing in our public worship." English Methodism had banned the organ in 1806, but within a few years, as we know from the troublesome "Leeds Organ Case" in the late twenties, the organ was permitted under rather stringent voting procedures. In the Methodist Episcopal Church musical instruments were never forbidden by legal enactment, but in early days it was assumed that their use was contrary to Methodist principles of worship.

The stand of early Free Methodism against choirs and instrumental music is explained by the historic Methodist position against them, and the deterioration of congregational singing and the increase of formalism in worship that accompanied, if they were not caused by, the introduction of these features in major Methodism about the time of Free Methodism's origin.

Restrictions slowly relax

For many years there was little if any agitation in the Free Methodist Church for choirs and musical instruments in worship. Not until ninety-five years had passed were all restrictions lifted. Following is a summary of General Conference attention to the music issue.

1860. The church was launched with both instrumental music and choirs in public worship forbidden.

1898. The church's historic position against instrumental music was strongly endorsed by the committee on reforms and its report was adopted. This may indicate that promotion of the cause of music had begun.

1903. The Southern California Conference asked General Conference to leave unchanged the disciplinary restrictions on music, which it did. Evidently agitation for instrumental music then existed.

1907. A ruling by Bishop B. R. Jones in the New York Conference of 1903 was sustained by the General Conference, that ruling having declared that the use of instruments of music in the Sunday school came under the restriction of the *Discipline.* It would appear that the same General Conference discerned the prudential nature of the issue when it refused to take steps to place the prohibition of instrumental music in the "restrictive rules," which would then require concurrent action of General Conference and the annual conferences to change the rule.

1931. The proposal to strike from the *Discipline* the rule against instrumental music and choirs was defeated by a vote of 45 for, 98 against. A resolution was then adopted confirming the *status quo,* but in the case of instrumental music, exempting "foreign-speaking churches or missions in the United States, Mexico and Japan." The exemption was listed as a foot-note qualifying the prohibitive rule. This step, exempting certain churches from the prohibition of instrumental music, committed the Free Methodist Church to the position that its restrictions were prudential, and not based upon the claim that the use of instruments in divine worship was inherently sinful or worldly.

During the quadrennium following the 1931 General Conference, the Board of Administration called for a referendum on the question of music, and votes were taken in the local membership of the denomination.

1935. The General Conference declared the referendum unwise and unauthorized, and the results of the voting were never disclosed. This General Conference defeated a proposal to approve instrumental music by a vote of 43 for approval and 112 against—a definitely lower ratio for the instrument than in 1931.

1939. This General Conference rejected a proposal to permit the use of instrumental music on a local option or congregational basis, the vote standing 61 for, 98 against.

1943. General Conference voted 88 to 84 to approve instrumental music on a two-thirds vote of the local church, if the conference in which the church was located had approved music by a majority vote. Choir singing was forbidden, and only one instrument could be used—organ or piano.

1947. General Conference removed the requirement that an annual conference must first approve instrumental music before a church within its bounds could vote to have an instrument.

1955. General Conference deleted the rule forbidding choirs, and left the use of musical instruments to majority vote of the local church, without restriction as to number and kind, but stipulating that change of policy concerning the use of instruments "may not be considered twice in the same conference year."

Although General Conference lifted the specific restrictions governing instrumental music, at the same time it declared the following principle for the guidance of the church's worship through music:

> The purpose of music in divine service is to inspire and to sustain worship. Therefore participation in musical exercises, vocal and instrumental, shall seek to contribute to reverent and exalted worship and not to the display of talent, however excellent. The primary purpose of musical instruments in divine service is to support and guide the human voice, whether in congregational or special singing. Only man of all earthly creatures can worship, and those responsible for planning the church's program of music and those directing the same will therefore subordinate the instrument to the human voice as a means to the worship of God in the congregation.

With the adoption of this statement, the transition from legal restrictions to the declaration of a principle had been made without rupture or crucial tension; but the effectiveness of a guiding principle is yet to be measured.

Several years after the General Conference had broken a long-guarded tradition, a brother, who acknowledged that he had been in the conservative camp on the music question, expressed the magnanimous spirit of one whose cherished tradition had been shattered by an unwelcome innovation, but who recognized that the heart of vital religion had not been sacrificed along with the tradition. There can be no schism in a church where such a spirit prevails. He said:

> The attitude which some of us have had concerning instrumental music may illustrate how sacredly one may hold a tradition. We have to concede that it is not forbidden in the Holy Scriptures. We should call to mind that there have been men

all throughout our history who favored having music, and so long as they were in the minority, they conceded to the will of the majority and did not allow these differences to break their fellowship. Now that we are in the minority, the Lord give us grace to do as well as they. A minority group still feel that there is nothing comparable to good singing without instruments, and that although the rule was only a tradition, the change should not have been made.[24]

We repeat the comment made in Chapter Nine, that only in its removing the restrictions against instrumental music and choir-singing has the Free Methodist Church officially reversed a major position established by the founders in 1860. Although this change has been made, may the church never forget that congregational singing holds first place in Free Methodist worship through music. In the words of B. T. Roberts, "singing is as much an act of worship as prayer."

The Growth of a hymnody

During the years of exclusively congregational and unaccompanied singing, the Free Methodist Church was not indifferent to music as an essential element of worship. The early *Disciplines* called for the cultivation of singing in every society, and congregational singing itself developed both singers and leaders of congregational singing. Moreover, the schools and colleges of the church gave excellent training in practically all fields of music, and in later years they have featured a cappella singing and have developed choirs that excel therein.

Any account of the place of music in Free Methodist worship would be incomplete without at least a brief survey of the development of its hymnody. In the earlier years of its history, the church rather generally used the *Methodist Episcopal Hymn Book* of 1849. The General Conference of 1878 designated a committee of fifteen to compile and edit a hymn book, but stipulated that the project must not involve the church in a financial way. Perhaps for this reason at the close of the quadrennium, although six hundred hymn selections had been gathered, the book had not been published. The 1882 General Conference appointed another and a smaller committee, and

---

24. D. N. Thomas, "Phariseeism and the Holiness Movement," in *The Free Methodist;* July 29, 1958; p. 470.

the following year *The Hymn Book of the Free Methodist Church* was published by the committee's chairman, B. T. Roberts. The book was a word edition of 868 selections. The General Conference had instructed the committee to base the book upon the *Methodist Episcopal Hymn Book* then in use among Free Methodists, and the *Wesleyan Hymnbook* of England. This the committee did, but drew also on the *Wesleyan Canada Hymn Book*, the *Primitive Methodist Hymn Book of Canada*, Ray Palmer's collection, and others.

It is evident that the church continued to use other hymn books after 1883, for the committee on publications of the 1886 General Conference commented on the unfortunate lack of uniformity through the church in the matter of hymn books, and commended the *Hymn Book* of 1883. The committee urged, however, that future publications be more substantially bound and typographical errors be avoided. But the church now had its own *Hymn Book* containing many choice hymns, a book that did splendid service for several years. The 1898 General Conference made it the duty of pastors to see that the *Free Methodist Hymn Book* was used in the regular services.

It seems that a *Metrical Tune Book* had appeared in 1874, edited by Philip Phillips, but so far as we have determined, this first edition was quite outside Free Methodist influence and patronage. It carried standard tunes, but without hymns, and was described in the Preface as "containing all the popular tunes from every source, which can be used with any Hymn Book, and from which the Chorister can select a tune of his own choice." Another edition appeared in 1890 with J. G. Terrill's name connected with that of Philip Phillips. This edition was in use among Free Methodists at the time of Terrill's death in 1895, according to Hogue.[25] Terrill was in process of revising the book when he died, and the work was completed by T. B. Arnold and published by him in 1896. Arnold had been the church's first publishing agent, and when the third edition of the *Tune Book* appeared, he was owner and publisher of the church's Sunday-school publications. The title of this edition was, *Metrical Tune Book with Hymns and Supplement*. This and the *Hymn Book* still belong to the treasury of childhood memories of our older generation.

---

25. W. T. Hogue, *History of the Free Methodist Church*, Free Meth. Pub. House, Winona Lake, Ind.; v. 2, p. 209.

FREEDOM OF THE SPIRIT IN WORSHIP

The early half of the *Tune Book* carried the entire 868 hymns of the 1883 *Hymn Book,* grouped in pages each of which carried at the top the musical staff of the tune by which the several hymns printed on the same page were to be sung. The hymns carried the numbers assigned them in the *Hymn Book,* the sequence of course being confused by the classification of the hymns on pages according to their proper tunes; but the tunes were numbered consecutively. The minister announced a hymn by the number it carried in the *Hymn Book,* and also by the number of its tune in the *Tune Book.* Thus the congregation was adequately guided even if some members carried *Hymn Books* and others *Tune Books!*

The second portion of the *Tune Book,* called *Supplement of Light and Life Songs,* was entirely different. The songs were arranged in the customary fashion, words within the staff and the songs numbered consecutively. As the title suggests, the *Supplement* was a gospel song book, probably the forerunner of the series of *Light and Life* song books which the church itself published later.

In 1903 the General Conference authorized a Sunday-school song book and created a committee to prepare it. There began a series of worthy gospel song books which we shall not take space to name or describe.

In 1910 appeared the first hymn book published by the church itself. Its title was *Free Methodist Hymnal,* and it carried 738 selections with music, in regular hymn-book style with words directly accompanying the musical staff. About this time a commission on union with the Wesleyan Methodist Church became active, and it may be that the interest in union was expressed by the inclusion on the hymnal commission of a representative of the Wesleyan Methodist Church. That church also made this book its official hymn book, under the title *Wesleyan Methodist Hymnal.* This was a practical hymnal, serving well its generation of forty-one years.

In 1951 the church published its present hymnal, this one likewise in cooperation with the Wesleyan Methodist Church with which again a commission on union of the two churches was active. The title of this book is *Hymns of the Living Faith.* It carries 579 hymns and in addition has sections both of responsive and unison readings. The late Dr. George McCutchan, editor of *The Methodist Hymnal,* evaluated it in the highest terms. We take the following from a personal letter dated July 9, 1953:

> I want to congratulate you on your *Hymns of the Living Faith;* it is one of the finest hymnals which has appeared in this century. And when I say that I am saying a great deal for there have been some very fine ones issued. Not only have you remained true to your traditions but you have kept abreast with the best that has developed in the hymnological field.

The Free Methodist Church, committed from its origin to earnest congregational singing, a decade before the close of its first century had developed a hymnody ranking with the best in musical excellence and which, at the same time, was faithful to the church's rich heritage in doctrine and experience.

Church architecture

Another important influence on worship is the architecture and interior furnishings of the house of worship. Following the change in Methodist church music during the second quarter of the nineteenth century, a new era in Methodist church architecture came in the third quarter which replaced the plain meetinghouse or chapel with costly edifices having sky-reaching steeples.

The first *Discipline* of American Methodism, adopted by the Christmas Conference of 1784 which organized the Methodist Episcopal Church, contained the following declaration on church architecture:

> Let all our chapels be built plain and decent; . . . but not more expensively than is absolutely unavoidable: Otherwise the Necessity of raising Money will make Rich Men necessary to us. But if so, we must be dependent upon them, yea, and governed by them. And then farewell to the Methodist-Discipline, if not Doctrine too.[26]

It is not without significance that the 1872 General Conference deleted all of this declaration but the first two clauses. American Methodism by then had become essentially a middle-class church, and the "Gilded Age" was dawning. Consequently the church was far from indifferent to the influence of men of wealth. The legalizing of

---

26. Quoted by David Sherman, *History of the Revisions of the Discipline of the Methodist Episcopal Church.* Nelson & Phillips, New York; p. 85.

"pewed" churches in 1852 had already marked an important step toward changing the character of Methodist church buildings. Encouraged by Bishop Simpson, who began his episcopal career in 1852, Pittsburgh in 1855 built American Methodism's first gothic temple.[27] In connection with the centenary celebration of Methodism's introduction into America, the influential Abel Stevens in 1866 named improvement in church architecture as the responsibility of Methodism in ministering to the public culture. He wrote:

> True art should be recognized as one of the noblest handmaids of religion; elevating impressions and associations, through the senses in our temples, may ennoble even divine worship; and imposing monuments of taste, consecrated to piety, are among the highest means of national culture, and the highest proofs of advanced civilization.[28]

Such sentiments pointed the way to extravagant displays of church architecture and art during the latter part of the century, which further restrained the freedom of spiritual worship. With Stevens' advanced ideas of sensate worship, contrast Robrts' convictions expressed five years earlier:

> Expensive, splendid churches are the offspring of pride. And they in their turn beget pride. Pride keeps out the Spirit of God, and engenders formality. You need never expect to see a simple-hearted, spiritual people, worshipping in a magnificent temple.[29]

The founding fathers of Free Methodism held to the simplicity of the early Methodist meetinghouse. Studying the structure and design of older Free Methodist churches still standing, one notes their solid strength, their simple lines, their attractive proportions, and their utility for the period in which they were built—an era that knew little of the departmentalized church of today and its architectural demands. One of our congregations, which was organized as a Free Methodist Church in 1860 and worships today in the building erected in 1863, has architect's plans for a new church that incorporate the original structure as a wing of the new edifice. It may well be that those early reformers built for two centuries!

---

27. See Robert D. Clark, *The Life of Matthew Simpson*. The Macmillan Co., New York; p. 192.
28. Abel Stevens, *The Centenary of American Methodism*. Carlton & Porter, New York; p. 235.
29. *The Earnest Christian*; v. 2, March 1861; p. 100.

It is unfortunate that an intermediate era of fragile, box-like structures succeeded the earlier and more substantial church buildings, but we are now passing into a third era wherein those fragile shelters are giving way to modern, functionally designed churches. Our founding fathers did not foresee our day's architectural developments, but they built to meet the simple needs of their day even as we should build to meet the diversified needs of ours.

In the early years the Free Methodist Church enacted no legislation concerning church architecture. Simplicity was taken for granted as an essential of historic Methodism, and, in any case, for reasons of economy elaborateness was out of the question. But after the passing of two decades the General Conference of 1882 deemed the following safeguard necessary:

> Let all our houses of worship be built plain, and decent, without steeples, and not more expensive than is absolutely required for comfort, convenience, and stability, and with all seats free.[30]

Other than editorial changes, this continued as originally adopted until 1955 when the provision of a divided chancel in two or three new churches of the denomination created an issue that became acute in the General Conference. Unable to reach satisfactory wording to express the consensus of the body, the General Conference broke all precedent by referring to the Board of Administration the drafting of a statement on an unsolved issue. To the existing statement quoted above, the Board of Administration added the following:

> Let the architecture and interior arrangements of our churches be planned and constructed to contribute to a distinctively evangelical simplicity and reverence in worship which make the preaching of the Word central in the service.

The 1955 General Conference had regularly adopted the following statement which is incorporated with both the foregoing statements as one section of the 1955 *Discipline*:

> It is understood that we will build in keeping with prevailing architecture of the surrounding area and with such attractiveness as to commend the gospel to the community.

The present era of church building is witnessing unprecedented

---

30. The requirement last named, free seats, had been in force since the church's founding in 1860.

expansion in the church structures of Free Methodism across the continent. The new functional architecture of today is a radical departure from the traditional architecture of yesterday, but while attractive and in some cases striking in appearance, it is economical and highly adaptable to growing programs. Rapid and radical changes make it the more urgent that the Free Methodist Church be alert to the principle of simplicity, lest competition for community prominence or conference pre-eminence, or the persuasiveness of nonevangelical architects, lead to a greater interest in the structure in which we worship than our concern for the spirit of worship itself. The Free Methodist standard in architecture calls for simple, economical, Word-centered and appropriately designed church buildings.

Believers' meetings

In major Methodism after mid-century, marked changes took place in the services conducted within its high-arched gothic structures. When circuits and itinerant preachers gave way to stations with resident pastors, class meeting and class leader lost their former spiritual importance. With the development of religion as big business, making rich men necessary to support the church and calling for their help in places of administrative control, trustees tended to replace stewards in church management. More and more the exercises of worship passed from lay into professional hands. Love feasts, class meetings and prayer meetings lost their appeal, and religious services tended to become more a performance on a stage before spectators, less a society engaged in communal worship. As someone has said, business meetings came to replace prayer meetings. In fact, a speaker in the Sixth Ecumenical Methodist Conference of 1931 could say the word "society" was no longer appropriate in Methodism, for the "society" had become a "congregation." The society, he said, "is maintained by the activity of its members, everyone bringing something of spiritual help and sustenance for the good of the whole," whereas a congregation "is a gathering of people who attend upon the ministry of a preacher." [31]

When a society changes to a congregation, believers' meetings go into decline and the weekly program of group devotion and wor-

---

31. R. H. B. Shapland, "The Outlook," in *Proceedings of the Sixth Ecumenical Methodist Conference* (1931). M. E. Church South, Nashville; p. 305.

ship is continued with difficulty. The importance placed on the class meeting until mid-century, and its defensive battle at that time to maintain an existence, are reflected in these words of Bishop Morris written in 1851:

> To change the rule so as to allow its professors to attend class meeting or not, at their own option, and still remain members of the church, would be practically to abolish the institution itself; and to abolish class meeting would be virtually to abolish Methodism, and let our church members fall into lifeless formality. . . . Let no one, under a mistaken notion of improving Methodism, seek to have this test of membership done away, unless he prefers careless and worldly-minded professors of religion to living stones of the temple of God.[32]

Thirty years ago Merrill Gaddis wrote of the Free Methodist Church, "Its pietistic technique is shown in the important place assigned to believers' meetings, particularly the class-meeting, for the development and maintenance of the perfect life." [33] How valid is this appraisal in 1960?

Our Methodist heritage included such believers' meetings as the class meeting, the love feast, and the prayer meeting. The general quarterly meeting developed under Loren Stiles in 1855 when he was presiding elder over the Genesee District of the Methodist Episcopal Church. It quickly won the support of the reformers and was carried over by them into the young church where it rapidly became an established institution. It continues today as the district quarterly meeting. Although this three- or four-day event was an occasion when preachers from the district brought the sermons, it was so characterized by warm fellowship among the people, both in informal association and in organized services, that we mention it here in connection with believers' meetings. And much the same could be said of the camp meeting which ran for eight or ten days, and drew family groups and individuals from a district or conference area to reside on the grounds as a miniature community for that period.

Economic and household changes in more recent years have operated against large attendance at district quarterly meetings today,

---

32. Thomas A. Morris, in the Introduction, John Miley's *Treatise on Class Meetings*. Swormstead & Poe, Cincinnati; pp. 20, 21.
33. M. E. Gaddis, "Christian Perfectionism in America." University of Chicago, doctoral thesis; p. 438.

except for special rallies scheduled on a particular day of the period. There has been a tendency to shorten the span of the district quarterly meeting, even to a single day in some areas. Then the event takes on the character of a general rally featuring different interests in different services of the day's program, including a session of the district quarterly conference. The district quarterly meeting is still an important occasion of spiritual fellowship among us.

The camp meeting has been an outstanding agency both of evangelism and Christian nurture. In early days it might change its location from year to year, seeking as principal needs of the encampment a good grove of trees, water, and accessibility to people, but needing no permanent structures. In recent years a camp meeting is usually established in one location with permanent and well developed facilities. Its program is diversified to meet the needs of different age-groups, and sometimes an annual conference operates separate camps for the different groups.

Increasingly the camp meeting is becoming an institution enlisting in residence the Christian community of an extensive denominational area, and no longer draws the immense crowds of "out-siders" that characterized the evening and Sunday services of former generations. This fact means the reduction of the opportunities for revival evangelism, but increases the opportunities for evangelizing the children and youth of the church and developing them through Christian nurture.

One of the best accounts of the old-fashioned Free Methodist camp meeting is J. G. Terrill's *The St. Charles Camp Meeting*, covering that historic camp meeting from 1860 to 1882. From this story one gets the picture of the early camp meeting as including such features as an earnest Christianity; revival power, attended at times by emotional excess; episodes of rowdyism; a great Sunday crowd of many thousands requiring a check-stand for lunch baskets, umbrellas and parcels; a varied program adapted to the needs of varied groups; spiritually powerful preaching on a high intellectual level; a concern for social and benevolent causes; a Christian fellowship that crossed denominational lines, even in the selection of a noted Methodist evangelist for the preaching staff.

The founders of Free Methodism maintained also the people's meetings inherited from Methodism at the local society and circuit levels. The prayer meeting was well established from the beginning and has continued a vital force to this day. But there has been decline both in the class meeting and in the love feast.

The class meeting was organized by John Wesley early in Methodism's history, as related in Chapter Nine. Wesley was criticized for introducing a novelty. He answered the criticism by pointing out that the class meeting was simply a prudential, and not an essential or divine institution; and that there was advantage in maintaining flexibility in the prudentials of the work. "We are always open to instruction," he said; "willing to be wiser every day than we were before, and to change whatever we can change for the better." [34]

Today we criticize the church for neglecting what Wesley was criticized for initiating! If the class meeting is indeed outmoded, as so many claim, is there no one with John Wesley's open mind and practical imagination to point the way to something that will do for the church today what the class meeting did for it yesterday? The class meeting had something the church needs today, whether that benefit is to return through the revival of the class meeting or through some new channel.

Features of Free Methodism's early class meeting included: (1) attendance by members of the church only, except by consent of the leader; (2) a general class meeting held every month for all classes of the society; (3) examination by the leader of every person in his class as to how his soul prospers, "not only how each person observes the outward rules, but how he grows in the knowledge and the love of God"; (4) admonition by the pastor of those who wilfully persist in neglecting the meetings of the class, and bringing them to trial "for neglect of duty" if there is no improvement. Excepting the closed feature of (1), these features obtain in principle today with minor changes, but are inadequately practiced.

In the beginning, love feasts were to be held every three months on each circuit, with closed doors, and non-members of the church were to be admitted only with the pastor's consent. The requirement of a love feast every three months still stands in the *Discipline*, but

---

34. J. Wesley, "A Plain Account of the People Called Methodists," in *Works* (Emory ed. 1853); v. 5, p. 180.

is not consistently exercised. When held, it usually is a general testimony meeting on a quarterly meeting occasion, without the personal greetings and symbolic breaking of bread and sharing of water which were wont to be attended by the melting of differences if such existed, and a closer fellowship among Christians.

The spirit of such early institutions as the class meeting and the love feast must continue to flow through the church, if necessary through modified or new forms, if we are to conserve that lay participation in the church's fellowship and devotion which is essential to free worship. Even a professor in Boston University has been aroused to sound this warning to major Methodism: "Communal prayer and testimony must be restored somehow to a prominent place among us, lest we cease not only to be Methodists but to be Christians." [35]

The graver danger

With major Methodism generations since, Free Methodism now faces "the graver danger." Free Methodist worship is a going concern with worship-centered music, reverent and simple sacramental ritual, simplicity of physical arrangements with a quickening concern for attractiveness, believers' participation with freedom of spiritual spontaneity expected and appreciated—all providing a warm setting for the ministry of the Word as the focal feature of the service.

But certain changes have occurred, some of them changes that brought alarm to sober Methodists a century ago. Instrumental music and choirs are accepted—and who will say that, in general, they are not remaining within bounds of the church's clearly defined principle? Standing for prayer in public worship instead of kneeling is increasingly common: God forbid the time should ever come when Free Methodists are content to remain seated! Seldom now is a worshiper seen to kneel quietly in his pew when he takes his place—or even to bow his head, for a moment of silent prayer.

Harmon notes that the musical "Amen" came into Methodist worship with the hymnal of 1905 and its publication of an order of worship that made place for the singing of "Gloria Patri" and the recital of the Apostles' Creed. In the back of the book was a section of

---

[35]. L. Harold DeWolf, "The Doctrine of the Church," in *Methodism*. Wm. K. Anderson, Editor. The Methodist Publishing House, Nashville p. 217.

responsive readings. Harmon states that the publication of this hymnal and the adoption of the orders of worship it carried "caused a storm in many Methodist churches" "It not only smacked of formality," he says, "it *was* formality." [36] Our purpose in citing these innovations which were introduced into Methodist worship in 1905, is not to condemn any particular form mentioned up to this point, but to throw into bold relief the rapidity with which forms can invade free worship.

Paving the way for such an order of worship, according to Harmon, was the influence of the Protestant Episcopal Church whose form of worship is the standard toward which other churches are moving, "so that today the worship service as conducted in any regular church of one of the great denominations is very much like that of any other."

Then came the liturgical upsurge a score of years after the Methodist order of worship was published in the 1905 hymnal, and under the inspiration of that upsurge, Harmon reports, some pastors ventured a formal call to worship and a prayer over the offering, even before these were placed officially in the Methodist order of worship. Under liturgical influence came also architectural changes, and "the divided chancel appeared for the first time in Methodist buildings," Harmon reports. "Up to that time," he explains, "the pulpit had been central with the Communion table and the 'altar' below it. After that, in certain churches the pulpit was moved to one side and through the divided chancel one saw the lifted altar," after the Protestant Episcopal pattern.[37]

Because it is the inwardness of worship rather than its outward form that counts, Harmon says, adding to the service what he terms "liturgical odds and ends" for the purpose of enriching it, is pointless. Who does not know ministers such as Harmon describes, who carry God's presence with them into the pulpit and from the first moment communicate a sense of that Presence to the congregation? These preachers do not wait upon "liturgical odds and ends" to induce an instinctive religious awe which may be quite devoid of the grace of God. Such a religious mood may be aroused in even the most

---

36. Nolan B. Harmon, "Methodist Worship: Practice and Ideals," *ibid.*, p. 234 *et seq.*
37. *Ibid., loc. cit.*

secularly minded by spacious architecture, artistic symbolism, the moving strains of organ music, the chant of robed choir, and the sepulchral intonations of a read liturgy. But this mood is far other than the spontaneous outgoing of a devout soul in praise and worship of God. One is sensate, induced by aesthetic surroundings; the other is spiritual, the active response of "the heart."

Elmer T. Clark claims that "the emotional element has all but passed from the religion of the great Churches." As it stands, his statement is hardly true. The liturgical appeal is primarily emotional, but at the level of induced mood rather than outgoing passion. But Clark makes clear that he means that these churches lack the latter when he notes that it is pathetic to watch them, "developing puny 'worship programs' and impotent 'decision day services' and 'religious emphasis weeks' in an endeavor to make up for the passing of great emotional experiences that plumbed the depths of men's souls, changed lives, emotionalized conviction and attitude, and left the irreducible appreciation of spiritual values."

In the foregoing words Clark very well expresses the futility of formalism, but the rest of the paragraph gives one pause: "The naive and simple people of the sects cling to the feeling element. They deliberately adopt devices to stir the emotions and attribute the results to the direct operation of the Holy Spirit." [38] But such a statement can with greater accuracy be applied to the refined liturgist than to the "naive and simple people of the sects"—excepting perhaps those of the frankly charismatic groups.

At this point we ask two questions of those who scornfully ascribe the yearning for "heart religion" to the mentally retarded, the culturally impoverished and the emotionally starved unfortunates whose low economic level precludes their indulging in "worldly" amusements, and who therefore seek emotional release in demonstrative religion: (1) Are the patrons of the movie-house, the race track, the night club, and the tavern, chiefly those of affluence, intelligence and refined tastes? Again, (2) who in this period of American plenty has not the means—or the credit—with which to indulge his desires, and therefore must resort to "cheap" religion for emotional excitation?

---

38. Elmer T. Clark, *The Small Sects in America*. Cokesbury Press, Nashville; p. 274

None other than the late W. W. Sweet, authority on religious sects in America, reversed the aim of the weapon of scorn when he said that "emotion has been so completely squeezed out of present-day Protestant worship that the people are becoming emotionally starved," and suggested this as a possible cause of the popularity of motion pictures.[39] Sweet made this suggestion in 1945, before our crop of television antennae had appeared as by magic above practically every American home, rich or poor.

"Errors of thought are as frequent and profound as errors of emotion," wrote Sweet, and related revivalism to intellectualism by saying, "Strange as it may seem to those who think of revivalism only in terms of ignorance, superstition, and an exaggerated emotionalism, there is a very close relationship between the history of higher education in America and revivalism." [40] And then he enumerated several outstanding colleges of the country that have been established by the impetus of religious revival.

By way of conclusion

Free Methodism today holds a strategic position in the area of worship. It maintains simplicity and earnestness, with restraint against an undue liberty that sacrifices true devotion by exalting the flesh on the one hand, and maintains a vitality that resists the creeping death of ritualistic formalism on the other. There seems to be little danger now that the church will veer from its course into the extravagances of the former, but may it guard against the subtle pull of the liturgical current, and refuse to take on forms and symbols to induce the mood of worship while allowing the fire of devotion to die down on the altar of the heart. Only thus can it minister to the inner experience of cleansing and power in the individual, and insure simplicity of worship in the freedom of the Spirit in the congregation.

---

39. W. W. Sweet, *Revivalism in America*, Charles Scribner's Sons, New York; p. 181.
40. *Ibid.*, p. 145.

CHAPTER NINETEEN

Disciplined Living

Christian discipline

The Christian life is a way of discipline. John Wesley recognized this truth and set himself with all the moral force of his strong character against those who taught or practiced the opposite. He could not brook the ethics of a religion that "made void the law through faith." After reporting his interrogation of a libertarian whose so-called freedom in Christ led him to claim as his right "every thing in the world," including the bodies of consenting women and the material possessions of his neighbor, Wesley exclaimed in righteous indignation against such antinomians, "Surely these are the first-born children of Satan!" [1]

Wesley's standard of Christian discipline banned not only the morally repugnant license which such deluded souls claimed as their privilege under the freedom conveyed by grace, but it extended even to what popularly are considered harmless peccadillos, such as wasteful personal habits, the extravagant or immodest fashion of one's dress, and the types of worldly amusements in which he indulges.

Synthesis of belief and life

From its beginning the Free Methodist Church has sought to correlate belief and life, after the example of Wesley. The church has held that affirmations of a creed are of little worth unless they are demonstrated in Christlike living. In the effort to set conduct in its proper relationship to doctrine, the emphasis may have shifted sometimes toward legalism, and minor particulars may have displaced vital principles at the center of Christian concern. But the synthesis of Christian belief and Christian practice has ever been sought as the ideal.

In line with this ideal, the Free Methodist Church holds that it is the responsibility of a Christian denomination to define, as a condition of membership in the church and as a witness to the world, not

---

1. J. Wesley, *Journal*. Epworth Press, London; v. 3, 238.

only what a Christian should believe, but as well how a Christian should live. Some denominations exact a confession of faith but ignore or neglect the life witness. Free Methodism emphasizes both, belief and life.

Therefore, seeking to promote and maintain the early Methodist emphasis on simplicity and purity of life and conduct, the Free Methodist Church has made certain requirements of its members, practically all of which are in line with Wesley's General Rules which still are embodied in the Free Methodist *Discipline* as valid and binding principles of Christian conduct. Free Methodists are to abstain from all use, processing or merchandising of tobacco, opiates, and alcoholic beverages; dress plainly and inexpensively; carefully observe the Lord's Day; avoid worldly amusements; refrain from membership in the oath-bound lodge; avoid profane language and evil speaking; maintain business integrity; and follow other regulations based upon the General Rules.

A church which seeks to maintain such principles, which are so contrary to popular practices, may easily become too exclusively negative in emphasis; but rightly understood, Free Methodism's distinctives in the area of conduct are rooted, not in negatives, but in this great affirmation, *The Christian should be Christlike.* In the perspective of this affirmation such questions, for example, as, *Can one smoke and be a Christian?* become mere quibbling. The proper question is rather, *Is smoking Christlike?* If first one makes the great affirmation, the answers to many questions concerning a Christian's behavior become self-evident.

Freedom through discipline

The stoutest contenders for "Christian liberty" in matters of personal conduct, strangely enough, are often those who are most insistent upon rigidity in matters of doctrinal belief. But the liberty of conduct they claim so often tends to the license of self-indulgence, whereas true liberty is possible only through restraint. Long ago the Psalmist discerned this paradox, and declared, "So shall I keep thy law continually forever and ever. And I will walk at liberty: for I seek thy precepts." [2]

---

2. Psalm 119:44, 45.

The validity of this principle that liberty comes only through law, is daily demonstrated in the realm of human relations. Where is liberty when the motorist demands the freedom of the road to drive as he lists? Or when the merchant asserts his freedom to choose his own weights and measures? Liberty then becomes license, and the outcome is not freedom, but confusion and bondage. Law properly is not the expression of tyranny, but the technique of order by which alone true freedom may be achieved.[3]

Christian discipline at its best is not legalism, but love seeking the pattern of God's will. As Fenelon put it, "Christian perfection is not the harsh, wearisome constraint which you imagine. It requires us to belong to God with our whole heart; and when once that is the case, whatever we do for him becomes easy."[4] And Bishop William T. Watkins has beautifully explained why Wesley's rigorous requirements were not galling to early Methodists: "Only burdens which men lack the power to carry seem burdensome. A religion which lays burdens on men but gives them power to carry these burdens is not a burdensome religion." The change of the inner life which changes a man's desires, says Bishop Watkins, "takes the strain off the will."[5]

Chaos is come again

A swelling tide of libertarianism in America, beginning almost a century ago, has now reached tidal-wave destructiveness in dissipation and debauchery, sexual immorality, broken homes, unnatural affection, lawlessness, crime, juvenile delinquency, and widespread psychosis.

How has this come about? The self-expressionism of America's "gilded age" of the last quarter of the nineteenth century, blossoming from the Darwinian hypothesis which had broken upon the intellectual world in the late fifties, was rationalized in the early decades of the present century by Freudian psychology and made palatable by the theories of "progressive education." But after the passage of a century, expressionism has not yielded the promised Utopian society

---
3. See L. R. Marston, *From Chaos to Character;* Light and Life Press, Winona Lake, Ind.; p. 116 *et seq.*
4. *The Spiritual Letters of Archbishop Fenelon,* translated by Sidney Lear; Longmans, Green & Co., London; p. 246.
5. William T. Watkins, "Wesley's Message to His Own Age," in *Methodism,* Wm. K. Anderson, Editor. Methodist Publishing House, Nashville; p. 26.

of well-adjusted and integrated personalities. Instead of that, we are nearing the bedlam of tooth-and-claw individualists who prefer chaos to order.

It is not without significance that history synchronized the birth of a spiritual movement, channeled through firm disciplines, with the beginning of vigorous dissemination of a devastating materialism which was to work havoc with morals and religion throughout the century. B. T. Roberts was contemporary with Darwin, Huxley and Spencer. In 1859 appeared Darwin's *Origin of Species*. In 1860 occurred the historic Oxford debate between Bishop Wilberforce and Thomas Huxley on the validity of Darwin's book, a debate in which the cause of the spirit fared ill at the hands of an arch-devotee of naturalism. It was also in 1860 that the Free Methodist Church was launched on a sea it must navigate through a hazardous channel against heavy headwinds. Many doubted its ability to keep afloat.

The young church was only well started on its voyage when "the gilded age" of America's fantastic materialistic growth set in—an era of selfish capitalism, corrupt politics, cheap culture, and degrading amusements. "Freedom had become individualism," writes Parrington, "and individualism had become the inalienable right to preempt, to exploit, to squander. Gone were the old ideas along with the old restraints." Indeed, only the fittest could survive, the fittest in tooth-and-claw and in clever cunning. Parrington phrases a devastating summary of "the gilded age" by saying, "It was an anarchistic world of strong, capable men, selfish, unenlightened, amoral—an excellent example of what human nature will do with undisciplined freedom." [6]

The authors of *The Rise of American Civilization* tell us what "the gilded age" offered in commercialized amusements, a description differing little from the bill of fare of our own age, but without today's low culture piped into every living room through radio and television.

> Vaudeville shows, prize fights, circuses, dime museums, and cheap theaters, like the spectacles of ancient Rome, kept count-

---

6. From *Main Currents in American Thought*, Volume 3, by Vernon L. Parrington, copyright, 1930, by Harcourt, Brace and Company, Inc.; renewed 1958, by Vernon L. Parrington, Jr., Louise P. Tucker, Elizabeth P. Thomas. Reprinted by permission of the publishers; p. 17.

less millions happy in penury.... The Paris can-can was imported in 1872, becoming quickly a high favorite and bringing heavy revenues into the pockets of promoters. Whole armies of scribblers were kept busy plotting hair-raising melodramas based on love, suicide, rum and murder. "Cheap and nasty" were the watchwords of the new festivity and nothing could break the spell.[7]

How could a small, pietistic group propagate itself and maintain its discipline against worldliness in such areas as personal habits, attire, amusements, and business dealings in a period of moral and spiritual decadence, without resorting to such protective measures as secluded colonization, uniformed garb, and a rigid ban against participation in political affairs and public education? In the next chapter it will appear impossible that Free Methodism could ever have resorted to such withdrawal from the world to protect its piety, while it had the leadership of a man of B. T. Roberts' broad and intelligent social comprehension and interests. That Free Methodism's standard of piety was maintained through its first half-century, without recourse as a group to defensive withdrawal from the social order, is attested by Professor J. A. Faulkner of Drew, a man well acquainted with Free Methodism, who included the following statement in his contribution on American Methodist history to an extensive two-volume English work published in 1909:

> Compared with the great American churches, the Free Methodists are a feeble folk, but they have proved that in the midst of our naturalistic and pleasure-loving age, whose spirit—none will deny—has infected the churches, it is possible for a church, founded on the self-denying ordinances of Wesley, both to live and to thrive.[8]

Character through conflict

But the severest testing of Free Methodism's discipline was yet to come, for although rampant materialism had prevailed in society through much of the young church's first half-century, the more stealthy influences of Freud's naturalistic psychology and Dewey's humanistic educational theory were yet to be encountered. These

---

7. Charles A. Beard and Mary A. Beard, *The Rise of American Civilization*. The Macmillan Co., New York; v. 2, 398.
8. W. J. Townsend, H. B. Workman, and Geo. Eayrs, *A New History of Methodism*. Hodder and Stoughton, London; v. 2, 134.

influences opposed discipline—in fact, they all but drove it from the American scene.

We would not anticipate too fully in this chapter what properly belongs to another, but discipline is so inextricably interwoven with education that we venture a few educational considerations in an effort to make clear the present confused state of discipline in general.

For decades education has been dominated by the dogma that no restraints should be imposed on children and youth lest violence be done to the developing personality. Educators have sought as major goals the integration of personality and its adjustment to society. To reach these goals, they held, conflict must carefully be avoided.

Even the church's educational program has tended to focalize the child's immediate experience and interest, moulding him to conformity with the world rather than seeking the transformation of his nature by divine grace and the shaping of his character through sturdy Christian nurture.

What have been the results of such teaching on adjustment and avoidance of inner conflict? Our young people today, in general, are neither adjusted nor are they free from conflict. Because of the basic twist of human nature to selfishness, many of them in this era of individual freedom and relaxed moral restraints have disregarded or defied the law of society, and in consequence we have a broken social order, shattered by delinquency and crime.

But such obvious consequences of freedom turned into license, heralded in daily headlines and published abroad at stated intervals in mounting statistics of social and moral tragedies, tend to obscure other unhappy results of our American libertarianism. Not only is society being broken, but youthful personalities are being broken by our patternless morals in ways unforeseen when Freud and Dewey held the field of ethical and educational theory against contenders for disciplined restraint. In 1946 a psychologist, addressing a group of scientists in St. Louis, broke into the daily news with the doctrine, strange for that day, that children and youth need discipline if they are to be saved from uncertainty, frustration and fear. In line with this doctrine, there recently came to the writer's attention the case of an eleven-year-old girl who confided to her playmate, a disciplined child of a minister's family, that she wanted to run away from home because her mother didn't love her—this she knew because her mother let her do and have everything she wanted! Because of human nature's craving for security and its longing for guidance, some young people—and even young children, react to the present confusion and collapse of moral standards with a sense of lostness, and turning inward upon themselves, they develop anxieties, frustrations, and haunting feelings of guilt. In some children and youth conscience will not down!

Contrary to the claim of the late Dr. Freud, high priest of expressionism, there is an increasing realization among psychologists and educators that moral standards are not hazards but helps to mental health; that man's highest pleasure is not the pleasure of instinct but the pleasure of conscience; that frustrations and anxiety neuroses come, not so much from self-restraint and repression as from self-indulgence and expressionism.[9]

But there is another consequence of the selfish paganism of the present era. Because of human nature's craving for a cause greater than self, some young people react against selfishness to espouse some challenging ideology which they promote with supreme devotion. Such idealistic youth would revolutionize society. They provide fertile soil for such militant paganism as Communism, and unless captured by a worthy cause will rebuild society on undemocratic and non-Christian foundations.

Will *rebellious* and *fearful* and *idealistic youth*—and their elders of the same categories—respond to the discipline of the Cross? Note a few observations that point to an affirmative answer.

The late Clarence E. Macartney, for many years pastor of Pittsburgh's First Presbyterian Church, made the discovery several years ago that "the churches which are holding their young people best are those very churches which say to their young people, 'As members of the Church of Christ, Thou shall not do this. Thou shalt not do that.'" Dr. Macartney concluded that "when Christian standards are set high, and separation from the world is demanded, you give young people a banner about which they can rally and a platform upon which

---

9. See the report of a paper by Orval Hobart Mowrer presented to a section of the American Association for the Advancement of Science, in *Time*, Jan. 12, 1948.

they can stand." [10] The record of youth's loyalty to the Free Methodist Church and its disciplines tends to confirm this judgment of Dr. Macartney. And experienced observation suggests that pressures to compromise our disciplines do not come chiefly from the youth group.

After administering five annual conferences in 1873, finding in each the work prospering and in a healthy state, Bishop Roberts wrote the following:

> In this age of compromise, when the difference between the church and the world is so small as to be nearly imperceptible, the wonder is that any church can maintain a denominational existence, which insists that its members shall not stand connected with any secret societies, that they shall dress plain, not indulge in the use of tobacco, allow no seats in their houses of worship to be rented or sold, nor permit any appeals to be made to pride or love of pleasure to raise funds for the promotion of the cause of Christ. But this church not only stands, but is spreading quite as rapidly as is consistent with a healthy growth, and what is quite remarkable, it makes most progress where its peculiar principles are insisted upon with the greatest tenacity, and the work promoted is most radical and thorough.[11]

The bishops' address to the Free Methodist General Conference of 1907, nearing the mid-point of the church's first century, drew conclusions concerning the relationship of discipline to healthy growth similar to those B. T. Roberts had reached in 1873 when the church was very young. The bishops in 1907 said:

> We have noted with much sorrow in some parts of our work what appears to be the beginnings of defection from our original plainness, simplicity and unworldly mode of life. Wherever the primitive standard of Free Methodism is lowered in these respects, spirituality declines and frigid formality steals over the people. Nor does this method of compromise succeed, even as a policy for winning popular favor. The facts show the contrary to be true. Wherever in a true evangelical spirit, our people have been most loyal to the principles of Free Methodism, there they have drawn the largest following, have been most successful in gathering and holding the young people, and have generally realized the greatest prosperity. While we would not be legalists

---

10. *The Presbyterian*, May 3, 1945.
11. B. H. Roberts, *Benjamin Titus Roberts*. The Earnest Christian Office, North Chili, N. Y.; p. 438.

on the one hand, neither should we be latitudinarians on the other. When plainness, simplicity and spirituality cease to differentiate us from the worldly conformed masses in other churches, there will be no longer an excuse for our separate denominational existence.

Elton Trueblood has reported the discovery, by those dealing with the maintenance of spiritual life during the period of World War II, that "in most instances, it was the people with a strict or even narrow faith who kept the best grip on themselves in the chaotic days through which all were forced to live," and "those of fundamentalist tendencies were more likely to keep up the practice of their religion in camp than were the modernists and liberals." [12]

Elmer T. Clark has remarked on the vigorous growth of the sects, and, notwithstanding their ignoring "nearly all the principles of modern religious education," that they "not only survive, but flourish and often out-strip denominations that employ them all." This leads Clark to question if, "after all, the modern developments are really as efficient as they are claimed to be, and whether the sects do not possess elements of value which others have omitted and might well incorporate." [13] The explanation is simple: the sects have the discipline of a cause, for as Trueblood has said, "Powerful groups, for whatever ends, are disciplined groups, whereas libertarian movements end in futility." [14]

Fittingly enough, in his devotional reading one morning in the period of his preparation of this chapter, the writer came upon this statement of rugged truth: "There must be resistance, struggle, conflict, or there can be no development of strength." [15] Character is developed through conflict, and Christian character through the disciplines of the Cross.

Methodist discipline, 1900 and 1956

In the episcopal address to the 1900 General Conference, the bishops of the Methodist Episcopal Church recognized that many changes had occurred in the outward forms of Methodism, and asked,

---
12. Elton Trueblood, *Alternative to Futility*. Harper & Bros., New York; pp. 82, 83.
13. Elmer T. Clark, *The Small Sects in America*. Cokesbury Press, Nashville; p. 288.
14. Elton Trueblood, *Alternative to Futility*. Harper & Bros., New York; p. 91.
15. J. R. Miller, *Making the Most of Life*. Little, Brown, and Co., Boston; p. 63.

"Which do they indicate, growth or decay?" They listed some of these changes, after each asking if it indicated growth or decay, but weighting, it would seem, the "growth" inquiry to receive the affirmative answer. A part of the series follows:

> The rigid and minute church discipline of former years is relaxed: is this a sign of pastoral unfaithfulness, or is it a sign of growing respect for individual liberty and a better conception of the function of the church? The plainness of the early Methodist congregations has disappeared: is this simply vanity and worldliness, or is it, in part, the natural and justifiable development of the aesthetic faculty under more prosperous external conditions? The strenuous contention for this or that doctrine or usage of Methodism, once common, is now rarely heard: is this indifferentism, or is it, in part, a better discernment of that which is vital to the Christian faith, and, in part, the result of an acceptance by others of the disputed opinion? [16]

But after more than a half-century of libertarian infiltration from materialistic and pagan sources, the bishops in the episcopal address of the 1956 Methodist General Conference were more realistic concerning what had happened to Methodist discipline. After noting Wesley's program of discipline and the resistance it met in eighteenth-century England, the bishops said:

> Today the Church faces a similar mood in the popular attitude toward Christian discipline and its influence upon the lives of Christian people. Self-imposed and church-imposed restrictions are alien to the popular mentality. Spiritual oversight is resented and the admonition of one by another through testimony and correction is a vanishing practice in human relations. The cult of freedom, by which its adherents distort the word to mean the lack of all restraint, has become the real competitor to the disciplined life which is the badge of a redeemed society. It has proven also to be the Trojan horse by which pagan attitudes have infiltrated the Christian fellowship.[17]

Answering by implication at least the questions raised by their predecessors, the bishops of 1956 frankly faced the situation of mid-century:

---

16. *Journal of the General Conference of the Methodist Episcopal Church*, (1900). Eaton & Mains, New York; 60.
17. *Journal of the 1956 General Conference of the Methodist Church*. Methodist Publishing House, New York; p. 231.

The time is upon us to take our bearings and to observe the effect which this libertarian mood is having upon the character of our people and the direction of their life. Studies reveal that the onset of personality and character disintegration under the pressure of modern living is greatest among those of indefinite faith and of laxness in the observance of Christian disciplines. The vitality and productivity of newer and smaller religious groups bear a striking relation to the restrictions imposed and the demands made upon their members. Educators agree that the breakdown of discipline is now their "number one problem."

In the success of rival philosophies and secular activities the Church sees its own earlier strategy of the disciplined life taken over and used against it. . . .

The recovery of discipline will bring the Church again to the narrow gate and the straight way which the Master said would lead to life. What in Methodism has been thought of as archaic must in Methodist pragmatic fashion be put beside the needs of our daily living. What is expected of a Methodist, how should a Methodist act and what are the compulsions of his conduct, are questions which must again take definite form if a Church which has the organization and resources for establishing the Christian fellowship shall come to its full strength of influence. . . .

The hope for the survival of Christianity as a distinctive way of life lies in its power to discipline at a time when the popular mood would erase identifying marks of Christian conduct.[18]

A century's adventure in Christian discipline

We are now to review the course discipline has taken in the Free Methodist Church from its founding in 1860. Some will think the people called Free Methodists peculiar indeed to legislate on picayunish matters such as amusements, organized secret associations, personal adornment, the use of tobacco and alcohol, and perhaps a half-dozen other restraints on personal liberty. We remind the reader of the earlier statement of Free Methodism's purpose to correlate Christian belief and Christian life; of the church's conviction of its responsibility to define how a Christian should live as well as what he should believe. Free Methodism stands in the tradition of historic Methodism which sought this synthesis more than two centuries ago, and realized it to a degree superlatively beyond the achievement of any later era in any division of the Methodist movement. Humbly,

---

18. *Ibid.*, p. 231 *et seq.*

therefore, we undertake the task of tracing Free Methodist discipline through the span of one century.

In the General Rules mentioned earlier in this chapter and the membership covenant quoted in Chapter Fifteen, brief summaries of what Free Methodism requires of its members in matters of Christian discipline have been sketched. Principles underlying some of the church's rules are elaborated briefly in a chapter of the *Discipline* entitled "Christian Conduct." Two paragraphs of this chapter, Par. 84, on "Labor and Industrial Relations," and Par. 85, on "Militarism and War," are more closely related to the next chapter of this book dealing with social concern and stewardship. The paragraphs of the 1955 *Discipline* which are most pertinent to Christian discipline are:

   50 to 56, the General Rules;
   57, the Special Rules;
   87 and 88, the membership covenant;
   80, Temperance;
   81, Marriage and Divorce;
   82, Dress;
   83, Secret Societies.

Many of the significant changes in the *Discipline* and of the actions of General Conference affecting Christian conduct are reviewed in the following several pages under three classifications, (1) revisions of the General Rules and the Special Rules; (2) other revisions related to Christian discipline; and (3) General Conference actions on rulings, appeals, resolutions, and committee reports.

Revisions of General and Special Rules

Few changes have been made in the General Rules, amendments to which require the concurring votes of the annual conferences and the General Conference. The 1951 General Conference, with the concurrence of the annual conferences, transferred the few amendments that had been made in the General Rules to a separate division called Special Rules. This left the General Rules exactly as they were adopted by the Pekin Convention in 1860; and that body had taken over, intact, the General Rules of the parent church save for substituting an unequivocal rule prohibiting *the buying, selling, or holding of a human being as a slave.* The Methodist Episcopal Church's amendment of its slavery rule in 1864, after the Emancipation Proclamation had been issued, and the restoration by the Free Methodist Church in 1951 of its General Rules to their 1860 form, brought item-by-item agreement of the two churches in their General Rules on Christian conduct.

Following is the record of changes in the General Rules of the Free Methodist Church over the course of one hundred years, and the recent establishment of a list of four Special Rules supplementing the General Rules or making specific application of some of them.

1870. An amendment to the General Rules was initiated by General Conference which would prohibit, as falling under *Softness and needless self-indulgence,* "especially snuffing, chewing or smoking tobacco, for the gratification of a depraved appetite." This was duly enacted into law by the confirming votes of the annual conferences. Until this time, the new church had continued with no specific legislation against the use of tobacco.

1878. An amendment to the General Rules was enacted which prohibited, under *Doing what we know is not for the glory of God,* "belonging to secret societies." However, from the beginning the renunciation of membership in secret societies had been included in the church's membership covenant.

Because of its relationship to the 1870 tobacco amendment we call attention at this point to the 1878 report of the committee on reforms which expressed regret that some members of the church were taking advantage of the qualifying clause in that amendment which read, "for the gratification of a depraved appetite,"—these members probably claiming medicinal reasons for using tobacco. The committee called for conscientious observance of the rule.

1882. The General Conference initiated an amendment which would substitute for the 1870 wording, "the habitual use of tobacco or opiates, in any form whatever," but this was never carried into law.

1886. The 1870 amendment was changed to read, "snuffing, chewing or smoking tobacco or the habitual use of opiates." This wording prohibited even the occasional use of tobacco, but made possible the medicinal use of opiates.

1951. The General Conference of 1951 initiated a major revision of the church's Constitution, which was confirmed as law by the concurring votes of the annual conferences. By this revision the General Rules were restored to their original form of 1860. The two revisions that had been made, one prohibiting all use of tobacco and habitual use of opiates, and the other declaring against Free Methodists belonging to secret societies, were incorporated in a new portion of the Constitution designated Special Rules. Here they are protected against impulsive change under Restrictive Rule 1, just as formerly they were protected when embodied in the General Rules. The Special Rules, adopted in the 1951 revision and now standing in the Constitution, are:

1. Members shall conform to the scriptural standards of attire, adorning

themselves in a meek and quiet spirit, not with gold, pearls, and costly array.

2. The church forbids its members the using, growing, processing, buying or selling of tobacco; the habitual use of opiates; and the processing, buying, selling or using intoxicating liquors unless for mechanical, chemical, or medicinal purposes, or in any way intentionally and knowingly aiding others to do so.

3. The church condemns secret societies on scriptural grounds and as contrary to the glory of God, and forbids membership in them.

4. The church recognizes no other ground for divorce than that permitted by the Word of God (Matt. 5:32; Mark 10:11, 12).

Other revisions related to Christian conduct

Revisions of General and Special Rules, as parts of the Constitution, and its Restrictive Rules can be made only by concurring action of the General Conference and the annual conferences. Revisions of the *Discipline* outside the Constitution, now to be reviewed, can be made by the General Conference acting alone. These revisions also have been few in number.

1866. A brief chapter on secret societies was inserted in the *Discipline*, stating the basis of the church's rule against membership in them.

1874. A statement of the church's position on divorce was added to the section on marriage. This was the church's first legislation recognizing this problem.

1886. The question asked preachers joining the conference in full relationship, "Do you use snuff, tobacco, or drams?" was stricken. This had survived to this point as an anachronism.

1911. The question in the membership covenant concerning dress was amended by deleting the words, "with shamefacedness and sobriety, not with broidered hair."

1915. To the introductory section of the *Discipline* which carried the title, "The Free Methodist Church—Origin and Character," a paragraph was added which stated the stand of the church against entertainments in church buildings and by church organizations which are "contrary to the spirit and letter of our Discipline."

1923. The General Conference enacted regulations for the church's educational institutions in line with the church's standards of Christian discipline.

1951. The requirement that Wesley's Sermon on Dress be read at least once a year in each society was deleted.

The General Conference also deleted all references to the wedding ring. These were three in number, (1) a resolution adopted by the General Conference of 1874, carried in the Appendix to the *Discipline* under Constructions of Law, which declared the sense of that Conference that the rule against the wearing of gold applied to the wearing of gold wedding rings; (2) a similar resolution adopted by the 1939 General Conference, recorded likewise in the Appendix, which dealt with but went beyond the resolution against wearing gold as applied to the wedding ring, and brought "any kind of finger ring or jewelry" under the pledge of the membership covenant to lay aside all superfluous adornment; and (3) a footnote to the rule against the wearing of gold, inserted by the 1943 General Conference, which declared that this rule applied to "the wearing of finger rings of all kinds." Since these three items were not constitutional amendments, but resolutions of preceding General Conferences, the Conference of 1951 had authority to delete them, notwithstanding the fact that they referred to a general rule.

1955. The paragraph on Marriage and Divorce in the chapter on Christian Conduct was extended to embody the import of previous rulings on the subject, and to provide for a solemn declaration by a candidate for membership in the church, whose divorce had been granted technically on other grounds when scriptural grounds actually existed, that these grounds did exist and were a cause of separation and subsequent divorce.

The relatively few changes dealing with Christian conduct made in a hundred years point to the stability of the church's discipline. Checking both types of changes, those requiring concurrent action by the annual conferences and those needing only the action of General Conference, we find that modifications in the conservative direction have fairly well balanced in number those made in the liberalizing direction. This seems the more significant because the church began as a reform movement with high initial requirements in the area of conduct, which in the normal course of such movements might easily have been lowered.

Miscellaneous actions of General Conference

The actions of General Conference through appeals, rulings, resolutions and committee reports through a century, having to do with Christian discipline, are too numerous for complete summary. Those cited here throw additional light on the development of the church's thinking on Christian life and conduct.

1866. A resolution against hop-growing was adopted, as conflicting with the general rule prohibiting "evil of every kind," and "doing what we know is not for the glory of God." The General Conference disapproved the action of an annual conference in passing a resolution against the use of tobacco and claiming authority to enforce the same, on the ground that the conference transcended its powers in attempting to enact laws. Not until 1870, a decade after the church was founded, did it legislate concerning the use of tobacco.

1870. The expulsion of a minister for immorality and imprudence was sustained against his appeal from the action of his annual conference. Also, the expulsion of a minister for alleged erroneous teachings, contrary to resolutions adopted by his annual conference on the details of dress and adornment with which he did not agree and which he would not teach, was sustained. He declared his agreement with the Scriptures and with the *Discipline* on the subject of dress, but protested the resolutions of his conference. This was the case of D. W. Thurston, referred to in Chapter Sixteen. It is not clear why the attempt of an annual conference to legislate against tobacco by resolution was disapproved by the General Conference of 1866, and the attempt of the same conference (Susquehanna) to legislate against particulars of adornment by resolution was sustained by the 1870 General Conference.[19]

1878. Growing of hops and barley for the general market was disapproved. Sunday cheese- and butter-making, and the use of such public conveyances as are run with no regard for the sanctity of the Sabbath were discountenanced. The committee on reforms called attention to the fact that "we as a people are almost alone for plainness of dress, in opposition to the extravagant fashions of the times, and earnestly exhort our people to guard against the introduction little by little of innovations and practices calculated to foster conformity to the world."

1886. A resolution was adopted declaring the opinion that "the growing, manufacture and sale of tobacco is a violation of the Discipline prohibiting 'evil of every kind.'" The use of tobacco had been prohibited by amendment of the General Rules in 1870, but not its processing and merchandising.

The Prohibition Party was endorsed by the General Conference, but B. T. Roberts, an ardent temperance advocate, protested the action because it committed the church politically. A resolution was adopted, disapproving the Sunday sale of ice cream, lemonade and like refreshments by boarding stands on campgrounds, and instructing Free Methodist preachers not to participate in camp meetings where such things were allowed. Evidently these Sunday sales did not occur on Free Methodist campgrounds.

1890. The committee on reforms supported emphatically Free Methodist principles of simplicity in dress, but warned that "we should avoid weakening our influence on this line of reform by manifesting an unwise and unscriptural spirit of judging and condemning each other for things that are not clearly contrary to the Word of God." The report was adopted.

Two resolutions were adopted relating to the Chicago World's Fair,

---

19. The General Conference Journal of 1870, strangely enough, does not give the specifications in the charge of "erroneous teachings" upon which D. W. Thurston was tried by his annual conference, but these and other details have been supplied by the secretary of the Susquehanna Conference, the Rev. Clark W. Snyder, and by the Rev. D. Stiles, Jr., from the Susquehanna Conference Journal of 1869.

one against the sale of liquor on the grounds, the other against operation of the Fair on Sundays.

1894. The General Conference refused to approve a proposal that a footnote be appended to the general rule against profaning the Sabbath, which would declare, as a violation thereof, "carrying or selling milk to factories, or delivering it to railroad stations" on that day. Another indication of the growing reluctance to multiply legalisms was the response made to a memorial concerning the wearing of neckties, declaring such to be a matter in which "every man should be fully persuaded in his own mind and guided by his personal convictions." This as an issue seems not to have existed in the church's early history, but to have been introduced later.

1898. A resolution was adopted disapproving the selling of liquor in army canteens. No doubt this was prompted by the outbreak of the Spanish-American War. The committee on the state of the work noted the aggravation of the problem of Sabbath observance by the universal use of bicycles!

1903. A resolution was adopted which would leave to the conscience of a clerk in a general store his handling tobacco for his employer. The resolution was ordered published in the Supplement of the *Discipline* under Decisions and Rules, but the order was never carried out. Twenty-eight years later, probably in ignorance of this 1903 resolution, the 1931 General Conference declared a contrary opinion, that a clerk could not handle tobacco for his employer under the rules governing church membership.

1907. The message of the bishops ably dealt with the church's problems and the challenge facing it. A portion of the address was quoted in an earlier section and further portions appear in the following section.

1911. The committee on reforms presented resolutions protesting worldliness, tobacco, liquor, moving pictures, trusts, divorce, secrecy, covetousness, light conversation, too long sermons, social evils—and all were adopted!

1947. A strong resolution was adopted, urging the invoking of spiritual resources to correct worldliness of dress. A committee was selected to examine anew the church's principles and its prudentials, and to report to the next General Conference.

1951. Important recommendations of the committee on principles and prudentials were adopted. Portions of its report are given in the following section.

1955. The address of the bishops to the 1955 General Conference sounded the call to renewed loyalty as the church approached the close of its first century. Here are their words: "Your bishops recommend that this General Conference call the ministry, the laity, and every organization of the church to renewed and undivided loyalty to the historic principles of the church in all four areas of doctrine, experience, worship, and standards of holy living; and further, to a like loyalty to the church's approved program of advance at every level from local congregation, through district and conference channels, to general church departments."

The content of the foregoing pages, by the very nature of its theme of discipline, could only be restrained in emphasis; and that in spots the emphasis was definitely negative should not be surprising. But scanning these pages brings now and again a note of affirmation as with the passing of years, the church turned from its absorption with the past to view its present responsibility and the challenge of its future. To clarify this note of affirmation we draw upon the address of the bishops as the church in 1907 approached its semi-centennial, and likewise upon the report on principles and prudentials adopted early in the closing decade of the church's first century, in 1951.

Calling the church to its twentieth century task

The bishops' message to the General Conference of 1907 frankly dealt with the negativism of some who were impeding the church's progress. After reviewing some of the hindrances to advance, the bishops said:

> Still more damaging to our cause has been the influence of those here and there among our own people who, however well intentioned may have been their zeal, have acted without discretion, in that they have mistaken the negative and subordinate truths we preach for the fundamentals of Free Methodism, and have so constantly exploited and magnified the non-essentials of Christianity in the name of the church as to leave the general impression on the public that the Free Methodists are a class of narrow extremists and ranting enthusiasts, with no issues to present of sufficient merit to engage the consideration of intelligent men, or to justify their existence as an ecclesiastical body.

The firmness of the bishops on the essential principles of the church they make clear in that portion of the address quoted on page 366 *et seq.* What they point out in the foregoing paragraph, therefore, was in no sense the exhibition of a leaning toward compromise. They were concerned with the mission of the church in the world of the twentieth century, and courageously called the church to its task, saying:

> Each succeeding generation of mankind is compelled to meet and grapple with problems altogether peculiar to its own time. The church that forgets this, and gives itself to living chiefly in the past, and simply to reaffirming its attitude regarding the issues it was called to support and defend at the time of its origin, will soon be regarded by the general public as a belated institution,

and in the same measure will have ceased to be a potent factor in the transformation and spiritual uplift of society.

The address declared that Bible religion never changes in principles with changing fads and fashions, but does have in great degree the characteristic of adaptation, "and thereby is always abreast of the new problems that from time to time arise in every department of human affairs." The message sounded this challenge:

> Our people must not, on the one hand, be visionaries, vainly occupied with the hidden things of the future and the impracticable things of the present, nor on the other hand, allow themselves to become mere fossilized specimens of a bygone age or generation. Rather should they be, even above others, a practical people, dealing in a masterful way with the great, vital problems of their own time, and gathering inspiration from both past and future for doing heroically what the present time demands.

Such was the high point of vision and challenge reached by the bishops of the church more than a half-century ago. To that height they would call the people from their legalisms and their pietistic withdrawal from the fields of service and duty. But the church, too long on the defensive, was slow to move its forces from their scattered redoubts into line of action on the field of battle.

Principles and prudentials

With the passing of the years, however, certain matters became troublesome to the smooth functioning of the church, due to conflicting concepts of what constituted principles essential to Free Methodism and earnest Christianity, and what were matters of method and sphere of application of those principles to current needs and problems. The question of instrumental music was an area of tension for some years, as the preceding chapter has related. This was not an issue involving the general rules, and therefore could be settled by direct vote of the General Conference. This settlement of the issue occurred in principle in 1943 when the General Conference by a narrow margin deleted the rule against instrumental music and permitted an organ or a piano in public worship. The prolonged course of events to this change, and the further liberalizing of the church's program of music until 1955, have been reviewed step by step in the preceding chapter. In the minds of many, here was an issue involving principle, but the church generally now sees it as a prudential matter, even including some of those who still maintain that the change was not a prudent one.

About the time the crucial phase of the music issue had passed, another issue developed. This concerned the wedding ring, the prohibition of which was not specified in the general rules but had been attached thereto by the resolutions adopted by two General Conferences, and a footnote to the rule inserted by a third. The setting was favorable to a sharp contest, and the lines were clearly drawn.

It was in this situation, the music issue partially settled and the wedding ring issue developing to an early climax, that the bishops proposed in their message to the General Conference of 1947 the appointment of a committee to reaffirm the church's principles and to re-examine its prudentials. Out of the work of that committee there came to the 1951 General Conference a thoughtfully conceived and clearly worded report which the Conference unanimously adopted. Because of their relevance to a clear understanding of Free Methodism's accepted philosophy of Christian discipline, we venture to reproduce portions of that document. The report asserted. "The church needs rules," and proceeded to define their legitimate place:

> The Free Methodist Church is established on the principle that a denomination has the responsibility to offer guidance to its members in the realm of ethics and conduct, as well as in doctrine and belief. In the espousal of this position, the Free Methodist Church avoids both the doctrinal vacuum of the creedless and the ethical looseness of those who scorn or neglect rules for methodical Christian living. In so doing, the Free Methodist Church has followed the well balanced division between doctrine and conduct of the apostolic church and early Methodism. The history of Christendom shows that churches lacking sufficient guidance in either area have had corresponding weakness.
>
> Wesleyan doctrine with its emphasis upon the purification of personality through the filling of the Holy Spirit, demands the witness of a life lived according to the highest standards of Christian love in practice.
>
> Rules have a further and broader social function. Well-defined standards of Christian conduct, consistently maintained by its membership, are essential to a church's corporate witness. By such standards the church seeks to carry out its prophetic mission in rebuking sin and confronting the sincere with the challenge of a righteous cause.

The rules of the church also provide clear-cut boundaries for the guidance and discipline of its members where uncertainty or perplexity might otherwise prevail. They likewise represent an effort to maintain a climate of Christian living conducive to growth in grace by excluding the unwholesome and the unworthy from fellowship.

The report next distinguished principles and prudentials. "Principles of conduct," said the committee, "are clearly taught in Scripture, or are directly implied in the Word"; but, "Prudentials are those rules formulated by the church and required of its members as aids to godliness." In areas not specifically covered by rules of either class, the individual must decide the course he should take.

The report pointed out that the General Rules formulated by Wesley "are clear-cut examples of scriptural principles related to conduct," which "are either found in the Word or are logical extensions of Scripture applied to specific problems." These broad rules of Wesley have in general provided adequate guidance for members of the Free Methodist Church, without further elaboration or enumeration of items specifically prohibited. But according to the committee, enumeration of prohibited items, even where prohibition may be advisable, will not alone solve the problem. The church "must provide a spiritual atmosphere and place its emphasis upon general principles having a broad base in Scripture." Furthermore, "These principles must be applied to life and conduct through consciences quickened by the Holy Spirit and nurtured by earnestness and prayer."

"The Scriptures are the reference point of faith and the norm of practice." With this "nail in a sure place" the committee closed this section of its report. Near this nail is another, driven long ago by B. T. Roberts, but still holding, firm and sure: "Where God's Word speaks out explicitly even conscience must keep silence."[20] Thus, Free Methodism maintains the supremacy of the Scriptures.

Toward the solution of the problem

The problem of Christian discipline is well on the way to solution in any life or in any group that can sincerely join with Charles Wesley's longing uttered in these lines of an old, old hymn sung by our fathers a century ago:

---
20. *The Earnest Christian*, v. 9, Feb. 1865; p. 63.

> *I want a principle within,*
> *Of jealous, godly fear;*
> *A sensibility of sin,*
> *A pain to feel it near.*

But with "a principle within," discipline still is needed. Even under grace, law is necessary to teach man the pattern of God's will. Discipline is a continuing and growing experience when it moves from the compulsion of outer constraint to the impulsion of inner principle and the purpose of a sanctified will. Roberts was right in teaching that the Christian's progress in holiness comes through obedience and suffering. But the suffering that perfects a saint is not the suffering the ascetic legalist devises as an automatic and artificial means of perfection, or a bargaining demand on God's favor because of the merit of his good works. It is rather the suffering of our common lot, not presumptuously sought but serenely accepted by a faith—

> *That will not murmur or complain*
> *Beneath the chas'ning rod.*

In the growing and healthy Christian, discipline, then, means the rallying of obedience from reluctant compliance with onerous demands of imposed rules, to ready acceptance of God's will, prompted by conscience or revealed by the Spirit in line with the Word; God's will, accepted as the challenge of the Cross to give oneself and one's all, even beyond the reasonable call of duty. This last is self-discipline going the second mile, yielding even the good in life to God's best.

Bishop Kennedy probed to the moral quick when, discussing discipline in *The Methodist Way of Life*, he said that submitting to regulations for the sake of great convictions is the pathway to freedom, and added:

> When men chafe under restrictions, they have lost sight of the purpose the restrictions are supposed to serve. When we lack commitments to mighty goals, then we seek a liberty which turns into license.[21]

Entering its second century, let the Free Methodist Church con-

---

21. Gerald Kennedy, *The Methodist Way of Life*. © 1958 by Prentice-Hall, Inc., Englewood Cliffs; p. 191.

tinue the disciplines that have given it character, and let its members accept these disciplines, not reluctantly as imposed legalisms, but joyously in willing acceptance of the challenge of the Cross. Thus, they will obey, not from the fear that torments, but from that perfect love which casteth out fear.

Chapter Twenty

Faith Working by Love

We come to the concluding chapter on the church maintaining its witness. Previous chapters have traced Free Methodism's course of a century in *doctrine*, or defining our faith; in *experience*, or possessing our faith; in *worship*, or expressing Godward our faith; in *discipline*, or witnessing our faith in personal restraint. The present chapter explores the church's course in *stewardship*, or expressing our faith in social concern.

The outward reach

Social concern is no minor area of Christian responsibility. To a scribe who asked Jesus to state the first commandment, He declared it to be that a man relate himself to God through a love that harmonizes all his powers with God's will. But Jesus also gave the second commandment, by which He declared man's proper relationship to man as the horizontal or social reach of love. There is no commandment greater than these, He said. Accordingly, approached from any angle, the heart-center of our Christian faith is a love that reaches upward to God, and outward to man.

There are those to whom mention of Wesley's General Rules means only the restrictive rules of personal discipline, such as came under review in the preceding chapter. But these rules also contain positive commands to stretch forth the hand of helpfulness to all. Note a portion of them:

It is expected of all who continue in these societies, that they should continue to evidence their desire of salvation,

Secondly, By doing good, by being in every kind merciful after their power, as they have opportunity, doing good of every possible sort, and as far as possible, to all men.

To their bodies, of the ability which God giveth, by giving food to the hungry, by clothing the naked, by visiting or helping them that are sick or in prison.

To their souls, by instructing, reproving, or exhorting all we have any intercourse with; trampling under foot that enthusiastic doctrine, that "we are not to do good unless our hearts be free to do it."

And John Wesley was as vigorous in promoting these positive, socially beneficial requirements as he was in enforcing the restrictive personal demands of the General Rules. His own activities in social welfare and the social benefits of the revival he led have received extended consideration in Chapter Seven.

Free Methodism's heritage of social concern

The upward reach of Free Methodism has been vigorous and sometimes strenuous. How extended and how effective has been its outward reach? Some may say that Free Methodists have been less effective in a fruitful social concern than in any other area of their heritage. This may be so, but the social concern of minority religious groups generally has been underestimated, and such have been compelled to labor under the charge of social indifference. In any event, for the Free Methodist Church a foundation deep and strong was laid by Roberts' alert interests and intelligent activities, both in the area of moral and religious concern and in the broad fields of government and economics.

Social experts of the modern variety hold earnest Christianity in low regard, "playing down" the social significance of that Christian piety which calls forth industry, frugality, sobriety, and personal righteousness. Such piety they brand as individualistic, socially negative, other-worldly; and they ridicule it as a compensatory reaction of narrow-mindedness whereby withdrawal from society and deprivation of worldly pleasures now will yield "pie in the sky by and by." But there is a powerfully positive social force in true piety, for it keenly senses social obligation and relates personal habits and daily conduct to social need. Roberts answered the cynics when he wrote in *First Lessons on Money*, a little book on economics that he published in 1886, "It is a gross caricature of Christianity to represent that it teaches that happiness in the future world is to be secured by negating the duties which we owe to our fellow men in the present world."[1]

The moral, social, economic, and political concerns that engaged Roberts' interests and energies included such varied causes as "free"

---

1. B. T. Roberts, *First Lessons on Money*. Rochester, N. Y.; p. 143.

churches, abolition of slavery, education, temperance, anti-secrecy, money and banking reforms, taxation, and federation of farmers. In addition to these, he sought reforms in ecclesiastical polity that had definite social bearings, such as the ordination of women and lay representation in the councils of the church equal to ministerial representation. His teachings on the stewardship of possessions and of earning abilities were a generation ahead of his day.

Only a few of these areas of social concern, which entered Free Methodism's heritage through its founder, can receive here extended attention. Some not dealt with in this chapter receive either incidental or major attention in other chapter divisions of this book.

The gospel for the poor

The founder of Free Methodism, even as the founder of Methodism, had a social passion that stamped his ministry. Roberts' reforming zeal and his activities in the cause of "free" churches already have been reviewed prominently in the pages of this book, but it is further worthy of note that he placed the cause of "free" churches even above the success of the Free Methodist Church as an organization. In 1862, when the denomination was but two years old, he expressed the desire to solicit wealthy men in Syracuse for funds, "enough to build a free church, not a Free Methodist Church, but a free church," and added, "It seems to me that God wants *free* churches in all our cities." [2] In an editorial in *The Earnest Christian* several months earlier, after reporting more calls for "free" churches than there were qualified preachers to supply them, he disclaimed "the slightest ambition to build up a new denomination," and declared that his desire was for spiritual churches, "in which all seats shall be free and no respect paid to persons on account of wealth or social position." And he said that it was his preference that existing denominations take and hold the position of spiritual religion, with seats free to all, rather than "to see a new denomination raised up to spread these Scriptural principles." [3]

In 1866 the introductory address of the Free Methodist *Discipline*, which previously had detailed the ecclesiastical conflict out of which

---
2. B. H. Roberts, *Benjamin Titus Roberts*. Earnest Christian Office, North Chili, N. Y.; p. 294.
3. *The Earnest Christian*, v. 2, June 1861; p. 192.

the church had its origin, was replaced by a clear-cut statement of the principles upon which the new church was founded. In this 1866 address we find the following reasoned and forceful declaration of concern for all classes and races of men, which placed the young church at the forefront in social idealism among all denominations of that or later generations:

> All their churches are required to be as free as the grace they preach. They believe that their mission is two-fold—to maintain the Bible standard of Christianity—and to preach the Gospel to the poor. Hence they require that all seats in their houses of worship should *be free*. No pews can be rented or sold among them. The world will never become converted to Christ, so long as the Churches are conducted upon the exclusive system. It has always been contrary to the economy of the Christian Church, to build houses of worship with pews to rent. But the spirit of the world has encroached by little and little, until, in many parts of the United States, not a single free church can be found in any of the cities or larger villages. The pew system generally prevails among all denominations. We are thoroughly convinced that this system is wrong in principle, and bad in tendency. It is a corruption of Christianity. *Free churches are essential to reach the masses.* The provisions of the Gospel are for all. The "glad tidings" must be proclaimed to every individual of the human race. God sends the true light to illuminate and melt every heart. To civilized and savage, bond and free, black and white, the ignorant and the learned, is freely offered the great salvation.
>
> *But for whose benefits are special efforts to be put forth?* Who must be *particularly* cared for? Jesus settles this question. "The blind receive their sight, and the lame walk, the lepers are cleansed, and the deaf hear, the dead are raised up," and as if all this would be insufficient to satisfy John of the validity of his claims, he adds, "and the poor have the gospel preached to them." This was the crowning proof that He was the One that should come. In this respect the Church must follow in the footsteps of Jesus. She must see to it that the gospel is preached to the poor. Thus, the duty of preaching the gospel to the poor, is enjoined by the plainest precepts and examples. If the gospel is to be preached to all, then it follows, as a necessary consequence, that all the arrangements for preaching the gospel should be so made as to secure this object. If it be said that seats would be freely given to those who are unable to pay for them, we answer, this does not meet the case. But few are willing, so long as they are able to appear at church, to be publicly treated as paupers.

Rented pews are no longer an issue in maintaining the freedom of the gospel, but the principle involved is now attacked from other quarters, and Free Methodism's position on the principle remains unchanged.

The freedom of the slave

The issue of human slavery was a more significant factor in the origin of Free Methodism than has commonly been understood. The long record of Methodist compromise on slavery issues was reviewed in Chapter Ten. In the Genesee Conference the changing climate toward slavery added to the tension between the Regency and the reform party, and prepared the way for the political alliance between the pro-slavery Border and the historically abolitionist Genesee, as was mentioned in Chapter Fourteen. Roberts' stand against slavery was well known and certainly intensified the opposition he met in Genesee, if indeed it did not affect the handling of his appeals by the General Conference.

At its organization, the Free Methodist Church changed but one stipulation in the General Rules of the parent church. This was its substitution for the nebulous prohibition, "The buying and selling of men, women, or children, with an intention to enslave them," the unequivocal prohibition of "The buying, selling, or holding of a human being as a slave." Not until the General Conference of 1864, when, as previously noted, there was not a legally held slave anywhere in the United States, did the Methodist Episcopal Church amend its slavery rule to a like unequivocal statement, which read, "Slaveholding; buying or selling slaves," and so it appears today in the Methodist *Discipline*.

Discussing the long record of slavery compromise of Northern Methodism, J. Minton Batten has said, "The one uncompromising method of dealing with slavery as an evil would have been the adopting of the simple policy of making slaveholding a bar to membership in the Methodist societies or churches and then enforce this rule, allowing no exceptions of its application." [4]

This is the course Free Methodism took. From the address quoted above from the 1866 *Discipline*, the following likewise is taken:

---
4. J. Minton Batten, "Divisions in American Methodism," in *Methodism*, Wm. K. Anderson, Editor. Methodist Publishing House, Nashville; p. 61.

The Golden Rule, [Free Methodists] hold, applies equally to the colored as to the white race. The first Free Methodist Church ever organized was in St. Louis, a slave-holding city, and at a time when slaveholders were freely admitted to the churches generally. Yet they made non-slaveholding a test of membership, prohibiting, as they ever have done, "the buying, selling, or holding a human being as a slave."

This earliest of all Free Methodist churches was organized in the early spring of 1859, more than a year before the denomination was launched. Chapter Fourteen told of the event and the part B. T. Roberts had in completing the organization and seeing that slaveholding was made a bar to membership. This Free Methodist congregation set the pattern against slaveholding.

At different times during the course of the years the attempt has been made to delete the anti-slavery rule from the *Discipline* as no longer relevant and an unpleasant reminder of the sectional conflict which all but dissolved the Union. All such efforts have failed, and rightly so, for the rule is a memorial to the wisdom and courage of the church's fathers and a testimony to a world that still needs the clear affirmation of the principle of human freedom.

Passive and active holiness

One of the mysteries of that mid-century period was the failure of outstanding spiritual leaders in Methodism to take a vigorous stand against slavery. Timothy L. Smith traces the growth of abolitionism well into the fifties until finally religious sentiment had rallied behind the reform effort. "Abolition was no longer the hobby of fanatics," he says, "but the moral objective of the greatest preachers in the free states," and, "Revivalists of all persuasions contributed to the goal for which . . . anti-slavery editors were striving in the cities of the North." Then he adds:

> The only major exceptions were the Methodist perfectionists surrounding Phoebe Palmer. Her fast friends, Bishops Edmund Janes and Leonidas Hamline, were the architects of the policy of silence which later became the regret of Northern Methodism. George and Jesse Peck, Nathan Bangs, Alfred Cookman, and a host of her other admirers supported it fully.[5]

---

5. Timothy L. Smith, *Revivalism and Social Reform*. Abingdon Press, Nashville; pp. 210, 211.

Issues of the *Northern Independent* appearing late in 1859 and early in 1860 made references to Dr. Bangs as president of the Ministers' and Laymen's Union of the M. E. Church, organized a few months before the General Conference for the purpose of working for moderation in handling the slavery issue and opposing abolitionism.

The following revealing incident, of which Dr. Bangs was a principal, is taken from the *Northern Independent* about a year after the Civil War had broken out. The Doctor was presiding at the Tuesday Meeting in New York, as frequently occurred in Mrs. Palmer's absence. We follow the account as reported in the *Northern Independent*:

> Presently the speaker arose to speak, and alluded to the subject of slavery. In an instant, the good Doctor informed him that he must not introduce the subject. The stranger seeming disposed to proceed, was at length told, in Dr. Bangs' style, to *"sit down!"* And finally he submitted to the gag. The same rule prevails in the celebrated "Fulton-Street Prayer-Meeting," in this city, and we believe in the John Street meetings. No man must speak or pray against the great American abomination.

The reporter makes this sobering comment: "It is just such religion, falsely so called, that has kept slavery in countenance, made the slave interests impious and rebellious in Church and state, and brought all our present troubles upon us. And still Methodist D.D's. are tender of the feelings of slave-holders." [6]

The same journal reported another prayer meeting, this one in Philadelphia. A brother prayed, "Oh, Lord, forgive us our great national sin"— and at that point was interrupted by the leader's bell! After the service the brother explained to the leader that he was about to ask forgiveness for our national sin of *swearing*. The leader apologized, and explained that by "our great national sin," slavery is usually meant. The brother was puzzled, not understanding why if slavery were the great national sin, one could not pray about it! [7]

According to Smith, Mrs. Palmer and her associates "were laggards in whatever demanded stern attacks on persons and institutions," and,

---

6. *Northern Independent*, v. 5, June 13, 1861.
7. *Ibid.*, Jan. 17, 1861.

"Denouncing social and political injustice remained for them a prerogative of divinity." [8] These good people placed peace and unity above righteousness, a not unusual sin of other-worldly saints whose passive holiness awaits the orderings of Providence and lets evil take its course, trusting God to right matters in the end—even if He must then visit judgment upon both the just and the unjust, upon the latter for aggressive wickedness and the former for peace-loving acquiescence.

On the slavery issue, as other areas of evil, B. T. Roberts' holiness was of the practical sort, and he could brook no pious passivity when confronted with wrong. His loneliness as a reformer was the greater because those spiritually akin to him, including even Mrs. Palmer whose ministry at the Collins camp meeting helped him into full surrender and consecration, stood aloof from courageous participation in the conflict for social righteousness to which that consecration in 1851 had committed him. That Roberts was acutely aware of this moral passivity of leaders in pious spirituality, is disclosed in the following excerpt from his pen on "Hatred of Sin":

> Holiness is not indifference. One who is truly holy does not feel that he has done his duty by simply abstaining from sin. True holiness is not that easy, good-natured disposition that smiles at sin, and gives it ample toleration, especially if it is fashionable, or popular, or capable of being turned to account in "building up the church," that is, adding to its members and influence. There was a great deal of this spurious kind of holiness in this country in the palmy days of slavery. You may search volume after volume of its literature, designed for circulation in the South, without finding one bold, manly, outspoken denunciation of the sin of slave-holding. You might have attended the "holiness meeting," week after week, without hearing one prayer offered for the liberation of the slave, or one testimony borne against the "sum of all villainies." No farther south than the city of New York, at no later a date than soon after President Lincoln's emancipation proclamation, you might have heard a brother called to order in the leading "holiness meeting" for thanking God for this proclamation which struck the fetters from three million bondmen.[9]

---

8. Timothy L. Smith, *Revivalism and Social Reform*; Abingdon Press, Nashville; p. 212.
9. B. T. Roberts, *Holiness Teachings*. Earnest Christian Publishing House, North Chili, N. Y.; p. 57 *et seq.*

The active holiness of early Free Methodism found expression in pungently worded resolutions adopted from time to time by the Illinois Conference during the nation's conflict over slavery and the period of reconstruction. So indicative are these of the young church's vigorous concern to secure and guarantee human rights to all, that some of them are printed for preservation and dissemination in Appendix C of this volume. There may they serve, not only as interesting comments on a past generation's social conscience, but to monitor the church's conscience in future generations.

Bishop Roberts and economic interests

That B. T. Roberts wrote a book on economics has been stated. Not inappropriately, for the governmental context of money was prominent therein, the book carried a front-page quotation from William Penn, reading, "A man should make it a part of his religion to see that his country is well governed."

Looking back to his own college course in economics, the present writer can very well believe that a preliminary canter through Roberts' book at the opening of the course could have eased the shock of his plunge into the depths of Ely's *Principles*. And mentioning Ely—Roberts quoted him in 1866 as one of his authorities. Was Roberts so alert in this field that he had discovered a young and brilliant economist in the making? Or was Ely an aged man when the writer studied his text nearly thirty years later? Investigation discloses that when Roberts wrote *First Lessons on Money*, Richard T. Ely was a young professor shortly past thirty in Johns Hopkins University, and the alert Roberts already was reading after him.

We make no effort to summarize Roberts' interesting and alluminating book, but would suggest his reason for writing it and the point of view held by the author. He wrote *First Lessons on Money* in the interests of economic reform. He hoped to instruct the common people in the elementary principles of economics, for, as stated in his Preface, he was convinced "that the money question will not be settled until the People settle it." He was a bimetalist, convinced that the demonetization of silver and the adoption of a single gold standard played into the hands of capitalists and against the poor and those who owed money. He called for laws to make it difficult for one man to amass an immense fortune to be passed down in the family through successive generations, and urged that the people see to it that their representatives in Congress pass laws in the interests of the people, "and not in favor of the moneyed class and rich corporations." Let us recall that 1886 was in the "gilded age" of large capitalist empires and rampant materialism, in the bounty of which the poor had little share. Bishop Roberts was alert to the moral and spiritual bearings of the era and sought reform of its evils.

He had a keen interest in the welfare of the farmer. When the Agricultural Society of Western New York in 1872 asked him to speak at a fair in the neighborhood of Rochester, he did so, speaking on the subject, "A Conspiracy Against Farmers." The address was published and received considerable attention. In it, he discussed railroad grants, the bonding system, and national banks, all as they adversely affected the farmer. On this occasion he promoted and with his son helped organize the Farmers' Alliance in New York State, an organization that had been initiated in Chicago two years earlier. In 1880 he wrote his son the following letter concerning the progress of the movement:

> Our Farmers' Alliance that you assisted me to organize has already become a formidable power in the politics of the state. Through their influence a Bill has been introduced into our Legislature requiring the railroads of the state to carry a car load of the same freight between the same places for the same price for all parties. It is making a great stir. The Railroads oppose it with all the influence they can control. But it will ultimately carry, if not at this occasion, then at a future one.[10]

While in St. Louis in March, 1874, he wrote, "Went with Brother Lovejoy to a meeting of the Farmers' Club at the court house. I spoke by invitation and urged upon them the importance of a general organization throughout the country." [11]

Bishop Roberts did not hesitate to write extensively on economic and political issues in the religious journals he edited, *The Earnest Christian* and *The Free Methodist*. In 1876 he wrote on "Business Stagnation," asserting that the country had all the elements of national prosperity, "Yet, in the midst of plenty," he said, "we are in

---
10. C. H. Zahniser, *Earnest Christian: Life and Works of Benjamin Titus Roberts*; p. 256 *et seq.*
11. B. H. Roberts, *Benjamin Titus Roberts*; p. 467.

want." According to his analysis the causes of this condition were mainly three: (1) *Over-production,* the cause of which had been the seven-day week, especially in the great iron and oil industries which now were in depression; (2) *Extravagance,* on the part of rich and poor alike; and (3) *Conspiracies to keep up prices,* rather than letting them be regulated by the law of supply and demand. "Interfere with this law," he said, "and confusion follows." Other than farmers, all the great industries and labor had conspired to create fictitious prices which have "practically shut us out of the market of the world." [12]

In *The Free Methodist,* Roberts ventured a lengthy editorial on Henry George's *Progress and Poverty,* published in 1889. In this volume George had developed his theory of a single tax on land to correct the inequalities of wealth and poverty. He held that the unearned increment of unimproved land is the product of society itself and not of the efforts of the owner, and therefore the state may justly appropriate through taxation the appreciated value. Roberts was in full sympathy with George's purpose, but objected that the single tax on land, exempting from taxation the processes and products of labor, far from relieving inequities in the distribution of wealth, would aggravate them by confiscatory taxes and drive farmers from their farms. The actual causes producing immense estates, he said, were the granting of unfair public franchises and the watering of corporation stock. Reform must come from correcting these evils.[13] That George's theory has not generally been accepted by economic science or in taxation procedures after seventy years, and the subsequent history of capitalistic monopolies, tend to confirm the position taken by Roberts.

In the same publication Bishop Roberts advocated bringing down extortionist prices by a "do-it-yourself" economy. The following excerpt shows that he could be humorous as well as practical:

> Bring the old spinning wheel down from the garret and let the grandmothers teach the girls how to run it. It will be better for them to spin stocking yarn than "street yarn." Darn and patch the old clothes instead of buying the new ones on credit. Wear on the farm, or in the shop, the old-fashioned, homemade blouse

---

12. *The Earnest Christian,* v. 31, Feb. 1876; p. 64.
13. B. T. Roberts, "The Single Tax," an editorial in *The Free Methodist,* v. 23, Sept. 10, 1890; p. 8.

instead of a coat. Hire a carpenter to make the coffin; and leave the undertaker to his grave reflections.[14]

Industrial relations

For a church with the early leadership of a Roberts, the concern of Free Methodism for social and economic reform has been moderate. One of its principal areas of resolution and legislation has been that of industrial relations. The church has kept in view the evils both of capital and labor, but much of its conservatism on the issues involved has resulted from the secrecy feature of unionism, along with the unfortunate episodes of violence that have accompanied labor's efforts to force its demands. These factors of secrecy and violence have kept the Free Methodist Church from lending fuller support to the labor cause.

One of the church's early censures against labor was countered with a rebuke to capitalism. This was in 1878 when the committee on reforms expressed regret "that there is a Communistic element among our workers" and condemned "the lawless acts of violence inspired thereby in the recent railroad strike," but severely censured "the oppressions of capitalism and business corporations."

The committee on reforms of 1894 made the following analysis:

> Capital unites to control prices which, as is often observed, makes the rich richer and the poor poorer. Then labor combines to forcibly redress its grievances and we have the strike which results in an appalling loss of life, obstruction to traffic, and, perhaps more than all else, the flooding of our country with an injured and idle class of men who are activated by anarchistic doctrine.

The committee on reforms of 1903 well expressed the church's conflicting sympathy for labor and abhorrence of the flagrant evils persisting within its organized efforts to secure its rights. The report said:

> We as a church are in hearty sympathy with the laboring man in his struggles with greedy capital and capitalistic trusts to secure his share of the profits accruing from his labor, and extend him our hearty Godspeed, but deprecate and deplore the un-American and despotic methods resorted to and employed by many labor unions in strikes and lockouts, and are more and more persuaded

---

14. *Ibid.*, v. 23, Nov. 5, 1890; p. 8.

that secret orders are detrimental to the true and lasting interests of the working man.

This General Conference declared its opinion that membership in trade unions contravened membership in the church because of their general character as secret societies, confirming an interim pronouncement of the church's executive committee. The decision of the executive committee was printed in the Supplement of 1903 as the first specific mention of labor unions in the *Discipline*. This ruling embodied a caution against anyone's concluding that the church was unfriendly to labor, by saying:

> We cannot, however, allow this position to be misinterpreted and misconstrued as opposition to organized labor as such. We are not opposed to such proper organizations as seek to promote the interests of the laboring man. It would be unreasonable for us to do so as fully three-fourths of our membership are found among the laboring classes. To oppose organized labor that seeks the betterment of the laboring classes would be to oppose our own interests.

The General Conference of 1915 for the first time brought into the *Discipline* definite legislation on the question of labor unions. The close relationship of the problem to secrecy is suggested by the placing of this legislation under Secret Societies, as well as by its wording. Discrimination against nonunion workers in the employment practices of Free Methodist employers was forbidden, as well as membership of Free Methodists in the union. Following is the statement of the 1915 legislation:

> We would not oppose the open and honest organization of the laboring classes seeking in a proper way their betterment without injuring others or violating the inherent rights of any, but we are opposed to the element of pledged or oath bound secrecy, the policy of coercion, the practice of lawlessness, or any other evil in such organizations, and we prohibit our members from membership in labor unions or other societies where such evils exist. We hold that labor unions as now generally constituted are secret societies and that membership therein is a bar to membership in the church.
>
> We also declare that discrimination in favor of unionsim as against non-unionism on the part of contractors or employers is a violation of Par. 44 of our General Rules. Any contractor or any employer of labor found guilty, according to the process of

disciplinary trial, of thus discriminating shall be debarred from membership in the Free Methodist Church.

The 1919 General Conference added to the church's statement forbidding membership of Free Methodists in labor unions the following adjustment, which was adopted by a very close Yea and Nay vote, 56 to 55:

> If a union consents to give a person the privilege of working, upon the payment of the regular dues, without taking an oath or pledge of secrecy or attending the meetings of the union, such person accepting employment under this provision shall not be debarred from membership in the church.

The 1923 General Conference, however, deleted this provision, and also the rule forbidding discrimination in favor of union labor by Free Methodist employers. Action was taken by this Conference to establish an Industrial Commission to investigate the entire industrial situation and report to the next General Conference. But no activity was reported by this commission in 1927, the lame reason offered being the fact that no funds had been provided for the investigation.

In 1939 the *Discipline* was revised in more affirmative terms in its statement on labor, and in 1951 for the first time were labor considerations given a section separate from Secret Societies, under the heading, Labor and Industrial Relations. The 1939 statement, edited but not changed in principle, stands as follows in the present *Discipline*:

> We would not oppose the open and honest organization of the laboring classes seeking in a proper way their betterment without injuring others or violating the inherent rights of any. But we are opposed to pledged or oath-bound secrecy, coercion, lawlessness, or any other evil in their organization; and we prohibit our members from joining labor unions or other societies demanding an oath-bound pledge of secrecy as a condition of membership. Yet, otherwise, we recognize their inherent right to hold membership in labor organizations. And wherever they cannot on account of required oath-bound pledges of secrecy be members of the labor union, if merely upon the payment of regular dues they are allowed to work free from the use of coercion, we grant them the privilege of doing so.

The Executive Commission of the Board of Administration shall constitute a Board of Industrial Relations the duty of which is to furnish information and render decisions upon all matters of industrial relations. To this Board should be committed all questions, communications, and papers relating to labor unions or membership in them. This Board shall, wherever practicable, constitute a collective bargaining agency on behalf of the members of our church.

At last the church had reached a generally constructive position on organized labor, while maintaining its position against secrecy and violence.

In 1947 the General Conference made a comprehensive statement on labor which (1) condemned "any group or system which would tend to oppress or enslave the laboring man, . . . or which would prevent him from using any proper, right or lawful means of improving the conditions under which he must labor"; (2) rejoiced in reforms making for health and safety in the conditions of labor; (3) condemned communistic agitation within labor's ranks, and limiting the amount of work a laborer may perform; and (4) declared un-American and wrong "any principle which denies workers the right or privilege to work at a chosen vocation, or which would set aside his democratic rights or cause him to set aside or violate his God-given convictions."

By 1955 the committee on reforms had become the committee on social, moral and economic action, and in that year recommended that labor and management cooperate to check the loss of time from employment and inconvenience to the public caused by strikes; declared that requiring a person to join a union as a condition of his employment is contrary to the fundamental principles of freedom for which the nation stands; and declared that both organized labor and management should be required to live up to their contracts with each other, and each be held financially responsible for breaches of the same.

Secret societies

That the Free Methodist Church disapproves secret societies has repeatedly been indicated in this and former chapters. It is obvious that compromising associations with a quasi-religious organization cannot but dull the spiritual life of a born-again Christian, not to mention the loss of spiritual power resulting from social activities of a worldly character in which the lodge will involve him. He must accept the most intimate, oath-bound fellowship of those who, unknown to him when he joins, are completely alien to his Christian culture and ideals.

Perhaps someone will say that these objections are largely of personal concern to the Christian, such as normally come within the purview of the preceding chapter on Christian discipline. But strangely enough, there are those, even ministers among them, who justify their membership in the lodge on the ground that it extends their reach of Christian helpfulness and influence to others. But what a contradiction: a Christian joining a limited and exclusive secret order for the purpose of extending his Christian ministry! Can one conceive that Jesus would have joined a group in an intimate fellowship which arbitrarily excluded all others but those with whom he shared certain secrets under oath? The exclusiveness of the secret order is one of the features that makes it a hindrance to the Christian's social witness.

Then there is the further risk—one that a devout Christian should hesitate to venture—of being compelled to swear to guard secrets and to follow procedures in conduct of which he has no knowledge at the time, even taking oaths that may require him to place his allegiance to his lodge above his family, his church, and his country. The social bearing of this risk is obvious enough.

Secrecy makes possible, and therefore encourages, machinations that reach into and corrupt society in what should be its legitimate and open associations, as happened a century ago in the lodge-cloaked operations of the Regency party of the Genesee Conference.

About ten years ago, in the context of Stanley High's "Pink Fringe of Methodism," the late Bishop Frederick DeLand Leete wrote of the dangers involved in the membership of church leaders in propaganda organizations, and the need for reserve even in fraternity relationships. He gave point to the latter caution by stating that the Free Methodist Church never would have left the parent church but for the pressure of fraternity influence exerted by the Genesee and the General Conference.[15] The report on secret societies to the 1866 General Conference similarly pointed out that, but for the secret society evil,

---

15. Personal Letter, dated Feb. 5, 1950.

there would have been no necessity for the Free Methodist Church. It was this General Conference of 1866 that enacted legislation on the secrecy issue and inserted the same in a section of the *Discipline* where it has remained through ninety-four years, unchanged but for minor editing. We reproduce it here in its present form:

> Voluntary associations are not necessarily sinful because they are secret. But secrecy is always a ground of suspicion. Evil works instinctively incline to darkness. Good works grow up in light. God commands us to let our light shine. Even a good cause under the shadow of secrecy invalidates its claim to the confidence of open and honest men. Grace and guile can have no affinity. All secrets necessary to be kept can be kept without an oath. A bad institution should not, and a good one need not, be secret. Philanthropic associations claiming our cooperation on Christian grounds must do so with open face. They must lift the veil while demanding our salutation, or we cannot salute them by the way. Therefore, all secret societies are to be eschewed.
>
> Any society requiring an oath, affirmation, or promise of secrecy, as a condition of membership, is held to be a secret society; and any member joining or continuing in one violates his covenant obligations as set forth in Pars. 57, Sec. 3, and 87, Sec. 5, and shall in due form be excluded from the church; and the preacher shall report that he is excluded for infraction of our rules and regulations.

On the basis of a General Conference ruling in 1927, there was added to the above paragraphs on secret societies in 1951 the following provision:

> Nothing herein shall prevent one's paying dues in a secret society to keep in force insurance contracted for before becoming a member of the church.

It was noted in the preceding chapter that secret society membership was barred from the beginning of the church by the membership covenant, and the prohibition of membership in secret societies was added to the General Rules in 1878, and transferred to the Special Rules in 1951.

Militarism and war

The Free Methodist Church stands firmly against militarism without, however, holding the position of nonresistance to armed evil, or of pacifism as universally binding upon the Christian conscience.

In 1911 the General Conference adopted a memorial appealing for universal peace, and ordered that copies of the same be sent to government officials. In 1935 a new section was inserted in the *Discipline* under the caption, Militarism and War, which declared that militarism was contrary to the spirit of the New Testament; disapproved military training in schools as fostering the spirit of militarism; declared against compulsory military training and bearing of arms except in case of national peril; and in these matters called for respect for the individual conscience of members of the Free Methodist Church. In 1939 this sentence was added in further support of conscientious objectors: "Therefore we claim exemption from the bearing of arms for all members of our church who are conscientious objectors." In 1947 the statement disapproving military training in schools was deleted, and a clause was added setting up the machinery for registering Free Methodists who are conscientious objectors. This is the church's position as now defined in the *Discipline*:

> Militarism is contrary to the spirit of the New Testament and the teachings of Jesus Christ. Even from humanitarian principles alone it is utterly indefensible. It is our profound conviction that none of our people should be required to enter military training or to bear arms except in time of national peril, and that the consciences of our individual members should be respected. Therefore we claim exemption from the bearing of arms for all members of our church who are conscientious objectors.

Temperance and prohibition

The Free Methodist Church has always stood for temperance, as was clearly indicated in the preceding chapter's report of its demands for personal abstinence from alcoholic beverages and other physically hurtful indulgences. But the church from the beginning went far beyond personal restraint in these matters to expressions of strong concern over the evil effects of intemperance upon society. Reformers engaged in this area testify that they always can depend upon Free Methodist support of their endeavors, either by local option or Prohibition party methods, to combat the manufacture and sale of liquor.

The 1882 General Conference introduced a section in the *Discipline* headed "On Temperance" which included a general statement of the evils of strong drink, and stipulated that only unfermented wine should be used in the sacrament of the Lord's Supper. It defined political responsibility as follows:

> Let every man of God break away from the trammels of party, and never knowingly give his vote or influence to elect any man to office, who will use his official or personal influence to legalize the traffic in intoxicating liquors as a beverage. As Christians, we are bound to do all we can to prohibit by law this nefarious traffic.

The entire section as adopted in 1882 remains unchanged in the 1955 *Discipline* of the Free Methodist Church.

The next General Conference, in 1886, adopted a long report on reforms which included endorsement of the Prohibition Party. So committed was B. T. Roberts to the principle of independence of party control adopted in 1882, and now violated in the adoption of the 1886 resolution, that he and three other signers presented a protest against the action. This protest read in part as follows:

> We believe that, as the representative body of the church, we have no right to seek to commit the church to any political party. Our members should be left free to vote for the prohibition of the liquor traffic in that manner that in their judgment is best calculated to promote the cause of prohibition, as they are left to do by the Discipline.

Earlier in that conference Roberts had made a generous offer of copyrights, type and printing fixtures in view of the proposal now before the conference to order the establishment of a denominational publishing house. This offer he now withdrew and asked that the following statement be placed on record:

> As the Report on Reforms adopted by a majority of the members of this Body this morning unqualifiedly commits us as a Church to a Political Party as such, which action I conscientiously hold to be wrong; and as the Paper to be established by this Body will probably be our exponent of the views of the majority, and so become the *organ of a political party*, and as I cannot in conscience give my countenance or support to such a measure; I hereby withdraw the offer which I made toward the establishing of a "Book Room," and hold myself free to act in the matter as my judgment shall dictate and God shall lead. Signed, B. T. Roberts.

The same evening the following resolution was adopted by the General Conference:

> Whereas, This General Conference has endorsed the existence of the Prohibition Party and commended it as the most efficient agent in procuring both state and national prohibition; and, Whereas, There has arisen in the minds of some a fear that, in the establishment of a Church Paper, it will be issued as an organ of the Prohibition Party; Therefore, Resolved That it is the sense of this General Conference that while our Church Paper should advocate the principle of Prohibition, it is not to be committed to the advocacy of any Political Party.

In the same sitting, the General Conference elected this busy bishop, already editor of *The Earnest Christian*, the editor of *The Free Methodist!* Thus was expressed the church's high confidence in its senior leader, notwithstanding his strong disagreement on occasion with the majority.

The strong commitment of the church to the Prohibition Party that has existed through the years may be gathered from the fact that its members have been Prohibition candidates in various state and in national elections, and the General Conference frequently has scheduled an evening speaker of prominence in that party to represent the cause of temperance.

Position on racial discrimination

This courageous declaration of the 1866 General Conference still stands in the *Discipline* of 1955: "To civilized and savage, bond and free, black and white, the ignorant and the learned, is freely offered the great salvation." In the latter year, momentous in the nation's history because of the Supreme Court Ruling of May 17 which declared that racial segregation is unconstitutional, the General Conference adopted the following resolutions which had been submitted by the committee on social, moral and economic action:

> WHEREAS, the Word of God clearly states that "God . . . hath made of one blood all nations of men" (Acts 17:26) and that "there is neither male nor female; for ye are all one in Christ Jesus" (Galatians 3:28), and
>
> WHEREAS, one of the disruptive forces which hinders revival and the working of the Holy Spirit is prejudice and discrimination in human relations, and

WHEREAS, the acts of racial prejudice as manifested by segregation in America have been exploited by the leaders of godless communism to strengthen their appeal to the masses, and

WHEREAS, the Supreme Court of the United States has declared that legal segregation is contrary to the Constitution of the United States and has forbidden discrimination on public transportation, in public buildings, and public schools, and

WHEREAS, the Free Methodist Church of North America has declared that the "glad tidings must be proclaimed to every individual of the human race—to savage and civilized, bond and free, black and white—"

BE IT THEREFORE RESOLVED, that the General Conference of the Free Methodist Church of North America recognize the May 17 Supreme Court decision as being in harmony with the constitutional guarantees of equal freedom to all citizens and with the Christian principle of perfect love, and

BE IT FURTHER RESOLVED, that this body commend the Free Methodist laymen, pastors, superintendents, and general officers who by their efforts and influence have endeavored to maintain our original convictions by keeping the doors of our churches and general gatherings open to all people regardless of race, class, or color, and with special commendation to those pastors and laymen who have successfully integrated into their membership born-again Christians of various races and nationalities, and

BE IT FINALLY RESOLVED, that we urge Free Methodists across the nation to continue to witness to the Bible standard of brotherhood both in word and deed and to lend their support to other religious bodies and suitable secular organizations in an effort to combat racial discrimination.

This forthright resolution of 1955 confirmed the position Free Methodism had declared in the *Discipline* of 1866 nearly a century earlier, and had repeated in succeeding *Disciplines* to the present.

Other reform interests

The concern of Free Methodism in civic and national problems has been expressed at different times and in different ways. How far Bishop Roberts was influential in the incident we are about to relate we do not know, but he ministered in the St. Charles camp meeting of 1862 when an unusual thing happened. It was found that an Illinois election was to be held during the scheduled period of the meeting, the purpose of which was to vote on the adoption of a proposed new and iniquitous constitution which would favor the pro-slavery interests of southern Illinois and prohibit the entry of Negroes into the State. The election was to be held on Tuesday of the camp meeting, but the camp meeting was concluded on Monday, Roberts reported, "in order to give the voters time to get home and deposit their emphatic protest against this anti-Christian project." Then Roberts commented, "Faith and works must go together. We must not only pray for righteousness to prevail, but do all we can in a Christian manner to make it prevail." [16] The civic conscience that would adjourn a camp meeting early for an election is as commendable as it is unusual.

The committee on reforms of the 1882 General Conference reported the Christian's responsibility for his vote in these words: "And while we rely upon God for success, we will respect His glory in the use of the elective franchise, voting only for such men irrespective of party as we believe will promote and maintain righteousness instead of mere party interests."

In the General Conference of 1886, the committee on the state of the work warned against losing sight of the true nature of the church's task and becoming mere reformers. The report said:

> While the religion we teach will make us take our stand on the side of every great moral reform, yet it will not permit us to make zeal for reforms a substitute for vital godliness. Christian efforts, put forth in a Christian spirit to promote reforms, will be but one of many fruits borne by the tree of righteousness of God's own planting.

The 1943 General Conference adopted a resolution supporting the separation of church and state, and opposed the continuance of the Vatican embassy. Again in 1951, through its committee on social, moral and economic action, the church declared vigorously for the separation of church and state, especially disapproving a president having a personal representative at the Vatican, and the support of parochial schools from public revenues.

It is worthy of note that Bishop Roberts' leadership in reforms was recognized and appreciated by the church. Shortly after his

---
16. *The Earnest Christian*, v. 4, July 1862; p. 30.

death, through its committee on reforms the General Conference of 1894 declared:

> It is encouraging to observe that the wisdom of the founder of our Zion, with respect to reformative principles, is confirmed by the development of the times. We now, as from the inception of our church, stand in the front rank of America's reformative organizations.

Free Methodist stewardship

For all his concern for the poor, Bishop Roberts was not opposed to wealth as wealth, but against unfair methods employed in its accumulation, and against its abuse and perversion to selfish ends. In two successive issues of *The Earnest Christian* in 1865, articles appeared from his pen on the stewardship of wealth and the ability to make money. "A talent for business is as much the gift of God as a talent for preaching," he maintained. Therefore it follows, "If it is wrong to bury it in one case, it is in the other. If God gives you the ability to get wealth, use it,—not for self-aggrandizement but for the good of your race." Such was Roberts' "gospel to the rich," which carried the responsibility to devote to doing good all wealth above that sufficient to enable a man and his family "to live in a comfortable, plain, Christian manner." [17]

Again, he wrote, "A talent to make money should be devoted to the service of God just as much as a talent to preach or write. You have no more right to employ it for your own special advantage in the one case than the other." He exhibited his practical sense in a brief exegesis of I Thessalonians 4:11, 12. "God does not require his people to take upon them the vows of voluntary poverty," he said; "Nor would he have them dependent upon others," he added. It is your duty to earn all you can, and further, "It is as much your duty to work, when able, as to pray." If with God's blessing a man "is enabled to procure a good home, and lay by property sufficient to provide for his wants in case of old age or disability to labor," he is encouraged in this by God's Word as given us in I Timothy 5:8. But, Roberts added, this "does not give permission to lay up treasures on earth—to heap up riches. This, God plainly forbids." [18]

---

17. *Ibid.*, v. 9, Feb. 1865; pp. 62, 63.
18. *Ibid.*, v. 9, March 1865; p. 94.

Such, in brief, were the principles of stewardship, both of money and talents, taught by the founder of the Free Methodist Church.

Indicative of a church's outward reach is the faithfulness of its members in their stewardship of material goods. As early as 1886, the General Conference adopted a resolution condemning covetousness as equally evil with secrecy, pride, worldliness, the use of tobacco and other items forbidden in the *Discipline*, and recommended that tithing be taught. A quarter-century later the General Conference added to the duties of the pastor stipulated in the *Discipline* the following responsibility:

> To warn people of the evil consequences to themselves and the Church of God of covetousness and withholding of their means from supporting the Gospel, and to urge upon all systematic and proportionate giving, and to preach upon the same, encouraging our people to tithe their income.

Except for a simple editorial change, this statement has stood in successive issues of the *Discipline* for nearly half a century, and undoubtedly has influenced the remarkable growth in recent years of a stewardship consciousness in Free Methodism.

Free Methodist stewardship today, however far it falls short of its full Christian responsibility, favorably compares with the stewardship of other and larger groups when measured on a *per capita* basis of giving to Christian and benevolent causes. In fact, minority religious groups generally exceed in this regard the major denominations, leading Bishop Kennedy of the Methodist Church to acknowledge, "Those sects which have placed tithing at the center of their way of life shame us with their giving in proportion to their wealth." [19] In line with this admission, the stewardship report on American Protestant denominations for 1958[20] lists the Free Methodist Church in *per capita* giving to foreign missions at a figure six times the *per capita* giving of major Methodism to the same cause. It may be assumed that comparisons would also favor, perhaps in lesser ratio, the giving of the Free Methodist Church to other benevolent causes.

The giving of Free Methodists, it should be noted, is on a voluntary

---

19. Gerald Kennedy, *The Methodist Way of Life*; © 1958 by Prentice-Hall, Inc., Englewood Cliffs, N. J.; p. 166.
20. Report, "Statistics of Church Finances," Department of Stewardship and Benevolences, N. C. C. C., Nov. 1, 1959.

basis, and not required by a legal exaction of tithes.

Reaching upward and outward

The horizontal reach to others should be strong in a church that had its origin in issues that involved, among others, such social problems as freedom of the slaves and preaching the gospel to the poor. Conservative in matters of doctrine and firm in the discipline of conduct, the church may have lagged for a time behind the socially progressive pace of its reforming pioneers, but whatever degree of social indifference may have affected the Free Methodist Church in its mid-period or earlier, evidence points to a present effort to maintain the outward, social reach of the gospel, along with the upward reach of a personal faith.

CHAPTER TWENTY-ONE

The Church as a Channel

While following sections of the Wesley trail in England, it was once the writer's privilege to visit the countryside parish church of South Leigh, near Oxford, where John Wesley preached his first sermon in 1725 shortly following his ordination as deacon. Inscribed on the pedestal of the pulpit is the record of Wesley's preaching there, as also is this statement made by Wesley only two years before his death: "I declare once more that I live and die a member of the Church of England and that none who regard my judgment or advice will ever separate from it."

Not long after this interesting visit to South Leigh, in quest of Wesleyana in the British Museum, by rare good fortune the writer discovered a letter addressed to one of Wesley's preachers named Samuel Bradburn. It was dated in 1783 when Wesley was eighty years old. After advising a Brother Ridel "not to please the Devil by preaching himself to death," Wesley had turned abruptly to write, "I still think, when the Methodists leave the Church of England, God will leave them." Even good men can be mistaken, as was John Wesley in this prediction.

It was never John Wesley's purpose to withdraw Methodism from the Church of England to establish another denomination. Until his death, although providential events began to point toward separation, Wesley held firmly to the idea of Methodism as a "society," organized for the spiritual discipline of its members, the evangelization of others, and good works in behalf of all, which should continue to operate within the aegis of Anglicanism but not as an official adjunct of the Church of England.

But God had another purpose, and contrary to Wesley's design but largely in consequence of some of the policies he had introduced in Methodism, the movement shortly after his death would completely release its tenuous tie to the Church of England to become a separate denomination. As expressed by Bishop Kennedy, "when the tide of a mighty spiritual power begins to run, it is almost impossible to control or confine it within existing conditions." [1]

Free Methodist founders not seceders

Nor did B. T. Roberts and his fellow reformers in the century following Wesley design to withdraw from the Methodist Episcopal Church to organize another Methodist denomination. Repeatedly the reformers had declared their purpose not to secede but to remain with the church—although a secession was, in fact, what many of their opponents desired! Even after their exclusion from the Genesee Conference, we have noted, they assumed that the General Conference would resolve the difficulties and they would be restored. We have also seen that one of the resolutions adopted by the West Sweden Laymen's Convention, called to plan their course after the unexpected refusal of the General Conference to hear the reformers' appeals, urged the people to adhere to the Methodist Episcopal Church wherever possible; but where this was impossible without strife, then, "for the sake of Christian peace and order" they were to organize themselves "into bands and societies, under the name 'Free Methodist Societies.'" [2]

At some point, perhaps after this convention, B. T. Roberts concluded, quite contrary to his former inclination, that the only proper course now was to organize a new denomination. It may be that he reached his decision only in the apple-orchard council the morning of the organizing convention. Anyway, later that day in the convention itself he could say, "We are ready. . . ." [3]

What else could be done? The dispossessed preachers and laymen were Methodists, and there was no other Methodist body that stood firmly with them on all issues involved in their rejection by the parent church. Nearest them was the Wesleyan Methodist Connexion that had separated seventeen years before on the issue of slavery, episcopal autocracy, and uncharitable dealings with abolitionist reformers. Although the doctrinal issue of entire sanctification was not a formally stated factor in its separation, and the doctrine was not included in its

---

1. Gerald Kennedy, *The Methodist Way of Life*. © 1958 by Prentice-Hall, Inc.; Englewood Cliffs, N. J.; p. 1.
2. *Supra*, p. 249.
3. *Supra*, p. 254.

original Articles of Religion, the Wesleyan Methodist Connexion after organizing proceeded promptly to frame and adopt such an article. The two groups were in close accord on the issue of slavery, but on other matters of reform, such as rejection of secrecy and certain restrictions against worldliness which were a part of Christian discipline among those who were to be Free Methodists, they were rather far apart at that time. Peters has caught the distinction between them which undoubtedly explains why the reformers of the sixties did not seek fellowship within the same communion with the reformers of the forties and their descendants. Peters stated that distinction in these words:

> The history of these two churches illustrates the growing tendency of the holiness emphasis of this period to identify sanctification with an individualistic puritanism. . . . Thus the Wesleyan Methodist Church, organized in the early flush of the revival of the 1840's, reflects in its history, a system relatively liberal at the outset but which grew increasingly insistent upon the observance of rules as it became a more distinctively holiness church. The Free Methodist Church, on the other hand, coming out of a later phase and self-consciously identified as a holiness church, began with a fully enunciated set of stringent regulations.[4]

After a century, however, the two churches are now close together in matters of Christian discipline, as likewise in doctrine and social reform. Their present differences are principally in the area of organization and government, but here also the distance between them has grown less with the passing of the years.

What is the church?

To this question the founders of Free Methodism gave an answer, inherited from the Thirty-Nine Articles of the Church of England by way of John Wesley and the Methodist Episcopal Church. Article xvi of the Free Methodist *Discipline* reads:

> The visible Church of Christ is a congregation of faithful men, in which the pure word of God is preached, and the sacraments are duly administered, according to Christ's ordinance, in all those things that of necessity are requisite to the same.

---

4. John L. Peters, *Christian Perfection and American Methodism*. Abingdon Press, Nashville; p. 130.

The emphasis of this declaration is spiritual, stressing faithfulness of the congregation, preaching the Word, ministering the sacraments. And properly so, for the essential character of the church is its spiritual quality, and not its material and organizational features which, when unchecked, have choked the vital spiritual principle or have cramped, dwarfed and distorted it within rigid, man-made forms. Paul well understood this problem when he wrote, "the letter killeth, but the spirit giveth life."

But granting the danger inherent in organization and regulation, we must keep in view another side of this complex problem. In their emphasis on the Spirit, some would shackle neither mind with doctrine nor conduct with discipline, while still others disclaim all ecclesiastical order as of the devil himself. We do well to recognize that without organizational forms, modes of worship, standards of faith, and principles of conduct, only confusion can result—be it irresponsibility, fanaticism, liberalism, or licentiousness. Even the above-quoted Article of Religion combines with its major spiritual emphasis a measure of order by making the Word of God the standard of preaching and the ordinances of Christ the basis of the sacraments.

The crucial task is rightly to assess organization and order as means rather than end—as a channel that provides the Spirit free passage rather than a reservoir in which the Spirit is held prisoner. Several years ago P. T. Forsyth thought he discerned a turning of the religion of the day from the quest for freedom to a quest for authority, and he rejoiced in the prospect, saying, "Every church in so far as it is a true church, must welcome the change which turns the question of the age from a freedom to an authority that creates freedom." [5]

Ecclesiastical authority, church organization, religious ordinances—all are for this purpose, to provide conditions favorable to the transmission of spiritual grace and power from their source in God to the individual and the church, and through them to the whole world.

Necessary to any adequate understanding of a church, is knowledge of its standards of Christian faith, Christian conduct, and church government. So basic are these that the principles underlying each have been set forth in a special section of the Free Methodist *Dis-*

---

5. P. T. Forsyth, *Faith, Freedom, and the Future.* Hodder and Stoughton, New York and London; p. 290.

cipline called the Constitution. One division of this Constitution declares the essentials of the church's faith in a series of twenty-three Articles of Religion; another division sets forth the principles and basic requirements of Christian living in terms of Wesley's General Rules and a brief collection of supplementary Special Rules; a third establishes the over-arching polity of the church in thirteen Articles of Organization and Government to which is attached a set of three Restrictive Rules.

Free Methodism's standards of doctrine and of Christian discipline have received our attention in previous chapters; its government is to be considered in this. It is this area which provides flexibility and adaptability to changing needs and conditions by processes of amendment in all three areas of the Constitution, processes more simple in the general area of government, more difficult in the area of Christian doctrine and Christian discipline. This adaptability in church government derives naturally from historic Methodism which developed, not as a sect claiming the authority of an apostolic pattern of government, but as a spiritual fellowship within the Church of England. And because Methodism developed from such beginnings rather than as an effort to establish a sect on someone's idea of the New Testament Church as the pattern decreed for all Christian groups, Methodist communions have never been rigidly sectarian in claiming for their polity apostolic validity and denying to other groups the right to existence.

It is true that John Wesley once held the episcopal form of church government to be mandatory in Scripture, but later became thoroughly convinced, "that neither Christ nor His Apostles prescribed any particular form of Church government, and that the plea for the divine right of the Episcopacy was never heard of in the primitive Church." But he continued to believe that the episcopal form was that followed by the apostles and reflected in their writings.[6]

Free Methodism, in line with the tradition of Methodism, does not maintain that its organization and government derive their pattern in any detailed sense from the apostolic church, but conceives of the varied forms of church government, such as Episcopal, Presbyterian, Congregational, as different plans chosen by God as human means

---

6. J. Wesley, *Letters*. Epworth Press, London; v. 3, 182.

through which to build His church on earth. In harmony with this view, the founders of Free Methodism provided means of amending previous legislation to meet changing conditions and needs. As will shortly be noted, the one fixed and unalterable principle they established was the right to impartial trial and of appeal.

Early organizational features

The organizing convention at Pekin took over the main features of the parent church's polity, but placed curbs on clerical control at all levels, local church, conference, and general. The principal checks were earlier discussed but some of the changes in church organization and function during the century past are yet to be reviewed.[7]

Because they appear at different points in this review and are basic to the church's legislative pattern, we first note what are called the Restrictive Rules. The church's founders embodied in the *Discipline* rules whereby the legislative powers of General Conference were limited so that it could not alter two vital areas of the church's laws by a simple majority vote, but must pass the proposition by a two-thirds vote, and further, secure a three-fourths vote of the members of the annual conferences. Moreover, another area of legislation was so protected that no change therein could be made by any means. The three rules thus restricting change were called the Restrictive Rules, and were the nearest a written constitution the church could boast until 1915.

The items which at Free Methodism's founding required, for change or amendment, two thirds of the votes in General Conference and three-fourths of the votes in the annual conferences were those restricted by:

Rule 1, which included standards of conduct and doctrine as declared in, (1) the General Rules, (2) the Articles of Religion, and (3) other doctrinal standards of the church;

Rule 2, which included the laws requiring, (1) lay representation, (2) an intinerant ministry, and (3) free seats in all the churches.

Rule 3, for which no amending provision was made, guaranteed to ministers and laymen the right to an impartial trial and the right of

---

7. *Supra*, p. 256 *et seq.*

appeal. The special care to protect these rights arose from the fact that many of the reformers had been denied them by the parent church in New York and Illinois, and several of these reformers were among those who framed the laws for the new church. Thus they sought to protect a principle of elemental human justice by an inviolable law more binding than any by which they would protect even standards of conduct and doctrine.

Organizational developments of a century

Summaries of some of the more important organizational acts of the General Conferences follow, in some instances accompanied by comments of the author.

1862. The first General Conference of the Free Methodist Church was held in 1862, after the young church had operated for two years under the *Discipline* adopted by the Pekin Convention of 1860. This General Conference revised the original *Discipline* in line with historic Methodism by substituting the term "conference" for "convention" to designate the church's official assemblies at general, annual and district levels.

The definition of voting membership in the annual conference was broadened to include preachers "on trial." In the early days when ordained ministers were limited in number and many pastoral charges were supplied by unordained preachers, this extension of the vote may have seemed advisable to balance the lay vote which was given to all pastoral charges whether served by ordained preachers or those licensed only. But the next General Conference restored the original basis of membership, including as voting members only preachers in orders with full conference relationship.

An executive committee of the General Conference was established to care for the following interim business: (1) advising the general superintendent concerning the organizing of new conferences, and approving the same in the interim of General Conferences; (2) electing a general superintendent in the event of a vacancy; and (3) fixing the salary of the general superintendent. The first item had been enacted to settle a legal issue precipitated by the general superintendent's organizing the Susquehanna Conference six months prior to the convening of the 1862 General Conference. The first *Discipline* had not defined the authority for organizing new conferences, and serious conflict developed which threatened the unity of the young church, especially when the Genesee delegates challenged the right of the Susquehanna delegates to seats, and the Genesee delegation withdrew from the General Conference in protest when those delegates were seated. The difficulty extended long beyond the adjournment of the General Conference, but was finally settled, in large part by the clear logic and Christian restraint of the general superintendent who was the principal target of the attack by the Genesee group.[8]

The executive committee set up by the first General Conference with such limited powers—powers having to do only with the affairs of the one executive then serving the church—was the beginning of an interim machinery of government that during the years ahead would develop into a complex system of many wheels, and wheels within wheels.

This General Conference provided that the circuits of a district should share the support of a district chairman who was not assigned to a pastorate but gave himself fully to evangelism in his district. Thus early, the development of a traveling superintendency was under way.

Following the Methodist Episcopal *Discipline* in setting up Restrictive Rules and provisions for their amendment, the organizing convention of 1860 had failed to restrict also the method of amending the amending provision itself. Accordingly, the Restrictive Rules were vulnerable to simple amendment of the amending process by any General Conference. In fact, the General Conference of 1862 did take action deleting all provisions for amending the Restrictive Rules. Perhaps the purpose of this Conference was to "freeze" these Rules and the items they covered against any possibility of future change. It appears that the Conference acted within its authority, however unwise its action may have been.

1866. This Conference declared that the 1862 Conference had acted beyond its authority in deleting the provision for amending the Restrictive Rules, but in this it was mistaken. However, it restored the provision. Interestingly enough, the 1947-1951 committee on principles and prudentials, without discovering that the 1862 General Conference actually had deleted the provision by which the Restrictive Rules could be amended, came to the conclusion that the Restrictive Rules were vulnerable. Why? Because the restrictions on the powers of the General Conference were so worded as to apply only to amending the Restrictive Rules and not to amending the provisions by which they could be amended. The 1951 General Conference, with the concurrence of the annual conferences, then restricted the provision for amending the Restrictive Rules as well as the Rules themselves.

The effort to eliminate deacon's ordination and retain only the order of elder in the ministry resulted in a tie, which the president's vote decided in the negative.

1870. One of the restraints against centralization of authority established by the Pekin Convention was the requirement that district chairmen be elected by the annual conferences rather than appointed by the general superintendent. The 1870 General Conference provided that the president, who normally of course would be the general superintendent, should make appointments to fill vacancies in the office of

---

8. See B. H. Roberts, *Benjamin Titus Roberts*. Earnest Christian Office, North Chili, New York; chs. 22, 23. Also, W. T. Hogue, *History of the Free Methodist Church*. Free Meth. Pub. House, Winona Lake, Ind.; v. 1, ch. 35.

district chairman, the appointment to be confirmed by the ensuing district quarterly conference. This provision still is in effect.

This General Conference voted by the required two-thirds majority to place under Restrictive Rule 2 a fourth item, the general superintendency. This action was referred to the annual conferences whose members concurred by the required three-fourths majority, and the general superintendency was thereby established as an item of government which could not be changed by General Conference, except under the proviso attached to the Restrictive Rules. This is the only item added to those protected by Rule 2 in the history of the church, although as will later be noted, an item likewise has been added to the protected list of Rule 1.

1874. For the first time, two general superintendents were ordered elected. E. P. Hart was the one chosen to serve with B. T. Roberts.

1878. The pastoral time limit of two years was removed in cases of colored and foreign-language churches. Efforts to extend the time limit in all cases would soon follow. This General Conference authorized the editorial substitution of "Free Methodist" for "Methodist" wherever the latter still lingered in the *Discipline.*

1882. The effort to lift the pastoral time limit from two to three years was defeated. This General Conference took action whereby a conference, upon the unanimous recommendation of the stationing committee, could leave a preacher without appointment. This rule is still in effect. To some the rule may seem autocratic, but under the appointive system some protection against the necessity of appointing inacceptable men seems advisable.

This General Conference recommended that the general superintendents arrange a general plan of superintendency, "so that the labors of each superintendent shall be within the territory in which the conferences are located over which he is to preside the ensuing year." This is the reverse of the present plan, according to which each bishop serves during the year the conferences over the sessions of which he last presided, or over which his appointed supply presided for him.

1886. Three general superintendents were ordered, and G. W. Coleman was added to the board. Again, the move to have but one order of ministers by eliminating the order of deacon was unsuccessful. Pastoral appointments for a third year to the same place were authorized in special cases, by unanimous vote of the stationing committee, but the two-year limit was retained.

1890. The Conference recommended that the general superintendents organize a board and so arrange their schedules that each conference would have a pastoral visit every two years. The superintendents were authorized to appoint supplies to serve as presidents of annual conference sessions in their absence, an action precipitated by B. T. Roberts' appointment of Wilson T. Hogue to supply the Canadian Conference for him when, at that time, the only disciplinary provision for securing a president *pro tem* in the absence of the general superintendent was the election by the body of an elder from its own number. Roberts' appointment of Hogue had been challenged, and General Conference agreed that the appointment had been undisciplinary, but proceeded to revise the *Discipline* to make such appointments legal thereafter.

At this General Conference Roberts presented a strong resolution by which he sought to secure the ordination of women. The failure of his effort was one of the keenest disappointments of his later years. He died during the following quadrennium, and it was to be several quadrenniums yet before the church would grant to women this right.

After the defeat of the Roberts resolution on the ordination of women, a motion was brought before the Conference to disapprove such ordination. In sardonic humor someone moved to amend the proposal by adding, "when called of God and duly qualified." The proposed amendment drove home its barbed point, but failed of course to win enough support to prevail. The original motion was passed by a narrow margin, 35 to 29.

1894. This General Conference convened without B. T. Roberts, who had deceased February 27, 1893. Wilson T. Hogue had been appointed by the executive committee to complete the quadrennium as general superintendent in his place. Burton R. Jones was elected to the place thus left vacant, to serve with E. P. Hart and G. W. Coleman who were continued in office.

This General Conference was confronted with a resolution to group the annual conferences in three districts and appoint a superintendent over each for a period of four years. The measure lost, the vote being 8 to 64. The proposal to change the title "general superintendent" to "bishop" was defeated by a vote of 45 to 48. The proposal to change the title "district chairman" to "presiding elder" lost by a tie vote, but a later proposal carried to change the title to "district elder."

A vote was taken in this Conference on the question, "Do you believe in the ordination of women?" The presiding officer made clear that a vote on a motion so phrased could enact no legislation. The results seemed to indicate a declining sentiment for the ordination of women, with 35 affirmative and 65 negative judgments recorded.

1898. For the first time, four general superintendents were ordered, and W. A. Sellew was added to the board. Again the attempt to change "general superintendent" to "bishop" failed. A three-year pastoral limit was approved.

1903. A vacancy occurring on the board of general superintendents by the retirement of G. W. Coleman because of age, Wilson T. Hogue was elected to succeed him. The third attempt to adopt the title "bishop" to replace "general superintendent" failed by a large margin, 38 to 79.

1907. But the fourth attempt succeeded by a similar margin, 83 to 40. From that time the title "bishop" has prevailed, although in the 1911 General Conference there was an unsuccessful attempt to return to the former title.

A resolution to approve the ordination of women was rejected in committee, but its rejection in committee by less than a two-thirds vote permitted it to come before the General Conference itself. There the resolution passed, worded as follows:

"Whenever any annual conference shall be satisfied that any woman is called of God to preach the gospel, that annual conference may be permitted to receive her on trial, and into full connection, and ordain her a deacon, all on the same conditions as we receive men into the same relations; provided always that this ordination of women shall not be considered a step toward ordination as elder."

These terms of ordination still govern, and women ordained as deacons may not proceed to full ordination in the Free Methodist Church.

1915. Until the General Conference of 1915, the Free Methodist Church had a *Discipline* with Restrictive Rules guarding vital areas, but had no formal constitution. The 1911 General Conference appointed a committee to draft a proposal, which was submitted to and approved by the 1915 General Conference. No concurring vote of the annual conferences was required because the new Constitution embodied intact the Restrictive Rules which alone, under the rules then operative, required concurring vote of the annual conferences for amendment or revision. This Constitution left all areas not covered by the Restrictive Rules open to simple amendment by vote of the General Conference. This situation was to be changed in the constitutional revision of 1951.

1923. The attempt to increase the pastoral time limit failed, as did also a proposal to establish a general church budget to be known as the General Stewardship Fund.

1927. The pastoral time limit was increased to four years in those cases unanimously approved by the stationing committee, still leaving the standard limit at three years.

1931. The central church organization was revised to replace separate boards administering the different departments of the church by a Board of Administration designed to function through four departmental Commissions. This reorganized general church plan is described in a subsequent section.

1939. The action of 1890 proposing the organization of a board of bishops was a recommendation, and not a revision of the *Discipline.* The 1939 *Discipline* was amended to provide such a board, and to define its sphere of operations. The pastoral time limit was raised to four years, a fifth-year appointment to be permitted by unanimous vote of the stationing committee.

1947. The effort to remove completely the pastoral time limit failed, 85 to 80, but was reconsidered, and passed 90 to 71. A general budget was approved, known as the General Service Fund, which continues in effect to the date of this writing.

1951. A major revision of the church's Constitution was passed by the 1951 General Conference and referred to the annual conference for concurrence, which was voted. The revision, based in part upon the work of the 1947-1951 committee on principles and prudentials, sought to insure greater stability of the church's basic law, both in those areas covered by the Restrictive Rules and elsewhere in the Constitution. The revised Constitution made uniform the requirement of a two-thirds majority of the votes, both of the General Conference and the annual conferences, to amend the Restrictive Rules and the process of their amendment. It will be recalled that formerly the required majorities were two-thirds for the General Conference and three-fourths for the annual conferences. Further stabilization of the church's basic law was accomplished by requiring for amendment of the non-restricted areas of the Constitution, not simply a two-thirds vote of the General Conference as formerly had sufficed, but a majority vote of annual conferences and General Conference. Of special note in connection with the 1951 revision of the Constitution was the placing under the protection of Restrictive Rule 1 of all conditions of church membership.

The revised Constitution was approved 103 to 27 by the members voting in the General Conference; 1959 to 51 by the members voting in the annual conferences, except two sections on which the negative votes ran somewhat higher, 83 against the Special Rule on dress and adornment (probably because not stringent enough for these voters); 146 against the provisions for a Judicial Council. Thus, the entire Constitution was adopted by votes well above the required two-thirds.

1955. For the first time in a century, the General Conference permitted the posting of nominations for general elective officers, excepting bishops. The effort to place the bishops in areas for a four-year term failed by a vote of 108 to 62.

One of the measures provided by the 1951 revision of the Constitution for the stabilization of the church's legislative and judicial procedures was the creation of a Judicial Council with rather broad functions. By action of the 1955 General Conference and the concurring action of the annual conferences, these functions were amended to commit to the Judicial Council "authority to determine the constitutionality of any acts or proposed legislation of the General Conference body upon appeal of one-fifth of the members of said General Conference," during its session.

This General Conference made possible the election of district and conference superintendents from outside the conference and anywhere within the denomination, upon the nomination of the bishop or the nominating committee, with the previous consent of the one nominated. Another departure concerning superintendents was the provision for fixing the term of a superintendent for three years by a two-thirds vote of the conference, the term to be considered after the election.

A move to recognize more fully congregational judgment in the matter of pastoral appointments was made by this Conference in its authorizing a confidential vote on the return of a pastor, such vote to be advisory to the stationing committee and not determinative.

THE CHURCH AS A CHANNEL

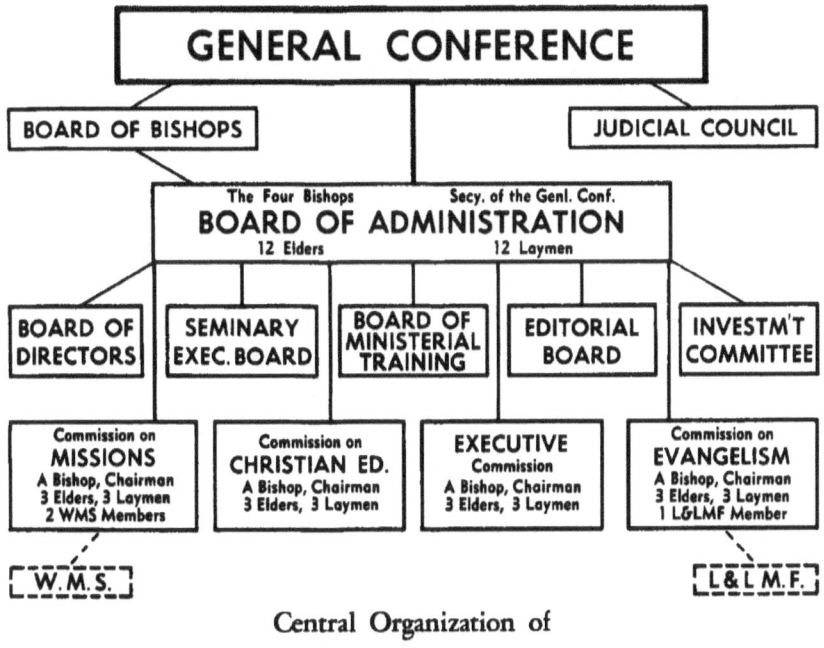

Central Organization of
The Free Methodist Church

The central organization of the church in 1960

The foregoing summary of governmental changes has not included the departmental developments of the general church as they have taken shape with the steady denominational growth of Free Methodism. Such majority developments are reported in later chapters, and the following paragraphs summarize the present structure of the general church. The chart above has been designed to clarify the relationships of different units.

General Conference. The supreme law-making and governing body of the Free Methodist Church is the General Conference. It is composed of an equal number of ministerial and lay delegates, and the bishops, who are co-chairmen. The delegates are elected by the annual conferences on a basis proportionate to membership. The acts of the General Conference are subject to the provisions of the Constitution.

421

Board of Bishops. The bishops, elected by the General Conference for a term which is the interval between sessions thereof (usually four years), are organized as the Board of Bishops for counsel, general church planning, and tasks assigned to it by the General Conference and the Board of Administration.

Each bishop has dual areas of responsibility, in one direction a geographic area of the church at the level of the annual conferences; in another direction a functional area of the general church in his capacity as chairman of a Commission of the Board of Administration. In connection with the former, each bishop presides in turn over the sessions of a group of annual conferences, the groups in number equaling the number of bishops. During the year following his administration of the sessions of a group of annual conferences, he maintains general supervision of them as the president of each. In connection with the area of the general church structure to which he is assigned, his responsibilities vary with the nature of the work of the Commission he heads, and with its staff organization and program.

Judicial Council. The Judicial Council determines the constitutionality of any act or proposed legislation of the General Conference, upon request of one-fifth of the members of the Conference while in session. The other judicial functions belonging to the jurisdiction of the general church are performed by the General Conference, the Executive Commission, and the bishops (through their decisions on points of law). The General Conference determines the number, qualifications, terms of office, and mode of selection of the members of the Judicial Council.

Board of Administration. The Board of Administration is elected by the General Conference according to twelve administrative districts (a minister and a layman from each), with the bishops and the secretary of the General Conference members *ex officio.* This Board is the official church in the interim of General Conferences, with broad powers defined by the *Discipline* in these terms:

> The Board of Administration shall have general organizational, promotional, and supervisory powers over all the activities of the church during the intervals between General Conference sessions.

Commissions. From its membership the Board of Administration sets up four Commissions as its subsidiaries in distinctive functional areas to carry on the program of the general church. Membership on the Board of Administration thus is basic and primary; Commission membership is derived and secondary. Actions of the Commissions are in the nature of committee recommendations to the Board of Administration, by it to be adopted, rejected, or re-committed.

Each Commission is made up of a bishop as chairman, and three elders and three laymen from the membership of the Board of Administration. The Commission on Missions has two additional members who represent the Woman's Missionary Society as an auxiliary of that Commission; the Commission on Evangelism has one additional member who represents the Light and Life Men's Fellowship as an auxiliary of that Commission. Members of the Commission representing auxiliary bodies are not members of the Board of Administration.

The areas assigned to the four Commissions as now constituted, briefly described, are:

1. The *Executive Commission,* which is, (1) the executive committee of the Board of Administration, caring for concerns of the church that arise in the interim of Board meetings; (2) the Commission having budget supervision of the general church and its departments, including retirement plans; (3) the Board of Directors of the Publishing House; (4) the Court of Appeals, with other judicial responsibilities in the interim of General Conferences; (5) the Radio Board; (6) the responsible committee for Church and Parsonage Aid; and (7) the committee on Benevolent Institutions. Present chairman, Bishop L. R. Marston.

2. The *Commission on Missions,* whose work covers the vast missionary enterprise of the denomination in foreign countries and among foreign-language peoples in North America, and other groups as designated by the Board. Present chairman, Bishop W. S. Kendall.

3. The *Commission on Christian Education,* which operates through five departments, (1) Sunday Schools; (2) Educational Institutions; (3) Young People; (4) Intermediate Youth; and (5) Service Training. Also, it has close relationship to inter-Commission bodies such as the Central Board of Ministerial Training and the Executive Board of John Wesley Seminary. Present chairman, Bishop C. V. Fairbairn.

4. The *Commission on Evangelism and Church Extension,* the work of which is to promote evangelism throughout the church, aid in establishing new congregations, and assist in building new church structures. A department of this Commission engages in inter-racial evangelism. Present chairman, Bishop J. Paul Taylor.

Board of Directors. The members of the Board of Administration constitute the members of the corporation, The Free Methodist Church of North America. The affairs of the corporation are conducted by a Board of Directors, made up of five members of the Free Methodist Church elected by the corporation from the church at large. This Board functions similarly to boards of trustees of church bodies at conference, district and local levels.

Investment Committee. Five businessmen are chosen by the Board of Administration from the church at large to have charge of the investment of the funds of the general church and of its Commissions and Departments.

Executive Board of John Wesley Seminary. The Board of Administration is the Seminary Board of Control. A Seminary Executive Board plans and directs the institution, subject to the approval of the Board of Control. This Executive Board is composed of the members of the Commission on Christian Education, plus the chairman and one additional member from each of the other three Commissions.

Central Board of Ministerial Training. The Board sets up, approves and supervises the program of the church for the education and training of ministers, subject to the provisions of the *Discipline*. It is composed of thirteen members, some serving *ex officio*, the rest chosen by the Board of Administration.

Editorial Board. The function of this Board is to coordinate the publications of the general church, and to approve the character of each.

Auxiliary Organizations. The Woman's Missionary Society and the Light and Life Men's Fellowship are organizations related or auxiliary to the central organization of the church, with appropriate Commission representation as previously noted.

Executive Personnel. No attempt has been made to include in the chart the administrative and executive offices serving the general church. Some members of the general church staff are elected by General Conference, and some are appointed by the Board of Administration. The relationship of all staff members to the Board of Administration is defined by the *Discipline* as follows:

> All general officers, departmental executives and promoters,

elected or employed, shall serve under the Board of Administration, through the appropriate Commission, to whom they shall be directly amenable.

Free Methodist organization a woven pattern

We have not presented the structure and operations of the church at levels below the central organization, assuming that most of our readers will have become acquainted with local church, district, and conference operations through participation and observation.

Scanning Free Methodism's entire machinery of ecclesiastical operation and control in the light of church history and contemporary practice, one is convinced that in general it is inherently functional and not static, and that the church's growth, especially in the home area, although steady and at periods gratifying, has not been as large as vigorous use of the organizational means provided in the church's structure should yield.

The polity of the church falls between a stringent episcopacy on the one hand and a *laissez-faire* congregationalism on the other. The church's governing bodies, from local official boards up through quarterly and annual conferences to the Board of Administration and to General Conference, provide a desirable flexibility of procedure which is responsive to the wishes of the majority, within limits set by the *Discipline*. Free Methodist polity provides also an executive and administrative personnel, paralleling the boards of control, to carry out the programs of action planned and approved by these boards. This personnel includes pastors, answerable immediately to their official boards and their people, to the district conference and superintendent, and ultimately to the annual conference; district and conference superintendents, answerable to the district quarterly and the annual conference; bishops and general secretaries, answerable immediately to the Board of Administration through their respective Commissions, and ultimately to the General Conference.

The foregoing in briefest outline sketches the vertical organization of the church in terms of authoritative relationships of boards and their executives. But these boards and their executives have spheres of lateral or horizontal functioning which are to be developed in succeeding chapters to portray the extension of the church's ministry through different channels, which reach practically every level of authority. We venture to suggest that the vertical or authoritative relationships are the warp, and the horizontal or functional spheres of action are the woof, of the pattern of Free Methodism as a denomination.

No one will maintain that this organizational pattern is perfect, and General Conferences in the church's second century will be making readjustments and revisions of the pattern, even as General Conferences in the church's first century have done. But in its basic features the legislative, administrative and departmental organization of Free Methodism provides an instrument of denominational progress, even in an era of ecclesiastical change when major denominations are obliterating their historic patterns in mediating mergers; when the conservative doctrinal movement is veering away from denominationalism to independency; and when a strong subjectivism is luring many into unrestrained sectarian and even into cultist groups.

* * * * *

Officers of the general church other than bishops are listed at the conclusion of later chapters in which the departments they served are reviewed. The bishops as general, rather than departmental, officers are listed, with their terms of service, at the close of this chapter on the general church.

General Superintendents

* B. T. Roberts	1860-1893	E. P. Hart	1874-1908
	George W. Coleman 1886-1903		

Bishops

B. R. Jones	1894-1919	* G. W. Griffith	1927-1936
* W. A. Sellew	1898-1929	* B. J. Vincent	1931-1931
W. T. Hogue	1903-1919	* R. H. Warren	1935-1938
William Pearce	1908-1947	L. R. Marston	1935-
† J. S. MacGeary	1911-1915	‡ M. D. Ormston	1936-1958
* W. H. Clark	1919-1925	C. V. Fairbairn	1939-
D. S. Warner	1919-1927	J. Paul Taylor	1947-
* A. D. Zahniser	1927-1935	W. S. Kendall	1958-

The schedule of General Conferences of the Free Methodist Church appears on page 589.

---

* Service in office terminated by death.
† Missionary bishop.
‡ Bishop emeritus since 1958.

CHAPTER TWENTY-TWO

Outreach Through Evangelism

Since 1862 the Free Methodist Church has carried in succeeding issues of its *Discipline* the following commitment to world-wide evangelism:

> The provisions of the gospel are for all. The 'glad tidings' must be proclaimed to every individual of the human race. God sent the true light to illuminate and melt every heart. To savage and civilized, bond and free, black and white, the ignorant and learned, is freely offered this great salvation.

In the same context is declared Free Methodism's two-fold mission, "to maintain the Bible standard of Christianity, and to preach the gospel to the poor." The church, then, is to be both a witness and a herald; it is to venture forth in untried paths to carry the gospel to those that sit in darkness.

Free Methodism on the march

The Free Methodist Church was evangelistic from its origin. This was demonstrated by its breaking through barriers of prejudice, and withstanding the opposition of established religion and worldly-mindedness in both church and society, to carry the gospel far and wide.

The map of early Free Methodism's march across America is a stirring symbol of its early evangelism. Beginning with the Genesee Conference in western New York and with the Illinois Conference, the work spread from each as a source. From Genesee the cause marched eastward, with the Susquehanna and New York conferences soon planted, the latter including the nation's metropolis and the area northward and southward into adjacent states. In time, the southward extension saw Maryland and Virginia separated to form a southern conference.

Again from Genesee the work spread southward into Pennsylvania and West Virginia, the Pittsburgh Conference first being organized, and later from it the Oil City Conference—the two making western Pennsylvania one of Free Methodism's strongholds. After some delay,

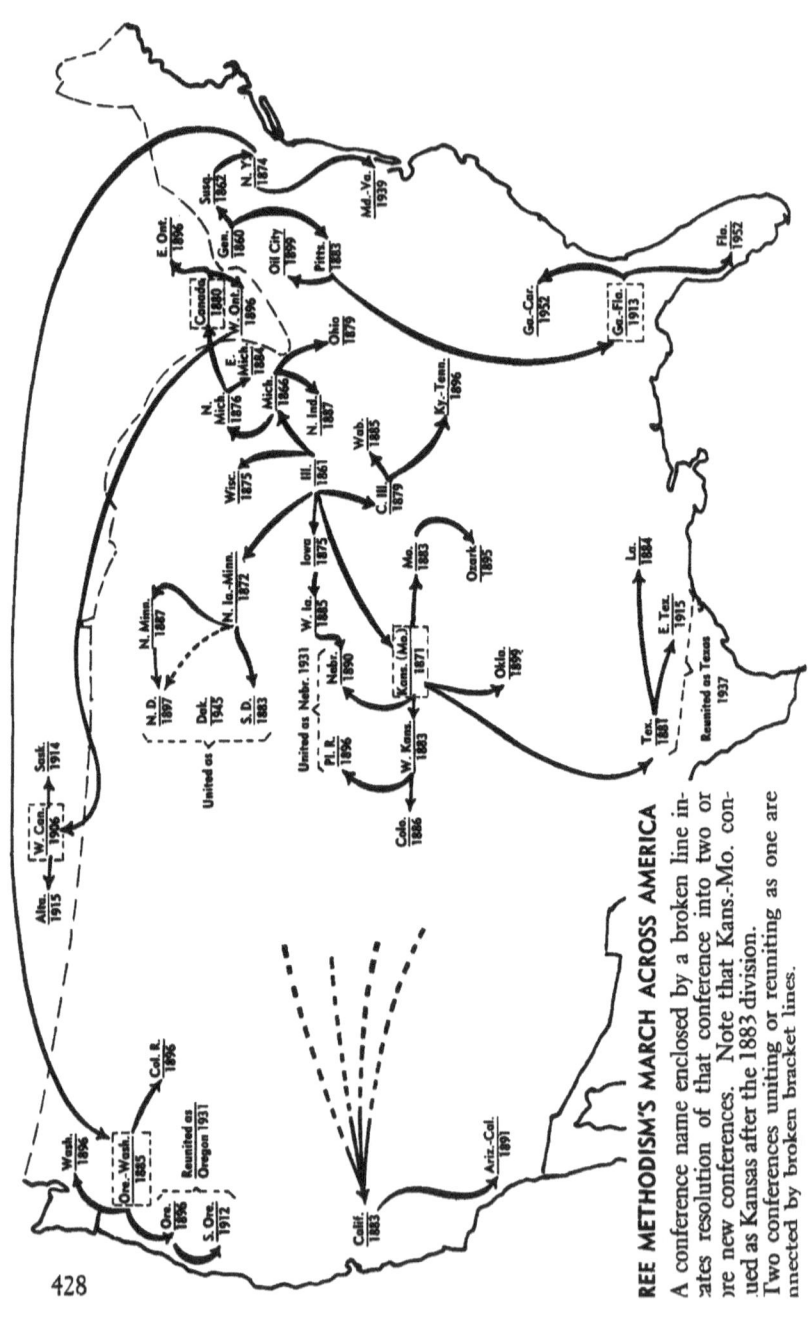

FREE METHODISM'S MARCH ACROSS AMERICA

A conference name enclosed by a broken line indicates resolution of that conference into two or more new conferences. Note that Kans.-Mo. continued as Kansas after the 1883 division. Two conferences uniting or reuniting as one are connected by broken bracket lines.

the course of evangelism from the Pittsburgh Conference overleaped the Appalachians into Georgia and Florida, which now form two conferences with North Carolina combined with Georgia.

From the Illinois source, the message was carried into Michigan, an area destined to become another stronghold where, by 1884, there were three conferences, Michigan, North Michigan, East Michigan. From Michigan the work spread southward into Ohio and North Indiana.

From North Michigan, prior to the division which provided an East Michigan Conference, the march crossed into Canada and in time the Canadian Conference was formed. This shortly divided its vast territory and became two conferences, East Ontario and West Ontario. Missionaries principally from West Ontario trekked across the plains to form the Western Canadian Conference which in turn developed into the Saskatchewan and Alberta conferences.

Starting again from Illinois, there came from it the Indiana and Central Illinois Conference which later divided into the Central Illinois and the Wabash conferences. From Central Illinois the movement crossed the Ohio River, and the Kentucky and Tennessee Conference resulted.

Another line of advance from the Illinois Conference pushed westward to form the Kansas and Missouri Conference, from which a triple division produced the Missouri, Kansas, and West Kansas conferences. From Missouri the move southward produced the Arkansas and Southern Missouri Conference, now called the Ozark Conference. From West Kansas the march led westward to the organization of the Colorado Conference, and northward to form the Platte River Conference. From Kansas the cause moved southward to yield the Texas Conference, and then spread to form East Texas and Louisiana. The two Texas conferences are now one again. Later, from Kansas, was developed the Oklahoma Conference.

Taking another westward course from Illinois, the trail leads to Iowa and then West Iowa. Nebraska was formed from portions of the West Iowa and Kansas conferences. The Nebraska conferences are now united as one.

Still another course from Illinois led northward to Wisconsin, and northwestward to Northern Iowa and Minnesota, Dakota (later known as South Dakota), North Minnesota, and North Dakota. The Dakota conferences have since merged.

Overleaping much of the Rocky Mountain area, the trail again appears in the Pacific Northwest, the initial move to evangelize this area having been made from New York, nearly three thousand miles distant. The Oregon and Washington Territory Conference resulted in due time, and from it by a triple division came the Oregon, Columbia River and Washington conferences. Later the Southern Oregon Conference was separated from the Oregon Conference, but they have again become one.

More difficult to trace is the evangelistic source of the California Conference, which drew upon several eastern conferences. Bishop Roberts spent nearly six months in the area around San Francisco in 1879. When organized in 1883, six of its seven ordained preachers had transferred from five different eastern conferences, and the source of the seventh preacher we do not know. From California was later organized the Southern California Conference, now known as the Arizona-Southern California Conference.

By the time of B. T. Roberts' death in 1893, when the church was thirty-three years old, thirty-three annual conferences had been organized. Five more were to be formed before the close of the nineteenth century. Many of these conferences were struggling frontier holdings, representing Free Methodism's march with the westward tide of migration during the later nineteenth century. We may say that these conferences—some of them at least—were homestead claims staked out by pioneer evangelists for clearing and development, later to yield their harvests under pastoral cultivation in more settled times.

Of whom the world was not worthy

The far-reaching ministry of some of the pioneers of early Free Methodism causes one to marvel, even in this day of rapid and easy transportation and communication. As only one example of many pioneers, we select Thomas S. LaDue[1] who, in 1861 when about thirty years of age, left the St. Charles pastorate of the Congregational

---

1. John LaDue, *The Life of Thomas S. LaDue*. Free Meth. Pub. House, Chicago, Ill.

Church to enter the Free Methodist ministry in the Illinois Conference.

After a brief pastorate with the Free Methodists in St. Charles, General Superintendent Roberts asked him to go to Rochester, New York; and again in less than a year to a pioneer ministry in southern Michigan where he developed a circuit that extended into northern Indiana. From there he was returned to Illinois where his ministry was interrupted by a call into the Union Army, and shortly he was made a chaplain.

After the war he returned to work in Illinois and later was sent by the Conference to pioneer work in Wisconsin; then to a circuit straddling the Wisconsin and Minnesota line. He was made chairman of the Minnesota District of the Illinois Conference in 1868, and largely out of his labors, which extended in northern Iowa, came the organization of the Northern Iowa and Minnesota Conference in 1872.

In 1874 he was called to Brooklyn, New York, and from the geographically extensive and physically arduous labors of a western frontier itinerant, LaDue was plunged into the maelstrom of a city pastorate. This was the year the New York Conference was organized. Following Brooklyn, he was assigned to other pastoral work in the Pennsylvania portion of the Conference, and later he became chairman of the Northern District. For two years he was pastor in Philadelphia. His health was breaking, and the way opened in 1882, while he was serving a second time as pastor at Allentown, to answer an urgent call to Oregon. Here the later years of his life were spent in another pioneer field, and here again he was to serve as district chairman. He helped form the Oregon and Washington Territory Conference in 1885, out of which in 1896 came the Oregon, Washington and Columbia River conferences. T. S. LaDue died in 1888, at fifty-six years of age, after twenty-seven years of heroic ministry of the gospel through the Free Methodist Church. That ministry covered areas of the Midwest in the states of Illinois, Michigan, Indiana, Wisconsin, Minnesota, and Iowa; areas of the East in the states of New York and Pennsylvania; areas of the Pacific Northwest in the states of Oregon and Washington.

Some of his experiences, typical of the experiences of other hardy pioneers of that day in Free Methodism, remind one of the early days of Methodism in England. This educated and eloquent minister had been victimized, slandered, egged, assaulted, falsely accused, arrested and fined, but he never wavered in "maintaining the Bible standard of Christianity" and "preaching the gospel to the poor." Of Thomas S. LaDue, and of many like him who joined in Free Methodism's valiant march into strange and hostile regions, it may in all truth be said, "The world was not worthy." And we ask, soberly and humbly, is the church they planted on that march across America in Free Methodism's first generation, worthy of them in this generation at century's end?

> *They climbed the steep ascent to heav'n*
> *Thro' peril, toil, and pain:*
> *O God, to us may grace be given*
> *To follow in their train!*
> —Reginald Heber

The General Conference and evangelism: earlier period

In the early years, when the young church was primarily an evangelistic movement, little legislation on evangelism was necessary. Every pastor, district chairman and general superintendent was an evangelist, and the principal task of the church was evangelism of a very direct, revivalistic type. General Conference legislation at that period was more largely engaged with matters of church polity by which to govern the growing church, and with defining standards by which those evangelized and brought into the church were to be guided in the Christian way.

1860. The first *Discipline* and several thereafter carried a brief chapter on "Missions," but the contents dealt with establishing new work and supporting the extension of the church into new areas. For many years the church's concept of missions was home missions and church extension, and the first *Disciplines* included in connection with missions no reference to carrying the gospel to other lands. Those early *Disciplines* gave each annual conference "charge of all missions within its bounds," and authority "to employ missionaries to labor within its bounds." Such missionaries, with the concurrence of the conference president, were to "establish new churches, where the interests of the cause of God require." The support of such work was to be provided from funds raised through the classes by the leaders to the amount of a cent a week from each member willing to contribute, and from a public missionary offering to be taken on each preaching point. These funds were to be turned over to the annual conference "and applied according to its direction."

Nothing appears in these early *Disciplines* concerning any such class of workers as "evangelists," although the district chairman "was to labor as an Evangelist within his district," if so directed by the annual conference. When so directed, he became in effect a traveling chairman, supported by district apportionments to all the circuits, rather than an appointed pastor supported by his pastoral charge. Only in this connection do we find the term "evangelist" employed in the early *Disciplines*.

1874. For the first time in 1874 was provided a class of lay workers called "evangelists." These were defined as "a class of preachers called of God to preach the gospel, to labor to promote revivals of religion, and to spread abroad the cause of Christ in the land; but not called to a pastoral charge, or to government in the church." No provision for their ordination was made, as in the case of local preachers who from the beginning had a defined status and a route by following which they could qualify for ordination.

Also in 1874 for the first time reference is made in the *Discipline* to a "General Missionary Board," but only in connection with the transmittal to it of general mission funds and the distribution of those funds. Previously, funds for conference missions [home evangelism] had been administered by the annual conferences. There is no further statement concerning the Board or its purposes in the *Discipline*, but turning to the General Conference Journal we read this statement:

"It shall be the duty of this Board to take charge of all the monies raised for General Mission purposes in the several annual conferences and appropriate the same to the foreign missions or to the several annual conferences for home missions within its bounds as in their judgment the cause of God can best be promoted."

The church's program of foreign missions was yet to be launched, but there now was dawning a sense of responsibility for general missions to include foreign as well as home expansion, and practical steps and active promotion would follow.

1882. Hogue first mentions the organization of a General Missionary Board in 1882 which, according to him, was the church's first definite step looking toward foreign missions. "Until then," wrote Hogue, "its organized missionary efforts had been confined to what might more properly be called Home Missions." [2] He omits all mention of the organization of the General Missionary Board in 1874, and of the action of General Conference which gave that board authority over foreign work on the same basis as the home fields. But even the 1882 *Discipline*, which should have reflected the active concern of the new program of foreign missions, makes reference only to "General Missions" as had previous *Disciplines*. Foreign missionary effort is not specified, even in the provisions for missionary offerings, of which one was mandatory for general missions, to be not less than twenty-five cents per member, and

---

2. W. T. Hogue, *History of the Free Methodist Church*. Free Methodist Publishing House, Winona Lake, Ind.; v. 2, 255.

a second offering, likewise mandatory, for the support of missions within the bounds of the annual conference. "General Missions" was then general indeed, covering the interests of both home evangelism and foreign missions.

In 1882 for the first time reference was made to "general evangelists." These were to be appointed by General Conference "to travel through the country at large" in developing new fields and organizing new churches. The General Missionary Board was authorized to make appropriations for the support of these evangelists. Home evangelism and foreign missions were alike to be under the General Missionary Board.

1886. This General Conference amended the chapter on Missions to differentiate contributions to "foreign missions" from contributions to "general missions," and for the first time in the *Discipline* the term "foreign mission" appears. The differentiation of efforts to expand abroad and at home was now under way, but the latter program was to suffer by being called "general missions" after foreign missions had become firmly established as the leading concern of the General Missionary Board.

1890. The 1890 General Conference ordered the General Missionary Board to "have charge of all the General and Foreign Missions of the Church established by the Board"; and now an offering specifically for foreign missions, with subscriptions, was ordered and at the same time the stipulated offering for general missions [home evangelism] was reduced to fifteen cents per member.

This General Conference authorized the creation of conference missionary societies, "which shall have charge of all missions within its bounds," with "power to employ missionaries to labor within its bounds." This appears to have been the predecessor of what we now designate the conference board of evangelism.

The committee on missions of the General Conference recommended that the General Missionary Board be permitted to organize a Women's Foreign Missionary Society as auxiliary to the board, and the organization of the same took place at the next General Conference, in 1894, further emphasizing foreign missions in the program of the General Missionary Board.

This General Conference enacted legislation for the regulation of evangelistic bands, the occasion of such legislation being the development of the Pentecost Bands within the church but with inadequate church control. Here we digress to give a brief summary of the Pentecost Bands and their final separation from the church to become an independent movement.

The Pentecost Bands

The 1890 General Conference was a disappointment to General Superintendent Roberts at three points, (1) the failure of his efforts

OUTREACH THROUGH EVANGELISM

to secure for women preachers the right to ordination;[3] (2) the adoption of the majority recommendation in the case of R. W. Hawkins' book, Redemption, in preference to his more lenient proposal;[4] (3) what seemed to him the rigorous handling of the Pentecost Bands.

These bands had developed under the ardent and devoted leadership of Rev. V. A. Dake, but along lines outside the established channels of church authority. In time they developed a strenuous if not strained spiritual emphasis and a growing resistance to denominational control. According to Bishop Hogue, the movement became essentially a church within the church.[5] The 1890 General Conference attempted to bring these bands into line with church authority by adopting a set of rules to govern bands and their operations, but these regulations were unsatisfactory to the leadership of the movement and conflict continued into the following quadrennium. Efforts were renewed by the General Conference of 1894 to bring the recalcitrants into line, not by further legislation, for the 1890 rules were considered adequate if cooperation could be secured. To this end the Conference declared its fellowship and its good will toward the Bands. But the Bands were now on their way to schism, and a separate organization was established known as the Missionary Bands of the World. According to the *1959 Yearbook of American Churches* the membership of the organization in 1956 was one hundred and forty, grouped in eleven congregations. The *1960 Yearbook* reports their merging with the Wesleyan Methodist Church in 1958.

In its dealings with the Pentecost Bands, the Free Methodist Church came the nearest repeating Methodism's historic pattern of action against "irregulars." A more moderate course might have conserved to Free Methodism the zeal of this movement which had been fruitful in bringing a considerable harvest into the church. V. A. Dake utilized talents, especially of the young, in the cause of evangelism. In this he was ahead of his generation, for Free Methodism then had no channels of service through which to direct the energies of its youth.

---

3. *Supra,* p. 418.
4. *Supra,* p. 296.
5. W. T. Hogue, *History of the Free Methodist Church;* v. 2, 194.

Benson Roberts evaluated as follows his father's attitude toward the conflict precipitated within the church by the Pentecost Bands:

> He recognized the power of good that was in them, yet saw that their plans and methods were not wise, and that their leaders were headstrong. He was in favor of conserving their spiritual life and force to the church; others were for excluding them. He himself had, no less than others, been made to feel humbled and hurt at the course their leaders had taken. But he was ready to lay aside all personal feelings, and work in harmony, if possible, with them for the sake of Christ's cause. It was not possible, however, to reconcile the opposing sentiment, owing to the unwise and harsh utterances of their leaders respecting the church and leading men in it. They had openly characterized as persecution whatever did not approve of their methods. They courted opposition, and were very ready to be martyrs. He saw here disintegrating forces that would tear down what had been built up at the expense of much toil.[6]

* * * *

And now we return to summarize General Conference actions concerning evangelism.

1894. The committee on the state of the work in 1894 reported the tendency of the church to extend itself too far before establishing firmly what had been started. The report pointed out that the eagerness of our people "to push out into new territory has too often been a powerful temptation to leave old circuits unsupplied, resulting in serious loss numerically, financially, and we believe spiritually." In some instances, the committee feared, this had meant more loss than gain.

Perhaps the time had come for a more settled pastoral ministry, but the earlier pattern set by the pioneers in venturing into new fields now interfered with the church's meeting the new pastoral need. Anyway, the report warned, "There are too many preachers who, instead of devoting themselves to earnest, faithful pastoral work, and to feeding the flock of God, want to be running hither and thither as evangelists."

This General Conference elected W. G. Hanmer general conference evangelist.

1898. Again four years later the same note of warning against too strong a dispersion of efforts was sounded by the committee on the state of the work. "We are compelled to admit that our work does not grow internally as fast as we desire," the committee said. "We often enter new fields to the loss of the old ones: thus we expand rather than grow."

---

6. B. H. Roberts, *Benjamin Titus Roberts.* Earnest Christian Office, North Chili, New York; p. 556.

1903. This General Conference ordered two general conference evangelists, and provided the same by continuing W. G. Hanmer in office and electing C. W. Stamp to serve with him. The committee on the state of the work discerned the need for greater urgency in evangelism, and called attention to the greater progress of the foreign over the home work by saying, "The foreign work makes a better showing than the home work in every particular."

Declining progress in evangelism

At this point we turn for a time from summaries of General Conference actions affecting evangelism, to consider one reason for evangelism's low state in Free Methodism's mid-era. Home evangelism had been the principal if not sole missionary concern of the church during its early years, and yet by 1903 foreign missions had far outstripped home evangelism along all lines. Such, at least, had been the judgment of a committee appointed by General Conference to evaluate the church's progress.

A full explanation of the lag in home evangelism must include a complex of factors, but one factor seems to have been the name under which evangelism had operated for so long a period—a name that better described the newer foreign missionary enterprise of the church than home evangelism. The term "missions" may have been satisfactory enough so long as it meant home evangelism and church extension, and there was no foreign missions activity in the church. But with the development of a vigorous program of foreign missions operating under the same board, "general missions" came to mean a system of doles for weaker home conferences, whereas "foreign missions" was an energetic outreach to new and distant lands offering the lure of romance and the challenge of sacrifice and heroism.

Fortunately for foreign missions, no stipulated amount per member was set when in 1890 offerings for this cause were ordered on each pastoral charge. For general missions there had been a stipulated minimum for some time. This minimum was dropped from twenty-five to fifteen cents per member when the offering for foreign missions was made an independent call. And general missions was continued on an assessment basis of collection and a dole system of distribution under the General Missionary Board, even after the General Board of Aggressive Evangelism had been organized by the General Conference in 1919. With the reorganization of the general church under a Board of Administration in 1931, the general mission fund was administered by the Commission on Evangelism, and then, with the inauguration of the General Service Fund in 1948 the item disappeared as an assessment.

The psychology of a stipulated assessment worked against generous giving to the cause of general evangelism and church extension. Had not one done his duty to the cause of extending the church at home when he paid his conference claims? There were other factors crippling the cause of evangelism, but here we find a serious handicap to home expansion.

When the Church Extension Society was created in 1886, it also came under the administration of the General Missionary Board, and so continued until its transfer to the Executive Committee of the general church in 1919.

Status quo or advance?

Statistics disclose that the rate of the church's growth percentagewise had been slowing down prior to 1903, the year in which the committee on the state of the work made its disturbing comparison of home and foreign expansion. It is not unusual for a movement to decline in rate of membership gain after the first few years of its existence, but the deceleration of Free Methodism's growth rate immediately prior to 1903 had been acute. During the eight years from 1886 to 1894, the church had increased 51 per cent in membership; in the nine years following, closing with 1903, the increase in membership had been only 15 per cent! Had the rate of increase from 1886 to 1894 continued to 1960, Free Methodism in America at its centenary would number 650,000. Something more than an unfortunate name and the stronger competitive appeal of foreign missions was wrong with home evangelism in Free Methodism's mid-period. What was it?

The suggestion insistently nudges consciousness that the warnings of 1894 and 1898 to General Conference, against too rapid expansion lest esablished work be jeopardized, may have been a factor in slowing the momentum of the church's earlier growth to near-stagnation. For it is true of a church as well as an individual, that hoarding life is to lose it but losing it for Christ and the gospel is to find it.

Anyway, as our introductory chapter asserted, there was a period in Free Methodist history in which a transition occurred from crusading reform and evangelizing zeal to settled denominationalism. During this transition the church held firmly to its original distinctives while losing some of its former urgency. Intent upon maintaining its witness, the church's campaign spirit of the first generation waned, and a defensive attitude developed which sought to "hold the fort" rather than carry on a campaign in the field. From conquest to protest, from advance to defense, from facing the future to looking to the past—thus may be described the changes that crept over the church and all but paralyzed it for several years. Such was the condition against which the bishops warned the church in their 1907 message.[7]

Interpreting in purely negative terms the church's mission "to maintain the Bible standard of Christianity" may lead a church to neglect its further mission of heralding abroad the good news of salvation, of "preaching the gospel to the poor." It is possible to witness *against* so many things that are wrong in the world until courage is drained away and faith is paralyzed. And without the zest of heroic adventure and the thrill of conquest, witnessing loses its urgency and its power to convince.

The progress of evangelism, later period

In Free Methodism's turning from the conflict to an increasing introversion lay the major cause of the church's lower rate of growth beginning in the nineties and becoming painfully apparent by 1903. This introversion of interest and energy was to continue many years.

We resume the review of general conference actions affecting home evangelism:

1907. A problem that has handicapped evangelism in recent time seems to have appeared more than a half-century ago, leading the 1907 General Conference to insert in the *Discipline* the stipulation that "no conference preacher shall be granted an evangelistic relation to the conference who does not intend to devote all his time to evangelistic work." In 1939 this requirement was changed to an intention to devote three-fifths of the year to evangelism. As condition of renewal of the relationship, the preacher must give a satisfactory account of the time actually spent in the evangelistic field during the year. The change was a move, not so much to relax the standard as to define it in terms that

---

7. *Supra*, p. 376.

made its administration easier. To this revision was added in 1955 the requirement of five years of pastoral ministry for conference preachers appointed as evangelists, except by approval of the stationing committee and the conference board of evangelism.

The 1907 General Conference felt the stirring of agitation to do something to stimulate evangelism. An elaborate plan for a "Commission on Aggressive Evangelism" was proposed, but was tabled. Three general conference evangelists were ordered, and S. K. Wheatlake and J. H. Flower were elected to serve with C. W. Stamp, who was continued in office. General conference evangelists were to work under the General Missionary Board, as in the past.

1911. The desire to see evangelism quickened throughout the church led to a proposal to the 1911 General Conference that a general solicitor be employed to raise a million dollars for the cause. This measure was not supported by the committee on aggressive evangelism, but the offer of W. B. Bertels to attempt to raise fifty thousand dollars was approved by the committee and accepted by the Conference. Interestingly enough, Bertels was a layman, a manufacturer of tinware in Wilkes Barre, Pennsylvania.

1915. The *Discipline* was revised in 1915 to require each annual conference to organize a conference evangelistic board "to carry on aggressive evangelistic work within its bounds." The challenge of home evangelism was arousing the church. The General Missionary Board still served as the administrative board in the field of evangelism at the general church level, and constituted the Church Extension Society.

1919. The General Conference of 1919 transferred the Church Extension Society to the Executive Committee of the general church, and established a General Board of Aggressive Evangelism. At last the promotion and administration of home evangelism, with the exception of so-called "general missions," had been transferred from the General Missionary Board which now had in its care a growing foreign missionary enterprise that demanded its major time and energy.

1931. In 1931, with the reorganization of the general church program in terms of a Board of Administration with subsidiary Commissions to function in departmental areas, evangelism became the core of the Commission on Evangelism, Charities and Benevolences, and Church Extension. At a later date the department of Charities and Benevolences was transferred to the Executive Commission. The present scope of operations of the Commission on Evangelism and Church Extension was briefly outlined in the previous chapter.

1935. This General Conference provided for a general evangelistic secretary to serve as the executive of the Commission. The late Rev. R. B. Campbell was elected to this office and served therein for twenty years.

1947. Provision was made in 1947 for the election of general evangelists. These as a rule have been appointed to geographic areas as their fields of principal ministry.

1955. The General Conference of 1955 placed home evangelism in the center of the session's emphasis. On the opening day, the message of the bishops dealt largely with the evangelistic mission of the church, and recommended that during the quadrennium then beginning, "evangelism and church extension be the major program of all agencies and departments of the church, and that our entire membership plan its stewardship of finances, time and talent in line with this emphasis." The Rev. L. W. Northrup was elected general evangelistic secretary, and led in an unprecedented promotion of the cause of evangelism throughout the church in America.

The Light and Life Men's Fellowship

In the preceding chapter, the pattern of the organization of the general church portrayed the Light and Life Men's Fellowship as an auxiliary of the Commission on Evangelism. This is one of the newer movements within the church. It began with a call to the laymen of the church and a preliminary organization in 1947, following which local and area units were affected. The movement was organized nationally at the General Conference of 1951, and now employs an executive director, Rev. Charles W. Kingsley.

The movement is related to the church officially by membership of the local president on the official board of the local charge, and by representation at the general level on the Commission on Evangelism.

The principal emphasis of the organization is personal witnessing and soul winning, with other emphases including fellowship, stewardship, and service. In areas, the young movement already shows encouraging vitality and promises to be an effective means of directing the energies of the church outward to the neighborhoods in which our churches and our members are located.

The gospel witness through philanthropy

Before concluding the chapter with an account of the church's "Forward Movement" of recent years, it seems appropriate to insert a section on the church's gospel witness through organized concern for the unfortunate as a means of "preaching the gospel to the poor."

Notwithstanding the church's commendable record of giving to causes such as involve programs of the local congregation and the extension of the gospel at home and abroad, its record of interest and support of welfare causes, such as may be described as more philanthropic than religious, is less outstanding. During the early years of the church's history the heavy demands for leadership personnel and for funds to develop the denominational program restricted the sources both of personnel and money to be channeled into organized philanthropy.

In time, however, a few institutions were developed under regional church sponsorship, and these have rendered valuable social and spiritual service. But to this day the general church has provided to these area institutions little more than an inspecting and accrediting service, and the allotment of "patronizing territory" to each from which it may solicit support. While no denominational funds subsidize these institutions and their church support must come from the churches in their patronizing territories, denominational accreditation benefits them by stabilizing public confidence and giving them standing with welfare agencies and state authorities.

The institutions now accredited by the Free Methodist Church are here briefly described.

The Gerry Homes, located at Gerry, New York, minister both to the aged and to children needing institutional care. To Anna Chesbrough, wife of S. K. J. Chesbrough and a member of the first society organized after the Pekin Convention, is ascribed credit for stirring up such interest in establishing an institution that the Genesee Conference in 1885 took steps to that end. The institution was incorporated in 1886, the site was purchased in 1888, and the Homes were opened in 1889 in what had been the facilities of Gerry Seminary, owned by the Rev. W. A. Sellew who later became a bishop of the Free Methodist Church. The cost of the property was a small fraction of its value, W. A. Sellew contributing all of his personal investment therein.

Today there are two main buildings, one housing the aged, the other housing the children There are also a central heating plant, an infirmary (a memorial to W. A. Sellew), two modern duplex units for retired ministers and their wives, and other facilities. The institutional plant adjoins a well stocked and productive farm of one hundred and fifty acres. The net assets of the institution amount to more than $400,000, and the annual operating budget is about $85,000. The normal capacity of the home for the aged is fifty; for the children's home, forty-three.

Woodstock Homes include the Children's Home and Sunset Manor, located at Woodstock, Illinois. The former was organized as the Chicago Industrial Home for Children in 1886 by Rev. T. B. Arnold who had for years been the proprietor of *The Free Methodist* before the publication was taken over by the denomination in that year, at which time he became the church's first publishing agent. Free Methodist headquarters then were in Chicago. Mr. Arnold, homeward bound one winter evening, discovered two boys foraging their suppers from garbage cans. When he learned that they were homeless waifs who slept at night in boxes or doorways, he took them to his own home and kept them. Within three months he was sheltering seventeen such children!

In 1888 he incorporated the Chicago Industrial Home for Children, and in 1900 it was moved to Woodstock. The institution has cared for a multitude of children through nearly three-quarters of a century. Its present ministry in large measure is to children from broken homes, a fact reflecting one of the serious social problems of our day.

In 1903 Rev. J. D. Kelsey, while manager of the Children's Home, founded what was then called the Old People's Rest Home as a corporation separate from the Children's Home. The two institutions, although still separate corporations, are now under the same administration.

Sunset Manor, as the Old People's Rest Home has been renamed, is equipped to care for sixty residents with facilities which include two large buildings, a duplex and other apartment provisions for eight retired couples, an annex for residence of staff members; and a dwelling house for managerial personnel. The Children's Home has a capacity of fifty-two. The plant includes a main building, dormitory for older children, laundry, superintendent's residence, and a staff cottage. The combined net assets are about $210,000, the combined operating budgets approximately $160,000. The combined staff numbers about thirty.

Life Line Children's Home of Kansas City, Kansas, was founded by Rev. and Mrs. S. V. Coe in 1907, and was chartered in 1908. The institution developed out of city mission work of the Coes and the calls that came to them to find babies for adoption and foster homes for babies. The adoptive function of the institution has declined with the lifting of the lower age limit for admission to five years. The upper limit is sixteen years; the average population is about forty children. More than five thousand children have received the ministry of the institution in the past fifty-two years. Housing includes four buildings, a main structure for general family living, a gymnasium with a residence area for older boys, a combined laundry and heating plant, and a modern home for the superintendent. The operating budget is between $40,000 and $50,000; the net assets are above $260,000.

The Deaconess Hospital of Oklahoma City was first organized as a rescue home for unfortunate girls in Guthrie in 1900, and was moved to its present location in 1910. A hospital building was constructed in 1931 which for a time was used for maternity cases. In 1944 this became a general hospital and was opened to the public. The unwed mother program was continued as a department of the hospital. In 1955 the hospital was enlarged, remodeled, and equipped with new surgical and obstetrical facilities. In 1959 the hospital was further enlarged to provide two emergency units and other facilities. The capacity of the hospital now is forty-four beds.

The unwed mother program carries the name "Home of Redeeming Love." Since 1910 there have been more than eight thousand girl patients, and the babies placed since 1928 number about two thousand.

The net assets of the Home and the Hospital are $465,000, and the combined operating budget exceeds $400,000. The Hospital has twenty acres of land, with several buildings in addition to the main hospital building. These include a nurses' and workers' home, girls' dormitory for the Home of Redeeming Love, an arts and crafts building, and three cottages. Further planning is under way for an enlarged ministry by this institution.

The Jolley Home of Conyers, Georgia, is the youngest of the church's benevolent institutions. It was established under the leadership of Rev. George A. Gaines in 1947, and is controlled by the Georgia and Carolina Conference of the Free Methodist Church. Between ninety and one hundred children are in residence. The physical plant serving these children includes the mansion of the late Colleen Moore from whose estate it was purchased, a large double garage remodeled to pantry use and guest entertainment, an office building which once contained the famous Colleen Moore Doll House (which is now on exhibition in Chicago), a boys' dormitory, a dining hall, combined laundry and heating plant, and a gymnasium. A farm is operated in an extensive program of raising hogs, cattle, and their feed. The annual budget is $77,000, and net assets are approximately $160,000. The institution receives only children surrendered to its complete care by the courts or written agreement of parent or guardian.

A spiritual emphasis in philanthropy

The church's institutions are developing, not only in material facilities, but also in their professional ministries to the psychological and spiritual needs of those in their care. A new interest in social work as a profession is growing among young people in our colleges. Already this is reflected in the programs of the institutions. Reports submitted by the institutions reflect a genuine concern for the whole person, with moral and spiritual values dominant. With the far-reaching growth of the welfare state, Christian philanthropy faces peculiar difficulties, and will survive only by the favor of God and the help of His people. Christian philanthropy has a ministry to earth's unfortunates the state cannot give. Here are fragments gleaned from the reports.

From the Gerry Homes: Adverse to the "social gospel" that neglects the spiritual needs of man in deference to meeting his social and material needs, Bishop Sellew sought to integrate a program of spiritual and social service by establishing the Gerry Homes. How to integrate the "Gospel of Grace" and the "Social Gospel," without compromising our convictions or sacrificing our prudentials, has always been one of the crucial problems of our church. Our founding fathers, I believe, successfully met this problem by neither denying nor defying the material aspect of life; rather, they dedicated the material to God by founding and maintaining our charitable institutions. The test of reality in the spiritual in this materialistic age is whether it functions in temporal and social areas of human living.

From the Woodstock Homes: We seek to provide for more than custodial care. We offer redemptive care—a Christian environment where tender love and devotion on the part of a dedicated staff help in leading these children to Christ. Many of these children from broken homes have deep problems and resentments that frequently take months to change. One forgotten area of Christian service is provided in such homes as this. It takes dedication, sacrifice, faith, and a genuine love for children, but the rewards are great when young lives can be redirected and transformed by the Friend of all children who said, "Suffer the little children to come unto me, and forbid them not."

From Life Line Children's Home: Family worship each morning and bed-time devotions in small groups help the children to grow and develop spiritually. The aim of the staff is not only to teach the children about the love of God, but to manifest that love in daily living so that each boy and girl will have a true knowledge of God and His love for them. The majority of the children coming to the Home have had no previous knowledge of God. This is truly "home missions" at work in an area of great need and rich returns.

From the Deaconess Hospital and the Home of Redeeming Love: The object of our spiritual guidance program is to assist all of the girl patients to become Christians. Religious services are held three times a week and family devotions every day. While casework includes the total picture of counseling and rehabilitation, we endeavor to make this field contribute to the dominance of strong Christian influence. The employment of a full-time chaplain for the Deaconess Hospital and the Home is now under serious consideration.

From the Jolley Home: The Jolley Home is dedicated to serving the youth of today by providing them with a sense of well-being and security, thereby elevating their ideals and reinspiring the enthusiasm that is found in normal youth. Generally, an effort has been made to diagnose all newcomers to find how they respond to love. If this is lacking, the ministry of trying to understand is begun which often produces confidence. New horizons are opened, and in many cases the child continues to pursue Christian objectives. The nature of the service rendered the child is connected with all parts of his being, the physical, the mental, and the spiritual. It is the purpose of the Home to keep a child in its care until it is felt he can adust and contribute to the welfare of society.

City missions

We have not mentioned city missions and other agencies operated under the sponsorship of Free Methodists, some of them connected officially with Free Methodist organizations. These agencies have done a work of inestimable value, not only in ministering to the unfortunate but likewise in providing earnest Christians with avenues for the exercise of their stewardship, both of financial means and of personal service.

In the beginnings of Free Methodism, B. T. Roberts took a course that made him, as a follower of his Lord, an example worthy of emulation in this area of evangelism. Earlier in these pages[8] was noted his love for the poor that led him, at great personal sacrifice, to purchase a theatre building in downtown Buffalo and open it as a "free" church. This was in the spring of 1860. But his concern for preaching the gospel to the poor, not exhausted by this fruitful effort, led him further to establish a mission above a saloon in Buffalo's most morally polluted area. This was in 1862 when the burdens of the new church rested heavily on his shoulders. The neighborhood was the then notorious Five Points, between the canal and the lake, where nearly every building housed a brothel and a bar. It was not long until several youthful derelicts had been converted to Christ and to pure living. Roberts wrote about the project in an editorial, "Mission Field." This item of his account startles one: "To the young women who become converted we furnish a home in our family, until the way is opened for them to take care of themselves in a respectable manner." [9] And so it appears that the church's first "Home of Redeeming Love" was the private home of the church's amazing founder who opened his own family circle to take in strangers, even the world's outcasts.

Evangelism is heralding the good news to make Christ known. Its avenues are more than the ministry of preaching, although the spiritual must always be the ultimate objective. Evangelism means also a compassion in which the Christian identifies himself with another's varied needs and which moves him to share whatever he has of moral, social, and psychological, as well as spiritual resources, to relieve the distressed in body, mind and spirit. Note the clear teaching of Jesus

---

8. *Supra*, p. 236.
9. *The Earnest Christian*, v. 3, June 1862; p. 187.

in his account of the final reckoning. Those who have so loved their Lord that with self-forgetting concern they shared with the unfortunate of earth their food and clothing, shelter and nursing, hospitality and consolation, and even a cup of cold water in His name, in glad surprise will hear their Master's voice claiming these acts of love as done in His behalf: "Inasmuch as ye have done it unto the least of one of these my brethren, ye have done it unto me." [10]

The Forward Movement

An earlier section of this chapter noted a decline in the rate of the church's expansion which became critical about 1903. A major explanation offered of the church's slowing down was the subsidence of the aggressive evangelistic spirit that had characterized the first generation, as the church withdrew into itself to devote its energies more to saving itself and conserving the past than to saving sinners outside its pale. This introvertive tendency seems to have affected most of a half-century of Free Methodism's history, roughly defined as extending from 1894 to 1944. In the fall of the latter year, stirred by the church's slow progress in face of the spiritual need of the times and the church's inherent but latent resources, Dr. C. Hoyt Watson, then president of Seattle Pacific College, led in the launching of the Forward Movement of Free Methodism. Originally authorized by the Board of Administration at its inception in 1944, the Forward Movement was sanctioned by the approval of the General Conference of 1947, and has been continued by each succeeding General Conference.

The Forward Movement has challenged the church to make its positions more than something to be defended—to make them also means of advance. Those promoting the movement have held the clear conviction that Free Methodism must be more than a witness for the defense—its message and program must be employed in a great spiritual and evangelistic outreach. Accordingly, a program of inspiration and faith-building was first launched, with methods and policies subordinated to spiritual values.

Such encouragement and inspiration were needed to redirect outward the church's interest and energies, for sometimes our very

---

10. Matthew 25:31-46.

perfectionism[11] has brought defeat through our delay, while we despairingly wait to perfect the means we are to employ in the work of God. To reach our goal we must take to the open road and head for the far-off horizon. Detaining the car in the shop and tearing it down to find the source of every mystifying rattle and elusive squeak has meant paralysis, not forward movement. The church needed faith that there is no handicap inherent in its doctrines, standards of Christian living, or its polity that can explain failure or low achievement, and that the distinctives of the church are not only right in principle, but if rightly handled lead to success.

This claim in nowise blinks the fact that the church's machinery from time to time needs adjustment, and now and then may need radical repair. Some adjustments can be made on the road, and if more drastic repairs are necessary, there is the General Conference; and there are also the annual conferences when their concurrent action is required. The church needed the confidence that the day-by-day devotion of every member, working at whatever level of the church's structure with the means the church provided, would insure progress in that area of the Kingdom where God had placed the Free Methodist Church.

To abate any tendency to impose a program on the church, handed down from the headquarters departments which by this time were highly developed and strongly entrenched in their positions, conference superintendents and pastors were called to meet with the general men to work together in the cause of advance. The desire was to channel the resources of the general church to every level without quenching local and conference initiative, for this was to be a movement carrying no dead-heading passengers.

After acquaintanceships had been established among pastors and superintendents in different areas, after confidence in each other had been strengthened by these acquaintanceships, and after the Holy Spirit's melting presence had brought closer fellowship and sense of unity, the time came when the councils that were called could grapple with problems, policies, methods. By 1951 the bishops

---

11. The term as here used refers to standard of achievement, not to a doctrine of Christian experience.

as directors of the Forward Movement included in their report to General Conference the following paragraph:

> We are a conservative people and we have been rather slow in taking to the reconditioning of our old weapons and in laying hold of other good tools simply because they are new to our hands. Nevertheless, the Forward Movement is taking hold; it is getting a grip on our ministers and our members, on their minds and their hearts, on their imagination and their faith, on their planning and their efforts. There is evidence of definite progress—a real Forward Movement—on many lines.

The rate of growth since the launching of the Forward Movement has appreciably exceeded the rate in the quadrennium which immediately preceded it, but the gains have been far from commensurate with the church's potential, and far below the church's outreach in the first generation. In all humility we do well to pray,

> *Remember, Lord, the ancient days;*
> *Renew thy work; thy grace restore;*
> *And while to thee our hearts we raise,*
> *On us thy Holy Spirit pour.*

Although its membership gains have been modest in the closing quadrenniums of the church's first century, the spirit and ideals of the Forward Movement have now flowed through the church at all levels. General men who travel throughout the connection sense the impetus of new courage and confidence and action. In the report of the bishops to the General Conference of 1951 are these words, immediately following those quoted above from the same source:

> But we must push this battle harder than ever. This is no time to call a halt, much less to surrender ground already taken which was so hardly won, and especially with the total task yet so far from being done. The Forward Movement must constantly be kept before our people and our Church. This must not be the momentary flash of an emotional explosion, nor the dim flash of sheet lightning, reminding one of a preceding hot day; this must be the steady burning of "that flame of living fire," which shall characterize the people called Free Methodists until the return of our Lord and Saviour, Jesus Christ. Having put our hands to this plough, we must not—we will not—look back.

May the Forward Movement of the Free Methodist Church sweep across the threshold of the second century as an evangelizing crusade, even as the church's first century began!

The general evangelistic secretaries serving as executives of the Commission on Evangelism and Church Extension since its organization in 1931 have been:

R. B. Campbell   1935-1955   L. W. Northrup 1955-

CHAPTER TWENTY-THREE

The Outreach Through World Missions

The outreach of the Free Methodist Church through missions has been a vigorous one. It began with pioneer efforts in the eighties, and within three-quarters of a century the work has so increased that today two of every five Free Methodists live outside the United States and Canada where the church had its origin and early growth. Rapid expansion of the church abroad continues.

Organizational developments

Early organizational steps in the missionary enterprise of the church were sketched in the last chapter to show the development of foreign missions within "Missions," which in the beginning of the church's history had included only home evangelism. Once begun, the foreign missionary enterprise, and such home mission enterprises as were directed to foreign-language groups and to underprivileged areas of the home land, came to demand the full services of the General Missionary Board. And so, in time, home evangelism and church extension were transferred to the control of other agencies of the church. Note the following steps:

1860. The Free Methodist Church was founded with the adoption of a *Discipline* in which "Missions" was conceived in terms of home evangelism, with no reference to a ministry of the gospel in foreign countries.

1862. The first General Conference appointed a committee to draft the constitution of a missionary society and to incorporate the same in New York. B. T. Roberts was designated president, with Thomas Sully and Joseph Travis the other members of the committee. The only reference to this venture we have found is the record of this action in the 1862 General Conference Journal. Why nothing resulted from the action or what the society's area of concern was to be, foreign or home missions, is not disclosed.

1874. For the first time, in 1874, a General Missionary Board was organized. Reference to this Board in the *Discipline* merely defines its responsibility to receive and disburse monies collected for "general missionary purposes." Although the 1874 *Discipline* made no mention of foreign missions in connection with the Board or its funds, we find in the General Conference Journal that the action creating this Board assigned to it the duty of appropriating funds, both to foreign missions and to the annual conferences for their home missions.

1882. A complete reorganization of the General Missionary Board, or perhaps more accurately, the creation of a new board, was ordered by the General Conference. The *Discipline* stipulated in detail the personnel, and made the secretary of the Board an officer to be elected by General Conference by ballot. But still the term "foreign missions" did not appear in the *Discipline,* nor in this instance even in the General Conference Journal. A distinction between general missions and conference missions was made in the *Discipline,* and presumably the former included foreign missions and any home mission enterprises not conducted by the annual conferences. Offerings for "general missionary purposes" were made mandatory on the pastoral charges, these not to be less than twenty-five cents per member. Offerings for missions within the conferences were also to be taken by the pastors. During this quadrennium, in 1885, the Board was incorporated. In the same year it sent out its first foreign missionaries, the vanguard of a long line of hundreds of courageous and consecrated volunteers to begin and carry forward the foreign missionary enterprise.

1886. In differentiating contributions to "general missions" and "foreign missions," the latter term appeared in the *Discipline* for the first time. The General Missionary Board was made the Church Extension and Aid Society for the purpose of assisting in the building of new churches.

1890. Emphasis was given to foreign missions as a concern of the General Missionary Board by the stipulation in the *Discipline* that this board was responsible for "all the General and Foreign Missions of the Church established by the Board." This General Conference ordered that offerings specifically for foreign missions be taken. Further emphasis on foreign missions came with the authorization of a Women's Foreign Missionary Society as an auxiliary to the General Missionary Board. The organization was effected at the next General Conference, held at Greenville, Ill., in 1894.

1919. Church extension was transferred from the General Missionary Board to the Executive Committee of the Church, although this General Conference had established the General Board of Aggressive Evangelism. The administration of general missions, which by now meant home evangelism and excluded foreign missions, seems to have been continued by the General Missionary Board until the reorganization of the general church structure in 1931.

1931. Through reorganization of the general church to provide an inclusive Board of Administration, that Board became the General Missionary Board. Under the Board of Administration the Commission on Missions thenceforth would operate the church's program of missions. This program now includes foreign missions, home mission projects serving foreign-language groups, and such other special home fields as the Board of Administration has designated.

THE OUTREACH THROUGH WORLD MISSIONS

Missionary pioneers[1]

The record of heroic sacrifice of those who first offered themselves for service to their Lord and the church in foreign lands well matches that of home evangelists who earlier blazed a trail for Free Methodism across the American continent. We mention only a few of these pioneers who opened our earlier fields, and let the brief summary we give of their ministry represent the larger company of heroes, not a few of whom became martyrs for the cause of Christ.

In 1880, even before a missionary board existed that was adequately organized to appoint and send missionaries, Rev. Ernest F. Ward requested of the Illinois Conference, and was granted, appointment as a missionary in India. It is a matter of interest that it was the same annual conference that started Thomas S. LaDue on his far-journeyings across America nearly twenty years earlier.

Mr. and Mrs. Ward went out at their own expense, with no missionary board back of them but with the prayers and cordial support of many in the church. Later, they were appointed missionaries by the Free Methodist Board, and rendered long and faithful service. Father Ward lived to a ripe old age, and died in 1938.

The first Board appointment to India was in 1885. This was Miss M. Louisa Ranf who labored with the Wards until claimed by death due to burns received from a kerosene lamp, accidentally overturned in a Church of England service she was attending. She died in 1890, one of the first in a long line of missionary heroes who gave their lives while in foreign service. Later missionaries chose Yeotmal in the Province of Berar as the center of Free Methodist occupation in India, and from there the work has been administered to this date.

Also in 1885 the Board made its first appointments to Africa, a company of five. They landed in Durban, and Robert R. Shemeld and his wife remained in South Africa and established Bethany Mission. The others journeyed northward into Portuguese East

---

1. In preparing the summary statements concerning selected pioneer missionaries and the missionary fields of the church, the writer has found the following publications helpful: B. S. Lamson, *Lights in the World*. General Missionary Board, Winona Lake, Ind. B. S. Lamson, *1959 Annual Report, Free Methodist Missions*, and reports for years immediately preceding 1959. W. T. Hogue, *History of the Free Methodist Church*. Free Meth. Pub. House, Winona Lake, Indiana; v. 2, ch. 16.

Africa and established the Inhambane Mission Station which continues as an important center of our work in that country. Two of the three at Inhambane, Rev. W. W. Kelley and Mrs. Kelley, could not endure the climate and were forced to leave after a year on the field. W. W. Kelley later was elected missionary secretary.

Left alone at Inhambane was G. Harry Agnew, indomitable hero of Free Methodist Africa Missions. The Board sent others to assist him, but the climate was too severe for most of them. He served two terms as a single man. In 1894 this lonely man wrote:

> I have had lots of sickness lately, inflammation of the liver, jaundice, and inflammation of the kidney. . . . Since that I have had inflammation of the lungs, and a kind of pleurisy that still sticks to me. . . . When a white man is sick there is no native who has any idea of looking after him. Even the native Christians are utterly unable to grasp the situation. If you want anything cooked in the line of a delicacy, you must explain and explain. Finally the dish is brought in, burned or smoked or a failure in some other way. . . . I am here in the midst of millions of savages. I never expect to see America again.[2]

He was married in 1895 to Susie Sherman. She died that same year of African fever. In 1897 he married Lillie Smith, and together they went to Johannesburg. There he labored among the men in the gold mines and established firmly the work of the Free Methodist Church in that place. The Boer War interrupted his labors, and for a time he labored in Natal, but after the war returned to Johannesburg.

During eighteen years he had been home only twice. He was planning to return for the 1903 General Conference when fever laid him low. Soon another martyr had given his life to extend the Christian witness on foreign soil. His widow, devoted to his memory and to his Christ, died on the field in 1939.

One of the stark tragedies of those early years was the death in 1888 of father, mother and child in their first year of service in Portuguese East Africa. Abbie Lincoln gave birth to a child which did not live, and its death was followed shortly by the death of the mother. The husband and father, Arthur D. Lincoln, attempted to

---

2. Quoted in *Lights in the World*, p. 140 et seq.

THE OUTREACH THROUGH WORLD MISSIONS

return to America, as his dying wife had desired, that he might place another child in what later has been known as the Woodstock Children's Home. When he reached Natal he was stricken with African fever, and he also died.

The Free Methodist work in Japan was begun by a young man, Masazi Kakihara, renamed Paul by an American friend and benefactor. He was a product of Christian missions in Japan, and was sanctified on his way to America while clinging to a spar in the ocean following shipwreck. Desiring to get to Greenville College after his arrival, he walked six hundred miles of the distance from Arizona to Illinois. After two years in Greenville College he was accepted by the Board and appointed missionary to his homeland in 1895. He opened work on the Island of Awaji. There he encountered Rev. T. Kawabe, a man of strong character, superlative gifts, and deep devotion. Mr. Kakihara interested him in Free Methodist missions, and in 1896 Mr. and Mrs. Kawabe were accepted by the Free Methodist Board. Brother Kakihara had been effective as a missionary but was diverted to business by which he hoped so to prosper that he could support the cause of missions in Japan. In this he was disappointed, for his business venture failed. T. Kawabe served through long and critical years as one of the stalwarts of the Japanese Free Methodist Church.

Free Methodism's pioneer missionary in China was Clara A. Leffingwell, a survivor of the Boxer Uprising of 1900 during which crisis her life was in great peril. At that time she was serving under the China Inland Mission because there was no opportunity for the Free Methodist Church to commission her when first she was ready for appointment to the field. During a furlough in America in 1903, Miss Leffingwell was engaged to promote the cause of establishing a Free Methodist Mission in China. She returned to China under appointment of the Free Methodist Board in 1905, a few months after the Board had sent out C. Floyd Appleton and G. H. Schofield. Within a few weeks a fatal illness removed Miss Leffingwell from her work to her eternal reward.

The cause of Free Methodist missions in China had made great progress during the years until the coming of the Communist regime. The vicissitudes of our work in mainland China during the establish-

ment of the new order provide a saga of peerless courage on the part of Free Methodist missionaries, some of whom remained to the last. Women missionaries, true to the example of Clara Leffingwell a half-century earlier in the Boxer Uprising, suffered imprisonment and narrowly escaped death. We cannot know the steadying effect their devotion has had on the church in China during subsequent years.

It remains to mention the Mills family in another of our older fields, the Dominican Republic. Mr. and Mrs. S. E. Mills went to this Catholic country in 1889 and pioneered for many years, independent of Board support and, for a time, of Board connection. But the Mills were in sympathy with Free Methodist principles and accepted the assistance of Board missionaries. Their operation as independents tended to delay the organization of the work under Free Methodist auspices, but organization was effected in 1908. A few years after the death of the parents, George W. Mills and his wife, Ruth, were appointed by the Board and served from 1917 until their retirement in 1958. In terms of man-years, the four Millses gave a century and a quarter to missionary service in the Dominican Republic.

And what shall I say more? for the time would fail me to tell of all who lived and labored and died in far-off lands to fulfill their Lord's command to be witnesses unto Him "unto the uttermost part of the earth." They prayed—and God answered:

> Is there some desert, or some boundless sea,
> Where Thou, great God of angels, wilt send me?
> Some oak for me to rend,
> Some sod for me to break,
> Some handful of Thy corn to take
> And scatter far afield,
> Till it in turn shall yield
>   Its hundredfold
>   Of grains of gold
> To feed the happy children of my God?
>
> Show me the desert, Father, or the sea;
> Is it Thine enterprise? Great God, send me!
> And though this body lies where ocean rolls,
> Father count me among all faithful souls.[3]

---

3. Mrs. Chas. E. Cowman, Compiler, *Streams in the Desert*. Cowman Publications, Inc., Los Angeles; p. 329.

Women and Free Methodist missions

Women have more freely offered themselves for missionary service than have men, and those remaining at home have also been more active in promoting the cause of missions than have men. The chapter on missions of the Free Methodist Church would be dull reading without those pages the women have written by their consecration, their diligence, and their efficient organization.

It has previously been noted on these pages that the Women's Foreign Missionary Society was organized nationally at the General Conference of 1894. Prior to that date local societies had been formed, the first at Verona, Pa., in 1889 by Mrs. Ella MacGeary. To Miss Emma Freeland, who later became Mrs. C. W. Shay, much credit is due for devoting herself to promoting the support of missions among the women of the church. Miss Freeland was moved to this task by the impact of the Student Volunteer Band on the Wellesley campus while she was a student there. She drafted a simple constitution which guided the organization of local and conference societies until the national organization was set up, and her influence led many groups to organize. The first conference society to be formed was the Wisconsin.

Mrs. Ellen Lois Roberts, widowed a year earlier by the death of General Superintendent Roberts, was elected president of the national organization when it was formed in 1894. In the first quadrennial meeting in 1898, a constitution was adopted which gave as the society's purposes, (1) the promotion of missionary intelligence, (2) the deepening of interest in world evangelism, and (3) securing sympathetic contributions for missions.

By 1903 the national society had over five thousand members in 336 local societies. In 1959 the membership in the United States and Canada was twenty-six thousand, in other countries seven thousand.

In the raising of funds for missions, the organization, today bearing the official name, Woman's Missionary Society, has been highly successful. In recent years it has turned into the cause of missions an average well over $400,000 annually, and since 1894 the total raised has been $8,500,000.

Different projects of the Society contribute to interest in world evangelism and to missionary intelligence. First of these in importance should be placed *The Missionary Tidings*, a monthly periodical with few equals in its field. When publication began in 1897, the magazine had a thousand subscribers; today its circulation is above twenty-seven thousand.

The Woman's Missionary Society maintains departments of stewardship, literature, and mission study. The literature department has published more than fifty books on Free Methodist missions and missionaries. In a recent year the department of mission study reported nearly one hundred thousand books read by the women of the society.

The Woman's Missionary Society begins the process of missionary education early. A Junior Missionary Society was formed as an auxiliary of the adult organization in 1898. Its goals are to win children to Christ, instruct them concerning the church and its program of missions, and guide them into lives of service whether at home or abroad. There are now nearly nine hundred local societies with a total membership of approximately twenty-five thousand. In 1958 these children raised for missions $70,000.

The church's first missionary society for young people was organized by the Woman's Missionary Society in 1919 as the Young People's Missionary Society. The organization was transferred to the Commission on Christian Education when the structure of the general church was reorganized in 1931. It now operates as Free Methodist Youth, and will be described in Chapter Twenty-seven.

Outreach to world fields

Space permits but a bird's-eye glance at each field to give a sketchy concept of the world-terrain of Free Methodist missions at the close of the church's first century. Fields are presented in order of date of opening.

India, 1881. The beginnings of Free Methodist work in India have been noted in an earlier section of the present chapter. After moving slowly for years, the church in India now exhibits vitality and vigorous growth. Frontier evangelism is no longer the burden of the missionary but is being carried on by native evangelists. Full conference status bespeaks the self-governing and self-supporting progress of the Indian church.

The headquarters are at Yeotmal in Berar Province. Here is located Union Biblical Seminary, in the support and operation of which a dozen evangelical missions unite. This seminary is rapidly gaining standing among theological institutions in India. At Umri are located the central boarding school and the Umri Mission Hospital and clinic.

The past five-year gain of the church in India has been 45 per cent. Present membership, 1,430.

Portuguese East Africa, 1885. Free Methodism's oldest mission field in Africa, opened by G. Harry Agnew and the Kelleys seventy-five years ago, is now growing rapidly. An evangelist school trains native workers, and younger prospects for Christian service attend a youth Bible school. Increasing self-government is accompanying the rising tide of evangelism, and there is a growing interest in education. Schools and clinics are in great demand. This field is yielding a bountiful harvest. The gain of the past five years was 44 per cent. Present membership, 4,895.

Dominican Republic, 1889. The opening of work in this strongly Roman Catholic country by the self-supporting S. E. Mills was reported earlier in this chapter. This devout layman was the first Protestant missionary in the Dominican Republic. The first missionary assisted by the Board was Miss Esther D. Clark. A well-equipped and beautifully housed Instituto Evangelico trains native preachers and Christian workers. A grade school also is conducted. The spirit of evangelism is increasing, and church membership is growing. The past five-year increase has been 32 per cent. Present membership, 1,871.

South Africa, 1891. Rev. and Mrs. A. D. Noyes pioneered the work in South Africa. After an unsuccessful venture of our Board to establish them in Liberia, the Noyes labored for a time with the American Board, but in 1891 Mr. Noyes, to provide for a Free Methodist mission station, used his own funds to contract for a two thousand acre farm which later was taken over by the Free Methodist Board. Much of the Fairview farm is now owned in parcels by Christian natives. The work in South Africa through long years has meant much to the economic, educational, physical, and spiritual life of the area. Now serving the area is the Greenville Mission Hospital. Increased harvest should follow the increased emphasis on evangelism recently reported. Present membership, 1,442.

Japan, 1895. The origin of Free Methodist missions in Japan has been summarized earlier in this chapter. As the work was begun by the Japanese, so their leadership and initiative throughout the years have been of a high order. When the depression in the thirties seriously depleted the home treasury, the Japanese Church went on a self-supporting basis by its own choice, and asked the Board to direct its now restricted resources to other mission fields.

World War II wrought great destruction among our Japanese churches and virtually destroyed the Osaka Bible School. With energy and determination the Japanese church undertook reconstruction. Some of Japan's finest post-war church structures have been built by the Free Methodist Church. The rebuilt school is now Osaka Christian College with three hundred students in its arts and seminary departments. Along with the Japanese nation, the Free Methodist Church in Japan is spurred by a sense of destiny. The past five-year increase has been 19 per cent. Present membership, 3,899.

Transvaal, 1895. The church's mission in this northern-most province of the Union of South Africa centers around the gold mines of the Johannesburg area with its rapidly shifting population. Thousands yearly are drawn to the mines from other parts of Africa for employment, and many are constantly returning to their native regions. Opportunities for evangelism are vast, as likewise are the moral and spiritual needs of the people. The F. L. Baker Memorial Bible School, recently established in the eastern part of the Transvaal, is training much needed native evangelists. Present membership, 1,516.

Egypt, 1899. Our missionary enterprise in Egypt is a recent acquisition, coming by unanimous vote of a self-governing church in 1959 to follow its mother, the Holiness Movement Church of Canada, into union with the Free Methodist Church. There are eighty-two local churches in the connection, many of them in population centers with buildings seating four or five hundred people. This new Free Methodist Church in Egypt is aggressively evangelistic. A Bible school trains its workers. Membership, 5,000.

China, 1903. Following upon the labors of Clara Leffingwell, Free Methodist missions were established in the provinces of Honan, Shensi, and Szechwan. A Bible school in Kaifeng trained native workers. Kaifeng also was the administrative center of Free Methodist missions in China. The political situation in mainland China has necessitated the removal of missionaries, and communication with the Chinese church is broken. The latest report received listed the membership at 2,849, and that figure is used in Free Methodism's world statistics from year to year. By this token, the Free Methodist Church still claims its own children in Red China.

Brazil, 1928. Free Methodism in Brazil began in the labors of a Japanese missionary, released by the Free Methodist Church in Japan to carry the gospel to numerous countrymen in Sao Paulo. This missionary was Rev. Daniel Nishizumi, who supported himself in Brazil as a teacher while developing a congregation, organizing a Christian day school, and establishing a church. In 1946 the Board organized the work in Brazil as a mission field and sent missionaries. These missionaries had barely arrived when an automobile accident caused the death of Mr. Nishizumi. His dying message was, "My work is finished. Meet me in Heaven."

Many rallied to the support of the work the departed brother had so successfully started. Under the direction of capable missionaries, the church in Brazil has grown. In fact, during the past five years its membership has tripled. Two educational institutions are in operation, a

Christian day school in Sao Paulo, and the Free Methodist Seminary and Bible School a few miles out. Funds for the campus and buildings of the latter institution came largely from Spring Arbor Junior College—students, faculty and friends. The outlook is bright for building a substantial church in Brazil. Present membership, 1,062.

Congo Nile, 1935. The Free Methodist pioneer in this area, first explored by David Livingstone, was the late Rev. J. W. Haley, a missionary statesman who was led to enter the region in 1935 and to establish work at Muyebe in Urundi. The work extended rapidly from this point to other portions of populous Urundi and northward into likewise populous Ruanda. This new field is still in the stage of revival, and as always following revival, schools have been established. Five central primary schools enroll fifteen hundred pupils. The Mweya Bible School is a union enterprise of the Free Methodist Mission, the Friends Mission, and the World Gospel Mission. The Free Methodist Mission has provided Kibuye Hospital and two dispensaries. At one of the dispensaries a new child welfare building has recently been constructed. Congo-Nile is Free Methodism's numerically largest and one of its most rapidly growing mission fields. The past five-year increase has been 76 per cent. Present membership, 8,315.

Southern Rhodesia, 1938. In response to the call of natives and after investigation of the field by Portuguese East missionaries, Rev. and Mrs. Ralph Jacobs were appointed by the Board to enter Southern Rhodesia in 1938. From their second Sunday on the field and continuing for years, there was almost continuous revival. The field now has several stations, a Central Training School, a Bible School, a hospital, dispensary, and a first-aid station. In an area of ten thousand square miles of this primitive country, the Free Methodist mission is the only evangelical enterprise. Even this young church is growing in sense of Christian responsibility and the desire to become self-supporting. A large influx of Africans now coming from congested areas in other parts of the continent for resettlement here, makes the position of this mission strategic. The past five-year increase has been 57 per cent. Present membership, 1,277.

Paraguay, 1946. In the year the Board took over the work in Brazil, it launched a missionary program in neighboring Paraguay. The city of Asuncion is headquarters. From Encarnacion missionaries are evangelizing both Paraguayans and Japanese. The membership of the church in Paraguay is yet small—only fifty-two—but it is growing. The mission conducts a Bible school and a clinic. Rev. and Mrs. H. H. Ryckman were the first missionaries to enter this field.

Philippines, 1949. Free Methodism's interest in the Philippines as a field for missions grew out of the challenge this field presented Free Methodist chaplains stationed in the Islands during World War II. Their encouragement and contacts, along with internal conditions in China making necessary the reassignment of China missionaries, led to the appointment of Rev. and Mrs. Walter Groesbeck and Rev. and Mrs. John Schlosser to the Philippines in 1949. Mission stations were opened on the island of Mindanao. Already there is a Bible school at Butuan where a substantial church has been built. The church in the Philippines is making rapid progress in native leadership and in the direction of self-support, although the economic standard of the country is low. In the past year alone, the gain in membership was 20 per cent. Present membership, 453.

Hong Kong, 1951. Rev. I. S. W. Ryding in 1951, when compelled to leave China, devoted himself to mission work in Hong Kong until his death. In 1956, Free Methodist interests in this British Crown Colony, including the Third Street Chapel, were turned over to the Canadian Holiness Mission which had opened its work in Hong Kong in 1954. With the union of the Holiness Movement Church of Canada with the Free Methodist Church in 1959, the Canadian Holiness Mission has become one of Free Methodism's missionary outposts. Hong Kong, now a city of refugees from Red China, is in desperate spiritual and physical need. Present mission membership, 722.

Formosa, 1952. Our work in Formosa, with headquarters in Kaohsiung, opened in 1952 with missionaries who, for the most part, had been transferred from mainland China. The work is growing and a strong evangelistic spirit prevails. The Holy Light Bible Seminary, established in 1954, is preparing Christian workers for this vast field where many doors are wide open to the missionary enterprise.

In 1958 a high-ranking army officer was baptized and joined the Free Methodist Church. This was Lieutenant-General Chen Chihch'iang, who died shortly after this courageous step. He had requested a Christian funeral, and the same was conducted in a Free Methodist Church. These events brought the Christian religion to the attention of officer friends of the General, some of whom turned to Christ.

The membership gain in the one year of 1959 was 20 per cent. Present membership on Formosa, 1,115.

Outreach to needy fields in North America

The following areas of the North American continent are the responsibility of Free Methodist Missions.

Oakdale Mission, 1912. This is the Board's oldest home mission project. The work was begun in 1912 by the Board's appointment of J. M. Moore, M.D., to an area in the mountains of Eastern Kentucky. Miss Elizabeth O'Connor succeeded him and greatly developed the project. In 1921 the Oakdale Vocational School was organized, which is now accredited through the high school level. The years during which the Oakdale Mission has served this region have witnessed great changes, wrought by the gospel influences of the mission churches and the school.

Pacific Coast Japanese Conference, 1913. Free Methodist missionary work among the Pacific Coast Japanese began in 1913. The Conference was organized in 1932. World War II disrupted seriously the Japanese Church, but it is now prospering after reconstruction and is practically self-supporting. Under vigorous leadership, the church is growing with a gain during the past five years of 45 per cent. Present membership, 703.

Pacific Coast Latin-American Conference, 1917. The stimulus initiating Mexican missions in Southern California was a revival at Los Angeles Seminary (now Los Angeles Pacific College) which sent young people to "Dogtown" to work with Mexicans in a mission Sunday school. The Southern California Annual Conference and the General Missionary Board cooperated, and the project developed finally into a Mexican Provisional Conference in 1931. In 1958 the Pacific Coast portion of the conference and the inland portion were separated, the former becoming a full conference with twelve churches in California and six in Lower California (Mexico). Present membership, 637.

Mexican Provisional Conference, 1931. The division of the original Mexican Provisional Conference in 1958 was noted above. After the division, Free Methodist missions in the interior continued as the Mexican Provisional Conference. The area includes Arizona and Mexico east of the Gulf of California. One small district of this conference is situated along the Gulf and, strictly speaking, is not interior Mexico. The gain in this area during the past five years has been 138 per cent. The present membership, 752. Nogales Bible School is a well established training center for Mexican pastors and workers, located on the Arizona side of the international boundary.

Florida Spanish Mission, 1941. This mission was born of the inspiration and labors of Rev. and Mrs. E. E. Shelhamer. At first it was an independent venture, and later the Board assumed responsibility. The first worker to be assisted by the Board was Miss Ruth Landin, who is still with the mission. The mission property occupies a city block in Tampa. A broad program of education, evangelism, recreation and welfare is conducted.

Northern Ontario Mission, 1943. The mission program centers in Fort William on Lake Superior and in Timmins in the gold mining region. The former is within the West Ontario Conference, the latter within the East Ontario Conference. The General Missionary Board began its cooperation with these conferences at these points in 1950. Fort William in particular becomes a strategic base of mission operation with the opening of the St. Lawrence Seaway in 1959. Present membership, 66.

The Texas Latin-American Mission, 1948. The center of this field is San Antonio among 200,000 Latins. There are churches in two other Texas locations, and additional preaching points. The work is small but consistently growing. Present membership, 147.

Broadview Indian Mission, 1952. Mission work with the Cree and Chippewa Indians in Saskatchewan first received the support of the Board in 1952. During 1959 twenty-five Indians were baptized. Converts are doing missionary work with their own people. Church membership now numbers thirty-nine, and the number is increasing.

The challenge of our missionary opportunities

The church's missionary enterprise now surpasses in magnitude the home church of forty years ago, and is increasing much more rapidly than the home church. At present rates of growth for the two, within ten years the overseas churches will overtake the American church in membership and perhaps in enterprise for the Kingdom.

One of World Free Methodism's crucial needs in the decade immediately ahead is more rapid strengthening and expansion of the home base to insure financial support and missionary personnel commensurate with the world-encircling opportunities God has opened before the church as it looks down the vista of its second century.

Let the reader envisage an inclusive membership outside the United States and Canada exceeding 38,000; a staff of 200 missionaries to render expert services in preaching, church administration, medicine, surgery, nursing, teaching, engineering, farming and other professional and technical capacities; 1,400 mission pastors, evangelists, and Bible women; 585 organized churches and 1,250 outstations; 15,000 non-Christians receiving instruction in elementary Christian principles; 400 native teachers; 14,000 students in village day schools; 1,200 youth in boarding schools; 25,000 patients annually in our mission hosiptals; scores of thousands of the injured and ill receiving annually 325,000 dispensary and first-aid treatments—extend the list of ministries to the world's needy on and on. Such is Free Methodism abroad today; what will it be tomorrow?

Dr. B. S. Lamson, present Missionary Secretary, who came to this position sixteen years ago, gives in these brief words his reaction to the swift developments now transpiring in other countries, and what these developments betoken for tomorrow:

> Our mission fields are developing into conferences and national churches. Joint consultations now in progress anticipate a world Free Methodist organization. In this fellowship all our churches duly represented may pray and plan and labor together for the greater glory of God and the more rapid evangelization of the world. The missionary will be ready for new methods of evangelism, new types of service, and alert to the new fields ripe for the gospel. The home church will support missionaries and national leaders in the greatest world-wide evangelism crusade of our history. If we give ourselves without reserve to save the lost world, God will take care of our church.

It is now your turn . . .

The prolific burgeoning of Free Methodist foreign missions in the past decade or two, highlighted in this chapter's record of growth from small beginnings, and the tide of nationalism now sweeping around the whole world, have prompted a re-study of the entire strategy of foreign missions for the new era that so suddenly has broken upon us.

Note the strategy of Paul the Apostle, missionary statesman of the first-century church. The first church he planted on European soil was at Philippi. A decade later from prison in Rome he wrote that church, "It is now your turn to take part in that battle you once saw me engaged in. . . ."[4] Such was Paul's program, to evangelize a nucleus in one city and leave that "cell" to enlarge and develop and multiply by the inherent life and power of the gospel, while he moved on to new frontiers. We read with amazement the record of his missionary strategy. He lingered but a few days or weeks or months in a place to establish the beginnings of a church, and then courageously he left it to develop indigenously, returning only occasionally on a visit of supervision and administration. What confidence Paul had in the gospel as the power of God!

Will Paul's strategy of the first mid-century work in this twentieth mid-century? If it will, we must seize its advantage to evangelize the nations. Our world is in flux and turmoil. The upsurging independence of the colored races and other national groups makes precarious the position of missionaries in vast areas once open, it then seemed, to the leisurely processes of cultural missions.

But can there be evangelism without Christian culture to precede it and prepare the way? There is evidence that the moral impact of the gospel is effective even with untutored heathen. Note as only one example the report, given earlier in this chapter, of the revival that broke out in Southern Rhodesia on the second Sunday after the missionary's arrival, and which continued with power for years without cessation. We do not minimize the importance of Christian culture, but sometimes the missionary enterprise has made Christian culture

---

4. Philippians 1:30, as translated by J. B. Phillips, *Letters to Young Churches*. The Macmillan Co., New York; p. 117.

a substitute for evangelism. Christian fruit withers when its branch is grafted onto an unregenerate root. Paul expected the gospel root to produce Christian fruit, and Christian culture and Christian institutions to come in consequence of his evangelism. Christian institutions are then indigenous, growing out of the regenerate nature of the people, and not imposed upon their paganism. Note the observation made by William Arthur a century ago:

> Statesmen and philanthropists, occupied with the idea of forming happy nations, frequently look to good institutions as the means of doing so; but find that when the institutions are more than a certain distance in advance of the people, instead of being a blessing, they become a snare and a confusion. The reason of this is obvious: good institutions to a certain extent presuppose a good people. Where the degree of goodness existing in the people does not in some measure correspond with that presupposed in the institutions, the latter can never be sustained. . . The only way to the effectual regeneration of society is the regeneration of individuals; make the tree good, and the fruit will be good; make good men, and you will easily found and sustain good institutions.[5]

Increasingly the missionary aim must be the evangelization of groups of nationals in strategic centers, these to increase by indigenous evangelism and to be established by the development, indigenous so far as possible, of schools, hospitals, and other cultural resultants of Christianization.

This does not mean releasing the home church from responsibility for world missions, but rather increasing its responsibility if this eleventh-hour crisis is to be met successfully. Until blocked by national governments unfriendly to missionary enterprise, missionary supervision and encouragement must be continued; and most important of all missionary tasks will be the training of nationals as evangelists, pastors, teachers, nurses, doctors, administrators, and economic leaders in vast areas that missionaries can never reach in the fragment of time remaining for unhampered missionary activity. Then, when an unfriendly government erects barriers to keep the missionary outside, the native church will be established inside the country, and the missionary can say, "It is now your turn."

---
5. William Arthur, *The Tongue of Fire*. Light & Life Press, Winona Lake, Ind.; p. 91.

World Planning Council approved

In line with the foregoing interpretation of missionary strategy suited to present world conditions, the Commission on Missions presented the following statement and request to the Board of Administration in 1958:

> In view of:
>
> 1. The mounting tide of nationalism in practically all areas of our foreign missionary endeavor, the spirit and ideals of which have deeply affected Christian nationals in those areas;
>
> 2. The proper objective of missionary endeavor to develop the indigenous church as rapidly as possible wherever the Christian enterprise is planted; and
>
> 3. The gratifying development of Christian leadership and the capacity for self-direction among nationals in an increasing number of Free Methodist mission fields—
>
> — it has become clear to the Commission on Missions that the Free Methodist Church of N. A. is approaching the time when it must think in terms of a world church of related national churches, and plan with representatives of national Free Methodist groups looking toward the organization of largely autonomous national churches within the various countries now controlled in large measure by mission extensions of the home church.
>
> Therefore, the Board of Administration is requested to take steps toward setting up a World Planning Council for Free Methodism, the immediate nucleus of which shall be an American Panel of nine members, which panel shall study the plans of other American and also foreign churches now seeking to meet the same challenge we face. This panel should be invested with authority to affiliate with other national panels of Free Methodists in the proposed World Planning Council for Free Methodism.

This request was approved, and the North American Panel, as it was renamed, was increased to eleven members. The Panel called in as counselors several experienced missionaries from different fields who were in this country on furlough or special mission, and from them arrived at a better understanding of the peculiar problems which nationalism brings to any effort to organize such a World Planning Council, and of the processes involved in preparing national churches for greater autonomy. In consequence of their counsel, it was decided that the organization of a World Planning Council should not be the first step, but that there first should be a series of regional consultations in which representatives of national churches from large world regions could meet around the conference table with representatives of the North American Panel, and through fellowship, group worship, and full discussion of both national and world problems find the essential elements of a world Free Methodism and locate desirable adjustments to national needs, especially in the fields of church government and administration.

Early it was agreed that the first area conference should engage the Asia fields of India, the Philippines, Formosa, Hong Kong, and Japan; and also the national church of Egypt. As this chapter is being written, plans are nearing completion for the Asia Conference to be held, by invitation of the Japan church, at Osaka in April of 1960. Panels have been formed in the participating countries to study common topics, and to select for consideration by the conference the problems peculiar to each field. Delegates to the conference have been selected by and from the panels. The total delegation from all fields and the carefully restricted American representation will approximate thirty members.

This venture to develop a World Planning Council of Free Methodism has been presented in such detail because of its epochal significance in preparing for the church's further world expansion in its second century. A world-wide call for prayer has been issued that God will direct by His Spirit the Asia Conference. Upon the success of this conference will depend the perfecting of plans now in prospect for two further area consultations, one to engage the fields of Latin America and the other the Africa fields.

· · · · ·

Those who have been associated with the development abroad of world Free Methodism as the church's general missionary secretaries, with their terms of service, are:

C. B. Ebey	1882-1890	W. B. Olmstead	1919-1932
W. W. Kelley	1890-1893	*H. F. Johnson	1932-1942
* J. G. Terrill	1893-1895	*H. H. Winslow	1942-1944
B. Winget	1895-1915	B. S. Lamson	1944-
J. S. MacGeary	1915-1919		

* Service terminated by death.

CHAPTER TWENTY-FOUR

Outreach Through Press and Radio

From the beginning of the Free Methodist Church the printed page has been employed to convey the gospel and to promote the interests of the denomination, but not until more than a quarter-century had passed were means of publication provided under direct denominational control.

Earlier unofficial channels of communication

When the church came into being, B. T. Roberts already had published eight issues of the monthly journal, *The Earnest Christian*, frequently quoted in these pages and described in Chapter Sixteen.[1] Edited and owned by Roberts, this journal was fully committed to the principles upon which the new denomination had been founded, and those principles were ably expounded in its columns, albeit in no narrowly sectarian manner. Reports concerning revivals and the editor's wide travels throughout the country, as well as news of the young church's progress kept readers informed concerning Free Methodism and identified the editor with the movement. All these factors benefited the church but provided it with no official voice.

Likewise the *Northern Independent*[2] served as a medium of denominational news, official announcements, and reports, but its editorial policy, although friendly, was not fully in harmony with Free Methodist principles. Timothy L. Smith avers that Editor Hosmer was an ardent holiness advocate,[3] but examination of scores of issues of the paper has left us in doubt. Even if the editor-in-chief was fully committed to holiness doctrine, some of his staff were not agreed thereon, although B. T. Roberts and S. K. J. Chesbrough served terms as corresponding editors. Moreover, the *Northern Independent*, being primarily an organ of slavery reform, ceased publication shortly after the slaves were freed on January 1, 1863. Although of inesti-

---

1. *Supra*, p. 274 *et seq.*
2. *Supra*, p. 184 *et seq.*
3. Timothy L. Smith, *Revivalism and Social Reform.* Abingdon Press, Nashville; pp. 205, 203.

471

mable service to the cause which produced Free Methodism and to the young church during the earliest years of its existence, the *Northern Independent* could serve in no official sense as the voice of Free Methodism.

Church-related private ventures

We have noted the effort of A. A. Phelps to launch a denominational weekly to begin January 1, 1861, in which he was unsuccessful primarily because the Genesee Conference considered such a venture at that early date too great a financial undertaking for the young church. The reader will recall B. T. Roberts' fear that at that early stage a denominational paper would encourage controversy with the parent church when the need was revival.[4]

But the idea did not die. At the second session of the Genesee Conference a committee was appointed to work with a committee of the Illinois Conference in planning a denominational paper. Nothing resulted from this and other attempts until in the General Conference of 1866 Rev. Levi Wood was commissioned to raise five thousand dollars with which to launch a paper under his editorship. Not succeeding in raising this fund, Levi Wood assumed the project as a private venture. Upon pledge of support voted by the annual conferences of 1867, he published the first number of *The Free Methodist* on January 9, 1868. The project demanded herculean effort and drastic financial sacrifice. Unable to continue, the owner-editor offered the paper to the church at the General Conference of 1870.

The General Conference voted to accept the offer, and elected Rev. Epenetus Owen editor, but he resigned immediately. In this emergency, Mr. Joseph Mackey of New York City, a businessman, offered to assume the indebtedness against the paper and to publish it for the Free Methodist Church. The first issue under his ownership appeared on November 10, 1870. The paper was continued by Mr. Mackey for a year or more when the heavy loss he was sustaining on the paper, probably along with the demands of his own business which had suffered during the experiment, led him to sell.

The purchaser was Rev. Lewis Bailey of the Illinois Conference,

---

4. *Supra*, p. 266 *et seq.*

who removed the publication of the paper from New York City to Aurora, Illinois. After a successful editorship of two years at the cost of great labor, Mr. Bailey broke under the strain and shortly died. His widow sold the paper in 1874 to a partnership of Rev. D. P. Baker and Rev. T. B. Arnold, both ministers of the Illinois Conference. The subscription list then carried 3,200 names.

The new owners moved the publication of the paper to Sycamore, Illinois, where brothers of T. B. Arnold were engaged in the printing business. After years of deficits, the paper very soon was paying its own way. In 1880 the printing plant was removed to Chicago, in which city for more than a half-century *The Free Methodist* would be published.

The church acts[5]

Until the General Conference of 1882 there had been little interest manifested by the church in providing a publication department of its own, but in this Conference the matter received serious attention. It was at about this time that D. P. Baker, the editor-member of the partnership, retired and the paper became the sole property of T. B. Arnold. He was averse to the church entering the publication field at that time, pleaded for postponement of the step, and offered the General Conference the privilege of electing an editor to succeed D. P. Baker. Consideration for this worthy man who had invested so much labor and finance in the paper, and was succeeding where others had failed, no doubt entered into the decision of the General Conference that "it is not advisable to establish a denominational publishing interest at the present time." Accepting the offer that the General Conference elect the editor, that body chose Rev. Joseph Travis, another minister of the Illinois Conference whose members had been, and for many years yet were to be, active in the publishing interests of the denomination. The new editor was entirely satisfactory to the owner of the paper, and no changes were made during the quadrennium.

A vigorous group in the 1886 General Conference was determined

---

5. From this point and through the section, "Relocation at Winona Lake," the writer is indebted at several points to B. H. Gaddis, publisher from 1933 to 1954, for his research in the records and periodicals of the period which he has made available in an unpublished typescript containing a wealth of interesting detail.

that the time had come for the church to establish its own publishing department and take full control of denominational publications. The debate was long extended, and enlisted able men on both sides of the issue. Again, T. B. Arnold was determined if possible to prevent the move. A strong committee of twenty-five brought in the unanimous recommendation that a publishing house be established, and ably presented their reasons. A part of the preamble to the report follows:

> We believe an imperative demand exists for the General Conference to assume control of our denominational publishing interests. There is a tendency among us toward the multiplication of unauthorized individual publishing enterprises, claiming to represent the doctrines and issues of the Free Methodist Church. Various periodicals are already in the field, calling loudly for the patronage and support of our people. These are not agreed in their representations of Free Methodism, either as to its doctrines, discipline or spirit. In some instances we fear insubordination to wholesome order and discipline is directly encouraged. All this tends to produce confusion and to introduce distraction and division among us. The multiplication of hymn and song books by individuals, and their introduction among our congregations in the stead of church hymn books, though not designed to work injury, are nevertheless destructive of that uniformity in public worship which is highly desirable.

Briefly summarized, the report recommended: Immediate steps to establish a church paper; this to be accomplished by purchase of *The Free Methodist* if satisfactory terms could be arranged; the executive committee to be made the publishing committee; this committee to establish a publishing house when practicable and two-thirds of the necessary funds had been provided; pending the acquisition of a publishing house, the publishing of the church paper to be contracted, preference to be given T. B. Arnold if *The Free Methodist* should be purchased from him; the publishing committee to employ a manager; the General Conference to elect an editor, but to authorize the publishing committee to change editors and fill editorial vacancies; a campaign to be launched immediately to raise funds for a publishing house.

The opponents argued that private ownership meant greater efficiency and lower costs; that church ownership tended to centralization of power, restrictions on discussion, and corruption—the last objection prompted, perhaps, by memory of the Methodist Episcopal Book Room troubles of the late sixties. The advocates argued that only a church-controlled agency could insure an editorial policy in line with denominational principles; that church ownership would make for denominational unity; to avoid everything subject to abuse would mean abandoning religion itself, and church-ownership need not lead to abuse of power. The preamble of the publication committee's report was adopted and negotiations with T. B. Arnold for the purchase of *The Free Methodist* were undertaken.

The problem of the church's entering the publishing field and producing its own denominational paper presented one of the most crucial issues the denomination had faced. This issue was complicated further by the related issue B. T. Roberts had brought to a focus by his protesting the resolution adopted by the conference endorsing the Prohibition Party. This, he held, committed the church to a political party rather than to a principle. It will be recalled that he withdrew his offer of valuable printing equipment for the proposed publishing venture because a church-owned paper might become virtually an organ of a political party on the basis of this resolution.[6] Concerning the clash of opinions over the reform issue, the *General Conference Daily* reported the following:

> All the positiveness of Free Methodism's character came out in this discussion. That there were some things said that had better not have been said, is true. But the very heat of the discussion was a struggle to bring all to one view as to the means of warring against a common foe. Here was a mingling of fear and love. Fear that the position of the church on the question would be weakened, and the cause of temperance be injured thereby; of love for God and truth and humanity. The struggle was an exciting one, especially to such as were unable to see the deep moving of conscience and principle in both sides. Each tugged hard to pull the other over until finally the vote was called for, and it was found that the conference was largely in favor of acting with the Prohibition Party in political action against intemperance.[7]

The vote on the recommendations of the publication committee

---
6. *Supra*, p. 401
7. *General Conference Daily*, Oct. 27, 1886; p. 2.

had not yet been taken, and the atmosphere was tense. The sharp division over the reform resolution could defeat the proposal that the church now establish its own paper, and its venturing into further publication fields. In the evening sitting of the same day that Roberts had withdrawn his offer in protest against the resolution, the mediating resolution quoted in Chapter Twenty[8] was adopted. The vote was then taken on the report of the committee on publications—and the same was approved by a vote of 40 to 7.

Then, strange to relate, the General Conference elected B. T. Roberts editor of *The Free Methodist*, and T. B. Arnold was chosen as manager or publishing agent. Such was the confidence of the church in the two men who had so vigorously opposed the will of the majority. The *General Conference Daily* commented, "All felt that there had been an interposition of the divine mind in bringing all to a remarkable unanimity of sentiment in regard to the great matters of denominational interest." [9]

The incorporation of "The Free Methodist Publishing House" was effected before the year 1886 had expired.

Problems, personal and official

The office of denominational editor was costly to B. T. Roberts, both in finance and in energy. The nominal stipend he was allowed as editor was consumed in the rent he must pay in the large city when he had a comfortable home of his own in North Chili. According to Bishop Hogue, another financial loss to Roberts was the sharp decline in subscriptions to Roberts' personally owned monthly journal, *The Earnest Christian*, because now its readers could peruse Roberts' pungent editorials every week in *The Free Methodist*, the subscriptions to which increased under Roberts' editorship. The added load of editing *The Free Methodist*, Hogue believed, shortened Roberts' life.[10]

The church was slow in meeting its obligation to Mr. Arnold on its contract to purchase *The Free Methodist*, but he was patient and in time the account was settled. The debt had been a load which

---

8. *Supra*, p. 402.
9. *General Conference Daily*, Oct. 27, 1886; p. 2.
10. W. T. Hogue, *History of the Free Methodist Church*. Free Meth. Pub. House, Winona Lake, Indiana; v. 2, 245.

burdened Roberts who used the columns of the paper to urge the church to lift it. He and Arnold each contributed five hundred dollars.

There were annoying criticisms through the church of the step the General Conference had taken in establishing a publishing business and taking over *The Free Methodist*. With these criticisms the editor dealt frankly and fearlessly. One critic, who had objected that church ownership was a dangerous step toward centralization of power that would curb freedom, Roberts answered by publishing a statement concerning the critic's own unsuccessful venture in conducting a school in Kansas for liberated slaves according to his own ideas of the freedom necessary to succeed in the undertaking. "He wanted control," said Roberts, and continued, "It was given him. He selected his own teachers. The columns of the paper were opened to his appeals. Our people contributed money for his support. The mission died on his hands." [11]

The reaction against church ownership of the paper must have been pronounced to call forth such editorial severity, or to explain the editor's appeal to the conferences to vote their support of General Conference action in one matter and their disapproval in another. He said, "The measure is not of my devising. I spoke and voted against it. But I am now fully convinced that it is the best thing that could have been done. If the annual conferences are of this mind, and will take hold heartily to carry the measure through, I am willing to toil on as I am doing. If they are indifferent or hostile, it will be my duty to resign the editorial chair. Let us have a frank expression." The conferences voted with one exception, and all voting supported the General Conference decision that the church enter the publishing business and take the paper from private management.

More perplexing than his urging conferences to vote support of the action of General Conference, was Roberts' further request that the conferences vote approval of locating the publishing house in a suburb of Chicago where real estate cost less, whereas General Conference had specified its location in the city itself. His call for conference votes in earlier cases was irregular, of course, and must be considered the exercise of editorial liberty rather than episcopal authority.

---
11. *The Free Methodist*, v. 19, Nov. 24, 1886; p. 8.

Sunday-school literature

In 1888 T. B. Arnold resigned as publishing agent, and S. K. J. Chesbrough was the unanimous choice of the executive committee to fill the vacancy. The recently established Chicago Industrial Home for Children and his growing business in publishing Sunday-school literature now demanded Mr. Arnold's full time and attention.

But, as he had pioneered successfully a denominational paper for many years, only to turn it over to the church in the end—reluctantly, it is true, but with nobility of spirit—so Arnold was to pass through the same ordeal again, this time with reference to his ministry to the denomination in the area of Sunday-school literature. The new publishing agent had a vision broader than a denominational publishing house devoted merely to the publication of a weekly church paper. There was a growing sentiment in the church also for expansion into the Sunday-school field.

The problem came before the 1890 General Conference in the report of the committee on publications which endorsed the church's publication of its own Sunday-school literature. Again there was animated debate, with T. B. Arnold again urging that the time was not ripe for the venture, that his publishing concern could serve the church in this field better than the church could do in providing its own literature. Mr. Chesbrough protested, "I ask, in the name of common sense, do we want a publishing house with all of the machinery—an editor, an assistant editor, a publishing agent, just simply to publish one paper? If we are going to have a publishing house we ought to do all our publishing."

Very largely in deference to Mr. Arnold, it would seem, the conference decided that the "time had not yet come for the publication of our Sunday-school literature." Prior to final adjournment, however, the executive committee was authorized to proceed to arrange for the church's publication of Sunday-school literature should such a step become necessary.

Again in the General Conference of 1894 the subject of the church's publication of Sunday-school literature was earnestly debated. Negotiations were begun with T. B. Arnold, but he was reluctant to release the Free Methodist market. He made a proposition which was rejected. Decision in the matter was left with the executive committee and a sub-committee. In October, 1896, action was taken to proceed. Four monthly story papers were purchased from Arnold, and their titles were changed to the following: *Our Young Folks; Youth's Temperance Evangel; Rose of Sharon; Lily of the Valley*. These titles will stir pleasant childhood memories of quiet Sunday afternoons in the minds of members of the present older generation! In 1912 these four monthly papers were combined into a weekly which still is published as *Light and Life Evangel*.

A few months after acquiring these story papers, the church purchased Arnold's lesson helps, quarterlies, and like Sunday-school items. Continuing in the publishing business to supply other markets, T. B. Arnold now had relinquished the Free Methodist market entirely to the Free Methodist Publishing House. In 1902 the church purchased all rights to *Arnold's Practical Commentary*. This still is a leading publication in its field, now in its sixty-sixth year.

The church owes a debt of gratitude to T. B. Arnold for his courageous pioneering in religious publications, by which he prepared the way for the Free Methodist Church to enter a field which has played an important role in the church's subsequent history.

The first editor of Sunday-school publications was Rev. W. B. Olmstead, elected in 1898 and serving until 1907 when he accepted a second election, the full-time office of general Sunday-school secretary. Since 1931 the office of editor of Sunday-school literature has been ably filled by his son, Dr. B. L. Olmstead.

Publishing House and Church Headquarters

During the years 1886 to 1894 the publishing interests of the church occupied rented quarters on Franklin Street, Chicago. These soon became inadequate for the growing business, and the 1894 General Conference authorized the securing of a publishing house and the purchase for that purpose of the First Free Methodist Church at 14-16 May Street, Chicago. This was a substantial and fairly new brick structure which, after purchase, was remodeled for publishing and office purposes. An audience room had been reserved by the church for its own use, which was released for a consideration near the close of the occupancy of this site by the Publishing House.

With the further growth of the business there were those who desired a new building, to be constructed specifically for publishing purposes. The question came before the 1903 General Conference. Now we find the aging S. K. J. Chesbrough on the conservative side, insisting that the release of the First Church audience room would make the May Street quarters adequate. "Do not drive me out of the old Publishing House," he begged. "Let me live there as long as I live and, when I am dead and gone, you can go where you see fit—but let me occupy the old home and keep my old stool."

No action was taken by the General Conference of 1903, but that fall, in the first session of the executive committee, a sub-committee was appointed to explore the possibilities of enlargement at the May Street location or of purchasing and building on a new site. A location on Ogden Avenue was actually purchased and plans for a building were prepared, but construction was delayed. In part, the delay was due to reluctance to change location without a specific directive from General Conference.

When General Conference next met in 1907, it ordered that no change might be made in the location of the Publishing House without a three-fourths vote of the executive committee. The same General Conference ordered the construction of a new publishing house in the city of Chicago, and left large powers with the executive committee to carry through the project.

In the fall, when the executive committee would proceed with plans to build on the Ogden Avenue site, already purchased, it met with strong protest from the publishing staff, and this location finally was abandoned. It was then decided to purchase and build at the corner of Washington Boulevard and May Street. A substantial structure was erected, three stories and a basement, adequate at the time to house both publishing interests and general church headquarters. During the building, one of the bishops declared his belief that the structure would serve the church's needs for fifty years, and another bishop gave assurance that it would be adequate for generations to come. The building was completed in 1909 and dedicated at the time of the October board meetings. As its first half-century drew to a close, Free Methodism had reason to rejoice that its general publishing and administrative interests were established at the center of the nation in a representative building, and 1132-34 Washington

Boulevard became a symbol of the church's growing maturity.

But the building was to be outgrown by the church's bustling business within a quarter-century. Publishing needs increased along with other activities of the general church, the various departments of which required space. The building had not been equipped for extensive press operations and it was necessary to send out to commercial presses in the city much of the product of the composing room. There also were labor and other cost factors in a large city that led in time to investigation of possibilities of locating elsewhere.

Relocation at Winona Lake

In 1933, after carefully considering other possible locations, the board of directors of the Free Methodist Publishing House settled upon the purchase of a substantial building originally constructed for college purposes, set in an expansive campus acreage in the village of Winona Lake, Indiana.

The building readily lent itself to remodeling for publishing purposes. New equipment was installed in the mechanical department to make it a complete printing establishment. In February, 1935, the staff took possession of the new and spacious plant, with every department in operation. With the renovation of the intrinsically beautiful building accomplished, and with the landscaping of the campus that spring, the institution became a credit to the denomination whose publishing and general administrative interests it focused. This epochal transfer occurred early in the publishing administration of Mr. B. H. Gaddis, who was to direct the new development until 1954.

The church's publishing enterprise

The Free Methodist Publishing House in 1960 is operated through eleven departments which employ personnel exceeding eighty in number. The total volume of publishing business exceeds three-fourths of a million dollars annually. Its publications regularly go to fifteen countries scattered over every continent of the world.

Major items of printing equipment include four linotypes, a fully furnished composing room, two large letterpresses, five medium presses, a large offset press and complete auxiliary equipment, a flat cutter, four folders, a modern book bindery, and mailing machines.

The replacement cost of the plant's equipment exceeds a quarter-million dollars.

When the plant was opened in 1935, it provided 11,200 square feet of operating space without the offices. Additions to the building since 1935 have increased this space to 25,000 square feet, plus a connecting warehouse of 5,400 square feet. As this chapter is being written, plans are under way for the Publishing House to vacate 8,400 square feet of office space (not included in the above plant figures) by removal to a new office structure soon to be erected. The two office floors of the original building will then be given over entirely to the departmental offices of the General Church. This will permit departments previously housed elsewhere to be brought together in a General Church Headquarters. The spacious ground-floor of the original building will continue to house the printing plant, which will be connected with the new office building of the Publishing House by means of an enclosed corridor. For the first time in its history of a century, the Free Methodist Church will have a General Church Headquarters distinct from its Publishing House.

The printing plant produces the following periodical literature with circulation as indicated:

1. *Sunday-school literature*:
Four story papers	121,000
Uniform lesson quarterlies	96,600
Uniform lesson leaflets	24,300
Graded lesson quarterlies	83,750
2. General church and departmental periodicals:
The Free Methodist (weekly)	30,000
Youth in Action (monthly)	11,000
Missionary Tidings (monthly)	25,000
Sunday School Journal (monthly)	6,000
Transmitter (monthly)	17,000

The three periodicals last named are printed in the plant, but are published by the departments sponsoring them.

3. Annual and quadrennial publications:
Yearbook of the Free Methodist Church of N. A.	5,500
Arnold's Commentary on the International Sunday School Lessons, Uniform Series	15,500
Doctrines and Discipline of the Free Methodist Church of N. A.	3,879

4. Periodicals printed for outside agencies:
   Call to Prayer (monthly) 24,000
   Brethren Herald (weekly) 11,000

In addition to periodicals, books in increasing number are coming from the Free Methodist Publishing House, most of them under the trade name, Light and Life Press. At this writing, eleven books are in process or have been accepted for publication.

Worthy of note is the new Aldersgate Biblical Series, a cooperative venture of denominations in the Wesleyan doctrinal tradition. This series is graded for adult classes in the Sunday school. Every book in the Bible is covered in forty units, twenty from the Old Testament and twenty from the New Testament. A class covering a unit per quarter may thus complete a thorough study of the entire Bible in ten years. The series is being published by Light and Life Press.

The church's outstanding publication is *The Free Methodist*. We noted earlier in this chapter that this magazine began as a private venture in 1868, and after a hazardous history, with several changes in ownership, was taken over by the church in 1886. For the size of its denominational constituency, the circulation through many years has been large and the paper enjoys a wide reading beyond the church's membership. The present editor, Dr. James F. Gregory, states briefly as follows the editorial policy of the paper:

> It is the purpose of *The Free Methodist* to inform its readers doctrinally, to shed light on Christian experience, to enliven the truth of the Scriptures, to unify the church in a program of evangelism through every department, to act as an organ of promotion, and to cover the news of the church.
>
> Special attention is given to the centrality of the Bible as God's book. The importance of Christianity in family life is a major concern. Considerable attention is given to religious news that the denomination may be aware of its responsibility in the church universal.

In 1961 the Free Methodist Publishing House will celebrate the seventy-fifth anniversary of its founding. In little more than two generations the church has developed its publication ministry to a high level of communicative effectiveness, especially in nurturing the Christian life of the church's membership. The present challenges the church to extend its evangelistic outreach by means of the printed page, for reasons suggested in the following section.

The ministry of Christian publishing

Transmitted by voice or printed symbol, words are man's principal means of communication. Through the medium either of sound-waves or light-rays, words illuminate the mind, stir the heart, challenge the will. But sooner or later what has been heard or seen fades from memory, and because the mind's power of retention does not permanently fix the meanings conveyed by vocal or visual symbols, the message finally may pass beyond recall. At this point, history discloses that printed symbols have the advantage, for only those tribes and nations that have a written language rise above a primitive status of civilization. Whereas the stimulus of the spoken word ends with the speaking, the visual stimulus of the printed word abides, and may be renewed at will so long as one has access to the printed page which provided the original stimulus. The messenger may be dead, but he "yet speaketh." The printed page retains its primacy among the means of public communication, notwithstanding such modern inventions as radio and television.

The printed page has far-reaching significance for the extension of the gospel, especially in this era of growing literacy among formerly primitive peoples and of rising nationalism among them which tends to close the door to Christian missions. The printed page finds its way where preacher and missionary are forbidden, and will repeat its message again and again. The printed page provides the Christian enterprise its most effective means of keeping pace with the explosive population growth of the non-Christian world.

But the printed page offers these advantages as well to pagan religions and materialistic ideologies, and these are using this means as never before. If Christians fail to meet the challenge of the world's growing literacy by publishing afar the word of truth, the working of Satan will be the more effective because of our negligence. Christian publishing is the ministry of the printed word by which the church seeks to carry out the Lord's commission to extend the gospel witness to the ends of the earth.

But Christian publishing is more than processing periodicals, books, and promotional pamphlets of religious content from the raw materials of paper, ink, and "copy." A commercial plant will handle such religious jobs as will pay according to the ledger, and it is interested only in what will pay such profits. But as a preacher who is faithful to his calling will carry the message to those who cannot pay him in earthly coin, living meantime on the generosity of others who do support him, so denominational publishing renders its ministry in areas that involve deficit operations to produce the profits for which it exists. Christian publishing, especially if it is carried on by a denomination, does not eliminate financially unprofitable departments merely because "they don't pay." If the service is essential to the fulfillment of a need for which the denomination is responsible, profits from other publishing areas must replace the loss in the absence of subsidy or endowment. The end of Christian publishing is a ministry of the printed word no less commanding than the preacher's ministry of the spoken word.

The present publisher, Dr. Lloyd H. Knox, has made this comment on denominational publishing, referring especially to the favorable position of the Free Methodist Church in this field of endeavor:

> Familiarity with the contemporary situation in publishing among the denominations strengthens the conviction that a strong denominational publishing program is imperative in perpetuating Free Methodist distinctives and our essential message, and in promoting a wholesome denominational unity. Many publishers and denominational leaders have confided their distress and alarm at their own lack of a strong, centralized program of communication through printing. Especially is this true in the area of growing curriculum needs. Our friends congratulate our denomination for having been wiser. Considering our membership, the church's publishing program at its present level is by comparison outstanding, and the horizon of a new century presents almost limitless vistas.

By all means save some

We turn now to consider another medium of extending the gospel witness through words. These are times of rapid change when methods of past generations need to be amplified and revised to bring the never-changing message of the gospel into effective contact with the multitudes of a new generation.

Modes of transportation have changed, and thereby the spread of the gospel has been profoundly affected. Early pioneer preachers used the means at their command to reach those who needed their ministry. They trudged many a weary mile through winter storm and summer sun to search out their lost sheep. Horse and saddle on wilderness trails took them and their gospel to the settler's frontier cabin. Later, horse and cart or sled followed primitive logging roads to one-room schoolhouses in a clearing, that preachers might tell the news to eager listeners or rowdy disturbers of the meeting. Years passed, and the "horseless buggy" brought them—if providence rode with them—over mud-rutted and sand-drifted wagon-roads to the village church or crossroads chapel with the Word of God. And now, preachers reach their most distant circuit points in modern automobiles that clock sixty miles an hour or more, depending upon the vagaries of conscience and local speed laws. More progressive parsons take to the air and, after meeting the home congregation in the morning, appear that evening as guest-speaker hundreds of miles away. Our most modern transportation is used to the end that, by all means, some may be saved.

Social patterns also have changed. Fifty or sixty years ago the rural population was the dominant social force in American life. Since many rural communities were isolated from urban culture with its commercialized amusements, and the means of communication and transportation were limited, announcement of a preaching service in village chapel or country schoolhouse drew a crowd. Today it is different. Popular magazines, spicy fiction, news-magazines and newspapers flood even secluded communities. Few areas are too remote to be reached by television, and radio knows no bounds. The movie is within a fifteen-minute drive of nearly the entire population, and organized sports draw immense throngs from extensive interstate areas. Smaller but more numerous groups gather at the dance-spot and roadside tavern at country crossroads or in city outskirts. Crowds which two generations ago were drawn to religious services by social hunger now sate that hunger in social contacts far removed in place and kind from religious influences.

Because of this change in America's social pattern, evangelism seeks new channels to supplement but not supplant the traditional approach of mass revivalism. Of the new channels, radio is the most widely used and the most effective. Modern communication has transcended modern transportation, and without leaving his study or pulpit, the preacher may project his voice with the gospel message to the remote corners of the world. Those who never go to church hear him. Those who would go but are confined to sickbeds hear him. Those who answer the call of duty may hear while traveling on highway, train or plane. Radio carries the voice of the man of God with the message of the Son of God into nooks and crannies to charge the careless, rebuke the rebellious, instruct the ignorant, and lead the penitent to peace.

The Light and Life Hour

The General Conference of 1943 was challenged by the new developments in communications and took action providing a standing committee on radio. In consequence, the first broadcast seeking national coverage to be launched by official sponsorship of an entire denomination went on the air October 1, 1944. Dr. LeRoy M. Lowell was the speaker and director of music of the program which originated in the Ferndale Free Methodist Church of the Detroit area. Following the growing practice of attaching the phrase "Light and Life" to projects of the church, this radio program was named the Light and Life Hour.

Following the resignation of Dr. Lowell in 1945, Dr. Myron F. Boyd, then pastor of Seattle First Church, was appointed director and speaker, and Dr. Lawrence Schoenhals, the director of music. For a time the program originated in Seattle, and after the removal of the offices and recording studios to the church's Winona Lake headquarters, music production has continued on the campus of Seattle Pacific College. Boyd and Schoenhals are still with the program.

The quality of the program, both message and music, is measured by the awards of the trophy contest sponsored by the National Religious Broadcasters on the basis of all-around quality of religious programs submitted for competition. The first year of the contest, 1948, the Light and Life Hour tied for first place. Thereafter for four successive years, it won the trophy which became its permanent possession in 1952, when the contest was discontinued.

Foreign broadcasting has been stimulated by the director's tours abroad from time to time. The last tour, in 1959, took him into

Russia where the Light and Life program has been received with deep appreciation by evangelicals. The message was beamed to Russia in the Russian language in 1958, and a Latvian program was begun in 1959. Plans are under way and station time has been contracted for broadcasting to Europe in Spanish, French, and German.

From small beginnings, measured by the first annual budget of $60,000 in 1944-45, the Light and Life Hour has expanded its program until the budget for 1959-60 calls for $233,000.00 to support 160 weekly broadcasts over 135 stations. Free Methodism's outreach through radio has been extended far.

" . . . Hearken, ye people, from far . . ."

As was not possible when Isaiah thundered these words twenty-seven centuries ago, those "from far" now hear the good news of salvation as those who have the message give it wings on radio. Who can doubt, had God delayed the revelation of Himself in Christ to our day, that radio would be a chosen medium of Christ's ministry? Nor can we believe that the Apostle Paul, master strategist of the church, would neglect the use of radio were he now director of world evangelism.

We are amazed to read of Wesley's ability to reach the ears of thousands, his voice unaided by modern technology. Were he alive today Wesley would not travel by stagecoach nor astride a horse—he would fly. Nor would he limit the range of his voice to the thousands in his vast congregations; by radio he would address millions in many nations. How different might have been the history of Methodism could Roberts, a century after Wesley, have used radio to stir to action the faithful throughout the church of his day! That he would have used it were it then available, those familiar with his energetic and aggressive outreach will agree.

That which was unknown in the days of Isaiah, of Jesus and of Paul, of Wesley and of Roberts, is a commonplace today, and to keep faith with them the church must not neglect its means of reaching "people, from far."

* * * * *

From its establishment in 1886 the Free Methodist Publishing House has been directed by the following Publishers:

T. B. Arnold	1886-1888	N. W. Fink	1926-1933
S. K. J. Chesbrough	1888-1907	B. H. Gaddis	1933-1954
* W. B. Rose	1907-1926	L. H. Knox	1954-

The editors of *The Free Methodist*, with terms of service, have been:

Under private ownership—

Levi Wood	1868-1870	D. P. Baker	1874-1882
Joseph Mackey	1870-1871	Joseph Travis	1882-1886
* Lewis Bailey	1871-1873		

Under church ownership—

B. T. Roberts	1886-1890	G. W. Griffith	1923-1927
B. R. Jones	1890-1894	J. T. Logan	1927-1931
W. T. Hogue	1894-1903	C. L. Howland	1931-1955
C. B. Ebey	1903-1907	J. F. Gregory	1955-
J. T. Logan	1907-1923		

The Directors of the Light and Life Hour, with terms of service, have been:

L. M. Lowell	1944-1945	M. F. Boyd	1945-

* Service in office terminated by death.

CHAPTER TWENTY-FIVE

The Christian Nurture of Childhood

Under the caption "The Church as a Channel," Chapter Twenty-one sketched the structure of the Free Methodist Church as providing a channel for the transmission of the gospel witness, and then the three succeeding chapters proceeded to describe the church's outreach through home evangelism, world missions, and such means of communication as the printed page and radio. The present chapter and the following two are devoted to Christian nurture as the means of conveying the witness to the church's children and youth, and confirming that witness in their minds and hearts.

What is education?
Man is a learner, which means that he is changed by experience; that what happens to him and how he reacts thereto make a difference in the total complex of traits we call Willie Brown. In its broadest sense, human education is simply the changing of human nature through experience. Every school, existing anywhere, giving whatever level of instruction, and seeking to serve whatever cultural or vocational end, endeavors to establish and improve in its pupils certain traits considered desirable or necessary by the agency maintaining the school, and to eliminate or correct other traits the agency disapproves. Accordingly, the education of the school is the purposeful control of the learner's experience to the end that certain intended changes in his nature shall take place. Such directed learning is called *formal education*.

But not all learning occurs under the direction of the school. Education is as broad as life and its processes cannot be restricted to

---

1. Portions of this and following sections, through "Education and evangelism," reflect the thought and expression of Chapter Four and of section vi of Chapter Eleven of the book of Frank E. Gaebelein, *Christian Education in a Democracy*, published by Oxford University Press, New York; 1951. The similarities arise from the fact that the present writer collaborated in the preparation of these sections, as explained by Dr. Gaebelein in the Foreword. The present writer has permission of publisher and author to draw upon the material he contributed. Portions directly quoted are properly indicated.

a child's hours in the schoolroom. The undirected, give-and-take experiences of the street, the playground, and the home change or educate the child no less truly than do those experiences which are directed by the school. The undirected, incidental and even accidental learning of everyday living is called *informal education*.

It will be granted readily that both formal and informal education are important in shaping the character of the developing child. But there is a third type of education described by the present writer elsewhere as follows:

> Experiences which to the learner [in this third type of education] seem casual and uncontrolled are in reality planned by the agent of some organization or the apostle of some ideology. Quite unaware, the learner is gradually changed and imperceptibly conditioned to standards and practices toward which he was formerly indifferent, if not downright antagonistic. The subtle manipulation of the individual's experience without his awareness of such control is *propaganda*. Modern developments like the press, the motion picture, radio, and television may be used for propaganda. In fact, so educationally effective have these agencies become that they now challenge the long established primacy of home, church, and school as character-forming influences.[2]

Propaganda is a principal means of brain-washing and thought-control, with a potency that may spread throughout an entire nation, or around the world if the means of communication can be utilized, to change customs, basic attitudes, political principles, and even moral standards and religious convictions. Propaganda provides anti-Christian forces with their most effective weapon against the Christian witness—a weapon more dangerous than martyrdom. Perhaps never since the Graeco-Roman era, when the Apostle Paul uttered his warning against conforming to the world, has the threat to the Christian witness been so great.

Education as adjustment

The education of the schools for decades past has sought as its primary goal so to change human nature as to adjust the learner to the world of his physical and social environment. Modern education's underlying philosophy is a naturalism that conceives human

---

2. F. E. Gaebelein, *Christian Education in a Democracy*. Oxford University Press, New York; p. 69.

nature to be essentially good, and maintains that by the processes of education it will unfold into sweetness and light. Accordingly, man needs no Saviour and the universe needs no Sovereign—other than man himself! Man belongs to the temporal order and can ignore the eternal as unreal.

Guided by this false doctrine of human nature's innate goodness, the modern educator focalizes the child's immediate interests to set the goal of life in the direction of selfish desire rather than according to moral principle. Such an education of adaptation to the contemporary is satisfied to release the child's inner tension between duty and desire, not by moral conquest of desire, but by surrender to its urge. The outcome is a sophisticated paganism in some, a gross sensualism in others. We read the resulting record daily in the headlines of the morning paper and periodically in the mounting statistics of crime and delinquency released in bulletins of the Federal Bureau of Investigation. And everywhere are the evidences of sin's growing prevalence and of society's growing indifference to standards of righteous living. What once was called "soft pedagogy" has combined with insidious propaganda to corrode and weaken character, and to blur and all but obliterate the clearly etched patterns of established morality.

Education as adjustment and adaptation to the world-as-it-is has failed. The contemporary provides an inadequate basis for a sound education. After all, he is best adjusted to the age who has firm footing on the "Rock of Ages." We turn from naturalism and humanism to seek in Revelation a valid philosophy by which to guide the educational process.

Christian education as transformation

By the mind and pen of the Apostle Paul, God has declared that adjustment to the age is not life's great end, but that this end is rather the progressive realization of the divine will. Through Saint Paul, God also has declared that this end must be reached by way of a transformation of the nature and a complete renewal of the mind. Weymouth's version of Romans 12:2 yields an illuminating statement of the Christian basis of education. His rendering of the passage reads, "And do not conform to the present age, but be transformed [*in nature*, Moffatt inserts] by the renewal of your minds, so that you may learn by experience what God's will is, namely all that is good and acceptable to Him and perfect." [3]

Paul here has touched the crucial center of the problem of education. He has dealt, at least tacitly, with such up-to-date educational concepts as human nature, its adjustment, learning through experience, and ends. He has anticipated modern educational thought in his conceiving that education is not a static something, given or added to the learner, but that it is the learner's living and growing experience. But Paul's statement differs from the position of the moderns in its insistence that a transformation of human nature from sinfulness to righteousness is a necessity, and in its maintaining that from this point of transformation there is to follow a growth in Christian character according to a divine pattern. Paul's words bring to the reader sharp awareness of the antithesis of education as adjustment of the natural man to an evil world, and adjustment of the transformed man to the will of God.

Christian education and conflict

The section of Chapter Nineteen on "Character through conflict" anticipated in measure the present section, and what was there recorded need not here be repeated in detail. That earlier treatment of discipline, and the discussion of education in the opening sections of the present chapter, make clear that Christian education places strenuous demands upon human nature by challenging it to noble endeavor within the pattern of Christian righteousness. Far from seeking to conform youth to this world, Christian education precipitates in youth that crisis which comes with the discovery that a sinful self is in rebellion against a righteous God. But Christian education does not leave youth at this point of crisis, nor does it seek to relax the tension of conflict between evil desire and the Christian ideal by lowering the ideal in the pagan fashion of the age. It seeks rather the transformation of desire to accord with the ideal, and a surrender to the dominion of righteousness that brings peace with God and oneself.

Dr. Norborg, a Christian psychologist of standing, has said that a religious experience "without sin-experience, sin-feeling, sin-despair,

---

3. Richard Francis Weymouth, *The New Testament in Modern Speech*. Harper and Bros., New York; p. 375.

and sin-deliverance would not be Christian." [4] And yet how nervous at this point the Christian church has become, and how carefully does it attempt to ward off from youth the grip of conviction for sin! Youth counselors hasten to allay youths' tensions between the world and Christian ideals with distracting palliatives of service programs and with specious rationalizations of sin itself. But the Christian educator who grasps the essential facts of Christian life and experience knows that it is better that youth continue to old age the victim of inner turmoil than pay the price of a strangled conscience for a peace that is the sleep of death. Indeed, "Earth knows no tragedy like the death of the soul's ideal."

But the Christian educator also knows that youth may reach something better than inner turmoil and constant struggle ending in repeated failure; he knows that youth may come into a relationship to God through Christ which lifts life to the plane of victory. This adjustment to the will of God is the surest guarantee, both of right relationships in society and of progressive adjustment to self; of a conscience void of offense and of a peace that passeth understanding.

We have sought to make clear that Christian education does not seek to shape character to the present evil world, but to transform it to the moral image of God; and that this entails conflict because of the necessity of choice, especially of moral choice. Complete adjustment to the environment with absence of conflict, far from being a desirable end of education or goal of life, means either uninhibited impulsive behavior "with all the brakes off," or mental stagnation. A hint of what may happen through adjustment without conflict, as the goal of existence, appeared in a recent magazine article [5] concerning Sweden as a welfare state where financial problems have all but disappeared for the individual, and personal and family problems in large part have been taken over by society. The article raises the question if this paradise has not developed its own problems out of the very fact that the State has assumed such full responsibility for the material well-being of its citizens that they now are unprepared to cope with unusual vicissitudes of existence from which the State

---

4. Sv. Norborg, *Varieties of Christian Experience*. Augsburg Publishing House, Minneapolis; p. 137.
5. Peter Wyden, "Sweden: Paradise with Problems," in *Saturday Evening Post*; Dec. 19, 1959.

cannot shield them. Crime and delinquency are rising rapidly, and some ascribe suicides to the smooth adjustment of life that breaks down in emergencies with people who have never been trained to meet them. The author of the article cites a prominent Swedish psychiatrist as holding the view that the State's system of attempting to provide security has deprived the people of making decisions for themselves.

A mechanistic psychology will emphasize adjustment and adaptation as education's proper end, but a psychology that reckons with the spiritual nature of man sees conflict as a consequence of man's power of choice and as a necessity to moral, intellectual, and spiritual growth. The end of Christian education is not the resolution of conflict by adjusting the learner to things as they are, but is the development of Christian character which involves conflict between enduring Christian ideals and the fluid fashions of the world.

Education and evangelism

Central in the Bible's portrait of human nature is its exceeding sinfulness apart from divine grace. We have defined education as the changing of human nature through experience, which is a process on the human level. It is impossible for sin-corrupted human nature to attain to righteousness by its own inherent power—hence the incisive demand Jesus addressed to the learned and cultured Nicodemus, "Ye must be born again."

But if education is the changing of human nature through experience, what is the transformation of human nature mentioned by Paul in Romans 12:2, and what did Jesus mean by being "born again"? Both meant the changing of human nature by the grace and power of God. The renewed mind and transformed nature are preliminary to learning by experience what is the will of God. Another term for this change is regeneration. And this is the goal of evangelism, to see men's natures transformed from sin to righteousness by the touch of God. Although evangelism works on a divine level, let one never forget that in this working of divine power God employs human means.

Christian education also is the human means by which God works divine purposes. The Christian teacher directs the child's experiences to readiness for the new birth, leads him onward from that event through Christian nurture to full surrender to the claims of Christian holiness, and thereafter assists him "to learn by experience what God's will is, namely all that is good and acceptable to Him and perfect." Such nurturing of childhood and youth—and of adults as well, may rightly be called "educational evangelism."

In *Christian Education in a Democracy* we have offered the following statement of Christian education, placing the transformation wrought through evangelism at the center:

> From the evangelical point of view, religious education is (a) the transmission by the Christian Church or the Christian community of the Judaeo-Christian heritage, including the Bible as the record of God's will and His plan for man's redemption centering in the sacrificial gift of Jesus Christ; (b) the application of the specific teachings of the Bible to life and conduct, including the individual's relationships in society; (c) training in the approach to God through Christian worship; (d) directing the student to that transforming experience which comes only from personal contact by faith with Christ as Lord and Saviour; and (e) leading the student on in continuing nurture to increasing stature in Christian character.[6]

It thus becomes clear that education and evangelism are both essential in the Christian enterprise. When their respective roles and their close relationship in this enterprise are understood, any assumed antagonism of "either-or" yields to a synthesis of "both-and." Again in the source just quoted, we have attempted to express their relationship as follows: "The position of evangelism is central and crucial; of education, contextual and vital. It is Education▶ Evangelism▶ Education."[7] Another has phrased the appropriate union of education and evangelism in these words:

> Evangelism without education leads to superstition and fanaticism. Education without the warmth of spiritual appeal passes into cold formalism and skepticism. The two are united in the thought of God. They must be kept together in the work of men. To neglect either is to limit the usefulness and imperil the life of the church.[8]

---

6. F. E. Gaebelein, *Christian Education in a Democracy*. Oxford University Press, New York; p. 71 *et seq.*
7. *Ibid.*, p. 273.
8. Henry H. Sweets, Compiler, *Source Book on Christian Education*. Executive Committee on Christian Education, Presbyterian Church in the U. S., Louisville; p. 77.

Christian nurture in early Free Methodism

As noted in Chapter Twenty-two, Free Methodism's early emphasis was strongly evangelistic, because of which the movement rapidly spread across the continent. But with this strong evangelistic urge there was inadequate concern for Christian nurture. In the beginning the church recruited its members principally by evangelizing adults and receiving into fellowship believers who were dissatisfied with the formalism and spiritual decline of their former churches. It is unfortunate, although understandable, that the nurture of childhood and youth occupied only the margins of official church concern in those early days of itinerant evangelism.

Attention to Christian nurture in early Free Methodism was directed to institutions of general education, with training the ministry of the young church at least an implicit concern. The institutions that were established enrolled young people of Free Methodist families whose Christian nurture, in some instances, had been neglected by home and local church. Some of these were evangelized in the schools; others withstood the nurturing and evangelizing influences of the schools and were lost to the church. Consideration will later be given to the development of these institutions, most of which in time became junior or senior colleges.

Another direction of the church's early concern for Christian nurture was the Sunday school in which the children of Free Methodist families received a measure of Christian instruction. Direct results in childhood conversions were meager, perhaps due to the generally assumed hiatus between education and evangelism, in consequence of which conversions in a "school" were neither sought nor expected.

Evangelistic results with children seem to have been greater in the "children's meetings" of the district camp meeting which were directly evangelistic in purpose and method. But the fruitage too often was lost soon after a camp meeting revival through the neglect of Christian nurture of youthful converts by home and local church. The loss of generations of youth through failure to cultivate the beginnings of Christian life and faith is a dark page in Free Methodism's history.

Following are summaries of general conference actions and resolutions of the church's first half-century:

1878. As early as 1878 the importance of the Sunday school was highlighted when the General Conference gave over an afternoon to a Sunday-school conference which all delegates were requested to attend. The conference considered these questions: "1st. How can we make our Sunday schools more Free Methodistic? 2nd. How can we make them more attractive to children? 3rd. What can be done to develop greater efficiency in our Sunday-school teachers?"

The committee on Sunday schools of this General Conference recommended that preachers, at the time of the examination of their character by the annual Conference, be required to report the extent of their labors in the Sunday school; that general superintendents include attendance upon and assistance in Sunday-school conventions as a part of their work; that teachers' meetings be held weekly in all societies wherever practicable; that Sunday-school conventions be held in connection with one or more district meetings each year in all the conferences. These recommendations were approved.

The report of this committee carried this comment: "The labors and success of Mr. Moody have demonstrated what power and efficiency may be attained by one denied the knowledge of a liberal education, but who will make a good use of the Word of God."

The problem of conserving to the church its youth was recognized at this early date, the same report again emphasizing the importance of the Word, saying:

"It is a lamentable fact that many children of Free Methodist parents are being lost to the church. Even when converted many of them go to other denominations for their church homes. Is not the reason of this found in the lack of careful instruction in the Word of God? If our principles are unscriptural, let us throw them away; but if they are not, let us teach them to the children."

1890. Further concern for the Word as the basis of Free Methodist principles was manifested in 1890 when the General Conference appointed the general superintendents to prepare a catechism which should incorporate Scripture texts supporting the fundamental doctrines of the church. This catechism was intended for use in Sunday schools, the church's educational institutions, and the home circle.

1894. The Sunday-school committee of the General Conference of 1894 recommended that district elders arrange the quarterly meetings so as not to interfere with the Sunday-school hour, or schedule a children's meeting in place thereof. This General Conference provided also that a general Sunday-school secretary be elected as soon as possible, this officer to devote his entire time to the promotion of Sunday-school interests throughout the denomination. But not for nine years, in 1903, was the first full-time Sunday-school secretary to be elected.

This Conference faced frankly some of the weaknesses that impeded the progress of the church. The committee on the state of the work made these observations:

"We have not that firm hold upon our young people which we should have. We do not get as many into the fold of Christ, or even into our Sabbath schools as is our duty and privilege—they go elsewhere.

"A still further crying evil is the lack of parental government which prevails among us to an alarming extent. . . . This is a great reproach to the cause of God and an effectual barrier to our progress. . . ."

1898. This General Conference voiced the same lament, that the church was failing to hold its youth. The committee charged this "in part to a lack of parental government and godly training at home." Further, stated the report, "The tendency to worldliness in some parts of our Zion impresses the minds of our young people that the plainness of attire that marked us as a church in our early history is not as important now as then."

1903. The bishops' address noted a measure of failure with the church's young people and children. The bishops pointed out, "We are not at our best along this line, and it is our deliberate opinion that we have not as yet reached the measure of our duty nor realized the possibilities within our reach. It is a fact quite generally admitted and always regretted that many children from our families drift away from us into the world or into some form of wordly religious life."

The committee on the state of the work in the same General Conference reported, "The greatest problem before us, next to the maintenance of the experience and practice of holiness, perhaps, is the salvation of our children and young people. There are reasons why so few of our children are saved to God and the church. To our minds the main fault lies in the home. There is a lack of proper discipline in our homes. Children too frequently are not only allowed to do as they please, but even to run the family affairs. It could hardly be expected that children who are not taught to respect parental authority will submit to divine authority."

Yet another committee of this Conference was disturbed by the problem of the church's youth. The report of the committee on Sunday schools expressed surprise that so few Sunday-school children were converted, and attempted to suggest an explanation of the difficulty as follows: "It seems to indicate that the home life is not favorable or that the Sunday school should greatly improve in grace, or skill, or both. The fact of our being in an evil world does not fully account for it."

It is noteworthy that a Sunday-school convention and young people's meeting had been arranged in advance of General Conference, and that the General Conference approved the holding of the same.

The committee on young people and children, it seems, recommended the organization of a "Christian Helpers Society," which was approved by the narrow margin of 52 to 50! Nothing significant seems to have come from this action.

1907. The General Conference of 1907 made Rev. W. B. Olmstead the first full-time general Sunday-school secretary. For nine years he had been editor of Sunday-school literature and had been re-elected for another quadrennium in that relationship. When made general Sunday-school

THE CHRISTIAN NURTURE OF CHILDHOOD

secretary he promptly resigned the editorial office and Rev. D. S. Warner was chosen to fill the vacancy thus created.

That the Sunday school was coming into its own in Free Methodism is further suggested by the following excerpt from the address of the bishops:

"The Sunday-school work of the Free Methodist Church has come to such proportions, and also of such vital relation to our denominational growth and efficiency, that only the unenlightened among us can be indifferent to it, or regard it, in comparison with other departments of our work, as of secondary importance. . . . If, in our early history, the 'struggle for existence' made necessary by almost universal opposition, and by our limited numbers, resources and equipments, made us less attentive to the children and the Sunday-school work than we should have been, we are now largely redeeming ourselves as a denomination from that neglect and its unfavorable results."

In this address to the 1907 General Conference, the bishops urged the need of an organization in the church through which to channel the talents and energies of its young people in Kingdom service. Here is their plea:

"Let our young people be organized in such a way, and for such lines of action, as are in keeping with the spirit and determining purpose of the church itself, with provision for a periodical to represent them and their work as soon as a subscription list can be secured that will warrant the financial part of the enterprise, and a vast amount of buried talent will be brought into recognition, and most potential forces for good from which the church now receives practically but little benefit, for lack of concentration and organization, will be turned to united and constant advantages for the advancement of our work in city, town, and hamlet, and in home and foreign fields."

The realization of this vision of a youth organization with its own publication was to be delayed several years, but finally came to its fulfillment, as will be reported in the next chapter.

The church's lack of success in winning and holding its children and youth in its first half-century seems to have been due in no small degree to its failure properly to combine Christian nurture with the evangelization of the young. The claim that a sound conversion will settle the problems of childhood and youth has proved disastrous. That an experience of Christian conversion without Christian instruction is not enough has been tragically demonstrated again and again when some of our finest young people with a Christian experience, but with inadequate grounding in faith and knowledge, have lost their balance in the crosscurrents of unbelief, wrong belief, and worldly temptation. The Christian, young in years, can no more safely be left alone to find his way than can the redeemed derelict to whose help the entire congregation rallies lest he enter into temptation and lapse again into his old ways. Certainly, the Christian home and the Christian church owe the youthful convert no less careful guidance in Christian living and faith than they so readily offer the adult convert who has been saved out of years of sin.

The church in its earlier years neglected not only the Christian nurture of its youthful converts, but likewise the Christian training of its unconverted youth. They sadly err who hold that Christian training of the unregenerate avails nothing, and leave their children to be saved at last by some miracle of grace in spite of their habits of evil and their ignorance of the Word resulting from neglect by parents or church. Likewise sad is the contrary error, to which early Free Methodism was largely immune, which trusts in Christian training to induce Christian experience and develop Christian character apart from a miracle of regenerating grace to transform the nature and renew the mind. Let it be said again that the answer to youth's problem of becoming a mature Christian is not an alternative of *either* Christian nurture *or* evangelism, but is a synthesis of *both* Christian nurture *and* evangelism. This answer the church was to learn more perfectly as its second half-century progressed.

We turn now to consider developments during that period.

Education and church membership

Not until relatively recent years has the church officially recognized the place of specific Christian nurture in the preparation of converts for church membership, and placed responsibility for this nurture directly with the pastor. The General Conference of 1935 recommended that the pastor form classes for preparatory members wherever practicable, the same to meet monthly "for instruction in the *Catechism, Discipline* and history of the Free Methodist Church and such encouragement as will help probationers [now called preparatory members] to go on into a definite experience of entire sanctification."

The General Conference of 1947 went further, strengthening the 1935 provision to include among the duties of the pastor the following:

> To provide for the culture of converts by such instruction and encouragement as will help them go on into a definite experience of entire sanctification, and to inform probationers of the privi-

leges, duties, and responsibilities of full membership, using particularly the *Catechism,* the *Discipline,* the history of the Free Methodist Church, and such other materials as the church provides, and forming classes for the purpose wherever practicable, but in no case neglecting to see that each person receives this care.

This General Conference directed also that the president of the annual conference review this provision before the conference, along with "Rules for a Preacher's Conduct" and other items in the chapter on "Qualifications and Work" of the minister.

The 1947 statement of pastoral responsibility for the culture of converts and the instruction of preparatory members was not implemented by an outline of instruction or by the provision of texts, and little seems to have been done during the ensuing quadrennium. The 1951 General Conference took the further step of requiring three months of instruction as a condition for full church membership, and commissioned the Board of Bishops to prepare the course. A beginning was made by the provision of simple materials in the four fields of Christian life, Christian faith, the working of the church, and the history of the church. The course in a measure has met a real need, but should be amplified and graded for different levels of maturity.

Today our children and young people are bombarded, even in Christian homes, with confusing and often perniciously pagan propaganda from press, radio, and television. The formal education of the modern school, we have noted, is directed to adjustment to the age—even to some of its evils. The informal give-and-take of modern society is almost entirely non-Christian and sometimes even anti-Christian. Previous provisions which the church has made for Christian nurture, principally through the Sunday school and youth organizations, are necessary but not sufficient. The new course has been organized directly to build Christian character and to develop Christian faith for church membership. It is not a substitute for evangelism, but in the pastor's hands it is a preparation for evangelism and a conserver of its results.

Recent growth of the Sunday school

During the later period of Free Methodism's history has occurred the rapid growth of the Sunday school. During the church's first two decades, Sunday-school enrollment was below church membership. At the mid-point of the church's first century, Sunday-school enrollment was less than 40 per cent above the total church membership; now, that enrollment exceeds by 150 per cent the church's membership. This expansion of the Sunday school has profoundly affected the architecture of new church structures, and has necessitated the remodeling and enlargement of many older structures. In some instances the problem has been met by the building of detached church-school plants. In the last ten years the weekly attendance in Free Methodist Sunday schools has increased by 32,000.

Fortunately, the idea of the Sunday school as an evangelizing agency has gained ground in recent years, and the unusual growth of Sunday-school enrollment has been a response to the church's effort through the Sunday school to reach the children of unchurched homes, and their unchurched parents as well. But still it must be acknowledged that the recruiting of church members from our populous Sunday-school constituency continues on too low a level when that constituency includes the evangelistic challenge of nearly ninety thousand non-churchmembers. But this field is ripe unto the harvest, and the aggressive outreach of the church's Sunday-school program gives promise. The present general Sunday-school secretary recently stated his concept of the Sunday school as follows:

> Traditionally the Sunday school has been considered as a department of the church created to teach children and youth the ways of Christian faith and life while seeking to provide Bible classes for adults. Today a new Sunday-school concept has swept across America in all evangelical churches. While the traditional emphasis has remained, the Sunday school is being recognized as an effective channel to extend the church's full witness, reaching into the homes of the unchurched, teaching them the Word of God, imparting spiritual truth, and making possible effective evangelism. But it also has proved to be an effective agency to enlist and train workers for Christian service. To the aggressive, growing evangelistic church, the Sunday school has become the church at work.[9]

The present enrollment in Free Methodist Sunday schools is 146,000, with 17,000 officers and teachers. More than $725,000 a

---

9. R. S. Nelson, "Extending Our Witness Through the Sunday School," *The Free Methodist*; April 14, 1959; p. 3.

year is spent for operation of the Sunday schools and their related activities. The *Sunday School Worker,* a monthly magazine established in 1920, now has a circulation of 6,000 under the title *Sunday School Journal.* A General Sunday School Council made up of regional representatives relates the program of the headquarters to the needs of the local areas.

Christian Youth Crusaders

Different programs of organized activities for the earlier youth or intermediate period were launched in areas of the church in the late thirties, leading up to the official recognition of Christian Youth Crusaders by the General Conference of 1939. The organization began under the direction of the Sunday-school department of which at the time Rev. A. L. Brown was general secretary.

The General Conference of 1951 approved the appointment of a director of intermediate youth at such time as finances could be provided, and in 1953 Rev. Floyd M. Todd was placed in office and proceeded to develop a Department of Intermediate Youth for the direction and promotion of church-wide activities of the Christian Youth Crusaders.

This department now functions under the Commission on Christian Education, independently of the Sunday-school department. It has grown rapidly, from 1,200 registered members in 1954 to 8,400 in 1959. In addition to registered members, many children attend the activities of local organizations.

The organization seeks to promote the child's mental, physical, spiritual, and social development, and to lead the child to Christ and into church fellowship. Its most fruitful means of childhood evangelism is the program of summer C.Y.C. camps, of which seventy-eight were conducted in 1959 with more than seven thousand campers. The department promotes a broad range of activities. A beginning has been made in the development of a curriculum of instruction.

The organization has brought fresh vitality into the church's program for intermediates. It is winning general acceptance and offers great promise of holding them during their transition to young manhood and young womanhood, when they will be ready to enter the organization known as Free Methodist Youth.

The Christian elementary day school

During recent years a development in Christian nurture through general education at elementary and secondary levels has been making rapid progress. It is known as the Christian day school movement. Schools are established and conducted under Christian auspices, sometimes denominational, sometimes community. Under the name Light and Life Day Schools the movement was recognized at the elementary level by the General Conference of 1951, and the encouragement and promotion of such schools were committed to the responsibility of the Commission on Christian Education, to be handled through its department of educational institutions.

These schools are increasing in number and patronage under the sponsorship of Free Methodist congregations in certain areas, the southwest especially. They normally draw upon children of the community as well as the congregation. Special buildings for these schools are being built with grounds equipped for play activities. The extent and nature of the impact of such schools upon the church and its ministry to the community remain to be measured objectively, but the opinions of pastors of churches conducting the schools are generally favorable. The movement shows no signs of abatement and may develop to a point where it provides an enlarged opportunity for Christian nurture at the younger ages throughout many more areas.

The church must save its own

America's changing religious terrain over the century since the founding of the Free Methodist Church urges the necessity that the church save its own children and youth, and bring them into the church if Free Methodism is to advance. In 1860 the Free Methodist Church was the only denomination in America aggressively holiness in emphasis. The National Holiness Association had not then been organized. In consequence, Free Methodism's appeal to spiritually hungry members of the more formal churches was far broader than today. Furthermore, a higher percentage of the population was unchurched, and in consequence the field was more open for the evangelization of the unsaved than is now the case. For these reasons the Free Methodist Church then had opportunities for growth through winning adult recruits which more than offset its losses through neglect of its own children and youth. Its very success in winning adults tended to obscure those losses and to weaken concern for the Christian nurture and evangelization of the young.

Today, with several energetic holiness denominations in the field, and with the further evangelistic pull of pentecostal groups working the field of the lower and middle classes, Free Methodism's growth increasingly depends upon its bringing its own children and youth into established church membership. In this direction, the church's record is improving. After all, how can we ask God to give us the heathen for our inheritance if we neglect our own household and fail to hold the children God has given us?

This, then, is an area of insistent challenge as the new century of Free Methodism dawns: to bring into Christian experience and church membership the children and youth of the church's non-member constituency of ninety thousand, who already are under instruction in our Sunday schools. And the field is inexhaustible, for the world will never be evangelized as a task completed—another generation is always pressing upon the heels of the present. The task is an ever-recurring, never-ending one. We can change the world of tomorrow only by saving the youth of today.

By way of summary
In this chapter, dealing with Christian nurture in the earlier years, we first considered education in its broadest terms as the changing of human nature through experience, and proceeded to contrast the modern emphasis on education as adjustment of the learner to the world, with Christian education as adjustment of the learner, transformed in nature, to the will of God. We noted that Christian education, far from bringing adjustment to the present world, on occasion may actually entail conflict between the Christian's standards and the world. However, the grace of God enables the Christian to desire, not the way of the world, but the will of God. Thereby the conflict is resolved into moral victory.

Analysis next disclosed that the assumed antagonism between Christian education and evangelism does not exist, but that in fact the two are complementary. The preparation for the transformation of nature wrought by evangelism is facilitated by Christian training, and the transformation itself is confirmed and matured by a continuing Christian nurture.

We then turned our inquiry to discover the place of Christian nurture in early Free Methodism. The dominance of evangelism in the church at first, it was pointed out, tended to submerge or displace Christian nurture during the early decades. In time, however, the Sunday school gained in influence and there developed a growing concern for the children and youth the church had been failing to win and hold.

Although the earlier history of the church disclosed this weakness in its program of Christian nurture, later years brought a period of rapid expansion in Sunday schools and the development of organized activities for youth that are cause for hope of the future. We have reviewed, in addition to the growing place of the Sunday school in the Free Methodist Church, the recent organization of the Christian Youth Crusaders to provide varied activities for intermediate youth, the central aim being the conversion of these children and their training for responsible church membership. At the same time the church has provided for the culture of converts in preparation for church membership under the direction of pastors. Brief comment was offered concerning the Christian day school.

Finally, the children and youth of the church's nonmember constituency of ninety thousand have been presented as an evangelistic challenge to the church as it enters its second century.

The next two chapters, on Christian nurture in the later years, will survey the church's educational institutions and the organization of its older young people in Free Methodist Youth.

*   *   *   *   *

The officers that have directed and promoted the youth interests of the church surveyed in this chapter are listed below, with their terms of service. Perhaps logically the editors of Sunday-school literature should have been listed with the church's publishers and the editors of *The Free Methodist* at the close of Chapter Twenty-four. However, the concern of these editors has been the instruction of children and youth, and thus we justify their listing here.

Editors of Sunday-school Literature—
W. T. Hogue	1897-1898
W. B. Olmstead	1898-1907
D. S. Warner	1907-1919

G. W. Griffith   1919-1923
B. J. Vincent   1923-1931
B. L. Olmstead   1931-

General Sunday-school Secretaries—
W. B. Olmstead   1907-1919
J. B. Lutz   1919-1925
J. H. Whiteman   1925-1939
A. L. Brown   1939-1955
R. S. Nelson   1955-

Director of Intermediate Youth—
Floyd M. Todd   1953-

CHAPTER TWENTY-SIX

The Christian Nurture of Youth

Free Methodism's educational tradition

The late Bishop Wilson T. Hogue once wrote, "The men who were chiefly instrumental in founding the Free Methodist Church were, for the most part, men who had been trained in colleges and universities. They were not the men lightly to esteem intellectual training, or to suppose that, in the founding of His kingdom, God ever places a premium on ignorance." [1]

The educational tradition of Free Methodism is to be traced through general and liberal arts channels rather than, to any large degree, through restricted vocational and technical channels. This observation applies to the religious emphasis of the church's educational institutions as well as to the secular. A recent comprehensive study of these institutions reveals that in the earliest statements on education in the annual conferences which were looking toward the founding of Christian schools, the need for institutions combining general learning and Christian culture was declared. Also, it was discovered that in the official definition of the purposes for which the earliest schools were established, the training of the ministry was not prominent. Quoting this study by L. R. Schoenhals:

> It is evident that there was strong interest in founding schools under denominational auspices. These schools were not to be Bible schools in the sense that a liberal education was to be excluded. Certain tendencies in the public schools made the establishment of Free Methodist schools imperative. The interest was in terms of providing wholesome educational surroundings for the children of Free Methodist parents. .... It was noted that there was no expressed concern in establishing schools for the training of prospective ministers.[2]

---

1. Wilson T. Hogue, *History of the Free Methodist Church*. Free Meth. Pub. House, Winona Lake, Ind.; v. 2, 305.
2. L. R. Schoenhals, "Higher Education in the Free Methodist Church in the United States: 1860-1954." (Unpublished doctoral dissertation, University of Washington, 1955); p. 12 *et seq.*

FROM AGE TO AGE A LIVING WITNESS

Interest in general education grounded on Christian principles as essential in the program of the infant church was early manifested by B. T. Roberts in the founding of a school as the first benevolent institution to be established in Free Methodism. Although Roberts sensed keenly the church's mission to preach the gospel to the poor, he founded Chili Seminary only six years after the denomination was organized, and before a missionary board was functioning, or a board of charities to provide an orphanage or home for the aged had been established. Reflecting the broad concern of that first school of the church for Christian culture is the following statement Roberts published in the first catalogue of Chili Seminary, announcing its program for 1869-1870:

> While we cannot prize, too highly, the benefits of mental culture, we should not lose sight of that moral and religious culture, which lies at the foundation of correct principles and good character. Education and religion should by no means be separated. Indeed, to divorce them is dangerous, as is proved by the history of the past. Ignorance is the mother of superstition and religious error; and a system of education that does not comprehend the great truths of revelation, fosters skepticism and infidelity in the youthful mind. The teacher who is interested in the moral destiny of a pupil, and also in his usefulness to mankind will labor to show the harmony between science and Christianity—between the discoveries of the one and the doctrines of the other.

The church's tradition of general education has produced its present program of higher education as exhibited in the brief historical sketches of its schools about to be presented. In this tradition the personal factor has been of outstanding importance. What Mark Hopkins shares with the student is more significant than the material equipment, let it be a log or a thoroughly equipped campus. This may explain the passion of so many frontier conferences to have a Christian school, although the meager population, by any realistic appraisal, could never support it either with finances or students. But, all the same, the school is there after generations of struggle and sacrifice and failure—but miracle! Whatever happens by way of fire, drouth, depression, emigration from the area, Mark Hopkins remains and a succession of students will find places on the log. L. R. Schoenhals explains as follows the founding of a school on the bleak plains of the Dakota Territory in 1887, three years after the organization of its frontier Conference with a membership in the low hundreds:

> Anyone pointing to the seeming impossibility of founding a school there would have had to reckon with the intelligence, the courage, the imagination, and the religious faith of some of the Dakota pioneers. These people generated an enthusiasm that never acknowledged discouragement. If material resources disappeared they called upon spiritual reserves that impelled them with intense emotion to make even greater personal sacrifices. Speaking of the early days of the seminary, one person recalled such an incident:
>
> "Once when the school was so involved in debt, because of misfortune, that there seemed no way to meet its obligations, a few of God's saints gathered on the camp ground and prayed and sang and subscribed until eleven hundred and fifty dollars had been raised. One who had just 'proved up' on his homestead was so wrought upon by the Spirit that he deeded it outright to the seminary." [3]

Educational control in the Free Methodist Church

Another feature of education in the Free Methodist Church to be kept in mind, if one is to understand the development of its schools, is their local and regional character. The general church has not established schools but has left that enterprise to groups of individuals and to conferences. Had the denomination as such controlled the founding of schools, undoubtedly there would have been fewer of them. Whether the total contribution of the schools to the church and society would then have been greater, or less, is a matter of opinion. In its policy of leaving the organization and support of schools to local initiative, the denomination seems to have followed the pattern of the parent church which, Dr. Schoenhals has noted, had no central board of education until 1869, although by that time two hundred or more Methodist institutions of varying academic grade had been established. In 1894 was established the board of education of the Free Methodist Church. Until that date no mention of the schools of the church had appeared in the *Discipline*.

Early pronouncements of General Conference

Although leaving educational initiative to the conferences, the

---
3. *Ibid.*, p. 194. Quoted from C. W. Shay, *General Conference Daily*, June 18, 1903; p. 8.

General Conference repeatedly manifested its interest in Christian education and the church's educational institutions. The church had been in existence but a decade and had but one seminary of learning when the committee on education reported as follows to the General Conference of 1870:

> Though the illiterate may enjoy religion, they must enjoy it under great disadvantages which are felt more and more as the soul climbs heavenward, and labors to shed light upon the dark world. The leaven of salvation in such a one may use up his entire stock of knowledge to the best possible advantage, often making him the instrument of great good; but it cannot use what is not there. The leaven only affects the meal with which it is brought into contact.
>
> Hence our usefulness must depend largely upon our knowledge of science, as well as upon our knowledge of salvation. No amount of piety can atone for a want of mental culture; God never does for man what He has given him power to do for himself.
>
> To make a *man*, the head and heart must be properly trained. Educate the intellect *alone* and you are liable to make a tiger; cultivate the moral faculties *only* and you make a fanatic. The man who would survey the literal heavens, cannot dispense with the telescope however perfect may be his vision; neither can he dispense with eyes, because he holds in his hand the most perfect glass. His object can be reached only by combining the two.
>
> So must mental and moral culture be fully combined to fully reach the great end of human existence.

The committee on education in 1878 would see the interests of the two schools then in existence protected, and therefore said in its report, "We desire to see these seminaries more fully relieved from financial difficulties before recommending the establishment of others." The same committee declared for education in these forceful words: "Numerous illustrious examples in the Scriptures show that the Omniscient, in choosing agents for His work, had an eye not only to natural qualities, and those sanctified, but also to those improved by education and learning."

The schools of the church, although denominationally committed in principle, have generally been nonsectarian in spirit. This sectarian moderation was expressed by the report of the committee on education to the General Conference of 1874 when it recommended that it was "highly important that the teachers in our Seminaries be persons of sound piety, and that the principals at least, be members of the Free Methodist Church."

Already in 1882 the pressure to organize schools was being felt and three institutions already were in operation, Chili, Spring Arbor, and Evansville seminaries. The committee warned: "The magnitude of such undertakings should caution the annual conferences against hastily engaging in new school enterprises, unless the buildings are furnished gratuitously. Such opportunities will probably occur as often as the needs of our people require." Such warnings were little heeded, however. And the General Conference could do no more than warn!

On the same occasion Spring Arbor Seminary was reported to be in a prosperous condition, operating on the "self-supporting plan," which was explained very simply: "The principal having all the revenue from tuition and paying all salaries of teachers, and all incidental expenses. The plan works well although it yields but a meager income to the principal."

Eight years later, there were three more institutions officially sponsored by conferences, Orleans, Neosho Rapids, and Wessington Springs seminaries; another, sponsored by Free Methodists but not officially approved by any conference had come and gone, and another such was struggling for recognition. These were Gerry Seminary and Virginia Seminary. At this General Conference of 1890, Bishop Roberts proposed the following resolution which was adopted: "That no new school enterprise of the rank of academy or seminary shall be started without the consent of the Executive Committee." In the nature of the case, this action could only be advisory, although the implication that a school initiated without such consent could not be recognized as a Free Methodist institution by the General Conference no doubt served as a deterrent. The committee on education reported, "One of the most hopeful indications connected with our work, is the increasing sense of responsibility manifested throughout the denomination concerning the thorough Christian culture of the young." The *Discipline* was revised by this General Conference to include the recommendation that all pastors preach at least once a year in every congregation a sermon on Christian education and our schools. There being no section of the *Discipline* on educational institutions, this advice was appended to the list of duties "of those who have charge of circuits."

In the General Conference of 1898, the committee on education requested and received permission to have services on an afternoon and evening in the interests of education, and the General Conference of 1903 ordered an afternoon sitting to be devoted to the schools, and on that occasion representatives of the institutions addressed the body. The recognized institutions listed in the 1903 *Discipline*, were: *Colleges*, Greenville; *Seminaries*, A. M. Chesbrough, Spring Arbor, Evansville, Wessington Springs, Seattle, Orleans. All conference-sponsored institutions had survived but Neosho Rapids Seminary. Orleans had succumbed for a time, but again was functioning as a Free Methodist institution. This General Conference approved a recommendation to raise an endowment fund for the schools, to be no less than $25,000. The General Conference was giving more attention to the schools of the church. The committee on the state of the work asserted, "If we can bring our educational and our social capabilities to a high standard, and along with these maintain our principles which are embedded in truth, and which bring the fullness of the Holy Ghost, nothing can stand before us."

In the General Conference of 1907 the bishops' message made the following pronouncement on education and Christian culture:

> The Free Methodist Church has never worshiped at the shrine of illiteracy. While not accepting that doctrine of the supremacy of intellect, which anciently gave birth to the Gnostic, Ebionic, and various other heresies, and in more recent times has leavened the church with rationalism and destructive criticism, she has ever recognized the power and value of reverent and consecrated culture as an agency in securing the salvation of men, and in advancing the Kingdom of our Lord Jesus Christ in the earth."

This General Conference indicated further its interest in education by electing an educational secretary, but there is evidence of little activity in the office although the General Conference recommended that the secretary set as his financial objective the raising of a million dollars! The man elected was Alexander Beers who probably found

THE CHRISTIAN NURTURE OF YOUTH

little time for raising a million dollars for all the schools while attempting to establish on a secure financial basis Seattle Seminary, of which he then was the principal.

Against the background of these few observations on the educational tradition of Free Methodism and the actions of the various General Conferences that reflected interest in education and the church's schools during the first half-century, we now review in brief the history and character of each of the church's educational institutions in order of their founding, grouped as schools now existing, schools that have been closed, and non-official educational ventures.[4]

Roberts Wesleyan College (founded as Chili Seminary, 1866)

This was the first educational institution of the denomination, founded by B. T. Roberts at North Chili, New York. Its founding and successful direction through its early years added heavy burdens to a man loaded already with "the care of all the churches." Once when urged to take it easier, he replied, "I am bearing double burdens, and all because those whom the Lord calls to come to His help do not respond to His call; thus leaving me not only to bear my *own* burdens, but also to do the work *they* leave undone."[5]

B. T. Roberts turned in his own Rochester residence as initial payment on a farm at North Chili, where the institution was to be built ten miles west on the Buffalo Road. He also purchased and closed the tavern in North Chili to remove from the school community its evil influence. Until the seminary building was completed in 1869, classes were held in the Roberts home and in the former tavern. Appeals for financial assistance for the school and reports concerning its progress now and again appeared in *The Earnest Christian.*

For the first two years B. T. Roberts served as principal, and again

---

4. Many of the historical facts concerning Free Methodist schools in the summaries of this and the following chapter have been drawn from Wilson T. Hogue's *History of the Free Methodist Church*, v. 2, chs. 18, 19; and from L. R. Schoenhals, "Higher Education in the Free Methodist Church, etc." Typescript of a book by John Sigsworth now being printed, *The Battle Was the Lord's*, has supplied information concerning the Canadian schools. Contemporary factual information has been provided directly from the institutions.
5. Mrs. D. A. Jeffries Catton, "Early Days of the Seminary," *The Earnest Christian;* v. 65, April 1893; p. 128.

for the year 1874-1875; but for many years he seems to have carried major responsibility in directing the institution. During its varying fortunes a long succession of administrators served the school— nineteen different principals and presidents, stretching across most of a century. Only three of the nineteen served more than five years. These were Benson H. Roberts who first served a term of three years (1876-1879), and later for twenty-five years (1881-1906) as joint principal with his capable wife, Emma Sellew Roberts; George W. Garlock, who served eleven years (1919-1930), during which period, in 1921, the institution added junior college courses beyond the highschool department; and Merlin G. Smith who served twenty-four years (1933-1957), during which period, in 1951, the institution graduated its first class to receive baccalaureate degrees and in 1953 received its permanent charter as a senior college. Dr. Ellwood Voller, coming from the student personnel office at Michigan State University, took office as president in 1957.

In addition to having a bishop serve as principal, it is interesting to note, the institution also chose a principal who later became bishop, David S. Warner (1906-1908). Especially in the earlier years, Chili Seminary supplied principals for other schools of the church as they were established.

The name of the institution was changed in 1884 to A. M. Chesbrough Seminary, in honor of the man who had left the school a legacy of $30,000. Again in 1945, when the school was chartered as a junior college, the name was changed, this time to Roberts Junior College; as a college of senior grade the institution now is known as Roberts Wesleyan College.

Today an attractive thirty-acre campus adjoins a large modern college farm. There are five major buildings. Pearce Memorial, named in honor of Bishop William Pearce, is a commodious colonial structure combining a church with an educational plant. The sanctuary seats 500, and auxiliary rooms seat another 500 when needed. Carpenter Hall, named in honor of Adella P. Carpenter who taught in the institution for more than forty years, is a large building that houses a residence hall for women, social rooms, dining room, and gymnasium. Cox Hall is an administration and educational building, containing also an auditorium and the library. Roberts Hall, oldest building on the campus, has been reconstructed for administrative offices. Mersereau Science Hall is a substantial reconstruction of former military buildings. A quonset-type building serves as recreation center, and several near-campus houses serve as music hall, residences for men, apartments for families. Roberts Collegiate Industrial building, 80 x 120 feet, is rented to manufacturing concerns which in turn employ students of the college.

There are now in Roberts Wesleyan College 356 students, served by a faculty numbering 28.[6] From this oldest campus of Free Methodism have gone forth many servants of church and society to enter the Christian ministry, missions, law, medicine, education, business, government, social welfare, and other fields. The following paragraphs epitomize some of the institution's purposes and goals:

> Since it is axiomatic that the Christian college should produce Christians, it should acquaint students with the Bible, both Old and New Testaments, as the revelation of truth upon which the Christian faith is based, to the end that each student may be led to a personal acceptance of Christ as the way, the truth, and the life.
>
> A conviction of the desirability of the cultivation of the whole person persists as the over-all objective of the college. Academic training of quality is given within the matrix of a distinctly Christian philosophy which affirms the inestimable worth of every individual and gives meaning and purpose to life.

We close this brief sketch of the oldest educational institution in Free Methodism by citing the remarks made by the representative of the New York Board of Regents in presenting to Roberts Wesleyan its permanent senior college charter in 1953. Of a particular characteristic of this institution which had been recognized across the state, Dr. Frederick Ross said:

> ... This characteristic is one that many other institutions of higher learning are presently concerned to recapture for their own enterprise in order that their students may go out into later lives of usefulness, buttressed by that faith in God and belief in those elements of truth and character which for over almost a century have been inculcated here, and which have given to the graduates of this institution the strength and courage to face the complexities not only of modern life, but also the character to meet the trying and sometimes critical problems of personal relations.

---

6. Student enrollments and number of faculty in this and following reports have been computed as of mid-year, 1959-1960. Student enrollments in annual reports of these institutions will exceed the figures here given because they will include the number of students in all terms of the year. For emphasis and readier comparisons, numerals rather than spelled-out figures are employed in these reports generally, even where better form calls for the latter.

Here, an institution founded by men of faith has kept alive the teachings of our fathers; and it is with marked satisfaction that those of us who work in education elsewhere note the interest now being taken by other institutions in ways and means to foster in our youth the fundamentals of Americanism and allegiance to the things of the spirit.[7]

Spring Arbor Junior College (founded as Spring Arbor Seminary, 1873)

In 1835 a Methodist Episcopal institution was incorporated with view to building a college on the site of an old Indian village at a place known as Spring Arbor, about eight miles west of the city of Jackson, Michigan. Buildings were never erected and the school never opened. A short time later nearby Albion became the permanent site of the Methodist Episcopal college of that area. In 1844 the Free Will Baptists established Michigan Central College at Spring Arbor where it remained until 1855 when the institution was transferred to nearby Hillsdale where it continues today as Hillsdale College.

Free Methodism had entered Michigan in the early sixties, and the Michigan Conference was organized in 1866 largely from the labors of Rev. Edward Payson Hart of the Illinois Conference. Mr. Hart was continued in his aggressive leadership of the work in that area as district chairman after the Michigan Conference was organized. In 1870 he began promoting the idea of an educational institution to serve the rapidly growing conference.

In 1871 it happened that the Michigan Conference was held in the village of Spring Arbor. A committee on education was appointed which prepared and presented to the conference a proposal which was approved, and was then submitted to the citizens of Spring Arbor as the terms under which the Free Methodists would launch a school in the community. But matters did not move rapidly enough to permit final action by the Conference that year. At the 1872 session in Delta, Ohio, another committee was appointed with full power to proceed with the establishment of a school within the limit of funds it could raise and the subscriptions it could secure. This committee met at once and agreed upon Spring Arbor as its choice of location, and before Conference adjourned had taken pledges and

---

7. *The Free Methodist*; August 4, 1953; p. 6.

renewed old ones approximating a total of $2,000. Then Mr. Hart and the committee proceeded to Spring Arbor and pressed the community to give its decision on the terms proposed to it in 1871. Funds were promptly raised sufficient to meet the proposed agreement, and the committee purchased the old school buildings and ten acres of land. By late spring the campus was in readiness and a summer term of school was conducted by the first principal, Clark Jones. The dedication was held at the opening of the new school year, September 2, 1873, with General Superintendent Roberts the dedicatory speaker.

As the moving spirit in the founding and development of Chili Seminary was B. T. Roberts, the church's first general superintendent, so the moving spirit in the Spring Arbor venture was E. P. Hart who, a year after Spring Arbor's opening, was to become the church's second general superintendent. The founding of each institution awaited the leadership of a man of wisdom, determination, energy, and practical common sense. Both men laid strong foundations for the church's future educational structure.

Again, as in the first school of the church, administrative terms at Spring Arbor have been short. Seventeen principals and presidents have served Spring Arbor, among them, three who later became bishops of the church. These were Walter A. Sellew (1876-1877), David S. Warner (1893-1905), and Burton J. Vincent (1905-1909). L. M. Lowell, first director of the Light and Life Hour, served two terms as president (1935-1944 and 1955-1957). James F. Gregory, present editor of *The Free Methodist*, served also in this capacity (1944-1950). Others who have served five years or more have been Clark Jones (1873-1875 and 1877-1883); Albert Stilwell (1883-1893); H. S. Stewart (1911-1917 and 1920-1924); Merlin G. Smith (1926-1934); and C. D. Moon (1950-1955). The present incumbent, Dr. Roderick J. Smith, a public school administrator, took office in 1957.

The facilities of the Spring Arbor campus were meager when the Free Methodists took possession, and within a few years the arduous task of building was necessary to meet the needs of the growing institution. Building replacements and additions have continued through the years until now the Spring Arbor campus is one of the best in the church for meeting the needs of the constituency it serves. The major buildings are Smith Gymnasium; DeCan Hall, housing the science laboratories and the library; Sayre Hall, which is a classroom building; Muffitt Hall, a modern dormitory for women, housing also the dining room and kitchen; Ormston Hall, a modern dormitory for men matching Muffitt Hall; Post House, a dormitory for women; E. P. Hart Memorial Chapel, with a modern auditorium seating 1,000; The Maycroft, housing the administrative offices. There are also two supplementary dormitories and a new practical arts building.

Spring Arbor Junior College through the years has been definitely an institution of its church area, training young people for Christian service and lay callings, and returning them to their communities to contribute to society and the church. The institution is now a two-year junior college with an associated four-year high school, although steps are being taken looking toward expanding the college to senior level within the near future. The students now number 310, 86 per cent of whom come from a Free Methodist constituency. The faculty numbers 17.

The declared goal of the institution is to prepare its students for effective Christian living by assisting them—

(1) *Spiritually* to become mature, responsible Christians whose lives are dedicated to the service of God and man. This necessitates a personal experience of regeneration and sanctification, and is the basis of personal and social integrity.

(2) *Intellectually* to understand the world in which they live, including their fellow men. This requires guided exploration in all areas—scientific, social, cultural, and religious.

(3) *Vocationally* to make an occupational choice which takes into account their interests and abilities.

(4) *Personally and socially* to be able to live effectively, creatively and joyfully in the society in which they find themselves.

Central College 1914 (founded as Orleans Seminary, 1884)

This institution began in 1884 as Orleans Seminary, founded in Orleans, Nebraska, by pioneering homesteaders of the West Kansas Conference. Prominent in its beginning was Rev. C. M. Damon. Almost from the first this frontier institution suffered from lack of funds, but its loyal friends continued to sacrifice for its maintenance and to send their children to this struggling institution. In 1888 the trustees surrendered to the West Kansas Conference the power of electing trustees, and in 1889 the Conference appealed to the executive committee of the general church to take over the property and the operation of the school. The executive committee agreed, on certain conditions; and the ensuing General Conference approved its action in view of the emergency, but did not approve the operation of schools by the General Conference as a policy. There followed a period of confusion and distress, and finally the Methodists purchased the school. They likewise had financial difficulties and could not meet their obligations. In 1897 the institution reverted to the Free Methodist Church. In 1896 the Platte River Conference had been organized, and within its bounds were the village of Orleans and the Orleans Seminary Campus. This young conference purchased the school from the general church for $4,000, planning to operate it with the financial support and student patronage of adjacent conferences. The institution was re-incorporated, and for a period of years continued with a measure of success. A part of the time the enrollment was good. Several strong men were in its succession of principals, including N. B. Ghormley, Arthur J. Damon, and W. W. Loomis. Rev. L. Glenn Lewis became principal in 1912, and under his administration the school, renamed Central Academy and College, was transferred to McPherson, Kansas, where it was more centrally located within its patronizing area. Mr. Lewis continued as president of the reorganized institution, and later became general educational secretary of the denomination.

The removal of an institution from one locality to another is a hazardous venture, but in this instance was accomplished successfully. The new location was in a thriving county-seat city of the wheat-farming and oil-producing area of central Kansas, well placed with reference to the lower-central plains states which largely comprise the patronizing territory of Central College.

The administrators of the institution in its McPherson location who have served five years or more have been L. Glenn Lewis (1914-1919), the founding president; Chas. A. Stoll (1919-1939), who built soundly over a period of twenty years, and died in the service of the school; Orville S. Walters, M.D. (1939-1944), a competent organizer, now director of the University of Illinois health service; and Mendall B. Miller (1945-1953), experienced college educator, now on the faculty of Seattle Pacific College. Since 1955 the president has been Dr. Elmer E. Parsons, formerly in educational missions in Japan.

Central College campus, previously occupied by Walden College, is a fifteen-acre plot upon which had been constructed a substantial four-story brick building, now called the Administration Building. This houses offices, classrooms, laboratories, and library. In addition, there are: the Industrial Arts Building; the Home Economics cottage; Lewis Hall for high school girls, which houses also the kitchen and dining room facilities for campus residents; Stoll Hall, a residence for men; and the Elms, a residence for college women. A multi-function building is now under construction which will provide a gymnasium, auditorium, and music hall. There are six residences for faculty and student use. The McPherson Free Methodist Church, a large and attractive plant, adjoins the campus and renders invaluable service to the campus group.

Central College is the oldest junior college accredited by the state of Kansas. Its campus is superior for the size of its student body. Splendid as is the location of the school for the area it serves, that area does not include Free Methodism's larger conferences. However, the ratio of Central's enrollment to the Free Methodist population of its patronizing area is high. The present enrollment is 149, served by a faculty of 17. Seventy-four per cent of the students come from a Free Methodist constituency.

Many of the alumni of Central College are engaged in full-time Christian service. Twenty-eight of its alumni are doctors of medicine—a splendid record for a junior college of moderate size. There is an intense loyalty to the institution on the part of its graduates.

A brief statement declaring the purpose of the institution follows:

> Central College has always expressed its chief purpose in its intention to provide well integrated training for people to participate as Christians in the life of the nation and community. It has been its goal to maintain on the campus itself a model Christian community where young people can grow to the greatest advantage. Central College conducts a liberal arts program designed to develop the entire individual, intellectually, socially and spiritually.

Wessington Springs College (founded as Wessington Springs Seminary, 1887)

The Dakota Annual Conference was organized in 1883, six years before the admission of the two Dakotas as states. This Conference later became the South Dakota Conference. The North Dakota Conference was not organized until 1897.

In the eighties the Dakota Territory was a pioneer, homesteading area, as was the West Kansas Conference, including its part of Nebraska, when Orleans Seminary was established in 1884. Even more sparsely populated than Kansas and Nebraska, Dakota was not a promising field for a school under the auspices of a church whose membership in the vast Dakota Territory numbered in the low hundreds. But those hardy pioneers who had migrated from points "back East" desired the educational and religious privileges they had enjoyed in the more settled areas from whence they came to this new country.

The intelligent concern of these men of the frontier plains for Christian education was expressed in the very first conference session by the committee on education in the following words, gleaned by Dr. Schoenhals from the Minutes of 1883:

> The design of education should be to stimulate and lead out the mental and moral faculties to take active and earnest stand for truth and godliness. We approve of and are grateful for the general good done through the common schools. We regard them as a necessity, but deplore the many evils creeping into them, viz.: ignoring the fact that God rules and overrules in the affairs of men, the exclusion of the Bible in many places, and the little attention paid to the morals of pupils. We trust that the denominational schools of our own and some other churches will ever seek to make the matter of educating the heart of equal importance with that of the mind." [8]

The Dakota Conference took decisive action to establish a school of its own in its session of 1886, only three years after its organization. A Methodist Episcopal minister by the name of A. B. Smart of Wessington Springs, by working diligently with his community and with the conference committee on location, secured the institution for Wessington Springs. A building was begun, but before its completion Wessington Springs Seminary was opened in a vacant store building on November 15, 1887. The school was soon moved into the basement of the new structure, and into its upper floors as the building progressed and the school grew.

The faithful and persistent force that actually launched the institution and held it on its course during the early years was its first principal, Rev. J. B. Freeland, who served from 1887 to 1896.

---

8. L. R. Schoenhals, "Higher Education in the Free Methodist Church, etc.," p. 194 *et seq.*

Since Freeland, the school has had seventeen administrators, two of them later becoming bishops of the church. These were G. W. Griffith (1910-1915), and Burton J. Vincent (1920-1923). W. B. Olmstead, who already had filled important posts in the general church and was yet to serve as general missionary secretary, was president when the school became a junior college in 1918. His term as president was 1916-1920. One of Wessington Springs' early principals was to become one of the most distinguished educators of Free Methodism. This was Eldon Grant Burritt (1900-1902), who later became principal of Evansville Seminary (1902-1905), and still later, president of Greenville College (1908-1927). Others, who served presidential terms of more than five years and skillfully piloted the school through hazardous seas, have been Harry B. Ansted (1925-1936), W. A. Harden (1936-1943), and Geo. E. Kline (1945-1957). Dr. Philip Harden, son of President W. A. Harden, has served as president since 1957.

The campus of Wessington Springs College is a spacious one, including one hundred and twenty-five acres on the eastern slopes of the Wessington Hills. On the campus proper are the Administration Building, housing administrative offices, classrooms, laboratories, music studio, and library; the Gymnasium-Auditorium; Olmstead Hall, for women, and housing also the domestic departments serving campus residents; Greenwald Hall, for men; the chapel which also serves as the local church; Ann Hathaway Cottage, set in a Shakespeare Garden; two residences divided into faculty apartments; and G. I. apartments for veterans and other campus families.

Wessington Springs College has never been one of the church's larger institutions. Its growth has been restrained by sparsity both of general and of church population in its area; by weather hazards affecting farm production; and by migration westward. Its present enrollment is 102, served by a faculty of 12. Sixty-eight per cent of the students are drawn from a Free Methodist constituency.

All Free Methodist Schools are interdenominational in their ministry, but perhaps of them all Wessington Springs has belonged in the broadest sense to its geographic area. Early it became a teacher-training institution, and because of this has been identified with interests of the general public extending far from the campus. Its distance from other institutions, public and private, has broadened its ministry far beyond the denomination by which it is sponsored. Because of these wider connections, a type of educational evangelism has characterized the ministry of Wessington Springs College, and numbers have been evangelized on its campus who, in turn, have become bearers of the gospel witness to other areas and to other nations. For periods of years on end the school has known financial crisis, but after nearly three-quarters of a century it continues, a blessing to its own area, to the church, and to the world.

In addition to the large number of Christian ministers, missionaries, and educators that have come from its influence, its alumni include substantial laymen of different callings who also acknowledge indebtedness to Wessington Springs College for introducing them to the best things in life. In line with the school's motto, "Education for Character," is this declaration of the institution's purpose:

> Wessington Springs College places a positive emphasis on Christian training for Christian living. A principal objective of the institution is to educate for character. This is the world's need, as world leaders affirm who maintain that only the Christian spirit among men can save the world from ruin. Toward reaching this goal, the college provides religious instruction, student vespers, chapels, convocations, and special evangelistic services, all of which encourage spiritual meditation and devotion, and prompt to righteous living according to the Christian standard.

Seattle Pacific College (founded as Seattle Seminary, 1891)

The Oregon and Washington Territory Conference of the Free Methodist Church was organized in 1885, four years before Washington was made a state. Conference interest in planting a Free Methodist school on the Pacific Coast soon developed, leading in 1891 to decisive action in the incorporation of Seattle Seminary. The initial financial backing of the project came from subscriptions previously secured, largely through H. H. Pease who was himself a generous giver to the cause; and from the significant gift of five acres of land, deeded to the new corporation by Mr. and Mrs. Nils B. Peterson.

The Petersons stipulated that the institution to be established on the land they had given should provide for the training of missionaries. Interestingly enough, one of their daughters, Lily, after attending the institution, went to China and virtually gave her life, dying at an early age. Another daughter, Mattie, also was trained in Seattle Seminary and, after further education, took her sister's place in China, serving there for thirty-three years.

Shortly after the incorporation of Seattle Seminary, a contract for a building was let, but the contractor defaulted, causing loss of money and time. Alexander Beers was called as principal of the school, on the recommendation of B. T. Roberts who knew him as a student in A. M. Chesbrough Seminary. The school opened for classes in 1893.

When Mr. Beers took charge, there was already a heavy debt on the institution, but this man of genial optimism, dauntless courage, and dogged persistence was able to see the load of debt greatly reduced within a few years. According to L. R. Schoenhals[9] Mr. Beers was the dominating personality controlling, directing, and promoting Seattle Seminary from 1893 to 1916, although for the ten-year period 1894-1904 his official connection was not as principal but as board president and financial agent (with perhaps a brief intermission). During this period of ten years the titular principals were C. W. Shay (1894-1899); Chancellor N. Bertels (1899-1900); C. W. Shay (1900-1902); and A. H. Stilwell (1902-1904). In 1904 Mr. Beers resumed the principalship and continued therein to his retirement in 1916, with the title of president after 1913. During his administration, in 1910, a modest beginning in college instruction was begun. This developed to the point in 1915 when the institution was renamed Seattle Pacific College. In 1916 the college department enrolled nearly 30 students. In 1950 a graduate year was added.

From 1916 to 1959 Seattle Pacific College was served by only two presidents, O. E. Tiffany (1916-1926), and C. Hoyt Watson (1926-1959). The former established the institution educationally and financially on a more substantial collegiate basis. The latter saw the development of Seattle Pacific College from about 100 college students to full accreditation and an annual enrollment of nearly 1,800 students. Dr. Watson's term, never surpassed in length in the history of educational administration within the Free Methodist Church, was a period of student, curricular, faculty, campus, and financial expansion. Upon his resignation in 1959, C. Dorr Demaray was elected president. Dr. Demaray came to the position with years of experience in college teaching and administration, and for the eleven years immediately preceding his election had been vitally associated with the campus as pastor of the First Free Methodist Church of Seattle.

---

9. *Ibid.*, p. 257.

The campus of Seattle Pacific College holds fifteen or more major buildings, including those now under construction. The majority of the buildings are comparatively new, having been constructed during the current period of expansion. Outstanding among these buildings are McKinley Auditorium; Watson Hall, for women; Marston Hall, for women; Moyer Hall, for men; and the Royal Brougham Pavilion (gymnasium). Under construction are three major buildings, Health, Student Union, and Crawford Music Building. There are several other buildings on-campus and near-campus, small and larger. The President's Home is a residence of distinction, overlooking the campus and providing a panorama of the Lake Washington area of the city. Adjacent to the campus and cooperating in its spiritual life is the new First Free Methodist Church of Seattle, one of the largest in the denomination. On Whidbey Island in Puget Sound, the college has a 100-acre educational and recreational campus known as Camp Casey.

The present student body numbers 1,196; the faculty, 57. Twenty-four per cent of the students come from a Free Methodist constituency. Fifty-five per cent of the ministers of the three annual conferences of the Northwest are alumni of the institution, and 36 per cent of active missionary staff of the church are from its alumni. Other alumni, numbering more than 125, serve other missionary groups. Still other alumni have achieved distinction in education, business, the health professions, and other constructive callings. Two thousand students of the school have qualified for teaching certificates since 1922. The moral and Christian impact of such a stream of alumni upon the current of national and international affairs is incalculable.

The following paragraphs are excerpts from the institution's declared philosophy and objectives:

> The Christian way of life is centered in God as revealed in Jesus Christ. Any philosophy of education emanating therefrom should be so oriented. Basic to this idea is the fundamental faith that fellowship with God is not only a necessity to man's fullest self-realization, but also the strongest dynamic toward social living.
>
> The Christian philosophy recognizes the biological, psychological and social nature of man, but regards him as primarily a spiritual being created in the image of God and potentially a child of God, though in his natural state perverted by sin and requiring the power of God for the remedy of his condition and the realization of his potentialities. It holds that the process of education leads to and builds upon such transformation, seeing

in the fulfillment of the purposes of God the fullest development of the personality of the individual.

The college program in all its phases should be so organized and directed as to help students attain for themselves a completely integrated Christian life which issues dynamically in service and the acceptance of responsibility within the college, church, home, community and vocation.

It is the responsibility of Seattle Pacific College to assist each student to set for himself worthy goals and to help him attain them. Development is encouraged in areas which contribute toward the self-realization of the student and the maturing of his relationship to God and society. Therefore, attention is focused on intellectual growth, spiritual development, cultural appreciation, social awareness and competence, physical well-being, and vocational preparation.

Greenville College, 1892

The first educational institution to be established as a college in the Free Methodist Church was Greenville College of Greenville, Illinois, located within the bounds of the Central Illinois Conference which took the initiative in its founding. A devout member of the Methodist Episcopal Church, who had been impressed by the evidences of spirituality he discerned among Free Methodists, gave his farm for the purpose of establishing a Free Methodist school. The donor was James T. Grice, from whose farm was realized the sum of $6,000. For this amount he and his wife received an annuity contract.

The Central Illinois Conference had elected nine men as trustees, and authorized them to establish a college. Among these nine men was Rev. Franklin H. Ashcraft, a widely known evangelist who had been a principal contact with Mr. Grice and who had in view a property in Greenville which might be secured as a campus. In fact, negotiations had been carried to that point where, upon securing the Grice farm, the nine trustees proceeded promptly to purchase the campus of the former Almira College. This had been a Baptist college for women, established in 1855 and continuing until 1890. The cost of the campus of ten acres and a substantial four-story brick building was $12,200 cash, borrowed by the nine men from a Greenville bank. The campus was deeded to these men as individuals, upon advice that as a board their legal status was uncertain. The purchase was made in April, 1892, and a month later they deeded the campus to the Central Illinois Conference, probably to establish for the college sound public relations as a church-owned institution. School was opened that fall.

Greenville College was duly incorporated on May 31, 1893, but the campus remained for two more years the legal property of the Central Illinois Conference. On May 29, 1895, the College having cleared the original indebtedness, the Conference conveyed to the College corporation the title to the campus. And thus it came about that Greenville College began operating as a school nearly a year before incorporation and nearly three years before it had title to the campus which had been purchased specifically for its use.

The first president of Greenville College was Rev. Wilson T. Hogue, a minister of growing influence in the denomination and a prominent pastor in the Genesee Conference of the Free Methodist Church. President Hogue was a man of culture and competence, and during his administration of twelve years the institution acquired a character that has persisted. He resigned in 1904 because of his election to the office of bishop. However, throughout most of his presidency of Greenville College he also served the general church, first as interim general superintendent following the death of the senior superintendent, B. T. Roberts; and from 1894 to 1903 as editor of *The Free Methodist.*

Chosen to succeed Wilson T. Hogue was Rev. A. L. Whitcomb, pulpit prince and dynamic teacher under whose administration the College had gratifying growth. He resigned in 1908 to resume his pulpit ministry. His successor was Professor Eldon G. Burritt (1908-1927), cultured scholar, Christian gentleman, and wise administrator who gave the prime of his years to shaping Greenville College as an institution, distinctive in its emphasis on character and scholarship. His administration was terminated by death in 1927. His successor was the present writer, who served from 1927 to 1936. Formerly dean of the college, he came to the presidency from an executive position in child development with the National Research Council. During this period the institution sought to develop further its internal strength in faculty organization, curriculum, and definition of the purposes and aims of the institution. He resigned after his election as bishop of the church, and H. Johnson Long succeeded him in 1936. Dr. Long, with both baccalaureate and doctorate degrees from the University of Kansas, was chosen from the Greenville faculty with which he had served as professor of chemistry from 1927, and later in the administrative capacity of executive assistant. He is still president in 1960, and during his twenty-four years of vigorous leadership Greenville College has achieved full accreditation, and has experienced unprecedented expansion of student enrollment, financial resources, and campus facilities.

The principal campus facilities include: The historic Almira building, now Hogue Hall, which houses general administrative offices, classrooms, and, on the upper floors, men's residences; LaDue Chapel Building, to connect with a classroom unit which is projected for completion in 1960; the Memorial Library of more than 39,000 volumes; E. G. Burritt Gymnasium; a new gymnasium-auditorium building, now under construction, with which the original gymnasium will be integrated both structurally and functionally; Carrie T. Burritt Hall, and the two connecting structures, Dallas Annex and Burritt Annex, for women, and also housing social rooms and cafeteria; and Janssen Hall, for men. Near-campus are the Music Hall and several college houses adapted to dormitory use. Facing the campus is the new Free Methodist Church, built to serve college and community with a seating capacity of above 900.

The students of Greenville College number 590, the faculty, 37. Fifty per cent of the full-time students are drawn from a Free Methodist constituency. Strongly denominational in its constituency during the years, the institution nevertheless has been generously interdenominational in its ministry. Conservativism in matters of Christian belief, Christian idealism in life, and consecration to worthy causes have been cardinal concerns on the Greenville campus. In consequence, many of its alumni through the years have committed their lives to Christian service. More than 400, or better than one of every five of the 1905 ministers holding relationship to the Free Methodist conferences of the United States and Canada, have been students in the institution. A recent survey of the faculties of forty Christian colleges disclosed that more graduates of Greenville were on these faculties than graduates of any other institution of the group. Of the present active missionary staff of the denomination, numbering approximately 169, Greenville alumni and former students number 64. Many other alumni as Christian laymen are leading dedicated lives in public education, medicine, business, and numerous other callings.

Such alumni are the outcome of the following objectives Greenville College has held for its students through nearly seven decades:

1. *The development of the whole personality,* fostered through a balanced liberal arts curriculum; varied co-curricular activities, close faculty-student relationships; and emphasis on mature convictions which develop a firm loyalty to the Christian cause.

2. *Disciplined living,* sought through careful definition of Christian standards and their application to daily living; the maintenance of academic discipline as essential to the discipline of character; and joint participation of faculty and students in creating a Christian campus community.

3. *Dedication to Christ and His service,* as the outcome of a pervasive and compelling ideal of what it means to be fully Christian, whether the vocation the student chooses is secular or religious.

Sketches of the remaining schools of Free Methodism are continued in Chapter Twenty-seven.

CHAPTER TWENTY-SEVEN

The Christian Nurture of Youth
—continued

The preceding chapter, after presenting a summary statement of the church's educational tradition, has epitomized in order of their founding the stories of six of the church's present institutions. This chapter continues with statements concerning the remaining three existing schools, three schools that have been discontinued, and a paragraph each concerning four schools sponsored by Free Methodists but not officially recognized by the denomination. Further sections of this chapter present an account of the development and progress of the church's organized program for young people, now carried on by Free Methodist Youth, and of the church's program of ministerial training. A summary of the church's provisions for theological training at the seminary level concludes the chapter.

Los Angeles Pacific College and High School (founded as Los Angeles Free Methodist Seminary, 1903)

The prime mover in establishing Los Angeles Free Methodist Seminary was Rev. Clyde B. Ebey, editor of *The Free Methodist* from 1903 to 1907. The launching of the institution was financed with the gift of one hundred city lots by one Ralph Rogers. From this tract the campus area was reserved, and the remainder was sold and the proceeds were applied to the cost of the seminary building, an attractive mission-type structure. The character of the community that would grow up around the school was safeguarded by including in the deeds to the lots a clause forbidding the manufacture or sale thereon of intoxicating beverages.

The first principal, N. J. Davis (1904-1907) was brought from Evansville Seminary in Wisconsin, where he had been the vice-principal. The school opened in September, 1904, with both elementary and high school pupils. Before the close of the year the enrollment had reached 114. A beginning in college instruction was made in 1911, and by 1915 courses for two college years had been set up. By 1920 three students graduated from junior college, and the number increased thereafter. A four-year Bible college curriculum leading to the A. B. degree with a major in Religion was provided in the mid-thirties, and was approved by the denomination in 1936. In 1954, plans to proceed from junior to senior college status were authorized by the denominational board. A total of forty-six baccalaureate degrees have been conferred to date.

The roster of principals and presidents is a distinguished list—and a long one, eighteen having served in the school's fifty-six years. The terms of only four exceeded five years: Paul R. Helsel (1923-1929), now a retired professor of the University of Southern California; Byron S. Lamson (1930-1939), since 1944 the General Missionary Secretary of the Free Methodist Church; C. Dorr Demaray (1941-1948), now president of Seattle Pacific College; and the present incumbent, Robert J. Cox (1953-   ), who came to the position from the pastoral ministry in Oregon. B. J. Vincent (1910-1912) came to the principalship directly from the same position in Spring Arbor Seminary. He later was to become principal of Wessington Springs College, and still later, he would be elected a bishop. W. C. Mavis (1939-1941) was to serve many years as dean and director of John Wesley Seminary Foundation. The roster carries the names of many other outstanding personalities.

The campus is on two levels. On the upper campus are the original structure, now the Administration Building, housing offices, library, music rooms, print shop; the Student Center; a veterans' unit reconstructed as an apartment residence; Bagley Hall, for men; and Vincent Hall, for women. Under construction is a new classroom building for the high-school department. On the lower campus are the Auditorium-Gymnasium, with a seating capacity of 2,000; Demaray Hall, housing a spacious dining room and other facilities; and the new Science Building. Near the campus on this level is the attractive and commodious Hermon Free Methodist Church, recently constructed, which ministers to the campus group.

The present student body numbers 241, with 42 per cent coming from a Free Methodist constituency. The teaching staff numbers 23. This younger school, as the older schools of the denomination, has been productive in the training of ministers, doctors, missionaries, educators, businessmen, and members of other callings. It has served its church constituency of California and Arizona, along

THE CHRISTIAN NURTURE OF YOUTH—*continued*

with youth of many other groups, and has always welcomed other nationalities to share its privileges. Its objectives are here suggested:

Los Angeles Pacific College and High School seeks to transmit our heritage in the arts, sciences, and evangelical Christianity, to the end that the student will develop: 1. skill in communication, health, and use of leisure; 2. appreciation of beauty and a sense of wonder; 3. the practice of independent thought; 4. love as the central motivation of conduct; 5. cooperation and sympathy in human relationships; 6. economic understanding necessary to a skilled producer and a wise consumer; and, 7. intelligent willingness to assume social, civic, and religious responsibilities, through sensitive and unselfish participation in community life. These objectives are pursued in a social and academic atmosphere oriented to Christian beliefs, attitudes, and modes of conduct.

Lorne Park College (founded as Lorne Park Seminary, 1924)

For some time Ontario Free Methodism had been interested in a Canadian School. In fact a young woman named Martha Stonehouse, who died in 1889, had left a thousand dollars to assist worthy students preparing for the ministry in a Canadian Free Methodist school. Thirty-five years after her death Lorne Park Seminary was founded, and qualified to receive the legacy. In 1924 a campus, previously occupied by a Seventh Day Adventist school, was purchased near Port Credit, Ontario. On the land were a large brick house which became the main building of the new school, a small stone house, and a barn. The cost was approximately twenty thousand dollars.

The first principal was James F. Gregory who that year had graduated from Greenville College. Previously noted have been his later presidency of Spring Arbor Junior College and his present editorship of *The Free Methodist*. There were 25 students the first year, 52 the second. In 1927 the name of the institution was changed to Lorne Park College, and in 1928 it was granted a Provincial charter.

James F. Gregory served for eight years, and was followed by nine different administrators and twelve administrations. The late Alice E. Walls served three separate terms as principal, five years in all. Others who served five years are R. Barclay Warren (1946-1951), present editor of *Canadian Free Methodist Herald*; and K. Lavern

Snider (1951-1956), now a missionary to Japan. Recent administrators have borne the title of president. The present incumbent is Rev. Byron Withenshaw, a young minister of the West Ontario Conference and a recent graduate of Asbury Theological Seminary. He became president in 1959.

As the years passed and the institution grew, minor buildings were added to the original campus. Finally another campus area was acquired, located across Queen Elizabeth Highway, where the major campus developments have taken place. This campus is now an area of approximately twelve acres. In 1955 an administration building was constructed on the new campus, which was named in honor of the first principal. The sale of building lots and larger areas, carved from the original campus, has greatly assisted in the development of the school. The campus now is provided with J. F. Gregory Hall, housing offices, classrooms, library, dining room, and the auditorium-gymnasium; the Girls' Dormitory; the Boys' Dormitory, which is the original seminary building and soon to be replaced by a new dormitory; and several staff residences.

Students number 76, 54 per cent of them coming from a Free Methodist constituency. The school has served well its area, both in general training of its young people and in the preparation of its ministry. Nineteen of its alumni are now serving in the two Ontario conferences.

Two of the school's past principals have stated the objectives of the institution in the following paragraphs:

> To provide for youth the opportunity of securing mental training under conditions and influences most conducive to the development of pure, noble character, which finds its source in effective religious experience through saving faith in our Lord Jesus Christ, and which issues in practical service.—*Alice E. Walls.*

> The school has had two main objectives, the education of young men and women for the Christian ministry, and the education of high school students in a thoroughly Christian environment. The accomplishment of the first objective may be seen in well trained ministers, and ministers' wives, in all our Canadian conferences, and in missionaries now serving in China and Africa. ... No less have been the returns from the hundreds of young people of secondary school age who have not only found knowledge and training for life here, but through Christian experience have found the power to do that which is right. These have made their influence felt as leaders in Free Methodist churches on every district.—*J. F. Gregory.*

THE CHRISTIAN NURTURE OF YOUTH—*continued*

Moose Jaw Bible College (founded as Moose Jaw Bible School, 1940)

The Ontario school served the western conferences for several years, but the great distance made desirable a school in the west. After two years of Conference deliberation and no action, two score or more young people marched into a sitting of the 1939 Saskatchewan Conference singing, "I know the Lord will send a Bible school." The presiding bishop permitted the group to express its desires, and the Conference appointed a committee under the chairmanship of Rev. D. S. Wartman. A spacious sixteen-room house was soon found, well suited to the purpose, well located on an eminence overlooking the city of Moose Jaw, and reasonably priced. This was promptly purchased. Mr. and Mrs. Wartman were vigorously behind the project for several years, carrying much of the load of administration. The first principal was Miss Florence Pickert (1941-1947) from Cleveland Bible College, who served until her resignation to enter mission service. Succeeding her was Rev. M. C. Miller (1947-1954), a minister of the Washington Conference. Unusual for a small and young school, its two first administrations spanned fourteen years. Subsequent terms of two years have been that of Rev. Wilfred Kinney (1954-1956), a minister of the Saskatchewan Conference, and Rev. Louis Smith (1956-1958) of the New York Conference. In 1958 Rev. J. Wesley Stewart, recently graduated from Seattle Pacific College, became the president.

The campus of thirteen acres contains the original building, Frank's Hall, which is the men's dormitory; and the new Annex, a three-story structure housing offices, classrooms, dining room, and the women's dormitory. There is also a small staff home on the campus.

Students number 30; faculty, 5. All but three of the students come from a Free Methodist constituency. The school in the early years offered a three-year diploma course in Bible and a one-year Christian workers' course, and recently has ventured into the Bible college field with a curriculum leading to the degree Th. B. The first class to graduate with the degree will be the class of 1960. The institution is training ministers for the Saskatchewan and Alberta conferences, and some of its students proceed for further training to institutions of the church in the United States. The venture made in 1940 was a courageous one, but already the school has contributed much to the program of Free Methodism in Western Canada.

As the name of the institution indicates, its purpose is a practical one. The president writes, "Our basic purpose is to train our young people so well that they will be capable of carrying out the task God has for them."

Discontinued educational ventures

A few schools established under Free Methodist sponsorship have not survived the rigorous testing that time brings. The critical cause of the discontinuance of these schools has been a constituency inadequate in numbers and therefore weak in financial resources and student patronage. Those that became firmly established made worthy contributions to the church areas they served and to their communities until changing conditions terminated their ministry.

The Evansville Junior College (founded as Evansville Seminary, 1880). This was the third school to be sponsored by the Free Methodist Church. Some time after 1855 a school had been established under Methodist Episcopal auspices at Evansville, Wisconsin. Not succeeding, the institution passed into the hands of the Free Will Baptists. They in turn met failure and offered the campus to the Free Methodists. After amendment of the charter as proposed by the Free Methodists, the institution was turned over to them, and in 1880 it opened as a Free Methodist school.

J. Emory Coleman, son of G. W. Coleman who later became bishop, was the first principal and ably served until poor health compelled him to resign in 1884. Note the outstanding names in the list of principals and presidents succeeding him: Bertels, Whitcomb, Stilwell, Burritt, Sanford, Webb, Anna Burton, Blews, Cooper, Howard. The institution grew, and by 1885 the enrollment was 132. A new building was completed in 1890. In 1910 college instruction was added, and by 1912 the institution was offering two years as a junior college. Around 1920, out of negotiations of the general church with schools of the central area looking toward merger or readjustment of relationships among educational institutions in that area, Evansville returned to academy status under its original name, Evansville Seminary. In 1926 the board of trustees voted to discontinue the school, and the campus was sold to private school interests.

Evansville history is a record of heroic sacrifice and high achievement. The institution was a credit to the denomination, due both to the character and abilities of the men who directed its course and to the quality of its educational product. Among its alumni were men of distinction in public life, and its contribution to the territory of the church it served was large.

Neosho Rapids Seminary, 1887. Interest in the establishment of a school by the Missouri and Kansas Conference was expressed in 1882 by the appointment of a committee to raise funds for such a cause. The next year the conference was divided by separating from it the Missouri Conference and the West Kansas, leaving the Kansas Conference as the continuing body. During the period in which the newly organized West Kansas Conference was establishing and opening a school at Orleans, Nebraska, the parent conference was struggling with a similar task, but not until 1887 was Neosho Rapids Seminary opened at Neosho Rapids, Kansas. After a struggling existence of eight years, fire destroyed the Seminary building, and for lack of finances and sufficient interest in the continuance of the institution, it was closed in 1895. During its existence, it had been included by the General Conference in the list of recognized Free Methodist schools.

Campbell Free Methodist Seminary, 1910 (continued as McKinney Junior College, 1920.) In 1909 the Texas Conference appointed a committee to locate a site on which to establish a school. The campus of a previous educational institution at Campbell, Texas, was secured, and Campbell Free Methodist Seminary opened in 1910. Principals of the institution were, in order, N. W. Sanford, C. E. Harroun, E. A. Andrews. In 1919 the corporation was dissolved and it was planned that the school would reopen that fall as McKinney Junior College, McKinney, Texas. The removal was delayed a year by delay in completing the McKinney plant, and school was continued for 1919-1920 on the Campbell campus with the first year of college instruction added to the previous program. In 1920 the school was opened at McKinney with Rev. C. L. Howland, later an editor of *The Free Methodist*, as president. The unexpected additional costs of the McKinney college building so handicapped the project that the school was closed in its second year on the McKinney site. The territory of the institution became a part of Central College territory.

Non-official educational ventures

Schools of brief existence and tenuous connection with the Free Methodist Church include:

Gerry Seminary, 1884. Rev. W. A. Sellew and his wife established and operated a school called Gerry Seminary, at Gerry, New York, for the period 1884-1888. A factor in its discontinuance seems to have been its location near the officially recognized school of the church at North Chili. As noted in Chapter Twenty-two, W. A. Sellew contributed his personal investment in this seminary property when it was transferred to the Gerry Homes to become the first charitable institution of the denomination.

Virginia Seminary. Rev. W. A. Sellew, some time following the Gerry venture, established a school called Virginia Seminary at Spotsylvania, Virgina, to which, by the influence of B. T. Roberts, Alexander Beers was called as principal at midyear, 1889-1890. Mr. Beers remained in this position until shortly before he became principal of Seattle Seminary—again on the recommendation of B. T. Roberts. Although the school was never officially sponsored by the New York Conference whose bounds then extended southward to include Virginia, when the committee on education of the 1890 General Conference listed the recognized schools of the denomination without including Virginia Seminary, the Conference ordered it to be included with the others. Evidently there was then hope that this institution would become firmly established in the educational program of the church.

Lawrence Seminary, 1889. The published minutes of the 1888 Texas Conference reported preliminary steps to organize a school, and the 1889 minutes indicated the purchase of four acres of land in Lawrence, Texas, with buildings suitable for a school. The school was to open in December of that year. According to Dr. Schoenhals, reference to the institution does not appear in the published minutes thereafter, but the school is referred to in a Central Illinois Conference report on education in the published minutes of 1892. The minutes of the Texas Conference for that period have been destroyed by fire and any further information is lacking. It is clear that the project was conference-sponsored, but never established itself as a denominationally recognized school.

B. T. Roberts Seminary, 1907. This institution was founded in Atlanta six years before the organization of the Georgia and Florida Conference. Under the labors especially of Rev. E. E. Shelhamer several churches had been established in the area and these had been organized as the Atlanta District of the Pittsburgh Conference. The school served a need of the area at the time, especially in training workers for the church. Rev. N. L. Smith, Atlanta pastor, served as principal. In 1909-1910 the enrollment reported was 56. Not long thereafter the school closed.

Youth in action

From their beginnings, the schools and colleges of the church have provided young people with far more than the education of the classroom, library, and laboratory. On a Christian campus a young person has opportunities for Christian fellowship and worship with other young people, for wholesome recreational and social activities, and for varied types of directed Christian service not open in many instances to young people in the home community, the public school, or the non-Christian college, except as the church may provide for organized youth activities under appropriate supervision.

For many years the Free Methodist Church made no such provision, and there was a serious need that our young people outside our schools and colleges, greater by far in number than those within these institutions, should have opportunities for Christian fellowship and activity comparable to those offered by the schools to their students. But many leaders in the church feared that a youth organization would open the door to worldliness.

And worldliness will enter through that door if a church bargains for the lesser of two evils by compromising Christian standards in the effort to hold its youth. We offer an extreme example: the church that yields to the specious argument, "But young people *will* dance, and it is better that they dance under church supervision than in night club or tavern," overlooks two important points. First, social dancing cannot be justified as a Christian practice under either sponsorship, religious or commercial; second, young people educated in dancing by the church will the more readily dance elsewhere. The church can never win against the world in the world's own game.

The primary issue in the Free Methodist Church has not been a conflict between Christian and sinful activities under church auspices, but has concerned the length to which the church should go in meeting the legitimate activity needs of youth in a society more pagan than Christian, and organized to offer stones but not bread to meet those needs.

It was noted in the preceding chapter that more than a half-century ago general conference committees were lamenting the failure of the church to save and hold its youth, and that in 1907 the bishops called for a youth organization to enlist young people and channel their energies and talents in the cause of Christ. A dozen years passed before anything was done. And then it was not the general church that undertook the task, but the Woman's Missionary Society. In 1898 this society had organized the children as an auxiliary, with the name Junior Missionary Society. In 1919, twenty-one years later, the women organized a youth auxiliary, the Young People's Missionary Society. Although limited in scope principally to missionary education and activities, the organization during its first quadrennium grew to more than three thousand members, and during the next quadrennium doubled its membership.

The women had demonstrated that a youth organization could succeed without the dire consequences some had feared, and in 1927 there were those who worked for the establishment of a youth organization more general in the scope of its program. They succeeded, and the General Conference approved the organization of a Young People's Society. During the ensuing quadrennium both youth organizations were in operation and often in competition. As could have been foreseen, the arrangement was far from satisfactory. The 1931 General Conference sought the solution of the problem by making the Young People's Missionary Society the official youth organization of the church and permitting the Young People's Society to lapse. As the official youth organization of the church, the Young People's Missionary Society was no longer to be an auxiliary of the Woman's Missionary Society, but was to be integrated directly with the church organization at all levels. Consequently, its superintendent was now a general church officer, elected directly by the General Conference. Young people at a certain period have a way of breaking from a mother's solicitous care, and so it was with the Young People's Mis-

THE CHRISTIAN NURTURE OF YOUTH—*continued*

sionary Society and the Woman's Missionary Society. The time had come for youth to become a part of the official church. But let it not be forgotten that the church owes to the women the vigorous young adult now serving with such initiative and enthusiasm the cause of Christ.

During the twenty-nine years since 1931, the Young People's Missionary Society (renamed Free Methodist Youth in 1955) has practically doubled its active membership with a roll exceeding 13,000 in the United States and Canada. Free Methodist Youth has been organized also in Brazil, Paraguay, Formosa, the Philippines, the Dominican Republic, and Japan. In 1955 the estimated world membership of Free Methodist Youth was 30,000.

Some of the projects undertaken by Free Methodist Youth are summarized below to reflect the nature of the organization and to indicate the ways by which it enlists the interests and activities of young people.

Home Evangelism. Wide-spread house-to-house visitation by young people, open-air evangelism, tent meetings, and other evangelistic activities characterized the Mid-Century Youth Crusade of 1950.

Evangelism abroad. An evangelistic tour of the Dominican Republic was undertaken in 1950 by the superintendent and the four regional directors of Free Methodist Youth. In 1959 a plane load of young men flew to the Dominican Republic and there scattered to all parts of the country in evangelistic teams. These efforts, with the great evangelistic rally at Santiago, yielded gratifying evangelistic results. A church extension venture in Ireland is to enlist the cooperation of Free Methodist Youth in 1960.

Youth Camps. The youth camp movement in the Free Methodist Church began in the late thirties and was extended widely at conference and regional levels. These camps are evangelistically fruitful. In addition, a church-wide camp in recent years draws hundreds of young people from coast to coast to Camp Mack, near Winona Lake.

Bible Quiz. In 1953 began the Bible Quiz program in which local teams winning conference contests compete for international honors at the annual Youth Camp. The movement has spread to several national groups abroad.

Journalism and publications. The *Y.P.M.S. News* was launched in 1942 as a monthly. It was succeeded in 1956 by *Youth in Action*, a magazine with a circulation approaching the membership of the sponsoring organization.

Eight volumes of *Sunday Evenings with Jesus* have been produced, each a program series for a year of weekly local services of Free Methodist Youth. *Spirit Filled Songs for Singing Youth* and Bible Quiz text books have been published. An expansion of curriculum materials for youth is now being planned.

Service to servicemen. Following the outbreak of World War II, the Church Council for Men in Service was organized in 1943 to minister to the church's men in all branches of military service. The roster of those receiving the church's ministry through this Council reached 16,950 in 1947, but diminished after demobilization to 1,497 in 1950. The Council, no longer appearing to be an emergency need, was made a department of Free Methodist Youth for the post-war period of peace. Then came the Korean crisis which rapidly extended the list until in 1953 the number served mounted to 6,145. In 1958 what perhaps is to be close to a normal cold-war level of 3,286 was reached. Young people, taken from their homes, churches, schools, and normal employment by the peculiar necessities of an unpredictable world situation, have a claim upon the church for a spiritual ministry. The servicemen's department of Free Methodist Youth seeks to meet the need through Christian literature, direct mail communications, and personal counseling by mail and, when possible, on military installations.

Fund raising. For other than its own program, Free Methodist Youth raises funds for such causes as Missions, Evangelism, and Christian Education. Total funds raised have reached as much as $184,000 in a year.

The foregoing partial list of activities has dealt principally with general and headquarters projects, but nearly 900 local societies of Free Methodist Youth are functioning in the local churches of the United States and Canada. In the language of the Constitution of the organization, they are working "to promote the spiritual welfare of the young people connected with the Free Methodist Church, and to provide direction for their Christian activities, and to help them in their contribution to the church and the world." The more specific objectives of Free Methodist Youth, as detailed in its Constitution, are:

1. To seek and maintain among its members the highest type of Christian experience and life through regeneration and baptism of the Holy Spirit, to encourage growth in grace, and to prepare for efficient membership in the Free Methodist Church; 2. To enlist, inspire, and train young people to win the lost of their generation; 3. To study the needs of the various fields and become intelligent supporters of the full missionary program; and, 4. To encourage Christian stewardship and raise money for projects sanctioned by the general authorities of the church in ways consistent with the Discipline of the Free Methodist Church.

The organization of the church's youth is now generally accepted. Through it in recent years a loyal group of young people has been won to Christ and the church, and youth's talents and energies have been channeled in effective Christian service at home and abroad. In the following brief statement the present superintendent, Rev. C. Mervin Russell, shares the problem of his department and its challenge:

> It is well to bear in mind that since it is a youth organization, Free Methodist Youth never "arrives." Young people just pass through it. At best we barely have time to capture their interest, lead them to Christ, establish them spiritually and train them for leadership, and they are gone to bigger Kingdom tasks for God and the church. From its early predominant missionary emphasis, and without losing any of it, Free Methodist Youth has endeavored to develop a well balanced program by which to prepare young people to serve the total church.

Preparation for the ministry: early period

For many years from the church's founding, preparation for the ministry was an individual matter of home study, the satisfactory completion of which was determined by the annual conference through examinations. In the *Northern Independent* of October 17, 1861, shortly before the close of the first conference year and looking to the approaching session of the second annual conference, this announcement by Loren Stiles, Jr., appeared:

> NOTICE.—The several Classes in the Genesee Convention of the F. M. Church will meet for examination in the F. M. Church in Perry, Wednesday, the 23rd inst. at 1:00 o'clock p.m. Let all members of the Committee, and candidates for examination, be punctual at the hour.

The examinations thus announced were based upon the 1860 *Discipline*, adopted by the Pekin Convention. Candidates for admission to "the Traveling Connection on probation" were to be examined on what later came to be known as the preliminary course. At that time this course included English grammar, arithmetic, modern geography, spelling, and composition. The only subject of directly religious content was the Free Methodist *Discipline*. After completion of the preliminary course came a four-year course, the substantial content of which can be appreciated only by reading it. Because so few copies of the first *Discipline* are extant, and in order that the second century may know upon what meat the church's pioneer preachers grew strong in mind and spirit, we reproduce the outline of the course as it was published a hundred years ago.

COURSE OF STUDY FOR TRAVELING PREACHERS

First Year
The Bible—Doctrines

The Existence of God; the Attributes of God, namely, Unity, Spirituality, Eternity, Omnipotence, Ubiquity, Omniscience, Immutability, Wisdom, Truth, Justice, Mercy, Love, Goodness, Holiness; the Trinity in Unity; the Deity of Christ; the Humanity of Christ; the Union of Deity and Humanity; Personality and Deity of the Holy Ghost; Depravity; Atonement; Repentance; Justification by Faith; Regeneration; Adoption; the Witness of the Spirit; Growth in Grace; Christian Perfection; Possibility of Final Apostacy [sic]; Immortality of the Soul; Resurrection of the Body; General Judgment; Rewards and Punishment.

Watson's Institutes, First Part; Wesley's Plain Account of Christian Perfection; Cutter's Anatomy and Physiology; Caldwell's Elocution.

Composition

Essay or Sermon.

[Read Wesley's Sermons and Notes; The Life of Wesley; Platt's Gift of Power; Wayland's Political Economy.]

Second Year
The Bible—Sacraments

The Sacrament of Baptism—Its Nature, Design, Obligation, Subjects, and Mode; The Sacrament of the Lord's Supper—Its Nature, Design, and Obligation.

Watson's Institutes, Second Part to the 18th Chapter; Peck's Central Idea; Wayland's Moral Science.

Composition

Essay or Sermon.

[Read Bangs' History of Methodism; Johnston's Natural Philosophy.]

Third Year
The Bible—History and Chronology

Candidates are to be prepared upon the leading events in the Old and New Testament; Reference Books; Horne's Introduction; and Robinson's Palestine.

Watson's Institutes, Second Part, beginning with the 18th Chapter; Paley's Natural Theology; Ruter's Church History; Whateley's Logic; Boyd's Rhetoric.

Composition

Essay or Sermon.

[Read Fletcher's Works; Smith's Patriarchal Age; Wilson's Outlines of History.]

THE CHRISTIAN NURTURE OF YOUTH—*continued*

FOURTH YEAR

Review of the whole course. Watson's Institutes, Third and Fourth Parts; Butler's Analogy; Hitchcock's Elementary Geology.

Composition

Essay or Sermon.

[Read Smith's Hebrew People; Mosheim's Ecclesiastical History; Wayland's Intellectual Philosophy; History of the United States.]

Roberts on the minister's training

No doubt B. T. Roberts had an important part in planning this course, the mastery of which would assure a preacher's competence in the principal areas of ministerial preparation, with practical theology, Hebrew, and Greek excepted. Roberts, a student of both languages, exhorted preachers to study the Scriptures in Hebrew and Greek as well as in their English translations. In that admirable book of his authorship, *Fishers of Men*, Roberts goes so far in encouragement as to give assurance that "any ordinary person can gain such a knowledge of the Hebrew, or the Greek, by diligent study for three months, as to be able by the help of the Grammar and Lexicon, to study out to his satisfaction, the meaning of any text in either of these original languages." [1]

He would have preachers study also science, literature, mathematics —"in short," he wrote, "every branch of human knowledge can be used to advantage in the work of winning souls to God." [2] His advice is reminiscent of Wesley who in 1756 outlined the desirable qualifications of the minister to include the study of the Scriptures, both in English and the original languages, as well as history, geography, logic, mathematics, natural science, geometry, and the manners of a gentleman; for the minister, he said, should exhibit "all the courtesy of a gentleman, joined with the correctness of a scholar." Certainly, in the thinking of both Wesley and Roberts, education and evangelism were allies and not enemies.

Preparation for the ministry: middle period

The course of study for ministers continued according to the pattern set in 1860 well into the church's second half-century. There were, however, numerous changes in required texts and books to be

---

1. B. T. Roberts, *Fishers of Men*. G. I. Roberts & Co., Rochester; p. 254 *et seq.*
2. *Ibid.*, p. 258.

read. Some of the new titles were those books written by the church's own authors. Roberts' *Fishers of Men* and *Why Another Sect* appeared in the course in 1882; Hogue's *Hand Book of Homiletics and Pastoral Theology* and Terrill's *Life of Redfield* were added in 1890. *Fishers of Men* and *Homiletics and Pastoral Theology* remedied the earlier lack in the field of practical theology. Roberts' *Holiness Teachings* was added in 1894.

Other titles provided by the church's own writers as time passed included: Hart's *Reminiscences of Early Free Methodism*; Hogue's *The Class Meeting as a Means of Grace*; Sellew's *Clara Leffingwell, a Missionary*; Hogue's *Hymns that are Immortal*; MacGeary's *Outline History of the Free Methodist Church*; W. B. Olmstead's *Handbook for Sunday School Workers*; Hogue's *History of the Free Methodist Church*; Burritt's *The Pupil and How to Teach Him*; Baldwin's *The Indwelling Christ*; Hogue's *The Holy Spirit*; *Instrumental Music in Public Worship*; Howland's *The Story of Our Church*; Fairbairn's *Primer in Evangelism*; Watson's *Digest of Free Methodist Law*; Marston's *Youth Speaks!*; B. L. Olmstead's *A Brief Life of St. Paul*; Blews' *Master Workmen*; Marston's *From Chaos to Character*.

The last outline of the home study course, which appeared in the 1947 *Discipline*, in addition to several of the titles in the foregoing paragraphs, included Ralston's *Divinity*; Fisher's *Church History*; Jevon's *Logic*; Cannon's *Theology of John Wesley*; Wood's *Perfect Love*; Sampey's *The Heart of the Old Testament*; Stalker's *Life of Christ*; Hurlbut's *Biblical Geography*; Adams' *Ancient Records and the Bible*; Jones' *The Faith of Our Children*; Wesley's *Sermons*, and others.

Comparing the 1860 and 1947 courses of study, one gains the impression that the former was more basic and better focused, but by 1947 the home study course had been subordinated in importance to residence study in the church's schools. The trend from home study to residence study was accelerated by a significant action of the 1939 General Conference, marking a rather sharp transition to the contemporary period.

Preparation for the ministry: contemporary period

The General Conference of 1939 began the articulation of college studies with ministerial preparation by outlining a core curriculum at college level to meet the academic requirements for ordination of candidates pursuing an approved course in a Free Methodist institution. It is true that for many years it had been the practice of conference examining boards to accept college subjects for equivalent subjects in the home study program, but no equivalent college program as a substitute for the entire home study course had previously been planned and officially adopted. The *Discipline* of 1939 still carried the home study outline for candidates to follow who had not pursued the approved curriculum in college, and for a time many continued their training under the old plan. But the college plan came increasingly into favor.

In the 1939 plan, however, there was a difficulty that decreased its effectiveness. From the beginning the church had required not only the four-year course of study beyond the preliminary course for full ordination, but also a four-year period of itinerant service under conference appointment. Normally both study and itinerant requirements were carried simultaneously by the candidate, the latter being met by the young pastor's early ministry under conference appointment to a charge. The new plan provided for the completion in college of the candidate's academic preparation, but left him at college graduation no nearer ordination because he must yet serve under conference appointment two years before ordination as deacon, and another two years before ordination as elder.

The 1943 General Conference sought to remedy this weakness by adopting a plan whereby properly supervised Christian service in preaching, church school and youth work, pastoral visitation and the like, pursued during college training for the ministry, might be applied toward a portion of the itinerant requirement for ordination. During the four-year college course the ministerial candidate thus could earn two years of itinerant or practical credit and upon graduation be ready for ordination as deacon. Among other advantages of this plan was its provision for bringing the candidate more closely under the supervision of his annual conference during his college years.

In the *Discipline* of 1947, preference was given the four-year curriculum of ministerial training offered by the schools of the church by placing its publication ahead of the home study outline. The official seminary program of the church had been planned since the 1943 General Conference, and the 1947 *Discipline* gave recognition thereto by stipulating that the seminary graduate must have at least one year under pastoral appointment before ordination as elder. This allowed the seminary candidate to acquire three years of itinerant credit while in college and seminary.

The 1951 General Conference allowed study credits for ordination to be earned either by college study or by correspondence study administered by the Department of Service Training. No home study course was listed in the 1951 Discipline, but provision was made in exceptional cases for the conference board of examiners to direct that the course be taken by home study.

The 1955 General Conference replaced the Central Board of Conference Examiners with a Central Board of Ministerial Training of broader powers and functions. This General Conference encouraged ministerial candidates to complete college and, if feasible, seminary also. No provision of home study for traveling preachers was made other than the course outlined for local elders, by completing which an exceptional candidate of advanced years might qualify for conference admission and ordination as deacon if he had the unanimous approval of the conference board of ministerial training and the vote of three-fourths of the annual conference. To the one choosing this route to deacon's ordination, the way to ordination as elder was closed. The regular program of ministerial training was now to pursue studies in college or seminary, or to take correspondence study under the direction of the Central Board of Ministerial Training. The traditional home study course had practically disappeared in the sixteen years since General Conference took steps to articulate ministerial preparation with college study.

Great as are the advantages of the newer system, the disappearance of the old brings not unmixed gain. The administration of ministerial training by several institutions, and by even a larger number of instructors, must unavoidably sacrifice in some measure that early common core of knowledge and agreement in thought among the church's ministry such as had been insured by the prescription of books written by some of the best thinkers in the Methodist tradition. Any adequate conserving and unifying influence in the future training of the ministry of the church must now rest in large part with the Central Board of Ministerial Training in its control of the core curriculum and, perhaps in crucial areas, in its designation of approved texts. This board as now constituted is large and representative enough to safeguard the reasonable claims of institutional freedom. After all, it is the church itself that has the greater and more crucial interests to be safeguarded in the training of the ministry of the denomination.

Service Training

Closely related to ministerial training today is the Department of Service Training of the Commission on Christian Education. For many years Service Training has provided courses for Sunday-school workers and other lay leaders, but with the passing of the historic home study course for preachers, the Service Training Department has been expanded to provide, by correspondence, courses under qualified teachers for candidates who have not met full ministerial requirements by residence study in college or seminary. The department has rendered important service in both fields—training lay workers and instructing ministerial candidates.

John Wesley Seminary Foundation, 1947

In the period between 1925 and 1930 the trend toward advanced theological study increased among the church's young ministers, and within a few years a portion of the flow of college graduates to university postgraduate study was diverted to the theological seminaries. A few leaders in the church began to consider Free Methodism's need of an institution of theological seminary grade. In fact, Greenville College had established a department of advanced theological study but after graduating eight with the degree Bachelor of Divinity, terminated the department in the interests of its major task, the building of a strong liberal arts institution. But the seminary trend continued until in 1944-1945 there were well above twenty Free Methodist students in a single interdenominational seminary. It was increasingly clear that the time had come when the Free Methodist Church should consider gathering its scattered seminarians into a program of its own. A survey of conference leaders disclosed a surprising interest in this direction.

Accordingly, in 1945 the Board of Administration authorized the launching of a seminary, to open in the fall of 1947, under the control of that board. In the spring of 1946 a Free Methodist professor in Asbury Theological Seminary, Wilmore, Kentucky, suggested that the church seek affiliation with that institution, an independent seminary of conservative, Arminian and Wesleyan tradition, fully committed to the same doctrinal positions as those held by the Free Methodist Church. Such an affiliation would secure at once an established and rapidly growing campus, a larger faculty than the church would be able to assemble for many years, and other related advantages. After careful planning and consideration, the affiliation was approved by the Board of Administration in 1946, the program at Wilmore to be inaugurated in the fall of 1947. All arrangements were tentative, with freedom for the church to withdraw from affiliation at any time. From the brochure announcing the affiliation, we quote the following:

> John Wesley Seminary, a corporation of the Free Methodist Church, by action of the Board of Administration in October, 1946, affiliated with Asbury Theological Seminary, Wilmore, Kentucky. The affiliation functions through John Wesley Seminary Foundation which seeks to insure seminary training for ministerial candidates of the Free Methodist Church under denominational influence, guidance and control.
>
> Through its Dean, the Foundation provides guidance and counsel on education and personal problems, assists in directing student life and fellowship in harmony with Free Methodist standards, supervises the practical field activities of the students, and assists in placing the students, upon graduation, in positions of maximum Christian usefulness within the Free Methodist Church. The Foundation also provides financial assistance through scholarships for students who are qualified.

All facilities of the campus are available to students of the Foundation, and upon graduation these students receive the diploma and degree of Asbury Theological Seminary as well as a certificate from John Wesley Seminary Foundation. The Foundation maintains a center for Free Methodist students where social and reading rooms, library and offices are located. After thirteen years of mutually satisfactory affiliation of John Wesley Seminary Foundation and Asbury Theological Seminary, with greater permanence of the relationship now in view, the Foundation plans the erection of a substantial structure on its own property adjacent to the campus. This will provide better facilities for the items mentioned above, and also a sanctuary.

A distinct advantage in the affiliation is the presence on the Seminary faculty of several Free Methodist professors, approximating in number the staff which a separate institution would need in its beginning. A further favorable consideration is the fact that Foundation students are allowed, under the instruction of a Free Methodist pro-

THE CHRISTIAN NURTURE OF YOUTH—*continued*

fessor, to take courses in Free Methodist history, mission, and polity, the same to apply toward a degree. Differential courses in doctrinal subjects are unnecessary because of full agreement of the Foundation and the Seminary in the doctrinal area.

The alumni of John Wesley Seminary Foundation for the first twelve years of its operation number 218, of which number 179 have completed work for their post-college degrees in Asbury Theological Seminary. Of the 218, the 181 now serving in the Free Methodist Church or preparing for such service through further training are classified as follows: pastors and superintendents, 103; missionaries, 34; teachers, 24; general church and institutional executives, 6; chaplains, 5; ministers' wives, 6; in further advanced training, 3. In Christian service outside the denomination are 13 ministers and 6 missionaries, bringing the total in Christian service to 91.7 per cent. The remaining 18 of the 218 are a miscellaneous group made up of laymen, presently inactive preachers, deceased, unknown, and the like. This unusual record of persistence through the training period to enlistment in a field of service, and also the splendid accomplishments of these alumni in that service, bespeak the success of the Foundation in fulfilling its purpose of training effective and Spirit-filled ministers for the Free Methodist Church.

Throughout the thirteen years of the affiliation, Dr. W. Curry Mavis, professor of pastoral work in Asbury Theological Seminary, has directed the Foundation. Associated Free Methodist professors of the Asbury staff at present are Dr. George A. Turner, Biblical literature; Dr. Harold C. Mason, Christian education; and Dr. George Herbert Livingston, Old Testament.

General educational secretaries of the Free Methodist Church have been:

Alexander Beers 1907-1911   L. Glenn Lewis 1919-1933

In the later periods for which no general educational secretary was elected, the chairman of the Commission on Christian Education has acted.

The following have served as general superintendents of Free Methodist Youth:

Mrs. Emma L. Hogue   1919-1931   B. H. Pearson   1935-1943
Mrs. Lillian B. Griffith 1931-1935   Ernest Keasling   1943-1958
                    C. Mervin Russell 1958-

O. S. Walters, M.D., has served as general director of Service Training from 1937.

W. Curry Mavis has served as dean of John Wesley Seminary Foundation from 1947.

We have now all but completed the effort to present an interpretation of Free Methodism in the light of its backgrounds in Methodism and the history of its first century. To understand the church we first looked to John Wesley and his Methodism of the eighteenth century, and scanned its progress in America through transition to crisis, and the founding of the Free Methodist Church in 1860. We then examined the record of the new church to determine with what success it had maintained the Wesleyan witness in the areas of doctrine, experience, worship, Christian discipline, and stewardship, and followed Free Methodism's extension of this witness by means of home evangelism, world missions, communications, and the varied fields of Christian nurture. In the next and concluding chapter we are briefly to survey the century now completed, evaluate the present status of Free Methodism, and attempt to define the challenge and promise of the new century the church now enters.

CHAPTER TWENTY-EIGHT

A Century Ends — Another Dawns

The journey in retrospect

We began the search for Free Methodism's origins in eighteenth-century England when moral and spiritual forces were fast running out. It was then that John Wesley, from the futility of his own efforts to save his soul by devious routes of man's devising, at last made his escape by the highway of faith. Following that highway, he came to the place of inner poise and spiritual power.

We observed that under the earnest and effective preaching of Wesley, and of others who likewise had found the way of faith, light began to break over dark England. Many, long in despair under the guilt of their sins, could now sing hymns of glad assurance of forgiveness. Hope was kindled in others as they saw lives of sodden wretchedness transformed to radiant joy. The good news of salvation for all was proclaimed in sermon, testimony, and song in open fields, the market place, and the meetinghouse. The good news spread from neighbor to neighbor, and was confirmed by Christian fortitude under mob violence. Sobriety and frugality broke the grip of poverty, and men's bodies, created to be habitations of God's Spirit, took on new significance as the stark ugliness of man's inhumanity to man was seen in the light of a love that embraced the entire human race. In the span of half a century, and in large part because of one man's full surrender to the will of God, a nation was saved from revolution, and a religion near exhaustion if not extinction was revived to life and power.

The revival swept beyond England and the British Isles to American shores. Here Methodism was to grow up in a new country and become an inseparable part of it—a vital and spiritual part. Methodism shared with America its dynamic itinerant urge to new frontiers; America shared with Methodism its pioneer vigor. Both had great hopes and to realize them, both were challenged to large tasks.

This identity of Methodism with the life of young and self-reliant America was her strength, and yet in time it was to discover her weakness. So readily did Methodism adjust to the culture of America that she came to share an activism that could be busy with peripheral concerns and neglect the central things of life, and to share a pragmatism that on occasion could place success above principle. Herein appeared in American guise that encroaching worldliness which in England so deeply concerned John Wesley in his later years. He observed with dismay the trend in England when prosperity brought Methodism to kinship with the prevailing culture, refined to a degree of respectability by Methodism's own earlier reformation zeal.

In America for some time the constantly advancing frontier provided opportunity for the exercise of the vigorous zeal and the rigorous standards of primitive Methodism. Also, back of this frontier, in rural and more secluded areas, were left islands of simple culture favorable to the survival of earlier Methodist ideas and ideals. It was when urban and rural Methodism were brought together in close conference relationship that tensions developed, especially as the urban element became dominant and, by its avid efforts to adjust to an increasingly secular American culture, stirred the conservative element to vigorous reformation activity.

Such areas of close geographic association of urban and rural Methodism were western New York and northern Illinois at the mid-point of the last century. The rural strength had previously been dominant, but the cities in these areas now were rapidly growing. Buffalo numbered above 80,000 in population in 1860—not large compared with today's population centers, but at that time ninth in the nation in size. Buffalo Methodism could not completely submerge the rural areas of Genesee Methodism, but growing rapidly and freely imbibing worldly culture, it threatened the patterns of original Methodism and thereby stimulated the opposition of the conservative element. Likewise in Illinois the conflict erupted in the rural shadowland of a large and rapidly growing city. In 1840 Chicago had a population less than 5,000, but by 1860 this had increased to 109,000.

We have seen how the conflicts that developed within Methodism in these two areas during the fifties climaxed in forcible separation of the reformers from the Methodist Episcopal Church. They had been defeated in their efforts to restore and maintain the historic Wesleyan witness, for the church in these areas was too largely under the control of those committed to the church's eager pursuit of contemporary culture. The strange procedure that led to unjust expulsion of the reformers and denied them all redress made another Methodist church inevitable. Accordingly, the Free Methodist Church was organized in 1860 on the foundation of such distinctive principles of original Methodism as the doctrine and experience of Christian holiness, simplicity and freedom of the Spirit in worship, Christian discipline of daily life, and a devoted stewardship.

The church's footing on these principles has had a century's testing, and the record discloses few changes in the church's position. The judgment declared by the late Bishop William Pearce fifteen or twenty years ago, that the Free Methodist Church had held more firmly to its founding principles over a longer period of time than the parent church had held to its principles, still is valid. The principal visible changes have occurred in certain worship practices and in the relaxing of certain points of Christian discipline in matters of dress and personal adornment. Some would hold that these changes are in the direction of a transition from external to internal discipline, from control by legalisms to control by principles. Granting this, it still remains that at the close of its first century the Free Methodist Church faces the crisis of a transition that has meant in many another Christian group the surrender of the principles themselves. The church must not ignore Wesley's caution that Methodism's prudential regulations guard its essential principle, which is holiness of heart and life; if the prudentials are despised, he warned, the essential will soon be lost.[1]

If Free Methodism is to hold to its historic principles, there must be on the part of its membership generally a supreme loyalty to Jesus Christ as Saviour and example, a full obedience to the law of God as the Christian's guide, a quick responsiveness to the promptings and the checks of the Holy Spirit in areas of uncertainty, and a readiness to accept necessary controls by the church at points which cannot properly be left to individual choice if the church is to bear a consistent Christian witness.

It is gratifying to note that in the area of stewardship, the church has moved nearer the teachings of Scripture as emphasized by the

---

1. Wesley's statement was quoted on p. 169.

church's founder than it held in its mid-period, and perhaps in its beginnings; and this has been brought about without legal enactment of taxation or tithing. Here is encouragement that consistent emphasis on a principle, with clear instruction in its meaning and its application to life, can lead to a high level of practice.

Free Methodism's witness, maintained with a large measure of effectiveness through a century, has been extended through the church's outreach by means of home evangelism, world missions, communications, and the varied agencies of Christian nurture. The church's effectiveness in the use of some of these channels has varied with periods of its history. Through evangelism in the first generation the church experienced its most rapid growth of the century, but our survey has disclosed a sharp subsidence around 1900. More recent concern for home evangelism promises a revival quickening. The church's outreach through world missions, beginning seventy-five years ago, has been increasingly vigorous and fruitful, yielding now almost spectacular growth in the church abroad. Schools, publications, radio and other means of outreach have all made their contributions. A well organized denominational program now maintains channels for extending the church's witness through evangelism, missions, publications, radio, Sunday schools, youth organizations, and educational institutions. The church has never been better equipped to extend its witness than now, as it enters its second century.

The larger fellowship

One purpose of this concluding chapter is to define the position of the Free Methodist Church in the religious world, relating it especially to the evangelical movement of its period in history. What has been its spirit and attitude toward other Christian bodies?

The sectarian spirit tends to bigotry, and in its extreme manifestations holds that only those can be saved who belong to a certain church, and refuses fellowship to those of another name. At the other extreme, the ecumenical spirit inclines toward compromise of denominational distinctives and may seek agreement with all religious groups in terms of their lowest common denominator. Between these extremes can be found a sturdy denominational spirit, differing from ecumenical indifference by firmly holding to definite standards of faith and life, and from sectarianism by recognizing that there are sincere Christians in other groups. While the denominationalist has a personal conviction that his church is God's place for him, and through no other can he witness so clearly or serve so effectively, he recognizes, nevertheless, that there are devout Christians in many other churches and to them he gladly extends the right hand of Christian fellowship.

The history of the Free Methodist Church shows that its spirit is neither that of the bigoted sectarian nor of the indifferent ecumenicist, but is that of the loyal denominationalist. It must be granted that there have been Free Methodists of a sectarian spirit, but that these have betrayed the witness of the church is made apparent by such evidence as follows.

In the early years of Free Methodism's history B. T. Roberts stated that his difficult experiences with the parent church had cured him of sectarian bigotry. He said, "I feel a deep sympathy with every enterprise that has a tendency to promote the kingdom of Christ in its purity." [2] Not long thereafter, as noted in Chapter Twenty[3] he affirmed that he preferred that existing denominations should meet the purposes for which it had been necessary to organize the Free Methodist Church, which then would make a new denomination unnecessary.

Therefore it is not surprising that the very first General Conference, held in 1862, appointed a committee to negotiate union with the Bible Christians, should God's providences lead that way. These Methodists of a small English group, the General Conference declared, were "God's dear children," and if it were the Lord's will, union "would be to the benefit of both these branches of God's church." We have no record of further developments in the case, but this action exhibited the church's spirit of fellowship early in its existence.

The General Conference of 1882 adopted the following generous statement with reference to cooperation with other Christians, at the same time safeguarding Free Methodism's witness:

> We have Christian fellowship and love for all persons of whatever denomination who show by their lives that they "follow

---
2. *The Earnest Christian;* v. 9, Jan. 1865; p. 7.
3. *Supra,* p. 385.

peace with all men, and holiness without which no man shall see the Lord." We will unite with all well-disposed persons, in an open, Christian manner, in promoting social and civil reforms. But we cannot unite, where we are required to compromise our principles, in holding union meetings with any person, or denomination, whose practical standard of Christian character and church fellowship is obviously below that plainly set forth in the New Testament.

This declaration stands in the church's *Discipline* today.

The modern holiness movement began in the late sixties with the organization of various associations for the promotion of the Wesleyan doctrine and experience, and by 1886 the movement was well under way. Its constituency was drawn largely from those in major Methodism who desired to see Christian holiness restored to its historic place therein. In that year the General Conference of the Free Methodist Church adopted this resolution:

> Whereas entire sanctification gives the unity of the Spirit without regard to denominational preference, and, Whereas we recognize that God has greatly blessed the holiness movement both within and without the Free Methodist Church:
> Therefore: Resolved, that we extend hearty fellowship and cooperation to all churches, associations, or other agencies that are in harmony with the Word of God in teaching and practice.

Now, in the ninety-second year of the National Holiness Association, the Free Methodist Church is a denominational member of the organization.

A second interdenominational fellowship in which the Free Methodist Church has had a part is the National Association of Evangelicals, organized on a permanent basis in 1943. The Free Methodist Church was one of the early denominational affiliates of this agency, which was established for united evangelical action. The organization has been effective in representing evangelicals in a wide range of interests where Bible-believing Christians need to be heard as a united voice. Also, through the cooperation of many groups, the resources of each group have become more effective. Many of the varied thrusts of the current evangelical upsurge have originated with or gained momentum from the National Association of Evangelicals. Its statement of faith includes declarations of, 1. the inspiration and authority of the Scriptures: 2. the Trinity; 3. the deity of Jesus Christ, and His virgin birth, sinless life, miracles, atoning death, bodily resurrection, ascension, and "His personal return in power and glory"; 4. the necessity of regeneration to salvation; 5. "the present ministry of the Holy Spirit by whose indwelling the Christian is enabled to live a godly life"; 6. the resurrection of the saved to life, of the lost to damnation; 7. the spiritual unity of believers.

It is worthy of note that John Wesley in 1764 attempted to form a union of evangelical clergymen which was to be based, he said, not upon agreement in opinions, religious phraseology, or church order, but upon the member's acceptance of belief in three essentials, namely, original sin, justification by faith, and holiness of heart and life, "provided their life be answerable to their doctrine." Only three replied of the forty or fifty clergymen to whom he addressed his proposal.[4]

The Free Methodist Church is not a member of the National Council of the Churches of Christ in the U. S. A., principally because of the inadequate doctrinal position of the organization and the frankly liberal character of much of its leadership and constituency. But the church does not withhold fellowship from those who do belong to the Council, merely on the basis of their affiliation therewith.

In its earlier years the open fellowship of Free Methodism was expressed by such official actions as the appointment of B. T. Roberts and T. B. Arnold to represent Free Methodism at the Centenary Conference on Protestant Missions of the World, held in London in 1888; the election of B. Winget and J. S. MacGeary as delegates to the Ecumenical Missionary Conference in 1900, meeting in New York; the election of Benson H. Roberts to the Commission of the Ecumenical Methodist Conference and as delegate to the London Conference of 1901. And the Free Methodist Church is now a member of the World Methodist Council, with representation in the World Methodist conferences.

For extended periods on two occasions negotiations have been carried on, seeking union of the Wesleyan Methodist and the Free Methodist churches. The former period extended from 1911 to 1919, the latter from 1943 to 1955. The latter negotiations were terminated

---

4. J. Wesley, *Journal*; Epworth Press, London; v. 5, 60-66.

by action of the Wesleyan Methodist General Conference of 1955, and it may be that the two churches can better promote the gospel working separately than in union. In 1959 the Holiness Movement Church of Canada united with the Free Methodist Church, bringing into the union several hundred members from Canada, an Egyptian national church of 5,000 members which followed the parent by its own vote, and two other mission enterprises. The union has been marked by the warmest of Christian fellowship.

In concluding this section, let it be said that a Free Methodist cannot be sectarian in spirit and remain true to an essential principle of his church. The Preamble to the Constitution of the Free Methodist Church states the church's threefold purpose in framing the Constitution to be, 1. To "wisely preserve and pass on to posterity the heritage of doctrine and principles of Christian living transmitted to us as evangelicals in the Arminian-Wesleyan tradition"; 2. To "insure church order by sound principles of ecclesiastical polity"; and 3. To "prepare the way for evangelization of the world and a more effective cooperation with other branches of the church of Christ in the advancement of Christ's Kingdom among men."

Probably few groups have so clearly set forth this combination of denominational distinctives on the one hand and inclusive fellowship in the Christian faith on the other. This combination guards against both extremes—sectarian bigotry and ecumenical indifference. Only as the Free Methodist Church maintains both emphases, making its contribution to the inclusive fellowship without compromising its distinctives, will its witness be effective.

Sect or church?

Ernst Troeltsch[5] has traced the usual course by which what he calls the sect-type of religious organization in time moves to the established church-type of organization. This transition occurs through the sect's gradual absorption of the culture of contemporary society, and its surrender of those distinctives by which it originally maintained its separation from the world. The sect is the original religious type, from which the church-type develops as the sect's emphasis on personal relationship to God and individual holiness

---

5. Ernst Troeltsch, *The Social Teaching of the Churches*. The Macmillan Co., New York; v. 1, 331-342.

weakens, and the institutional emphasis comes to predominance. Then the church becomes the channel if not the source of grace, with its symbolism, sacerdotalism, and a professional clergy displacing the former sect's lay emphasis on personal piety and an inward faith as the normal possessions of every member of the fellowship.

The reader of that significant book, *Beyond Conformity*,[6] will sense the distinction between sect-type and church-type religion in the contrast the author draws between today's culture-Christianity and vital evangelical Christianity. Culture-Christianity is the church-type of religion that has absorbed modern secularism until it in turn has been all but absorbed by it; but evangelical Christianity begins with a radical change in a man's nature, a "new birth" that sets a man at variance with the world's culture. In Chapter Twenty-five of the present volume, the same distinction was drawn between an education that seeks the child's adjustment to the world's culture, and Christian education which seeks his adjustment on a higher and spiritual level, following the transformation of nature according to Paul's account in Romans 12:2.

Niebuhr[7] has said that a person enters the church-type of religion by natural birth rather than by spiritual rebirth; he is born into the church in the same sense that he is born into a particular social and economic culture. In contrast, one enters the sect by joining it, usually following a radical change of nature and purpose. But, Niebuhr points out, the sect-type begins to take on the characteristics of the church-type in one generation. The first generation seeks to nurture the second generation in the sect's culture, but convictions that were stamped deeply upon the souls of the parents by cataclysmic conversion are less clearly impressed upon their children by education and discipline. "Rarely does a second generation hold the convictions it has inherited with a fervor equal to that of its fathers, who fashioned these convictions in the heat of conflict and at the risk of martyrdom."[8] And thus it comes about that ideals and purposes transmitted to younger generations by the culture of a sect on its way to churchhood, are

---

6. W. Curry Mavis, *Beyond Conformity*. Light & Life Press, Winona Lake, Ind.; especially ch. 1.
7. H. Richard Niebuhr, *The Social Sources of Denominationalism*. Henry Holt & Co., Inc.; Hamden, Conn.; p. 17.
8. *Ibid.*, p. 19.

moderated and modified by the insidiously pervasive culture of the world until, within a few generations, the distance has disappeared that once separated sharply the sect from culture-Christianity.

In his message on the occasion of the centenary of the organization of the Methodist Episcopal Church by the Christmas Conference of 1784, Bishop Foster cited Isaac Taylor's claim, "that a moral wave measured eighty years—forty to reach its crest and break, and forty to subside and be lost. He allowed eighty years for the Methodist phenomenon, when he predicted it would vanish and disappear." The Bishop added, "He made a mistake." Then, with obvious foreboding, he asked, "Is it only the mistake of a few years?" [9]

The preceding section, "The larger fellowship," described Free Methodism as strongly denominational in emphasis but non-sectarian in spirit. We found that in the religious context of its period in history the Free Methodist Church has extended its fellowship to other sincere Christians and evangelical groups, seeking the mean between the extremes of sectarian exclusiveness and the surrender of its distinctive denominational witness. We may add also that to meet life's normal secular demands, the church has sought a discipline by which to prepare its members to live in the world and not to be of the world; to avoid monkish asceticism at one extreme and absorption by the spirit of the world at the other. These observations raise the question, Where, then, does Free Methodism measure on Troeltsch's scale of religious organizations ranging from the exclusive sect-type to the inclusive, comfortably adjusted church-type?

Free Methodism, as practically every religious movement, was more concerned with its differences from other groups in its earlier than in its later history. Accordingly it partook more of the nature of the sect-type then than it does now when the church seeks a basis of agreement with other groups within the evangelical family. But even in the beginning it was not fully the sect-type. This is suggested by its early deep concern for social, economic, and political issues. This concern is reflected in the annual conference resolutions that appear in Appendix C of this volume, and additional evidence is included in

---

9. R. S. Foster, *Centenary Thoughts for the Pew and Pulpit of Methodism*. Phillips & Hunt, New York; p. 167.

Chapter Twenty, "Faith Working by Love." Note the contrast of this evidence with the following statement concerning the sect-type by Troeltsch:

> Their attitude towards the world, the State, and Society may be indifferent, tolerant, or hostile, since they have no desire to control and incorporate these forms of social life; on the contrary, they tend to avoid them; their aim is usually either to tolerate their presence alongside their own body, or even to replace these social institutions by their own society.[10]

There is this consideration that may have contributed to Free Methodism's being at most only a modified sect-type in its beginning: The Free Methodist Church did not revolutionize the order of denominational existence its founding leaders had known in the larger group, but only modified Methodist Episcopal government and drew more firmly certain of its principles that it might more effectively continue that way of life which they had always known, but which recent innovators had distorted. The reformers neither claimed new revelations of truth nor sought to restore some ancient form of allegedly "pure" Christianity. These considerations, we suggest, tended to make a nonsectarian spirit compatible with sect-type firmness in doctrinal beliefs and standards of daily living. In fact, early Methodism, likewise sect-type in firmness of doctrine and practice, was not of the usual sect-type spirit, as its continuance within the Church of England for a half century or more suggests.

Free Methodism's course, attempting to function in the world's broad social context while trying to maintain sect-type controls of doctrine and life, has been a venture attended by great hazards to these distinctives. Such a balance is not easily achieved or maintained, and opinions will vary concerning the degree of compromise that has been entailed in the adjustments the church has made to changing conditions. Probably all will agree that during the century the Free Methodist Church has moved farther from the sect-type and nearer the church-type. Although there is cause for concern lest the shift continue to the point of no return, past which many groups have moved, the encouraging fact still remains that the Free Methodist

---

10. Ernst Troeltsch, *The Social Teaching of the Churches.* The Macmillan Co., New York; v. 1, 331.

Church has continued for a hundred years a clear denominational witness and a strong opposition to the secularism of its age.

Decline is not inevitable

The usual progressive fading of distinctives among religious groups with succeeding generations confronts the cause of earnest Christianity with a problem similar to John Wesley's perplexity over the seeming tendency of religious revivals to destroy themselves. The diligence and frugality that follow revival, Wesley had observed, normally yield prosperity and riches which engender pride and worldliness that cancel the benefits of revival. The only safeguard, said Wesley, is for the Christian not only to *gain* all he can, to *save* all he can, but also to *give* all he can![11] Therefore, the general rule of collapse after revival does not hold if the convert wills otherwise and pays the price of devotion and obedience.

Nor can we accept as holding in every instance Isaac Taylor's formula according to which a period of forty years marks the ascent of a moral or spiritual movement, and a like period its decline—even if we allow a decade's variation in the duration of each phase. History establishes the principle of the rise and fall of religious movements, even as the rise and fall of nations and empires. But to hold to the inevitability of any particular church's decline ignores spiritual laws which are not chained within statistical formulas. Such formulas express only what usually occurs and in a particular instance may be expected, but which cannot be predicted with certainty. When conditions are met, spiritual laws operate to bring revival. Otherwise there is no accounting for the Scriptures which abound in God's call to His people to return to first principles as the condition of restoration and renewal.

A splendidly realistic statement of the adjustments of recent years and the resulting problems appeared not long since in *The Free Methodist* from the pen of the church's general secretary of evangelism, Rev. L. W. Northrup. Extensive quotation of this article is justified by its pertinence to the church's position just now at the forks of the road, one way before it leading to decline, the other to greater conquests in the new century.

---

11. *Supra*, p. 153 et seq.

The last twenty-five years in the history of the Free Methodist Church have seen a series of startling changes. Beginning slowly at first, they have come with an unexpected swiftness and impact which have been disturbing to a large segment of our membership. Most of these have been in the realm of method, and are not related to our doctrine or our spiritual philosophy, except as each individual might read into these changes spiritual connotation and weight. . . .

To argue that there has been no loss of any kind in this painful realignment of our positions is naive. It is an unwarranted optimism. No church goes through an extended period without some losses. . . .

Two views predominate. One is that the changes made would sweep the church into a dazzling growth in membership, eliminate opposition, induce adherents, and enhance outreach to great proportions. The other is that these changes would plunge us into an irretrievable gulf of worldliness, apostasy, and ruin. *Neither view has been justified.* We have not had a sweeping growth in membership as a result of these changes, but neither have we been swept into a bleak apostasy. *We are not now in a retreat.* . . . A frank appraisal of the church, after having traveled the length and breadth of her borders, convinces us that we should gird on our armor and strengthen ourselves to do the task that God is calling us to do. . . .[12]

Second century advance

At the close of its first century the Free Methodist Church has the material and organizational equipment, and also the trained personnel adequate to the greatest forward and upward advance of its history. Its world membership is but slightly under a hundred thousand; its ministerial staff is in the neighborhood of two thousand, not including licensed and ordained nationals; its missionary staff is nearly two hundred. The church has nine schools and colleges in the United States and Canada, and a seminary program of merit. Its publishing house was never better equipped nor capable of better editing and publishing. Its headquarters' departments of finance, evangelism, missions, radio, Sunday schools, and youth are well organized and function effectively. Its benevolent institutions are better equipped than ever to minister to human need. The church at the local level is experiencing unprecedented expansion in sanctu-

---

12. L. W. Northrup, "Strengthen the Things that Remain," *The Free Methodist;* v. 90, March 26, 1957; p. 198.

aries of worship, Christian education plants, and parsonages to meet demands for more and better facilities for service to congregation and community.

And the church claims more than these material means and the excellence of human service. Through a century it has guarded the truths committed to its trust. Its doctrines are those of the Holy Scriptures as held in the Wesleyan tradition. Its principles of Christian practice challenge its members to holy living.

Thus equipped, advance is possible but not assured. A perfect automobile alone does not guarantee satisfactory transportation, even with a skilled chauffeur at the wheel. A car stalled at the roadside for lack of fuel in its tank is not in need of repair but of power. The perfectly organized and well equipped church may exhaust itself in turning the wheels of its own splendid and elaborate machinery, only to stall at the side of the road while some of the newer sects in their battered jalopies pass happily by, loaded with passengers on the way to the celestial city.

An experienced missionary secretary has said, "Some of our best organized fields are the most static." This might be said as well of some of the most completely organized home conferences. Organization with power is ideal, but the *sine qua non* of progress in the church is spiritual power. If Free Methodism should finally fail her mission, whatever may be the point of final collapse, the primary failure will be loss of power. Sound doctrine and strict piety are essential forms or directing restraints for the channeling of power to effective ends, serving as the banks of a river. Without the form of sound doctrine as one bank of the stream, and of piety as the other, religion flattens out and stagnates, even as a river without banks becomes a swamp. And yet the church may continue to the end a severe piety and a strict orthodoxy but die by losing the power of the Holy Spirit from its channel of most excellent forms. Should this happen, that the church maintain the form of godliness while denying the power thereof, it becomes a channel with no current, merely a dry river bed. To prevent this outcome, the Free Methodist Church must carry into the new century its witness of doctrine and piety, not as ends in themselves but as a channel for the passage of the Holy Spirit upon the world in revival power.

Because of the rapidly shifting tides of population today in America, the call to new fields comes from many directions. Due to the rugged demands Free Methodist standards make upon candidates for membership, its most propitious opportunities for evangelizing and recruiting new members of its fellowship come with the upheaval of social and economic changes where families are making adjustments to a new order of life and have not yet settled into established economic, social, and religious stratifications. The church's evangelistic strategy is now channeling evangelistic resources into these promising areas, and the returns should be large.

Looking upon the broad fields of the world's need beyond America, the church sees likewise unprecedented opportunities. The world is in unrest because of the ferment of nationalism, communism, and other ideologies that have taken advantage of the growing literacy of the masses and of modern means of communication. Free Methodism must do its part to insure that the world shall not settle from this unrest into the grip of communism, of apostate Christianity, or of its own past heathen bondage. The church's remarkable growth abroad in the last decade inspires faith that its part in the world task is an important aspect of its mission in its second century; that for the fulfillment of this mission God will supply His Spirit, a spirit not of fear, but of power, and of love, and of discipline.

Entering the new century, Free Methodism must view not only the far fields of the unchurched and spiritually hungry masses of America and the world, but also its own homestead enclosures—the children and youth of its families, its Sunday schools, its youth organizations, its colleges. Failure in its family circle will forfeit in large part the church's opportunities in its neighborhood and abroad. To repeat a question raised in an earlier chapter: If the church cannot win and hold its own, with what confidence can it claim the heathen for its inheritance?

But let the church never forget that to win its own means more than the nurture of its youth in the church's rich heritage, more than a "culture Free Methodism." It means leading youth to a crisis of repentance and of complete surrender to Jesus Christ as Lord of their lives, and God's answer by the Spirit's witness to their spirits that they are God's new creation. Nothing less than this will do on the bleak fields of world need; nothing less will do in the sheltered fold of Christian home and church.

The mission of the Free Methodist Church in the world will not close until Christ is King of Kings and Lord of Lords. As the church began a century ago, so let it continue to meet the perpetual need of the human spirit with the Bible's doctrine of full redemption; with the reality of an inner experience of cleansing and power that verifies the doctrine both in the inner consciousness and in the outward life; with the simplicity of spiritual worship untrammeled by elaborate ritual; with a life of daily devotion that separates from the world even in the world; with a full consecration of self and possessions to the service of God and man. All these principles are necessary to maintain *from age to age a living witness.*

* * * * *

It is the author's hope that from the pages of this book there may have emerged clearly in the mind of the reader the following conclusions:

The principles upon which Free Methodism was founded were accepted in major Methodism a century ago, but with increasing resistance in certain geographic areas; and accordingly the leaders in Free Methodist reforms sought to conserve as well as to restore historic Wesleyan values.

The progressive declension of major Methodism from its original emphases during the mid-era of the nineteenth century, points to a special providence in the development of Free Methodism at that time to help conserve and continue essential Wesleyan distinctives.

The founding principles of Free Methodism, still maintained by the denomination after a century, are still vital Christian issues, and therefore Free Methodism has a continuing mission.

Deviations of major Methodism and of other religious movements from their original principles provide warning, guidance and challenge to Free Methodism at critical points of its own present existence.

Appendices

APPENDIX A. NEW SCHOOL METHODISM

Following is the article written by Rev. B. T. Roberts, A.M., and published in the *Northern Independent* in 1857, which precipitated the crisis out of which in 1860 came the organization of the Free Methodist Church.

The best seed, sown, from year to year, on poor soil, gradually degenerates. The acorn, from the stately oak, planted upon the arid plain, becomes a stunted shrub. Ever since the fall, the human heart has proved a soil unfavorable to the growth of truth.

Noxious weeds flourish everywhere spontaneously, while the useful grains require diligent cultivation.

Correct principles implanted in the mind need constant attention, or monstrous errors will overtop them and root them out. Every old nation tells the tale of her own degeneracy, and points to the golden age when truth and justice reigned among men.

Religious truth is not exempt from this liability to corruption. "God will take care of His own cause," is a maxim often quoted by the cowardly and the compromising, as an apology for their base defection. When His servants are faithful to the trusts reposed in them, it is gloriously true; when they waver, His cause suffers. The Churches planted by the Apostles, and watered by the blood of martyrs, now outvie heathenism itself in their corruptions. No other parts of the world are so inaccessible to Gospel truth as those countries where the Romish and Greek Churches hold dominion.

As a denomination, we are just as liable to fall by corrupting influences as any were that have flourished before us. We enjoy no immunity from danger. Already there is springing up among us a class of preachers whose teaching is very different from that of the fathers of Methodism. They may be found here and there throughout our Zion; but in the Genesee Conference they act as an associate body. They number about thirty. During the last session of this Conference, they held several secret meetings, in which they concerted a plan to carry their measures and spread their doctrines. They have openly made the issue in the Conference. It is divided. Two distinct parties exist. With one or the other every preacher is in sympathy. This difference is fundamental. It does not relate to things indifferent, but to those of the most vital importance. It involves nothing less than the nature itself of Christianity.

In showing the doctrines of the New School Methodists, we shall quote from *The Advocate* of the sect, published at Buffalo. This is the organ of the party. It is sustained by them. They act as its agents. Where their influence prevails, it is circulated to the exclusion of other religious papers. Its former title was "*The Buffalo Christian Advocate.*" But since its open avowal of the new doctrines, it has significantly dropped from its caption, the expressive word, "*Christian.*" This omission is full of meaning. It is, however, highly proper, as we shall see when we examine its new theory of religion. We commend the editor for this instance of honesty. It is now simply "*The Advocate*"; that is, the only Advocate of the tenets it defends.

The New School Methodists affect as great a degree of liberalism as do Theodore Parker and Mr. Newman. They profess "charity" for everybody except their brethren of the Old School. In an article on "Creeds," published in *The Advocate* of April 16th, under the signature of W. the Rev. writer, a prominent New School minister, lays it on to "the sects whose watchword is a creed," in a manner not unworthy of Alexander Campbell himself. He says, "No matter how holy and blameless a man's life may be, if he has the temerity to question any tenet of 'orthodoxy,' he is at once, in due ecclesiastical form, consigned to the Devil—as a heretic and infidel. Thus are the fetters of a spiritual despotism thrown around the human reason. . . . And so it has come to pass that in the estimation of multitudes—the teachings of Paul are eclipsed by the theories of Calvin, and the writings of John Wesley are held in higher veneration than the inspired words of St. John." Is not this a modest charge?

But their theory of religion is more fully set forth in the leading editorial of *The Advocate* for May 14th, under the title—"*Christianity a Religion of Beneficence Rather than of Devotion.*" Though it appears as editorial, we have good reason to believe that it was written by a leading New School member of the Genesee Conference. It has not been disavowed by that party. Though it has been before the public for months, no one has expressed a dissent from its positions. It is fair to suppose that it represents the views of the leaders of this new movement.

It says, "Christianity is not, characteristically, a system of devotion. *It has none of those features* which must distinguish a religion grounded on the idea that to adore the Divine character is the most imperative obligation resting upon human beings. It enjoins the observance of but very few sacred rites; nor does it prescribe any *particular mode* for paying homage to the Deity. It eschews all exterior forms, and teaches that they who worship God must worship Him in spirit and in truth."

The Old School Methodists hold, that "to adore the Divine character" is the most imperative obligation resting upon human beings—that Christianity has *all* of those features that must distinguish a religion grounded on this idea. That he who worships God rightly, will as a necessary consequence, possess all social and moral virtues; that the Gospel does not leave its votaries to choose, if they please, the degrading rites of heathenism, or the superstitious abominations of Popery; but prescribes prayer and praise and the observance of the sacraments of baptism and the Lord's Supper, "as particular modes for paying homage to the Deity"; that there is no necessity for antagonism, as Infidels and Universalists are wont to affirm, between spiritual worship and the forms of worship instituted by Christ.

The following sneer is not unworthy of Thomas Paine himself. It falls below the dignity of Voltaire. "Christianity in nowise gives countenance to the supposition that the Great Jehovah is so affected with the infirmity of vanity, as to receive with *peculiarly* grateful emotions, the attention and offerings which poor, human creatures may pay directly to Him in worship."

The above may be sufficient to show what Christianity is not, in the opinion of these New School divines. Let us now see what it is. "The characteristic idea of this system is benevolence; and its practical realization is achieved in beneficence. It consecrates the principle of charity, and instructs its votaries to regard good works as the holiest sacrifice, and the most acceptable which they can bring to the Almighty. . . .

"Whatever graces be necessary to constitute the inner Christian life, the chief and principal one of these is *love to man.* . . . The great condition upon which one becomes a participant of the Gospel salvation, is—some practical exhibition of self-abnegation, of self-sacrifice for the good of others. *Go sell all that thou hast, and give to the poor,* were the only terms of salvation which Christ proposed to the young man, who, otherwise, was not far from the kingdom of heaven."

The Old School Methodists hold that benevolence is only *one of the fruits* of true religion, but by no means the thing itself. In their view, "The principal grace of the inner Christian life" is LOVE TO GOD; and the most acceptable sacrifice we can render HIM, is a broken and contrite heart. They teach that the great condition upon which one becomes "a participant of the Gospel salvation" IS FAITH IN CHRIST—preceded by repentance. They read in the Gospel that the young man referred to was commanded by Christ to "*come, take up the cross and follow me.*" The giving of his goods to the poor was only preparatory to this.

The New School Methodists hold that justification and entire sanctification, or holiness, are the same—that when a sinner is pardoned, he is at the same time made holy—that all the spiritual change he may henceforth expect is simply a growth in grace. When they speak of "holiness," they mean by it the same as do evangelical ministers of those denominations which do not receive the doctrines taught by Wesley and Fletcher on this subject.

According to the Old School Methodists, merely justified persons, while they do not outwardly commit sin, are conscious of sin still remaining in the heart, such as pride, self-will, and unbelief. They continually feel a heart bent to backsliding; a natural tendency to evil; a proneness to depart from God, and cleave to the things of earth. Those that are sanctified wholly are saved from all inward sin—from evil thoughts, and evil tempers. No wrong temper, none contrary to love, remains in the soul. All the thoughts, words and actions are governed by pure love.

The New School ministers have the frankness to acknowledge that their doctrines are not the doctrines of the Church. They have undertaken to correct the teachings of her standard authors. In the same editorial of *The Advocate,* from which we have quoted so largely, we read: "So in the exercises and means of grace instituted by the Church, it is clearly apparent that respect is had, rather to the excitation of the religious sensibilities, and the culture of emotional piety, than the development of genial and humane dispositions, and the formation of habits of active, vigorous goodness."

Here the evils complained of are charged upon *"the exercises and means of grace, instituted by the Church."* They do not result from a perversion of the means of grace, but are the effects *intended* to be produced in their institution. It is THE CHURCH, then, that is wrong—and so far wrong that she does not even *aim* at the development of proper Christian character. "The means of grace," in the use of which an Asbury, an Olin, a Hedding, and a host of worthies departed and living, were nurtured to spiritual manhood, must be abolished; and others, adapted to the "development of genial and humane dispositions," established in their place. The Lodge must supersede the class-meeting and the love-feast; and the old-fashioned prayer-meeting must give way to the social party! Those who founded or adopted "the exercises and means of grace instituted by the Church"—Paul and Peter, the Martyrs and Reformers, Luther and Wesley, Calvin and Edwards—all have failed to comprehend the true idea of Christianity—for these all held that the sinner was justified by *faith in Christ*, and not by "some practical exhibition of self-abnegation." The honor of distinctly apprehending and clearly stating the true genius of Christianity was reserved for a few divines of the nineteenth century!

USAGES—RESULTS

Differing thus in their views of religion, the Old and New School Methodists necessarily differ in their measures for its promotion. The latter build stock Churches, and furnish them with pews to accommodate a select congregation; and with organs, melodeons, violins, and professional singers, to execute difficult pieces of music for a fashionable audience. The former favor free Churches, congregational singing, and spirituality, simplicity and fervency in worship. They endeavor to promote revivals, deep and thorough; such as were common under the labors of the Fathers; such as have made Methodism the leading denomination of the land. The leaders of the New Divinity movement are not remarkable for promoting revivals; and those which do, occasionally, occur among them, may generally be characterized as, the editor of *"The Advocate"* designated, one which fell under his notice, as *"splendid revivals."* Preachers of the old stamp urge upon all who would gain heaven the necessity of self-denial—non-conformity to the world, purity of heart and holiness of life; while the others ridicule singularity, encourage by their silence, and in some cases by their own example, and that of their wives and daughters, "the putting on of gold and costly apparel," and treat with distrust all professions of deep Christian experience. When these desire to raise money for the benefit of the Church, they have recourse to the selling of pews to the highest bidder; to parties of pleasure, oyster suppers, fairs, grab-bags, festivals and lotteries; the others for this purpose, appeal to the love the people bear to Christ. In short, the Old School Methodists rely for the spread of the Gospel upon the agency of the Holy Ghost, and the purity of the Church. The New School Methodists appear to depend upon the patronage of the worldly, the favor of the proud and aspiring; and the various artifices of worldly policy.

If this diversity of opinion and of practice among the ministers of our denomination was confined to one Conference, it would be comparatively unimportant. But unmistakable indications show that prosperity is producing upon us, as a denomination, the same intoxicating effect that it too often does upon individuals and societies. The change, by the General Conference of 1852, in the rule of Discipline, requiring that all our houses of worship should be built plain, and with free seats; and that of the last General Conference in the section respecting dress, show that there are already too many among us who would take down the barriers that have hitherto separated us from the world. The fact that the removal is gradual, so as not to excite too much attention and commotion, renders it none the less alarming.

Every lover of the Church must feel a deep anxiety to know what is to be the result of this new order of things. If we may judge by its effects in the Genesee Conference, since it has held sway there, it will prove disastrous to us as a denomination. It so happened, either by accident or by management, at the division of the Genesee Conference eight years ago, that most of the unmanageable veterans, who could neither be induced to depart from the Heaven-honored usages of Methodism, by the specious cry of "progress" nor to wink at such departures, by the mild expostulations of Eli, "Why do ye thus, my sons!" had their destination upon the east side of Genesee River. The first year after the division, the East Genesee Conference had twenty superannuated preachers; the Genesee Conference had but five. "Men of progress" in the prime of life, went west of the river, and took possession of the conference. For the most part, they have borne sway there ever since. Of late, the young men of the Conference, uniting with the fathers, and thus united, comprising a majority of the Conference, have endeavored to stop this "progress" away from the old paths of Methodism. But the "progressives" make up in management what they lack in numbers. Having free access at all times to the ears of the Episcopacy, they have succeeded, for the most part, in controlling the appointments to the districts and most important stations. If, by reason of his obvious fitness, any impracticable adherent of primitive Methodism has been appointed to a district or first-class station, he has usually been pursued, with untiring diligence, and hunted from his position before his constitutional term expired.

In the bounds of the Genesee Conference, the people generally are prepossessed in favor of Methodism. During the past eight years there have been no external causes operating there against our prosperity that do not operate at all times and in all places. Within this period, the nominal increase of the Church in that Conference has been but seven hundred and eighty. The East Genesee Conference has had an increase, within the same time, of about two thousand five hundred. In order to have simply kept pace with the population, there should have been within the bounds of the Genesee Conference, one thousand six hundred and forty-three more members than there are at present. That is, in eight years, under the reign of new divinity, the Church has suffered, within the bounds of this one Conference, a relative loss of fifteen per cent in members.

The Seminary at Lima, at the time of the division, second to none in the land, has, by the same kind of management, been brought to the brink of financial ruin.

We have thus endeavored to give a fair and impartial representation of New School Methodism. Its prevalence in one Conference has already, as we have seen, involved it in division and disaster. Let it generally prevail, and the glory will depart from Methodism. She has a special mission to accomplish. This is, not to gather into her fold the proud and fashionable, the devotees of pleasure and ambition, but, "to spread Scriptural holiness over these lands." Her doctrines, and her usages, her hymns, her history and her spirit, her noble achievements in the past, and her bright prospects for the future, all forbid that she should adopt an accommodating, compromising policy, pandering to the vices of the times. Let her go on, as she has done, insisting that the great, cardinal truths of the Gospel shall receive a living embodiment in the hearts and lives of her members, and Methodism will continue to be favored of Heaven, and the joy of earth. But let her come down from her position, and receive to her communion all those lovers of pleasure, and lovers of the world, who are willing to pay for the privilege, and it needs no prophet's vision to foresee that Methodism will become a dead and corrupting body, endeavoring in vain to supply, by the erection of splendid Churches, and the imposing performance of powerless ceremonies, the manifested glory of the Divine presence, which once shone so brightly in all her sanctuaries.

"Thus saith the Lord, Stand ye in the ways, and see, and ask for the old paths, where is the good way, and walk therein, and ye shall find rest for your souls."—Jer. 6:16.

APPENDIX B. GENERAL CONFERENCE ACTION ON ROBERTS' APPEALS

Below is reprinted an excerpt from the report of the Committee on Appeals to the General Conference of the Methodist Episcopal Church, held in Buffalo, New York, in 1860. The excerpt is that portion of the report which deals with the two appeals of Benjamin Titus Roberts from the decisions against him by the Genesee Annual Conferences of 1857 and of 1858.

BUFFALO, May 30, 1860.

The Committee having heard and considered the Minutes, Documents, and Pleadings in the first appeal case of Benjamin T. Roberts, who appeals from the decision of the Genesee Conference whereby he was adjudged to be reprimanded before the Conference, proceeded to vote in the case with the following result: On the question of affirming, nineteen voted in favor and nineteen against it. On the question of remanding the case for a new trial, the Committee voted almost unanimously in the negative. On the question of reversing the action of the Conference, eighteen voted in favor and twenty against, a result which, as the General Conference has decided, leaves the decision of the Genesee Conference as the final adjudication of the case.

J. T. CRANE, Secretary.

BUFFALO, May 31, 1860.

The Committee have considered the second appeal of B. T. Roberts, who appeals from the action of the Genesee Conference, whereby he was expelled from the ministry and the Church.

The representatives of the Genesee Conference objected to the admission of the Appeal on the ground,

1. That B. T. Roberts, subsequently to his trial and condemnation, joined the Methodist Episcopal Church as a probationer, and thus, at least, tacitly confessed the justice of the action of the Conference of his case.

2. That B. T. Roberts, since he was deprived by his expulsion of his ministerial authority and standing, has continued to preach, and has thus rebelled against the authority of the Conference and the Church.

3. That B. T. Roberts, since he declared his intention of appealing to the General Conference has connected himself with another organization, contemplating Church ends independent of and hostile to the Church to whose General Conference he now appeals.

The Committee, after hearing the statements and pleadings of the representatives of the parties,

Resolved, That the Appeal of B. T. Roberts be not admitted.

J. T. CRANE, *Secretary*.

APPENDIX C. EARLY FREE METHODISM AND NATIONAL AFFAIRS

The deep and intelligent concern of the Free Methodist Church in national affairs during the critical decade of the church's founding is reflected in the following resolutions adopted from time to time during that decade by the Illinois Conference and duly recorded in its Journal.

Item 1. Report of the Committee on the State of the Country to the Third Annual Session of the Western Convention (Illinois Conference), October, 1862.

Whereas a wicked rebellion against the best government in the world is devastating our land, filling our homes with mourning on account of the loss of our brothers and sons; and whereas slavery, an institution abhorred of God, contrary to the Bible, revolting to every dictate of humanity, and justly denounced by John Wesley, the venerable founder of our common Methodism, as the source of all villainies, is the cause of all our calamities; and whereas it is our settled conviction that there can never be permanent peace as slavery exists; Therefore—resolved:

1. That we feel deeply grateful to God for giving the President, Abraham Lincoln, the love of justice, and the moral courage to issue his proclamation of 22nd of September 1862, giving freedom to the slaves of all rebels in arms the first of January next. We look upon this proclamation as the morning star which shall usher in the day of peace to our distracted country, and herald the advent of freedom to the oppressed of all nations, a document which will go down to posterity by the side of the immortal Declaration of Independence.

2. That the complicity of the churches with the crime of slavery, admitting slave holders to their communion, and apologizing for their enormous crimes, calls for the deepest humiliation on the part of every believer in the justice of God, and the most earnest prayer and supplication that He will, in His infinite mercy, bring the church of Christ to the purity of the Gospel.

3. That we recommend to all our people to observe Friday, the seventh day of November next as a day of fasting and prayer, that God will graciously pardon our flagrant offences as a nation, give to our rulers a love for righteousness which exalteth a nation, and firmness to avow and stand by the great principles of human equality; and that He will help our armies and give them success in battle, and restore peace on the basis of universal freedom to our country, and open the way for the proclamation of the gospel in all its purity from the Atlantic to the Pacific, and from the shores of the St. Lawrence to the Gulf of Mexico.

B. T. Roberts, Secretary   B. Hackney, Chairman

Item 2. Report of the Committee on the State of the Country to the Fourth Annual Session of the Illinois Conference, October, 1863.

Every attribute of God, every element of the Christian religion, every principle of humanity is opposed to the system of human slavery. Therefore we, the ministers and laymen of the Illinois Conference of the Free Methodist Church, unanimously resolve:

1st. That we cordially approve of the course of the President in emancipating the slaves and in arming the colored peoples and encouraging them to fight for the liberties of their race and for the existence of the nation.

2nd. That we are utterly opposed to any peace that leaves the least vestige of slavery in the nation. Such a peace would be virtually throwing away all the blood and treasure that have been expended, and laying the foundation for another war still more bloody and disastrous.

3rd. That we should have much more hope of the speedy and successful termination of the war if the President could see the way clear to remove General Halleck from the Chief Command of the Army, a man whose sympathies have on so many occasions and in so marked a manner been shown to be in favor of human slavery, and whose influence has on more than one occasion crippled the efficiency of our valiant soldiers.

We think that the necessities of the case demand that Generals of unquestioned loyalty and ability, like Tremont and Butler and Ligel, and whose career while in the field was distinguished by marked success, should be restored to commands suitable to their talents and the services they have already rendered their country.

4th. That we hereby pledge to the government our hearty cooperation in its efforts to suppress the gigantic and wicked rebellion now raging: And that our fervent prayers shall be offered to Almighty God for His gracious interposition in our behalf as a nation.

Committee: B. T. Roberts
James Powers
E. P. Hart

Item 3. Report of the Committee on the State of the Country to the Sixth Annual Session of the Illinois Conference, September, 1865.

Since the last session of our Annual Conference a sanguinary civil war has closed and we are blessed with peace. The fell spirit which originated the rebellion has met with a decisive overthrow. It appealed to the arbitrament of war and was defeated. It consummated its unnatural crime in the tragic scene at Ford's theatre, when a revered magistrate was smitten down. At first in the history of our country it was simply *tolerated*, but like every other sin it speedily claimed the *right* to exist, then it stood at the baptismal font, witnessed a good confession and was taken into the church; then it assumed the control of national affairs, and attempted the foul usurpation of power at the expense of right. Its power, its religious character, its right to exist are gone, and its presence is no longer tolerated in our land. We recognize the hand of God in our delivery and attribute all the glory and success to Him.

But the spirit of slavery still survives, and it is as cruel and as directly in antagonism with the Christian religion and the principles of a republican government as ever. It cannot be trusted. Our only safety as a nation is to render it powerless for mischief. Therefore

Resolved. That justice and safety demand that in the states lately in rebellion the ballot should be placed in the hands of the colored men, who as a body showed themselves in every possible way, loyal to the country in its hour of peril.

Resolved. That we are in favor of having the constitution so amended that nowhere in the United States shall the civil rights of any person depend upon his creed, condition or color.

Resolved. That inasmuch as we as a nation have been guilty of degrading the colored man by keeping the means of social, intellectual and spiritual culture out of his reach, and by crushing his aspirations after anything that can exalt or dignify our common humanity, it now behooves us, as a Christian people to use all the means in our power to educate him morally, socially, and religiously.

Resolved. That we approve that policy of Government which will tend to dislodge the remaining spirit of slavery from seats of power and place in positions of controlling influence those who stand on the broad platform of human rights, and who are animated by the indwelling spirit of human liberty; and that in the reconstruction of the South, sectional bigotry should be a disqualification for office, and adherence to those sentiments that originated and characterized, throughout, the rebellion should be sternly discountenanced and reprobated.

Committee: B. T. Roberts
C. H. Underwood
B. Hackney

Item 4. Report of the Committee on the State of the Country to the Eighth Annual Session of the Illinois Conference, September, 1867.

As Christian men and patriots we can but feel deeply interested in the affairs of our government. The number of preachers in this conference that have seen active service in our late conflict, some of whom are maimed for life and others have fallen, identify us as a conference with that conflict, and it is with pain that we see the results of it thrown away by the policy of the President, and we hope that congress as a body will stand by those men among them that care more for principles of righteousness than matters of policy, and if they cannot say who shall exercise the right of suffrage in the different states, they will at least forbid and prevent all class legislation relating thereto —and in our humble judgment the best and the only means to settle the troubles of our country is to place the control of our government in the hands of loyal men North and South.

Committee: J. G. Terrill
J. Catterlin
N. D. Fanning

APPENDIX D. GENESEE METHODISM MAKES AMENDS

In 1910, fifty years after Benjamin Titus Roberts was expelled by the Genesee Conference of the Methodist Episcopal Church and seventeen years following his decease, that Conference, in connection with the observance of its centenary, vindicated the character of B. T. Roberts by restoring his parchments to his son, Professor Benson Howard Roberts. The account of the event and the remarkable fraternal address delivered by Professor Roberts on that occasion are quoted below, as they were reported in *The Free Methodist* of October 11, 1910.

At this conference of 1910, Dr. Ray Allen, conference secretary and historian, delivered an address which briefly reviewed Genesee's record of a century. The portion of his message dealing with the midcentury conflict that gave rise to Free Methodism has already appeared in this volume, near the close of Chapter Fourteen. Review thereof in connection with the reading of the following address by B. H. Roberts is suggested.

Notwithstanding unfortunate details of the past recorded in the present volume, relationships of the Free Methodist Church with its parent, now The Methodist Church, have been maintained for years on a plane of Christian fellowship and cooperation in matters of inclusive Methodist concern. It is with pleasure, therefore, that we publish for permanent reference this appendix, recording the gracious act of Genesee Methodism a half-century ago in seeking to make amends for the injustice wrought by an earlier generation.

A SIGNIFICANT EVENT

At the session of the Genesee conference of the Free Methodist church, recently held at Silver Lake, New York, a communication was received from the secretary of the Genesee conference of the Methodist Episcopal church, requesting that a fraternal delegate be sent to the next session of the Genesee conference, to be held at Rochester in October, 1910.

In response to this invitation, Rev. Benson H. Roberts was selected to represent the Genesee conference of our church.

APPENDICES

He was most graciously welcomed and treated with the utmost cordiality. The day before his arrival the conference voted unanimously and with general applause to restore the parchments of the late Benjamin T. Roberts, his father, which had been taken from him when he was expelled from the church over fifty years ago.

Rev. C. W. Bacon, of the Genesee conference, was invited to the platform and was introduced to the conference by Bishop Warren.

After the fraternal address of Brother Roberts, the secretary, Dr. Ray Allen, in a touching speech, presented the parchments to him. This presentation occasioned great applause. Brother Roberts feelingly responded to Dr. Allen's speech.

The fraternal address was dignified, scholarly and uncompromising in its character. In the address, Brother Roberts, in a very able manner, justified the position taken by his father and others which led to their expulsion, and suggested the necessity of proclaiming the same truths and maintaining the same positions to-day as formerly. Owing to the peculiar circumstances of the case, the speaker occupied an extremely delicate position as fraternal delegate, but he performed the duty assigned him in a way wholly creditable to himself and to the church he represented.

The following is the excellent address of Brother Roberts:

FRATERNAL GREETING

To the Reverend Bishop presiding, the Ministers and Members of the Genesee Conference:

Greeting:

At the request of your body, and by the vote of my own conference, I am present to extend to the Genesee conference of the Methodist Episcopal church the Christian greetings of the Genesee conference of the Free Methodist church. The child of fifty years, begotten amid the stress and storm of divided opinion and stern antagonisms, of reluctant parentage, greets to-day the mother who has attained the century mark.

These two churches, with all the fifteen branches of Methodism in America, should have much in common. Begotten of the mighty force of English Methodism, which, not exhausted with awakening England from a fossilized formality to new spiritual life, manifested its virile power in that, wherever a Methodist crossed over seas to the wilderness of America, there he found, or became the nucleus of, a Methodist society.

We of the various branches of Methodism have a common root in the past. The writers and thinkers of early Methodism touch us all alike with the fire of their testimony, the cogency of their reasoning, the depth of their learning, and with the dynamic force of personal experience. The Wesleys, by their sermons, and perhaps more by their hymns, Adam Clarke, Fletcher, Watson, have been your teachers and ours. Together as loyal Methodists we drink at the same wells of learning and inspiration.

We not only have a common origin, a common root in the Methodism of the past, but we, in particular, stand committed by our past, by our hymns,

583

and by Methodist writings, to a common advocacy of experimental religion. The Methodist has a creed, he has the ordinances and the sacraments, but the Methodist bases his salvation not on intellectual assent to a creed, however orthodox, nor does he rest upon submission to an ordinance, however scriptural, nor upon participation in a sacrament, however solemn. Rather he goes to the fountain head, and, as he presents himself at the bar of the church, to the question, "Have you the witness of the Spirit that you are a child of God?" he answers, "I have." His soul exultant sings:

> "My God is reconciled,
> His pardoning voice I hear:
> He owns me for His child;
> I can no longer fear."

Perhaps the particular and definite contribution of early Methodism, as it should be that of the present day, to the religious life of their age and ours also, is the insistence laid upon the necessity of the new birth, upon the fact that a personal experience of religion is not only possible but essential. That a man could and must have a personal experience of the work of the Holy Spirit in conviction, in regeneration and in sanctification, as the foundation of all acceptable Christian life was the preaching and the practise of early Methodists. This insistence of the Wesleys and their coadjutors upon a vital, personal touch with God produced such a renaissance of spiritual life and force in the days of the Wesleys as the world has not seen since the early centuries of the Christian church.

To-day the church and the world need a revival of the supernatural in religion. The so-called scientific spirit, coupled with the rationalizing and materialistic tendency, so prevalent in the last fifty years, has so permeated society and the church, pulpit and pew, that there is need of a supernatural religion to lift men to the plane of spiritual contact with God. Too long have Nature and natural law been allowed in the current thought to supersede the divine One, who is the only source whence emanate Nature and natural law. The miracle of the New Testament has been too long relegated to the background in too many pulpits for preacher or people to expect the miracle of conversion in the pew. The result is that church rolls are padded with the names of those who know not the work of the Spirit in their own hearts. This lack is so manifested in their lives that many have ceased to look to the church for spiritual help. Indeed, the confidence of many in the vitality of what the church stands for has passed with the passing of Christian experience and personal testimony.

Is there not a call for Methodism in all its branches to rally to the advocacy of a supernatural religion that is more than a psychological effect of reflex action of nerve centers? Twice-born men are the hope of Christianity to-day, as they have been the instruments under God of its spread in the past.

The church today needs men who know God. The contest is between an intellectual and a spiritual religion, between a religion that is a result of a syllogism and a religion that is a result of experience.

As at the council of Nicea there was danger of following the intellectual methods of pagan philosophy, so to-day there is danger of following a materialistic philosophy. To quote the words of Professor Armitage in the *Hibbert Journal*, "Early Christianity lay in devotion to a person, and in an experience of joy and confidence flowing into life out of that devotion. In some way or another Christ had made men whole. Those men might have very vague ideas as to who He was, or by what powers He had healed them, and they might stumble and fall into confusion when they expressed themselves about Him; but they confidently called Him Lord, and sang hymns unto Him as God, without knowing how or why they believed that in Him they had seen the Father, and in His name they found power to walk as sons. They were so transmuted by the sense that this ever-living Lord had set His love upon them that they never again could despair of themselves, and they turned back to the tasks of life with new motives for duty, or faced its trials as men who could even rejoice in tribulation. Their experience carried its own vindication to that distracted later empire, for joy and strength justify themselves, and men joined their company that they, too, might pass out of weakness and fear."

Is there not need to-day that all the forces of Methodism unite in rallying the church around a risen Lord who is divine, who is the Son of God, and who will manifest Himself in the lives and hearts of men?

There was a marked line of separation between the church and the world in the early days of Methodism. Should this line be less distinct now? If so, why? Has Christ and His cause changed? Is self-denial any more pleasing? Is the world less proud, less selfish? Is the common life of the people less burdened with the extravagance and the folly of fashion-mongers? Is the theater become so refined that the pure-minded find no longer cause to blush? Is gambling in polite circles robbed of its baneful results? Is there not a difference between the child of God born of the Spirit and the one who knows not God? Has the world yet learned to do business according to the Golden Rule? Are the wage earners less burdened? Do not our corporations still need men of the Zaccheus type, who will restore fourfold? Does not our state need men who will govern righteously, scorning the bribe? Surely here, in the uplift of society, is common ground for the forces of Methodism to work together.

You will expect me at this time to say something of the Free Methodist church. It was cradled in adversity, nursed in poverty, scorned by many, derided by others, and by some branded as fanatic. Its founders became such unwillingly, but they were shut up by events to this course alone.

This is not the time to recount the excitement, the antagonism, the fierce opposition engendered in the fifties of the past century in the Genesee conference which finally resulted in the expulsion of six ministers and several hundred lay members from the Methodist Episcopal Church. Sorrowful and heavy were the hearts of these whose offense was that they were too Methodistic, too zealous. Surely the Christian church has need in our day for even the zeal that is sometimes extreme. These men insisted that it was Methodistic to be born again; that holiness of heart became the children of God; that there would be a line of separation between the church and the world; that thus the rules of the Methodist Discipline and the vows of membership should be kept. By a majority they were voted disturbers in Israel, and were dismissed from the church of their choice in many cases, as they claim, illegally. Thrust out, having no home, it was natural that they should organize into bands which later became the Free Methodist church.

The new church was few in numbers, rigid in its rules, interpreting the Scriptures literally. They adopted as their Discipline the Discipline of the Methodist Episcopal church, modifying it in few respects. Especial emphasis was laid upon the rules respecting plainness of dress and amusements. Rules were adopted forbidding membership in secret societies, slave holding, the use of tobacco in any form, the use of musical instruments in the church, and providing for free seats. Surely they were not bidding for popularity, nor did they gain it. The preachers insisted upon repentance; their services were marked by fervor, and often by demonstrations, affording a strange sight to the on-lookers. Excesses followed, as they always will follow such a movement, yet these instances were local, or isolated, and did not deter the mass from sober sanity in their determination to follow God and be led by His Spirit. As time passed on the numbers grew, and the church spread, until now after a lapse of fifty years the church that was organized after painful deliberation and much hesitancy, numbers over thirty thousand. It has educational institutions from the Atlantic to the Pacific, a publishing house, a goodly force of missionaries on the foreign field, in Africa, India, China and Japan.

The unpopular truths of Christianity are ours to advocate and defend. To these the Free Methodist church stands committed. That a child of God, born of the spirit, will live a godly life, abstaining from worldly amusements, the theater, card playing, and in such matters giving God the benefit of the doubt; that women, born of the Spirit, will not adorn themselves with gold or costly array; that the churches shall be free to all, rich and poor, sweeping away all fortuitous distinctions in the house of God; that its members shall abstain from the use of tobacco, from membership in oath-bound secret orders, but be brothers to all men; that the child of God shall seek holiness of heart as a second work of grace received by faith on the Son of God—to these truths this church stands committed. Is it any wonder that its growth is slow, that only here and there one is found who will submit to such rules of living, and that few wealthy or renowned will accept such restrictions? Yet, are they not based on the teachings of Scripture and the spirit of the gospel as understood from the beginning? Moreover, with the Holy Spirit dwelling within, does not such a life become one of perfect freedom where the soul chooses denial and rejoices in fellowship with Christ?

Do not the Christian churches at large owe a debt of support to the church that will openly and avowedly adopt and advocate such truths, truths that are so unpopular and so generally disliked that they are never preached in many pulpits and are openly repudiated in some? To advocate these truths aright requires a deep baptism of the spirit of love, lest the preacher become censorious or Pharisaical. Will you not pray that a mighty baptism of divine love and a spirit of holy wisdom may so rest upon our preachers and members that they may become true ministers of the Spirit of our Christ?

The child has a complaint and a request to make of this the parent conference. Demosthenes, in his speech On the Crown says, "In the first place, O men of Athens, I ask of you that you will not make my enemies my judges."

APPENDICES

The feeling prevails in the Free Methodist church that in the matters incident to the formation of the church those hostile to it have become the historians of the events.

In several incidents of note the historical accuracy of your writers is challenged, and in other instances their reflections on the character of the men who became the founders of this church are resented as being both unwarranted and unworthy. I do not desire at this time to provoke discussion. The whole matter at issue is set forth at length in Bowen's "Origin of the Free Methodist Church" and in "Why Another Sect?" written by B. T. Roberts, in which the subject is discussed at length, with evidence adduced. The attention of one of your authors was called to some of the most glaring inaccuracies in his work. In his reply he stated that the matter would have attention when a second edition was called for. This second edition has never been published.

Further, and I know you as Christian men, many of you the sons of Christian ministers, will pardon me for submitting the following at this time in detail, which, for years, I have wished to bring to the attention of your conference, as a loyal son out of love and affection to a noble father, as a member of the Christian church, the great body of Christ, who prayed for His disciples that they all may be one, as a member of the Free Methodist church, who values the good name of its founders.

In your conference minutes you publish a necrology list. In this list of your honored dead occur the names of our honored dead whom you, I am sure unwittingly, dishonor. Against the names of B. T. Roberts, Loren Stiles, Joseph McCreery, and the others who were expelled in those troublesome times, is the word "expelled." The statement squares with the fact. But there are instances, as you know, where the truth unexplained becomes misleading and injurious to the uninformed because of the inevitable inference. The statement is true, the inference erroneous, false. Hence, the statement becomes a source of error. The inevitable inference from the word "expelled" against the names of these men is that they were unworthy, of doubtful morality, unfit to hold a place in the Christian ministry. It is, in effect, to brand them with ignominy throughout posterity. But these men were not so esteemed by those who knew them best. Loren Stiles, the polished orator, immediately after his expulsion from your body, was invited to become pastor of an independent church in the community where he was best known. Joseph McCreery, a wit, eloquent with a native genius that was inimitable, a hymn writer, who gave to the world that well known song with the refrain, "I'm glad salvation's free," was elevated to the judgeship in Kansas because of his integrity and moral probity. B. T. Roberts, during the very conference session when he was on trial, was appointed to preside at one of your board meetings, and also to preach a memorial sermon at the same session, as your minutes will show. After his expulsion he was invited to join the New York conference and take an important church in Brooklyn. His life was in the limelight of publicity for many years. His character as a Christian gentleman, as a worthy minister of Jesus Christ, was never questioned.

> "He preached Christ and His apostles twelve,
> But first he followed it himself."

Others of these men lived noble, self-denying lives. These facts are unquestioned. It may be said they opposed proper authority, but Methodism owes too much to men of initiative to condemn too seriously independence of conviction.

Brierly, the English essayist, says, speaking of Wesley, "Have we noticed that strange piece of undefined ethic which arises on the question of his relation to authority? He himself finds no way of carrying out his mission, but by disobeying the bishops and breaking the rules of his church. From his own followers, on the contrary, he requires a strict obedience. 'Do not seek to mend our rules, but keep them.' The man whose whole strength lay in a daring initiative desires as the very last thing to see that character reproduced in his converts. The ecclesiastical rebel founds the severest and best obeyed ecclesiastical rule of modern times. It is an illustration of the maxim familiar to the student of history but not found in the text books that the morality which makes a great leader is something quite other than that which makes a good follower." And yet despite the rebellion of Wesley, the church of England honors him by placing the beautiful medallion of the Wesleys on the walls of Westminster Abbey.

The request I have to make is this, that after the word "expelled" some explanatory clause be inserted, as, "For violation of ecclesiastical censure." Thus the statement will be true both as to fact and as to inference.

This I ask not in the name of justice, for the men of the past are before the throne of God, who metes absolute justice to all. Not in the name of sweet mercy, whose quality is not strained, but rather in the name of Christian courtesy, that spirit begotten of Christ which honors God, ennobles him who exhibits it, and marks him as Godlike, which enriches humanity in its bestowal, and affords to the world evidence that His kingdom is coming who shall reign forever.

To-day are fulfilled the words of the prophet, "Before they call I will answer." My heart is full as I pause to give recognition to your most gracious attitude, manifested by the tone and temper of your historian, by the conclusion of the matter reached by his survey of those troubled days, and still further made evident by your vote to restore the parchments of B. T. Roberts, which decision, by its spontaneity, by its unanimity and heartiness evinces the fulness of grace and kindly spirit.

Gentlemen, brethren of the Genesee conference, a world-wide opportunity is before the Methodist Episcopal church in her vast numbers, her network of missions and the influence of her educational institutions. Your opportunity is magnificent, your responsibility is colossal. To you are especially committed the oracles of God. You are leaders. Often you become the source of public opinion. The needs of our day are urgent, and the demand upon pulpit and pew is imperative that we in our generation do the work of our Lord as did the fathers in their generation. We are called with a high calling, but God's callings are God's enablings. Faithful is He who calleth us, who also will do it.

APPENDICES

APPENDIX E. GENERAL CONFERENCES, SECRETARIES, TREASURERS

The bishops co-chairmen, ex officio

Session	Year	Date	Place	Secretary
1	1862	(Oct. 8	St. Charles, Illinois)	Joseph Travis
		(Nov. 4	Buffalo, New York)	
2	1866	Oct. 10	Buffalo, New York	J. W. Reddy
3	1870	Oct. 12	Aurora, Illinois	W. Gould
4	1874	Oct. 14	Albion, New York	J. W. Reddy
5	1878	Oct. 9	Spring Arbor, Michigan	W. Gould
6	1882	Oct. 11	Burlington, Iowa	W. Gould
7	1886	Oct. 13	Coopersville, Michigan	S. K. J. Chesbrough
8	1890	Oct. 8	Chicago, Illinois	S. K. J. Chesbrough
9	1894	Oct. 10	Greenville, Illinois	S. K. J. Chesbrough
10	1898	Oct. 12	Chicago, Illinois	S. K. J. Chesbrough
11	1903	June 10	Greenville, Illinois	S. K. J. Chesbrough
12	1907	June 12	Greenville, Illinois	M. B. Miller
13	1911	June 14	Chicago, Illinois	M. B. Miller
14	1915	June 9	Chicago, Illinois	M. B. Miller
15	1919	June 11	Greenville, Illinois	J. T. Logan
16	1923	June 14	Corunna, Michigan	J. T. Logan
17	1927	June 8	Rochester, New York	J. T. Logan
18	1931	June 10	Greenville, Illinois	J. T. Logan
19	1935	June 13	Winona Lake, Indiana	J. T. Logan
20	1939	June 14	Winona Lake, Indiana	J. T. Logan
21	1943	June 2	Greenville, Illinois	J. T. Logan
22	1947	June 11	Winona Lake, Indiana	R. B. Campbell
23	1951	June 13	Hillsdale, Michigan	C. A. Watson
24	1955	June 7	Winona Lake, Indiana	C. A. Watson

The general treasurers of the Free Methodist Church have been:

S. K. J. Chesbrough	1907-1909	N. W. Fink	1921-1932
Thomas Sully	1909-1915	B. H. Gaddis	1933-1944
G. W. Saunders	1915-1921	J. M. Daniels	1944-1948
	A. S. Hill	1948-	

589

Bibliography

Principally included in the following list are books and periodicals referred to or quoted in this volume.

Allen, Ray; *A Century of the Genesee Annual Conference of the Methodist Episcopal Church: 1810-1910*. Rochester: Published by the author. 1911.

Anderson, William K.; *Methodism*. Nashville: The Methodist Publishing House. 1947.

Asbury, Francis; *Journal of Rev. Francis Asbury*, 3 vols. New York: Lane & Scott. 1852.

Atkinson, John; *Centennial History of American Methodism*. New York: Phillips & Hunt. 1884.

Bangs, Nathan; *Prospects and Responsibilities of the Methodist Episcopal Church*. New York: Lane & Scott. 1850.

———; *The Necessity, Nature and Fruits of Sanctification*. New York: Phillips & Hunt. 1851.

Barclay, Wade Crawford; *Early American Methodism, 1769-1844*; v. 2, *To Reform the Nation*. New York: Board of Missions and Church Extension of the Methodist Church. 1950.

Beard, Charles A., and Mary R. Beard; *The Rise of American Civilization*, 2 vols. New York: The Macmillan Co. 1930.

Berkeley; *The Works of George Berkeley*, 4 vols. Alexander Campbell Fraser, editor. New York: Oxford University Press. 1901.

Birrell, August; *Essays and Addresses*. New York: Charles Scribner's Sons. 1901.

Brailsford, Mabel Richmond; *A Tale of Two Brothers: John and Charles Wesley*. New York: Oxford University Press. 1954.

Brash, W. Bardsley; *Methodism*. New York: Harper & Brothers. 1928.

Bready, John Wesley; *This Freedom—Whence?* Winona Lake, Indiana: Light and Life Press. 1950.

Cambridge Modern History, 13 vols. Lord Acton et al, editors. New York: Cambridge University Press. 1909.

Cannon, James, Jr.; *Bishop Cannon's Own Story: Life as I Have Seen It*; Richard L. Watson, editor. Durham, N. C.: Duke U. Press. 1955.

Carter, Henry; *The Methodist Heritage*. Nashville: Abingdon Press. 1951.

Cartwright, Peter; *Autobiography of Peter Cartwright*. Nashville: Abingdon Press. 1956.

Cell, George Croft; *The Rediscovery of John Wesley*. New York: Henry Holt & Co., Inc. 1935.

Chesbrough, S. K. J.; *Defence of Rev. B. T. Roberts, A.M.* Buffalo: Clapp, Mathews & Co. 1858.

Chorley, E. Clowes; *Men and Movements in the American Episcopal Church*. New York: Charles Scribner's Sons. 1946.

Christian Advocate, The; New York. Sept. 9, 1926. (Centennial Number, Section Two.)

Church, Leslie F.; *The Early Methodist People.* New York: Philosophical Library. 1949.

Clark, D. W.; *The Life and Times of Elijah Hedding.* New York; Carlton and Phillips. 1856.

Clark, Elmer T.; *Charles Wesley, Singer of the Evangelical Revival.* Nashville: The Upper Room. 1957.

———; *The Small Sects in America.* Nashville: Cokesbury Press. 1937.

———; *The Warm Heart of John Wesley.* New York: Association of Methodist Historical Societies. 1950.

———; "The Three Roots of American Methodism"; *Together,* v. 3, no. 11, November 1959.

Clark, Robert D.; *The Life of Matthew Simpson.* New York: The Macmillan Co. 1956.

Conable, F. W.; *History of the Genesee Annual Conference of the Methodist Episcopal Church, 1810-1872.* New York: Nelson & Phillips. 1876.

Cowman, Mrs. Charles E., compiler; *Streams in the Desert.* Los Angeles: Cowman Publications, Inc. 1925.

Crooks, George R.; *The Life of Bishop Matthew Simpson.* New York: Harper & Bros. 1891.

Cross, Whitney Rogers; *The Burned-Over District; The Social and Intellectual History of Enthusiastic Religion in Western New York, 1800-1850.* Ithaca: Cornell Press. 1950.

Dargan, E. C.; *A History of Preaching,* 2 vols. (in one). Grand Rapids: Baker Book House. 1954.

Doctrines and Discipline of the Free Methodist Church. (A complete file since the church's origin in 1860 is at Free Methodist Headquarters, Winona Lake, Indiana.)

Earle, Ralph; "John Wesley's New Testament," *The Seminary Tower.* Kansas City, Missouri. Spring 1959.

Earnest Christian, The; B. T. Roberts, editor 1860-1892. Rochester and North Chili, New York.

Edwards, Maldwyn; *After Wesley.* London: The Epworth Press. 1935.

Emory, Robert; *History of the Discipline of the Methodist Episcopal Church.* Revised to 1856 by W. P Strickland. N. Y.: Carlton & Porter. 1843.

Faulkner, John Alfred; *The Methodists.* New York: Eaton & Mains. 1903.

Fenelon; *The Spiritual Letters of Archbishop Fenelon.* Translated by H. L. Sidney Lear. London: Longmans, Green, and Co. 1898.

Fitchett, W. H.; *Wesley and His Century: A Study in Spiritual Forces.* New York: Eaton & Mains. 1903.

Fletcher, John; *Checks to Antinomianism,* 2 vols. New York: Phillips & Hunt.

Foster, R. S.; *Centenary Thoughts for the Pew and Pulpit of Methodism.* New York: Phillips & Hunt. 1884.

BIBLIOGRAPHY

Free Methodist, The; Winona Lake, Indiana: Free Methodist Publishing House. (Weekly.)

Gaddis, Merrill E.; "Christian Perfectionism in America." (Unpublished doctoral dissertation, University of Chicago, 1929.)

Gaebelein, Frank E.; *Christian Education in a Democracy.* New York: Oxford University Press. 1951.

Gorrie, P. Douglass; *Episcopal Methodism as It Was and Is.* Auburn and Buffalo: Miller, Orton & Mulligan. 1854.

Gould, N. S.; "Free Methodism," *Cyclopedia of Biblical, Theological and Ecclesiastical Literature,* v. 6. John M'Clintock and James Strong, editors. New York: Harper & Bros. 1876.

Green, J. R.; *A Short History of the English People.* New York: Harper & Bros. 1886.

Hart, Edward Payson; *Reminiscences of Early Free Methodism.* Chicago: Free Methodist Publishing House. 1913.

Henry, Stuart C.; *George Whitefield: Wayfaring Witness.* Nashville: Abingdon Press. 1957.

Hibbard, F. G.; *Biography of Rev. Leonidas L. Hamline.* New York: Eaton & Mains. 1880.

Hogue, Wilson T.; *History of the Free Methodist Church,* 2 vols. Winona Lake, Ind.: Free Methodist Publishing House. 1915.

Hosmer, William; *Slavery and the Church.* Auburn, N. Y.: W. J. Moses. 1853.

Hyde, A. B.; *The Story of Methodism.* New York: The M. W. Hazen Co. 1888.

Hymns of the Living Faith. Winona Lake, Ind.: Light & Life Press. 1951.

Jackson, Thomas; *The Centenary of Wesleyan Methodism.* New York: Mason & Lane. 1839.

James, William; *Varieties of Religious Experience.* New York: Longmans, Green, & Co. 1902.

Jones, E. Stanley; *Victorious Living.* Nashville: Abingdon Press. 1936.

"Journal of the General Conference of the Free Methodist Church" (unpublished) from 1862 to 1955. Filed at Free Methodist Headquarters, Winona Lake, Indiana.

Journal of the 1956 General Conference of the Methodist Church. Nashville: The Methodist Publishing House. 1956.

Journal of the General Conference of the Methodist Episcopal Church.
For 1860, New York: Carlton & Porter.
For 1900, New York: Eaton & Mains.

Joy, James Richard; *John Wesley's Awakening.* New York: The Methodist Book Concern. 1937.

Kendall, William C.; ("Diary." Unpublished. 1857).

Kennedy, Gerald; *The Methodist Way of Life.* Englewood Cliffs, N. J.: Prentice-Hall, Inc. 1958.

Kern, Paul B.; *Methodism Has a Message.* Nashville: Abingdon-Cokesbury. 1941.

Kirby, Ralph, compiler; *The Methodist Bedside Book*. New York: David McKay Co., Inc. 1954.

LaDue, John; *The Life of Rev. Thomas Scott LaDue*. Chicago. Free Methodist Publishing House. 1898.

Lecky, William E. H.; *A History of England in the Eighteenth Century*, 8 vols. New York: D. Appleton & Co. 1888.

Lee, Jesse; *A Short History of the Methodists in the United States of America*. Baltimore: Magill & Clime. 1810. (Limited reprint by Cokesbury.)

Lee, Umphrey; *The Historical Backgrounds of Early Methodist Enthusiasm*. New York: Columbia University Press. 1931.

Leete, F. D.; Personal Letter, May 18, 1943.

Lorimer, George C.; *Christianity in the Nineteenth Century*. The Lowell Lectures for 1900. Philadelphia: Griffith & Rowland Press. 1900.

Luccock, Halford E., and Paul Hutchinson; *The Story of Methodism*. Nashville: Abingdon Press. 1954.

McConnell, S. D.; *History of the American Episcopal Church*. New York: Thomas Whitaker. 1890.

McDonald, W., and John E. Searles; *The Life of Rev. John Inskip*. Boston: McDonald & Gill. 1885.

McLean, A., and J. W. Eaton, editors; *Penuel; or Face to Face with God*. New York: W. C. Palmer, Jr. 1869.

Marston, Leslie R.; "What it Means to Love God Perfectly," *The Holiness Pulpit*, James McGraw, compiler. Kansas City, Mo.: Beacon Hill Press. 1957.

Methodist Quarterly Review. v. 41, 1859.

Miller, J. R.; *Making the Most of Life*. Boston: Little, Brown, and Co. 1927.

Moore, Henry; *The Life of the Rev. John Wesley, A.M.*, 2 vols. London: John Kershaw. 1824.

Neely, Thomas Benjamin; *Doctrinal Standards of Methodism*. New York: Fleming H. Revell Co. 1946.

Niebuhr, H. Richard; *The Social Sources of Denominationalism*. Hamden, Conn.: Henry Holt & Co., Inc. 1956.

Norborg, Sv.; *Varieties of Christian Experience*. Minneapolis: Augsburg Publishing House. 1937.

Northern Independent. Wm. Hosmer, editor. Auburn, N. Y. (The author's search covered available numbers in Garrett Biblical Institute, University of Minnesota, and Wisconsin State Historical Library.)

Norwood, John Nelson; *The Schism in the Methodist Episcopal Church, 1844: A Study of Slavery and Ecclesiastical Politics*. Alfred, N. Y.: Alfred University, The Alfred Press. 1923.

Nottingham, Elizabeth K.; *Methodism and the Frontier: Indiana Proving Ground*. New York: Columbia University Press. 1941.

Our Church in This Age. Pastoral Address. Winona Lake, Ind.: Free Methodist Publishing House. 1939.

Overton, John Henry, and Frederic Relton; *A History of the English Church.* London: The Macmillan Co., Ltd. 1924.
Paine, Robert; *Life and Times of William McKendree,* 2 vols. Nashville: Publishing House of the Methodist Episcopal Church, South. 1874.
Parrington, V. L.; *Main Currents in American Thought,* 3 vols. (in one). New York: Harcourt, Brace & Co. 1958.
Peters, John L.; *Christian Perfection and American Methodism.* Nashville: Abingdon Press, 1956.
Phelps, A. A.; "Memoir of Rev. Wm. C. Kendall, A.M.," *Guide to Holiness,* v. 34, 1858. Boston: Henry V. Degen.
Piette, Maximin; *John Wesley in the Evolution of Protestantism.* New York: Sheed & Ward. 1937.
Presbyterian, The. May 3, 1945.
Proceedings of the Sixth Ecumenical Methodist Conference (1931). Nashville: M. E. Church, South. 1932.
Proceedings of the Ninth World Methodist Conference, 1956. Elmer T. Clark and E. Benson Perkins, editors. Nashville: The Methodist Publishing House. 1957.
Roberts, Benjamin T.; *Holiness Teachings.* North Chili, N. Y.: Earnest Christian Publishing House. 1893.
———; *Why Another Sect.* Rochester; Earnest Christian Publishing House. 1879.
———; *First Lessons on Money.* Rochester, N. Y. 1886.
———; *Fishers of Men.* Rochester: G. L. Roberts & Co. 1878.
Roberts, Benson Howard; *Benjamin Titus Roberts: A Biography.* N. Chili, N. Y.: The Earnest Christian Office. 1900.
Santayana, George; *Poems.* New York: Charles Scribner's Sons. 1923.
Schoenhals, L. R.; "Higher Education in the Free Methodist Church in the United States; 1860-1954." (Unpublished doctoral dissertation, University of Washington. 1955.
Sherman, David; *History of the Revisions of the Discipline of the Methodist Episcopal Church.* New York: Nelson & Phillips. 1874.
Simpson, Matthew; *A Hundred Years of Methodism.* New York: Nelson & Phillips. 1879.
Smith, Timothy L.; *Revivalism and Social Reform.* Nashville: Abingdon Press. 1957.
Stevens, Abel; *A Compendious History of American Methodism.* New York: Eaton & Mains. 1867.
Stoughton, John; *Religion in England,* v. 6. New York: A. C. Armstrong & Son. 1882.
Sweet, William Warren; *Methodism in American History.* New York: Methodist Book Concern. 1933.
———; *Revivalism in America.* New York: Charles Scribner's Sons. 1945.

Sweets, Henry H., compiler; *Source Book on Christian Education.* Louisville: Executive Committee on Christian Education, Presbyterian Church in U. S. 1942.
Taylor, Jeremy. *The Whole Works of the Right Rev. Jeremy Taylor, D.D.* London: Longmans, Green, and Co. 1883.
Tenney, Mary Alice; *Blueprint for a Christian World.* Winona Lake, Ind.: Light & Life Press. 1953.
Terrill, J. G.; *The St. Charles Camp Meeting.* Chicago: T. B. Arnold. 1883.
———; *The Life of John Wesley Redfield, M.D.* Chicago: Free Methodist Publishing House. 1899.
Tileston, Mary W., compiler; *Daily Strength for Daily Needs.* Boston: Little, Brown, and Co. 1927.
Townsend, W. J.; H. B. Workman and Geo. Eayrs; *A New History of Methodism*, 2 vols. London: Hodder & Stoughton. 1909.
Toynbee, Arnold; *A Study of History.* New York. Oxford University Press. 1947.
Troeltsch, Ernst; *The Social Teaching of the Churches*, 2 vols. New York: The Macmillan Co. 1931.
Trueblood, Elton; *Alternative to Futility.* New York: Harper & Brothers. 1948.
Turner, George Allen; *The More Excellent Way: The Scriptural Basis of the Wesleyan Message.* Winona Lake, Ind.: Light & Life Press. 1952.
Tyerman, Luke; *The Life and Times of the Rev. John Wesley.* 3 vols. New York: Harper & Bros. 1872.
Wakeman, H. O.; *An Introduction to the History of the Church of England.* London: Rivingtons. 1938.
Wesley, Charles; *The Journal of Charles Wesley: The Early Journal, 1736-1739.* London: Robert Culley. 1909.
Wesley, John; *Explanatory Notes Upon the New Testament.* London: The Epworth Press. 1948.
———; *The Journal of the Rev. John Wesley, A.M.*, 8 vols. (Standard Edition) Nehemiah Curnock, editor. London: The Epworth Press. 1938.
———; *The Letters of John Wesley*, 8 vols. (Standard Edition) John Telford, editor. London: The Epworth Press. 1931.
———; *John Wesley's New Testament.* Anniversary Edition. Philadelphia-Toronto: The John C. Winston Co. 1953.
———; *A Plain Account of Christian Perfection.* London: The Epworth Press. 1952.
———; *Sermons on Several Occasions*, 2 vols.; New York: Phillips & Hunt, n.d.
———; *The Works of the Rev. John Wesley*, 7 vols. Robert Emory, editor. New York: Carlton & Phillips. 1853.
———; *The Works of the Rev. John Wesley, A.M.*, 14 vols. 3rd. ed., Thomas Jackson, editor. London: Wesleyan-Methodist Book-Room. 1829-31.
Weymouth, Richard Francis; *The New Testament in Modern Speech.* Boston: The Pilgrim Press. 1939.
Zahniser, Clarence Howard; *Earnest Christian: Life and Works of Benjamin Titus Roberts.* Published by the author. 1957.

Index

A

Abell, Asa, 268-70, 320, 335-36
Abolition, 156, 173-74, 220, 388-89
Agnew, G. Harry, 454
Albion, 183, 200, 218, 237, 240, 264, 268-70
Albion Laymen's Conventions
  First, 211-12
  Second, 216, 232-34
  Third, 238-40
Aldersgate, 26, 30, 34, 36, 41-47, 53-54, 59-62, 91, 302, 483
Allen, Ray, 246-47
American Revolution, 110, 122, 125
Amusements, 149-50
Andrew, Bishop, 157
Anglican Church (see Church of England)
Annual Conferences (FM)
  Alberta, 429
  Arizona-Southern California, 430
  California, 430
  Central Illinois, 429
  Colorado, 429
  Columbia River, 430-31
  Dakota, 430
  East Michigan, 429
  East Ontario, 429
  Florida, 429
  Genesee, 265-67, 427
  Georgia and Carolina, 429
  Illinois, 265, 267-68, 427
  Iowa, 429
  Kansas, 429
  Kentucky and Tennessee, 429
  Louisiana, 429
  Maryland and Virginia, 427
  Michigan, 429
  Missouri, 429
  Nebraska, 429
  New York, 427, 431
  North Indiana, 429
  Northern Iowa and Minnesota, 430-31
  North Michigan, 429
  North Minnesota, 430
  Ohio, 429
  Oil City, 427
  Oklahoma, 429
  Oregon, 430-31
  Ozark, 429
  Pittsburgh, 427
  Saskatchewan, 429
  Susquehanna, 415, 427
  Texas, 429

AM—American Methodism
EM—English Methodism
FM—Free Methodism

  Wabash, 429
  Washington, 430-31
  West Iowa, 429
  West Kansas, 429
  West Ontario, 429
  Wisconsin, 429
Ansted, Harry B., 526
Antinomianism, 93-95, 97-98, 316
Appeal of Roberts, 242-45, 578-79
Appleton, C. Floyd, 455
Architecture, 128, 148, 262, 348-51
Arminianism, 94, 97, 274
Arnold, T. B., 442-43, 473-78, 489, 563
Articles of Religion
  (AM) 123, 131
  (FM) 257-59, 273-74, 289-90
Asbury, Francis, 122-23, 125-26, 130, 135, 158, 165
Ashcraft, Franklin H., 530
Assurance, doctrine of, 89-91, 124, 302, 305-6, 312-13

B

Bailey, Lewis, 472-73, 489
Baker, D. P., 473, 489
"Bands," 229-30, 232-35, 238, 249, 410, 434-36
Bangs, Nathan, 139-42, 162-63, 310, 388-89
Baptism, 35, 125, 128, 291-92, 340-41
Barclay, W. C., 128, 159
Batten, J. Milton, 147, 154, 220, 387
Beecher, Henry Ward, 75, 144
Beers, Alexander, 528, 555
Benevolent institutions, 442-47
Benson, Joseph, 93
Berkeley, George (Bishop), 26
Betts, Henry, 77
Bible Christians (EM), 222
Birrell, August, 113-14
Bishops, 420, 422
  Board of, 419, 422, 503
  Roster, 426
  Title of
    FM change to, 418
    Wesley's objection to, 123
Board of Administration, 419, 422, 440, 452, 553
Board of Directors, 423-24
Boardman, Richard, 122
Bohler, Peter (Moravian), 37-38, 48, 68
Bond, Thomas E., 143
Booth, William, 224
Bourne, Hugh, 221-22
Bowen, Elias, 267
Bowman, John, 203-4
Boyd, Myron F., 487, 489
Brailsford, Mabel Richmond, 61, 111-12
Brainerd, Claudius, 213
Brash, W. Bardsley, 78

Bready, J. W., 114
Bristol, 54-57, 62, 69-71, 82, 92, 111
Brockport, 181, 217-18
Brooks, C. D., 268, 270, 322
Brooks, James H., 214
Brown, A. L., 505, 509
Buffalo Advocate, 180, 184, 186, 194-96, 217
Buffalo, N. Y., 235-36
Buffalo Regency, 182, 189, 191-92, 217, 240-41, 398
Bunting, Jabez, 223-24
Burlingham, C. D., 210, 215, 218, 243, 320
Burritt, Eldon Grant, 526, 531
Bushnell, Horace, 326
Butler, Joseph (Bishop), 24-25, 89-90

C

Caldwell, Merritt, 137, 139
Calvinism, 77-78, 91-95, 97, 103, 108, 126
Cambridge, Modern History, The, 70, 113
Campbell, R. B., 440, 589
Camp meeting, 136, 145, 176, 221, 264, 321-22, 324-26, 330-31, 333, 352-53, 390
Cannon, Bishop, 324
Carlton, Thomas, 192
Carter, H., 116
Cartwright, Peter, 141-42, 146-47, 155, 162
Caryville, 175
Catechism (FM), 296, 499
Cell, G. C., 94
Central Board of Ministerial Training, 424, 552
Central College, 522-24
Charges
 Against Kendall, W. C., 190
 Against Roberts, B. T., 190, 192
Charities and benevolences, 440, 442-47
Chesbrough, Isaac M., 211, 254
Chesbrough, S. K. J., 185, 197, 202-3, 211, 253-54, 471, 589;
 Publishing Agent, 478, 480, 489;
 Mrs. Anna, 442
Choirs, (AM) 143-44, 199
 (FM) 261, 342-45
Chorley, E. Clowes, 124
Christian day schools, 506
Christian Education
 Christian Youth Crusaders, 505
 Commission on, 423, 452
 Conflict in, 494-96
 Day schools, 506
 Educational evangelism, 496-97
 Educational institutions, 511-543
 Free Methodist Youth, 544-47
 Membership training, 502-3

Ministerial training, 547-55
Sunday schools, 499-501, 503-5
Transformation, 493-94
Christian Education in a Democracy, 497
Christian experience
 Assurance, 302, 305, 312-13
 Conviction for sin, 313
 Faith, 306-7
 Fanaticism, 309-12, 315-16
 and formalism, 325-27
 and mysticism, 311-12
 Fervor, 317-19
 Heart-religion, 307-9
 Inner cleansing, 303, 305
 Inner conflict, 302-3, 305
 Outbreaks of religious feeling, 314-15
 Testimony of Christian church, 305
Christian Helpers Society, 500
Christian nurture, 498-508
Christian perfection, 97-102, 108, 110, 124, 126, 133-42, 285-88, 305, 310
Christian Youth Crusaders (see also Intermediate Youth), 505
Christmas Conference, 1784 (AM), 123-24, 129-30, 348, 566
Church Council for Men in Service, 546
Church Extension Society, 438, 440, 452
Church Membership (FM), 259-61, 293, 502-3
Church of England, 20-21, 24, 35, 37, 72, 74, 78, 85-86, 89-91, 115, 122-23, 409
Church, S. C., 320
Circuit Riders, 130, 142
Clark, Elmer T., 42-43, 122, 357, 367
Clark, Esther D., 461
Clark, W. H., 426
Class meeting, 82, 136, 146, 221, 352, 354
Clowes, William, 221-22
Coe, S. V., and Mrs., 443
Coke, Thomas, 36, 123, 126, 128, 130
Cokesbury College, 123
Coleman, G. W., 417, 426
Coleman, Seymour, 250
Commissions
 Christian Education, 423
 Evangelism and Church Extension, 423, 438, 440
 Executive, 396, 423
 Missions, 423, 452
Communion (see Lord's Supper)
Conable, F. W., 196, 200-1, 204-5, 269
Conferences (see Annual Conferences)
Congregational Free Methodist Church, 218, 237, 240, 270
Congregational singing, 144-45, 253, 261-62, 341-42, 344-45
Conscientious objectors, 400

598

INDEX

Constitution, (FM) 413, 419
  Revision, 420
Cooley, William, 218, 255
Court of Appeals (AM), 242-43
Cox, Robert J., 536
Crawford, J. F., 322
Cross, W. R., 167-68
Curry, A. F., 270

D

Dake, V. A., 435
Damon, C. M., 522
Daniels, J. M., 589
Dargan, E. C., 21
David, Christian, 49-50, 98, 302
Davis, N. J., 535
Deaconess Hospital & Home of Redeeming Love, 443-45
Deism, 22-24, 87, 89, 307
Demaray, C. Dorr, 528, 536
Denominational paper, 265-66, 401-2, 472-77
Discipline
  (AM) 127-30, 146-50, 348, 367-70
  (FM) 259-61, 289-98, 342, 411
    Belief and life, 359-60
    Christian conduct, 372
    General Conference actions, 373-75
    Needed, 380
    Principles and prudentials, 377-79
    Rules, 370-72;
      Place of, 378-79
    Twentieth-century task, 376-77
  Liberty through law, 369-67
  Wesley, 359
District quarterly meeting, 352-53
District superintendency, 416, 418, 420
Divided chancel, 350, 356
Divorce, 372-73
Doctrine
  (AM) 124-26, 134-42
  (FM) Beginning emphases, 273-74
    Changes in *Discipline*, 289-98
    Holiness teachings, 276-89
    Millennial doctrine, 298-99
    Resolutions on, 294-98
  Wesley:
    Assurance, 89-91, 302
    Christian perfection, 97-102
    Decline in England, 133-42
    Salvation for all, 91-95
Dorsey, Dennis B., 220-21
Downing, M. N., 255, 259, 330
Dress, 127, 146-49, 187, 253, 260, 374-75, 559
  Changes in *Discipline*, 372, 420

E

Earle, Ralph, 79
Earnest Christian, The, 176, 215, 236, 244-45, 252, 266, 268-69, 274-76, 331, 336, 385, 471, 476

Ebey, C. B., 470, 489, 535
Editorial Board, 424
Education (see also Christian Education)
  as adjustment, 492-93
  Formal, 491-92
  Progressive, 361, 364
Educational institutions, 511-43
  Control, 513
  Discontinued ventures, 540-41
  Doctrinal standards for, 293-94, 372
  General Conference actions, 514-17
  Non-official ventures, 542-43
  Roster
    Central College, 522-24
    Greenville College, 530-33
    John Wesley Seminary, 553-55
    Lorne Park College, 537-38
    Los Angeles Pacific College, 535-37
    Moose Jaw Bible College, 539-40
    Roberts Wesleyan College, 517-20
    Seattle Pacific College, 487, 527-30
    Spring Arbor Junior College, 520-22
    Wessington Springs College, 524-27
Edwards, Jonathan, 308-9
Edwards, Maldwyn, 110, 112, 164
Election, doctrine of, 93-95
Ely, Richard T., 391
Embury, Philip, 121
Emory, John, 219
Emotionalism, 307-19
England (eighteenth century)
  Age of Reason, 22
  Church and clergy, 20-21
  Deism, 22-26
  Morals, 19-20, 25-26
  Preaching, 24-25
  Results of revival, 105-7, 112-14
  "Enthusiasm" and "Enthusiasts," 23-24, 43, 48, 66, 87-89, 211, 307, 319
Epworth, 27-28, 31-32, 55
Estes, George W., 203-4
Eternal security, 95
Evangelism (FM)
  Benevolent institutions, 442-47
  Church Extension Society, 438, 440, 452
  Commission on, 423, 438, 440
  Conferences organized, 427-30
  Declining progress, 437-39
  Finances, 437-38
  Forward Movement, 447-49
  General Conference actions, 432-34, 436-37, 439-41
    Conference evangelistic boards, 440
    General Conference evangelists, 436-37, 440
    General Missionary Board, 433-34
    Missions-home evangelism, 432-33
  General Evangelistic Secretaries, 440-41, 589

599

Light & Life Men's Fellowship, 424, 441
Pioneers, 430-32
"Evangelists," 433-34, 439;
  General Conference, 436-37, 440
Evansville Junior College, 535, 540-41
Executive Committee, 415, 452
Executive Personnel, 424-25
  Bishops, 420, 422, 426
  Dean, John Wesley Seminary, 555
  Director, Intermediate Youth, 509
  Director, Light and Life Hour, 489
  Director, Dept. of Service Training, 555
  Editor—*Free Methodist, The*, 489
    —Sunday-school literature, 588-89
  Educational secretaries, 555
  General evangelistic secretaries, 589
  General missionary secretaries, 470
  General Sunday-school secretaries, 509
  General superintendents, FMY, 555
  General treasurers, 589
  Publishers, 489
Expulsion of reformers, 200, 204, 211, 213-14, 218, 220-24, 228-30, 241-44

F

Fairbairn, C. V., 426
Faith, 38, 306-7
  and works, 107-8, 110, 116
Fanaticism, 72, 307, 309-12, 315-16, 325-27, 335
  and fervency, 317-19
  and formalism, 326-27
  and Genesee Reformers, 320-22
  Nazarites, 330-33
  Roberts, 320, 322, 337
  Wesley, 309-11, 315-16, 318
Farmers' Alliance, 392
Farnsworth, H. H., 218
Faulkner, J. A., 85, 155, 363
Fervor in religion, 317-19
  (AM) 323-25
  Genesee Reformers, 320-22
  Roberts, 327, 332-37
Fetter Lane Society, 54-58, 72, 95-96, 315
Field-preaching, 57, 69-75
Fink, N. W., 489, 589
Fisk, Wilbur, 162
Fitchett, W. H., 19, 27, 37, 65, 114
Fletcher, John, 94-95, 310
Flower, J. H., 440
Forward Movement, 447-49
Foster, R. S., 151-52, 566
Foundery, 58, 80, 96
"Free" churches, 163, 166, 179, 196, 234-36, 238, 385-86
Freedom through law, 360-67

"Free Grace," 92, 95
Freeland, J. B., 525
Free Methodist, The, 266, 270, 402, 472-77, 482-83
  Editors, 489
Free Methodist Church
  Central Organization, 421-25
    Auxiliary organizations, 424
    Board of Administration, 419, 422, 440, 452, 553
    Board of Bishops, 419, 422, 426 (roster)
    Board of Directors, 423-24
    Central Board of Ministerial Training, 424
    Commissions, 422-23
      Christian Education, 423
      Evangelism and Church Extension, 423, 438, 440
      Executive, 396, 423
      Missions, 423, 452
    Editorial Board, 424
    Executive Board, John Wesley Seminary, 424
    Executive personnel, 424-25
    General Conference, 421; 589 (roster)
    Investment Committee, 424
    Judicial Council, 420, 422
  Denominational paper, 265-66
  Discipline, 411
    Belief and life, 359-60
    Christian conduct, 372
    General Conference actions, 373-75
    Needed, 380
    Principles and prudentials, 377-79
    Rules, 370-72;
    Place of, 378-79
    Twentieth-century task, 376-77
  Doctrine
    Beginning emphases, 273-74
    Changes in *Discipline*, 289-98
    Holiness teachings, 276-89
    Millennial doctrine, 298-99
    Resolutions on, 294-98
  Education
    Christian nurture, 498-508
      Christian Youth Crusaders, 505
      Day schools, 506
      General Conference actions, 499-501
      Membership training, 502-3
      Sunday schools, 499-501, 503-5
    Educational institutions, 293-94, 372, 511-43, 553-55
    Free Methodist Youth, 544-47
    Ministerial training, 547-55
    Servicemen's Department, 546
    Service Training, Dept. of, 552, 555
  Evangelism
    Benevolent institutions, 442-47
    Conferences organize, 427-30

INDEX

Declining progress, 437-39
Finances, 437-38
Forward Movement, 447-49
General Conference actions, 432-34, 436-37, 439-41
General Missionary Board, 433, 451
Light and Life Men's Fellowship, 441
Missions—home evangelism, 432-33, 451
Pioneers, 430-32
General Church Headquarters, 480, 482
Larger fellowship, the, 560-64
Merger, 462, 464, 563-64
Missions
  Foreign missions, 433-34, 437, 451-52
    Fields, 460-64
    Junior Missionary Society, 460
    Pioneers, 453-58
    Woman's Missionary Society, 424, 434, 452, 459-60, 544-45
  General Missionary Board, 451-58
  General missions, 433-34, 437, 451-52
  Home evangelism, 432-33, 437, 451-52
  Home missions, 464-65
  World Planning Council, 469-70
Organization, 253-54, 256, 331-32
  Articles of Religion, 257-59, 273-74, 289-90
  Church name, 264-65
  Conferences organize, 265-68
  Democracy, 256-57
  Issues of origin, 13-16, 252, 559
  Roberts, B. T., General Supt., 264
  Standards, church membership, 259-61, 293, 502-3
  Standards, local churches, 261-63
Polity, 414-26
  General Conference actions, 415-20
  Organizational features, 414
  Restrictive rules, 414, 416, 419-20
Publishing ministry, 472-85
  Free Methodist, The, 472-77, 483
  Publications, 482-83
  Publishing House, 474-76, 479-82
  Sunday-school literature, 478-79, 482, 500-1
Radio ministry, 485-88
Recruits, 268-70
Schism, 435-36
Social Concern
  Elections, 403-4
  Gospel for poor, 386, 441-47
  Industrial relations, 394-97
  Militarism and war, 399-400
  Racial discrimination, 402-3
  Secret societies, 397-99

  Separation of church and state, 404
  Slavery, 387-88, 391
  Temperance and Prohibition, 400-2
Stewardship, 252-53, 405, 559-60
Worship
  Architecture, 262, 348-51
  Believers' meetings. 351-55
  Hymn Books, 345-48
  Music, 341-45
  Restraint of undue fervor, 332-39
  Ritual and sacraments, 290-93, 339-41
Free Methodist "Societies," 231-32, 234-35, 238, 249, 410
Free Methodist Youth, 460, 501, 544-47;
  Superintendents, 555
Free seats (see also pew rentals), 253, 262, 264, 414
Furley, Samuel, 102

G

Gaddis, B. H., 481, 489, 589
Gaddis, Merrill E., 134-36, 145-46, 352
Gaines, George A., 444
Garlock, George W., 518
Garretson, Freeborn, 126
General Conference
  (AM) 240-44
  (FM) Architecture, 350
    Christian conduct, 372
    Christian nurture and Sunday schools, 499-503
    Educational institutions, 514-17
    Evangelism, 432-36, 439-41
    Foreign missions, 451-52
    General rules, 371
    Industrial relations, 394-97
    Miscellaneous actions, 373-75
    Polity, 415-20
    Racial discrimination, 402-3
    Roster, 589
    Secretaries of, 589
    Secret societies, 399
    Special rules, 372
    Temperance, 400-2
General Missionary Board, 451-55, 458
  General missionary secretaries, 470
  Home evangelism, 433-34, 437-38, 440
General rules, 82-83, 161, 249, 261, 360, 370-72, 383-84
General Service Fund, 419, 438
General superintendents (FM) 257, 264, 417, 418;
  Roster, 426
  Title changed to Bishop, 418
Genesee Conference (FM), 265-67, 427
Genesee Reformers
  Charges against, 190-92

601

Expulsion, 200, 204, 211, 213-14, 218, 220
Fervor vs. fanaticism, 320-22
  Loyalty to Methodism, 233-34, 410-11
  Restraint of undue fervor, 332-35
  Trials, 191-94, 201-5
Georgia, 32-35, 38, 44, 46, 67, 69
Gerry Homes, 442, 444-45
Gerry Seminary, 542
"Gilded Age, The," 361-62, 392
Good works, 107-8
Gould, N. S., 275, 337
Gould, W., 589
Green, J. H., 114
Greenville College, 530-33
Gregory, James F., 483, 489, 521, 537
Griffith, G. W., 426, 489, 509, 526
Griffith, Lillian B., 555
Groesbeck, Walter, and Mrs., 463

H

Haley, J. W., 463
Hamline, L. L., 323
Handel, George Frederick, 77
Hanmer, W. G., 436-37
Hard, Amos, 321
Harden, Philip, 526
Harden, W. A., 526
Harmon, Nolan B., 355-56
Hart, Edward Payson, 230, 333-34, 417-18, 426, 520-21
Hawkins, Richard W., 295-96
Heck, Barbara, 121
Hedding, Elijah, 137, 149
Helsel, Paul R., 536
Henry, S. C., 93
Hibbard, F. G., 184-86, 209-10
Hicks, Charles, 235
Hill, A. S., 589
Hogue, Emma L., 555
Hogue, Wilson T., 238, 240, 417-18, 426, 476, 489, 508, 531
Holiness, 97-102, 108, 124, 228, 252, 299, 391
  Fanatical holiness, 336-37
  New School Methodists, 187
  Roberts—experience, 176; teachings, 276-89, 390
  Wesley's witnesses, 303-5
Holiness Movement Church of Canada, 462, 464, 564
Holy Club, 28, 31, 34, 36, 68
Hosmer, W. C., 137, 158, 184-85, 207, 210, 213, 219, 243-44, 471
Howland, C. L., 489, 541
Hymnody (FM), 261-62, 345-48
Hymns of Methodism, 75-78
Hyde, A. B., 275

I

Illinois Conference (FM), 265, 267-68, 427

Independent Methodist Church (EM), 220-21
Industrial relations, 394-97
Industrial Revolution, 112
Infant baptism, 35, 291-92, 340-41
Inskip, John S., 323-24
Instrumental music, 143-44, 253, 261, 341-45, 377
Intemperance, 128-29, 160-63
Interdenominational cooperation, 560-64
  N.A.E., 562-63
  N.C.C., 563
  N.H.A., 562
Intermediate Youth, 505
  Directors, 509
Investment Committee, 424
Irving, Edward, 334
Issues of origin (FM), 13-16, 252, 559
Itinerant ministry, 73, 122, 125, 130, 142, 152, 222, 414
Ives, B. I., 322

J

Jackson, Thomas, 164
Jacobs, Ralph, and Mrs., 463
James, William, 326
Jarratt, Devereux, 124-25, 130, 308, 314
Johnson, H. F., 470
Jolley Home, 444-45
Jones, Burton R., 418, 426, 489
Jones, Clark, 521
Jones, E. Stanley, 302-3
Judicial Council, 420-22
Junior Missionary Society, 460

K

Kakihara, Paul, 455
Kawabe, T., and Mrs., 455
Keasling, Ernest, 555
Kelley, W. W., and Mrs., 454, 470
Kelsey, J. D., 443
Kendall, William C., 174, 177, 183, 189, 190-91, 198-201
Kendall, Mrs. William C., 199, 240
Kendall, W. S., 426
Kennedy, Gerald, 127-28, 163, 224, 380, 406, 409
Kent, J. P., 204, 321
Kern, Paul B., 86, 91
Kingsley, Charles W., 441
Kingsley, I. C., 183-84, 191, 320
Kingswood, 106, 111
Kinney, Wilfred, 539
Kline, George E., 526
Knox, Lloyd H., 485, 489

L

Labor unions, 394-97
LaDue, Thomas S., 430-32

INDEX

Lamson, B. S., 466, 470, 536
Landin, Ruth, 465
Lawrence Seminary, 542
Lay representation, 208, 253, 256-57, 414
Laymen's conventions, 211-14, 216
  Pekin, N. Y., 231, 252-65
  Second annual convention, 216, 232-34
  Third, 238-40
    Petitions to Genesee Conference, 238-39
    Western, 231
    (St. Charles) 250-52
  West Sweden, 249, 410
Lee, Jesse, 164-65, 314
Lee, Umphrey, 319
Leete, Frederick D., 13, 247, 398
Leffingwell, Clara A., 455, 458
LeRoy Conference, 189-94
Lewis, L. Glenn, 523, 555
Life Line Children's Home, 443, 445
Light and Life Day Schools, 506
Light and Life Hour, 487-88; Directors, 489
Light and Life Men's Fellowship, 424, 441
Lincoln, Arthur D., and Mrs., 454-55
Lincoln College, 28, 31
Liquor, 109, 128, 160-63, 375, 400-1
Livingston, George Herbert, 555
Lloyd, Daniel, 252
Logan, J. T., 489, 589
Long, H. Johnson, 532
Lord's Supper, The, 21, 35, 36, 125, 128, 130, 238, 290-91, 339-40
Lorimer, George C., 326-27
Lorne Park College, 537-38
Los Angeles Pacific College, 535-37
Love Feast, 53, 199, 304, 315, 352, 354-55
Lowell, LeRoy M., 487, 489, 521
Luther, Martin, 107, 243
Lutz, J. B., 509

M

Macartney, Clarence E., 365-66
McCreery, Joseph, Jr., 182, 204, 211-12, 255, 329-30
MacGeary, J. S., 426, 470, 563; Mrs. Ella, 459
McKendree, William, 165
Mackey, Joseph, 472, 489
McKinney Junior College, 541
Marston, L. R., 426, 531
Mason, Harold C., 555
Masonic lodge, 167-68
Mavis, W. Curry, 536, 555
Membership training, 502-3
Merchandising, 262-63

Merger, 462, 464, 563-64
Merritt, Timothy, 136
Methodism (AM)
  Amusements, 149-50
  Articles of Religion, 123, 131
  Christian perfection, 134-42
  Discipline, 127-30, 146-50, 348, 367-70
  Dress, 127, 146-49
  Fervor at mid-century, 323-25
  General Conference (1860), 240-44
    Slavery & Nazaritism, 241
    Genesee problem, 241-44
  Genesee Conference
    Autocratic government, 219-20, 224-26
    Brockport Conference, 217-18
    Buffalo Regency, 182, 189, 191-92, 217, 240-41, 398
    Centennial Conference (1910), 246-47
    Expulsion of Reformers, 200, 204, 211, 213-14, 218, 220
    Laymen expelled, 213-14
    Laymen's convention, 211-12
    LeRoy Conference (1857), 189-94
    Membership decline, 214
    Nazarites, 185, 189, 192, 194, 200-1, 204, 209-11, 217-19, 234, 241, 246-47, 268-69
    Niagara Street Church, 178-81, 195-96, 236
    Resolutions of protest, 207-8
    Restoration of parchments, 246, 582-88
    Trial of Roberts, 191-94, 201-5
  Intemperance, 128-29, 160-63
  Lay representation, 257
  Origins in America, 121-23, 131, 152
  Pew rentals, 128, 146, 163-67, 179, 188, 262, 349
  Problem of prosperity, 153
  Rock River Conference
    Expulsion of members, 228-29
    Redfield revivals, 228
  Sanctification, 125-26, 135, 137, 139-41
  Secrecy, 167-68
  Simplicity of architecture, 128, 148, 348-49, 356
  Slavery, 128-30, 136, 154-60, 184, 387-89
    Compromise on, 156-57, 387
    Dissension feared, 158-60
    Schism, 160
  Wesleyan in doctrine, 124, 126
  Worship, declining simplicity, 142-46, 351-52, 355-56
    Camp meeting, 145
    Choirs, 143-44
    Class meeting, 351-52

603

Instrumental music, 143-44
Love Feast, 146
Methodism (EM)
  Autocratic government, 223-24
  Decline in doctrine, 133-42
  Expulsion of reformers, 220-24
  Fervor in religion, 318-19
  Field-preaching, 69-75
  Hymns, 75-78
  Intemperance, 161
  Message, 85-103
  Name "Methodist," 28
  Pew rentals, 163-64
  Prison evangelism, 67-69
  Publishing ministry, 78-81
  Results of revival, 105-7, 113-15
  Secessions, 220-24
  United Societies, 81-83
Methodist Episcopal Church, South, 160
Methodist New Connexion (EM), 224
Methodist Protestant Church, 220, 222-23
Middleton, Conyers, 87
Militarism and war, 399-400
Millennial doctrine, 298-99
Miller, M. B., 589
Miller, Mendall B., 523
Miller, M. C., 539
Mills, G. W., and Mrs., 458
Mills, S. E., and Mrs., 458
Ministerial Training (FM), 547-55
  Central Board of, 424, 552
  Contemporary period, 550-52
  Course of study (1860), 547-48
  John Wesley Seminary Foundation, 553-55
  Middle period, 549-50
  Roberts' views, 549
Missionary Bands of the World, 435
Missionary Tidings, The, 460, 482
Missions, 451-70
  Commission on, 452
  Foreign Missions, 433-34, 437, 452
    Fields, 460-64
    Junior Missionary Society, 460
    Pioneers, 453-58
    Woman's Missionary Society, 424, 434, 452, 459-60, 544-45
  General Missionary Board, 451-58
  General missionary secretaries, 470
  General missions, 433-34, 437, 451-52
  Home evangelism, 432-33, 437, 451-52
  Home missions, 464-65
  World Planning Council, 469-70
Moon, C. D., 521
Moose Jaw Bible College, 539-40
Moravians, 34-38, 48-50, 53, 58, 68, 72, 95-98, 315
Morgan, murder of, 167-68
Morris, T. A., 352

Music, 143-44, 187, 253, 261-62, 341-45, 377
Mysticism, 31-34, 58, 311-12

N

Naming church (FM), 264-65
Nash, Arnold, 25
Nash, Beau, 71-72
National Association of Evangelicals, 562-63
National Council of the Churches of Christ in the U.S.A., 563
National Holiness Association, 562
Nazarite Bands (Extremists), 255, 329, 330-33
Nazarites (Reformers), 185, 189, 192, 194, 200-1, 204, 209-11, 217-19, 234, 241, 246-47, 268-69
Nazarite Union, 182, 320
Neely, T. B., 85-86
Nelson, R. S., 504, 509
Neosho Rapids Seminary, 541
Newgate Prison, 50, 67, 69
New Room (EM), 82, 96
"New School Methodism," 184-88, 191-92, 194-95, 202-3, 211, 252, 573-78
Niagara Street Church, 178-81, 195-96, 236
Niebuhr, Richard, 110, 112, 154, 565
Nishizumi, Daniel, 462
Northern Christian Advocate, 158, 180, 184-85, 209, 321
Northern Independent, 184-86, 193, 207, 209-10, 213, 218, 233, 237, 241-43, 249, 266, 271, 320, 389, 471-72, 547
Northrup, L. W., 441, 568, 589
Nottingham, E. K., 225-26
Noyes, A. D. and Mrs., 461

O

O'Bryan, William, 222
O'Connor, Elizabeth, 464
Olin, Stephen A., 172-73, 175, 188
Olmstead, B. L., 479, 509
Olmstead, W. B., 470, 479, 500, 508-9, 526
Ordination
  (AM) 128
  (FM) 341, 416-17
    Ordination of women, 418-19
  Roberts, 176, 178
  Wesley, John, 28
  Wesley's followers, 36, 123
Ormston, M. D., 426
Oxford, 27-29, 30-34, 49-50, 55-56, 68, 73

P

Palmer, Phoebe, 136, 176, 388-90
Parsons, Elmer E., 523

Pastoral time limit, 417, 419
  Vote by congregation, 420
Pearce, William, 14, 426, 518
Pearson, B. H., 555
Pekin, 196-98, 209-10
Pekin Convention (1860), 252-54, 547
Pentecost Bands, 434-36
Perfect love, 277, 283-84, 288, 293, 303-4
Periodicals, 482-83
Perry trial (1858), 201-5
Peters, J. L., 100, 126-27, 134-37, 287, 411
Peterson, Nils B., and Mrs.; Mattie and Lily, 527
Petitions to General Conference (AM), 238-39
Pew rentals (see also Free seats), 128, 146, 163-67, 179, 188, 262, 349
Phelps, A. A., 265-66
Pickert, Florence, 539
Pickett, Deeks, 162
Piette, Maximin, 20, 21, 29, 43, 81
Pike, 175-76, 200
Pilmoor, Joseph, 122
Polity (FM), 414-26
  Central organization, 421-25
  District superintendency, 416, 418, 420
  General Conference actions, 415-20
    Board of Administration, 419, 422, 440, 452, 553
    Board of Bishops, 419, 422
    Constitution, 420
    General Service Fund, 419, 438
    General Superintendents, 417-18, 426
      Title changed to bishop, 418
    Ordination of women, 418-19
    Pastoral time limit, 417, 419
      Vote by congregation, 420
  Judicial Council, 420, 422
  Organizational features, 414
  Restrictive Rules, 414, 416, 419-20
Pope, Alexander, 26
Prayer meeting, 352, 354
Primitive Methodist Church (EM), 220-22
Principles and prudentials, 375, 377-79
Prison evangelism, 50, 67-69
Progressive education, 361, 364
Prohibition Party, 374, 401-2, 475
Prosperity vs. spirituality, 153-54
Protestant Episcopal Church, 123-24, 356
Publishing House, 401, 474-76
  Chicago, Illinois, 479-81
  Publishers, 489
  Winona Lake, Indiana, 481
Publishing ministry
  (EM) 78-81

(FM) 472-85
  Free Methodist, The, 472-77, 483
  Publications, 482-83
  Publishers, 489
  Publishing House, 474-76, 479-82
  Sunday-school literature, 478-79 482, 500-1
Purdy, Fay, 217-18, 322

R

Racial discrimination, 402-3
Radio ministry, 485-88
  Directors, 489
  Light and Life Hour, 487-88
Ranf, M. Louisa, 453
Reddy, J. W., 218, 322, 589
Redemption, or the Living Way, Hawkins, 295-96
Redfield, John Wesley, 172, 179, 215, 227-28, 230-31, 250-52, 254, 258-59, 322, 334-35
Reform efforts, 171-73, 179, 184-88, 219-20, 223-34, 238-39
Reforms in England, 113-15
Rental of pews (see Pew rentals, Free seats)
Resolutions
  Albion Laymen's Convention, 212, 232-33, 239-40
  Brockport Conference (AM), 218
  Doctrinal, 294-98
  Illinois Conference, 579-82
  of protest, 207-8
  West Sweden Convention, 249, 410
  Western Laymen's Convention, 250-51
Restoration of reformers' parchments, 246, 582-88
Results of revival (Wesley)
  Lives changed, 105
  Moral standards raised, 112-13
  Reform in England, 113-15
  Revolution averted, 107, 114
  Society changed, 106-7
"Revivalists," 221
Ritual, 290-93, 339-41
Roberts, Benjamin Titus
  Abilities and leadership, 274-76
  Albion Laymen's Convention, 211-12
  Appeal to 1860 General Conference, 242-45, 578-79
  Charges against, 190, 192
  Chili Seminary, 512, 517
  Chooses ministry, 175
  Church architecture, 349
  Conviction, expulsion, 200, 204
  Editor—Earnest Christian, The, 215, 266, 274
    —Free Methodist, The, 402, 476-77, 489
  Education, 172

605

Elected General Superintendent (FM), 264
Fervor vs. fanaticism, 320, 327, 332
Formalism, 327, 337
Founder, not seceder, 410-11
Holiness received, 176, 264, 390
Holiness teachings, 276-89
Hope of restoration, 227, 234
Labors following expulsion, 215-16
Marriage and early ministry, 175-77
Memorial sermon, 200-1
Ministers' training, 549
Nazarite fanaticism, 330-32
Niagara St. appointment, 178-81
Ordination, 176, 178
Organizes "free" societies, 231, 235-36
Pekin pastorate, 196-99
Restoration of parchments, 246, 582-88
Restraint of undue fervor, 332-33, 336-37
Social concern
  Economic interests, 391-93
  Elections, 403-4
  Gospel for poor, 385-86, 446
  Prohibition Party and temperance, 173-74, 401-2, 475
  Slavery, 173-74, 387-88, 390
Stewardship, 405
Trials
  LeRoy, 191-94
  Perry, 201-5
Writings, 180, 184-88, 471, 573-78
Roberts, Benson H., 182, 246, 436, 518, 563, 582-88
Roberts, Ellen Lois, 175, 240, 459
Roberts, Harold, 149, 340
Roberts Seminary, B. T., 543
Roberts Wesleyan College, 517-20
Robie, John, 194-95, 217
Rochester, N. Y., 235
Rose, W. B., 489
Ross, Frederick, 519-20
Rules
  (AM) 127-28, 161
  Discipline needed, 380
  (FM) 360, 370-72, 378-79
  Restrictive, 414, 416, 419-20
  United Societies, 82-83, 161
Russell, C. Mervin, 547, 555
Ryckman, H. H., and Mrs., 463
Ryding, I. S. W., 464

S

Sabbath observance, 374-75
St. Charles, Illinois, 228-29, 267, 333, 403-4, 431
St. Louis, Missouri, 215, 230-31, 264, 388
Salvation Army (England), 224

"Salvation By Faith" (Wesley), 30, 37-38, 49, 68, 70, 72, 108, 111
Salvation for all, 91-95, 124, 130
Sanctification, 97-102, 108, 295-297, 303-5, 321, 410-11
  (AM) 125-26, 135, 137, 139-41
  (FM) 252-53, 258, 268, 273-74, 293-94
  Roberts, 276-89
  Testimony of Christian Church, 305
Saunders, G. W., 589
Schlosser, John, and Mrs., 463
Schoenhals, Lawrence R., 487, 511-13
Schofield, G. H., 455
Schools (see Educational institutions, Christian day schools, Sunday schools)
Scripture (Wesley), 87-89
Seattle Pacific College, 527-30
Secession not intended, 233-34, 409-11
Second crisis experience (Wesley), 100-2, 125
Secrecy, 167-68, 183, 253, 260, 264, 371-72, 394-97, 411
Secret societies, 397-99
Sellew, W. A., 418, 426, 442, 521, 542
Seminary, John Wesley, 553-55;
  Executive Board, 424
Separation of church and state, 404
Service Training, Department of, 552
  Director, 555
Servicemen's Department, 546
Shay, C. W., and Mrs. 459, 528
Shelhamer, E. E., and Mrs., 465
Shemeld, Robert R., and Mrs., 453
Simplicity
  architecture, 128, 148, 262, 349, 381
  worship (decline), 142-46, 351-52, 355-56
Simpson, Matthew, 148-49, 156, 160, 205, 213, 217-18, 228, 234, 315, 324, 349
Simpson, Mrs. Matthew, 148
Slavery, 229, 231, 241, 253, 261, 264, 390-91, 410-11, 579-80
  Abolition, 156, 173-74, 220, 388-89
  (AM), 128-30, 136, 154-60, 184, 387-89
  Roberts, 173-74, 387-88, 390
  Wesley, 109-11
Smart, A. B., 525
Smith, Louis, 539
Smith, Merlin G., 518, 521
Smith, Roderick J., 521
Smith, Timothy L., 134-35, 138, 165-66, 200, 275-76, 320, 388-89
Snider, K. Lavern, 537-38
Social concern
  (FM), Elections, 403-4
  Gospel for poor, 386
  Industrial relations, 394-97

Militarism and war, 399-400
  Racial discrimination, 402-3
  Secret societies, 397-99
  Temperance and Prohibition, 400-2
Roberts, 384-85
  Economic interests, 391
  Freedom of slave, 387-88, 390-91
  Gospel for poor, 385
  Wesley, 107-10, 115-17, 383-84
    Critics of, 110-12
"Spiritual Gifts," 267
Spring Arbor Junior College, 520-22
Stamp, C. W., 437, 440
Steele, Daniel, 174
Stevens, Abel, 124-25, 208, 319, 349
Stewardship, 116, 187-88, 252-53, 405, 559-60
Stewart, H. S., 521
Stewart, J. Wesley, 539
Stiles, Loren, Jr., 183, 191, 218, 237, 240, 258-59, 267, 321, 335, 352, 547
"Stillness," doctrine of, 34, 95-96, 312
Stilwell, A. H., 521, 528
Stoll, Charles A., 523
Strawbridge, Robert, 122, 125
Sully, Thomas, 589
Sunday-school literature, 478-79, 482, 500-1
  Aldersgate Biblical Series, 483
  Arnold's Commentary, 479, 482
  Editors, 479, 500-1, 508-9
  Graded Lessons, 482
  Light and Life Evangel, 479
  Uniform Lessons, 482
Sunday schools
  General Conference actions, 499-501
  Growth, 503-5
  Sunday School Journal, 482, 505
  Sunday-school secretary, 479, 499, 500, 509
Supreme Court ruling, 402-3
Sweet, Wm. W., 136, 162, 358
Syracuse, New York, 235

T

Taine, M., 114
Taylor, Isaac, 567-68
Taylor, J. Paul, 426
Taylor, Jeremy, 60
Temperance, 160-63, 173, 400-2, 475
Tenney, M. A., 87-88, 111, 116, 133
Tenure, pastors, 417, 419
  Vote by congregation, 420
Terrill, J. G., 229, 353, 470
Thomas, Eleazar, 176
Thurston, D. W., 218, 295, 374
Tiffany, O. E., 528
Tobacco, 372-75
Todd, Floyd M., 505, 509
Toynbee, Arnold, 325-26
Transcendentalism, 139, 190

Travis, Joseph, 231, 473, 489, 589
Treasurers (general), 589
Trewarvas, Richard, 312-13
Trial of Roberts
  LeRoy (1857), 191-94, 202
  Perry (1858), 201-5
Troeltsch, E., 14, 117, 319, 564
Trueblood, Elton, 367
Turner, George A., 100, 555

U

United Methodist Free Churches (EM), 223-24
United Societies, 81
  General Rules of, 82-83
Universal redemption, 124, 259

V

Vincent, B. J., 426, 509, 521, 526, 536
Virginia Seminary, 542
Voller, Ellwood, 518

W

Wakeman, H. O., 23, 115
Walls, Alice E., 537
Walters, Orville S., 523, 555
Ward, Ernest F., and Mrs., 453
Warner, D. S., 426, 501, 508, 518, 521
Warren, R. Barclay, 537
Warren, R. H., 426
Wartman, D. S., 539
Watkins, William T., 361
Watson, C. A., 589
Watson, C. Hoyt, 447, 528
Wealth, threat of, 153-54
Webb, Thomas, 121-22
Wedding ring, 372-73, 378
Wells, J. A., 209, 218
Wesley, Charles, 27-28, 36-37, 41-42, 55-56, 92, 96, 106, 111, 201
  Field preacher, 72-73
  Hymn writer, 75-78
  Prison evangelist, 67-68
Wesley, John
  Aldersgate experience, 41-42
    Before, 43-46
    Struggles following, 47-53
  Blazing trail of Christian experience, 59-61
  Break with Moravians, 58, 96
  Bristol,
    Call from Whitefield, 54-55
    Change in ministry, 54, 56-57, 59, 61-62
  Church government, 413
  Class meetings, 82, 354
  Concern for effect of riches, 80-81, 153-54
  Discipline, 359
  Early Life, 27-28

607

Experience of holiness, 97-99
Faith, 306-7
Fanaticism, 309-11, 315-16, 318
Field-preaching, 57, 70-75
Loyal to Church of England, 409
Marriage, 73
Message
  Based on Scriptures, 87-89
  Christian perfection, 97-102
  Doctrine of Assurance, 89-91, 302
  Free Grace, 91-95
Mission in Georgia, 32-35, 44
Moravian tutor in faith, 37-38
Prison evangelism, 50, 68
Quest for faith
  by way of legalism, 34-35
  " mysticism, 31-34, 60
  " reason, 29-30
  " ritualism, 35-36
Reformer, 113-16
Religious feeling, 315
Romance, 42, 44
"Salvation by Faith," 30, 37-38, 49, 68, 70, 72, 108, 111
Secret of success, 65
Social Concern, 107-10, 115-17, 383-84
  Critics of, 110-12
  Liquor, 109, 160-61
  Slavery, 109-10
Stewardship, 116
"United Societies," 81-83
Worship, 309
Writings, 35, 75, 78-81
Wesley, Samuel, Jr., 27, 31-32, 51, 105
Wesley Society, The, 118
Wesley, Susanna Annesley, 27
Wesleyan Methodist Church, 157, 220, 410-11, 435, 563-64
Wesleyan University, 172, 190
Wessington Springs College, 524-27
West Falls, 198-200
Western Laymen's Convention, 250-52
Wheatlake, S. K., 440
Whitcomb, A. L., 531
Whitefield, George, 28, 68-73, 91-93, 121-22, 308, 313-14
Whiteman, J. H., 509
Why Another Sect, 194, 196, 204-5
Wilbor, A. D., 203
Wilcox, Russell, 203-4
Wiley, Allan, 146
Williams, Robert, 122, 124
Winget, B., 470, 563
Winslow, H. H., 470
Withenshaw, Byron, 538
Witness of the Spirit, 89-91, 260
Woman's Missionary Society, 424, 434, 452, 459-60, 544-45
Women, ordination of, 418-19
Wood, Abner I., 216
Wood, Levi, 270, 472, 489
Woodstock Homes, 442-43, 445
World Methodist Council, 340, 563
World Planning Council, 469-70
Worship, 187, 252, 261-62, 264, 309
  (AM) 142-46, 351-52, 355-56
  (FM) Architecture, 348-351
  Believers' meetings, 351-55
  Hymn books, 345-48
  Music, 341-45
  Restraint of undue fervor, 332-39
  Ritual and sacraments
    Baptism, 340-41
    Lord's Supper, The, 339-40
    Ordination, 341
Wroote, 28, 31, 65

Y

Young people, 435, 460, 499-503, 543-44
Young People's Missionary Society (see Free Methodist Youth)
Youth in Action, 482, 545

Z

Zahniser, A. D., 426
Zahniser, C. H., 180, 216-17
Zinzendorf, Count, 49, 96-98, 137, 141, 276

This book is set in 11 point Electra type
and printed on Warren's Antique Text

www.ingramcontent.com/pod-product-compliance
Lightning Source LLC
Chambersburg PA
CBHW030211170426
43201CB00006B/56